Communications in Computer and Information S

Tomas Skersys Rimantas Butleris
Rita Butkiene (Eds.)

Information and Software Technologies

18th International Conference, ICIST 2012
Kaunas, Lithuania, September 13-14, 2012
Proceedings

Volume Editors

Tomas Skersys
Rimantas Butleris
Rita Butkiene

Kaunas University of Technology
Studentu g. 50-313a
LT-51368, Kaunas, Lithuania
E-mail: {tomas.skersys, rimantas.butleris, rita.butkiene}@ktu.lt

ISSN 1865-0929 e-ISSN 1865-0937
ISBN 978-3-642-33307-1 e-ISBN 978-3-642-33308-8
DOI 10.1007/978-3-642-33308-8
Springer Heidelberg Dordrecht London New York

Library of Congress Control Number: 2012946354

CR Subject Classification (1998): D.2.1, D.2.4-5, I.2.4, J.1, K.3.1, H.4, H.3.5, I.2, D.2

Typesetting: Camera-ready by author, data conversion by Scientific Publishing Services, Chennai, India

Printed on acid-free paper

Springer is part of Springer Science+Business Media (www.springer.com)

Preface

The International Conference on Information and Software Technologies—ICIST (formerly known as the IT Conference)—is hosted by the biggest technical university in the Baltic States, the Kaunas University of Technology. First organized as a part of the "Lithuanian Science and Industry" conference series in 1995, in Kaunas, Lithuania, this annual event became international in 2008, immediately attracting attention from academicians from all over the world.

The volume of *Communications in Computer and Information Science* series marks a new step for the conference. Having the proceedings published by Springer has raised the bar for our authors and will undoubtedly contribute to our on-going aim of improving the quality of the event by promoting the best research available not only in Lithuania but also internationally.

Thematically, the 18th iteration of the conference remained true to its original mission. The goal is to bring together practitioners and researchers in the field of software, hardware, and information systems engineering aiming at the everlasting convergence between business, software, and system requirements as well as application of new supporting technologies. At the same time, we strive to promote interdisciplinary approaches and multidisciplinary ways of thinking that could help achieve these aims. Although research takes central stage, the need to bring the theory and practice together calls for additional measures. Therefore, all conference participants are encouraged to attend the full-length advanced industrial tutorials on software development practices by well-known practitioners. The event was co-located with the conference for the third year in a row.

The papers were selected by the Program Committee consisting of 70 reviewers (supported by 12 additional reviewers) representing 45 academic institutions and four companies from 26 countries. Each submission was reviewed following a double-blind process by at least two reviewers, while borderline papers were evaluated by three or more reviewers. The quality of papers this year was quite high, as only 40 of 81 submissions were accepted for publication. We believe the selection of 40 accepted papers presented in this book is a good reflection of the latest research on the selected topics.

Finally, we would like to express our gratitude to the Lithuanian State Science and Studies Foundation and the Faculty of Informatics of the Kaunas University of Technology whose support made this event and this book possible.

Tomas Skersys
Rimantas Butleris
Rita Butkiene

Organization

The 18th International Conference on Information and Software Technologies (ICIST 2012) was organized by the Kaunas University of Technology and took place in Kaunas, Lithuania (September 13–14, 2012).

General Chair

Rimantas Butleris	Kaunas University of Technology, Lithuania

Local Organizing Committee

Rita Butkiene (Chair)	Kaunas University of Technology, Lithuania
Tomas Skersys (Co-chair)	Kaunas University of Technology, Lithuania
Darius Silingas (Industrial Tutorials Chair)	No Magic Europe, JSC, Lithuania
Lina Nemuraite	Kaunas University of Technology, Lithuania
Gintare Bernotaityte	Kaunas University of Technology, Lithuania
Tomas Danikauskas	Kaunas University of Technology, Lithuania
Kestutis Kapocius	Kaunas University of Technology, Lithuania
Jonas Ceponis	Kaunas University of Technology, Lithuania
Mikas Binkis	Kaunas University of Technology, Lithuania
Gytis Vilutis	Kaunas University of Technology, Lithuania

Program Committee

Jan Aidemark	Vaxio University, Sweden
Vassil Alexandrov	University of Reading, UK
Eduard Babkin	Higher School of Economics, Russia
Marko Bajec	University of Ljubljana, Slovenia
Rimantas Barauskas	Kaunas University of Technology, Lithuania
Ana Sasa Bastinos	University of Ljubljana, Slovenia
Joerg Becker	University of Münster, Germany
J. A. Rodrigue Blais	University of Calgary, Canada
Bernd Blobel	University of Regensburg, Germany
Albertas Caplinskas	Vilnius University, Lithuania
Sven Carlsson	Lund University, Sweden
Joanna Chimiak-Opoka	University of Innsbruck, Austria
Vitalij Denisov	Klaipeda University, Lithuania
Kiss Ferenc	Budapest University of Technology and Economics, Hungary
Hamido Fujita	Iwate Prefectural University, Japan

Anna Grabowska	PRO-MED Co. Ltd., Poland
Saulius Gudas	Vilnius University, Lithuania
Remigijus Gustas	Karlstad University, Sweden
Vladimir Hahanov	Kharkov National University of Radioelectronics, Ukraine
Mirjana Ivanovic	University of Novi Sad, Serbia
Alvydas Jaliniauskas	SubscriberMail, A Harland Clarke Company, USA
Raimundas Jasinevicius	Kaunas University of Technology, Lithuania
Andras Javor	McLeod Institute of Simulation Sciences, Hungary
Hai Jin	Huazhong University of Science and Technology, China
Vacius Jusas	Kaunas University of Technology, Lithuania
Egidijus Kazanavicius	Kaunas University of Technology, Lithuania
Marite Kirikova	Riga Technical University, Latvia
Jerzy Korczak	Wroclaw University of Economics, Poland
Tsvetanka Kovacheva	Technical University Varna, Bulgaria
Dieter Kranzlmueller	Ludwig Maximilian University Munich, Germany
Dejan Lavbic	University of Ljubljana, Slovenia
Rob Mark	Queens's University Belfast, UK
Raimundas Matulevicius	University of Tartu, Estonia
Arturas Mazeika	Max-Planck-Institut für Informatik, Germany
Pramod Kumar Meher	Institute for Infocomm Research, Singapore
Lina Nemuraite	Kaunas University of Technology, Lithuania
Jyrki Nummenmaa	University of Tampere, Finland
Toshio Okamoto	University of Electro-Communications, Japan
Stephan Olariu	Old Dominion University, USA
Tero Paivarinta	Agder University, Norway
Algirdas Pakstas	London Metropolitan University, UK
Marcin Paprzycki	Systems Research Institute, Polish Academy of Science, Poland
Michael Petit	University of Namur, Belgium
Henrikas Pranevicius	Kaunas University of Technology, Lithuania
Abhijit Ray	ST Electronics, Pte. Ltd., Singapore
Dalius Rubliauskas	Kaunas University of Technology, Lithuania
Rok Rupnik	University of Ljubljana, Slovenia
Giedre Sabaliauskaite	Lund University, Sweden
Marco Sajeva	Palermo University, Italy
Rimantas Seinauskas	Kaunas University of Technology, Lithuania
Darius Silingas	No Magic Europe, JSC, Lithuania
Kulwinder Singh	University of Calgary, Canada
Ilmars Slaidins	Riga Technical University, Latvia
Janis Stirna	Stockholm University, Sweden

Darijus Strasunskas	Norwegian University of Science and Technology, Norway
Giancarlo Succi	Free University of Bozen-Bolzano, Italy
Aleksandras Targamadze	Kaunas University of Technology, Lithuania
Laimutis Telksnys	Vilnius University, Lithuania
Peter Thanisch	University of Tampere, Finland
Babis Theodoulidis	University of Manchester, UK
Sofia Tsekeridou	Athens Information Technology, Greece
Raimund Ubar	Tallinn Technical University, Estonia
Olegas Vasilecas	Vilnius Gediminas Technical University, Lithuania
Radu Adrian Vasiu	Politehnica University of Timisoara, Romania
Damjan Vavpotic	University of Ljubljana, Slovenia
Benkt Wangler	University of Skovde, Sweden
Stanislaw Wrycza	University of Gdansk, Poland
Zheying Zhang	University of Tampere, Finland
Antanas Zilinskas	Vilnius University, Lithuania

Additional Reviewers

Linas Ablonskis	Kaunas University of Technology, Lithuania
Tomas Blazauskas	Kaunas University of Technology, Lithuania
Jonas Ceponis	Kaunas University of Technology, Lithuania
Robertas Damasevicius	Kaunas University of Technology, Lithuania
Virginija Limanauskiene	Kaunas University of Technology, Lithuania
Audrius Lopata	Kaunas University of Technology, Lithuania
Gytenis Mikulenas	Kaunas University of Technology, Lithuania
Alfonsas Misevicius	Kaunas University of Technology, Lithuania
Sarunas Packevicius	Kaunas University of Technology, Lithuania
Bronius Paradauskas	Kaunas University of Technology, Lithuania
Danguole Rutkauskiene	Kaunas University of Technology, Lithuania
Bronius Tamulynas	Kaunas University of Technology, Lithuania

Table of Contents

Artificial Intelligence and Knowledge Engineering

Business Process Modelling, Analysis and Design

Formal Analysis and Design Methods

Information and Software Systems Engineering

Information Technology Applications and Computer Networks

Information Technology in Teaching and Learning

Ontology, Conceptual Modelling and Databases

Requirements Engineering and Business Rules

Automation of Merging in ERP Revision Control

Algirdas Laukaitis

Vilnius Gediminas Technical University, Sauletekio al. 11,
LT-10223 Vilnius-40, Lithuania
algirdas.laukaitis@vgtu.lt

Abstract. In this paper, we describe a model for extracting rules that describe enterprise resource planning (ERP) system upgrade process. The rules are extracted automatically by analyzing programming code from completed ERP systems upgrade projects. Later those rules are verified and tuned by experienced programmer. The rules that we are extracting are described in the language equivalent to the first-order logic (i.e. expressivity of Turing machine). Nevertheless, we put a constrain on the rules description language by defining how knowledge base is used to define these rules. We require that ERP system code and ERP upgrade knowledge base must be transformed to a series of aligned strings without lost of expressivity. Such strong requirement ensures that we are able to use existing machine learning algorithms in the process of software development and upgrade. These series of strings are compared by strings manipulation algorithms and then differences are resolved by merge algorithm presented in this paper. We used Microsoft Dynamics NAV as an example to test usefulness of presented method but other systems can be used as well if they can be presented as series of code strings.

Keywords: rules induction, system simulation, business system upgrade, knowledge representation, automatic code generation.

1 Introduction

The Process of software upgrade is often highly complex in the Enterprise solution space. Many ERP products like Microsoft Dynamics Nav [16] or Microsoft Dynamix AX [8] include high level programming languages as an option for standard version modification to reflect local customer requirements. These programming languages allow for rapid customizations of the products at a very affordable price. It is important to emphasize that the customization projects are usually carried and implemented by a certified channel of value added resellers (VAR) worldwide, and then the process is highly decentralized. All that adds additional level of complexity when it comes to ERP system upgrade project.

In this paper we present the method and the system that allows us to manage this complex process of customization and upgrade. Particularly we focus on the following process:

T. Skersys, R. Butleris, and R. Butkiene (Eds.): ICIST 2012, CCIS 319, pp. 1–14, 2012.

1. We have the standard version of ERP system (we refer to it as OldBase) and we have a customized ERP system (we refer to it as OldCustom).
2. As technology changes over time, ERP systems providers are developing a new version of the system where new technology trends are reflected (we refer to it as NewBase).
3. At this moment a business company that runs its customized old version (OldCustom) of ERP system is faced with dilemma of adapting its old version system (OldCustom) by creating the new one (we refer to it as NewCustom).

Often it is an expensive and long term (up to the several month) project. It can be solved automatically if we use formal software specifications as it was suggested in [20]. Nevertheless, in practise, ERP business systems formal specifications are difficult to create and we don't know any ERP system that has a complete formal specification.

The problem that we are solving in this paper is closely related to the problem of software merge. As pointed out by [15] software merging remains complicated and error-prone process because software components that are involved in merging process depends on both the syntax and semantics of those elements. Nevertheless, many available software merge tools like Unix *diff* or *diff3* are based on textual merge techniques [11], [12] without consideration of software syntax and semantics. Several methods that considers syntax in software merging can be found in [5] and methods for semantic merge of programs can be found in [10]. There has been number of research projects that tried to consider domain independent syntax and semantics dimensions for software merging [14]. But all those approaches often doesn't suit well for ERP systems upgrade and then we need to develop the method for this ERP domain-specific task that we present in this paper.

The rest of the paper is structured as follows. In section 2 we present an architecture of semi-automatic ERP upgrade system that reduces the cost and time of the business system upgrade projects and increases the quality of the final system (i.e. NewCustom). In this section we present general framework of migration process to the new ERP version which supervised by IT expert. Next, in sections 3 , we present our attempt to investigate the possibility of applying artificial intelligence techniques and machine learning algorithms to increase the productivity of this semi-automatic ERP upgrade process. There are many ways to approach this task and we chose to investigate the possibility of learning from already completed projects. Those results are presented in section 4. In section 5 we present evaluation of suggested method. Finally, concluding remarks are provided.

2 Management of ERP Systems Upgrade

In this section we present the high level architecture of ERP management integrated development environment (IDE) in order to understand the complexity of

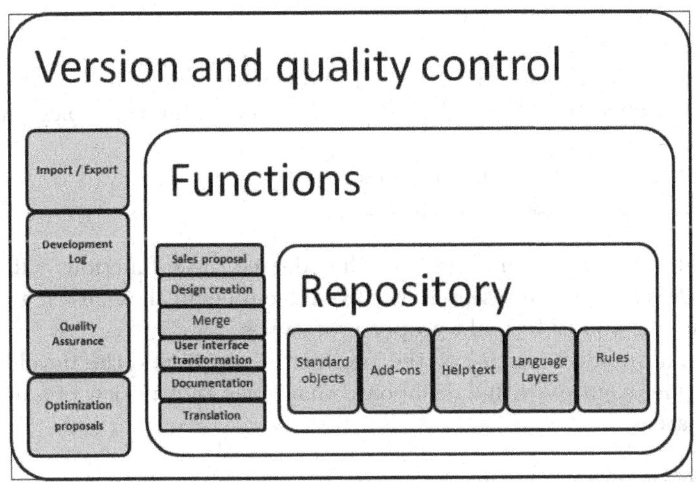

Fig. 1. High-level design of the the ERP management IDE

ERP upgrade process and design of algorithm presented in the following section. The Figure 1 shows the initial high-level design of the ERP management IDE.

The core of the system is the repository of all objects and data on the ERP products and there the following objects are presented:

1. All standard ERP system versions.
2. All customized ERP system versions.
3. All standard online help by standard version.
4. All add-ons that are part of the customers solutions.
5. All customized online help by customer version.
6. Rules and knowledge about ERP objects transformation efforts and knowledge about the complexity of an object.

The functions are the tools that help developers be more productive in their work. The typical process that we should be supporting is that a function runs and comes up with a proposal in each of the areas that the developer can then work further on or use as is. The functions that we look at prototyping as part of the project are:

1. Web-Service interface to receive information on the application that needs upgrade.
2. The knowledge base rules to calculate the estimated hours it will take to upgrade a customized application based on any later standard version.
3. Rules to calculate estimates for user interface and report transformation.
4. Rules to calculate estimates for documentation.
5. Rules to make a standardized proposal.
6. Rules to create standardized design document proposal.
7. Compare and Merge Tool for any two versions of an object: Generate a new target version of a customized object based on a later standard version:

   - Automatically - drafted version
   - Manually using tool
8. Rules to create transformation of UI and reports proposals.
9. Rules to generate online help skeleton for new columns, tables and forms automatically.
10. Rules to generate basic user manual.
11. Rules to make translation proposals.

Which functions can be build and to what degree these functions will be able to realize, depends on the research, the available tools in the market, the design options and our ability to build proper prototypes.

Version and quality control of the product is to provide the developer of a given customer solution with a dashboard that gives an overview of a number of important areas:

1. How far the project is and the status of each task in the project.
2. How much code optimization can still be done on the application according to LightTouch and the economic effect of maintaining the application going forward.
3. Which optimizations can be done on performance (SQL and native databases).
4. Which quality optimization processes still needs to be run in order to ensure high quality.

The version control part of the ERP management IDE manages the different developers and the jobs they are working on. The key functionality is about creating overviews on the consistency of the code, documentation, translation that is to be supplied in a given project:

1. Support version control, branching, check in and out of objects during a development project in a distributed environment.
2. Overview of the developers and which objects they are currently working on.
3. Completion Status overview of code, documentation and translation for a project.

We presented general architecture the ERP management IDE and upgrade processes. Next we present more detailed algorithm of software merge and final version generation. It is the most important component of ERP management IDE because it creates the biggest added value to value added resellers of ERP system.

3 Uniform Knowledge Representation

Most rule induction algorithms are closely related to the format of knowledge representation. We can see from the section above that our domain of interest (i.e. ERP upgrade) is closely related to the more general question of automatic software generation from informally or semi-formally defined business system requirements. We know that in order to get formal structure (i.e. computing program) by using an algorithms (i.e Turing machine that always halts within a finite time) we need that the input source or data to be defined by the formal structure. Then we have the problem of how to transform ERP upgrade expert knowledge and competed ERP upgrade projects code to the set of formally defined examples. Additionally, we require to reuse algorithms and software that already has sound representation in the field of artificial intelligence.

All those requirements that we defined for the knowledge and programm code representation language can be restated as the requirement to remove any domain specific knowledge on the language syntax level [13]. In this paper we suggest to transform all knowledge base to the set of rules that transforms program code (i.e. ERP system code) to the form of multi-aligned string sequences on several levels of abstraction i.e. we must transform our knowledge base in such way that for learning algorithms it will appear as simple string of symbols. In the Figure 2 we present general scheme of such multi-aligned string sequences as the set of paired strings.

The first set of paired strings $f1$ and $e1$ represents an ordinary programm code i.e. two versions of the ERP system. On this level of abstraction we have standard task of comparing two versions of program code. The tasks is to find differences in code and align semantically and syntactically equal segments of code. Usually this task is approached by using dynamic programming and sequence alignment algorithms such as Needleman-Wunsch algorithm [17] or Smith-Waterman algorithm [19].

Next, on other levels of abstraction we transform program code using knowledge base and we show how the final representation will look for learning algorithms. This is done using following procedure.

The pair of strings that represents some aspects from knowledge base is received in the following way: we take a word, line or segment of programme code and decide to replace or not to replace it by the label from knowledge base. For example we can replace all the objects descriptions in the code file by the labels like '*Table:Currency*','*Form:Transaction*' etc. We can take one of the parsers and replace some code by its documentation or some logical formal representation. We can take a language parser and replace all code lines in parse subtree by the subtree label. Even in the simples case when we consider only single word replacement by one possible label there is 2^n possible string pairs representations. Which one to choose we model as the hidden parameter.

Another hidden parameter that we introduced in our model is alignments. In the Figure 2 they are represented by the labels (a, b). Label a represents direct mapping of code segment to code segment in two versions of the program code and labels b represents splitting boundaries between code segment chunks. The parameters b can have another interpretation. As we mentioned earlier we don't know exact mechanism on how decoding is done. Then we can only guess the model structure which is used by ERP system upgrade expert. Then in the broad sense parameters b represents mechanism of transformation given that we learned transformation patterns base i.e. parameters a. Another important fact about parameter b is that

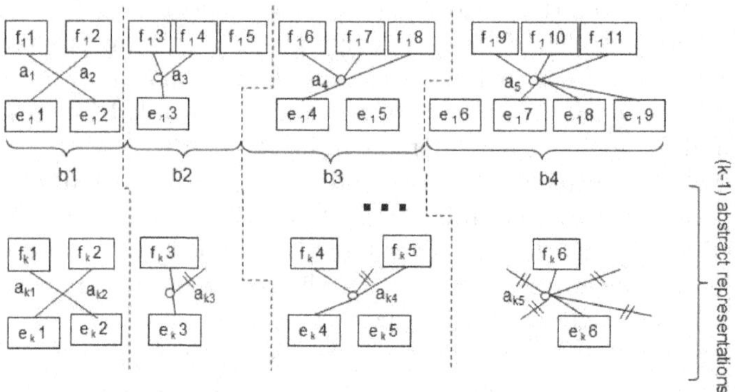

Fig. 2. Alignments within two versions of the ERP systems code

it incorporates our knowledge about context which ERP system upgrade expert takes into account. And again, it is a hidden parameter which we model.

Then, we can choose some model from machine leaning theory which we believe can be used in the decoding process i.e. final code generation from e to f , if we assume that we accumulated sufficient amount of ERP system upgrade projects code and learned parameters a with high accuracy. In this paper we chose to investigate a simple model of decision tree and noisy channel model [2], [6]. We use noisy channel model to align two versions of ERP systems code and decision tree model to extract upgrade rules from aligned ERP systems code. From the theoretical leaning we know that given enough data we can use greedy approach to learn such models [1], [7].

4 Learning of Code Upgrade Rules

4.1 Noisy Channel Model for Software Upgrade

The statistical approach for comparison of several sets of strings has widely used in such areas as spell checkers, question answering, speech recognition, and machine translation [3], [4]. It is an attractive method because it suggests fully automated process of learning and inference. Nevertheless, *"pure"*(i.e. using only data and model) statistical methods are insufficient for practical ERP systems upgrade . Then, hybridization by incorporating knowledge into statistical framework can be the answer. In the following model the idea of factoring probability distribution of one program code given another is extended by incorporating knowledge base description framework presented in previous section.

Let e stands for one program code and f for another version of the same program. Then the starting point for the probability representation can be expressed with alignment a as the hidden parameter:

$$P(f|e) = \sum_{a} P(f, a|e). \tag{1}$$

Probability $P(f,a|e)$ can be modeled in many ways. In our framework we suggest to modify it in such a way that knowledge from various knowledge bases will be included.

Let $e = e_1e_2...e_l$ be a programme code with l segments and $f = f_1f_2...f_m$ be a programme code with m segments. Let D be a knowledge bases representing the map $(\dot{e}, \dot{f})$, where $\dot{e}$ is a code in one version and $\dot{f}$ in another. Let $dictranslate(\cdot)$ be a function that returns the set of the code segments from knowledge base D. We define the function $match(codeset1, codeset2)$ which returns true if there is at least one code segment in the set $codeset1$ and in the set $codeset2$.

Then, with system codes e and f from existing projects database we consider the set of alignments $A = \{i,j\}$, $i \in [1,..,l]$, $j \in [1,..,m]$ where followings holds:

$$match(dictranslate(e_i), f_j) = true.$$

Let d_i be the distance between code segment e_i and its aligned counterpart f_{a_j}. Then, probability $P(f,a|e)$ can be decomposed as follows:

$$P(f,a|e) = \epsilon \prod_{j}^{m} \frac{1}{d_{a_j}} t(f_j|e_{a_j}). \tag{2}$$

By defining indicator function $I(a_j)$ which is equals 1 when function $match(\cdot,\cdot)$ is equal to $true$ and 0 otherwise we write

$$P(f|e) = \epsilon \sum_{a_1}^{l} ... \sum_{a_m}^{l} \prod_{j}^{m} \frac{1}{d_{a_j}} t(f_j|e_{a_j}) I(a_j),$$

subject to

$$\sum_{f} t(f|e) = 1.$$

Unconstrained auxiliary function

$$h(t|\lambda) = \epsilon \sum_{a_1}^{l} ... \sum_{a_m}^{l} \prod_{j}^{m} \frac{1}{d_{a_j}} t(f_j|e_{a_j}) I(a_j) -$$

$$\sum_{e} \lambda_e (\sum_{f} t(f|e) - 1).$$

The partial derivative of h with respect to $t(f|e)$

$$\frac{\partial h}{\partial t(f|e)} = \epsilon \sum_{a_1}^{l} ... \sum_{a_m}^{l} \sum_{j}^{m} \delta(f, f_j) \delta(e, e_{a_j}) t(f|e)^{-1}$$

$$\prod_{k}^{m} \frac{1}{d_{a_k}} t(f_k|e_{a_k}) I(a_k) - \lambda_e.$$

If this partial derivative is zero then

$$t(f|e) = \lambda_e^{-1}\epsilon \sum_{a_1}^{l} ... \sum_{a_m}^{l} \sum_{j}^{m} \delta(f, f_j)\delta(e, e_{a_j})$$

$$\prod_{k}^{m} \frac{1}{d_{a_k}} t(f_k|e_{a_k}) I(a_k). \quad (3)$$

Alignments A that maximizes $P(f, a|e)$ are called Viterbi alignments. An iterative estimation of Viterbi alignments by using (3) we mark as $V_1(f|e)$. There can be a question : do we need to search for Viterbi alignments when in most cases there is enough to search for longest common subsequence (LCS) in programs code as it is done in most software configuration management tools ? Our arguments for search of the Viterbi alignments are:

- it is possible to have a case when comparing two program codes the LCS problem doesn't makes sense (e.g. code "*Table1 Table2*" vs code "*Table2 Table1*");
- Viterbi alignments allow us to incorporate the knowledge as the hidden factor by using multi-abstraction layers of string set ;
- by searching Viterbi alignments we have a probability estimation of matching between various segments of code.

4.2 Algorithm for ERP Upgrade Rules Induction

Viterbi alignments allow us to determine differences and alignments between several versions of the ERP system code. The next step that we need to model is an induction of decision rules that together produce new version of upgraded ERP system (i.e. NewCustom). For that purpose we used decision trees [18] as an exploratory tool for an interactive inductive logic programming module that we developed during this research project.

The idea behind such approach is that at first we tried to induce simple attribute based rules by using completed ERP system upgrade projects as the data and decision tree rules as an algorithms. We found that those rules are not well suited to generate the final version of upgraded ERP system. We made a hypothesis that this can be attributed to inadequate amount of data due to high dimensionality of attribute space. Then, we tried to use a different approach, which we report in this paper. We generate the final system by using decision rules that are checked and modified by professional programmer. Such approach allows us to achieve more robust results and better quality of final ERP system code.

That approach requires that we produce a table where rows represent examples of decisions manually made by an expert responsible for ERP system upgrade. All columns except one in that table represents attributes upon which decision is made. The last remaining column represent decision code. The following list presents those attributes we used in this research project: 1. Version class. It is the class attribute we presented earlier i.e. OldBase, OldCustom, NewBase. 2. Object type e.g. Table, Form etc. 3. Version number. 4. Change size. 5. Is it a separate object. This attribute value is defined by programming code parser and it is equal true if code fragment represents separate object. 6. Is it a separate subobject. 7. Code segment: does it have a manually written comment. 8. Code segment: does it have a programm flow control element.

Next, we present more details on the upgrade process that was implemented at the current stage of this research project.

1. We start by loading all three versions of ERP system (i.e. OldBase, OldCustom, NewBase). The load is using regular expressions to structure code into segments and to extract features of code segments. The component for loading ERP system is similar to the compiler who compiles ERP system because it must structure the code by producing a parse tree. Additionally, the loading component must have semantic parser to extract semantic features of the code.
2. Find Viterbi alignments between pairs of ERP system code.
3. Find differences between pairs of ERP system code. We compute alignments A_s on sequences β_1 and β_2 by finding the longest common subsequence τ_β. We run Needleman-Wunsch algorithm [17] on β_1 and β_2 to find LCS. Needleman-Wunsch algorithm is most know in the field bio-informatics for Deoxyribonucleic acid (DNA) sequence analysis but we found it can be used successfully for programing code sequences, as well.
4. Generate a new version of ERP system. Pseudo code of this step looks as follows.

$NewCustom \Leftarrow''$ {initially we set NewCustom program code to empty strings}
for each OldBase, OldCustom, NewBase code sequence i such that $1 \leqslant i \leqslant number\_of\_code\_alignments$ **do**
  if $OldBase_i = OldCustom_i = NewBase_i$ **then**
    $NewCustom = NewCustom + OldBase_i$
  else
    for each $(OldBase_i, OldCustom_i, NewBase_i)$ match in knowledge base **do**
      get match with highest probability for $CodeSegment$
      if $CodeSegment$ probability $\geqslant$ $threshold$ **then**
        $NewCustom = NewCustom + CodeSegment$
      end if
    end for
  end if
end for

5. Formal verification of generated ERP system code. This step means that we automatically compile new ERP system code and run automated tests. If compilation and automated tests are OK then we proceed to the next step , otherwise, an expert responsible for upgrade project review failed code segments by rewriting transformation rules.
6. Verification of generated ERP system code by an expert. We need human-expert approval in the ERP upgrade project even if formal verification is OK. The ERP upgrade system produce prioritized list of decisions it made and human-expert review those decisions.
7. Report generation. The report is used by ERP system customer as the document on transformations done to the original ERP system.

5 Evaluation

In this paper we suggested the algorithm for Viterbi alignments between different versions of programm code, then we suggested the algorithm for induction of code upgrade rules and we suggested the framework to manage ERP system upgrade project. Then there are three questions that we must answer in evaluation part of this paper: 1. What is performance of suggested alignments algorithm when we compare it with longest common subsequences algorithm [12] used in most version control systems? 2. How much we can reduce error rates of automatically merged ERP OldBase, OldCustom and NewBase code if we use upgrade rules that were received by suggested rules induction algorithm? Can we generate positive return on investments if we use suggested framework instead of current approach in software upgrade projects?

In order to answer first two questions we incrementally selected 17 Microsoft Dynamics NAV completed projects for the evaluation of suggested algorithms. Each project has 4 files (OldBase.txt, OldCustom.txt, NewBase.txt and NewCustom.txt). Each file contains all data structures and business logic code from one version of Microsoft Dynamics NAV system. On average each file has size of 4.3 megabytes and 66198 code lines. Due to the amount of data we decided to verify alignments were there is conflict between our alignment algorithm and standard software merge tool kdiff3. Table 1 shows the results.

The following expression has been used to estimate error rate:

$$AlignmentsError = \frac{A_{mismatched}}{N}$$

Table 1. ERP management IDE Viterbi alignments error rates dependency from number of completed projects

/ Num. of projects	1	2	5	7	9	11	13	15	17
Error rate	0.0014	0.0012	0.0011	0.0005	0.0001	0.0001	0	0	0

where N is the total number of alignments, $A_{mismatched}$ number of mismatched alignments between our alignment algorithm and standard software merge tool kdiff3. The Table 1 shows the error rate progress as the number of completed projects, available for Viterbi alignments induction, increases. We can see that error rate approaches to zero when number of projects exceeds 11. With this evaluation we proof that suggested Viterbi alignments can detect all mismatches between sequential code lines. But this does not suggest that alignment method suggested in this paper is better then standard programm code alignments tool like kdiff3. The advantages of suggested method are reveled when we look at code that has non-sequential alignments or at code that is different from point of view of string match but is equivalent from point of view of code semantics. Table 2 shows the results for semantic and non-sequential alignments error rate. We used the same expression for error rate calculation as above, but for this time, $A_{mismatched}$ was number of mismatched alignments between our alignment algorithm and alignments made manually by programmers and N - the total number of such alignments.

Table 2. ERP management IDE Viterbi alignments error rates for non-sequential alignments and alignments equivalent from point of view of code semantics

/ Num. of projects	1	2	5	7	9	11	13	15	17
Error rate	0.32	0.30	0.30	0.27	0.26	0.26	0.27	0.26	0.25

The second question in our evaluation is about quality of new program version NewCustom that we generate from OldBase , OldCustom and NewBase (i.e. a 3-way merge). There is number of reliable 3-way merge tools on the market, but in order to compare them with our algorithm, we chose kdiff3 as standard plain text file comparison tool and Navision Developer's (ND) Toolkit as an intelligent merge tool that has some knowledge of program syntax and semantics. As an error rate we use ratio between number of erroneous conflict resolutions and number of all conflicts in the code. Table 3 shows error rates that we received for 17 already completed projects. We can see, that on average we achieve about 10 % reduction in error rate if we use ERP upgrade management IDE. Additionally, we can see that as number of projects that are completed increase the error rate of automatic code merge reduces to 0.12.

Table 3. Error rates for different products

/ Num. of projects	1	2	5	7	9	11	13	15	17
kdiff3	0.34	0.37	0.35	0.35	0.34	0.35	0.35	0.34	0.35
(ND) Toolkit	0.24	0.25	0.24	0.23	0.23	0.24	0.24	0.25	0.25
ERP management IDE	0.22	0.22	0.20	0.18	0.15	0.14	0.14	0.12	0.12

Presented method and software upgrade toolkit requires significant investments from company that decides to use it. We would like to be able to generate positive return on investments from method presented in this paper if we want it to be accepted by business. Even if we get ERP upgrade management IDE for free, there will be additional expenses to parameterize it and to develop knowledge base for a particular ERP system. Then the main objective in evaluation of the method, is to measure productivity change of the programmer who is responsible for the ERP upgrade project. One way to measure effectiveness of suggested method is to measure the time that we can save to complete the ERP system upgrade project. To do this, we have taken six programmers group that learned basic ERP upgrade skills and suggested to proceed with upgrade project during one week period using standard tools: kdiff3 and Navision Developer's Toolkit. Next week, we suggested to proceed the project with the tool developed during this research project. The productivity was measured by counting increase in the number of resolved conflicts. Table 4 shows results that we received. We can see that productivity increased about 25.29 %.

Table 4. Increase in productivity

	No. of conflicts 1	No. of conflicts 2	Increase in productivity
Programmer 1	128	145	13.28 %
Programmer 2	173	214	23.8 %
Programmer 3	267	312	16.85 %
Programmer 4	187	242	29.41 %
Programmer 5	197	273	38.58 %
Programmer 6	191	248	29.84 %

There is inevitable subjectivity in the experiments that we have done to measure productivity of the suggested method. Nevertheless, we believe that, even if results have been received on the small group of programmers we can still claim that we can improve such complex information systems processes as the ERP systems upgrade by using methods of artificial intelligence.

6 Conclusion

In this paper we described our research results on how to increase productivity of programmers in the ERP system upgrade projects. One conclusion that follows from our research is that we have presented the algorithm for Viterbi alignments to detect differences in program code. We have provided evidence that Viterbi alignments can integrate syntactic and semantic information of program code and improve the quality of software upgrade projects.

Next, we can conclude that it is possible to induce programm code upgrade rules from completed upgrade projects that can improve quality of automatically merged software. Nevertheless, we have shown that, at the current stage of research, there is no possibility to receive 100 % correct version of program code without programmers intervention.

In this paper we have shown that it is possible to build a business system upgraded tool that increases productivity of programmers when they are resolving conflicts in automatically merged software. The suggested framework can increase speed of learning and quality of code in ERP upgrade projects, but in order to achieve this, developers must invest their time to refine automatically induced rules that transforms code from one version to another.

In general, our research shows that artificial intelligence methods can be used in such projects to increase human-experts productivity but in order to develop such upgrade tools we need investments and dedication of programmers and analysts team. Additionally, we would like to point out that we reported in this paper the progress that we received at the first stage of the project. We think that as the company that is involved in the ERP upgrade projects will gain more experience and as the knowledge base become more mature we will be able to report more positive results on presented method.

References

1. Angluin, D., Smith, C.H.: Inductive Inference: Theory and Methods. ACM Computing Surveys 15(3), 237–269 (1983)
2. Baum, L.E.: An inequality and associated maximization technique in statistical estimation of probabilistic functions of a Markov process. Inequalities 3, 1–8 (1972)
3. Berger, A.L., Della Pietra, V.J., Della Pietra, S.A.: A maximum entropy approach to natural language processing. Computational Linguistics 22(1), 39–72 (1996)
4. Brown, P.F., Della Pietra, V.J., Della Pietra, S.A., Mercer, R.L.: The Mathematics of Statistical Machine Translation: Parameter Estimation. Computational Linguistics 19(2), 263–311 (1993)
5. Buffenbarger, J.: Syntactic Software Merging. In: Estublier, J. (ed.) ICSE-WS 1993/1995 and SCM 1993/1995. LNCS, vol. 1005, pp. 153–172. Springer, Heidelberg (1995)
6. Dempster, A.E., Laird, N.M., Rubin, D.B.: Maximum likelihood from incomplete data via the EM algorithm. Journal of the Royal Statistical Society 39(B), 1–38 (1977)
7. Gold, E.M.: Language identification in the limit. Information and Control 10(5), 447–474 (1967)
8. Ehrenberg, M.: Microsoft Dynamics AX 2012. A New Generation in ERP (2011)
9. Gold, E.M.: Language identification in the limit. Information and Control 10(5), 447–474 (1967)
10. Horwitz, S., Prins, J., Reps, T.: Integrating Noninterfering Versions of Programs. ACM Transactions on Programming Languages and Systems 11(3), 345–387 (1989)
11. Hunt, J.W., McIlroy, M.D.: An algorithm for diferential file comparison. Computer Science Technical Report 41, Bell Laboratories (1975)
12. Hunt, J.W., Szymanski, T.G.: A fast algorithm for computing longest common subsequences. Commun. ACM 20(5), 350–353 (1977)
13. Laukaitis, A., Vasilecas, O.: Multi-alignment templates induction. Informatica 19(4), 535–554 (2008)

14. Mens, T.: A Formal Foundation for Object-Oriented Software Evolution. PhD thesis, Vrije Universiteit Brussel - Faculty of Science - Departement of Computer Science - Programming Technology Lab (August 1999)
15. Mens, T.: A state-of-the-art survey on software merging. IEEE Transactions on Software Engineering 28(5), 449–462 (2002)
16. Microsoft Corporation. Microsoft Dynamics NAV (2012)
17. Needleman, S.B., Wunsch, C.D.: A general method applicable to the search for similarities in the amino acid sequence of two proteins. Journal of Molecular Biology 48(3), 443–453 (1970)
18. Quinlan, J.R.: C4.5: Programs for Machine Learning. Morgan Kaufmann Publishers (1993)
19. Smith, T.M., Waterman, M.S.: Identification of Common Molecular Subsequences. Journal of Molecular Biology 147, 195–197 (1981)
20. Zaremski, A., Jeannette, M.W.: Specification Matching of Software Components. ACM Transactions on Software Engineering and Methodology 6(4), 333–369 (1997)

A Variable Neighbourhood Search Enhancement for the Shift Sequence Based Method of the Personal Scheduling in Hospitals

Mindaugas Liogys and Antanas Zilinskas

Institute of Mathematics and Informatics, Vilnius University, Vilnius, Lithuania
m.liogys@eif.viko.lt, anatanas.zilinskas@vu.mii.lt

Abstract. The problem of personal scheduling in hospitals is an important problem of applied combinatorial optimization. Numerous specialized heuristics as well as metaheuristic methods have been proposed for solving that problem. The recently proposed shift sequence based method is one of the most efficient. In the present paper we propose an enhancement making that method faster, and improving its general performance. The original and enhanced versions of the algorithm have been compared using the real data from one of the main Lithuanian hospitals.

Keywords: shift sequence, medical staff scheduling, variable neighbor search.

Introduction

Large numbers of articles have appeared during the last decade which propose different algorithms supposed for the personal scheduling in hospitals, e.g. Genetic Algorithm (GA) [1], [3], Estimation of Distribution Algorithm (EDA) [2], Goal Programming (GP) [4], Shift Sequence Based Method [5], Hybrid heuristics (Hybrid Ordering and Variable Neighbourhood Search) [6], Branch and Bound [7], Bayesian Optimisation Algorithm (BOA) [8], Simulated Annealing (SA) [9]). As shown in [5] the shift sequence based method is one of the most efficient. In the present paper we propose an enhancement making that method faster, and improving its general performance. The original and enhanced versions of the algorithm have been compared using the real data from one of the main Lithuanian hospitals.

1 Problem Statement

We consider the problem of the personal scheduling for a month period in a hospital where 28 doctors, 42 nurses, and 19 members of the auxiliary staff are involved. The data is taken from a major Lithuania hospital. The schedules have to satisfy working contracts, and to meet as much as possible the requests of the health care workers (HCW). The working contract regulations are considered as hard constraints, and the personal preferences are considered as soft constraints [4].

T. Skersys, R. Butleris, and R. Butkiene (Eds.): ICIST 2012, CCIS 319, pp. 15–23, 2012.

1.1 The Hard Constraints

The hard constraints must be satisfied without any exceptions. If a hard constraint is violated then the solution to the problem is not acceptable, and therefore it is considered as infeasible.

The following hard constraints are imposed in the considered problem:

1. The shift coverage requirements must be fulfilled.
2. After night shift or duty shift must be at least for 24 hours rest time.
3. Duty shift must be assigned only on weekends.
4. HCW cannot be assigned to different assignments on the same time.
5. Only duty shifts can be assigned on weekends.

The hard constraint No. 1 states that the total number of shifts on the certain days must satisfy the coverage requirements. The hard constraint No. 2 states that there must be at least 24 hours time difference (according to the Lithuania law) between the night shift and any other shift. The hard constraint No. 3 states that the duty shifts must be assigned only on weekends or on bank holidays. The hard constraint No. 4 states that for the HCW, having more than one skill, the assignments must not overlap on the same day. The hard constraint No. 5 states that no morning, day and night shifts are allowed to be assigned on weekends.

1.2 The Soft Constraints

The soft constraints preferably should be satisfied, but their violation doesn't make the roster infeasible. The violations of the soft constraint are taken into account by penalties. The violations of the more important (for the considered hospital) soft constraints are penalized more severely.

The following soft constraints are considered in the paper:

1. Maximum number of consecutive work days.
2. Minimum number of consecutive work days.
3. Maximum number of shift assignments.
4. Maximum number of consecutive non-working days.
5. Minimum number of consecutive non-working days.
6. Maximum number of a certain shift worked.
7. Maximum number of consecutive working weekends.
8. Maximum number of working weekends in a month.
9. Requested days off.
10. Requested days on.
11. Requested shifts on.
12. Requested shifts off.
13. Requested shifts for each weekday.

1.3 Notations

The roster starts on the first day of the month ,and ends on the last day of the same month. There are 4 types of shifts that have to be assigned: morning shift (07:30 –

15:12), day shift (15:12 – 20:36), night shift (18:48 – 07:30) and duty shift (07:30 – 07:30 of the next day). Duty shift must be assigned only on weekends; the other shifts must be assigned only on workdays. The following notation will be used:

n – Number of days in a roster (it may vary from 28 to 31 days)
m – Number of HCW of specific skill available
i – Index of days, $i=1, 2, ..., n$
j – Index of HCW, $j=1, 2, ..., m$
M_i – Staff requirement for morning shift of day i
D_i – Staff requirement for day shift of day i
N_i – Staff requirement for night shift of day i
T_i – Staff requirement for duty shift of day i
$X_{i,j}$ – Decision variable. If HCW j is working on day i, then its value is 1, 0 otherwise.
$XM_{i,j}$ – Decision variable. If HCW j is assigned for morning shift on day i, then its value is 1, otherwise 0.
$XD_{i,j}$ – Decision variable. If HCW j is assigned for day shift on day i, then its value is 1, otherwise 0.
$XN_{i,j}$ – Decision variable. If HCW j is assigned for night shift on day i, then its value is 1, otherwise 0.
$XT_{i,j}$ – Decision variable. If HCW j is assigned for duty shift on day i, then its value is 1, otherwise 0.
$P_{i,j}$ – Penalty cost of HCW j working on day i
Max_A_j - Preferred maximum number of assignments for HCW j
Max_W_j – Preferred maximum number of working weekends for HCW j

1.4 The Mathematical Model

Since all hard constraints must be fulfilled, the main task is to minimize penalty cost related to the soft constraints. Problem can be formulated as follows [3]:

$$min \sum_{i=1}^{n} \sum_{j=1}^{m} P_{ij} X_{ij}. \tag{1}$$

The optimization should be performed taken into account the following constraints:

- The shift coverage requirements must be fulfilled [4]:

$$\sum_{j=1}^{m} XM_{ij} \geq M_i, \text{ for each } i = 1, \dots, n, \tag{2}$$

$$\sum_{j=1}^{m} XD_{ij} \geq D_i, \text{ for each } i = 1, \dots, n, \tag{3}$$

$$\sum_{j=1}^{m} XN_{ij} \geq N_i, \text{ for each } i = 1, \dots, n, \tag{4}$$

$$\sum_{j=1}^{m} XT_{ij} \geq T_i, \text{ for each } i = 1, \dots, n. \tag{5}$$

- After the night or duty shift must be at least 24 hours of rest time

$$XN_{ij} - X_{i+1,j} \geq 1, \quad \text{for each } i = 1, \dots, n, j = 1, \dots, m \text{ and } XN_{ij} \neq 0. \tag{6}$$

- Maximum number of shift assignments should be restricted

$$\sum_{i=1}^{n} X_{ij} \leq Max\_A_j, \text{ for each } j = 1, \dots, m. \tag{7}$$

- Maximum number of working weekends in a month should be restricted.

$$\sum_{i=1}^{n} XT_{ij} \leq Max\_W_j, \text{ for each } j = 1, \dots, m \tag{8}$$

2 The Shift Sequence Based Method

Shift sequence is a series of shifts (assignments) for each HCW. The shift sequence based method deals with scheduling problem using sequences rather than single shifts. Below we briefly review the method proposed in [5].

That method consists of two stages: the generation of shift sequences, and formation of the schedule according to the generated shifts.

Construction mechanism is discussed later in this chapter.

The hard and soft constraints are additionally categorized to the sequence, the schedule and the roster:

- Sequence constraints are applied when constructing shift sequences for each HCW.
- Schedule constraints are applied when combining schedule for each HCW.
- Roster constraints are applied when constructing an overall solution – roster.

Categorized constraints are listed in the following tables. Last column describes which category of constraints, listed above, it applies to.

Table 1. Hard constraints categorized to schedule and roster constraints

Hard Constraint	Category
1. The shift coverage requirements must be fulfilled. 2. After night shift must be at least 24 hours of rest time.	Roster Schedule
3. Duty shift must be assigned on weekends.	Schedule
4. HCW cannot be assigned to different assignments on the same time.	Schedule
5. Only duty shifts can be assigned on weekends.	Schedule

Table 2. Soft constraints categorized to sequence, schedule and roster constraints

Soft Constraint	Category
1. Maximum number of shift assignments.	Schedule
2. Maximum number of consecutive work days.	Sequence / Schedule
3. Minimum number of consecutive work days.	Sequence / Schedule
4. Maximum number of consecutive non-working days.	Schedule
5. Minimum number of consecutive non-working days.	Schedule
6. Maximum number of a certain shift worked.	Schedule
7. Maximum number of consecutive working weekends.	Schedule
8. Maximum number of working weekend in a month.	Schedule
9. Requested days off.	Schedule
10. Requested days on.	Schedule
11. Requested shifts on.	Sequence
12. Requested shifts off.	Sequence
13. Requested shifts for each weekday.	Schedule

2.1 The Construction of the Shift Sequences

In this stage, the shift sequences are constructed for each HCW, considering sequence constraints. Shifts sequences are ranked and sorted by their penalties so that firstly the best sequences would be considered in later stage.

To decrease the complexity, it is possible to limit the number of possible valid shift sequences by either considering only sequences with a penalty below a certain threshold, or by selecting the certain amount of the best sequences for each HCW in the second stage of the approach.

According to a number of usual number working days in a week, shift sequence length is up to 5 shifts. If there is the need of constructing sequences of length greater than 5, such sequences are constructed using combination of sequences of length up to 5 shifts. This combination is performed in the schedule and roster construction stage.

2.2 The Conctruction of Schedules

In the second stage of the approach, schedules for each HCW are constructed iteratively, using the shift sequences produced in shift sequences construction stage. Only schedule constraints are under consideration then constructing schedule for HCW. Roster constraints are applied then schedule is added to roster.

Basic algorithm of shift sequence based method:

Firstly HCW are ordered randomly later on, they are ordered by schedules penalty in a non-increasing order so that HCW who received the highest schedule penalties in the previous iteration are scheduled first at the current iteration.

```
Algorithm 1. Construct_Roster()
  construct and rank the shifts sequences for each HCW
  iteration = 0
  set max no. of iterations (MaxNoIter)
  randomly order HCW
  while (iteration < MaxNoIter)
    for each HCW ∈ ordered list of HCW
      Construct_Schedule(HCW, partial_roster)
      greedy local search to improve partial roster
    end of for
    store the best roster constructed so far
    calculate the penalty for the schedule of each HCW
    sort the HCW by their schedule's penalty in a non-
    increasing order
    increase iteration counter
  end of while
```

```
Algorithm 2. Construct_Schedule(HCW, partial_roster)
  set final threshold (f_threshold)
  set current threshold (curr_threshold = 0)
  while (curr_threshold ≤ f_threshold)
    for each sequence ∈ ranked list for the HCW do
      for each day in the planning period
        assign the sequence's  corresponding shifts based
        on the partial _roster if it does not violate any
        hard constraints and the penalty ≤ curr_threshold
    increase the value of curr_threshold
  return schedule
```

Schedule construction algorithm constructs schedule for HCW using low penalty shift sequences. Variable *curr_threshold* points what kind of sequences to use, i.e. if its value is 0, then only those sequences are used that has penalty equal to 0. If no valid assignment can be made for the current HCW, the shift sequence with the second lowest penalty is considered and so on.

During the roster construction, and after a schedule has been generated for the current HCW, an improvement method based on an efficient greedy local search is carried out on the partial roster. It simply swaps any pair of shifts between two HCW in the partial roster, as long as the swaps satisfy hard constraints and decrease the roster penalty. After all the schedules have been constructed and a roster has been built, there may still be some shifts for which the coverage is not satisfied. To repair this, a greedy heuristic is used. Each extra shift to be assigned is added to the HCW schedule whose penalty decreases the most (or increases the least if all worsen) on receiving this shift. After this repair step, the local search is applied once more to improve the quality of the overall roster.

3 Variable Neighbourhood Search in Shift Sequence Based Method

Shift sequence based method proposed in [5] builds schedule for HCW during a current iteration from scratch, only the order of HCW has changed. Variable neighbourhood search method builds schedule during current iteration according to results of previous iteration. During previous iteration used shift sequences are memorised and during next iteration schedule is build using memorised shift sequence's neighbour. The basic algorithm is presented by the following pseudocode:

```
Algorithm 3. Construct_Roster()
  construct and rank the shifts sequences for each HCW
  construct initial roster (curr_roster)
  set initial iteration counter (iteration = 1)
  set max no. of iterations (MaxNoIter)
  while (iteration < MaxNoIter)
    new_roster = mutate(curr_roster)
    if (penalty(new_roster) < penalty(curr_roster))
      curr_roster = new_roster
    else
      if (P > Random(0, 1))
        curr_roster = new_roster
    iteration = iteration + 1
  end of while
```

```
Algorithm 4. mutate(curr_roster)
  select HCW with worst schedule
  randomly select previously assigned shift sequence
  (prev_sequence)
  find suitable neighbour of prev_sequence
  (neighbour_sequence)
  replace prev_sequence with neighbour_sequence
  if some hard constraints are violated
    repair (add or remove shifts) using greedy local
  search
  return schedule
```

For creation of initial roster a unmodified shift sequence based method is used. Next rosters are created using variable neighbourhood search method.

Function *mutate* creates neighbor roster of previously built roster. We pick HCW with worst schedule (highest penalty value) and randomly select previously assigned shift sequence (*prev_sequence*). Then we search for suitable (no violations on hard constraints No.3 and No. 5) its neighbour shift sequence (*neighbour_sequence*). If neighbour_sequence is suitable we assign to HCW schedule and memorise the sequence, for later use. If *neighbour_sequence* is not suitable we look for another one (next closest neighbour), this process repeats until no suitable shift sequence can be found.

In case, then the *neighbour_sequence* cannot be found, shift sequence is replaced with empty shifts (days off).

In case, the neighbour sequence is shorter in length than previously assigned sequence, then the uncovered part of previously assigned sequence is replaced with empty shifts.

In case, the neighbour sequence is longer in length than previously assigned sequence and covers the part of the next sequence, then remainder of uncovered next sequence is replaced with empty shifts also.

For memorising of sequences used in schedule construction, schedule pattern is used. Schedule pattern is one dimensional array that has the same length as the schedule itself. Schedule pattern's items possible values:

- If scheduled free day (no shift) then item's value in pattern is -1
- If scheduled the *n*-th shift sequence from set of feasible shift sequences, then first item's value is number *n* and the rest of items (depends on sequence length) have assigned values -2.

For example, let's say 1 – morning shift, 2 – day shift, 0 – no shift. The *3-rd* shift sequence in ordered set of feasible shift sequences is (1 1 2 1) and schedule pattern is (-1 -1 3 -2 -2 -2 -1 -1). The schedule in this case would be (0 0 1 1 2 1 0 0).

Usually after replacement of shift sequences, appears hard constraints violations in the roster. To deal with this problem greedy local search method was used [10] that fixes violations to hard constraints. It adds additional shifts to HCW schedule whose schedule is under workload and removes shifts whose schedule is over workload.

In order to avoid the lack of hill climbing methods, i.e. do not to get stuck in local minima, the worse roster is accepted with a certain probability [9]

$$P = e^{-\frac{\text{new\_roster\_penalty} - \text{current\_roster\_penalty}}{iteration}} > Random(0,1) \quad (9)$$

4 Experimental Results

Experiments there made using Double Core 2.16 GHz processor. Software is written using C# programming language, each sub problem (doctors rostering, nurse rostering and auxiliary staff rostering) there solved in parallel (both methods) using different threads.

Tests were ran, separately, 100 times, using 500 iterations in each run, using the same initial roster.

Experimental results are listed in the following table.

Table 3. Experimental results

Method	Average Execution time (s)	Average Penalty Cost	Best Penalty Cost	Penalty Cost Deviation
Shift Sequence Based	500	17960	16540	879
Shift Sequence Method with Variable Neighbourhood Search	120	16825	14945	917

The results in Table 3 show that the shift sequence based method with variable neighbourhood search is faster than the original shift sequence based method without variable neighbourhood search. The experimental results also show that the shift sequence based method with variable neighbourhood search gives rosters of the better quality (less penalty cost) .

5 Conclusions and Further Work

The proposed in the present paper enhancement of the shift sequence based method by the variable neighbourhood search has improved the quality of the found rosters as well as the roster processing time.

Some of the soft constraints of the problem considered are better interpretable as the objectives than as the constraints. Therefore the proposed algorithm is planned to modify to be suitable for the multi-objective problems of the personal scheduling in hospitals.

Acknowledgements. The authors thank two unknown reviewers for their helpful suggestions. A.Žilinskas acknowledges the support by the Research Council of Lithuania under Grant No. MIP-063/2012.

References

1. Aickelin, U., Dowsland, K.: An Indirect Genetic Algorithm for a Nurse Scheduling Problem. Computers and Operations Research 31(5), 761–778 (2004)
2. Aickelin, U., Jingpeng, L.: An Estimation of Distribution Algorithm for Nurse Scheduling. Annals of Operations Research 155(1), 289–309 (2007)
3. Aickelin, U., White, P.: Building Better Nurse Scheduling Algorithms. Annals of Operations Research 128(1-4), 159–177 (2004)
4. Azaiez, M.N., Al Sharif, S.S.: A 0-1 goal programming model for nurse scheduling. Computers and Operations Research 32, 491–507 (2005)
5. Brucker, P., Burke, E., Curtois, T., Qu, R., Vanden Berghe, G.: A shift sequence based approach for nurse scheduling and a new benchmark dataset. Journal of Heuristics 16(4), 559–573 (2010)
6. Burke, E., Curtois, T., Post, G., Qu, R., Veltman, B.: A hybrid heuristic ordering and variable neighbourhood search for the nurse rostering problem. European Journal of Operational Research 188(2), 330–341 (2008)
7. Ikegami, A., Niwa, A.: A subproblem-centric model and approach to the nurse scheduling problem. Mathematical Programming 97(3), 517–541 (2003)
8. Jingpeng, L., Aickelin, U.: Bayesian Optimisation Algorithm for Nurse Scheduling. In: Scalable Optimization via Probabilistic Modeling, pp. 315–332 (2006)
9. Kundu, S., Mahato, M., Mahanty, B., Acharyya, S.: Comparative Performance of Simulated Annealing and Genetic Algorithm in Solving Nurse Scheduling Problem. In: IMECS 2008, vol. I (2008)
10. Selman, B., Kautz, H.A.: An Empirical Study of Greedy Local Search for Satisfiability Testing. In: Proceedings of the Eleventh National Conference of Artificial Inteligence, pp. 46–51 (1993)

Computational Study of Four Genetic Algorithm Variants for Solving the Quadratic Assignment Problem

Alfonsas Misevicius[1] and Evaldas Guogis[2]

[1] Kaunas University of Technology, Department of Multimedia Engineering, Studentų st. 50–400a/416a, LT–51368 Kaunas, Lithuania
alfonsas.misevicius@ktu.lt

[2] Singleton Labs, Narucio st. 31, LT–51405 Kaunas, Lithuania
evaldas.guogis@singleton-labs.lt

Abstract. Genetic algorithms (GAs) are a modern class of the metaheuristic methods that have been applied for the solution of different combinatorial optimization problems, among them, the quadratic assignment problem (QAP). Various modifications and alternatives of the genetic algorithms have been proposed in the artificial intelligence literature, and in many cases they performed quite successfully and efficiently. In this paper, we describe four variants of the genetic algorithm and some more or less slight variations of these variants. We also present the results of the computational experiments with both the real life like and randomly generated instances from the library of the benchmark QAP instances – QAPLIB.

Keywords: artificial intelligence, metaheuristics, (hybrid) genetic algorithms, combinatorial optimization, quadratic assignment problem.

1 Introduction

The quadratic assignment problem (QAP) [6, 17] can be formulated as follows. Given two integer matrices $\boldsymbol{A} = (a_{ij})_{n\times n}$ and $\boldsymbol{B} = (b_{kl})_{n\times n}$ and the set Π of permutations of the integers from 1 to n, find a permutation $\pi \in \Pi$ that minimizes

$$z(\pi) = \sum_{i=1}^{n}\sum_{j=1}^{n} a_{ij} b_{\pi(i)\pi(j)} \,. \tag{1}$$

The QAP belongs to an important and prolific domain of optimization problems known as combinatorial (discrete) optimization. Formally, these problems can be represented by a pair (S, f), where S corresponds to the set of feasible solutions (search space) and $f\colon S \to R^1$ denotes the objective function. In the case of the QAP, the solutions are represented by permutations (i.e., $S \equiv \Pi = \{\pi \mid \pi = (\pi(1), \pi(2), ..., \pi(n)), \pi(i) \in \{1, ..., n\}, i = 1, ..., n, \pi(i) \neq \pi(j), i, j = 1, ..., n, i \neq j\}$) and the objective function (denoted as z) is described as given above in formula (1).

The quadratic assignment problem also serves as a suitable and convenient platform for testing various optimization techniques, both exact and heuristic. Among

T. Skersys, R. Butleris, and R. Butkiene (Eds.): ICIST 2012, CCIS 319, pp. 24–37, 2012.

variety of heuristic methods, the genetic algorithms (GAs) – which are the main interest of the current work – have been proven to be extremely efficient, in particular, for the QAP [10, 20, 21, 32, 34].

This paper is structured as follows. In Section 2, we briefly review the GA variants that have been presented in the relevant literature. In Sections 3 and 4, we describe the basic features of the general framework of GA and propose our four GA variants. Further, we outline the experimental environment and present the results of the computational experiments with the proposed variants. The paper is completed with concluding remarks.

2 Related Work

Very briefly speaking, genetic algorithms are based on Darwinian notion of natural selection and follow an analogy with the Mendel's laws of transfer of traits [15]. In the context of combinatorial optimization, the GAs operate with populations of discrete solutions (like permutations of the QAP) so that the solutions correspond to (chromosomes of) individuals of a biological system[1] and the cost of a solution (the value of the objective function) is associated with the individual's fitness. The goal is to find high quality (if not optimal) solutions by applying an iterative process of succeeding virtual generations, which consists of the four basic operators: "selection", "crossover" ("recombination"), "mutation", and "replacement" ("update", "culling")[2].

For thorough studies on the principles of GAs, the interested readers are referred to [13, 26, 30].

To overcome the existing drawbacks and pitfalls and to enhance the performance of the early versions of GAs, the attention of the researchers has initially been paid to the fine-tuning of the parameter settings of GAs [28]. Later, several more deep conceptual improvements have been suggested, among them, compounded GAs [9], island-based GAs [5], messy GAs [14], parallel GAs [2]. Extensive research was carried out on the amendment of the particular components of GAs, including special parents' selection rules [11], innovative crossover operators [1, 8, 20], new population replacement strategies [33]. Considerable work has also been done on developing other specific modifications and extensions (see, for example, adaptive GAs [27], affinity GAs [36], double GAs [3], restart-based GAs using population diversification tools [22], GAs with random immigrants [7], GAs on graphics processing unit (GPU) [19], etc.).

The recent modern approaches rely on the inclusion of heuristic improvement algorithms into the traditional structure of GAs. The key goal here is to increase the GA efficiency by joining the explorative and exploitative forces of both the conventional GA operators and the incorporated heuristic optimizers (like descent/greedy local search (LS), simulated annealing (SA), tabu search (TS)). This

[1] In this case, the solution (permutation) π can be directly associated with a chromosome so that the single solution's element $\pi(i)$ corresponds to a gene occupying the ith locus of the chromosome.

[2] The crossover and mutation are also known as reproduction.

class of advanced GAs is commonly known as hybrid genetic (or memetic) algorithms (HGAs) [12, 18, 25] and the great potential of these algorithms has been revealed in various applications of computer science [29].

Further in this paper, we describe, in particular, the basic hybrid genetic algorithm and its variants to solve the QAP. We also present the experiments where the proposed variants are computationally tested and compared with each other.

3 Framework of the Hybrid Genetic Algorithm for the QAP: Main Features

The main features of the general framework of our genetic algorithm are as follows (these features are valid for all its variants).

- Our proposed algorithm is essentially the hybrid genetic algorithm in its nature, with the incorporated heuristic algorithm for the improvement of individuals (solutions)[3]. As a heuristic optimizer, we appply the iterated tabu search (ITS) algorithm [23], which may be seen as a series of runs of the self-contained tabu search procedure coupled with random mutations. The run time of the ITS algorithm can be fine-tuned by the controlling parameters Q and τ, where Q is the number of iterations (i.e., the number of calls to the self-contained TS procedure) within a single application of the ITS algorithm, and τ is the measure of search depth, i.e., the depth of the neighbourhood in the tabu search procedure. Note that, in the TS procedure, the variable oscillating tabu tenure is maintained. For more details, see [23].

  There are three usage modes of the ITS procedure: IteratedTabuSearch($\omega_1 Q$, τ), IteratedTabuSearch($\omega_2 Q$, τ), and IteratedTabuSearch($\omega_3 Q$, τ), where ω_1, ω_2, ω_3 serve as improvement factors, i.e., modifiers of the number of improvement iterations in different situations (in particular, initial population construction, post-reproduction and post-restart improvement/refinement (also see Fig. 1)).
- The population initialization is carried out in two phases. In the first phase, the population individuals (in fact, their corresponding chromosomes) are created in a pure random way. During the second phase, the population members produced in the first phase undergo a refinement process, with the intention of preparation of good starting conditions for the fast convergence of the GA. For the refinement, we employ the ITS procedure IteratedTabuSearch($\omega_1 Q$, τ), where the number of improvement iterations and the depth of search are equal to $\omega_1 Q$ and τ, respectively. The modifier $\omega_1 > 1$ is used to increase the number of iterations and extensify the search at the cost of smaller number of the future generations.

  It should be emphasized that our algorithm is implemented to operate with highly compact populations. With this model, we try to focus on the economy of

[3] Other terms can also be applicable when it comes to improvement of individuals, for example, "enhancement of individuals", "refinement of individuals", "upgrading of individuals". We will use some of them interchangeably.

computational resources when faced with time-consuming improvement algorithms. This concept is not new and it is in connection with what is known in the literature as "microgenetic algorithms" [16].

- Some variations of the extensified population initialization, at the cost of the decreased number of generations, are possible. The following are two proposed strategies, which have some relationship to so-called compounded GAs [9].
  - In the first, one-stage improvement strategy, the random population, P, of size $\alpha \times PS$ is initially generated, which is then improved and truncated by removing $(\alpha - 1) \times PS$ worst members. As a result, the size of the population, $|P|$, is equal to PS and it is not affected during the execution of the algorithm. The value of the regulatory parameter (coefficient) α is subject to the user's preference.
  - The second, two-stage improvement strategy is similar to the first one, except that an extra step of post-refinement is added before truncation. In our implementation, only half the population members are involved in the post-refinement process. Note that, in both strategies, we stick to increased number of improvement iterations, i.e., $\omega_1 > 1$.
- Regarding the reproduction process, we discuss our proposed different scenarios in Sect. 4. The differences are mainly due to variations in mating (recombination) tactics. Meanwhile, the mutation mechanism is retained the same in all variants, although it is implemented in a rather extraordinary way. Notice that mutations play very significant role in our GA in balancing the exploitative abilities of the aggressive heuristic algorithm. They are based on controlled randomized interchanges of genes (elements of a permutation) and are "tweaked" in the heuristic optimizer (i.e., the ITS algorithm), instead of being directly a part of the genetic algorithm itself. The mutation process is regulated by two main parameters: the frequency of mutations and the mutation strength. Remind that the tabu search process is "quantized" so that the number of "search quanta" is equal to Q ($Q > 1$) and the "quantum size" is equal to τ (in terms of the number of the search iterations). Then, the mutation procedure takes place every τ iterations and the mutation frequency within the ITS procedure is thus determined by the ratio $\frac{1}{\tau}$.
On the other hand, there are λ calls to the ITS procedure per one generation, which results in $\lambda(Q - 1)$ mutations per generation. The other regulatory parameter is the mutation strength, ρ, which is formally defined as:

$$\rho = HD(\pi, \tilde{\pi}) = \left|\{i \mid \pi(i) \neq \tilde{\pi}(i)\}\right|, \tag{2}$$

where $HD(\pi, \tilde{\pi})$ denotes the Hamming distance between permutations, and π, $\tilde{\pi}$ are the permutations (chromosomes) before and after mutation, respectively.

During the preliminary experiments, we found that the best results are achieved when ρ varies from $\lfloor c_1 n \rfloor$ to $\lfloor c_2 n \rfloor$, where n is the problem size and the values of the coefficients c_1, c_2 appear between 0.3 and and 0.9, depending on the problem instance.

- For the population replacement, we apply the generational update strategy, in particular, the so-called "$\mu + \lambda$"-scheme. In this case, it is assumed that the size of the parents' population, P, is equal to μ ($\mu = |P| = PS$) and the number of the offspring produced at the current generation (i.e., the size of an offspring pool, P^*) is equal to λ. We do not care about the duplication of individuals in the offspring pool for at least two reasons: 1) our randomized tabu search based optimizer can find different solutions even though the "starting point" is the same; 2) a special kind restart (diversification) procedure is included to reorganize the identical individual's chromosomes in the cases of the loss of genetic variance (see below). Another fact yet to mention is that the newly created offspring are not allowed to interact with the members of the parents' population until the current generation is completed and the pool becomes full. The population replacement is then carried out by removing λ worst individuals from the union of P and P^* to get a new population. (For example, if $\lambda = 1$, then the single offspring simply replaces the worst member of the population (provided that the offspring is better than the worst population member; otherwise, the offspring is disregarded).) In this way, the population size is kept fixed (i.e., $|P \cup P^*| - \lambda = PS + \lambda - \lambda = PS$); at the same time, the elitism is maintained, i.e., the population leader safely survives through all generations.
- As mentioned above, our GA employs a restart (diversification) mechanism to avoid the loss of genetic variability and premature convergence. The restart mechanism takes place in the cases only when the entropy of the population falls down below the specified limit (entropy threshold, ET). The population entropy $E(P)$ serves as a quantitative indicator of the population diversity and is calculated according to the following formula [31]:

$$E(P) = \sum_{i=1}^{n}\sum_{j=1}^{n} e_{ij} \Big/ n\log_2 n, \tag{3}$$

where $e_{ij} = \begin{cases} 0, \kappa_{ij} = 0 \\ -\frac{\kappa_{ij}}{PS}\log_2\frac{\kappa_{ij}}{PS}, \kappa_{ij} \neq 0 \end{cases}$ (here, κ_{ij} represents the number of times that the gene whose value is equal to i occupies the jth locus in the individuals' chromosomes of the current population P).

There are two main restart steps [22]. In the first step, we apply the mutation procedure with the maximally available mutation strength ($\rho = n$). Mutations are applied to all individuals but the best. This is to prevent going back to the visited solutions and to bias the search process into yet undiscovered search regions. At the same time, the elitism is preserved. The aim of the second step is to keep the high fitness of the solutions of the restarted population. For this purpose, we use the procedure IteratedTabuSearch($\omega_3 Q$, τ) with a somewhat increased number of the improvement iterations. This is easy to do by taking the coefficient ω_3 greater than 1 (we used $\omega_3 = 2$). After the restart, the genetic process proceeds in the ordinary way.

The whole genetic algorithm is continued until a pre-defined number of generations, N_{gen}, have been performed.

The description of the general framework of our genetic algorithm in the high-level pseudo-code form is presented in Fig. 1.

```
procedure HybridGeneticAlgorithm;
//input: n (the problem size), A, B (matrices),
//       N_gen – # of generations, PS – population size,
//       λ – # of offspring per generation, Q – # of improvement iterations, τ – depth of the search,
//       α – regulatory parameter for the population initialization,
//       ω1, ω2, ω3 – modifiers of the number of improvement iterations, ET – entropy threshold
//output: p* – the best solution found
begin
  create the random starting population P of size α×PS (P⊂Π);
  apply improvement procedure IteratedTabuSearch(ω1Q, τ) to
  the population members;
  in case of α>1, truncate the population P so that |P|=PS;
  π* := argmin_{π∈P} z(π) ; //π* – denotes the best so far solution
  for i := 1 to N_gen do begin
    P* := ∅;
    for j := 1 to λ do begin //λ offspring are created at each generation
      randomly select parents π′, π″ ∈ P for reproduction;
      get the offspring π‴;
      apply improvement procedure IteratedTabuSearch(ω2Q, τ)
      to the offspring π‴;
      if z(π‴) < z(π*) then π* := π‴; //the best so far solution is archived (saved)
      P* := P* ∪ {π‴}
    endfor;
    get new population P from the existing parents' population
    and the offspring pool P* (such that |P|=PS);
    if entropy of population P is less than ET then begin
      apply random mutations to all members of the current
      population, except the best one;
      apply improvement procedure IteratedTabuSearch(ω3Q, τ)
      to every (mutated) population member;
      if z(argmin_{π∈P} z(π)) < z(π*) then π* := argmin_{π∈P} z(π)
    endif
  endfor
end.
```

Notes. 1. The procedure IteratedTabuSearch serves as a heuristic optimizer for the improvement of the individuals (solutions). 2. The size of the starting population is regulated by the coefficient α ($\alpha \geq 1$). 3. The extensity of the improvement is controlled by the parameters Q (number of iterations), τ (search depth), and ω_1, ω_2, ω_3 (improvement factors).

Fig. 1. High-level pseudo-code of the hybrid genetic algorithm

4 Four Hybrid Genetic Algorithm Variants for the QAP

4.1 Variant 1 – Basic Hybrid Genetic Algorithm

Let us start with the basic hybrid genetic algorithm variant presented in Fig. 1. Note that, in variant 1 (and also in the remaining variants altogether), we use the extensified population initialization, as described above in Sect. 3. The iterated tabu search procedure with the embedded mutations acts as a heuristic improvement algorithm.

In variant 1, we make usage of the so-called cohesive crossover (COHX), which rationally exploits the problem-specific knowledge. The principle of COHX was originally proposed by Z. Drezner in [8], whereas we use our own COHX implementation [24]. The number of crossovers per single generation is handled by the parameter λ, whose value can vary between two opposites, 1 and *PS*, where *PS* is the actual population size. Also notice that the parents for crossover are selected randomly, uniformly. Of course, every offspring produced by COXH is subject to improvement by the procedure IteratedTabuSearch($\omega_2 Q$, τ) to ensure the permanent high quality of the individuals (solutions).

4.2 Variant 2 – Modified Hybrid Genetic Algorithm

This variant is almost identical to variant 1, with the exception of slightly modified cohesive crossover operator. The main steps of the modified COHX operator are as follows:

1) Check if the Hamming distance $HD(\pi',\pi'')$ between selected parents π' and π'' is below the specified distance threshold, *DT*. If this is the case, then go to step 2; otherwise, go to step 3.

2) Apply the mutation procedure to the worst parent (ties are broken randomly). After the mutation is completed, submit the mutated parent to the cohesive crossover procedure. The opposite parent remains unchanged.

3) Continue with the cohesive crossover procedure in the ordinary way.

The motivation of the current modification is to try to avoid potential negatives effects in the situations of mating of the parents, which are very similar to each other in terms of the genetic code.

We may think of the variants 1 and 2 as the artificial analogues of what the life scientists call sexual reproduction of organisms, whereas the rest of the variants (variants 3 and 4) are based rather on an emulation of asexual reproduction[4] in biological evolution.

---

[4] The Wikipedia article on asexual reproduction says: "Asexual reproduction is the process by which an organism creates a genetically similar or identical copy of itself without a contribution of genetic material from another individual." (see webpage: Reproduction - Wikipedia, the free encyclopedia, `http://en.wikipedia.org/wiki/Reproduction`).

4.3 Variant 3 – Asexual (Self-replicating) Hybrid Genetic Algorithm

This variant is obtained from the basic HGA version by simply eliminating the crossover operator and using the straightforward replication of the parent's (predecessor's) genetic material (i.e., the exact copy of the parent) as an offspring. We call the resulting algorithm with no recombination as an *asexual* (*self-replicating*) *hybrid genetic algorithm* (ASHGA). Doing so is not an original idea; however, we do not dispose of knowledge that such an approach has been examined in the hybrid-genetic-algorithm-for-the-QAP context. Note that this approach resembles the well-known particle swarm optimization (PSO) and artificial bee colony (ABC) algorithms.

4.4 Variant 4 – (Asexual) Hermaphroditic Hybrid Genetic Algorithm

Our fourth genetic algorithm variant turns out to be somewhere between the above asexual replicating algorithm and usual sexual variants, which use the recombination of the genetic information. The main distinguishing feature of the variant 4 is that the crossover operator is substituted by the mutation procedure identical to that embedded in the ITS algorithm. Instead of merging two parents, the mutation is applied to the single selected parent (predecessor), which is the one who is responsible for producing of the offspring. So, we feel that the metaphor "(*asexual*) *hermaphroditic hybrid genetic algorithm*" (HHGA) reflects the approach's nature quite adequately in this circumstance.

5 Computational Experiments

In order to evaluate the performance of the proposed genetic algorithm variants, the extensive computational experiments have been carried out on the benchmark QAP instances from the QAP library QAPLIB [4] (also see the web site `http://www.seas.upenn.edu/qaplib`). In particular, the following QAP instances were examined:

a) random instances (in QAPLIB, they are denoted by tai20a, tai25a, tai30a, tai35a, tai40a, tai50a, tai60a, tai80a, and tai100a; the numeral in the instance name indicates the size of the problem);

b) real-life like instances (these instances are denoted by tai20b, tai25b, tai30b, tai35b, tai40b, tai50b, tai60b, tai80b, tai100b, and tai150b).

These representative types of the QAP instances have been proposed by E. Taillard in [30] and [31].

We have experimented with the following four algorithm variants: BHGA – basic hybrid genetic algorithm; MHGA – modified hybrid genetic algorithm; ASHGA – asexual (self-replicating) hybrid genetic algorithm; HHGA – (asexual) hermaphroditic hybrid genetic algorithm. In addition, we were concerned with the following three variations of the population initialization: [1] one-stage improvement, $\alpha = 1$; [2] one-stage improvement, $\alpha = 4$; [3] two-stage improvement, $\alpha = 4$. On the whole, 12 modifications (variations) have been designed: $BHGA^1$, $BHGA^2$, $BHGA^3$, $MHGA^1$, $MHGA^2$, $MHGA^3$, $ASHGA^1$, $ASHGA^2$, $ASHGA^3$, $HHGA^1$, $HHGA^2$, $HHGA^3$. All the algorithms were implemented in the programming language Pascal (using Free Pascal compiler). The main controlling parameters of the algorithms used in the experiments are as shown in Table 1.

Table 1. Main controlling parameters

Parameter	Value		Remarks
	Random instances	Real-life like instances	
Population size, *PS*	30	10	
Number of generations, N_{gen}[†]	20	30	
Number of offspring per generation, λ	1	10	
Number of improvement iterations, Q[††]	20	5	
Search depth, τ[††]	$0.75n^2$	n	n is the size of the problem
Mutation strength, ρ[†††]	$[\lfloor 0.3n \rfloor, \lfloor 0.6n \rfloor]$	$[\lfloor 0.4n \rfloor, \lfloor 0.8n \rfloor]$	
Entropy threshold, *ET*	0.01	0.01	
Distance threshold, *DT*[††††]	$\lfloor 0.15n \rfloor$	$\lfloor 0.15n \rfloor$	
Modifiers (improvement factors):			
ω_1	10	5	
ω_2	1	1	
ω_3	2	2	

[†] In the extensified population initialization variants, the number of generations is correspondingly decreased so that the total CPU time is kept roughly the same.

[††] The most suitable values of the parameters Q and τ were determined during massive preliminary experiments whose results are omitted for the sake of brevity.

[†††] The mutation strength varies in the given interval, depending on the instance size.

[††††] This parameter is used in the variant 2 (MHGA).

The experiments were performed on four personal computers, each with an Intel Pentium 3 GHz single-core processor. So, all variants utilize approximately similar CPU times.

As a main performance criterion of the algorithms, we use the average relative deviation ($\bar{\delta}$) of the obtained solutions from the best known (pseudo-optimal) solution (BKS). It is defined by the formula: $\bar{\delta} = 100(\bar{z} - z^{\Diamond})/z^{\Diamond}\ [\%]$, where $\bar{z}$ is the average objective function value over 10 runs of the algorithm and $z^{\Diamond}$ denotes the best known value (BKV) of the objective function. (BKVs are from QAPLIB.) We also used two additional criteria: the number of the best known solutions found over 10 runs (C_{bks}) (in the cases of $\bar{\delta} > 0$) and the best found value (BFV) of the objective function (in the cases of $C_{bks} = 0$).

The results of the experiments with the different twelve GA variations on both the random and real life like QAP instances are presented in Tables 2–4.

Table 2. Results of the experiments with the different variants of HGA (I)

Instance	BKV	$\bar{\delta}$ / C_{bks} /BFV				Time‡ (sec.)
		BHGA^1	MHGA^1	ASHGA^1	HHGA^1	
tai20a	703482	**0.000**	**0.000**	**0.000**	**0.000**	3
tai25a	1167256	**0.000**	**0.000**	**0.000**	**0.000**	9
tai30a	1818146	**0.000**	**0.000**	**0.000**	**0.000**	13
tai35a	2422002	**0.000**	**0.000**	0.025/9	**0.000**	27
tai40a	3139370	0.093/0/ 3141702	0.083/0/ 3141702	**0.079**/0/ 3141702	0.114/0/ 3141702	280
tai50a	4938796	0.275/1	0.270/1	0.281/1	**0.260/1**	720
tai60a	7205962	0.251/0/ 7217850	**0.247**/0/ 7217850	0.258/0/ 7217850	0.250/0/ 7217850	1600
tai80a	13499184	**0.397**/0/13539166	0.404/0/13539166	0.415/0/13539166	0.399/0/13539166	4300
tai100a	21052466	**0.271**/0/21088768	0.304/0/21099586	0.294/0/21099586	0.291/0/21099586	11000
tai20b	122455319	**0.000**	**0.000**	**0.000**	**0.000**	0.4
tai25b	344355646	**0.000**	**0.000**	**0.000**	**0.000**	0.7
tai30b	637117113	**0.000**	**0.000**	**0.000**	**0.000**	1.6
tai35b	283315445	**0.000**	**0.000**	**0.000**	0.029/8	3
tai40b	637250948	**0.000**	**0.000**	**0.000**	**0.000**	4
tai50b	458821517	**0.000**	**0.000**	0.001/9	**0.000**	15
tai60b	608215054	**0.000**	0.003/9	0.003/5	0.000/7	28
tai80b	818415043	0.028/7	**0.000/9**	0.005/7	0.005/6	35
tai100b	1185996137	**0.010/9**	0.040/6	0.027/7	0.052/5	60
tai150b	498896643	**0.010/**1	0.047/1	0.028/**2**	0.047/0	1300
Average for tai*a:		**0.143**	0.145	0.150	0.146	
Average for tai*b:		**0.005**	0.009	0.006	0.013	
Cumulative average:		**0.070**	0.074	0.075	0.076	

‡ Average CPU time per run is given.

The following are the average deviations averaged over all three variations: BHGA – 0.0704; MHGA – **0.0698**; ASHGA – 0.0718; HHGA – 0.0723. From these summarized results and the results in Tables 2–4, it could be seen that the sexual reproduction variants appear slightly better than those of the asexual reproduction.

On the other hand, we obtain the following results if the average deviations for different population initialization modifications are averaged over four reproduction variants: ^{1} one-stage improvement ($\alpha = 1$) – 0.0736; ^{2} one-stage improvement ($\alpha = 4$) – 0.0719; ^{3} two-stage improvement ($\alpha = 4$) – **0.0676**. This time, we can observe that it is preferable to apply more extensive population initialization phase, sacrificing a certain amount of generations of the GA. Overall, the extensified variant of the algorithm MHGA (MHGA^3) appears as the best-ranked variant among all the variants studied.

It is also discovered from the experiments results that the real life like problems are quite easily solvable by our all genetic algorithm variants from both the solution quality and CPU time point of view. The CPU time for the random problems is, however, considerably larger than for the real life like problems. Despite this fact, the quality of the results for the larger random instances ($n \geq 40$) is relatively unsatisfactory and illustrates the evident hardness of the internal structure of random instances.

Table 3. Results of the experiments with the different variants of HGA (II)

Instance	BKV	$\bar{\delta}$ / C_{bks}/BFV				Time (sec.)
		BHGA^2	MHGA^2	ASHGA^2	HHGA^2	
tai20a	703482	**0.000**	**0.000**	**0.000**	**0.000**	*3*
tai25a	1167256	**0.000**	**0.000**	**0.000**	**0.000**	*9*
tai30a	1818146	**0.000**	**0.000**	**0.000**	**0.000**	*13*
tai35a	2422002	**0.000**	**0.000**	**0.000**	**0.000**	*27*
tai40a	3139370	**0.074**/0/ 3141702	**0.074**/0/ 3141702	**0.074**/0/ 3141702	**0.074**/0/ 3141702	*280*
tai50a	4938796	**0.275**/0/ 4941410	0.284/0/ 4950220	0.279/0/ 4941410	0.278/0/ 4941410	*720*
tai60a	7205962	0.264/0/ 7217850	0.271/0/ 7217850	**0.238**/0/ 7217850	0.251/0/ 7217850	*1600*
tai80a	13499184	0.427/0/13546150	0.422/0/13546150	0.424/0/13546150	**0.421**/0/13546150	*4300*
tai100a	21052466	0.281/0/21093586	0.278/0/21093586	**0.275**/0/21093586	0.289/0/21093586	*11000*
tai20b	122455319	**0.000**	**0.000**	**0.000**	**0.000**	*0.4*
tai25b	344355646	**0.000**	**0.000**	**0.000**	**0.000**	*0.7*
tai30b	637117113	**0.000**	**0.000**	**0.000**	**0.000**	*1.6*
tai35b	283315445	**0.000**	**0.000**	**0.000**	**0.000**	*3*
tai40b	637250948	**0.000**	**0.000**	**0.000**	**0.000**	*4*
tai50b	458821517	0.001/9	0.000/9	0.001/8	**0.000**	*15*
tai60b	608215054	**0.000**	**0.000**	0.005/8	0.005/8	*28*
tai80b	818415043	0.003/7	**0.000/8**	0.011/2	0.008/3	*35*
tai100b	1185996137	0.027/6	0.020/**8**	0.033/5	**0.012/8**	*60*
tai150b	498896643	0.023/2	**0.015/4**	0.023/**4**	0.027/0	*1300*
Average for tai∗a:		0.147	0.148	**0.143**	0.146	
Average for tai∗b:		0.005	**0.004**	0.007	0.005	
Cumulative average:		**0.072**	**0.072**	**0.072**	**0.072**	

Table 4. Results of the experiments with the different variants of HGA (III)

Instance	BKV	$\bar{\delta}$ / C_{bks}/BFV				Time (sec.)
		BHGA^3	MHGA^3	ASHGA^3	HHGA^3	
tai20a	703482	**0.000**	**0.000**	**0.000**	**0.000**	*3*
tai25a	1167256	**0.000**	**0.000**	**0.000**	**0.000**	*9*
tai30a	1818146	**0.000**	**0.000**	**0.000**	**0.000**	*13*
tai35a	2422002	**0.000**	**0.000**	**0.000**	**0.000**	*27*
tai40a	3139370	0.074/0/ 3141702	**0.067/1**	0.079/0/ 3141702	0.074/0/ 3141702	*280*
tai50a	4938796	0.229/1	**0.203/2**	0.236/1	0.223/1	*720*
tai60a	7205962	0.270/0/ 7218346	**0.225**/0/ 7208572	0.264/0/ 7218346	0.269/**1**	*1600*
tai80a	13499184	0.400/0/13544750	0.406/0/13543828	**0.396**/0/13544750	0.398/0/13544750	*4300*
tai100a	21052466	0.297/0/21106038	**0.283**/0/21102250	0.284/0/21102398	0.291/0/21102398	*11000*
tai20b	122455319	**0.000**	**0.000**	**0.000**	**0.000**	*0.4*
tai25b	344355646	**0.000**	**0.000**	**0.000**	**0.000**	*0.7*
tai30b	637117113	**0.000**	**0.000**	**0.000**	**0.000**	*1.6*
tai35b	283315445	**0.000**	**0.000**	0.019/9	**0.000**	*3*
tai40b	637250948	**0.000**	**0.000**	**0.000**	**0.000**	*4*
tai50b	458821517	0.000/9	0.000/9	0.001/8	**0.000**	*15*
tai60b	608215054	0.003/9	**0.000**	0.002/9	0.001/7	*28*
tai80b	818415043	**0.001/7**	0.008/4	0.005/6	**0.001**/6	*35*
tai100b	1185996137	0.019/**8**	0.014/7	**0.008**/7	0.012/**8**	*60*
tai150b	498896643	0.011/**1**	**0.010/1**	0.017/**1**	0.038/0	*1300*
Average for tai∗a:		0.141	**0.132**	0.140	0.139	
Average for tai∗b:		**0.003**	**0.003**	0.005	0.005	
Cumulative average:		0.069	**0.064**	0.069	0.069	

6 Concluding Remarks

In this work, we were concerned with studying the performance of the hybrid genetic algorithms for the hard combinatorial optimization problem, the quadratic assignment problem.

Four basic variants of the hybrid genetic algorithm and some variations were computationally tested and compared with each other with respect to the solution quality and run time.

The results from the computational study on the QAP instances from the QAP library QAPLIB show a potential of using the extensified heuristic search at the early phase of the population initialization. Also, it is demonstrated that the sexual way of reproduction of the offspring is slightly preferable to asexual reproduction.

We emphasize that the efficiency of the tested algorithm variants depends to large extent on the parameter calibration. This is especially important in the design of the hybridized algorithms, where more controlling parameters are involved to regulate the algorithms' behaviour.

The very significant learned fact is that the influence of the incorporated ad hoc heuristic algorithm becomes crucial within the hybrid GA architecture, where the explorative GA operators are effectively combined with exploitative heuristic improvement algorithm. It seems that the suitable heuristic optimizer – especially if it takes into account the problem-specific knowledge – controls the "fate" of the whole genetic algorithm.

References

1. Ahuja, R.K., Orlin, J.B., Tiwari, A.: A greedy genetic algorithm for the quadratic assignment problem. Comp. & Oper. Res. 27, 917–934 (2000)
2. Alba, E., Tomassini, M.: Parallelism and evolutionary algorithms. IEEE Trans. Evol. Comput. 6, 443–462 (2002)
3. Barrios, A., Ballestín, F., Valls, V.: A double genetic algorithm for the MRCPSP/max. Comp. & Oper. Res. 38, 33–43 (2011)
4. Burkard, R.E., Karisch, S., Rendl, F.: QAPLIB – a quadratic assignment problem library. J. Glob. Optim. 10, 391–403 (1997), `http://www.seas.upenn.edu/qaplib` (cited April 25, 2012)
5. Cantú-Paz, E.: Migration policies, selection pressure, and parallel evolutionary algorithms. J. Heurist. 7, 311–334 (2001)
6. Çela, E.: The Quadratic Assignment Problem: Theory and Algorithms. Kluwer, Dordrecht (1998)
7. Cheng, H., Yang, S.: Genetic algorithms with immigrants schemes for dynamic multicast problems in mobile ad hoc networks. Eng. Appl. Artif. Intel. 23, 806–819 (2010)
8. Drezner, Z.: A new genetic algorithm for the quadratic assignment problem. INFORMS J. Comput. 15, 320–330 (2003)
9. Drezner, Z.: Compounded genetic algorithms for the quadratic assignment problem. Oper. Res. Lett. 33, 475–480 (2005)
10. Drezner, Z.: Extensive experiments with hybrid genetic algorithms for the solution of the quadratic assignment problem. Comp. & Oper. Res. 35, 717–736 (2008)

11. Drezner, Z., Marcoulides, G.A.: A distance-based selection of parents in genetic algorithms. In: Resende, M.G.C., de Sousa, J.P. (eds.) Metaheuristics: Computer Decision-Making (Applied Optimization), pp. 257–278. Kluwer, Norwell (2003)
12. El-Mihoub, T.A., Hopgood, A.A., Nolle, L., Battersby, A.: Hybrid genetic algorithms: a review. Eng. Lett. 13, 124–137 (2006)
13. Goldberg, D.E.: Genetic Algorithms in Search, Optimization and Machine Learning. Addison-Wesley, Reading (1989)
14. Goldberg, D.E., Deb, K., Korb, B.: Messy genetic algorithms: Motivation, analysis and first results. Compl. Syst. 3, 493–530 (1989)
15. Holland, J.H.: Adaptation in Natural and Artificial Systems. University of Michigan Press, Ann Arbor (1975)
16. Kazarlis, S.A., Papadakis, S.E., Theocharis, J.B.: Microgenetic algorithms as generalized hill-climbing operators for GA optimization. IEEE Trans. Evol. Comput. 5, 204–217 (2001)
17. Koopmans, T., Beckmann, M.: Assignment problems and the location of economic activities. Econometrica 25, 53–76 (1957)
18. Hart, W., Krasnogor, N., Smith, J. (eds.): Recent Advances in Memetic Algorithms. STUDFUZZ, vol. 166. Springer, Heidelberg (2004)
19. Luong, T.V., Melab, N., Talbi, E.-G.: Parallel hybrid evolutionary algorithms on GPU. In: Proceedings of the IEEE World Congress on Computational Intelligence (CEC 2010), pp. 2734–2741. IEEE Press, Barcelona (2010)
20. Merz, P., Freisleben, B.: Fitness landscape analysis and memetic algorithms for the quadratic assignment problem. IEEE Trans. Evol. Comput. 4, 337–352 (2000)
21. Misevicius, A.: An improved hybrid genetic algorithm: new results for the quadratic assignment problem. Knowl.-Based Syst. 17, 65–73 (2004)
22. Misevicius, A.: Restart-based genetic algorithm for the quadratic assignment problem. In: Bramer, M., Coenen, F., Petridis, M. (eds.) Research and Development in Intelligent Systems, Proceedings of AI 2008, the Twenty-Eighth SGAI International Conference on Innovative Techniques and Applications of Artificial Intelligence, pp. 91–104. Springer, London (2008)
23. Misevicius, A.: An implementation of the iterated tabu search algorithm for the quadratic assignment problem. OR Spectrum 34, 665–690 (2012), doi:10.1007/s00291-011-0274-z
24. Misevičius, A., Rubliauskas, D.: Testing of hybrid genetic algorithms for structured quadratic assignment problems. Informatica 20, 255–272 (2009)
25. Moscato, P.: Memetic algorithms. In: Pardalos, P.M., Resende, M.G.C. (eds.) Handbook of Applied Optimization, pp. 157–167. Oxford University Press, Oxford (2002)
26. Reeves, C.R., Rowe, J.E.: Genetic Algorithms: Principles and Perspectives. Kluwer, Norwell (2001)
27. San José-Revuelta, L.M.: A new adaptive genetic algorithm for fixed channel assignment. Inform. Sci. 177, 2655–2678 (2007)
28. Schaffer, J.D., Caruana, R.A., Eshelman, L.J.: A study of control parameters affecting online performance of genetic algorithms. In: Schaffer, J.D. (ed.) Proceedings of the 3rd International Conference on Genetic Algorithms, pp. 51–60. Morgan Kaufmann, San Mateo (1989)
29. Sivanandam, S.N., Deepa, S.N.: Introduction to Genetic Algorithms. Springer, Heidelberg (2008)
30. Taillard, E.D.: Robust taboo search for the QAP. Parallel Comput. 17, 443–455 (1991)
31. Taillard, E.D.: Comparison of iterative searches for the quadratic assignment problem. Locat. Sci. 3, 87–105 (1995)

32. Tang, J., Lim, M.H., Ong, Y.S., Er, M.J.: Parallel memetic algorithms with selective local search for large scale quadratic assignment problems. Int. J. Innov. Comput., Inform. Control 2, 1399–1415 (2006)
33. Wu, Y., Ji, P.: Solving the quadratic assignment problems by a genetic algorithm with a new replacement strategy. In: Proceedings of World Academy of Science, Engineering and Technology, WASET, vol. 24, pp. 310–314 (2007)
34. Xu, Y.-L., Lim, M.H., Ong, Y.S., Tang, J.: A GA-ACO-local search hybrid algorithm for solving quadratic assignment problem. In: Keijzer, M., et al. (eds.) Proceedings of Genetic and Evolutionary Computation Conference, GECCO 2006, vol. 1, pp. 599–605. ACM Press, New York (2006)
35. Zhao, X., Gao, X.-S.: Affinity genetic algorithm. J. Heurist. 13, 133–150 (2007)

Generating Xpath Expressions for Structured Web Data Record Segmentation

Tomas Grigalis and Antanas Čenys

Department of Information Systems,
Vilnius Gediminas Technical University,
Vilnius, Lithuania
{tomas.grigalis,antanas.cenys}@vgtu.lt

Abstract. Record segmentation is a core problem in structured web data extraction. In this paper we present a novel technique that segments structured web data into individual data records that come from underlying database. Proposed technique exploits visual as well as structural features of web page elements to group them into semantically similar clusters. Resulting clusters reflect the page structure and are used to segment data records. During the segmentation process the technique also generates Xpath expressions. These expressions can be later used to directly extract data records from same template generated web pages without need to redo all the clustering and segmentation processes. Extracted structured data can be reused in wide range of applications, such as price comparison portals, meta-searching, knowledge bases and etc. The experimental evaluation results of proposed technique system on three publicly available benchmark data sets demonstrate nearly perfect results in terms of precision and recall.

Keywords: web data segmentation, structured web data, web data extraction, wrapper induction.

1 Introduction

Web page designers optimize representation of structured data for the human reader. An ability to segment and extract such data from the Web and represent it in a machine readable format would enable automatic population of knowledge bases. These, in turn, would advance the Web search engines towards the more expressive semantic level. Existing approaches typically search for repeating patterns in a web page by calculating the similarity between HTML tag tree nodes [1–5]. They do not show consistent results on different benchmark datasets and are prone to errors when dealing with contemporary WEB 2.0 pages.

We introduce a conceptually different structured web data segmentation approach. It clusters visually and structurally similar repeating web page elements to identify the underlying data records (DRs). Evaluation of the proposed technique on three public benchmark data sets demonstrates that the new method is consistent across all of them and produces remarkable results.

T. Skersys, R. Butleris, and R. Butkiene (Eds.): ICIST 2012, CCIS 319, pp. 38–47, 2012.

The technique is based on an observation that *structural* and *visual* properties are common to all web pages that represent data records from underlying databases. First, since a template is applied for each data record, the resulting HTML tag tree has repeating structural patterns. Second, the same visual style is used to represent an attribute of each data record to the viewer because it holds the same semantic meaning throughout the page. The resulting web page has structural and visual patterns that make interpretation of data easy for the human eye.

(a) Structured web data as input

Attribute	Xpath	Font	Color
£ 140	/html/body/div[1]/div[3]/a	Arial	EB103B
£ 105	/html/body/div[2]/div[3]/a	Arial	EB103B
£ 105	/html/body/div[3]/div[3]/a	Arial	EB103B
Xstring	htmlbodydivdiva-Arial,EB103B		
Xpath Rule	/html/body/div[*]		

(b) Cluster of price elements

IMG1; Panasonic Lumix DMC-SZ1...;	140 Inc. VAT; IN STOCK; Free delivery	
IMG2; Sony Cyber-shot DSC-W630...;	105 Inc. VAT; IN STOCK; Free delivery	
IMG3; Canon PowerShot A2400 IS...;	105 Inc. VAT; IN STOCK; Free delivery	

(c) Final segmentation result

Fig. 1. Example of segmentation process

The proposed technique combines structural and visual properties of each visible page element into a string representation, an *Xstring.* The structural property is represented by the path from the root node in the HTML tree to that particular element, i.e. its Xpath. Visual property is represented by formatting attributes of the element, e.g. font, color, etc. A cluster of similar Xstrings is formed from visually similar page elements, located in the same region of a web page, and, therefore, represents one data attribute. The set of clusters on the page represent the structure of underlying data records. Therefore, subsequent segmentation of relational data becomes straightforward.

As an example consider an excerpt from an online store of digital cameras in Fig. 1. The input consists of three data records represented using an unknown to us style template. Yet it is obvious that elements corresponding to the same attribute have the same visual appearance. For example, prices are shown using red Arial font. Fig. 1(b) shows the Xpath, font and color of the three elements corresponding to camera price. All the elements have the same Xstring representation and, therefore, fall into one cluster that represents the Price attribute. Xpath of the clustered elements is transformed into a data record segmentation rule (Xpath expression) as shown in the Figure. The segmentation rules are used to produce the final output as shown in Fig. 1(c). It is worth mentioning that segmentation process only segments data records. In other words, we find the boundaries (the start and the end) of each data record. After data records are segmented an extraction process usually follows.

2 Related Work

Since web data extraction has received a lot of attention there are proposed many approaches to segment and extract structured web data from web pages. All those methods can be divided into two broad categories: supervised learning approaches like Wien [6] or LiXto [7], which require some manual human effort to derive the segmentation and extraction rules, and automated data extraction systems like RoadRunner [8], DEPTA [5], VIDE [9], VINTS [10], which typically rely on the repetitive patterns in the HTML tags, work automatically and need no manual intervention to extract data. In this work we focus on the latter as we believe that only fully automatic systems can be applied for web-scale data extraction. Our proposed system belongs to this category.

One widely adopted technique to automatically detect, segment and extract data records is to search for repetitive patterns in HTML source code by calculating the similarity of HTML tree nodes. Variations of simple tree matching algorithm [11] are employed for this task [5, 1]. However, this technique finds it difficult to deal with structural irregularities amongst DRs , such as lists inside DRs [2].

Contrary to the above recent system VIDE [9] tries to not tie itself to HTML tree at all and instead depends purely on visual features of a web page. It builds a visual containment tree of a web page using patented VIPS [12] algorithm and then uses it instead of HTML tree. However if there are some unloaded images or missing style information in a web page VIPS may fail to build correct visual containment tree which leads to data segmentation and extraction problems [9].

Combining previous two approaches ViNTs [10] and DEPTA [5] systems try to exploit visual features of web pages to aid structural based data segmentation and extraction process. However, ViNTs system has not been reevaluated on WEB 2.0 pages, and evaluation of DEPTA demonstrated, that it cannot handle contemporary pages efficiently [2].

There is also relation to systems like TextRunner [13], which try to extract entities and their relationships from web pages using natural language processing and machine learning approaches, but those techniques usually work on regular text and are not suitable for dealing with structured data in web pages. By contrast, WebTables [14] extracts entities from structured web tables enclosed in <`table`> HTML tags. However, it would miss structured data presented in other form of html tags.

In summary, current algorithmic approaches often fail to achieve satisfactory performance in real-world application scenarios due to abundant structurally complicated WEB 2.0 pages. The system proposed in this work fully exploits visual and structural information and achieves remarkable results.

3 Structural and Visual Features of a Web Page Used in Data Record Segmentation

It is becoming very difficult to access and extract structured data from Web 2.0 pages, where many parts of page content are generated dynamically with Java scripts. This leads to a necessity to first of all render a web page in a contemporary web browser which executes all embedded Java scripts, applies cascading style sheets and etc. Only then we can leverage visual features of a web page, such as font color, font size for structured web data extraction. In this section the main visual and structural features of a web page are presented. We exploit these features for segmentation of structured web data records.

3.1 Structural Features of a Web Page

Each web page can be represented as a tree structure which is a fundamental data structure in XML documents. See Fig. 2 for an example. Thus a very useful approach for segmenting and extracting structured data from Hypertext Markup Language (HTML) documents is to employ Extensible Markup Language (XML) technologies to translate HTML to valid XML code. In this approach, HTML documents are first normalized into Extensible HTML (XHMTL) and then then processed by XML applications [15]. Xpath is a language used to navigated XML

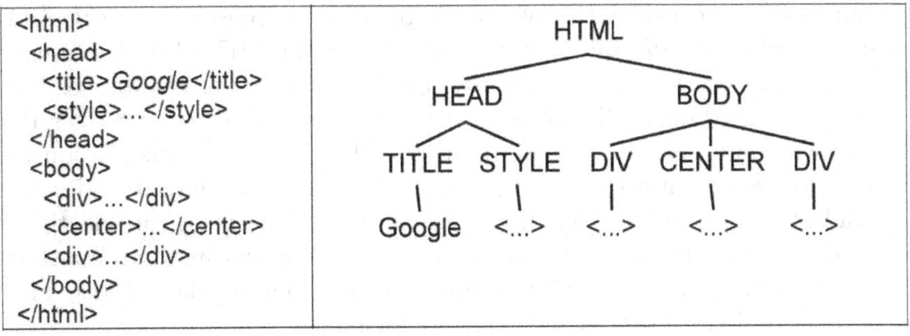

Fig. 2. HTML source code on left represented as tree structure on right

tree structure. The primary purpose of Xpath is to access parts of an XML document. Xpath is the result of an initiative to create a common syntax and semantics for functionality sharing between XSL Transformations and XPointer. Xpath operates on the abstract, logical structure of an XML document, rather than its underlying syntax (source code). Xpath gets its name from its use of a path notation as in URLs for navigating through the hierarchical structure of an XML document.

Xpath engine sees an XML document as a tree of nodes (see Fig. 2). The modeled HTML tree is widely used in structured data segmentation and extraction algorithms [5, 2], where very commonly dynamic programming is used to find similar branches of the tree. Similarity is determined by comparing every tree nodes with each another and if calculated similarity is higher than a predetermined threshold, then two branches of the tree are similar. Contrary to this comparison based approaches for searching similar trees, in this paper proposed algorithm employs location path enhanced with visual features of an element. A location path (Xpath) is one of most important kind of expressions in Xpath language. An Xpath locates and selects a set of nodes relative to the context node (usually a root node of the tree). The result of evaluating an Xpath is the node-set containing the nodes selected by the Xpath. Every Xpath can be expressed using a straightforward but rather verbose syntax. There are also a number of syntactic abbreviations that allow common cases to be expressed concisely [15].

There are two kinds of Xpath: relative location Xpath and absolute location Xpath. A relative Xpath consists of a sequence of one or more location steps separated by /. The steps in a relative location path are composed together from left to right. Each step in turn selects a set of nodes relative to a context node. Relative Xpath can improve the robustness of extraction wrapper. However, relative Xpath a not used in this paper proposed algorithm. Instead we exploit the absolute Xpath, which lets us better to compare HTML elements and find similar ones. An absolute Xpath consists of / optionally followed by a relative location path. A / by itself selects the root node of the document containing the context node. If it is followed by a relative location path, then the location path selects the set of nodes that would be selected by the relative location path relative to the root node of the document containing the context node [15].

For an example, consider the two kinds of Xpath expressions: *//title* (relative) and */html/head/title* (absolute). Both evaluated on HTML tree presented in Fig. 2 would return the same results: text node with string Google. XML documents operated on by Xpath must conform to the XML Namespaces Recommendation. The document tree contains nodes. In data segmentation and extraction process we use four kinds of nodes: root nodes, element nodes, text nodes and attribute nodes. Root node is regarded as the most top location of the HTML tree and is accessed every time we start evaluating and Xpath expression. Element nodes are the main nodes, which contains data items. There is an element node for every element in the document.

The task of structured data segmentation and extraction is to find data regions containing similar sets of data items (element nodes), group them into the sets (data records), segment and extract. Each element node has an associated set of attribute nodes, where the element is the parent of each attribute node. However, an attribute node is not a child of its parent element [15]. In the web page preprocessing stage we gather many visual clues about each element in the page and embed that information to the attribute nodes of each particular element.

3.2 Visual Features of a Web Page

HTML code together with images and visual style information is rendered in a web browser engine. The whole rendering process consists of computation of style data, frames construction, constant reflowing to represent changes or adding newly downloading information. The result is a web page as we see it in a web browser window. It has been showed [5] that using that computed visual information can improve data segmentation and extraction process. In this section we describe the two main visual features of a fully rendered web page, which helps to extract data: web page layout and elements font features. Each web page element let it be an image, a text string, or a white space, in a rendered web page takes some place. The whole web page can be seen as a coordinate system where x axis describes horizontal position and y axis describe vertical position. The most left top corner of a web page is a starting point, where x and y are equal to zero. The more some element is down in the page the bigger x value it has. And similarly the more some element is to the right in the page the bigger y value it has. The visual place each element takes in a page is bounded by a rectangular box and is called bounding rectangle. The left top corner of a bounding rectangle is positioned at an exact coordinate (x, y) in a web page. Each rectangle box, according to W3 specifications [16], has the following attributes: top, right, bottom, left, width, height. So the left, top, right and bottom properties are describing the bounding rectangle, in pixels, with the top-left relative to the top-left of the page view. Combined view of all rectangles makes a web page view. The proposed system makes use of these visual attributes to determine visual positions and sizes of extracting elements. In a rendered web page each visible HTML element has a rectangular bounding box. This box determines the spatial relations among web page elements. In clustering process we exploit the attributes of rectangular bounding box to determine the visible of the web page element. This is important, because we are only interested in

Table 1. An example of visual font features in a web page

HTML Font attribute	Attribute example	Rendered Text
size	15pt	text sample
color	red	text sample
weight	strong	**text sample**
underline	boolean: true	text sample
italic	boolean: true	*text sample*

visible web page elements. A text element in a web page can be modified by many different means. For example it is possible to set individual size, color, weight, strikethrough for each text word. Tab. 1 shows those features and theirs effects on text appearance in a web page. The change of any of mentioned font features, changes the visual representation of that text element. This is mainly used to discern one semantic type of text from another. Knowing these features and using them in the clustering process helps the proposed system to more effectively group semantically similar text to same clusters.

4 The Architecture of Proposed System

The object of structured web data segmentation is to segment all data records in a given web page. We assume that the web page is dynamically generated and hence an underlying template exists. Data items are usually located in data records, which all together make a data region. An ideal data record segmentation process identify (segment) all data records in the data region and no data record is missed or incorrectly segmented (for example, split apart).

The general architecture of our proposed system is presented in Fig. 3. Web page renderer is used to download HTML code from a web server and fully render web page in a browser window. That means that all JavaScript code is execute, Ajax request are called, all additional information of a web page, such as CSS (Cascading Style Sheets) files, images and etc., are downloaded. Our web page renderer is based on Mozilla Firefox web browser. In Web page preprocessing stage a JavaScript code injected into the web page to be able to extract visual features, such as font size, font style, font color and etc., of a web page. The extracted visual features of each HTML element node are then embedded into itself. The HTML tree with embedded visual data, enclosed text tags is passed to Xstring generation stage. Xstrings are modified Xpath location

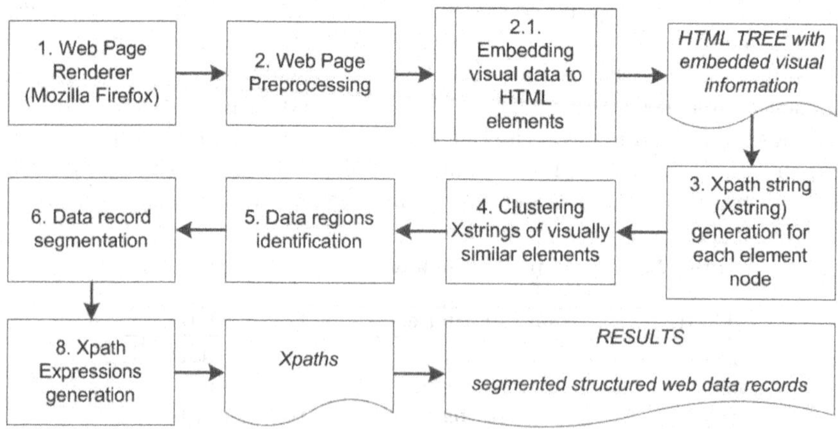

Fig. 3. The architecture of proposed system

strings with added visual data. So Each visible web page elements is represented by a Xstring, by which the elements are later clustered. As we see in Fig. 1(b) Xstring consists of a) tag names from Xpath b) visual features of that element (font style, color, weight, etc.). Structural features (string of tag names) identifies position in HTML document. Visual features enhance understanding of semantic similarity between web page elements. Clustering stage clusters Xstrings into separate clusters, i.e. all visible web page elements are clustered according to their Xstring. The resulting clusters contain only semantically similar web page elements Data records extractor using from clustering stage inherited information identifies data regions available on the web page. Each data region gets rules (Xpath expressions) to segment data records, which are inside particular data region.

5 Experimental Evaluation

To evaluate proposed approach we use the following three publicly available benchmark datasets containing in total of 7098 data records: 1) TBDW Ver. 1.02 [17], 2) ViNTs dataset 2 [10], 3) M. Alvarez et al. [1]. See Tab. 2 for details.

Table 2. The details of three public benchmark data sets used in experimental evaluation

Data Set	TBDW [17]	ViNTs-2 [10]	Alvarez [1]
Sites	51	102	200
Pages per site	5	11	1
AVG records	21	24	18
Total records	1052	2489	3557

These data sets contain web pages retrieved from different web sites. Each web page contains DRs, which should be extracted. During evaluation we take only one web page per site because all pages in one site use the same template. Websites were rendered using Mozilla Firefox web browser. Since some of the web pages from the data sets had malformed HTML source code we also ran the Tidy program [18] to clean some of the pages as it was done in RoadRunner [8] and DEPTA [5] experiments.

Following the works of other authors [1, 2, 9, 5, 10] in structured data extraction we use three evaluation measures which come from information retrieval field: precision, recall and F-score. For web data record segmentation, the recall and precision are computed based on the total number of correctly segmented data records in all pages and the actual number of data records in these pages. See (1) formula for precision, (2) for recall and (3) for F-Score calculation. In these formulas CSDR is correctly segmented data records, SDR is segmented data records, ADR is actual data records that are on particular web page.

$$Precision = \left(\frac{CSDR}{SDR}\right) \quad (1)$$

$$Recall = \left(\frac{SDR}{ADR}\right) \quad (2)$$

$$F - Score = \left(\frac{2 \times Precision \times Recall}{Precision + Recall}\right) \quad (3)$$

Table 3. Experimental evaluation results of proposed system on three public benchmark data sets

Data Set	TBDW	VINTS-2	Alvarez
Precision	99.81%	98.57%	98.20%
Recall	99.52%	98.51%	99.69%
F-Score	0.997	0.985	0.99

As we can see from Tab. 3 proposed approach consistenly on all three data sets demonstrate very high precision, recall and F-Score. The main problems that occurred while empirically evaluating structured web data segmentation our proposed technique are related to malformed HTML source code, extreme similarity (visual and structural) between records and non-records and incorrect segmentation of data region. Also we ran into web page rendering time problem. The time needed to render a contemporary web page may take around 10 seconds which becomes a bottleneck in whole structured data extraction process. We will address these issues in our future work.

6 Conclusions

In this paper we have addressed the problem of structured web data record segmentation. While reviewing the current state-of-the-art work we concluded that there is a need for scalable effective automatic structured web data segmentation and extraction system. To deal with segmentation problem we propose a novel technique, that exploits visual and structural features of a web page to segment structured data records from web pages. Experimental evaluation of proposed system on three publicly available data sets, containing more than seven thousand actual data records, revealed, that our solution achieves nearly perfect results, where precision and recall are higher than 98% on all of three public benchmark data sets.

References

1. Álvarez, M., Pan, A., Raposo, J., Bellas, F., Cacheda, F.: Extracting lists of data records from semi-structured web pages. Data & Knowledge Engineering 64(2), 491–509 (2008)

2. Jindal, N., Liu, B.: A generalized tree matching algorithm considering nested lists for web data extraction. In: The SIAM International Conference on Data Mining, pp. 930–941 (2010)
3. Kayed, M., Chang, C.: Fivatech: Page-level web data extraction from template pages. IEEE Trans. on Knowl. & Data Engineering 22(2), 249–263 (2010)
4. Su, W., Wang, J., Lochovsky, F., Liu, Y.: Combining tag and value similarity for data extraction and alignment. IEEE Trans. on Knowl. & Data Engineering 99, 1 (2011)
5. Zhai, Y., Liu, B.: Web data extraction based on partial tree alignment. In: Proc. of the 14th International Conference on World Wide Web, pp. 76–85. ACM (2005)
6. Kushmerick, N.: Wrapper induction for information extraction. PhD thesis, University of Washington (1997)
7. Baumgartner, R., Flesca, S., Gottlob, G.: Visual web information extraction with lixto. In: Proc. of the International Conference on Very Large Data Bases, pp. 119–128 (2001)
8. Crescenzi, V., Mecca, G., Merialdo, P., et al.: Roadrunner: Towards automatic data extraction from large web sites. In: Proc. of the International Conference on Very Large Data Bases, pp. 109–118 (2001)
9. Liu, W., Meng, X., Meng, W.: Vide: A vision-based approach for deep web data extraction. IEEE Transactions on Knowledge and Data Engineering 22(3), 447–460 (2010)
10. Zhao, H., Meng, W., Wu, Z., Raghavan, V., Yu, C.: Fully automatic wrapper generation for search engines. In: Proc. of the 14th International Conference on World Wide Web, pp. 66–75. ACM (2005)
11. Yang, W.: Identifying syntactic differences between two programs. Software: Practice and Experience 21(7), 739–755 (1991)
12. Cai, D., Yu, S., Wen, J., Ma, W.: Vips: a vision based page segmentation algorithm. Technical report, Microsoft Technical Report, MSR-TR-2003-79 (2003)
13. Banko, M., Cafarella, M., Soderland, S., Broadhead, M., Etzioni, O.: Open information extraction for the web. University of Washington (2009)
14. Cafarella, M., Halevy, A., Wang, D., Wu, E., Zhang, Y.: Webtables: exploring the power of tables on the web. Proc. of the VLDB Endowment 1(1), 538–549 (2008)
15. Clark, J., Derose, S., Corp, I.: XML Path Language, XPath (1999), `http://www.w3.org/TR/xpath/`
16. van Kesteren, A.: CSSOM View Module (2011), `http://www.w3.org/TR/cssom-view`
17. Yamada, Y., Craswell, N., Nakatoh, T., Hirokawa, S.: Testbed for information extraction from deep web. In: Proc. of the 13th International World Wide Web Conference on Alternate Track Papers & Posters, pp. 346–347. ACM (2004)
18. Paehl, D.: HTML Tidy Library Project Table of Contents (2012), `http://tidy.sourceforge.net/`

News Media Analysis Using Focused Crawl and Natural Language Processing: Case of Lithuanian News Websites

Tomas Krilavičius[1], Žygimantas Medelis[2] Jurgita Kapočiūtė-Dzikienė[1], and Tomas Žalandauskas[1]

[1] Baltic Institute of Advanced Technology, Saultekio 15, Vilnius
{t.krilavicius,j.kapociute-dzikiene}@bpti.lt, tomas@bpti.lt
http://www.bpti.eu
[2] UAB "Tokenmill"
zygimantas.medelis@tokenmill.lt
http://www.tokenmill.lt

Abstract. The amount of information that is created, used or stored is growing exponentially and types of data sources are diverse. Most of it is available as an unstructured text. Moreover, considerable part of it is available on-line, usually accessible as Internet resources. It is too expensive or even impossible for humans to analyze all the resources for a required information. Classical Information Technology techniques are not sufficient to process such amounts of information and render it in a form convenient for further analysis. Information Retrieval (IR) and Natural Language Processing (NLP) provide a number of instruments for information analysis and retrieval. In this paper we present a combined application of NLP and IR for Lithuanian media analysis. We demonstrate that a combination of IR and NLP tools with appropriate changes can be successfully applied to Lithuanian media texts.

Keywords: Information Retrieval, Natural Language Processing, stemming, focused crawl, Lithuanian language.

1 Introduction

The amount of information that is created, used or stored is growing exponentially and types of data sources are diverse. Most of it is available as an unstructured text. Considerable part of information today is created and accessible on-line, usually via Internet. However, it is too expensive or even impossible for humans to search for required information in such huge amount of different resources. Classical Information Technologies are not ready to cope with such amounts and heterogeneity of information as well [1]. *Information Retrieval* (IR) and *Natural Language Processing* (NLP) provide a number of instruments for information analysis and retrieval [2,3]. *Text analytics* [4] combine both these both fields as well as *Data Mining* [5] and *Knowledge Management* [6]. Text analytics embodies such applications, as machine translation, opinion mining and

T. Skersys, R. Butleris, and R. Butkiene (Eds.): ICIST 2012, CCIS 319, pp. 48–61, 2012.

sentiment analysis, media monitoring, semantics aware information retrieval and much more. There exists different techniques [2,3] and tools [7,8,9] that can be applied to develop text analytics applications. Most of them support only English and other popular languages, such as Spanish, French or German. Solutions for Lithuanian language are under development or in future plans only. Lithuanian (as well, as Latvian, some Slavic and other languages) differs substantially from English: it is highly inflective (e.g, declensions for nouns and adjectives), has many diminutives, reflexives, hypocoristic and pronominal words, does not have strict sentence structure, etc. It is recommended incorporating mechanisms, considering language specific, to achieve higher accuracy for highly inflective languages.

In this paper we are trying to kill two birds with one stone: investigating applicability of existing techniques and identifying the main missing solutions and in such a way drawing future research plans for Lithuanian language. We combine it with a development of Lithuanian media monitoring application prototype. Such system could be used for a set of different tasks: from a trivial tracking of some advertisement or political elections campaign to identifying selected adds with illegitimate content and their authors.

Of course, there are quite a few interesting results that discuss specifics of Lithuanian language. In [10] the way of building cache-based statistical model is discussed. Formal description of Lithuanian language is given in [11]. Several different approaches for classifying Lithuanian documents is discussed in [12] and [13]. A morphological annotation tool *Lemuoklis* is presented in [14]. General overview of Lithuanian NLP infrasture development is given in [15]. However, neither of results cover the whole chain of tools, most of them take an academic standpoint and do not discuss application of the proposed solutions in practice.

We start the paper from the concise description of the problem in Sect. 2. Usually, such solutions involve a chain of tools [2,3] that are used stepwise to achieve an anticipated result. Therefore, we define basic media monitoring system, and go through all the steps investigating their readiness for Lithuanian language in Sect. 3. Then we describe implementation and experimental results in Sect. 4. In Sect. 5 we give conclusions and draw future research plans.

2 Problem

The goal of the proposed system is to perform monitoring of Lithuanian news media, identifying main topics and facts. Work focuses only on Lithuanian web pages. Moreover, only media articles are considered, social media generated content is omitted in the current system. Articles from given sources should be downloaded and selected content should be annotated. Sample text is presented in Fig. 1.

3 Architecture and Tools

The purpose of Internet media monitoring and analysis system is to collect *relevant information* from the Internet, *prepare* text for analysis, extract relevant

Prokurorai pripažino: sąsajomis su čečėnų teroristais įtariama klaipėdietė ketino įvykdyti teroro aktą Rusijoje (papildyta, video) (147)

BNS ir lrytas.lt inf. 2010-05-04 15:49

Teisėsaugos pareigūnams pernai rudenį pavyko užkirsti kelią teroro aktui, kurį Lietuvos pilietė Eglė Kusaitė ketino įvykdyti Rusijoje - susisprogdinti kariniame objekte ir nusinešti su savimi kuo daugiau žmonių gyvybių, antradienį pranešė prokuroras.

Balandžio mėnesį mirtininkės susisprogdino Maskvos metro. Per sprogimą žuvo 40 žmonių. „Reuters"

Žiūrėkite reportažą.

Tokias detales antradienį per Lietuvos Apeliacinio teismo (AT) posėdį atskleidė Generalinės prokuratūros prokuroras Justas Laucius.

Fig. 1. Sample Article

information from the text and store it in the semantic document database. System user interface should provide convenient tools for search and analysis of documents stored in the database, e.g. *faceted search* and visualizations. We define all the components depicted in Fig. 2 in detail and indicate those parts that need further investigation.

A Focused Crawler is a web crawler that attempts to download only web pages that are relevant to a pre-defined topic or set of topics. This strategy serves two purposes in the context of media monitoring.

Firstly, it allows ignoring irrelevant content like advertisements or topics of no interest to a particular business domain. Secondly, it allows partitioning content by topic and applying the most suitable text analysis strategies to a given topic.

It employs several types of filters discriminating relevant information.

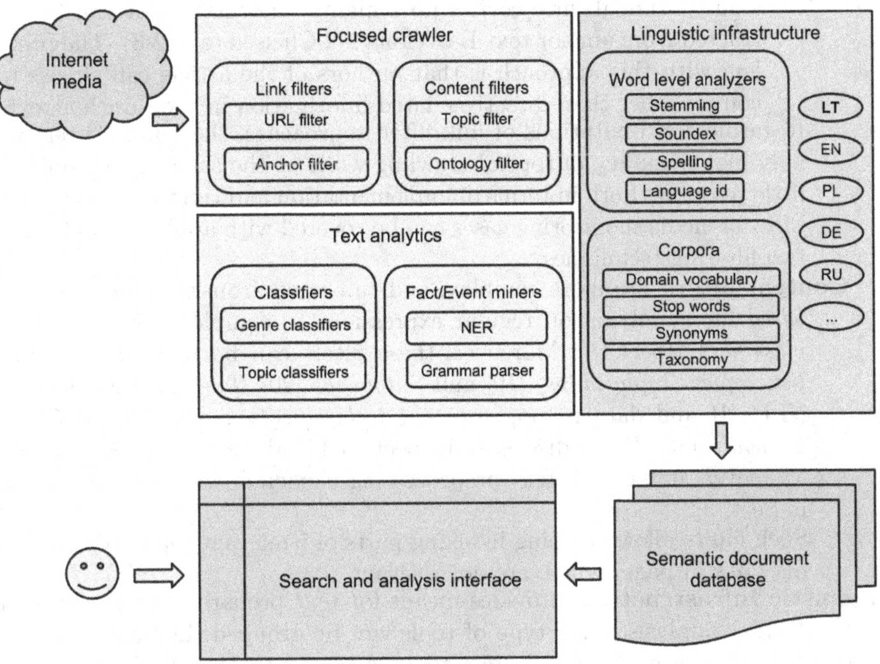

Fig. 2. General Architecture of Media Analysis System

Link filters are simplest way to separate relevant content.

Web crawler expands its crawl frontier by analyzing links present on currently processed pages. Thus, by controlling which links are added to the crawl frontier, crawler can be guided towards fetching only relevant links.

Links carry two attributes which can be analyzed for their suitability: `a.href` HTML element and anchor text.

URL filter processes `.href` elements, thus based on the content of address URL filters prohibit or allow certain links to be passed to crawl frontier. For example, if we are dealing with *sports* domain then only links which contain sports related vocabulary will be passed on. The following addresses will be considered as acceptable: `www.example.org/sports`, `www.example.org/barcelona's-ep-guardiola-on-brink-leaving-club`; while `www.example.org/food` will not. Obvious limitation of URL filter approach is that it will not work with sites where URLs carry no topical information, e.g. `www.example.org/17855980`. In this case other link filtering techniques must be applied.

Anchor text filter works in exactly the same manner except that it is not the content of address which is analyzed but anchor text. Anchor text is expressed in the following HTML code

```
<a href="www.ex.org/17855">Barcelona 2-2 Chelsea (agg 2-3)</a>
```

Thus, although href carries no semantic information, it can be extracted from anchor text Barcelona 2-2 Chelsea (agg 2-3). The problem with this approach is that authors of the article can choose to convey other than directly related information in their anchor text.

Regardless of limitations of link filter approaches, they provide reasonably high accuracy of topical crawling while at the same time requiring little resources both in terms of implementation and run time processing. Most of media monitoring cases can be covered with application of those two filtering techniques.

Content filters are more complex, and can range from the simple *terms-based* filters relying on regular expressions to complex *text documents classifiers* [16,17,18]. Moreover, these filters can be based on a *words list*, *topics (topic maps)* [19] and *ontologies* [20]. They combine several NLP, IR and data mining topics, i.e *classification* and *Named Entity Recognition (NER)*, discussed in Sect. 3.3 and Sect. 3.4, respectively. Moreover, it includes text preprocessing elements, which are discussed in Sect. 3.2.

Such filters allow skipping indexing parts of irrelevant topics or discarding links in pages which are not relevant.

Linguistic Infrastructure provides means for text preparation and usage in the further analysis. Such type of tools can be grouped differently, we set apart *corpora*, *word level* and *other* tools. All these tools are language-based and usually can not be directly applied to other language. Relevant aspects of such tools are discussed in Sects. 3.2 and 3.1.

Corpora vary in size and type can be used for different tasks. *Stop words* (Sect. 3.2) can be used to get rid of irrelevant words minimizing dictionary in such way. *Thesaurus* (or *dictionary of synonyms*) allows identifying/looking not only for the required terms, but for their synonyms, in such a way improving recall [2,3].

Word level analyzers operate at the word level. Some of them, e.g. *stemmer* [21] or *Soundex* [22] are used for identification of the basic word form. Spellcheckers are used to alter misspelled words with the correct ones.

Other tools provide additional information about the text, e.g. *language identifier* detects language and *sentence splitter* detects sentence boundaries.

Text Analytics describe a set of linguistic, statistical and machine learning techniques that model and structure information content of textual sources.

Classifiers usually assign particular meaning (certain category or topic) to the document. See Sect. 3.3 for more details.

Fact/Event miners usually operate in phrase or word level. *Named Entity Recognition* (NER) tools (Sect. 3.4) usually search for location names, person names, organization names, and miscellaneous types of entities.

Grammar Parsers There definition of *grammar* is somehow lax or broad. There by grammar we understand any patterns in the text which can be identified by a set of rules, e.g. grammar rule to identify person names would be defined along the following lines:

- Tokenize text;
- Seek two or up to four consecutive tokens which start with a capital letter;
- If the words are not surrounded by quotes and are not followed by company identification like Ltd or UAB, then mark that sequence as person name.

Semantic document database is used to store not only documents, but other relevant information, e.g named entities, basic word forms, classes, etc. However, it is language agnostic and, therefore, is not a part of our research.

Search and Analysis Interface allows exploring and analyzing information in a convenient manner [2,3]. Whereas a particular domain and language should be considered while designing it, in general, methods are language agnostic and are omitted from this research.

In the above list we provide a concise and by no means complete list of methods relevant for media monitoring tasks. In the following sections we continue analyzing the most relevant elements of text analytics chain.

3.1 Corpora

Quite a few Lithuanian language corpora are collected already, see [23] for a comprehensive review, and the number of corpora is increasing. However, most of the corpora are proprietary, i.e. created and owned by different institutions (usually universities or institutes), and the conditions for using them, getting support, up-times warranties are not usually clear. Some corpora for Lithuanian language are freely available:

Stop words list is provided in TokenMill's Lithuanian language pack [24]. See Sect. 3.2 for application of stop words.

Hunspell spell checking dictionary is freely available, see [25] and [26] for the details.

Dictionary of Synonyms (Sinonimų žodynas) is a small thesaurus, available at `http://sinonimai.lt/`

3.2 Text Preprocessing

Text preprocessing takes raw text in text, Word document, PDF or some other format and produces a document in the chosen document representation form. It takes a lot of steps, and some of them are rather complicated. We are not getting in details here (see [2,3] for the details), because it is not an object of this project, however some steps or aspects are quite important in our context.

Document and Structure. Documents are provided in some electronic format, that should be recognized first. Sentences and other structural elements should be detected also. Then words/terms should be separated. Mix of encodings and different languages used in the same document can complicate words, or even, sentences detection process.

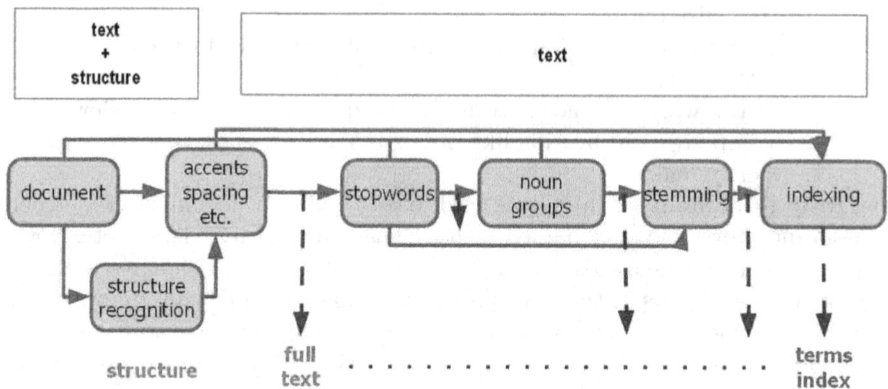

Fig. 3. Text Preprocessing Steps

Language identification [27] is the process of determining which natural language given content is in. Traditionally, identification of written language - as practiced, for instance, in library science - has relied on manually identifying frequent words and letters known to be characteristic of particular languages. More recently, computational approaches that view language identification as a special case of text categorization and rely on statistical methods, have been applied to the problem.

Lithuanian language identification package is available as a part of TokenMill's Lithuanian language pack [24].

Diacritical signs. Diacritical signs can be removed, left or two forms of term stored.

Stopwords. In computing, *stop words* [28] are words which are filtered out prior to, or after, processing of natural language data (text). It is controlled by human input and not automated. There is no one definite list of stop words which all tools use, if even used. Some tools specifically avoid using them to support phrase search.

Any group of words can be chosen as the stop words for a given purpose. For some search machines, these are some of the most common, short function words, such as the, is, at, which and on. In this case, stop words can cause problems when searching for phrases that include them, particularly in names such as 'The Who', 'The The', or 'Take That'.

Lithuanian stop words list is available in TokenMill's Lithuanian language pack [24]. However, the list should be tuned for a specific task, and often it is easy to generate a list just by analyzing word frequency in corpora.

Noun groups and stemming. Words can be reduced to their base forms, that is especially important for Lithuanian language, because it is highly inflective. One of the serious complications in case of customer care messages is that language is usually non-normative (in the sense of alphabet, abbreviations, pictograms, etc.), therefore some of current techniques can be useless.

Soundex [29,30,22,31] is a phonetic algorithm for indexing names by sound, as they are pronounced. General version of Soundex [22] is a part of most of the database management systems, and often used in census and other similar systems. For Lithuanian language at least two versions of Soundex are proposed. In[29,30] speech analysis techniques were used to group Lithuanian vowels by their pronunciation. In [31] a version of Lithuanian Soundex for geocoding is presented, i.e. for conversion of a textual address to a geographical locations. However, it is a combination of several different phonetic algorithms that ignores diacritics, i.e. it is rather "typex" algorithm that reflects spelling rather than pronunciation.

In linguistic morphology and information retrieval, *stemming* is the process for reducing inflected (or sometimes derived) words to their stem, base or root form. A working version of Lithuanian language stemmer [32] is available as a part of TokenMill's Lithuanian language pack [24].

Indexing produces a bag of words or other chosen document representation.

3.3 Classification and Clustering

Text classification is the process assigning particular category (or class label) (topic, genre, style, etc.) to an incoming classifiable text document, therefore it is possible only if solution is based on the certain rules (defined as a *model*). The model is usually created beforehand (during the learning phase of classification process) and then is used (during testing and operation phase). Depending on the training data (labeled or unlabeled) available during the learning phase, classification process can be performed differently and thereby have different automation levels. On purpose to operate with the labeled data, it has to be manually prepared beforehand: i.e. the class of each text document in the training data must be predefined by human expert. After that the significant features, associated with the different classes are extracted from the labeled data and integrated into the model. Usage of labeled training data requires human intervention, but guarantees that created model will have human desirable classes and will be based on the same perception about classification technique. Usage of unlabeled training data allows full automation, but requires additional stage, defined as clustering . The outcome of clustering process is the training data containing text documents with the automatically attached class labels. Automatically attached class labels sometimes differ from the human perception of classification, besides class labels often do not have associative meanings with the class. Mentioned shortcomings do not shade the main advantage to save much time and human resources.

Despite many surveys [16,17,18] on the different text clustering and classification methods and recommendations about the optimal methods, none of them we can implicitly follow, because our aim is to survey text classification methods focusing on the several important aspects their relevance to Lithuanian and other highly inflective languages (hence taking into account this language specifics).

The main goal of clustering is to group a set of documents into a subsets, so called clusters. Documents in cluster should be similar to each other while documents in different clusters should maximally dissimilar.

Clustering, which can be seen as a special case of classification, is an *unsupervised learning* technique, i.e. humans do not supervise the processes. Algorithm decide number of clusters (in some cases, number of clusters is predefined) assigns documents to them based on some predefined criteria, usually similarity functions.

Usually clustering is used to cluster search results for more effective information presentation to user, provide an alternative user interface for document set browsing or general exploratory browsing, provide faster and more efficient search, etc. In our case clustering would allow to find similar customer requests and answers to such requests. That would allow to use already existing answers as templates.

More formally clustering can be defined as follows [2]. Given as set of documents $D = \{d_1, d_2, \ldots, d_N\}$, a desired number of clusters K and an *objective function* that evaluates the quality of a clustering, the clustering algorithm should compute a cluster assignment $\gamma : D \rightarrow \{1, 2, \ldots, K\}$ that minimizes (maximizes) the objective function. Usually, the objective function is defined as a similarity or distance between documents. Resulting assignment allows assigns documents to clusters.

See [33,34,35] for comprehensive overviews. Very general overview of document clustering is provided in [36]. It gives a wide overview of different clustering techniques, but do not discuss quality and performance issues.

General classification and clustering techniques can be applied to Lithuanian language, however no research was performed to see, what quality can be achieved. However, some results show, that language specifics play important role for such highly inflected languages, like Lithuanian. Some theoretical results are already available [12,13], but more research is required.

3.4 Named Entity Recognition

The task of *Named Entity Recognition* [37] (NER) is to categorize particular words (usually proper nouns) in the text document into predefined classes like person names, location names, organization names, and miscellaneous (abbreviations, time, currency, etc.). The miscellaneous type in different NER tasks can include different types of named entities: it depends on further applications. NER has many applications in natural language processing like machine translation, question-answering systems, indexing for information retrieval, data classification and automatic summarization.

The methods, solving NER tasks, can be grouped into two main categories: *rule-based methods* and *machine learning methods*. Rule-based NER methods require comprehensive linguistic analysis of its application field (for ex.: the texts taken from such fields as science fiction, records, legal texts, etc.), followed by manual creation of rules presented as search patterns and gazetteers (for person names, location names, etc.). Rule-based methods are fastened to the particular application field they were created for; therefore they are very sensitive to changes of application field (in the same field, or when transferred to different application fields). For these reasons, rule-based methods are recently replaced by different machine learning methods: HMM, Maximum Entropy, Decision Tree, Support Vector Machines, Conditional Random Fields and different hybrid approaches. Machine learning methods do not require manually performed linguists analysis and search pattern creation, because they are forced all these tasks to do automatically. Besides they can be created in the way that their learning process would be continual (incremental), thereby ensuring their incremental adaptation to the application field and growth in accuracy also. Despite the major part of methods are proposed for English, much is done even for such languages as Punjabi [38], Arabian [39], Vietnamese [40], etc. Lithuanian is not exception in this case. The name entities such as person names, location names, acronyms, contractions, dates, foreign language insertions, sentence boundaries are presented in [41], dates [42] , citations [43]. Unfortunately, NER tasks for Lithuanian are solved using only rule-based methods.

4 Implementation and Experimental Results

The media monitoring solution is based on well supported open source tools. All of those tools support plug-in architecture, thus any modifications and or extensions needed to fulfill particular needs of the project, can be introduced without altering source code of those tools.

Crawling component is implemented using Apache Nutch [44]. Nutch is coded using Java programming language. Crawl data is written in language-independent formats. It has a highly modular architecture, allowing creating plug-ins for media-type parsing, data retrieval, querying and clustering. Main advantages provided by this software package:

1. highly scalable and feature rich crawler;
2. features like politeness which obeys `robots.txt` rules;
3. robust and scalable - Nutch can run a cluster of 100 machines;
4. quality it is possible to direct crawler to fetch "important" pages first.

Natural language processing is implemented with help of a set of different tools. GATE (General Architecture for Text Engineering) [9] is the main "umbrella" component working to tie together all other text processing components into text analysis engine. GATE provides the following advantages:

1. open source software capable of solving almost any text processing problem;
2. a mature and extensive community of developers, users, educators, students and scientists;
3. a defined and repeatable process for creating robust and maintainable text processing workflows;
4. in active use for all sorts of language processing tasks and applications, including: voice of the customer, cancer research, drug research, decision support, recruitment, web mining, information extraction and semantic annotation.

Apache Mahout [45] provides implementation of machine learning algorithms needed for text categorization and classification.

The results of crawl and text processing components are written to semantically enriched index which is accessed through search server. Search server is implemented on top of Apache Solr project [46]. Solr [46] is an open source enterprise search platform from the Apache Lucene project [47]. Its major features include powerful full-text search, hit highlighting, faceted search, dynamic clustering, database integration, and rich document (e.g., Word, PDF) handling. Providing distributed search and index replication, Solr is highly scalable (`http://en.wikipedia.org/wiki/Apache_Solr`).

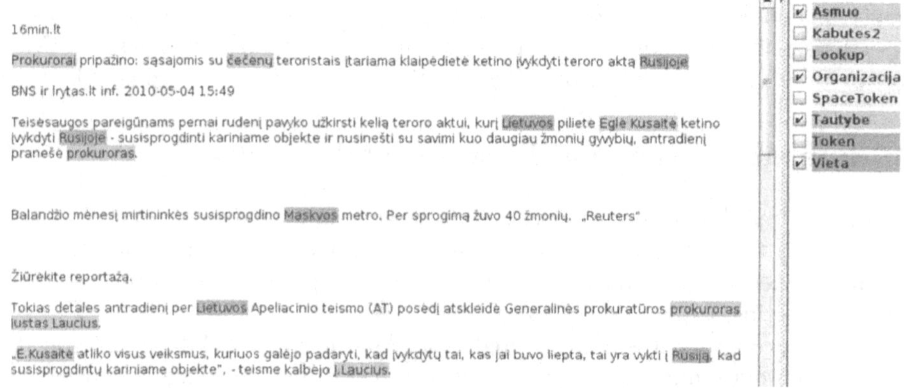

Fig. 4. Results

Results of annotated article from Fig. 1 are presented in Fig. 4. In general, results are encouraging, but further research and development are necessary.

5 Conclusions

We presented a work in progress, a case study of application of NLP and IR tools for Lithuanian News Media monitoring. As a part of this work we had to inventory Lithuanian language resources. A considerable number of such resources already exists (especially corpora), and the number is growing quite fast. Available resources can be used in building working applications for Lithuanian language. However, most of the resources are not ready for production, because legal and commercial aspects are not sorted out and formalized yet.

We would like to emphasize, that a production level morphological annotator and thesaurus for Lithuanian language are missing. Such tools would really improve situation a lot.

Our future plans include several NLP and IR related topics.

1. Analysis and development of classification and clustering techniques for Lithuanian language.
2. Improvement of the existing stemmer.
3. Developing techniques and methods for Machine Learning and Artificial Intelligence based NER.

Acknowledgments. This research was financed by *Development of Automatic Grouping and Topic Recognition of Customers Requests Systems Prototype*, High Technology Development Programme for 2011-2013, Nr. 31V-146. We thank Raimondas Širvinskas and Justas Balčas for their help in the technical development of the system.

References

1. Plana, A.: Text/content analytics 2011: User perspectives on solutions and providers. Technical report, Alta Plana (September 2011)
2. Manning, C., Raghavan, P., Schütze, H.: Introduction to Information Retrieval. Cambridge Univ. Press, New York (2008)
3. Baeza-Yates, R., Ribeiro-Neto, B.: Modern Information Retrieval. Addison Wesley (1999)
4. Natural Language Access to Structured Text. In: Coling 1982: Proceedings of the Ninth International Conference on Computational Linguistics (1982)
5. Tan, P.N., Steinbach, M., Kumar, V.: Introduction to Data Mining. Addison-Wesley (2005)
6. Rösner, D., Grote, B., Hartmann, K., Höfling, B.: From natural language documents to sharable product knowledge: A knowledge engineering approach. Journal of Universal Computer Science 3(8), 955–987 (1997)
7. Apache Foundation: Apache Tika. Web page (2011), `http://tika.apache.org` (last visited: December 10, 2011)
8. LingPipe: Lingpipe. Web page (2011), `http://alias-i.com/lingpipe/` (last visited: December 10, 2011)
9. Cunningham, H., Maynard, D., Bontcheva, K., Tablan, V., Aswani, N., Roberts, I., Gorrell, G., Funk, A., Roberts, A., Damljanovic, D., Heitz, T., Greenwood, M.A., Saggion, H., Petrak, J., Li, Y., Peters, W.: Text Processing with GATE (Version 6) (2011)
10. Vaičiūnas, A., Kaminskas, V., Raškinis, G.: Statistical language models of lithuanian based on word clustering and morphological decomposition. Informatica 15(4), 565–580 (2004)
11. Šveikauskienė, D.: Formal description of the syntax of the lithuanian language. Information Technologies and Control 34, 245–256 (2005)
12. Bevainytė, A., Butėnas, L.: Document classification using weighted ontology. Materials Physics and Mechanics 9(3), 236–245 (2010)
13. Tomović, A., Janičić, P.: A Variant of N-Gram Based Language Classification. In: Basili, R., Pazienza, M.T. (eds.) AI*IA 2007. LNCS (LNAI), vol. 4733, pp. 410–421. Springer, Heidelberg (2007)
14. Zinkevičius, Z.: Lemuoklis - tool for morphological analysis. Darbai ir Dienos (24), 245–274 (2000)

15. Marcinkevičienė, R., Vitkutė-Adžgauskienė, D.: Developing the human language technology infrastructure in lithuania. In: Proceedings of the 2010 Conference on Human Language Technologies – The Baltic Perspective: Proceedings of the Fourth International Conference Baltic HLT 2010, pp. 3–10. IOS Press, Amsterdam (2010)
16. Pandey, U., Chakravarty, S.: A survey on text classification techniques for e-mail filtering. In: Proceedings of the 2010 Second International Conference on Machine Learning and Computing, ICMLC 2010, pp. 32–36. IEEE Computer Society, Washington, DC (2010)
17. Baharudin, B., Lee, L.H., Khan, K.: A review of machine learning algorithms for text-documents classification. Journal of Advances in Information Technology 1(1), 4–20 (2010)
18. Harish, B.S., Guru, D.S., Manjunath, S.: Representation and classification of text documents: A brief review. IJCA, Special Issue on RTIPPR (2), 110–119 (2010)
19. Maicher, L., Park, J. (eds.): TMRA 2005. LNCS (LNAI), vol. 3873. Springer, Heidelberg (2006)
20. Yang, S.Y.: Ontocrawler: A focused crawler with ontology-supported website models for information agents. Expert Systems with Applications 37(7), 5381–5389 (2010)
21. Porter, M.F.: Snowball: A language for stemming algorithms. Published online (October 2001), `http://snowball.tartarus.org/texts/introduction.html` (accessed March 11, 2008)
22. The National Archives: The soundex indexing system. Web page (May 2007), `http://www.archives.gov/research/census/soundex.html`
23. Centre of Computational Linguistics: Lithuanian digital resources. Web page (2011), `http://sruoga.vdu.lt/lituanistiniai-skaitmeniai-istekliai`
24. TokenMill: Lt language pack. Web page (2012), `https://github.com/tokenmill/ltlangpack`
25. Németh, L.: Hunspell. Web page (2012), `http://hunspell.sourceforge.net`
26. Lukaševičius, R., Agejevas, A.: ispell-lt. Web page, `ftp://ftp.akl.lt/ispell-lt/`
27. Wikipedia: Language identification — wikipedia, the free encyclopedia (2012) (Online; accessed April 30, 2012)
28. Wikipedia: Stop words — wikipedia, the free encyclopedia (2012) (Online; accessed April 30, 2012)
29. Krilavičius, T., Kuliešienė, D.: Soundex for lithuanian language. Internal report, UAB TokenMill (2010)
30. Krilavičius, T., Baltrūnas, M.: Soundex for lithuanian language. Internal report and bachelor thesis, UAB TokenMill and Vytautas Magnus University (2012)
31. Paliulionis, V.: Lietuviškų adresų geokodavimo problemos ir jų sprendimo būdai. Informacijos Mokslai, 217–222 (2009)
32. Krilavičius, T., Medelis, V.: Porter stemmer for lithuanian language. Internal report and bachelor thesis, UAB TokenMill and Vytautas Magnus University (2010)
33. Ghosh, J., Strehl, A.: Similarity-Based Text Clustering: A Comparative Study. In: Kogan, J., Nicholas, C., Teboulle, M. (eds.) Grouping Multidimensional Data, pp. 73–97. Springer, Heidelberg (2006)
34. Zhong, S., Ghosh, J.: Generative model-based document clustering: a comparative study. Knowledge and Information Systems 8, 374–384 (2005), doi:10.1007/s10115-004-0194-1
35. Steinbach, M., Karypis, G., Kumar, V.: A comparison of document clustering techniques. In: KDD Workshop on Text Mining, vol. 400(X), pp. 1–20 (2000)
36. Andrews, N.O., Fox, E.A.: Recent developments in document clustering. Technical report (2007)

37. Nadeau, D., Sekine, S.: A survey of named entity recognition and classification. Journal of Linguisticae Investigationes 30(1), 1–20 (2007)
38. Kaur, D., Gupta, V.: A survey of named entity recognition in english and other indian languages. IJCSI International Journal of Computer Science Issues 7(6), 239–245 (2010)
39. AbdelRahman, S., Elarnaoty, M., Magdy, M., Fahmy, A.: Integrated machine learning techniques for arabic named entity recognition. IJCSI International Journal of Computer Science Issues 7(4), 27–36 (2010)
40. Nguyen, D.B., Hoang, S.H., Pham, S.B., Nguyen, T.P.: Named Entity Recognition for Vietnamese. In: Nguyen, N.T., Le, M.T., Świątek, J. (eds.) ACIIDS 2011, Part II. LNCS, vol. 5991, pp. 205–214. Springer, Heidelberg (2010)
41. Kapočiūtė-Dzikienė, J., Raškinis, G.: Rule-based annotation of lithuanian text corpora. Information technology and control. Technologija 34, 290–296 (2005)
42. Balčas, J., Krilavičius, T., Medelis, V.: Lithuanian date and time identification using GATE and Jape. Internal report and bachelor thesis, UAB TokenMill and Vytautas Magnus Unviersity (2012)
43. Širviskas, R., Krilavičius, T., Medelis, V.: Lithuanian citations identification using GATE and Jape. Internal report and bachelor thesis, UAB TokenMill and Vytautas Magnus University (2012)
44. Apache Foundation: Apache Nutch. Web page (2011), http://nutch.apache.org (last visited: December 10, 2011)
45. Apache Foundation: Apache Mahout. Web page (2011), http://mahout.apache.org (last visited: December 10, 2011)
46. Apache Foundation: Apache Solr. Web page (2011), http://lucene.apache.org/solr (last visited: December 10, 2011)
47. Apache Foundation: Apache Lucene. Web page (2011), http://lucene.apache.org (last visited: December 10, 2011)

Generating High Quality Candidate Sets by Tour Merging for the Traveling Salesman Problem

Andrius Blazinskas and Alfonsas Misevicius

Kaunas University of Technology, Department of Multimedia Engineering, Studentu St. 50–401, 416a, LT–51368 Kaunas, Lithuania
{andrius.blazinskas,alfonsas.misevicius}@ktu.lt

Abstract. One of the most important improvements for the Traveling Salesman Problem (TSP) heuristics is usage of limited size candidate sets, also known as candidate lists (CLs). CLs help to effectively reduce the search space and appropriately sorted biases the search in a more gainful direction. Besides the best known nearest-neighbor, quadrant, Delaunay or leading Helsgaun's alpha CLs, other effective CLs can be constructed. We revise tour merging technique proposed by Applegate et al. and using multi-random-start procedure with incorporated fast 3-opt and simplified Lin-Kernighan-Helsgaun (LKH) algorithm modifications, generate tour union CLs and analyze them by comparing with the most common alternatives. In addition, we propose a criteria indicating when merging procedure should be terminated to form high quality CLs. Finally, we show a high potential of such CLs by performing the experiments with our modified LKH variant.

Keywords: traveling salesman problem, candidate list, tour union, 3-opt, LKH.

1 Introduction

The traveling salesman problem (TSP) is one of the most popular combinatorial optimization problems [9]. It can be formulated as finding shortest tour (Hamiltonian cycle) on a set of nodes (cities) visiting every node only once when costs between all nodes are defined. If distance does not depend on the edge direction between two nodes problem is called symmetric TSP (STSP), otherwise it is asymmetric (ATSP).

TSP is NP-hard. The total number of possible tours for STSP is equal to $(n-1)!/2$ (n – the number of nodes) [7]. Clearly for such a search space it is relatively difficult to find good quality tours in short time. Exact methods for solving bigger problems are inappropriate because of enormous amount of time needed. As a result a lot of various heuristic algorithms and search space reduction techniques for them are proposed [6]. One of these reduction methods is usage of limited size candidate sets also called candidate lists (CLs).

Generally, candidate list for a particular node is a list of other graph nodes which are relevant or closest according to some criteria. For Euclidean TSP instances this criteria can be Euclidean distance. All node CLs put together essentially represent a graph, to which in this document we refer as candidate graph (CG). Quality of CG is

T. Skersys, R. Butleris, and R. Butkiene (Eds.): ICIST 2012, CCIS 319, pp. 62–73, 2012.

very important for search heuristics. The better CLs are the greater chances for search algorithm to find better solutions in shorter times. Generally, CG can be considered good if it has decent number of common edges with optimal tour, is relatively sparse and can be generated in a short time. Obviously, optimal tour for unsolved TSP problems is unavailable and so it is complicated to determine essential edges for inclusion in CLs. While edge cost (or distance) itself is a good indicator other effective criteria for edge fitness exist [7], [18].

Solving TSP with iterated local search (ILS), where in every iteration only the best solution is chosen, a lot of valuable information of rejected tours is discarded. Applegate et al. [1] have proposed to utilize this information in further search for a better final tour by merging previously generated tours. They called their technique *tour merging*. Using Lin-Kernighan (LK) heuristic [11] modifications – *Chained* LK [2] and Helsgaun's LK (LKH) [7], they generated good tours and successfully improved by searching created tour union graphs with exact algorithms found in *Concorde* code [22].

It should be noted, that tour union was also used earlier by Padberg and Rinaldi [14], where they also generated tours by LK and used union product for initialization of *branch-and-cut* algorithm. Tour merging recently is being widely explored in various ways and resulting graph is also used to identify pseudo backbone edges [18], [5]. Similarly, Lin and Kernighan initially have proposed that common edges of previously LK generated tours can be fixed in further LK searches [11]. Genetic algorithms [6] is another powerful algorithm class having the same goal – to form better derivative solutions utilizing previously generated ones by various crossovers. Helsgaun, in his LKH 2.0.5 version package, also uses tour merging extensively [7].

Merging the best tours found by effective algorithms is a good idea. Good tours usually have a lot of common edges with optimal tour. This allows to construct sparse graphs with good optimal tour coverage. But good solutions usually are in deep local optimum and are very similar to each other, so the lack of diversity sometimes cause a considerable amount of important edges to be missing in the resulting graph. Furthermore, it usually takes a lot of time to generate high quality solutions. For these reasons, we utilize faster and more diverse algorithms to construct merged tour graphs and use them as initial candidate lists for the modified version of LKH algorithm. We show that such CLs in some cases can be even more favorable than effective Helsgaun's alpha variant, since they can provide better initial edge set giving greater chances for optimum to be discovered. While in this document we will be analyzing only symmetric Euclidean instances, tour merging technique is not limited for this particular class of problems and is applicable in general.

2 Generating Candidate Sets

Various CL types have been proposed [6]. Most common of these are: nearest-neighbor, quadrant nearest-neighbor (or simply quadrant), Delaunay and others (see [22] for available different CL implementations in *Concorde*). Figure 1 illustrates differences between these types of CLs.

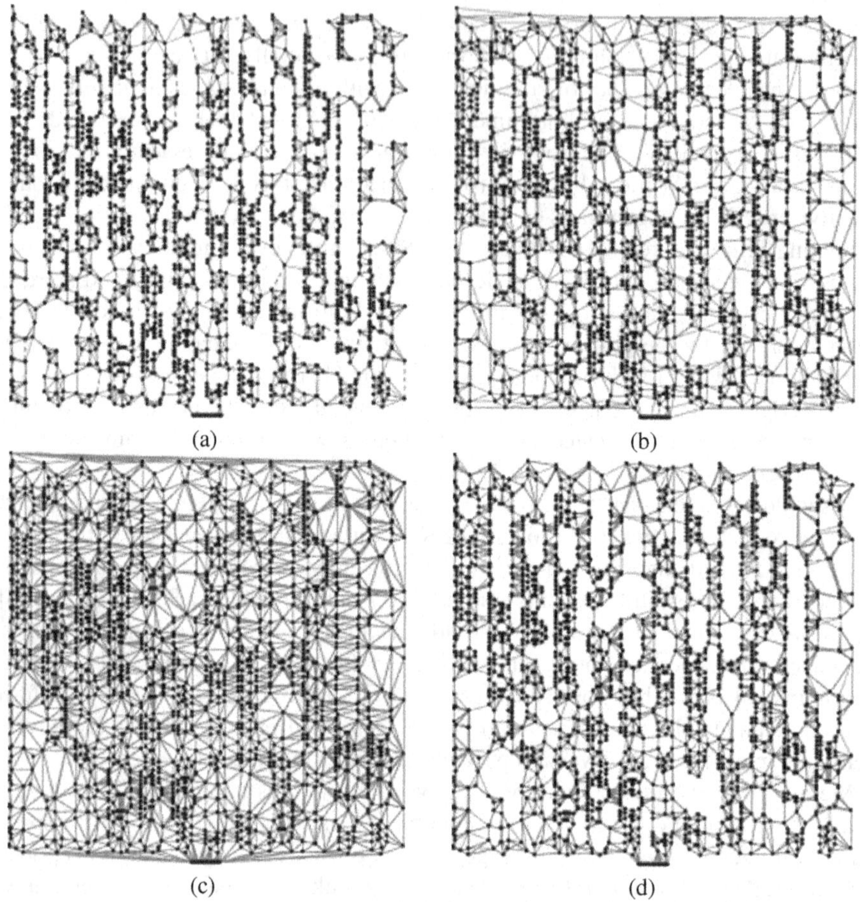

Fig. 1. Different candidate sets for *xqc2175* problem: nearest-neighbor (a); quadrant nearest-neighbor (b); Delaunay (c); Helsgaun's alpha (d). |CL|=5 (not applicable to Delaunay). Visible dashed edges depend to optimal tour and are missing in CLs.

Graph produced by tour merging process can successfully be used as CG in local search (LS). Tours for merging can be generated using various TSP algorithms, including LS heuristics. As mentioned before, LK and its modifications with classical CLs were used for this in the past. However, popular relatively small CLs, typically used for LK, usually are missing important edges contained in optimal solutions (see Table 1). It is not always an easy task for LK to discover such edges and therefore resulting found tours also may not contain them. Using bigger CLs may help, but in this case, for big problems LK becomes slow and generation of several tours may take a lot of time, so other faster methods should be considered. In particular, additionally to LK we are also interested in faster and still relatively strong 3-opt LS. Fast 3-opt implementations are possible [9]. What is more important, 3-opt is not so sensitive to big CL sizes when bigger problems are solved. For example, while original LKH (with default parameters and 5-opt moves) is starting to significantly slow down with |CL| > 6, 3-opt can easily handle |CL| = 40 or greater. CLs with such sizes cover a large neighborhood and with high probability contain most optimal tour edges. It is easy to foresee, that using 3-opt with big CL size, generated tour union graphs will have higher diversity and will not be as sparse as the ones generated using LK variants. However, they are likely to have much smaller CL size than the one used for 3-opt itself. So it may be reasonable to additionally pass this graph as CG further and repeat the search process with stronger LK modification. This proposes an idea, that CLs for stronger algorithms can be generated using weaker algorithms with bigger CL size, hoping that resulting merged tour graph will have important high quality edges. In next sections we will test these ideas and see if in such a way generated CLs can be practically useful.

2.1 Tour Generation Procedure

For tour generation we are utilizing simple multi-random-start scheme, similar to the one used by Boese et al. [4] (see Fig. 2). Using random starts in multi-start search may not be very efficient [10]. Faster approach would be using some greedy randomized initial tour and improving it with local search. Such scheme is proposed by Feo and Resende and named GRASP [15]. Another effective way is using so called *k-swap-kick* perturbations [17], when an existing good tour is only slightly perturbed. However, our experiments indicate, that even with higher runtime penalty, random starts give best diversification and enables to construct better quality CLs. Still, using *k-swap-kick* perturbations may also be useful, but in this case best perturbation size must be determined. Using small perturbations, like *double-bridge* move [8], CG generation converges slowly. Our experiments indicate, that for big problems like *pla85900*, most effective *k-swap-kick* perturbation size can be nearly as large as 1000 or even more. However, if right perturbation size is chosen, running times in some cases can be cut by half and nearly as good as multi-random-start quality can be achieved.

```
Repeat
   Generate random solution t;
   Find local optimum t1 with local search starting from t;
   Merge t1 into graph G;
until a stopping criterion is satisfied;
```

Fig. 2. Multi-random-start procedure used to generate tour union graphs

Another potentially important property of CLs is symmetry. Nearest-neighbor, quadrant and Helsgaun's alpha candidate sets typically are semi-symmetric: if node A is in CL of node B, B not necessarily will be in CL of A. These candidate lists can be easily symmetrized at a cost of slightly increased average CL size. Naturally, symmetric candidate lists can be considered being better than asymmetric or semi-symmetric, since they provide better possibilities on exploring neighborhood for the algorithm. However this is another possible topic for research, which is not covered in this work. We just mention that in our experiments with LKH modifications, highly artificially asymmetrized CLs had given much worse results than symmetric or semi-symmetric variants. Delaunay and merged tour CLs analyzed here are all fully symmetric.

For successful CL application, arrangement of its elements by some criteria typically should be made. In our case, we are using simple increasing edge cost sorting, though during the search process we additionally adjust them (see section 3 for details).

2.2 How Many Tours to Merge?

When to stop in tour merging procedure – is another important question. One simple way to determine approximate tour count needed to form good graph is to perform an experiment on solved TSP instances trying to determine best matched number by problem size. However, in this case problem specific aspects are not evaluated. Problem configuration has great influence on the search process and results. For example, it is well known that clustered TSP instances are more complicated to solve using LK [8]. Merging too few or too many tours may negatively impact quality of generated CLs. Instead of using predefined tour count, we propose relatively simple but effective criteria indicating when tour merging should be stopped. We offer to use added unique edge count (AEC) as an indicator. During merging procedure merged tour graph becomes enough steady at some point and AEC becomes small and relatively stable. When such point is reached, merging procedure can be terminated. To control when termination should take place, two parameters may be used: newly added unique edge count limit (AEL) and AELRep – parameter indicating how many subsequent iterations AEC should be lower than AEL. Parameter AELRep is necessary for more stable results, since the first occurrence of AEC < AEL may take place too early, especially if for some reasons multi-random-start procedure produces initial random tour similar to the one previously generated. Both parameters are predefined by the user before CG formation.

We will illustrate this idea by an example. Suppose we have chosen AEL to be 0.4% of problem size (n) and AELRep = 5. For problem *fnl4461* we have AEL = $4461 \times 0.004 = 17.8$. So if during merging procedure we encountered AEC < 17.8 five times in a row, CG generation is terminated.

2.3 Candidate Set Generation Results

For test problems we have chosen several instances from TSPLIB [16], [19] and VLSI [20] data sets available online. Most of them are at least partly clustered and not always trivially solved till optimality even by modern heuristics [1], [8], [13]. We also include several large instances to show how various characteristics of CG change with the increase of problem size. To compare generated tour union based CLs (Table 2) we additionally provide parameters of other well known CL types (Table 1).

The following parameters are used in below tables: NCOV – optimal tour edge count not covered by CG (alternative good tour is used if optimum tour is unavailable, see remarks for details); ANC – average neighbor count in CG (average CL size); MTC – merged tour count; TIME – CG generation time in seconds (or hours – h).

Table 1. Parameters of different popular candidate sets and their union

Problem	**Candidate set type**												
	Nearest-neighbor (5)	**Quadrant (5)**	**Delaunay**		**Alpha (5)**			**Quadrant (5) + Delaunay**		**Quadrant (5) + Alpha (5)**		**Delaunay + Alpha (5)**	
	NCOV	**NCOV**	**NCOV**	**ANC**	**NCOV**	**ANC**	**TIME**	**NCOV**	**ANC**	**NCOV**	**ANC**	**NCOV**	**ANC**
fl1577	34	23	10	5.9	9	5	3	9	7.3	6	6.1	2	6.8
d1655	39	29	17	5.9	12	5	3	13	7.4	12	6.2	6	6.8
vm1748	50	33	16	5.5	13	5	3	7	7.1	7	6	3	6.7
u2152	69	26	13	5.9	2	5	5	6	7.4	1	6.4	1	6.8
xqc2175	59	52	50	5.9	7	5	5	17	7.2	4	6.2	4	7
fl3795	66	58	45	6	35	4.9	15	28	7.6	24	6.2	22	7.1
fnl4461	36	27	17	6	4	5	23	6	6.5	2	5.8	2	6.4
rl5934	149	115	51	6	37	5	42	46	7.9	31	6.5	21	7.2
pla7397	65	53	44	5.9	15	4.9	66	29	7.1	11	5.8	7	6.8
d18512	152	136	74	5	22	5	489	37	6.5	10	5.8	5	6.4
pla33810	127	106	64	6	54	5	1652	36	7	38	5.9	22	6.7
pla85900	198	194	125	6	86	4.8	13887	76	7	66	5.6	46	6.7
ara238025	7751	6399	3900	6	1283	5	~34h	1943	7	799	6.2	618	6.8
lra498378	17980	13856	8174	6	-	-	-	3668	7.3	-	-	-	-
lrb744710	21089	17735	12270	6	-	-	-	5386	6.9	-	-	-	-

Table 2. Parameters of generated tour union candidate sets

Problem	**Candidate set type**											
	3-OPT (|QCL|=40)				**LKH3 (Delaunay)**				**3-OPT → LKH3**			
	NCOV	**ANC**	**MTC**	**TIME**	**NCOV**	**ANC**	**MTC**	**TIME**	**NCOV**	**ANC**	**MTC**	**TIME**
fl1577	0.6	5.2	132	2	0.9	3.1	55	5	1.1	3.1	61	5
d1655	0.2	5.1	104	1	1.5	3.3	60	6	0.1	3.2	61	4
vm1748	0.2	3.9	56	1	0	2.9	47	5	0	2.9	49	3
u2152	0	6.4	146	2	3.2	3.6	97	11	0.3	3.5	77	9
xqc2175	0.6	6.2	130	2	15	3.9	99	12	1.1	4	100	14
fl3795	0.2	4.8	104	4	22	3.3	55	15	2.1	3.5	61	13
fnl4461	0.1	5.1	74	2	0.2	3.6	75	33	0.1	3.6	68	23
rl5934	0	4.4	98	5	2.1	2.8	66	50	0.1	2.7	57	24
pla7397	0.7	5.8	109	8	9.2	3.6	75	66	4.9	3.6	75	56
d18512	0.5	5.2	73	13	1.6	3.6	71	413	0.2	3.6	73	318
pla33810	1.6	5.8	183	89	31.7	3.4	66	709	18.2	3.4	71	704
pla85900	2	6	163	254	42	3.6	61	3877	27	3.5	58	3264
ara238025	12.5	7.2	230	1528	752	4.5	106	~18h	46	4.5	107	~21h
lra498378	24.3	6.8	225	4749	1810	4.1	106	~95h	143	4.1	103	~99h
lrb744710	41	7.4	233	8460	-	-	-	-	-	-	-	-

Tours for merging are generated using fast 3-opt and LKH LS heuristics incorporated in multi-random-start procedure (Fig. 2). Implementations of 3-opt and LKH are based on Helsgaun's code and are fully coded in Java. It is important to note, that our LKH implementation is based on core search procedure only and essentially considers searching for sequential and non-sequential moves [8]. It does not contain other improvements from original code. For details about runtime environment and machine used for experiments see section 3.

Other remarks:

- In Table 1, CL size (|CL|), if applicable, is provided in parentheses. For nearest-neighbor and quadrant ANC=|CL|=5. For alpha $|CL| \leq 5$.
- For alpha CLs, time column indicates overall preprocessing time, which also includes subgradient optimization [7] (default parameters used).
- In Table 2, quadrant CLs of size 40 (|QCL| = 40) were used to run 3-opt.
- Notation of LKH3 means that LKH LS with at most best 3-opt sequential moves is used.
- Notation 3-OPT → LKH3 denotes that CG generated by multi-random-start with 3-opt was used in construction of CG produced by multi-random-start with LKH3.
- Table 2 contains average values of 10 runs, except for problems starting from $n = 238025$, for which only one trial is performed since running times become quite large.
- Several optimum tours may exist, so NCOV parameter is ambiguous, though still indicating important and interesting information.
- For *d18512* problem we did not have optimum tour so for NCOV calculation, tour (found by LKH 2.0.5) of length 645241 (deviation = 0.00046%) was used.
- For problems *ara238025*, *lra498378* and *lrb744710* optimum is unknown so in calculation of NCOV optimum tour is substituted with good tours found by other authors provided at [20] (*ara238025* used tour cost is *579075*, *lra498378* – 2169314, *lrb744710* – 1612132).
- Generating tour union CLs, AEL was set to 0.2% of n, except for 3-opt, for which AEL = 0.4% for problems up to n = 18512 (inclusive). In all cases AELRep = 5.
- Implementation of algorithm for finding Delaunay graph is based on *Concorde* code [22]. Nearest-neighbor and quadrant CLs are calculated using LKH 2.0.5 code [21].
- Quadrant CLs are formed by choosing |CL|/4 nearest nodes from every quadrant and appending missing with nearest-neighbors to fully reach CL size.
- ANC value of tour union CLs, for average size instances, is usually relatively small (< 5), however min and max values for individual nodes can reach much bigger values – 10 or more.

The chain of CG generation can be continued further. However, as our experiments indicate, using LKH3 generated CLs for LKH5 (LKH LS with at most best 5-opt sequential moves) does not produce noticeable improvements in resulting CLs. Actually, the lack of edge diversity in source CLs sometimes even worsens the situation: ANC is slightly decreased at a cost of noticeably increased NCOV. This drawback together with significantly increased running time makes LKH5 usage less attractive in this case.

Figure 3 illustrates how generated tour union CGs differ from other well known CL types in Figure 1.

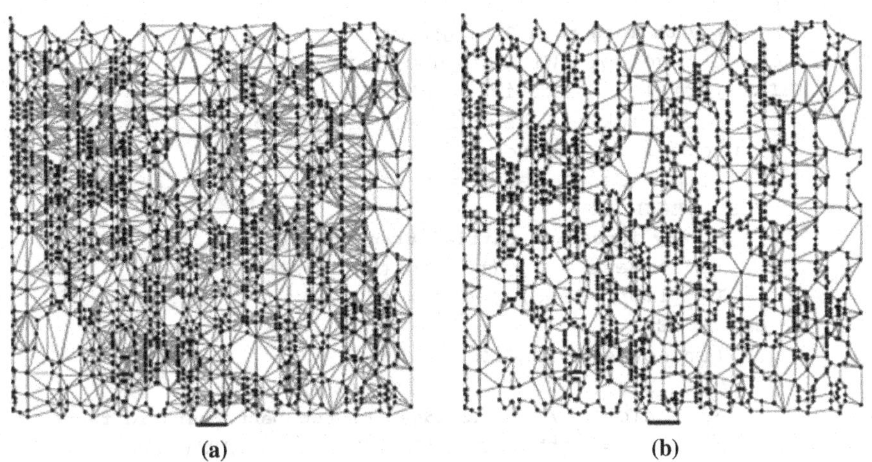

Fig. 3. Tour union candidate sets for *xqc2175* problem: generated by 3-opt (run with quadrant |CL|=40) (a); generated by LKH3 LS (using CG generated with 3-opt) (b)

3 Experimental Results

For experiments with generated tour union CLs we have constructed ILS scheme (see Fig. 4), which essentially is a modification (and simplification) of the ILS procedure used by Helsgaun [7]. All statements in previous section about modifications in core LKH LS function (in pseudocode denoted as *lkh5Mod*) are also valid here. Instead of multi-random-starts used for CG generation, *k-swap-kick* perturbations with dynamic kick size are incorporated in the main search scheme. Kick size is increased every *maxFails* = 5 non improving iterations. If any trial has improved or kick size has reached maximum and *fails* > *maxFails* – perturbation size is set back to minimum. In the experiments we were using predefined kick sizes in such order: 4, 16, 32, 64, 128. The most common type of random *k-swap-kicks* is used, but the set of nodes for kicking is limited to only those which have more than 2 neighbors in CG.

As can be seen from Figure 4, *iterative partial transcription* (IPT) [12] is retained in the main search procedure. For initial tour calculation Bentley's *multi-fragment* heuristic [3] was used. Main search procedure also utilizes *don't-look bits* [3]. During the search found better tours are added to CG, which is also adjusted the same way it is done in original LKH – common edges of two best tours are brought in front [7]. The iteration count limit (*maxTrials*) was set to *n*. The search procedure is terminated immediately if optimum is found.

```
PROCEDURE LKH-MOD-ILS (Tour t, CandidateLists cl, int maxTrials,
        int maxFails, int [] kickSizes)
    Tour bestt;  Node [] kickSet;  boolean improvBest;
    int trials = 0, fails = 0, kickIdx = 0;
    lkh5Mod(t, cl); // initial lkh5
    bestt = t;
    // nodes with more than 2 neighbors
    kickSet = getNodesWithNeighborCountGT2(cl);
    WHILE (trials < maxTrials) BEGIN
       kick(t, kickSet, kickSizes[kickIdx]);
       improvBest = lkh5Mod(t, cl);
       IF (improvBest) bestt = t;
       ELSE BEGIN
          // try iterative partial transcription
          improvBest = ipt(t, bestt);
          IF (improvBest) bestt = t;
       END ELSE
       IF (improvBest) BEGIN
          cl.add(t);
          adjust(cl); // bring edges of two best tours in front
          kickSet = getNodesWithNeighborCountGT2(cl);
          kickIdx = 0; // roll back to smallest kick
          fails = 0;
       END IF ELSE BEGIN
          fails++;
          IF (fails > maxFails) BEGIN
             // set next kick size
             kickIdx = (kickIdx + 1) % kickSizes.length;
             fails = 0;
          END IF
       END ELSE
       trials++;
    END WHILE
END
```

Fig. 4. Simplified and modified LKH ILS procedure used in experiments

Described ILS procedure (*LKH-MOD-ILS*) is implemented entirely in Java. IPT implementation is based on Helsgaun's code. Implementations of *two-level tree* (used for tour representation), *k-d tree* (used in *multi-fragment* heuristic) and *multi-fragment* heuristic itself are based on *Concorde* C code [22]. For compiling and running Java code *JDK 1.6* was used. Experiments were performed on the machine with Intel Core i7-860 processor and 8GB of RAM.

For comparison purposes the most recent unmodified Helsgaun's package version 2.0.5 was used. It was compiled and run using *Cygwin* [23]. Default parameters for LKH 2.0.5 were set.

Experiments were repeated for 10 times and averages for the following parameters were calculated: DEV – average deviation from optimal value:

$DEV = 100(z^* - z_{opt})/z_{opt}\ [\%]$, where z* – best found tour cost and z_{opt} denotes the optimal tour cost (optimal tour lengths can be found at TSPLIB [19] and VLSI [20] sites); OPTC – number of times optimum found; TIM1 – average overall running time; TIM2 – average running time until last improvement is made; TIMO – average running time when optimum was found. Parameters DEV, TIM1 and TIM2 are calculated only with data when no optimum was found. Tour union candidate sets for *LKH-MOD-ILS* were regenerated in every trial, therefore had slightly different properties. Average times provided in table do not include CG generation or preprocessing time.

Table 3. Experimental results with original implementation of LKH (version 2.0.5) and our LKH modification with tour union based candidate sets

Problem	Algorithm									
	LKH 2.0.5 (alpha (5) CLs)					LKH-MOD-ILS (3-opt → LKH3 CLs)				
	DEV	OPTC	TIM1	TIM2	TIMO	DEV	OPTC	TIM1	TIM2	TIMO
fl1577	0.056	3	156	87	110	0	10	-	-	2
d1655	0.002	0	18	3	-	0	10	-	-	2
vm1748	0.036	6	18	4	9	0	10	-	-	4
u2152	0.089	7	71	15	22	0	10	-	-	42
xqc2175	0.015	5	76	5	21	0	10	-	-	61
fl3795	0.045	3	724	90	329	0	10	-	-	67
fnl4461	0	10	-	-	28	0	10	-	-	169
rl5934	0.098	0	433	178	-	0	10	-	-	58
pla7397	0	10	-	-	212	0.001	2	4548	540	1570
d18512	0.002	0	9869	7590	-	0.027	0	23398	15343	-

4 Conclusions and Future Research

In this work, we performed a short analysis of different candidate list types and demonstrated that tour merging is one of the best techniques to generate CLs. Correctly formed, tour union CLs have low density and very good optimal tour coverage, compared to other CL types. Our proposed stopping criteria for tour merging procedure, based on newly added edge count, ensures that resulting CLs have high quality properties. Furthermore, utilizing fast 3-opt, CG generation times are quite decent even for very large instances. Even additionally "filtering" 3-opt generated CLs with simplified version of LKH3 (maximum of 3-opt sequential moves) overall generation times are noticeably lower than preprocessing stage of original LKH, during which subgradient optimization is performed and alpha CLs are generated. We also showed that CLs generated with 3-opt (quadrant CLs of size 40 were used for 3-opt) are better than Delaunay CG for further processing with LKH3. Our LKH ILS modification, based on dynamic *k-swap-kick* size, run with such CLs was able to give 100% success in finding optimal tours for problem range 1577-5934 we considered. However, Helsgaun's original implementation with alpha CLs is still undoubtedly powerful and may be more preferable for larger problems.

An interesting approach would be combining tour union and alpha CLs in a more elaborate manner so that resulting CLs would preserve best qualities of each. Of course, in this case for large instances overall generation times would be high, but it might be beneficial in searching for even higher quality solutions.

Usage of tour union based CLs is an effective way to reduce search space, however other reduction methods also exist. Another interesting idea for further improvement could be pseudo backbone edge contraction technique [5], where the problem size itself is effectively reduced.

References

1. Applegate, D.L., Bixby, R.E., Chvatal, V., Cook, W.J.: The Traveling Salesman Problem: A Computational Study. Princeton University Press, Princeton (2007)
2. Applegate, D., Cook, W., Rohe, A.: Chained Lin-Kernighan for large traveling salesman problems. INFORMS J. Comp. 15, 82–92 (2003)
3. Bentley, J.L.: Fast algorithms for geometric traveling salesman problems. ORSA Journal on Computing 4(4), 387–411 (1992)
4. Boese, K.D., Kahng, A.B., Muddu, S.: A new adaptive multi-start technique for combinatorial global optimizations. Operations Research Letters 16, 101–113 (1994)
5. Dong, C., Jäger, G., Richter, D., Molitor, P.: Effective Tour Searching for TSP by Contraction of Pseudo Backbone Edges. In: Goldberg, A.V., Zhou, Y. (eds.) AAIM 2009. LNCS, vol. 5564, pp. 175–187. Springer, Heidelberg (2009)
6. Gutin, G., Punnen, A.P.: The Traveling Salesman Problem and its Variations. Kluwer Academic Publishers, Dordrecht (2002)
7. Helsgaun, K.: An Effective Implementation of the Lin–Kernighan Traveling Salesman Heuristic. European Journal of Operational Research 126, 106–130 (2000)
8. Helsgaun, K.: General k-opt submoves for the Lin-Kernighan TSP heuristic. Mathematical Programming Computation, 119–163 (2009)
9. Johnson, D.S., McGeoch, L.A.: The traveling salesman problem: a case study. In: Aarts, E.H.L., Lenstra, J.K. (eds.) Local Search in Combinatorial Optimization, pp. 215–310. Wiley, Chichester (1997)
10. Li, W.: Seeking global edges for traveling salesman problem in multi-start search. Journal of Global Optimization 51(3), 515–540 (2011)
11. Lin, S., Kernighan, B.W.: An Effective Heuristic Algorithm for the Traveling-Salesman Problem. Operations Research 21, 498–516 (1973)
12. Mobius, A., Freisleben, B., Merz, P., Schreiber, M.: Combinatorial Optimization by Iterative Partial Transcription. Physical Review E 59(4), 4667–4674 (1999)
13. Marinakis, Y., Marinaki, M., Dounias, G.: Honey bees mating optimization algorithm for the Euclidean traveling salesman problem. Information Sciences 181(20), 4684–4698 (2011)
14. Padberg, M., Rinaldi, G.: A branch-and-cut algorithm for the resolution of large-scale symmetric traveling salesman problems. SIAM Rev. 33, 60–100 (1991)
15. Pitsoulis, L.S., Resende, M.G.C.: Greedy Randomized Adaptive Search Procedures. In: Pardalos, P.M., Resende, M.G.C. (eds.) Handbook of Applied Optimization, pp. 178–183. Oxford University Press (2002)

16. Reinelt, G.: TSPLIB — A Traveling Salesman Problem Library. ORSA Journal on Computing 3(4), 376–385 (1991)
17. Richter, D., Goldengorin, B., Jäger, G., Molitor, P.: Improving the Efficiency of Helsgaun's Lin-Kernighan Heuristic for the Symmetric TSP. In: Janssen, J., Prałat, P. (eds.) CAAN 2007. LNCS, vol. 4852, pp. 99–111. Springer, Heidelberg (2007)
18. Zhang, W., Looks, M.: A Novel Local Search Algorithm for the Traveling Salesman Problem that Exploits Backbones. In: IJCAI 2005, pp. 343–350 (2005)
19. TSPLIB Homepage, `http://elib.zib.de/pub/mp-testdata/tsp/tsplib/tsplib.html`
20. VLSI Homepage, `http://www.tsp.gatech.edu/vlsi/summary.html`
21. Helsgaun's Lin-Kernighan implementation (LKH) source code, `http://www.akira.ruc.dk/~keld/research/LKH/`
22. Concorde source code, `http://www.tsp.gatech.edu/concorde/index.html`
23. Cygwin homepage, `http://www.cygwin.com`

Towards Evaluating Efficiency of Enterprise Modeling Methods

Banafsheh Khademhosseinieh and Ulf Seigerroth

Jönköping University, School of Engineering
P.O. Box 1026, SE-55111 Jönköping, Sweden
{Banafsheh.Khadem,Ulf.Seigerroth}@jth.hj.se

Abstract. Each organization should make progress to remain competent in its business. Enterprise Modeling (EM) helps in understanding the current and planning the future states, followed by proposing improvement actions in an enterprise. To receive support from EM, we should start a process of using an Enterprise Modeling Method (EMM), that likewise any other process needs using resources. As resources are expensive, we prefer not only gaining results, rather using resources reasonably, i.e. performing an efficient process that supports the process quality. To realize if we have an efficient EMM, we should evaluate its efficiency. In this paper we present a method for efficiency evaluation of EMMs for general case of application. This method contains efficiency criteria and questions for evaluating their fulfillment. Then it is applied to the Enterprise Knowledge Development for appraising the evaluation method. The paper ends with a number of conclusions about the evaluation method.

Keywords: Enterprise Modeling, Enterprise Modeling Method, Efficiency.

1 Introduction

Any organization aims at making profit and progress to be able to survive in its business area. For this purpose, they have to keep improving different aspects of their business [1]. For making any kind of change or improvement in an organization, it is needed to understand the current (As-Is) state of the organization and figure out the desired/ future (To-Be) state. According to [2], Enterprise Modeling (EM) and Business Process Management (BPM) are two areas that for a long time have been part of a tradition where the mission is to improve business practice and management. EM supports understanding the "As-Is" processes and organizational structures in an enterprise, and developing and specifying the "To-Be" situation as support for process improvement of organizational change processes. A challenge in BPM, that can be found in EM too [3], is the need for moving beyond a narrow focus on one tradition or technology and actually dealing with a number of conceptual ways to slice the business in an integrated way. Performing such a slicing process aids in having knowledge about how an enterprise looks like from a specific viewpoint, followed by marking change needs and figuring out change measures, i.e. planning the improvement actions for the enterprise. In order to receive support from EM field, we

T. Skersys, R. Butleris, and R. Butkiene (Eds.): ICIST 2012, CCIS 319, pp. 74–86, 2012.

need an EMM. EMMs provide intuitive and understandable graphical languages to represent relevant concepts and their relationships, so modelers are able to explicitly and clearly capture and present domain knowledge using limited training in the corresponding methods and tools [4].

Process of applying an EMM, likewise any other process, requires having access to resources [5][6][7]. However, resources are usually scarce and using them is costly. Therefore, we require not only obtaining the intended output, which in this case are enterprise models, rather we would like to use resources in a reasonable and worthwhile way [8], i.e. have an efficient EMM application process.

Our desire is working with an EMM from high enough quality. Efficiency is a criterion for quality and its fulfillment supports fulfillment of EMM quality. To have an efficient EMM, we need to know what criteria should be fulfilled by that. A group of these criteria are called " criteria for general case of application" , i.e. criteria that their fulfillment do not depend on the case and should always be in a constant state. On the other hand we have "specific case of application" criteria, i.e. criteria that their fulfillment depends on the case of application. Criteria from the former group should be fulfilled prior to start any modeling case.

According to all above, the purpose of this work is shedding light on the efficiency issue in EM. This is done by explaining what an efficient EMM is, continued by presenting an efficiency evaluation method for general case of application. This method is then applied to Enterprise Knowledge Development (EKD) [9] for evaluating its efficiency in general case of application. This is done in order to support argument about helpfulness of the evaluation method.

The remainder of the paper is organized as follows: section 2 is about the followed research method, section 3 gives explanation about what the *Method Notion* and efficiency mean. This continued by presenting the efficiency evaluation method in section 4. In section 5 result of evaluating of EKD EMM in general case of application is presented. The paper finish by some conclusions about the method and suggestions for the future work in section 6.

2 Method

We started our work by literature review. By doing this, we found out that researchers in EM have worked widely on the issue of quality in EM and developed works for assessing and improving quality of EMMs and models (e.g. SEQUAL [10] and GoM [16]). But the subject of "efficiency" has not been taken into account by the researchers. We considered this as a starting point for a new work for studying efficiency in EM, and specifically EMMs.

The research methodology that we followed in this work was a combination of Deductive, Inductive and Codification. We, as EM experts, had gained some knowledge and anticipation about how an EMM should be by participating in research projects as well as teaching and supervising EM student projects. Based on this, the initial version of the evaluation method was developed by making the tacit knowledge, explicit. This was continued by an iterative cycle of development (build)-justification (evaluation). To carry out this cycle, we had to evaluate some EMMs, and a candidate in this way was EKD. This evaluation process helped in finding some of the strengths and weaknesses of the framework and making some conclusions on that.

3 Related Work

In this section we clarify what we mean by an EMM (3.1) and what efficiency is about (3.2).

3.1 The Method Notion

According to [11], all EMMs build on some implicit or explicit *Perspective* (philosophy). A *Perspective* is the conceptual and value basis of the EMM and includes value principles and categories (with definitions), which are more fully expressed in the EMM without being explicitly articulated. Parts of the *Perspective* can be inherent in the EMM in a rather tacit way.

An EMM involves procedural guidelines that show how to work and what questions to ask. This set of guidelines is called *Procedure*. Besides, there exist representational guidelines which is often called modeling techniques or *Notation*. A *Notation* prescribes how answers to the questions in *Procedure* should be documented. *Procedure* and *Notation* are tightly coupled to each other. *Concepts* are the cement and overlapping parts of the *Notation* and *Procedure*. When there is a close link between *Procedure*, *Notation* and *Concepts* we call this a *Method Component*. Different *Method Components* together form a structure called *Framework*, which includes the phase structure of the EMM. *Cooperation& Collection Principles* is about how different people interact and cooperate when performing the guided work. A *Method Component* can be used within several different *Cooperation Forms*. Figure 1 summarizes what each part of the *Method Notion* and is about how different parts are related to each other. Henceforth, to prevent confusion wherever we write *Method* (capitalized and italicized), it means we are referring to the *Method Notion* or any of its parts; whereas "method" (nor capitalized, neither italicized) means the contribution of the paper, i.e. the evaluation framework.

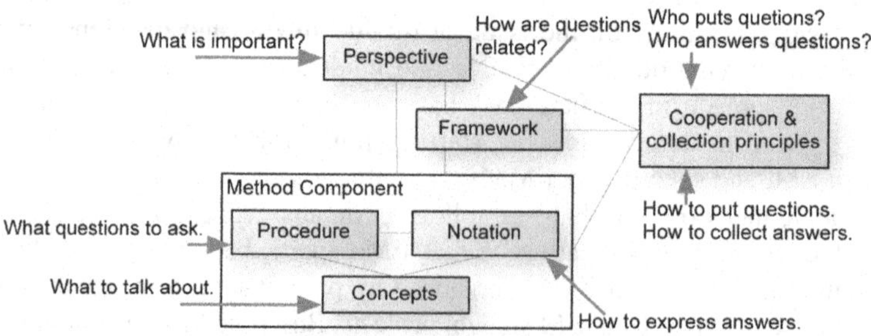

Fig. 1. Method Notion: Relationship between Perspective, Framework, Method Component and Cooperation Forms [11]

3.2 Efficiency

Any process is performed with the aim of gaining the expected results and it should be from high enough quality. On other hand, completion of a process requires using resources that are costly and not infinite. Therefore, people need to keep an eye on the resource usage, whilst carrying out the job. In fact, people would like to gain the maximum output in for the required input. This issue is discussed under the name of "efficiency". Efficiency is an aspect of quality and its fulfillment is a requirement for fulfilling quality of a process. Efficiency has been investigated by different people. By reviewing the works that define this term, we can see that efficiency has been commonly defined as the ratio between output and input [12].

On the other hand, there exists another type of attitude to efficiency that looks at this issue from the viewpoint of "working process and its foreseeability": Efficiency is used for passive or operational activity, which is usually defined technically so that the system and its behavior are foreseeable in advance [13].

Although in the first glance it looks that these two types of attitudes are different, they are not. They are two different ways of looking at efficiency and making it flexible to work about efficiency, based on the current work. Even having a foreseeable working process supports utilization of resources. An important point here is talking about any of "the used resources" or "foreseeability of the working process" has value only if the required results have been gained. Indeed, efforts in the way of having a foreseeable work process or reducing the amount of used resources should not result in sacrificing the results.

4 Efficiency of EMMs

In this section we shed light on the notion of efficiency in EMMs. To do this, we discuss what an efficient EMM is (4.1), continued by introducing the evaluation method. This method is comprised of a preparation stage (4.2) and its main body (efficiency criteria and their related questions) in 4.3.

4.1 What Is an Efficient EMM?

When we talk about an EMM, we are mainly interested in its application process. Therefore, when it comes to efficiency of an EMM, the sort of viewpoint to efficiency that talks about "working process and its foreseeability" is more helpful. Accordingly, we say that if behavior of an EMM (in use) is foreseeable, we firstly can get models closer to our desires, and secondly resources will be used in a more worthwhile way. Respecting [11], an EMM consists of different parts. If behavior of each EMM part is according to the confirmed characteristics (criteria), it supports foreseeability of the whole EMM in use. Fulfillment of these two supports gaining the expected results; and consequently, support its efficiency.

To assess whether the developed models match to the stakeholders' desires, we can use one of the existing frameworks. But for checking efficiency of the EMM we a method presented in section 4.2 and 4.3.

4.2 Preparation Stage

In the evaluation method that we have developed, each part of the EMM (respecting the *Method Notion* in [11]) should match to the efficiency criteria. However, EMM developers do not present their work in a way that these parts are differentiable. Thus, to do evaluation we, as EMM evaluators, have to reconstruct the EMM respecting this notion, i.e. finding out what the *Perspective*, *Framework*, *Method Component* (*Procedure*, *Notation* and *Concepts*) and *Cooperation& Collection Forms* are. Then we are ready to apply the main part of the evaluation method, that is comprised of efficiency criteria and questions for evaluating EMM parts.

4.3 A Method for Evaluating Efficiency of EMMs in General Case of Application

In this section, we introduce our method for evaluating efficiency of EMMs, for general case of application. Respecting the argumentation in 4.1, this method supports evaluating each part of an EMM. For this purpose, we give explanation about how an EMM part should be. These explanations embody in fact criteria that an EMM part should fulfill. If an EMM part conforms to the defined criteria, it has fulfilled the efficiency criteria. In addition, we require a concrete tool to evaluate whether efficiency criteria are fulfilled. Thus, we have defined a set of questions respecting explanations for each EMM to underline the most considerable points that should be taken into account. By applying these questions, we can discuss each EMM part and evaluate its efficiency. The result of these evaluations can be used to reach conclusion about efficiency of the whole EMM.

Here, we should note that the method applier is not restricted to the suggested explanations (criteria). Rather, (s)he based on his (her) needs can define more criteria and evaluation questions.

In the following, the main body of the framework, i.e. collection of explanation about each EMM part and questions, is presented. As the purpose of this framework is efficiency evaluation in general application case, our intent was towards a design that supports nor a subjective neither a case-dependent evaluation.

Perspective: In an EMM it should be specified what important in it is and can be expected from it. In other words, we need to know exactly what can be supported by the EMM. It is vital that *Perspective* be clear and understandable. Any change in the *Perspective* means the coverage of (and consequently the expectations from) the EMM should be reconsidered.

According to all these, we suggest the following evaluations:

- *Does the Perspective specify what can be supported by the EMM?* To find out if the EMM *Perspective* is clear enough, we have to assess if the developer has clarified for what purpose it can be applied and supports modeling the enterprise from what viewpoint
- *Does the Perspective clarify what cannot be supported by the EMM?* As a complement for checking the expressiveness of the *Perspective*, it is even supportive that the *Perspective* mentions what cannot be expected the EMM.

- *Has any explanation been given about the meanings that could be mixed up (with similar words)?* Although by reading the EMM *Perspective*, the user might think that (s)he has found the purpose of the EMM, similarities between close meaning can make confusion. Therefore, we should evaluate if any clarification about such issue is given in the EMM user guide. This evaluation can be done even as a part of the previous bullet point.

Framework: When a *Framework* is going to be applied in an EMM, it should support meeting the *Perspective*, i.e. achievement of the points that are determined in *Perspective*, fulfillment of *Perspective* goals and achieving the underlined results. Applying a non-relevant *Framework* might result in obtaining models which are out of stakeholders' focus point.

In addition to supporting the *Perspective*, it is expected that a *Framework* specifies what phases comprise the EMM, what the purpose of completing each phase is, what the inputs and expected outputs for each phase are. It is even necessary that the order of completing phases be prescribed. For example, we need to know whether we should complete the phases in sequence or in parallel and if it is possible to make changes in the order of phases or even perform some sequential processes in parallel.

According to all these, we suggest the following evaluations:

- *(Is it cleared) what type of EMM Perspective can be supported by this Framework*? This has to be checked in case that the *Framework* is an *External Framework*, i.e. the *Framework* is adapted (or imported) and is not specifically developed for the under discussion EMM. This evaluation is done by reviewing the *Framework* user guide and comparing it with the *Perspective*.
- *Does the phase structure of the Framework support meeting the Perspective?* In case of having an *External Framework*, we should assess suitability of its structure for the EMM and *Perspective*. The reason is that an *External Framework* (and its phases) is not developed for supporting this specific (EMM) *Perspective*. To address this question, we should work on the two following sub-questions:
    - *Are all the Framework phases needed for fulfilling the Perspective?* We should find out if completion of all phases of the *External Framework* are indispensable, or some of them should/ could be neglected.
    - *Are the needed phases able to support the Perspective fully?* After eliminating the unnecessary phases, it should be evaluated whether the set of remaining phases are strong enough to aid in holding up the *Perspective*, or not.
- *Is the structure of the Framework clearly defined?* Efficiency evaluation of a *Framework* structure means assessing if the comprising phases and relations between them match to the criteria . Hence, we break this question into the following sub-questions:

- *Is it cleared in what sequence the phases should be completed?* As working with a *Framework* means completing its phases, we should evaluate relations between different phases. This should aim at finding if it is cleared in what sequence they should be completed, and if any alternatives for that.
- *Is each phase of the Framework well-defined*? This evaluation has to do with the structure of each phase and encompasses issues such as if it is elucidated what the purpose of completing the phase is, what the input(s) and what the output(s) are.

Method Component: This part itself is comprised of *Procedure, Notation* and *Concepts*. Thus, for investigating efficiency of *Method Component* we should evaluate each of these three parts.

Procedure: In an EMM, *Procedure* is supposed to provide guidelines for modeling work. These guidelines should be represented / regarded as questions that help in gaining the required information on the enterprise. It is important that questions in a *Procedure* be clearly formulated and understandable to the readers. These are in fact questions that will be asked by the modeling expert(s) and answers to them are provided by the modeling participants.

Proper formulation of the procedural questions is not the only requirement in a *Procedure*. As it is mentioned in *Framework* section, completion of each *Framework* phase requires asking some procedural questions. And each of these questions should support/ be supported by the other procedural questions in the same phase, with the purpose of addressing the aim of the phase.

Therefore, evaluating *Procedure* means asking and addressing:

- *Are the procedural questions defined clearly?* Asking this question entails clarifying if each question is understandable. Moreover, we should assess if any question is vague and could be interpreted in various ways.
- *Is it cleared what Framework phase is supported by each question?* To clarify this, we should compare each procedural question and its expected answer with the *Framework* phase (the phase that it is specifically developed for, or even several phases) and their goals to find out if the question fits a phase, and consequently the EMM *Framework*.

Notation: By applying *Procedure* (and its questions) we gain some answers. These answers show which real world elements are related to each other and what the relations between them are. We might even need that documenting features of elements or relations be possible. A part of working with a *Method Component* is using *Notation* to document answers to the procedural questions. For applying *Notation* it is required to be familiar with its elements and relations. EMM workers might require to refer to the user guide from time to time and review elucidations on the *Notation* constituents, which are in general about how to present an element. Such a clarification could be in textual and visual form. Providing this information supports the user in selecting the correct elements and relations.

According to all above, we should answer:

- *Are the notational constituents elaborated?* To answer this question, we should consider both textual and graphical presentations and assess whether it is clarified how representation (and formulation) of each notational constituents (i.e. elements, relations and their features) individually and in relation with the other elements should be.
- *Do the Notation and its constituents support implementing answers to the procedural questions?* To answer this, each procedural question (and its expected answer) should be checked against the *Notation* constituents to find out whether the *Procedure* is supported by the *Notation.*

Concepts: As *Procedure* and *Notation* are applied together to produce models, it is needed to have knowledge about their mutual part, i.e. *Concepts.* Besides, as *Concepts* are the cement part between *Notation* and *Procedure*, there is a strong relation between *Concepts, Procedure* and *Notation.* Therefore, it is important that the EMM applier be able to find out what a *Concept* in this specific EMM means, by going through explanations about *Concepts.*

Application of *Procedure* and *Notation* should result in covering the *Concepts.* To support this, it is required to have one-to-one relation between *Concepts* and *Notation* as well as *Concepts* and *Procedure.* In other words, *Concepts* should be fully covered by both *Notation* and *Procedure* i.e., *Procedure* and *Notation* contain several meanings and abstractions that should be understood, either as they are or with the help of *Concepts.*

In order to evaluate if *Concepts* part in an EMM efficient is, we should ask and answer:

- *Are the conceptual elements elaborated?* To answer this question, we should investigate whether it is cleared what each *Concept* stands for in this EMM.
- *Are the defined Concepts covered by the Procedure and Notation?* In order to clear this question, from one side we should check if each *Concept* is covered by the *Procedure* part of the EMM; and from the other side, we check the *Concepts* against the *Notation* to find out if the *Notation* are taken into account in *Notation*, i.e. if *Notation* supports documenting the defined *Concepts.*
- *Are the meanings and abstractions pointed in Procedure and Notation covered by the Concepts?* We do not suggest asking this question as a separate evaluation task, rather we advise keeping an eye on it whilst working with *Procedure* and *Notation* to make sure that all terms used in them are understandable, either standalone or by reviewing *Concepts.*

Cooperation& Collection Forms: To work with an EMM, we should know what working way should be followed, i.e. what *Cooperation& Collection Forms* is appropriate (or even inappropriate). It is even preferred to have knowledge about weaknesses and strengths of the prescribed *Cooperation& Collection Forms.* The expectation is to see all these in the EMM user guide.

Accordingly, we should look for answer for the following questions:

- *Is it clarified what Cooperation& Collection Forms are for the EMM?*
- *Is it clarified what are pros and cons of the mentioned Cooperation& Collection Form?*

5 Efficiency Evaluation of "Enterprise Knowledge Development (EKD)" in General Case of Application

In this section we present results of applying the above introduced method for evaluating EKD. We assume that the reader is familiar with this EMM. Yet, (s)he can refer to the existing publications to get an overview (e.g. [7] and [14]) or deep understanding [9] about it. To carry out this evaluation work, we used [9], which is the complete user guide for it, and answered all questions based on that.

For using this method, first we completed the preparation stage, i.e. reviewed the user guide whilst keeping an eye on the *Method Notion* [11] and reconstructed EKD respecting this notion. This was continued by asking and answering evaluation questions. Results of the evaluation work is presented below. Result of addressing each questions starts with a short answer (Yes/ No/ Partially) to show what we have concluded about efficiency of each EMM part, followed by motivation around it. In this way, the questions were not applicable are determined.

Perspective

Does the *Perspective* clarify what can be supported by the EMM? Yes. In the EKD user guide , the authors have clearly stated how this EMM can support its potential users: "EKD is an approach that provides a systematic and controlled way of analyzing, understanding, developing and documenting an enterprise and its components, by using EM. The purpose of applying EKD is to provide a clear, unambiguous picture of: how the enterprise functions currently ,what are the requirements and the reasons for change, what alternatives could be devised to meet these requirements, what are the criteria and arguments for evaluating these alternatives".

Does the *Perspective* show what cannot be supported by the EMM? And has any explanation been given about meanings that could be mixed up (with similar words)? No. In the EKD user guide clarification about nor what is not supported by the EMM, neither the terms that have close or similar meanings is given.

Framework

(Is it cleared) what type of EMM *Perspective* can be supported by this *Framework*?

Does the phase structure of the EMM support meeting the *Perspective*?

As EKD is not developed on an *External Framework*, we do not need to answer any of these two questions.

Is the structure of the *Framework* defined clearly?

• **Is it cleared in what sequence the phases should be done?** No. According to the EKD user guide, six phases should be completed, each results in gaining a specific type of sub-model. By reviewing the user guide we can see that links between various sub-models are shown. Respecting these links we can conclude that relations between different phases are given. Nevertheless, no suggestion is given regarding the starting point, the sequence of performing the phases or the possible list of alternatives.

• **Is each phase of the *Framework* well-defined?** Partially. By going through the description of each phase we can see that the authors have explained what the purpose of each phase is (each phase is supposed to model the enterprise from a specific view point) and what output can be gained from each. On the other hand, it has not been cleared what inputs are required for completing each phase.

Method Component

Method Component in EKD supports developing six different sub-models: Goals Model (GM), Business Rules Model (BRM), Concepts Model (CM), Business Process Model (BPM) , Actors& Resources Model (ARM) and Technical Components& Requirements Model (TCRM). Therefore, evaluating the *Method Component* means evaluating each of these six *Method Components*. Summary of all these evaluations can be seen below:

Procedure

Are the procedural questions defined clearly? Yes. In the EKD user guide for developing each type of sub-model some driving questions are suggested. The reader is not restricted to these questions, but can use them for defining relevant questions. By going through the driving questions and evaluating them we found them understandable enough and not vague.

Is it cleared what *Framework* phase is supported by each procedural questions? Yes. In EKD each *Method Component* is developed to support a specific phase, aim of each is modeling the enterprise from a specific viewpoint. Therefore, it is clear what phase each *Procedure* (and its procedural questions) support.

Notation

Are the notational constituents elaborated? Partially. The EKD user guide contains enough graphical clarification (in the form of plain *Notation* and sample models) for developing all six *Method Components*.

On the other hand, textual clarification in different *Method Components* is poor or missing. In GM, BRM and TCRM the reader can find how to formulate labels of links by reviewing the general *Notation* and sample models. In GM a detailed explanation about how to write the "goals" and "problems" is given, whereas in TCRM just a small hint can be seen on this. In BPM, ARM, CM and BRM no textual clarification on respectively how to write the "business processes", "actors"& "resources", "concepts"& "attributes" and "business rules" has been given. In CM small notes can be seen beside the *Notation* about what each cardinality sign mean.

Do the *Notation* and its constituents support implementing answers to the procedural questions? Yes. The EKD *Notation* for CM fully supports its *Procedure*. Also, in GM, BRM and TCRM the *Notation* is general and can be specialized to the obtained answers, i.e. supports answers gained from the *Procedure*. Yet in ARM *Notation*, *Concept* PartOF has been left uncovered.

Concepts

Are the conceptual elements elaborated? Yes. In the EKD user guide all *Concepts* introduced for different sub-models are explained in detail.

Are the defined *Concepts* covered by the *Procedure* and *Notation?*

- **Are the defined *Concepts* covered by *Procedure*?** Partially. In all *Method Components*, except CM there exist *Concepts* that are not covered by *Procedure*: "Constraint" in GM, differentiation between different types of "rules" and "processes" in BRM and BPM respectively, "organizational unit", "non-human resource", "individual" and "role" in ARM, and finally "information system goal", "information system problem" and "information system requirements" ("information system functional requirements" and "information system non-functional requirements") in TCRM.
- **Are the defined *Concepts* covered by *Notation*?** Partially. In CM and BPM *Notations* support the *Concepts* fully. The general *Notation* in GM, ARM and TCRM can be specialized to support all *Concepts*, except "information system requirements" in TCRM, and different relationship types ("binary", "PartOF", ISA) in ARM. In BRM different types of rules are defined: "derivation rules", "event action rules" and "constraint rules", whereas they are not differentiated in the *Notation*.

Are the meanings and abstractions pointed in *Procedure* and *Notation* covered by the *Concepts*? Yes. Whilst working with different *Notations* and *Procedures*, we (as EM experts) did not find any term that seems to be vague, but is not elaborated by the *Concepts*.

Cooperation& Collection Forms

Is it clarified what Cooperation& Collection Forms are for the EMM? Yes. According to the EKD user guide, the suitable way for *Cooperation*, in contrast to consultative approach.

Is It explained what are the pros and cons of each? Partially. A list of advantages of participative approach is given in the user guide, which are "enhancement of models quality and consensus" and "achievement of acceptance and commitment". Nonetheless, it is not explained what are the disadvantages of this *Cooperation Form*.

6 Conclusions and Future Work

6.1 Conclusions

An EMM is comprised of different parts that are related to each other and should remain in coordination. This issue has been taken into account by the proposed evaluation method. This method includes two main sets of efficiency criteria and questions: one set supports evaluating each EMM part as an individual unit and the other set supports evaluating relations between different parts have are defined.

The evaluation questions are developed to help in conducting discussions around efficiency of an EMM part. This means, answers to these questions are preferred to be motivations about why the evaluating person believes this part efficient is or is not. For addressing these questions a "Yes/ No" (or in some cases "Partially") answer might be useful as an initial answer, but it is required to support it with more detailed clarifications. Although a "short" answer can be useful to show our conclusion about efficiency of that specific part, we should still present reasons to help the reader in understanding the logic of the reached conclusion.

After all these, the intention of conducting this work was developing a method that is not case-dependent or subjective. But by reviewing the framework and results of applying it to EKD we can see that there are questions that are inevitable to be subjective. In these questions, answers are mainly about EMM evaluator's deductions about a specific criterion. This means by involving another group of evaluators, the answers to the questions might differ.

6.2 Future Work

After defining efficiency criteria for general case of application, it is needed to be concerned about how to evaluate efficiency in specific application cases. Therefore, the future work will be finding out what criteria should be covered by an EMM to say it is efficient in specific case of application, plus questions that help in evaluating them.

References

1. Khademhosseinieh, B., Seigerroth, U.: An evaluation of enterprise modelling methods in the light of business and IT alignment. In: Zhang, R., Cordeiro, J., Li, X., Zhang, Z., Zhang, J. (eds.) Proceedings of the 13th International Conference on Enterprise Information Systems, pp. 479–484. INSTICC, Setubal (2011)
2. Harmon, P.: The scope and evolution of business process management. In: vom Brocke, J., Rosemann, M. (eds.) Handbook on Business Process Management, International Handbooks Information System, Germany. Springer, Heidelberg (2010)
3. Seigerroth, U.: Enterprise Modeling and Enterprise Architecture: The Constituents of Transformation and Alignment of Business and IT. International Journal of IT/Business Alignment and Governance 2(1), 16–34 (2011)

4. Tissot, F., Crump, W.: An Integrated Enterprise Modeling Environment. In: Bernus, P., Mertins, K., Schmidt, G. (eds.) International Handbooks on Information Systems. Springer, Heidelberg (2006)
5. Whitman, L., Huff, B.: On the Use of Enterprise Models. The International Journal of Flexible Manufacturing Systems 13, 195–208 (2001)
6. Larsson, L., Segerberg R.: An Approach for Quality Assurance in Enterprise Modelling. MSc thesis, Department of Computer and Systems Sciences, Stockholm University, No 04-22 (2004)
7. Stirna, J., Persson, A., Sandkuhl, K.: Participative Enterprise Modeling: Experiences and Recommendations. In: Krogstie, J., Opdahl, A.L., Sindre, G. (eds.) CAiSE 2007 and WES 2007. LNCS, vol. 4495, pp. 546–560. Springer, Heidelberg (2007)
8. Kaidalova, I.: Efficiency indicators for Enterprise Modelling Methods and Enterprise Models. MSc thesis, Jönköping University- School of Engineering (2011)
9. Bubenko, J., Persson, A., Stirna, J.: EKD user guide, Technical report. Royal Institute of Technology (KTH) and Stockholm University, Stockholm (2001)
10. Krogstie, J.: Quality of Models. In: Model-Based Development and Evolution of Information System, pp. 205–247. Springer, London (2012)
11. Goldkuhl, G., Lind, M., Seigerroth, U.: Method Integration: The Need for a Learning Perspective. Special Issue of the IEE Proceedings - Software and Distributed Systems Engineering Journal 145(4), 113–118 (1998)
12. Emrouznejad, A., Ali Emrouznejad's Data Envelopment Analysis Homepage. Warwick Business School, Warwick University, UK (1995-2001), `http://www.deazone.com/` (accessed February 26, 2012)
13. Kurosawa, K.: Productivity measurement and management at the company level: the Japanese experience. Elsevier, Amsterdam (1991)
14. Zikra, I., Stirna, J., Zdravkovic, J.: Bringing Enterprise Modeling Closer to Model-Driven Development. In: Johannesson, P., Krogstie, J., Opdahl, A.L. (eds.) PoEM 2011. LNBIP, vol. 92, pp. 268–282. Springer, Heidelberg (2011)
15. Persson, A., Stirna, J.: Towards Defining a Competence Profile for the Enterprise Modeling Practitioner. In: van Bommel, P., Hoppenbrouwers, S., Overbeek, S., Proper, E., Barjis, J. (eds.) PoEM 2010. LNBIP, vol. 68, pp. 232–245. Springer, Heidelberg (2010)
16. Becker, J., Rosemann, M., von Uthmann, C.: Guidelines of Business Process Modeling. In: van der Aalst, W.M.P., Desel, J., Oberweis, A. (eds.) Business Process Management. LNCS, vol. 1806, pp. 30–49. Springer, Heidelberg (2000)

On the Multi-objective Optimization Aided Drawing of Connectors for Graphs Related to Business Process Management

Vytautas Jancauskas[1], Ausra Mackute-Varoneckiene[2], Audrius Varoneckas[2], and Antanas Zilinskas[1]

[1] Vilnius University, Institute of Mathematics and Informatics, Vilnius, Lithuania
[2] Vytautas Magnus University, Faculty of Informatics, Kaunas, Lithuania
antanas.zilinskas@mii.vu.lt

Abstract. A problem of drawing aesthetically looking graphs is considered. We focus on graphs related to management of business processes. Vertices of a graph are visualized as rectangles (flow objects), and edges are visualized as rectangular connectors (sequence flow). A particular problem of aesthetic drawing is considered where location of vertices is fixed, and the lines representing the edges should be drawn. The latter problem is restated as a graphs oriented multi-objective combinatorial optimization problem. The generally recognized criteria of aesthetic presentation, such as the general length of lines, the number of crossings, and the number of bends, are considered as the objectives to be minimized. The attitude of the potential users of the supposed algorithms towards the relative importance of the considered criteria is elicited by a psychological experiment. The elicited information is used in the development of domain-specific multi-objective optimization algorithms. We propose for that problem a version of the metaheuristics of ant colony optimization. The efficiency is evaluated experimentally using randomized test problems of different complexity.

Keywords: visualization of graphs, multi-objective optimization, psychological experiment, business process diagrams.

1 Introduction

Problems of graph drawing attract many researchers, and plenty of publications on that subjects are available. Nevertheless special cases of that problem frequently cannot be solved by straightforward application of the known methods and algorithms. In the present paper we consider a particular problem of drawing graphs where criteria of aesthetics are crucial. Such problems are interesting with relation to the drawing of business processes diagrams. We state the problem as a multi-objective optimization problem where aesthetic criteria are optimized. Although the importance of the criteria of aesthetics to perception of information presented by graphs is thoroughly investigated, multi-objective optimization aided visualization algorithms, to our best knowledge, have not been proposed in, at least, open literature.

T. Skersys, R. Butleris, and R. Butkiene (Eds.): ICIST 2012, CCIS 319, pp. 87–100, 2012.

The Business Process Diagrams (BPD) are widely used in business process management. The Business Process Modeling Notation (BPMN) is accepted as a standard for drawing the Business Process Diagrams (BPD) [1]. According to the general opinion, the aesthetic attractiveness of the drawing of a BPD is especially important since the aesthetic layouts are also most informative and practical [2]. The graph drawing aesthetics is comprehensively discussed, e.g. in [3], [4], [5]. However, the criteria of the aesthetic attractiveness not always guarantee the informativeness of the diagrams drawn; we cite [4]: "Few algorithms are designed for a specific domain, and there is no guarantee that the aesthetics used for generic layout algorithms will be useful for the visualization of domain-specific diagrams". In the present paper we consider a particular problem of drawing graphs related to the business processes of SME: the algorithms of drawing the aesthetically pleasing sequence flows are considered assuming the flow objects fixed. The research is aimed at the substantiation of the algorithms supposed for including into a relatively simple and not expensive software package oriented not only to the consultants of business management but also to the managers of SMEs [6]. The original problem is reduced to a problem of the combinatorial multi-objective optimization. We start with the analysis of the attitude of the potential users of the supposed algorithms towards the relative importance of the widely acceptable criteria of BPD aesthetics. The latter are used as the objectives of the multi-objective optimization problem which formalizes the problem of BPD drawing as an optimization problem. For the general discussion on the synergy of optimization and visualization we refer to [7]. The stated multi-objective optimization problem related to BPD drawing is tackled by a version of the algorithm based on the ant colony metaheuristics.

2 An Original Problem of Visualization

In the present paper a particular problem of graph drawing is considered which is related to drawing of BPDs. Aesthetically pleasing lines, which represent the sequence flow, should be drawn assuming the fixed location of the flow objects. The problem of drawing is restated as a combinatorial multi-objective problem where the objectives correspond to the criteria usually used to assess the aesthetics of a BPD. The developed algorithms are supposed to be used interactively where the flow objects are located by a human user. We are going to continue this research and to develop an algorithm for the aesthetic re-location of the flow objects.

To enable a user completely percept the information, presented by the observable part of the BPD, the sub-charts which comprise up to 30 shapes, are drawn. A navigation tool aids a user to specify the sub-chart of interest. The more detailed information concerning the specified flow objects can be extracted by telescoping. To denote the flow objects in the considered diagrams, the notation of BPMN, namely the rectangles, the rhombs, and the circles, is used where these shapes represent the processes, the gateways, and the events correspondingly. The shapes are located in the pool lanes. The sequence flow is represented by the lines constituted of orthogonal

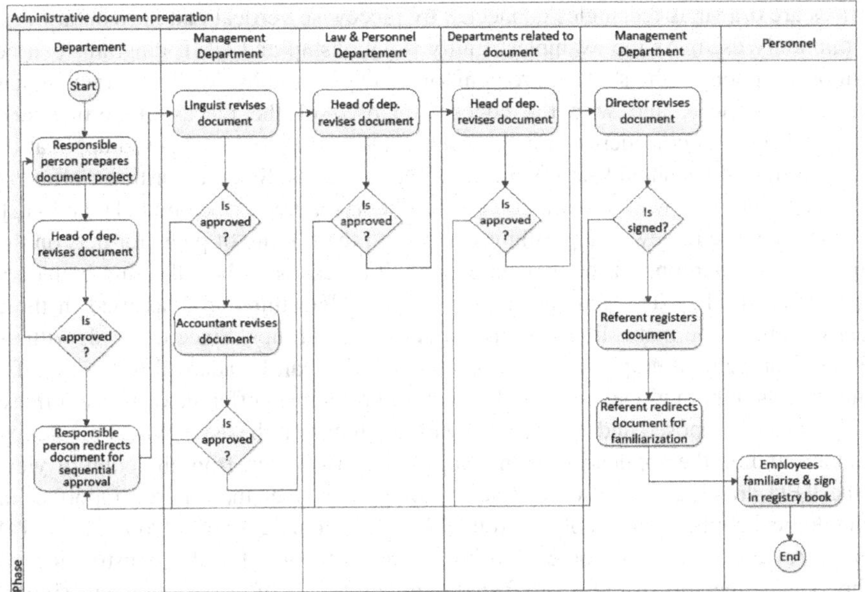

Fig. 1. An example of BPD

line segments. BPD can be augmented by the data objects and the data flows. An example of the diagrammatic visualization of a business process is presented in Fig. 1.

As the main criteria of aesthetics considered in the literature, e.g. in [2], [8], [9], [10], are: the total length of connectors, the number of crossings, the number of bends, the uniformity of the distribution of shapes in the area of the drawing, and the compatibility of the process sub-flows with the generalized top-down and left-right direction. However, the influence of these criteria to the perception of the information presented by the considered BPD is different, and depends on the user of the BPD. To implement a visualization method, which ensures the effective perception of a BPD, the attitude of potential users towards the listed above criteria is important. We propose to elicit the generalized attitude of a group of the potential users by means of a psychological experiment. Subsequently the elicited information supplements the statement of the optimization problem which solution is used to specify the drawing of the orthogonal connectors.

3 A Brief Overview of Single-objective Algorithms Aimed at Similar Problems

In the present paper we focus on the problem of the sequence flow visualization. Therefore the differences of the flow objects can be ignored, and a single rectangular shape is used below to represent the flow objects. The visualization of graphs, where vertices are drawn as rectangles connected by piecewise vertical and horizontal lines, is commonly used. As the examples, Entity Relationship and UML diagrams can be mentioned among others. The problem of drawing graphs, with the rectangular images of vertices, and with the edges composed of the pieces of vertical and horizontal lines, is considered in many papers. Depending on a supposed application area, the algorithms should satisfy different requirements. Some algorithms, efficient from the point of view of general complexity theory, are described by [11], and [12]. A comprehensive review of algorithms oriented to the routing of paths for nets on the chip layout to interconnect the pins on the circuit blocks or pads at the chip boundary is presented in [13]. The general purpose routing algorithms are classified in three groups, namely, the maze, line-search, and A*-search groups. Since those algorithms are based on general graph-searching techniques they can be adapted to the specific requirements of both global and detailed routing problems. Different versions of those algorithms are proposed and investigated with the focus on the asymptotic complexity estimates and on the application in the chip design. However, from the point of view of the BPD drawing, the criteria of aesthetics prevail over the criteria important in technological applications emphasized in [13]. In a recent paper by Wybrow et al [14] a brief review of the available algorithms and software, for the construction of orthogonal connectors, is presented from the point of view of the requirements similar to those stated above. The experimental testing performed by these authors has shown that some of the available software packages although provide the automatic orthogonal connector routing however produce the routes which may overlap other objects in the diagram. Popular software packages, Microsoft Visio 2007, and Concept Draw Pro5, provide the object-avoiding orthogonal connector routing, but in both cases the aesthetic criteria, such as minimizing distance or number of segments, are not taken into account. We cite the conclusion made in the introduction of [14]: "in all current tools that we are aware of, automatic routing of orthogonal connectors uses ad-hoc heuristics that lead to aesthetically unpleasing routes and unpredictable behavior". Agreeing with the latter conclusion as well as with the remarks cited in the Introduction we find the developing of new domain-specific algorithms reasonable.

4 The Description of the Psychological Experiment

The relative importance of the aesthetic criteria of BPD can be different for the different groups of professionals involved in the design and maintenance of business processes. We are interested in the attitude towards these criteria of the potential users of the algorithms in development. Therefore the pool of participants of the psychological experiments was selected from the master degree students in Business Informatics and in Applied Informatics, and of the businessmen who are professionals in information technology. The students have heard courses in software engineering, information systems, and data visualization at Vytautas Magnus University. These courses include themes on the visualization aesthetics, drawing of UML and CASE related diagrams as well as the business process modeling. The description of the assignments to the participants was in Lithuanian. For the repeating the experiment with a different pool of participants only minor revision would be sufficient to take into account education, practical skills, interests, and the other characteristics of the group of the respondents considered.

The psychological experiment is designed to elicit information on the relative importance of the criteria frequently used to evaluate the aesthetics and comprehensibility of BPD. Three criteria are considered: the total length of connectors, the number of crossings, and the compatibility of the process sub-flows with the generalized top-down and left-right direction. The criterion *number of bends* can be a priori accepted the most important one as it follows from [5], [10], [15]. The criterion of the uniformity of the distribution of shapes in the area of the drawing is not included into consideration since the shapes are supposed to be located by the human users. The goal of the psychological experiment is to rank the considered criteria and to evaluate their relative importance quantitatively.

4.1 The Application Domain

The process model used is of the type of models of administrative document preparation in a business enterprise. The document preparation process is maintained by the structure of the enterprise: the law and personnel department, the management department, the department responsible for document preparation, the other departments related to the documents and personnel. The structure of the enterprise is represented by the swimlanes of the BPD. The example of BPD is presented in Fig. 1.

4.2 The Design of BPD for Testing

The attitude of the participants towards the importance of the aesthetic criteria considered is analyzed using the results of the psychological experiment where the participants evaluated the esthetics of the specially drawn BPD. Following [4] the test diagrams have been drawn to represent three levels of the aesthetic appeal of BPD with respect to the criterion of interest:

– low – the reading and understanding of the process model becomes difficult, i.e., a lot of connector crossings puzzles perception of the BPD;

– middle – the process model is conceived without substantial difficulties but some effort is needed and some irritation related to the criterion considered is not avoided, i.e., the connector crossings somewhat disturb the perception of the considered business process;

– high – excellence with respect to the criterion of interest, i.e., BPD without of the unavoidable crossings of connectors.

One of the test diagrams is presented in the Fig. 1 where the criteria are of the following levels: crossings – high, length – middle, compatibility of sub – flows – middle.

4.3 The Implementation

The psychological experiment consists of two stages of 20 minutes duration.

The purpose of the first stage is to acquaint the participants of the experiment with the business process whose various BPDs are evaluated at the second stage. The respondents are given description of the business process and are asked to draw the BPD in the standard notations. All respondents have understood the business process properly since their drawings were correct.

At the second stage the participants are asked to evaluate the readability and comprehensibility of the received drawings with respect to the aesthetic criteria. Seven BPDs have been prepared for the experiment. Six of them represented either low or high level of the expressiveness of one of criteria, while the other two criteria were at the middle level of expressiveness. One drawing presented a BPD where all criteria were at the middle level of expressiveness. Each respondent has received six drawings of the former type and three drawings of the latter type. Nine drawings represent three levels of expressiveness of all three criteria considered. The diagrams have been presented to the respondents in the random order. The respondents have been asked to evaluate the comprehensibility and aesthetics of each BPD paying special attention to the criterion which level of expressiveness was represented by that BPD. The evaluation should be performed in scale between 0 and 1, where 1 means very good and 0 means very bad.

5 Results of the Psychological Experiment

The results of the psychological experiment consist of three lists where the assessments are related to three criteria of interest. Every list contains the assessments of three BPDs by 19 respondents. For example, the *i*-th line of the list related to the connector crossings (0.3 0.6 0.8) means that the *i*-th respondent has assessed the BPD of the low level of aesthetic appeal by the grade 0.3 in the scale between 0 and 1. The next numbers mean the grades of the BPDs of the middle and high level of aesthetic appeal correspondingly.

The attitude of a respondent towards the relative importance of two criteria is elicited by comparison of grades given to the pairs of BPDs of the same level. Let us assume that the grades given to BPDs with respect to the criteria C_1 and C_2 are (c_{11}, c_{12}, c_{13}) and (c_{21}, c_{22}, c_{23}) correspondingly. The inequality $c_{11} < c_{21}$ is interpreted as one yes-vote for C_1 as the criterion of the higher importance than C_2. The inequalities $c_{12} < c_{22}$ and $c_{13} > c_{23}$ have the same interpretation. Such a binary relation formalizes the notion that bad and medium expression levels of the most important criteria are graded worse than those of the least important criteria. The latter normally are graded rather permissively. The excellent alternatives of the most important criteria, contrary, are graded by higher grades than the excellent alternatives of the least important criteria.

The binary relation of importance among the criteria is defined according to the sums of yes-votes: $C_1 \succ C_2$ denotes that C_1 has got more yes-votes than C_2 implying that C_1 has been evaluated as more important than C_2. The application of that concept of ranking to the results of the psychological experiment implies the following result

$$\textit{the number of bends} \succ \textit{the number of crossings} \sim$$

$$\textit{the compatibility of sub-flows} \succ \textit{the length of connectors},$$

where the a priory assessment of the criterion the number of bends as the most important one is taken into account. To assess the relative importance of the considered criteria quantitatively we apply the method proposed by T.Saaty (see, [16], [17]) for the Analytic Hierarchy Process (AHP). That method requires representing the pairwise comparison of the importance of criteria as the ratio judgments. The five point scale is used to evaluate quantitatively the relative intensity of the importance of the criterion of the higher importance against the less important alternative. The evaluation is based on the percentage of the yes-votes collected according to the scale described by Table 1.

Table 1. Results of psychological experiment on BPD aesthetics

Points	Intensity of importance	Percentage of yes-votes
1	Insignificant	50% – 60%
2	Modest	61% – 70%
3	Strong	71% – 80%
4	Very strong	81% – 90%
5	Extreme	91% –100%

The matrix of the results of pairwise comparisons should include also the ratio judgments of less important alternatives against the more important ones; that part of the matrix is filled by the reciprocals of known symmetric elements. The weights of the alternatives compared are defined by the elements of the eigenvector of the matrix of pairwise comparisons which corresponds to the largest eigenvalue; see [17] for details. The matrix of the ratio judgments, which summarizes the results of the psychological experiment, and the weights of the criteria computed by the method used in AHP are presented below

$$\begin{pmatrix} C_k \setminus C_r & C_1 & C_2 & C_3 & C_4 \\ C_1 & 1 & 5 & 5 & 5 \\ C_2 & 0.2 & 1 & 1 & 4 \\ C_3 & 0.2 & 1 & 1 & 4 \\ C_4 & 0.2 & 1/4 & 1/4 & 1 \end{pmatrix} \Rightarrow \begin{pmatrix} w_1 \\ w_2 \\ w_3 \\ w_4 \end{pmatrix} = \begin{pmatrix} 0.60 \\ 0.16 \\ 0.16 \\ 0.06 \end{pmatrix} \qquad (1)$$

where the following notations for the criteria are used: C_1 – the number of bends, C_2 – the number of crossings, C_3 – the compatibility of sub-flows, C_4 – the total length of the connectors. The algorithmic evaluation of the quantitative value of the criterion C_3

for the given BPD is difficult. Therefore, the number of criteria in the statement of the multi-objective optimization problem is limited by three: C_1, C_2, C_4. The weights of these criteria are computed similarly to those in (2)

$$\begin{pmatrix} C_k \setminus C_r & C_1 & C_2 & C_4 \\ C_1 & 1 & 5 & 5 \\ C_2 & 0.2 & 1 & 4 \\ C_4 & 0.2 & 1/4 & 1 \end{pmatrix} \Rightarrow \begin{pmatrix} w_1 \\ w_2 \\ w_4 \end{pmatrix} = \begin{pmatrix} 0.69 \\ 0.21 \\ 0.10 \end{pmatrix} \tag{2}$$

The relatively large weight of the criterion *number of bends* is implied by its extreme intensity of importance set a priori. Such an evaluation is based on the widely recognized opinion substantiated, e.g. in [5], [10], [15]. It seems reasonable, however, to evaluate the weight of this criterion by a future psychological experiment equally with the other criteria.

6 The Proposed Algorithm

Let us specify the data which defines the problem of the visualization of a sequence flow. A usual for graph presentation data structure can be used here however the following specifics should be taken into account. The rectangle shapes are located at the nodes of a quadratic mesh. The segments of the orthogonal connectors can stretch along the borders of the pool lines and in the passages which are orthogonal to these lines, and interpose between the cells of the mesh. An example presented in Fig. 2 illustrates the permissible ways for routing: a connector starts at the point on the contour of the shape of origin and reaches the point on the contour of the destination shape, interconnecting only the neighboring thick points.

The construction of a desirable connector is a combinatorial optimization problem. The algorithms for the construction of the connectors optimal with respect to a single objective are discussed in Section 2. However, the formal involvement of all three criteria by a modification of a known, e.g. the shortest path type, graph algorithm seems difficult.

Let us start with the general comments on the validating the algorithm selection for a multi-objective optimization problem. The multi-objective algorithms of the type of the classical mathematical programming are efficient for the problems where the objective functions satisfy requirements very restrictive from the point of view of applications [18]. The stochastic algorithms are appropriate for single objective global optimization of the objective functions with various irregularities as discussed e.g. in [19]. The special case of stochastic algorithms, namely the evolutionary algorithms, is appropriate for solution of various applied problems of multi-objective optimization as shown in [20]. Therefore a stochastic metaheuristic algorithm seems appropriate for the development of an algorithm for the problem considered. The ant colony optimization (ACO) algorithms are especially oriented to search for short paths in

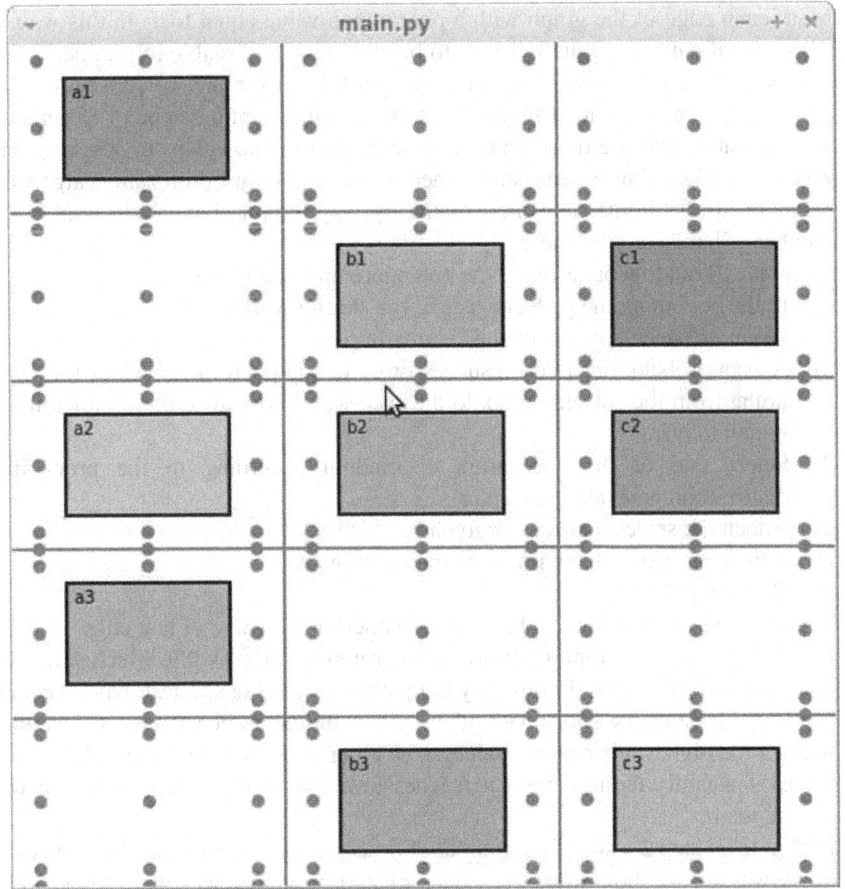

Fig. 2. A graphical illustration of data for solving the routing problem

complicated graphs [21], [22]. ACO algorithms are also efficient in solving bi-criteria traveling sales person problem as shown in the recent paper [23]. Following the arguments above we have developed two versions of ACO specified for the considered problem.

The first version differs from the standard version in the amount of pheromone placed on the path traveled by the ant:

$$\Delta_{pheromone} = \frac{w_L}{L - L_{\min} + 1} + \frac{w_b}{N_b - N_{b\min} + 1} + \frac{w_c}{N_c - N_{c\min} + 1}, \quad (3)$$

where L, N_b, N_c denote the total length, number of bends, and number of crossings of the considered connectors correspondingly; w with an index denotes weight of the corresponding criterion; min in the index denotes the current minimal value of the corresponding criterion. Below we present a description of the algorithm.

1) Mark each edge of the graph with a pheromone value equal to 1. In this way, at the start, all paths are equally likely to be chosen. It is possible to set pheromone values to something other than one at the start. For example we could use some other algorithm, or even ACO itself, maybe with different parameters, to generate a set of paths, and use those paths to modify pheromone values in advance, thus giving the algorithm a head start. Then, the ant colony optimization algorithm could be used to fine tune these paths by, say, emphasizing reduction in the number of bends or crossings.
2) Generate 10 random paths using the procedure outlined below.
   a) In the beginning the path consists of the starting vertex only.
   b) Generate successors for the last vertex in path.
   c) Assign probabilities to each successor by taking pheromone values for edges going from the current vertex to the successor. Normalize these probabilities to add to one.
   d) Select one of the successors at random according to the probability distribution generated in step (c).
   e) Attach the selected successor to path.
   f) If the new vertex is the final one then terminate.
   g) Go to step (b).
3) For each edge in path add Δ pheromone to pheromone value of that edge.
4) For each edge in the graph multiply the pheromone value by 0.9, which simulates pheromone evaporation. In this way the paths that are the shortest, have the least bends and least intersections with other paths will tend to be used most since they will get the highest pheromone values. The other paths will have their pheromone values constantly reduced until it reaches levels so low that almost no ant will choose them.
5) Repeat from step 2 a specified number of times. In the experiments the number of times was set to 500. However, values of 200 or even lower were found to be sufficient for the paths to settle.

The second version of the algorithm is developed implementing ideas of the Pareto Ant Colony Optimization (P-ACO) [24]. Here it is aimed at constructing a Pareto optimal set of paths in a graph, taking into account several criteria. As shown in [23] similar algorithm is efficient to solve bi-objective TSP problems.

A path is considered as a sequence of vertices. In the problems with weighted graphs, the sum of weights in the path can be considered as one of the path criteria. The algorithm uses pheromone matrices τ^k, $k=1,\dots,K$, where K denotes the number of objectives. The values of matrix elements τ^k_{ij} define the pheromone quantity corresponding to k-th objective placed on the edge connecting vertices i and j. These matrices are updated during the search, and they guide the ants along the edges of the graph. Different ants choose their way in the graph with different regard to the objectives. The algorithm is described below.

1) Initialize the pheromone matrix τ^k, placing on every edge the same quantity of pheromone; however ratio of pheromone quantity corresponding to different objectives (τ^k_{ij}/τ^h_{ij}) is equal to the ratio of weights in (2).

2) A specified number of paths n is generated. Each path should be taken by a single ant. Paths are generated as described below:
   a) An ant computes a vector of weights $p = (p_1, \ldots, p_k)$ for every objective. Value p_i, is chosen from uniform random distribution. These random weights serve to place emphasis on different objectives. This allows different ants to explore paths that are better in regards to some particular objective.
   b) If ant is at a node i, the next node is computed using formula (4), where Ω is the set of nodes directly reachable to from node i, q_0 is parameter of the algorithm, q is a random number from uniform distribution, η_{ij} is a priori attractiveness of edge from i to j, and α, β are parameters of the algorithm which evaluate importance of a priori knowledge or the pheromone matrix values:

$$j = \begin{cases} \arg\max_{h\in\Omega}\left[\sum_{k=1}^{K} p_k \tau_{ih}^k\right]^u \cdot \eta_{ih}^\beta, & \text{if } q \le q_0 \\ \hat{i}, & \textit{otherwise} \end{cases} \tag{4}$$

   where $\hat{i}$ signifies a node in Ω chosen using the probabilities calculated using formula (**5**):

$$p(h) = \begin{cases} \dfrac{\left[\sum_{k=1}^{K} p_k \tau_{ih}^k\right]^\alpha \cdot \eta_{ih}^\beta}{\sum_{h\in\Omega}\left[\sum_{k=1}^{K} p_k \tau_{ih}^k\right]^\alpha \cdot \eta_{ih}^\beta}, & \textit{if } h \in \Omega, \\ 0, & \textit{otherwise} \end{cases} \tag{5}$$

   c) Each ant, while travelling through edge $i \to j$ updates the pheromone values in each of the matrices. The update formula is $\tau^k_{ij} \leftarrow (1\text{-}\rho)\cdot\tau^k_{ij} + \rho\cdot\tau_0$, where ρ is evaporation rate. Parameter ρ is usually set to a value close to 0.1; this update function brings the pheromone value closer to initial value τ_0.
3) After all ants have finished their run two best ants are selected, separately for each objective k, i.e. two ants which found the smallest values of objectives. Then the pheromone matrices are updated using the following formula

$$\tau_{ij}^k \leftarrow (1-\rho)\tau_{ij}^k + \rho\Delta\tau_{ij}^k,$$

where

$$\Delta\tau_{ij}^k = \begin{cases} 15, & \text{if edge } i \to j \text{ belongs to the best and second - best paths,} \\ 10, & \text{if edge } i \to j \text{ belongs to the best path,} \\ 5, & \text{if edge } i \to j \text{ belongs to the second - best path,} \\ 0, & \text{0, otherwise.} \end{cases}$$

4) The current ants' solution is appended to the candidate set of Pareto optimal solutions if it is not dominated by the solutions in the stored candidate set. If it dominates some of the stored solutions, the latter are discarded.
5) This process is repeated from step 2 for a fixed number of iterations.

7 Computational Experiment

The proposed algorithm is implemented in C++, and its performance is evaluated experimentally. The statistics of the criteria of the constructed connectors is collected by the solution of randomly generated test problems. The locations of shapes are generated at the nodes of the rectangular mesh randomly with the uniform distribution. The randomly selected pairs of shapes are required to be connected. The size of the mesh is 3×5. The number of shapes is 6, 8, and 10, representing problems of increasing complexity. The mean values and standard deviations of the considered criteria are computed using the data of $m = 100$ solved test problems which are generated randomly as described above. The result of the solution of a particular problem is random since the ACO algorithm is randomized. Therefore, the optimization is repeated $k = 100$ times for each test problem.

The results of the experiments with the first version of ACO show that the most important criterion, namely the number of bends, for the medium dense diagrams can be reasonably improved by choosing the high value of the corresponding weight. The found values of the other two criteria are not sensitive with respect to the weights, and they are near optimal. The last lines in the tables present the results where 2/3 of cells are occupied by shapes. In the latter case only few indeed rational connectors are possible, and similar solutions are found with rather arbitrary values of weights.

Table 2. The mean values and standard deviations of the criteria of connectors found by the first version of ACO using the following weights: $w_L = 0.1$, $w_b = 0.69$, $w_c = 0.21$

k	L (means)	L (std)	N_b (means)	N_b (std)	N_c (means)	N_c (std)
6	7.832	3.092	9.825	3.856	1.437	1.594
8	10.103	3.512	12.622	3.838	3.451	3.610
10	12.680	3.704	15.770	4.307	5.483	4.763

Table 3. The mean values and standard deviations of the criteria of connectors found by the first version of ACO using the following weights: $w_L = w_b = w_c = 0.33$

k	L (means)	L (std)	N_b (means)	N_b (std)	N_c (means)	N_c (std)
6	7.871	3.143	11.958	5.084	1.369	1.505
8	10.050	3.593	15.165	5.344	3.003	3.075
10	12.631	3.721	16.771	5.102	5.166	4.532

The second version of ACO is more sophisticated. Here an ant chooses the direction to move from every node taking into account partial information on the objectives accumulated for all edges. Therefore different ants find sub optimal paths with respect to different objectives. The combination of parts of such paths is indeed more advantageous in constructing non-dominated solutions than combination of parts of paths which are sub-optimal with respect to a weighted sum of objectives. It could be expected that the more complete information about objectives implies the improvement of solutions with respect to the most important objective. The results of Table 4 show that the expectation was exceeded: the solutions are improved with respect to all objectives. The results of our experiments corroborate the conclusion of [23] on efficiency of the second version of ACO algorithm (called Pareto Ant Colony Optimization in [24]) for the solution of multi-objective graph optimization problems.

Table 4. The mean values and standard deviations of the criteria of connectors found by the second version of ACO

k	L (means)	L (std)	N_b (means)	N_b (std)	N_c (means)	N_c (std)
6	6.562	2.214	7.572	2.451	1.402	1.598
8	8.639	2.552	10.710	2.818	2.380	2.410
10	10.965	2.755	13.912	3.267	3.880	2.883

Both versions of ACO algorithm find the solution in time negligible from a human user point of view.

8 Conclusions

A problem of the aesthetical drawing of rectangular connectors, representing edges of graphs related to the BPD for small-medium enterprises, is re-stated as a combinatorial multi-objective optimization. The relative importance of the criteria of aesthetics is assessed by the results of a psychological experiment. A version of ant colony optimization algorithm is adapted to the considered problem, and its efficiency is evaluated by the solution of a set of randomly generated test problems. A natural continuation of this work is testing of the proposed algorithms with the graphs of real BPD of small-medium enterprises, and the comparison of the obtained quantitative results with the subjective assessments of experts.

Acknowledgements. The support by the Agency for Science, Innovation and Technology (MITA) trough the grant Nr.31V-145 is acknowledged.

References

1. Owen, M., Jog, R.: BPMN and Business Process Management, pp. 1–27 (2003), `http://www.bpmn.org`
2. Battista, G.D., Eades, P., Tamassia, R., Tollis, I.G.: Graph Drawing, Algorithms for the Visualisation of Graphs. Prentice Hall (1999)

3. Bennett, C., Ryall, J., Spalteholz, L., Gooch, A.: The Aesthetics of Graph Visualization. In: Cunningham, D.W., Meyer, G., Neumann, L. (eds.) Computational Aesthetics in Graphics, Visualization, and Imaging, pp. 1–8 (2007)
4. Purchase, H.C., McGill, M., Colpoys, L., Carrington, D.: Graph drawing aesthetics and the comprehension of UML class diagrams: an empirical study. In: Proceedings of the 2001 Asia-Pacific Symposium on Information Visualization, vol. 9, pp. 129–137 (2001)
5. Purchase, H.C.: Metrics for Graph Drawing Aesthetics. Journal of Visual Languages & Computing 13, 501–516 (2002)
6. ORGSOFT, `http://www.orgsoft.lt`
7. Žilinskas, A., Žilinskas, J.: Optimization based visualization. In: Floudas, C., Pardalos, P. (eds.) Encyclopedia of Optimization, pp. 2785–2791. Springer, Heidelberg (2009)
8. Purchase, H.C., Carrington, D., Allder, J.A.: Empirical evaluation of aesthetics based graph layout. Empirical Softw. Eng. 7(3), 233–255 (2002)
9. Kaufmann, M., Wagner, D.: Drawing Graphs: Methods and Models. Springer (2001)
10. Taylor, M., Rodgers, P.: Applying graphical design techniques to graph visualization. In: Proceedings of the 9th International Conference on Information Visualization, IV 2005, pp. 651–656 (2005)
11. Yang, C.-D., Lee, D., Wong, C.: Rectilinear Path Problems among Rectilinear Obstacles Revisited. SIAM J. Comput. 24, 457–472 (1995)
12. Lee, D., Yang, C., Wong, C.: Rectilinear paths among rectilinear obstacles. Discrete Applied Mathematics 70(3), 185–216 (1996)
13. Chen, H.-Y., Chang, Y.-W.: Global and Detailed Routing. In: Wang, L.-T., Chang, Y.-W., Cheng, K.-T. (eds.) Electronic Design Automation: Synthesis, Verification, and Testing, pp. 687–749. Elsevier/Morgan Kaufmann (2008)
14. Wybrow, M., Marriott, K., Stuckey, P.J.: Orthogonal Connector Routing. In: Eppstein, D., Gansner, E.R. (eds.) GD 2009. LNCS, vol. 5849, pp. 219–231. Springer, Heidelberg (2010)
15. Tamassia, R., Battista, G.D., Batini, C.: Automatic graph drawing and readability of diagrams. IEEE Trans. Syst. Man Cybern. 18(1), 61–79 (1988)
16. Farkas, A.: The Analysis of the Principal Eigenvector of Pairwise Comparison Matrices. Acta Polytechnica Hungarica 4(2) (2007)
17. Saati, T.L.: The Analytic Hierarchy Process: Planning, Priority Settings, Resource Allocation. RWS Publications, Pittsburg (2001)
18. Miettinen, K.: Nonlinear Multiobjective Optimization. Kluwer Academic Publishers (1999)
19. Törn, A., Žilinskas, A.: Global Optimization. LNCS, vol. 350. Springer, Heidelberg (1989)
20. Deb, K.: Multi-Objective Optimization using Evolutionary Algorithms. J. Wiley (2009)
21. Colorni, A., Dorigo, M., Maniezzo, V.: Distributed Optimization by Ant Colonies. In: Actes de la premiere Conference Europaenne Sur la vie Artificielle, pp. 134–142. Elsevier (1991)
22. Dorigo, M., Birattari, M., Stutzle, T.: Ant Colony Optimization. Technical Report No. TR/IRIDIA/2006-023 (2006)
23. Garcia-Martinez, C., Cordon, O., Herrera, F.: A taxonomy and an empirical analysis of multiple objective ant colony optimization algorithms for the bi-criteria TSP. European Journal of Operations Research 180, 116–148 (2007)
24. Doerner, K., et al.: Ant Colony Optimization: A Metaheuristic Approach to Multiobjective Portfolio. Annals of Operations Research 131(1-4), 79–99 (2004)

Evaluation of Elasticity Parameters for Heterogeneous Material with Periodic Microstructure

Dalia Calneryte

Kaunas University of Technology, Studentu str.50, Kaunas, Lithuania
dalia.calneryte@stud.ktu.lt

Abstract. Two approaches for evaluation of homogeneous elasticity parameters of heterogeneous material with periodic microstructure in linear elasticity are discussed in this paper. The two – scale modeling is used. Elasticity parameters for homogeneous material are evaluated in microscale and average stresses of three-dimensional heterogeneous and two-dimensional homogeneous models are compared in mezzoscale.

Keywords: Multiscale modeling, Linear elasticity, Homogenization, Finite element method.

1 Introduction

Many natural and artificial materials are not homogeneous in microscale level though modeling material in consideration of heterogeneity requires a lot calculations and computer memory. Regarding to a wide usage of heterogeneous materials there are numerical methods developed in order to reduce degrees of freedom.

The same structure is analyzed in two scales with different sets of assumptions (Fig.1). It is assumed that the tree-dimensional model in microscale is heterogeneous and composed of two isotropic materials. The elasticity parameters for equivalent

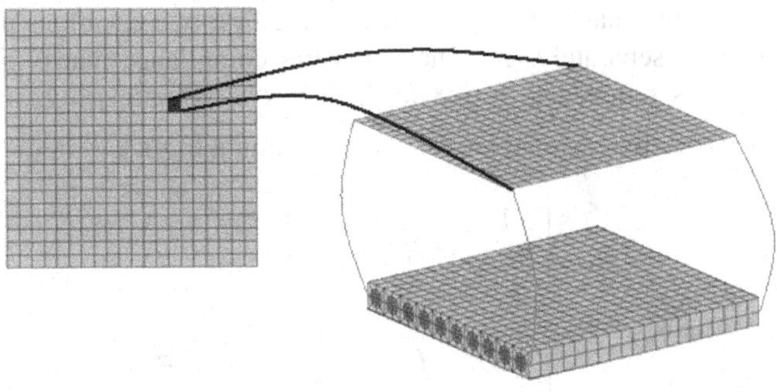

Fig. 1. Multiscale modeling scheme

T. Skersys, R. Butleris, and R. Butkiene (Eds.): ICIST 2012, CCIS 319, pp. 101–107, 2012.

homogeneous two-dimensional material model are evaluated in this scale. The orthotropic material in two-dimensional case has two axis of symmetry and is fully described with four elasticity constants: Young's modulus along the fibers E_x, Young's modulus in direction orthogonal to fibers E_y, Poisson ratio v_{xy} and in-plane shear modulus G_{xy}. The two-dimensional model is developed in mezzoscale with the assumption that the material is homogeneous. The behavior of two-dimensional homogeneous and three-dimensional heterogeneous models is compared if dimensions and loads for the models are equal in order to verify the ability to create a more complex model in macroscale.

The finite element method is used for the calculations. The continuous material model is converted to a finite number of simple shape geometrical figures which join at outer nodes. The finite element is described with its shape, elasticity parameters and constitutive laws [1].

Universal mathematical and programming language MATLAB and finite element modeling software LS-DYNA was applied to deal with the calculations.

2 From 3D Model to 2D Model

Linear elasticity only is discussed in this paper. It can be described using Hooke's law for stresses σ, strains ε and elasticity matrix *D* [7]:

$$\sigma = D\varepsilon \tag{1}$$

$$\varepsilon^T = \{\varepsilon_x \quad \varepsilon_y \quad \varepsilon_z \quad \varepsilon_{yz} \quad \varepsilon_{zx} \quad \varepsilon_{xy}\},\ \sigma^T = \{\sigma_x \quad \sigma_y \quad \sigma_z \quad \sigma_{yz} \quad \sigma_{zx} \quad \sigma_{xy}\}.$$

In order to reduce dimension of the model the inverse Hooke's law is used:

$$\varepsilon = S\sigma\,,\ S = D^{-1} \tag{2}$$

Considering the fact that dimension of the model in one direction is significantly smaller than in the others the plane stresses mode can be used. With the assumption that $\sigma_z = 0$ the third column and the third row of the 6x6 form compliance matrix *S* (the inverse of elasticity matrix *D*) is not used so the first two equations plus the last one can be rewritten separately [2]. The 6x6 form compliance matrix *S* for three-dimensional model is reduced to a 3x3 form matrix *S*'. Using $\gamma = 2\varepsilon_{xy}$ the inverse Hooke's law for a two-dimensional model is rewritten in a form:

$$\varepsilon' = S'\sigma',\ S' = \begin{bmatrix} \frac{1}{E_x} & -\frac{v_{yx}}{E_y} & 0 \\ -\frac{v_{xy}}{E_x} & \frac{1}{E_y} & 0 \\ 0 & 0 & \frac{1}{G_{xy}} \end{bmatrix},\ \frac{v_{yx}}{E_y} = \frac{v_{xy}}{E_x} \tag{3}$$

$\varepsilon'^T = \{\varepsilon_x \quad \varepsilon_y \quad \varepsilon_{xy}\}$, $\sigma'^T = \{\sigma_x \quad \sigma_y \quad \sigma_{xy}\}$. The elasticity constants can be easily expressed from the two-dimensional compliance matrix for orthotropic material.

3 Elasticity Parameters Evaluation by Modeling Pure Stresses

The first approach for evaluating elasticity parameters is modeling pure stresses. It is assumed that the bond between materials is perfect, the elasticity parameters and geometry of model are uniform, materials are linear elastic.

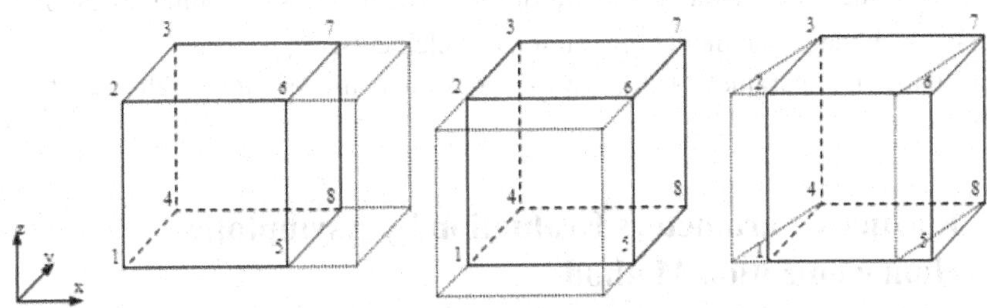

Fig. 2. Schemes for modeling pure stresses in LS-DYNA

The nodes in a plane 5678 are displaced in x direction and the nodes in a plane 1234 are fixed in x direction. All nodes of the model can move in other directions. With the assumptions that $\sigma_x \neq 0$, $\sigma_y = 0, \sigma_{xy} = 0$ from the inverse Hooke's law for plane stresses longitudinal Young's modulus E_x and Poisson's ratio v_{xy} are expressed [3]:

$$E_x = \frac{\sigma_x}{\varepsilon_x}, \; v_{xy} = -\frac{\varepsilon_y}{\varepsilon_x} \tag{4}$$

The nodes in a plane 1265 are displaced in y direction and the nodes in a plane 4378 are fixed in y direction. All nodes of the model can move in other directions. With the assumptions that $\sigma_x = 0$, $\sigma_y \neq 0, \sigma_{xy} = 0$ from the inverse Hooke's law for plane stresses transverse Young's modulus E_y and Poisson's ratio v_{yx} are expressed [3]:

$$E_y = \frac{\sigma_y}{\varepsilon_y}, \; v_{yx} = -\frac{\varepsilon_x}{\varepsilon_y} \tag{5}$$

The Poisson's ratio v_{yx} is not used because of the symmetry of elasticity matrix.

The nodes in a plane 1265 are displaced in x direction and the nodes in a plane 4378 are fixed in x direction. All nodes of the model can move in other directions. With the assumptions that $\sigma_x = 0, \sigma_y = 0, \sigma_{xy} \neq 0$ from the inverse Hooke's law for plane stresses the in-plane shear modulus G_{xy} is expressed [3]:

$$G_{xy} = \frac{\sigma_{xy}}{\gamma_{xy}} \tag{6}$$

The unidirectional fiber layer is modeled using pure stresses schemes (Fig. 2) in finite element modeling software LS-DYNA. The average strains and stresses are evaluated according to the following formulas:

$$\sigma = \sum_{i=1}^{n} \sigma_i \cdot \frac{V_i}{V}, \ \varepsilon = \sum_{i=1}^{n} \varepsilon_i \cdot \frac{V_i}{V} \tag{7}$$

σ_i - stress of the ith element, ε_i - strain of the ith element, V_i – volume of the ith element, V – volume of the model, n – number of elements.

The elasticity parameters for two-dimensional model are evaluated by 4-6 equations.

4 Elasticity Parameters Evaluation by Asymptotic Homogenization Method

The other approach for elasticity parameters evaluation is asymptotic homogenization. Only one periodic representative cell Y is analyzed. Elasticity parameters evaluation by asymptotic homogenization consists of two steps.

In the first step, the matrix of characteristic displacements χ which contains the eigendeformations in periodic cell Y is calculated from the relationship:

$$\left(\int_Y B^T DBdY \right) \chi = \int_Y B^T DdY \tag{8}$$

where D – elasticity matrix, B – matrix of partial derivatives of the shape functions [4]. Each shape function has a value of 1 at unique node and zero at all other nodes. This equation fits the standard form of the equilibrium of all elements:

$$KU = F \tag{9}$$

where K, U, F respectively global stiffness, displacement and load matrices [1].

In order the matrix χ is the only solution, the periodicity boundary conditions are imposed on the outer surfaces of the representative periodic element (Fig. 3). The periodicity conditions are enforced as multifreedom constraints by master-slave elimination method. At least one node of the periodic element must be fixed [5,6].

In the second step, the homogenized elasticity matrix is calculated [5,6]:

$$D^h = \sum_{k=1}^{n} \frac{V_k}{V} D_k (I - B_k \chi_k) \tag{10}$$

where lower index k signifies the quantities of the kth element, V – volume of the model, n – number of elements, I – identity matrix.

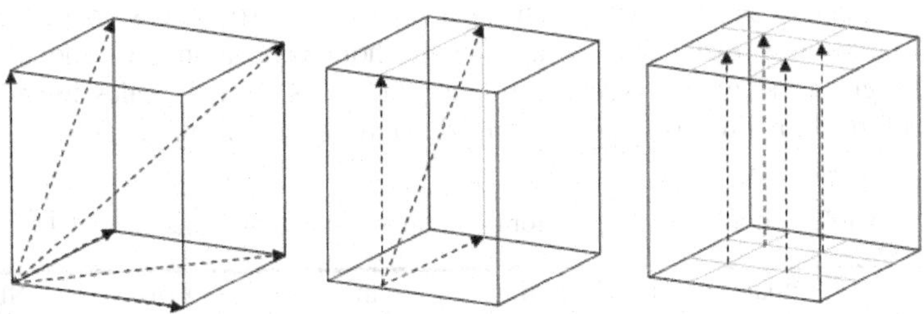

Fig. 3. Periodicity conditions for representative periodic element

Due to the fact that periodic element Y is three-dimensional, the transition from three-dimensional to two-dimensional model is applied, the compliance matrix is reduced and the elasticity parameters are evaluated.

5 Numerical Examples

The models with fiber volume fraction $f_r = 0.25$, $f_r = 0.35$, $f_r = 0.5$ (Fig. 4) are analyzed for a material composed of e-glass fibers and epoxy matrix (Table 1).

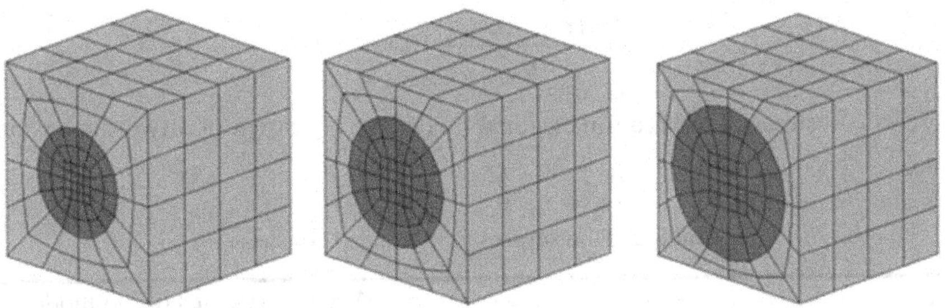

Fig. 4. Representative periodic elements with different fiber volume fractions

Table 1. Elasticity parameters of the composing materials

	E-glass	Epoxy
Young's modulus, E_x, N/m^2	$73{,}1 \cdot 10^9$	$3{,}45 \cdot 10^9$
Poisson's ratio, ν_{xy}	0,22	0,35
Shear modulus, G_{xy}, N/m^2	$29{,}96 \cdot 10^9$	$1{,}28 \cdot 10^9$

All elasticity parameters differ less than 10% in each case (Table 2). However, longitudinal Young's modulus evaluated in asymptotic homogenization were a little higher than evaluated with modeling pure stresses as a result of coarser discretization of the model used for modeling pure stresses.

The pure stresses of the three-dimensional model and two-dimensional models with elasticity parameters evaluated by asymptotic homogenization and modeling pure stresses are given in Table 3. Stresses in other directions are few scales lower than the stress in deformation direction so it is assumed that they differ insignificantly.

Table 2. Elastic parameters for two-dimensional homogeneous model

Fiber volume fraction f_r	Evaluation method	Longitudinal Young's modulus, E_x, N/m^2	Transverse Young's modulus, E_y, N/m^2	Poisson's ratio, ν_{xy}	Shear modulus, G_{xy}, N/m^2
0.25	I	1.9145E+10	5.8187E+09	0.3125	2.0593E+09
	II	2.0423E+10	6.0825E+09	0.3118	2.0362E+09
0.35	I	2.5445E+10	7.0087E+09	0.2993	2.4768E+09
	II	2.7256E+10	7.6505E+09	0.2976	2.4913E+09
0.5	I	3.4954E+10	9.5175E+09	0.2807	3.3254E+09
	II	3.7588E+10	1.1313E+10	0.2770	3.5234E+09

I – parameters evaluated by modeling pure stresses, II – by asymptotic homogenization.

The differences between stresses of two-dimensional and three-dimensional models are compared using relative value Δ:

$$\Delta = \frac{|\sigma_{3D} - \sigma_{2D}|}{\sigma_{3D}} \cdot 100\% \tag{11}$$

where σ_{3D} – stress of a three-dimensional model, σ_{2D} – stress of a two-dimensional model.

Table 3. Pure stresses for 3D and 2D models

Fiber volume fraction f_r	Average pure stresses	Average pure stresses of 3D model	Average stresses of 2D model			
			I	Δ, %	II	Δ, %
0.25	σ_x, N/m^2	1.91E+06	1.91E+06	0.00	2.04E+06	6.81
	σ_y, N/m^2	5.75E+05	5.82E+05	1.22	6.08E+05	5.74
	σ_{xy}, N/m^2	1.37E+05	1.38E+05	0.73	1.38E+05	0.73
0.35	σ_x, N/m^2	2.54E+06	2.54E+06	0.00	2.73E+06	7.48
	σ_y, N/m^2	6.97E+05	7.01E+05	0.57	7.65E+05	9.76
	σ_{xy}, N/m^2	1.67E+05	1.66E+05	0.60	1.70E+05	1.80
0.5	σ_x, N/m^2	3.50E+06	3.50E+06	0.00	3.76E+06	7.43
	σ_y, N/m^2	9.58E+05	9.52E+05	0.63	1.13E+06	17.95
	σ_{xy}, N/m^2	2.31E+05	2.24E+05	3.03	2.43E+05	5.19

I – parameters evaluated by modeling pure stresses, II – by asymptotic homogenization.

The stresses of a two-dimensional model with parameters evaluated by modeling pure stresses differed less than 10% compared with stresses for a tree-dimensional model in all cases. The stresses of a two-dimensional model with parameters evaluated by asymptotic homogenization differed more than 10% compared with stresses for a tree-dimensional model when the pure y stress was analyzed. On the other hand, the three-dimensional model was analyzed with a coarser mesh than the mesh for a representative periodic element for asymptotic homogenization. This fact may result the different behavior compared to the experimental model.

6 Conclusions

The elasticity parameters evaluated by two ways were compared in this paper. The behavior of two-dimensional model with parameters evaluated by modeling pure stresses agreed with behavior of three-dimensional model better than the two-dimensional model with parameters evaluated by asymptotic homogenization. In consideration of the mesh of three-dimensional model, the results should be examined experimentally.

References

1. Barauskas, R., Belevičius, R., Kačianauskas, R.: Baigtinių elementų metodo pagrindai. Technika (2004)
2. Barbero, E.J.: Finite element analysis of composite materials. CRC Press (2008)
3. Kaw, K.A.: Mechanics of Composite Material. CRC Press (2006)
4. Peng, X., Cao, J.: A dual homogenization and finite element approach for material characterization of textile composites. Composites: Part B 33 (2002)
5. Pinho-da-Cruz, J., Oliveira, J.A., Teixeira-Dias, F.: Asymptotic homogenisation in linear elasticity. Part I: Mathematical formulation and finite element modelling. Computational Materials Science 45 (2009)
6. Pinho-da-Cruz, J., Oliveira, J.A., Teixeira-Dias, F.: Asymptotic homogenisation in linear elasticity. Part II: Finite element procedures and multiscale applications. Computational Materials Science 45 (2009)
7. Zienkiewicz, O.Z., Taylor, R.L.: The Finite Element Method for Solid and Structural Mechanics. Elsevier Ltd. (2006)

Change Impact Analysis of Feature Models

Paulius Paskevicius, Robertas Damasevicius, and Vytautas Štuikys

Software Engineering Department, Kaunas University of Technology,
Studentų 50-415, LT-51368, Kaunas, Lithuania
paulius.paskevicius@gmail.com,
{robertas.damasevicius,vytautas.stuikys}@ktu.lt

Abstract. Changeability is a fundamental property of software systems. Every software system must evolve at all levels of abstraction (models, architecture, source code, documentation, etc.) to meet changing user and context requirements. To assess the extent of a change, change impact analysis must be performed. In this paper, we propose a taxonomy of change aspects in feature modelling domain, and analyse changeability of feature models, a high level representation of system's external user-visible characteristics. We propose the change impact model based on a feature dependency matrix to assess validity of feature change, to follow feature change propagation and to estimate changeability of a feature model using a Jaccard distance measure. The model is implemented using Prolog logic rules. A case study is presented.

Keywords: feature modelling, software evolution, changeability.

1 Introduction

Changeability is a fundamental property of all factors that influence software architecture [1]. Product requirements are often changed during development and over the lifetime of a product. Human-computer interaction is likely to change as users become more sophisticated in using the system and desire more effective ways of using it. In addition to implementing the system, a designer must prepare for the eventual change of the system during its lifetime. Change can be introduced by a number of factors such as changing domain requirements, physical characteristics of the system, different modes of user-system interaction, upgrade of hardware, etc. at different levels of software design including requirement specifications, high level models, architecture, source code, functional and non-functional characteristics. Software artefacts such as source code and design documents are commonly produced in an incremental manner via continuous change. Incremental change, as a process, adds new functionality and new properties to software. Change is an essential part of software processes such as maintenance, evolution, iterative development and enhancements, meta-design [2], anticipatory design and agile development [3]. Because of that, it plays an important role in practical software engineering. Thus software change as a part of software evolution is an inevitable process [4].

T. Skersys, R. Butleris, and R. Butkiene (Eds.): ICIST 2012, CCIS 319, pp. 108–122, 2012.

Preparation for anticipated as well as unanticipated changes is essential for reducing software maintenance costs and increasing maintainability, evolvability and lifetime of a software system. In fact, the role of changeability has been recognized as an important factor of software quality and maintainability in the ISO 9126 standard. The ISO/IEC 14764 standard identifies four types of change during software maintenance: corrective maintenance is a change (defined as modification) that fixes bugs in the code base; adaptive maintenance is a change that allows a system to run within a new technical infrastructure; perfective maintenance is a change intended to improve system characteristics, and preventive maintenance is a changed made to ease future maintenance and evolution of the system. The process and methodology for supporting software changes (e.g., maintenance plans, etc.) are decisive to increasing its longevity and avoiding the premature replacement of a software system.

Another important aspect of software change is software variability [5] at the software modelling and development stage. Variability is an important factor in Product Line Engineering (PLE) [6], which aims at creating an underlying architecture of a product's platform based on product commonality as well as planned variabilities. Variability is modelled using a feature modelling approach such as FODA [7] that uses graphical Feature diagrams [8] or a textual notation such as a Feature Description Language (FDL) [9] to express relationship between product features and compactly represent all products of a product line. Feature models are a representation of the software system's variability in terms of features, the external user-visible aspects of a system. Variability can be treated as an anticipated or easily predictable change, while changeability encompasses all aspects of change, anticipated, predictable and unpredictable.

Software change prediction is one of the essential activities for supporting software change [10]. To assess the impact of changes and the extent of change, change impact analysis of a software system must be performed. Knowledge gained from change impact analysis can be used to re-engineer the system. However, change impact analysis is not an easy task, because change factors can interact and may have different priorities when applied to a software system. When a change to a model of a system is considered, it is necessary to identify the parts of a model, which will be impacted as a result of that change to ensure that the model will still correctly represent the system after the change is implemented. Therefore, the development of methods to estimate, plan and implement changes of software system artefacts is required. Change impact analysis so far has been applied mostly to program code [11] or UML models [12]. In the context of PL modelling, change impact analysis is related to Abstract Delta Modelling [13]. Anquetil *et al.* [14] address traceability as part of change impact analysis of product lines. Catalogues and taxonomies of feature change operations to evolve a feature model are given by [15, 16, 17].

In this paper, we introduce a methodology for change impact analysis and change management of software product line feature models. We analyze how feature models react to a change, i.e. the changeability of feature models. We use change impact analysis of feature models as an approach to measure the evolution of product lines. A central problem is change propagation: given a set of primary changes that have been made to software features, the task is to establish additional features, which can be affected by primary change. To address this problem, we propose a method to evaluate change propagation of features based on a change impact model.

The structure of the paper is as follows. Section 2 discusses the context and concepts of software changeability and evolution research. Section 3 describes context and product modelling using feature diagrams. Section 4 discusses evolution and change of feature models, and proposes a change impact model for feature changeability. Section 5 presents a case study. Finally, Section 6 presents conclusions and discusses future work.

2 Software Changeability: Context and Concepts of Research

2.1 Taxonomy of Change

Due to the importance of program change, software changeability is researched in the variety of different contexts: component-based reuse, maintenance and evolution [15, 17], extreme programming [4], model and program transformation, generative technologies, including meta-programming [18]. One aspect of component-based reuse is to apply the white-box model and modify (i.e., change) the retrieved components in order to adapt them in another system. If component-based reuse focuses mainly on changes at the software development stage, maintenance deals with changeability at the evolution stage.

There are efforts to incorporate changeability into system architecture. For example, Fricke and Schulz [19] consider four key aspects of changeability (i.e., flexibility, agility, robustness, and adaptability) and propose some design principles to enable the incorporation of changeability aspects within systems. To analyze how individual changes are made to software systems, Benestad *et al.* [20] identify 43 attributes of changes. Another taxonomy of change, presented in [21], focuses on the how, when, what and where aspects of software change, and introduces 15 dimensions of change (change history, degree of automation, activeness, time of change, change type, change frequency, type of artefact, granularity, anticipation, impact, change propagation, availability, openness, safety and degree of formality).

Several of the dimensions of change are especially important at the software development time as follows:

Anticipation of change is an important attribute that facilitates maintenance and evolution. It refers to the time when the requirements for a change are foreseen. Some changes can be foreseen ahead during the initial development of a system and can be accommodated in the design decisions taken. Such changes should be captured at a high level of abstraction such as a feature model. The anticipated change typically involves much less effort to implement than the unanticipated changes. Anticipation is at the core of the product line development and evolution too, because a feature model of a product is an artefact that encodes the anticipated domain variability. Anticipation, however, is a costly activity and requires a great deal of effort from the designer. This effort increases costs, labour and contributes to increased complexity. However, anticipation can also be managed. For example, it can be introduced incrementally in the course of understanding of the state of the feature model as defined by features, feature relationships and feature constraints.

Granularity refers to the scale of artefacts to be changed and can range from a very coarse to a very fine degree of granularity. As granularity of features can range from software modules, to individual classes, class methods and attributes, granularity of feature model changes may encompass a wide range of underlying software change operations.

The impact of a change can span from local to system-wide changes. For example, renaming a parameter in a procedure definition would only be a local change (restricted to that procedure definition), while renaming a global variable would have, in the worst case, an impact on the whole source code. Sometimes, even local changes in the software may have a global impact. For example, deleting a procedure parameter might invalidate all call sites of the procedure. The impact of a change can span different layers of abstraction. For example, a source code change may require changes to the documentation, the design, the software architecture, and the requirements specification. Changes with a non-local impact require follow up changes in other encapsulated entities (procedures, modules, classes, packages, etc.). The process of performing such changes is called change propagation [22]. Mechanisms and tools that help with change propagation also need to perform change impact analysis, traceability analysis or effort estimation.

Change impact analysis aims to assess or measure the exact impact of a change. Traceability analysis can help with change impact analysis, since it establishes explicit relationships between two or more products of the software development process. Like impact, the traceability relationship can remain within the same level of abstraction (vertical traceability) or across different levels of abstraction (horizontal traceability). In many cases, changes with a high impact also require a significant effort to make the changes. This effort can be estimated using effort estimation techniques [23]. In some situations the effort can be reduced by automated tools. For example, renaming entities on the source code level is typically a global change with a high change impact, but the corresponding change effort is low because renaming can be done automatically.

Degree of Automation is also important dimension in this and many other contexts. Many researches propose to distinguish between automated, partially automated, and manual change support. In the domain of software re-engineering, numerous attempts have been made to automate, or partially automate, software maintenance tasks [21].

Change type is a dimension with variety aspects (values) to discuss (e.g., see typology of software changes in [24]). Here we make the distinction between structural and semantic changes only. This distinction is an important influencing factor on the change support mechanisms that can be defined and used. Structural changes are changes that alter the structure of the software. In many cases, these changes will alter software behaviour as well. A distinction can be made between adding new features to the software, deleting some elements from the software, and modifying an existing element in the software, e.g., renaming. Deleting and modifying suggests that changes will occur within the existing system, whereas addition suggests that extra functionality can be 'hooked' onto the existing system. Next to structural changes, a distinction should be made between semantics-modifying and semantics-preserving changes. Semantics-preserving changes are covered by software re-factoring [25]. In a wider context of re-engineering, semantics preserving changes are accommodated by restructuring activities such as loop enrolling (e.g., for better performance in compilers, etc.). Note that a change may only be semantics-preserving with respect to a particular aspect of the software semantics, while it is semantics-modifying when taking other aspects of semantics into account. For example, a typical re-factoring operation will preserve the overall input-output semantics of software, but may modify its efficiency or memory usage, which may be equally as important.

2.2 Change Impact Analysis and Evaluation of Changeability

Creating and maintaining software systems is a knowledge intensive task. The knowledge needed ranges in a wide spectrum, i.e., from a good understanding of the application domain, the system's architecture and how the different parts fit together, how the system interacts with its environment, the software process used, technical details of the programming language, etc. All this knowledge is difficult and costly to gather, store and maintain, because it usually resides only in the mind of software engineers who worked on a particular project. If this is a problem for development of new software, it is even more difficult for maintenance, when one must rediscover lost information of an abstract nature from legacy source code among a swarm of unrelated details. In this context, there is ongoing research on knowledge-based approaches such as the knowledge extraction technique adapted to the needs specific to software maintenance [26].

Change impact analysis is a part of incremental change design and it determines the full extent of the change, by finding all software components that will be affected by the incremental change. Change impact analysis is not homogeneous and has many aspects to be considered, such as technological (change propagation, concept location, impact measurement and assessment, availability of suitable tools, etc.) and non-technical (human factor, organizational issues, etc.). Different legal status of products and artefacts (open source, commercial), variety of systems and different views to treat them are inhibiting factors to software changeability. Impact analysis of a feature model includes checking validity of old constraints in the feature model (if any) and identification of possible new constraints. To obtain that, we need to consider a sub-task known as identification of concern location [27]. The outcome of impact analysis is the identification of induced constraints and relationships among features. This document is a part of input information for change implementation.

After the actual change in software is made, change propagation [22] finds all places, where secondary changes are to be made in order to complete the change. Change propagation to maintain consistency between software artefacts is one of the most critical problems in software maintenance and evolution. Although many approaches have been proposed (e.g., an agent-oriented approach [28]), automated change propagation is still a significant challenge in software engineering.

To evaluate and reason about changeability objectively, one should rely on the changeability measures [23]. To assess the changeability of evolving software systems one requires [29]: 1) taxonomy of changes, and 2) a catalogue of changeability criteria to enable the changeability assessment. Program dependency

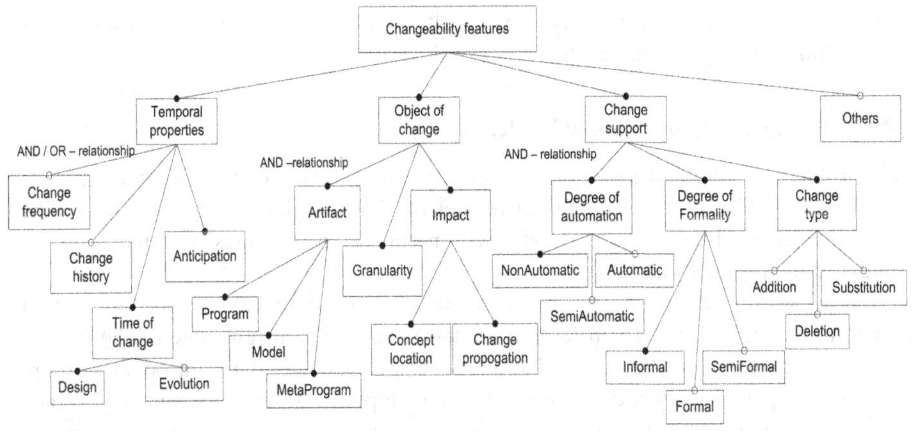

Fig. 1. Changeability features as a context model

analysis and changeability evaluation plays an important part in both impact analysis and change propagation. Finally, we summarize our taxonomy of change as a feature model (see Fig. 1) based on the taxonomy presented in [21].

3 Context and Product Relationship Modelling Using Feature Models

3.1 Context-Aware Feature Modelling

Software product line engineering is all about finding commonalities in products and managing variabilities. Feature modelling is used as a means to describe the variability of a product. While commonalities represent the intrinsic properties of the product itself, the exterior of the product (i.e., the context of its development, usage and maintenance) is the main source of its variability. The fundamental property of feature models (or, perhaps, models in general) is their dependency on the context, meaning that context change may cause changes in the base model semantics or structure. Though the role of context was known for a long time in system modelling (e.g., as a part of FODA [7]), context-dependency modelling as a powerful instrument for PLE was recognized only recently [30].

Context can be defined as a constraint of a problem, i.e. a kind of knowledge that is not explicitly used, but influences the problem solving process. While known and anticipated context information can be easily introduced into feature models to manage their variability explicitly either as a part of the model (e.g., as higher-level features with respect to the domain features), or as two separate models (domain feature model and context model, which is also expressed through features) in context-based feature modelling [30] and context lines [31], the unanticipated context changes require dynamic change of the feature model itself. Context modelling is essential for feature model understanding and development, because "the usage of context is a key driver for feature selections" [32].

A domain under analysis may have multiple contexts; these contexts may be related, thus making up a hierarchy of contexts (see Fig. 1).

3.2 Changeability of Feature Models

The problem of context-aware changeability analysis of feature models can be formulated as follows: to evaluate the impact of changes made to the features of the product described by the feature model with regard to the changes introduced by the context of the product line.

Before starting changeability analysis, first, we need to capture the context of change to be applied to a given feature model: what is the current state of the feature model, where it is applied, and what kind of changes are to be introduced (more formally a request for change is to be known and approved)? The changes may impact only the functionality or the structure of program instances to be generated from the changed feature model specifications, or both (functionality and structure). As a result, changes impact characteristics of the feature model, e.g., model complexity evaluated using the Cyclomatic Index can decrease or increase.

The change is not a solitary task but rather a set of related tasks such as: understanding of the feature model itself; understanding of the request for change; identification of changeable feature location; change propagation; implementation of the requested changes as a model evolution process; evaluation of change impact using quantitative model metrics.

The scope of changes may vary in a wide extent, but all of them can also be grouped in two categories:

1) Changes that are introduced through features only (e.g., to rename a feature, to change a feature value, to add a new value, or to delete feature value). This case can be considered as refactoring of a feature model [33]. The tasks such as a concern location and change propagation can be solved more easily, though it requires checking the consistence of constraints, if modified feature values were constrained.

2) Changes that cover also a change of the base program, its language or even a modelling language used to develop the feature model. The latter case is actually re-construction or re-design of the feature model.

The request for changes may include also the typical maintenance types (corrective, perfective, adaptive, preventive) identified for a target program rather than the feature model itself. If we need to change the program that is derived from the given feature model and is to be used in a narrow context (say one application) then we have program evolution rather than feature model evolution. The problem of understanding of request for change can be reformulated in terms of the feature model concepts. The software designer's task is to do so in order to facilitate other tasks such as to change a feature value, to add new feature value, to delete the old value or even the feature (with all values), to add a new feature and its values. However, the change of feature models (either at design or evolution stage) is a very complex task. Evolution of feature model is reasonable to apply if changes include a wider context rather than a stand-alone program. Next, we consider evolution of feature models and change impact analysis in more detail.

4 Feature Change and Changeability Analysis of Feature Models

4.1 Feature Change Operations

A feature model is a set of features, their relationships and constraints. Evolution of a feature model can be seen as its state change with the change propagation problem resolving for features, feature relationships and feature constraints. When analysing changeability and evolution of feature models, we adopt the taxonomy of changes proposed in [29]. The taxonomy is based on the abstract syntax tree (AST). Since feature models are also represented as a hierarchy of features (feature trees), we claim that parts of this taxonomy can be applied to feature model changes. A similar taxonomy [15] adopted for feature model change consists of atomic changes (rename feature, add leaf feature, remove leaf feature, and move feature), and composite changes (add feature sub-tree, remove feature sub-tree, split feature, and merge feature). Botterweck *et al.* [17] propose a more detailed set of evolution operators: add (optional|mandatory) feature *g* [below feature *f*], remove feature *g*, replace feature g_1 with (mandatory|optional) feature g_2, move feature *g* to *h*, rename f_1 to f_2, change feature *f* to (mandatory|optional), which are also based on the same core of tree edit operations (add, remove, move, replace).

The elementary tree edit operations are insert, delete, move and update of a tree node. Insert and delete operations are only allowed on leaf nodes (solitary features). Move operation moves a feature with all its children to another location in a feature tree. Update operation changes the value of a feature (e.g., characteristics or specific requirements associated with this feature). In a feature tree, the change of the value is represented by the change of feature name (label). Since feature trees also have decorations of tree nodes and edges representing different kinds of feature variability (*mandatory*, *optional*), feature selection rules (*all* features, *one of* feature, *more of* features) and feature constraints (*requires*, *excludes* or none), additional tree node and edge decoration change operations can be specified: update feature state, update feature selection rule and update feature constraint (for solitary features only).

Below, we specify feature model change operations more formally:

$INS(f_x, f_y)$: insert feature node f_x as the child of the feature node f_y.

$DEL(f_x)$: delete feature node f_x from a feature model.

$MOV(f_x, f_y) \rightarrow DEL(f_x), INS(f_x, f_y)$: move feature node f_x to the children of feature node f_y.

$UPD(f_x, f_y)$: update feature node f_x as f_y.

$STA(f_x, s)$: change the state of feature node f_x to *s*, where *s* is "mandatory" or "optional".

$SEL(f_x, r)$: change the selection rule of children of feature node f_x to *r*, where r is "all" (mandatory), "one_of" (alternative), or "more_of" (optional).

$CON(f_x, f_y, c)$: change the constraint between f_x and f_y to c, where c is "requires", "excludes" or "none".

We can summarize the feature model evolution process to the following stages:

a) Incremental change of the state of a feature model through the sequential introduction of a change increment. Incremental change [34] is a sequence of atomic actions: change increments (e.g., deletion, addition, substitution of a feature);

b) Resolving of the change propagation problem for the whole feature model for each change increment;

c) Iterative testing to be convinced in correctness of the incremental change.

4.2 Change Impact Analysis for Feature Models

The aim of change impact analysis is the determination of potential effects to a subject system resulting from a proposed change [35]. The premise of impact analysis is that a proposed change may result in undesirable side effects and/or ripple effects. A side effect is a condition that leads a system to a state that is erroneous or violates the semantics as a result of a change. A ripple effect is a phenomenon that affects other parts of a system because of a change.

The task of impact analysis is to estimate the ripple effects and prevent side effects of a proposed change. When a change to a feature model is considered, it is necessary to identify the elements of the feature model, which will be impacted as a result of ripple effect of change. The change also may lead to such side effects as feature mismatches, thus making a changed feature model invalid (e.g., describing an empty set of products).

Feature change may have an impact on an entire feature model. Therefore, change propagation and validity of the changed model must be considered. We formulate the following tasks for change impact analysis: 1) validation of changed feature model (change validity); 2) identification of other features in the feature model influenced by feature change (change propagation); 3) calculation of change of feature model metric (e.g., number of features, number of products, etc.) values (changeability). These tasks must be considered by a change impact model:

1) *Change validity.* We define a valid feature change as a change that given a valid featured model creates a valid changed feature model. Let F be a feature model. Let $F' \leftarrow \delta(F)$ be a changed feature model derived after application of change δ. Let valid be a predicate defined on a feature model F, which returns TRUE is a model is valid, and FALSE, if otherwise. Then let *validChange* be a predicate defined on F and δ, which returns TRUE is the changed model F' is valid, and FALSE, if otherwise: $validChange(F, \delta) \rightarrow valid(\delta(F))$.

2) *Change propagation.* To model change propagation, we adopt a commonly used model based on a component dependence matrix [36] to model changeability of feature models. We define a feature dependence matrix D, the elements thereof denote the probability of change between two features: If feature f_x is changed and if $D[f_x, f_y] = 1$, then feature f_y also must change. For each change operation, we construct a feature dependence matrix as described in Table 1.

Table 1. Construction of feature dependency matrices

Feature change operation	Values of feature dependency matrix elements
INS (f_x, f_y)	D [f_x, f_y] = 1
DEL (f_x)	D [f_x, *parent*(f_x)] = 1
MOV (f_x, f_y)	D [f_x, *child*(f_y)] = 1
UPD (f_x, f_x')	D [f_x, *child*(f_x)] = 1
STA (f_x, s)	D [f_x, *child*(f_x)] = 1, D [f_x, *parent*(f_x)] = 1
SEL (f_x, r)	D [f_x, *sibling*(f_x)] = 1
CON (fx_x, f_y, c)	D [f_x, f_y] = 1, D[f_y, f_x] = 1

After change dependence matrix is constructed, it is used to derive a change propagation matrix as follows: $\forall x, y,$ if $D(x, y) = 1$, then apply change $UPD(y, y)$ to D. The obtained change propagation matrix can be used to derive a list of features affected by change δ.

3) *Changeability.* We define changeability of a feature model as a distance between the original feature model and changed feature model.

Let F be a feature model. Let $F' \leftarrow \delta(F)$ be a changed feature model derived after application of change δ. Let C be a set of product instances described by F and C' be a set of product instances described by F'. Changeability of model F with respect to change δ is calculated as Jaccard distance between F and F':

$$ch(F, \delta) = J_\delta(C, C') = 1 - \frac{|C(F) \cap C(\delta(F))|}{|C(F) \cup C(\delta(F))|}.$$

The value of changeability ranges from 0 (none of the products change) to 1 (all products change). To evaluate changeability qualitatively, we propose using the following scheme (see Table 2).

Table 2. Evaluation of changeability

Changeability value	Changeability evaluation
0.0 – 0.2	Little impact
0.2 – 0.4	Some impact
0.4 – 0.6	Considerable impact
0.6 – 0.8	Significant impact
0.8 – 1.0	Very significant impact

4.3 Reasoning on Feature Models Using Prolog Rules

To estimate change validity, change propagation and changeability according to the proposed change impact model, we have implemented a feature model and changes on feature models as rules in Prolog logic programming language.

We define feature models as executable models in Prolog [38] using a subset of Prolog's grammar, which has been specifically formulated to have similarity with Feature Description Language (FDL) [9], because FDL is becoming more and more popular as a textual notation for feature model representation. The description of the grammar in BNF (Backus-Naur Form) is as follows:

```
<feature_model> ::= { <feature_definition> }
<feature_definition> ::= <rule> | <fact>
<fact> ::= <feature>.
<rule> ::= <feature> :- <rule_body>.
<rule_body> ::= <selector> {, <constraint>}
<selector> ::= <and_selector>
             | <or_selector>
             | <oneof_selector>
<and_selector> ::= all ( <alt_feature> { , <alt_feature> } ).
<or_selector> ::= more_of ( <feature> { ; <feature> } ).
<oneof_selector> ::= one_of ( <feature> { , <feature>} ).
<constraint> ::= <requires> | <excludes>
<requires> ::= requires ( <feature> , <feature> ).
<excludes> ::= excludes ( <feature> , <feature> ).
<alt_feature> ::= alt ( <feature> ) | <feature>
<feature> ::= <lower_case> {<char>}
```

The Prolog rules for expressing variability of features are defined as follows:

```
one_of(A, B) :- A -> not(one_of(B)); one_of(B).
more_of(A, B) :- A; B.
all(A, B) :- A, B.
alt(A) :- A; not(A).
requires(A, B) :- A -> B; not(fail).
excludes(A, B) :- A -> not(B); B.
```

In the Prolog executable specification, feature dependencies are specified as Prolog rules and solitary features are specified as facts. Additional rules specify feature selection rules. The implementation also allows to query feature models for their structure and properties, perform model validity checking as well as to compute basic metrics of a product line described by a feature model as well as feature model changeability metrics.

5 Case Study

As an example, we consider a cell-phone feature model [37] (see its graphic representation as a feature diagram in Fig. 2). Each cell-phone must have an accumulator cell (battery) and display, and may have an optional wireless connectivity. Wireless connection may be implemented using infrared connection or Bluetooth connection. Bluetooth connection requires lion (Lithium-Ion) battery. Display may be either monochrome or color, and the selection of color display excludes the usage of nica (Nickel-Cadmium) battery. Cell phone batteries may be either of liion, nimh (Nickel-Metal hydride) or nica type. This feature model has 10 features and describes a configuration space of 16 different valid products.

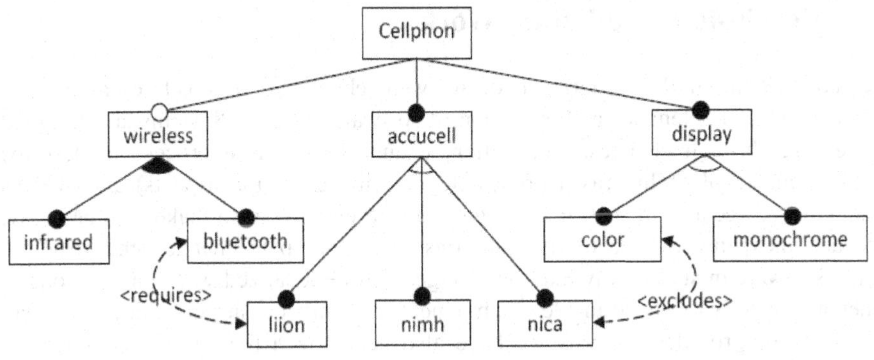

Fig. 2. Feature model of a cell phone

Using the Prolog rules given in subsection 4.3, we can describe a cell phone model (see Fig. 2) in Prolog as follows:

```
cellphone :- all(alt(wireless), accucell, display).
wireless  :- more_of(infrared, bluetooth),
            requires(bluetooth, liion).
accucell  :- one_of(liion, nimh, nica).
display   :- one_of(color, monochrome),
            excludes(color, nica).
```

The feature change operations and changeability computation also has been implemented as the Prolog rules. The results of change impact analysis of some changes applied to a cell phone feature model are summarized in Table 3.

Table 3. Examples of change operations and their effects

Feature	Feature change	Change propagation	No. of products in a new model	Change-ability value	Change ability impact
cellphon	UPD (cellphon, cellphone)	*none*	16	0	Little
wireless	STA (wireless, all)	infrared, bluetooth, liion	8	0.50	Consid-erable
RF	INS (RF, wireless)	*none*	32	0.50	Consid-erable
wireless	SEL (wireless, one_of)	infrared, bluetooth, liion	16	0.22	Some
bluetooth	CON (bluetooth, liion, none)	liion	16	0.40	Consid-erable
nica	DEL (nica)	color	16	0.67	Signifi-cant

6 Conclusions and Future Work

We have identified the importance of software change as a broad research topic within design, maintenance and evolution of software systems. Systems are designed and evolve through changes. Very often, changeability (as a process to describe changes) and evolvability (as a process to describe evolution aspects) are used as synonymous. Because of that, it is a significant research goal to make changes easy, safe and inexpensive. One of the solutions is to anticipate changes and structure within software in such a way that the changes will be localized within a component. When a change is localized inside a component, it is much easier to achieve the goal. Based on the provided analysis we have also generalized the definition of feature modelling as an evolutionary design paradigm based on model transformations to implement anticipated changes and variability. At the core of the processes is change anticipation that requires a great deal of analysis, domain modelling and its understanding. In this way our approach contributes to 'blurring boundaries between software development and evolution'. We have also identified that the feature model design and evolution processes can be described using the same approach that includes: a) incremental change of the previous state of a feature model; b) resolving of the change propagation task; c) iterative testing.

We have also proposed a change impact model for feature model. The change impact model allows to analyze effects of change on feature models, to research change propagation, to check the validity of changed feature model and to calculate changeability of feature model. We propose to estimate changeability of feature model to a change as a Jaccard distance between product sets described by an original and a changed feature model. The analysis of change performed on a simple feature model has shown what even a simple change of a single feature or relation between features can have a significant impact on the product configuration space. We hope that the proposed change impact analysis framework will help to better understand the feature model development and evolution and contribute to the construction of automatic (or semi-automatic) tools. Using the framework we are able to identify influential facts and draw the explicit relations between the context domain and the base domain to describe feature model changes in a well-established way. The implemented the framework in Prolog logic programming language to automate reasoning on feature models and their changeability.

Future work will focus on the extension of change impact model to source code artefacts. Given a knowledge base, where each feature is linked to corresponding source code implementing that feature, that task will be to research, how changes of the feature model of a system will affect the source code of the system itself.

References

1. Nord, R.L., Hofmeister, C., Soni, D.: Preparing for Change in the Architecture Design of Large Software Systems. In: The TC2 First Working IFIP Conference of Software Architecture (WICSA1), San Antonio, Texas (1999)

2. Fischer, G., Giaccardi, E., Ye, Y., Sutcliffe, A.G., Mehandjiev, N.: Meta-Design: a Manifesto for End-User Development. Communications of the ACM 47(9), 33–37 (2004)
3. Highsmith, J.: Agile Software Development Ecosystems. Addison-Wesley Professional (2002)
4. Beck, K.: The Inevitability of Evolution. IEEE Software 27, 26–29 (2010)
5. Bosch, J.: Software Variability Management. In: Proc. of the 26th Int. Conf. on Software Engineering (ICSE 2004), pp. 720–721. IEEE CS, Washington, DC (2004)
6. Pohl, K., Bockle, G., van der Linden, F.: Software Product Line Engineering. Springer, Heidelberg (2005)
7. Kang, K.C., Cohen, S.G., Hess, J.A., Novak, W.E., Peterson, A.S.: Feature-oriented domain analysis (FODA) feasibility study. Technical Report CMU/SEI-90-TR-021, SEI, Carnegie Mellon University (1990)
8. Schobbens, P.-Y., Heymans, P., Trigaux, J.-C.: Feature Diagrams: A Survey and a Formal Semantics. In: Proc. of 14th IEEE Int. Conf. on Requirements Engineering (RE 2006), Minneapolis/St.Paul, Minnesota, USA, September 11-15, pp. 136–145 (2006)
9. van Deursen, A., Klint, P.: Domain-Specific Language Design Requires Feature Descriptions. Journal of Computing and Information Technology 10(1), 1–17 (2002)
10. Kagdi, H., Maletic, J.I.: Software-Change Prediction: Estimated+Actual. In: Proc. of 2nd Int. IEEE Workshop on Software Evolvability, SE 2006, September 24, pp. 38–43 (2006)
11. Delamare, R., Munoz, F., Baudry, B., Le Traon, Y.: Vidock: A Tool for Impact Analysis of Aspect Weaving on Test Cases. In: Petrenko, A., Simão, A., Maldonado, J.C. (eds.) ICTSS 2010. LNCS, vol. 6435, pp. 250–265. Springer, Heidelberg (2010)
12. Briand, L.C., Labiche, Y., O'Sullivan, L., Sowka, M.M.: Automated impact analysis of UML models. Journal of Systems and Software 79(3), 339–352 (2006)
13. Clarke, D., Helvensteijn, M., Schaefer, I.: Abstract Delta Modeling. In: Proc. of Generative Programming and Component Engineering Conference GPCE 2010, Eindhoven, The Netherlands, pp. 13–22 (2010)
14. Anquetil, N., Kulesza, U., Mitschk, R., Moreira, A., Royer, J.-C., Rummler, A., Sousa, A.: A model-driven traceability framework for software product lines. Software and System Modeling 9(4), 427–451 (2010)
15. Xue, Y., Xing, Z., Jarzabek, S.: Understanding Feature Evolution in a Family of Product Variants. In: Proc. of 17th Working Conference on Reverse Engineering, WCRE 2010, Beverly, MA, USA, October 13-16, pp. 109–118 (2010)
16. Schmid, K., Eichelberger, H.: A requirements-based taxonomy of software product line evolution. Electronic Communication of the EASST 8 (2007)
17. Botterweck, G., Pleuss, A., Dhungana, D., Polzer, A., Kowalewski, S.: EvoFM: feature-driven planning of product-line evolution. In: Proc. of Workshop on Product Line Approaches in Software Engineering (PLEASE 2010), New York, NY, USA, pp. 24–31 (2010)
18. Damaševičius, R., Štuikys, V.: Design of Ontology-Based Generative Components Using Enriched Feature Diagrams and Meta-Programming. Information Technology & Control 37(4), 301–310 (2008)
19. Fricke, E., Schulz, A.P.: Design for Changeability (DfC): Principles to Enable Changes in Systems Throughout Their Entire Lifecycle. Systems Engineering 8(4), 342–359 (2005)
20. Benestad, A.C., Anda, B., Arisholm, E.: Understanding Software Maintenance and Evolution by Analyzing Individual Changes: A Literature Review. Journal of Software Maintenance and Evolution: Research and Practice 21(9), 349–378 (2009)

21. Buckley, J., Mens, T., Zenger, M., Rashid, A., Kniesel, G.: Towards a Taxonomy of Software Change. Journal of Software Maintenance and Evolution: Research and Practice 17(5), 309–332 (2003)
22. Rajlich, V.: A Model for Change Propagation Based on Graph Rewriting. In: Proc. of the Int. Conference on Software Maintenance, ICSM 1997, pp. 84–91. IEEE Computer Society, Washington, DC (1997)
23. Ramil, J.F., Lehman, M.M.: Metrics of Software Evolution as Effort Predictors - a Case Study. In: Proc. of Int. Confernce on Software Maintenance, pp. 163–172 (2000)
24. Chapin, N., Hale, J., Khan, K., Ramil, J., Than, W.-G.: Types of Software Evolution and Software Maintenance. Journal of Software Maintenance and Evolution 13, 3–30 (2001)
25. Fowler, M.: Refactoring: Improving the Design of Existing Programs. Addison-Wesley (1999)
26. Anquetil, N., de Oliveira, K.M., de Sousa, K.D., Dias, M.G.B.: Software Maintenance Seen as a Knowledge Management Issue. Information and Software Technology 49(5), 515–529 (2007)
27. Godfrey, M.W., German, D.M.: The Past, Present, and Future of Software Evolution. In: Proc. of Int. Conference in Software Maintenance (ICSM), Frontiers of Software Maintenance, vol. 10 (2008)
28. Dam, K.H., Winikoff, M., Padgham, L.: An Agent-oriented Approach to Change Propagation in Software Evolution. In: Proc. of Australian Software Engineering Conference, April 18-21, pp. 309–318 (2008)
29. Fluri, B., Gall, H.: Classifying Change Types for Qualifying Change Couplings. In: Proc. of 4th Int. Conference on Program Comprehension (ICPC 2006), Athens, Greece, June 14-16, pp. 35–45 (2006)
30. Fernandes, P., Werner, C.: Ubifex: Modelling context-aware software product lines. In: Proc. of 12th Int. Conference on Software Product Lines, SPLC 2008, Limerick, Ireland, vol. 2, pp. 3–8 (2008)
31. Ubayashi, N., Nakajima, S., Hirayama, M.: Context-Dependent Product Line Practice for Constructing Reliable Embedded Systems. In: Bosch, J., Lee, J. (eds.) SPLC 2010. LNCS, vol. 6287, pp. 1–15. Springer, Heidelberg (2010)
32. Lee, K., Kang, K.C.: Usage Context as Key Driver for Feature Selection. In: Bosch, J., Lee, J. (eds.) SPLC 2010. LNCS, vol. 6287, pp. 32–46. Springer, Heidelberg (2010)
33. Gheyi, R., Massoni, T., Borba, P.: Automatically Checking Feature Model Refactorings. Journal of Universal Computer Science 17(5), 684–711 (2011)
34. Rajlich, V., Gosavi, P.: Incremental Change in Object-Oriented Programming. IEEE Software 21(4), 2–9 (2004)
35. Bohner, S.A., Arnold, R.S. (eds.): Software Change Impact Analysis. IEEE Computer Society Press (1996)
36. Mao, C., Zhang, J., Lu, Y.: Matrix-based Change Impact Analysis for Component-based Software. In: Proc. of 31st Annual Int. Computer Software and Applications Conference, COMPSAC 2007, Beijing, China, July 24-27, vol. 1, pp. 641–642 (2007)
37. von der Maßen, T., Lichter, H.: Determining the Variation Degree of Feature Models. In: Obbink, H., Pohl, K. (eds.) SPLC 2005. LNCS, vol. 3714, pp. 82–88. Springer, Heidelberg (2005)
38. Paškevičius, P., Bindokas, M., Kasperavičius, A., Damaševičius, R.: Executable models and model transformations: a framework for research. In: Proc. of the 17th Int. Conf. on Information and Software Technologies, IT 2011, Kaunas, Lithuania, pp. 76–83 (2011)

A Graph Transformation Approach for Testing Timed Systems

Hiba Hachichi, Ilham Kitouni, Kenza Bouaroudj, and Djamel-Eddine Saidouni

MISC Laboratory, University Mentouri
Constantine, 25000, Algeria
{hachichi,kitouni,bouaroudj,saidouni}@misc-umc.org

Abstract. In this paper, we propose an approach based on the combination of Meta-modelling and Graph Grammars, to transform a Durational Action Timed Automata model (DATA*) into a timed refusal region graph (TRRG) for creating a canonical tester and generating test cases. However, our approach allows to generate automatically a visual modelling tool for DATA*, TRRG and the canonical tester. The cost of building a visual modelling tool from scratch is prohibitive. Meta-Modelling approach is useful to deal with this problem since it allows the modelling of the formalisms themselves, by means of Graph Grammars. Models manipulations are expressed on a formal basis and in a graphical way. In our approach, the UML class diagram formalism is used as meta-formalism to offer a meta-model of DATA*, TRRG and the canonical tester. The meta-modelling tool AToM^3 is used.

Keywords: AToM^3, DATA*, Formal testing, Graph transformation, Graph Grammars.

1 Introduction

Computer applications become increasingly involved in critical and real-time systems(e.g., automotive, avionic and robotic controllers, mobile phones, communication protocols and multimedia systems). These applications are known by their high complexity. Formal testing can greatly increase the confidence in the functioning of these applications. It allows checking the correctness of a system with respect to its specification.

In this work we are interested in formal testing approach [17], [10] where the temporal behavior of systems is taken into account. This approach is based on timed refusal. Testing based on timed refusal allows the comparison between the behavior of the specification and the implementation, if the implementation refuses an action after each timed trace, the specification also refuses this action. That means, *I* and *S* have the same refusals sets and the same timed traces. This theoretical approach is necessary to generate a canonical tester.

In this paper we use timed refusal region graph structure (TRRG). This structure allowed us to generate a canonical tester and test cases by several transformations on the Durational Action Timed Automata model (DATA*).

T. Skersys, R. Butleris, and R. Butkiene (Eds.): ICIST 2012, CCIS 319, pp. 123–137, 2012.

DATA* is a timed model, its semantic expresses the durations of actions and other notions for specifying the real-time systems such as urgency and deadlines [4].This model is based on a maximality semantic [18] and advocates the true concurrency; from this point of view it is well suitable for modelling real time, concurrent and distributed systems.

In this paper, firstly, we transform DATA* into timed refusal region graph (TRRG). Secondly, we transform this TRRG into canonical tester and we generate test cases using graph transformation [3],[13]. Indeed, we propose a DATA* meta-model and a TRRG /canonical tester meta-model. We use the meta-modelling tool $AToM^3$ [2],[5] to generate automatically a visual modelling tool to process models in DATA*, TRRG and the canonical tester. We also define a graph grammar to translate the models presented above.

This paper is organized as follows: section 2 outlines some related work. In section 3 we recall some basic concepts about DATA*, TRRG, canonical tester and graph transformation. In section 4 we describe our approach. In section 5, we illustrate our approach through an example. The final section concludes the paper and gives some perspectives.

2 Related Work

This paper deals with formal testing approach and model transformation, especially graph transformations.

Firstly we present several proposed works to tackle the problem of testing timed systems. Each of these works faces the problem from a different point of view. For instance, [16] uses the Extended Time Input Output State Machine to develop an algorithm for creating a canonical tester. It is used after for generating test sequences with time. In [17] they propose a fully automatic method for generating a real-time test sequences from a restricted sub class of dense time automata called event-recording automata which restricts how clocks are reset. This approach is based on de Nicola and Hennessy testing theory. A selection technique of timed tests is presented. This technique is based on symbolic analysis and coverage of a coarse equivalence class partitioning of the state space. The proposed conformance relation is a must/may preorder relation. In [6] authors present technique to testing real-time systems through the derivation of executable test cases on a specification modeled as a timed automata, this study deals with an equivalent representation of timed automata: Clock region graphs [1]. A test purpose is modeled by an acyclic graph: All paths of this graph which are found on the specification will be considered as a test case. [15] presents a framework for black-box conformance testing of real-time systems, specifications are modeled as timed automata and algorithms are proposed to generate two types of tests for this setting: Analog-clock tests, which measure dense time precisely, and digital-clock tests, which measure time with a periodic clock. A heuristic to generate a test case that covers all specification edges is briefly discussed.

Secondly we present some proposed tools in addition to AToM3 [5] that used meta-modelling concepts and visual tools like Generic Modelling environment (GME) [8] , MetaEdit+ [12] and other tools from the Eclipse Generative Modelling tools (GMT) project such as Eclipse Modelling Framework (EMF), Graphical Modelling Framework (GMF) and Graphical Editing Framework (GEF) [7]. There are also similar tools which manipulate models by means of graph grammars and none of these has its own meta-modelling layer, such as PROGRES, GReAT and AGG.

3 Background

In this paper, we interest in formal testing approach using graph transformation; we use a testing structure named timed refusal region graph (TRRG). This graph allows us to generate a canonical tester and extract automatically test cases after several transformations on specification graph, in our case specifications are modeled by Durational Action Timed Automata (DATA*).

The transformation process is performed by a graph grammar that takes the DATA* model as an input, executes the rules of the grammar, and generates the canonical tester as output passing by TRRG.

In the following, we recall some basic notions about DATA* model, TRRG, canonical tester and graph transformations.

3.1 DATA* Model

The DATA* model (Durational Action Timed Automata) [4] is a timed model defined by a timed transitions system over an alphabet representing actions to be executed. This model takes into account in the specification, the duration of actions based on an intuitive idea: temporal and structural non-atomicity of actions. This model seems interesting and funneling more and more research because it coated models of timed automata by maximality semantics [18].

The DATA* model, as the temporized models takes in charge the notions of urgency and deadlines as temporal constraints of the system. Fig.1 illustrates an example of this model:

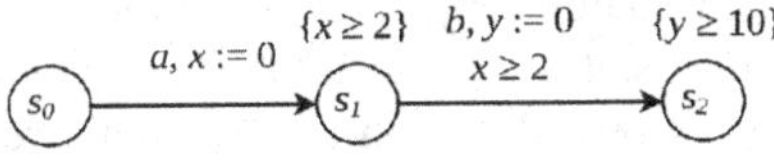

Fig. 1. DATA*

The durations associated to the actions are represented by constraints on the transitions and in the states targets of each one. In this sense, any enabled transition represents the beginning of the action execution. On the target state of transition, a timed expression means that the action is possibly under execution. From operational point of view, each clock is associated to an action. This clock is reset to 0 at the start of the action and will be used in the construction of the temporal constraints as guard of the transitions.

Fig.1 presents a system of two consecutives actions *a* and *b*, the clock x is associated to the action *a*, on the locality s_1 the temporal expression $\{x \geq 2\}$ represents the duration of action *a*. The end of the execution of an action is deduced implicitly in the case of an action that it is causally dependent.

The action *b* depends on *a*, so the transition is guarded by the relative duration constraint of *a*.

Formalization

Definition 1 : a DATA* *A* is a tuple (L, L_0, X, T_D, L_S) over *ACT* a finite set of actions, *L* is a finite set of states, $l_0 \in L$ is the initial state, *X* is a finite set of variables named clocks and T_D is a set of edges. A subset of *L* noted L_f for terminal states (final state).

An edge $e = (l, G, a, x, l')$ represents a transition from location *l* to location *l'* on input symbol *a*, *x* is a clock which is going to be reset with this transition. *G* is the corresponding guard which must be satisfied to launch this transition.

Finally, $L_S : L \rightarrow 2^{C(X)}_{fn}$ is a maximality function which decorates each state by a set of timed formula named actions durations; these actions are potentially in execution on it.

Definition 2: The semantic of a DATA* *A* is defined by associating to it a timed transitions system S_A over ACTUR+. A state of S_A (or configuration) is a pair $<l,v>$ such as *l* is a state of *A* and *v* is a valuation over *X*.

A valuation *v* is a mapping on *X* to R+. Let *x* be a clock, the valuation $v[x \leftarrow 0]$ resets clock *x* to 0 and each other clock *y* to $v(y)$. The valuation $v+d$ maps every clock *y* to $v(y)+d$ ($d \in$ R+). A configuration $<l_0, v_0>$ is initial if l_0 is the initial state of *A* and $\forall x \in X$, $v_0(x)=0$.

Two types of transitions between configurations of S_A are possible and correspond respectively to time passing thus the run of transition from *A*.

3.2 Timed Refusal Region Graph

Timed refusal region graph (*TRRG*) is generated from DATA*. It decorates aggregate regions automaton with refusals.

The aggregate regions automaton [9] provides a finite abstraction of DATA*; it consists of partitioning the states space into finite regions for reducing the combinatorial explosion of regions. A region is a symbolic representation of a clock valuations sets, regrouped in equivalence classes on clock valuations. The region concept was proposed by Alur and Dill in [1].

The proposed testing model (TRRG) introduces tow kinds of refusals on aggregate regions automaton, in addition to the classical refusals named forbidden actions (*Forb*). *Forb* is defined as a set of actions which cannot be permitted from one state. However, the two new kinds of refusals are named: permanent and temporary refusals.

The *Permanent refusals* are generated by the non-determinism in system behavior after the operation of determinization. The *temporary refusals* are provoked by actions which elapsed in time

Formalization

Definition 3: Let $D=(L,l_0,X,T_D,L_S)$ be a DATA* over *ACT.* Its aggregate regions automaton $ARA(D)=(S,s_0,T_R)$ over *ACT,* is defined as follows:

All states of *ARA(D)* are of the form $s_{ij} = (l_i, r_j)$ where l_i is a state and r_j is a clock region.

- The set of localities is noted S. The initial locality is $s_0 = (l_0, r_0)$.
- The set of transitions T_R is,

$$T_R = \left\{ t' / t' = (l,r) \xrightarrow{a} (l',r') \middle| \begin{cases} \exists l \xrightarrow{g,a,x} l' \in T_D \text{ and } \exists r'' \in succ(r) \\ \text{such as } r \subseteq g \text{ and } r' = r''[x \leftarrow 0] \end{cases} \right\} \quad (1)$$

$s_{ij}^f = (l_i, r_j)$ is a terminal locality iff $l_i \in L_f$, and $succ(r)$ is the set of all successors of the region r by lapsing time.

Timed refusal region graph (TRRG) extends aggregate regions automaton by sets of refusals defined as follows:

Definition 4: A timed refusals region graph of a DATA* *D*, (*TRRG(D)*) is a deterministic bi-labeled graph structure *A* constructed on the aggregate regions automaton of *D*, defined as structure $(S, s_0, T_R, \mathrm{Re}f_{TPR})$.

$$A = TRRG(D) = TRRG(ARA(D)) \quad (2)$$

With: $\mathrm{Ref}_{TPR} S \rightarrow P\left(P(\bar{V} \cup \bar{\bar{V}})\right)$ an application that associates for any $s \in S$ a set of refusals where:

$\bar{V} = \{\bar{a}(g): a \in ACT, g \text{ is gard}$ which must be satisfied to execute the action a $\}$ *and*

$\bar{\bar{V}} = \{\bar{\bar{a}}(g): a \in Act, g \text{ is gard}$ which must be satisfied to execute the action a $\}$ (3)

The semantic of $P\left(P(\bar{V} U \bar{\bar{V}})\right)$ is as follows:

$\bar{V} = \bar{a}(g) \in Ref_{TPR}(s)$: Permanent refusal means that the action *a* may be refused permanently form the state *s*, this refusal is possible but not certain. This certitude will take place after the satisfaction of guard *g*.

$\bar{\bar{V}} = \bar{\bar{a}}(g) \in Ref_{TPR}(s)$: Temporary refusal means that actions are refused as much as the guard *g* is not satisfied.

The determinization of TTRG is done according to the principle detailed in [14]; recall here that a determinization method is inspired from the classical one named subset construction.

As illustration, let consider the DATA* M of coffee machine depicted by Fig.2.

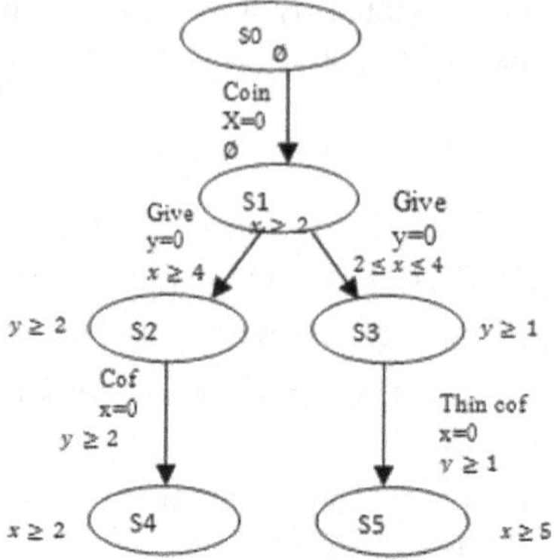

Fig. 2. DATA* M of coffee machine

The TTRG M' associated to DATA* M is depicted by Fig.3.

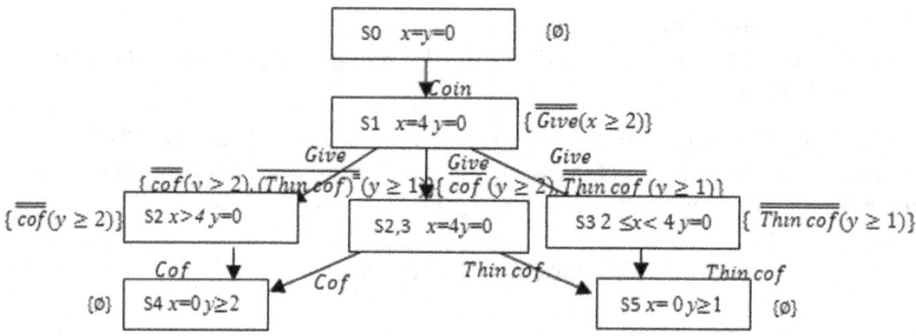

Fig. 3. TRRG M' associated to DATA* M

Timed Refusal Region Graph Generation. Based on Definitions above, a Framework to Create a TRRG Structure is Done in Five (05) Steps:

Input: Specification modeled in DATA*.

1- Determinate the DATA* structure,
2- Compute permanent refusals for all states,
3- Compute temporary refusals for all states,
4- Decorate every state by the tree sets of refusals (Forbidden, Permanent, and Temporary).
5-Calculete the aggregate regions automaton

Output: TRRG of the specification.

3.3 Canonical Tester

A canonical tester is able to detect every implementation that disagrees with a specification, thus if the implementation refuses an action after each timed trace, the specification also refuses this action. That means, *I* and *S* have the same refusals sets and the same timed traces. This theoretical approach is necessary to generate a canonical tester. In the proposed canonical tester, three verdicts $\{pass, incon, fail\}$ are used. At every step of the test computation if a locality is reachable so it is decorated by *pass* verdict. The inconclusive verdict *incon* is produced by the non-determinism present in the system, and captured by permanent refusals set. *Fail* is a new locality introduced to canalize transitions labeled by actions which are not permitted. Two cases of actions are not allowed: first, when an action is in the forbidden set of state. The second case, when an action is offered without respecting the guard. This action is in temporary refusals set.

A framework for creating the canonical tester of DATA* specification, takes as input the TRRG and generates test cases. Localities of the test case correspond to sets of localities of the TRRG graph and edges are labeled by actions in *ACT*. Therefore, all traces of the canonical tester will be considered as test cases. The concrete timed trace can be calculated by choosing specific time points in regions.

Fig.4 presents an example of a test case associated to the canonical tester generated from TTRG M'.

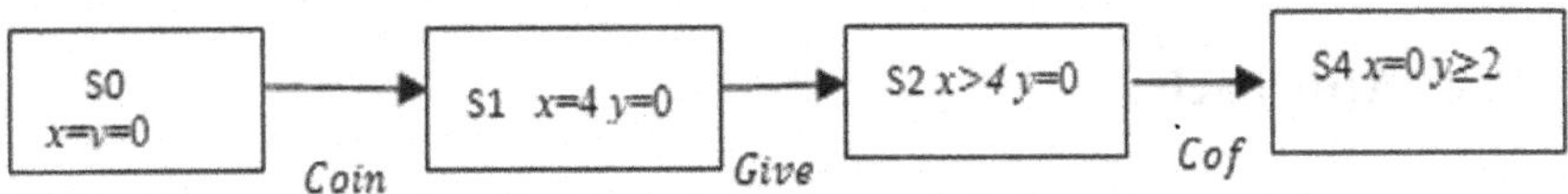

Fig. 4. Test case

3.4 Graph Transformation

A transformation between models is the automatic generation of a target model from a source model. This task requires a set of rules that describe how one or more constructs in the source language can be transformed to one or more constructs in the target language.

Graph Grammars [11] are used for model transformation. They are composed of production rules; each one have graphs in their left and right hand sides (LHS and RHS) (Fig.5). Rules are compared with an input graph called host graph. If a matching is found between the LHS of a rule and a sub graph in the host graph, then the rule can be applied and the matching sub graph of the host graph is replaced by the RHS of the rule. Furthermore, rules may also have a condition that must be satisfied in order to apply the rule, as well as actions to be performed when the rule is executed. A rewriting system iteratively applies matching rules in the grammar to the host graph, until no more rules are applicable. AToM^3 [2] is a graph transformation tool among others. In this paper we use it.

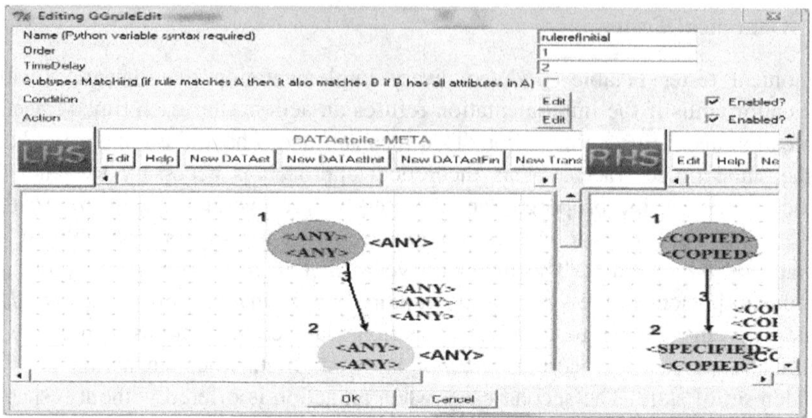

Fig. 5. A grammar rule (LHS and RHS)

AToM^3. AToM^3 is a visual tool for multi-formalism modelling and meta-modelling. It has been proven to be very powerful, allowing the meta-modelling and the transformations of known formalisms. AToM^3 is implemented in the language Python. Once we build meta-models for the interested models, AToM^3 can generate automatically a visual modelling environment, in which you can build and edit the new models.

4 The Approach

In order to perform the transformation of DATA* to the canonical tester using TRRG for generating test cases, we propose two meta-models; the first one associated to the DATA* model and the second one is associated with both TRRG and the canonical tester structures. We note here that the meta-models are described using UML class diagrams. Then we propose a grammar for the transformation. Meta-models and grammar are implemented in AToM^3 using python language.

4.1 DATA* Meta-model

The first meta-model proposed is a class diagram composed of the following classes (Fig.6):

- *DATAet class*: it represents the states of DATA*, each state has three attributes: a name (name), duration conditions (CD) and set of refusals (refusal).
- *TransitionD association*: it represents the transitions of DATA*, each transition is identified by an action, a clock and a guard.
- *DATAetInit class*: it represents the initial state of DATA*, it inherits the attributes from DATAet class.
- *DATAetFin class*: it represents the final state of DATA*, it inherits the attributes from DATAet class.

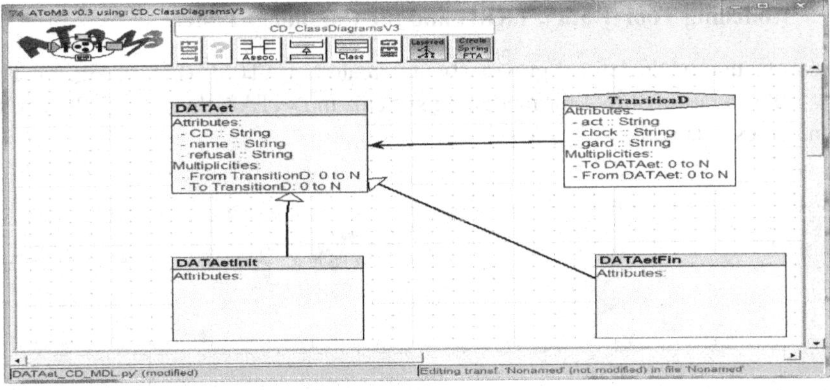

Fig. 6. DATA* meta-model

4.2 TRRG and Canonical Tester Meta-model

The second meta-model describes the TRRG and the canonical tester structures. In practical point of view, they have the same structure even if they differ semantically. This meta-model is a class diagram composed of the following classes (Fig. 7):

- *TRRG_Canonical_state class*: it represents the localities of TRRG and canonical tester structures, each locality has three attributes: a name (name), a clock region (clock_region) and set of refusals (refusal).
- *TRRG_Canonical_transition association*: it represents the transitions of TRRG and canonical tester, each transition is identified by an action.
- *TRRG_Canonical_StateInit class*: it represents the initial locality of TRRG and canonical tester; it inherits the attributes from TRRG_Canonical_state class.
- *TRRG_Canonical_StateFin class*: it represents the final locality of TRRG and canonical tester; it inherits the attributes from TRRG_Canonical_state class.

Each class has an only graphical appearance.

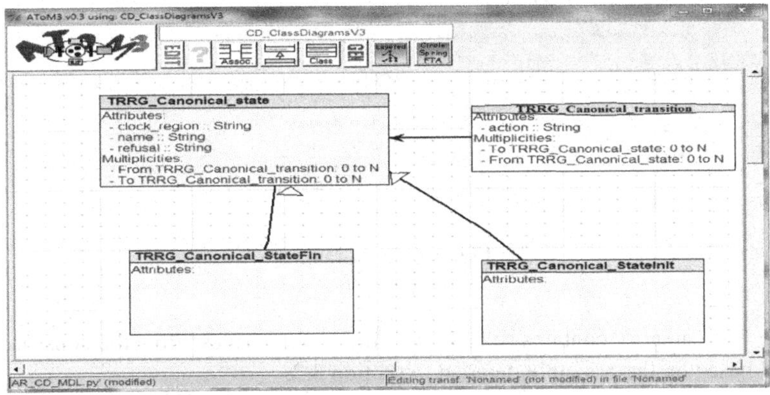

Fig. 7. TRRG and Canonical Tester Meta-Model

4.3 Modelling Tool (Data*, TRRG and the Canonical Tester)

The two meta-models defined previously are created in AToM^3 (Fig. 6, Fig. 7). They allow the generation of tool for modelling systems in DATA*, thus the TRRG and the canonical tester (Fig. 8).

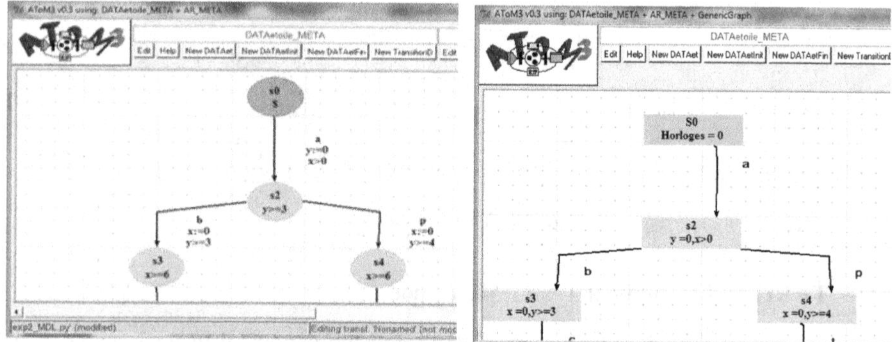

Fig. 8. Modelling tool of DATA* TRRG and Canonical Tester

4.4 Graph Grammar

The proposed graph grammar is composed by 23 rules organized in 2 categories (Fig. 9).

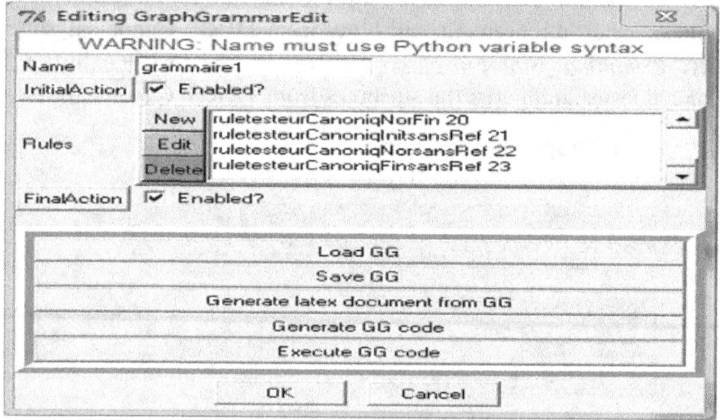

Fig. 9. Graph Grammar

The first category contains rules from 1 to 16; these rules allow the construction of TRRG based on the principle detailed in section 3.2.

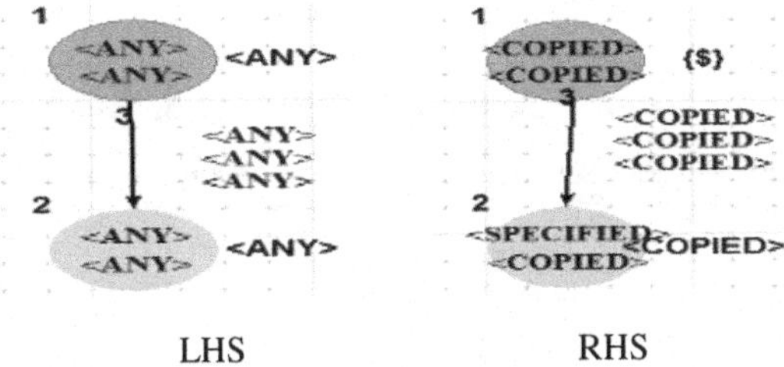

Fig. 10. Calculation of refusals associated to the initial state of DATA* (Rule 1)

- The 1st rule is used to calculate the set of refusals associated to the initial state of DATA* (Fig.10).
- Rules 2, determinizes and calculates the refusals set in the case of non-deterministic system.
- Rules 3 and 4 calculate respectively refusals of the rest and a final state of DATA*.
- Rule 5 is used to generate the first locality of TRRG associated to the initial state of DATA* where all clocks are reset to zero.
- Rules 6 and 7 generate the rest of TRRG.
- Rules 8 and 9 generate localities of TRRG in case of non-deterministic system.
- Rule 10 generates the final locality of TRRG associated to the final state of DATA*.
- Rules 11, 12 and 13 eliminate a generic links between DATA* and TRRG.
- Rules 14, 15 and 16 eliminate the graphical representation of DATA* model.

The second category contains rules from 17 to 23; these rules allow the construction of canonical tester and the generation of test cases based on the principle detailed in section 3.3.

- Rule 17 is used to generate the first locality of canonical tester associated to the initial locality of TRRG.
- Rule 18 generates localities of canonical tester in case of non-deterministic system.
- Rule 19 generates the rest of canonical tester.
- Rule 20 generates the final locality of canonical tester associated to the final locality of TRRG.
- Rules 21, 22 and 23 eliminate refusals of all localities and generate test cases.

5 Example

To illustrate our approach we propose the example of ATM system. This machine allows withdrawing money from account. Its behavior is as follow: Customer has to insert card in machine. After he has to type a code, if code is correct the machine delivers money and card. If the code is wrong, the machine can keep card or reject it.

Fig.11 presents a DATA* of ATM system. We have applied our tool on the DATA* model and obtained automatically the TRRG (Fig.12), the canonical tester (Fig.13) and we have selected an example of test case with pass verdict (Fig.14).

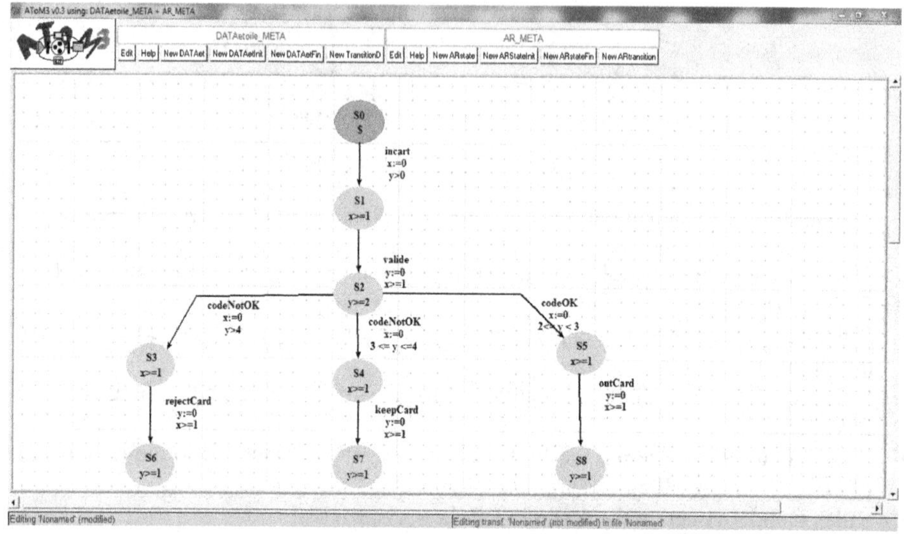

Fig. 11. DATA* of ATM system presented in AToM^3 tool

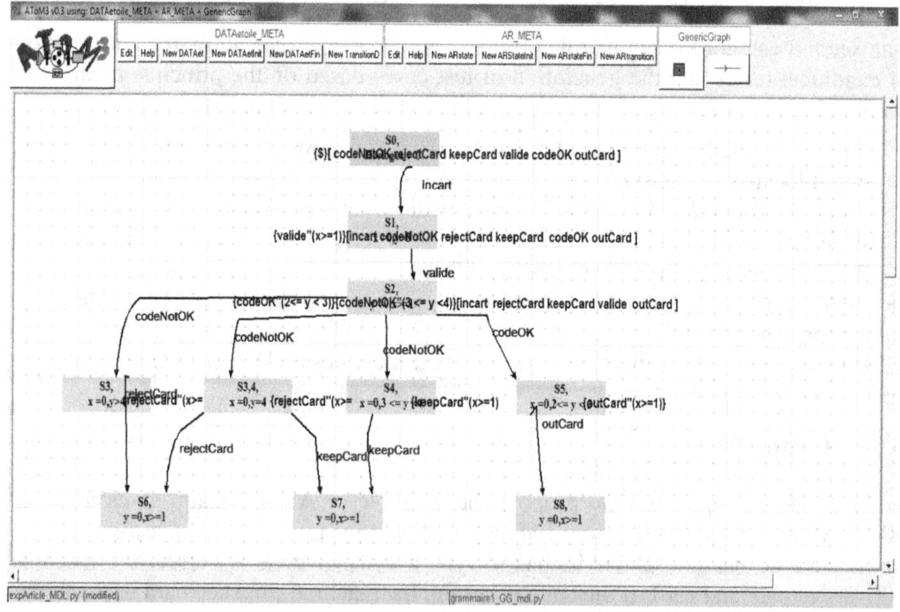

Fig. 12. TRRG associated to the DATA*

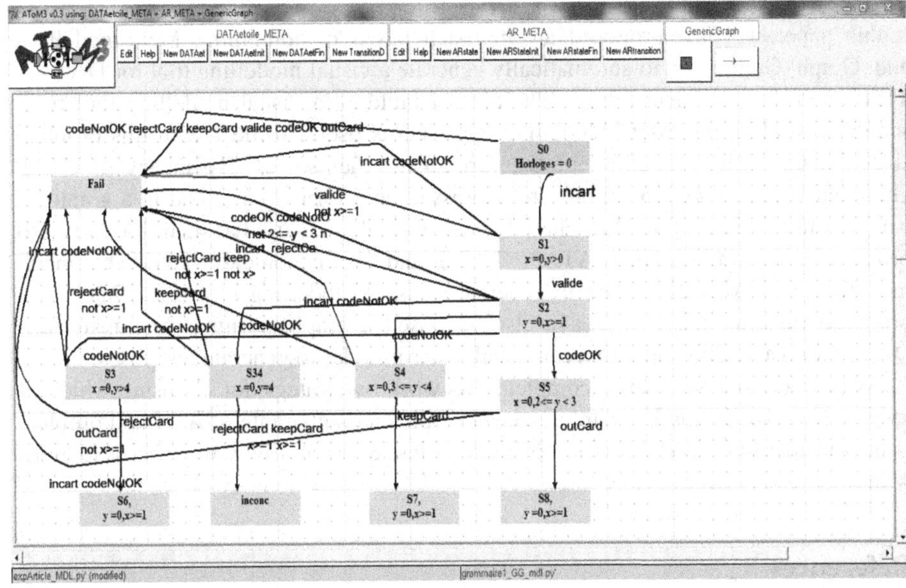

Fig. 13. The canonical tester

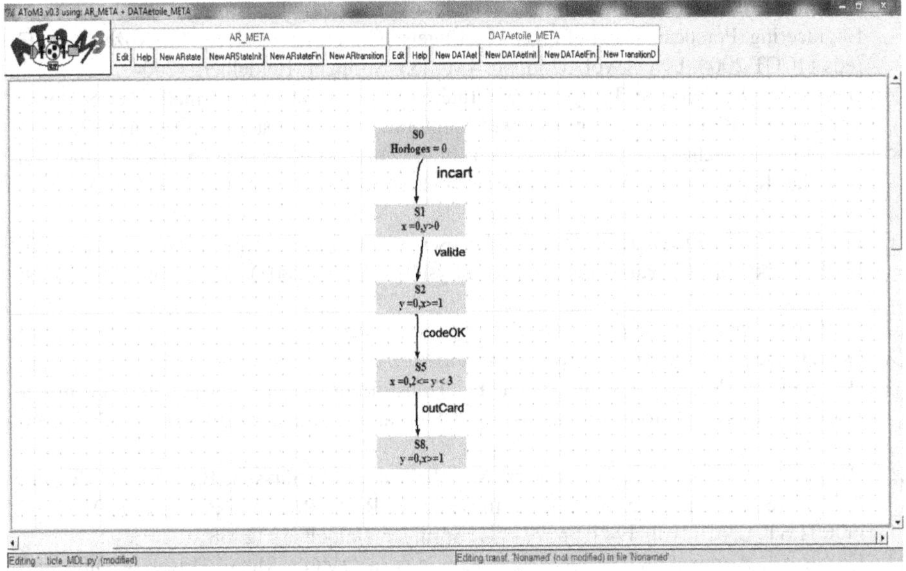

Fig. 14. Test case with pass verdict

6 Conclusion

In this paper, we have proposed an approach based on combining Meta-modelling and Graph Grammars to automatically generate a visual modelling tool for DATA*, TRRG and the canonical tester. The cost of building a visual modelling tool from scratch is prohibitive. Meta-Modelling approach is useful to deal with this problem since it allows the modelling of the formalisms themselves. By means of Graph Grammars, models manipulations are expressed on a formal basis and in a graphical way. In our approach, the UML class diagram formalism is used as meta-formalism to propose a meta-model of DATA*, TRRG and the canonical tester. The meta-modelling tool $AToM^3$ is used to generate a visual modelling tool according to the proposed meta-models. We have also proposed a graph grammar to transform a DATA* into a TRRG and into a canonical tester in order to generate test cases.

As perspective, we plan to complete this work by strategy for choosing which of test cases are sufficient for insuring some completeness guarantees. A related problem is how to measure the "goodness" of a set of test cases and how to select test suites with some good coverage measure.

References

1. Alur, R., Dill, D.: A theory of timed automata. Theoretical Computer Science, 183–235 (1994)
2. AToM3 Home page, version 3.00, `http://atom3.cs.mcgill.ca/`
3. Baresi, L., Heckel, R.: Tutorial Introduction to Graph Transformation: A Software Engineering Perspective. In: Ehrig, H., Engels, G., Parisi-Presicce, F., Rozenberg, G. (eds.) ICGT 2004. LNCS, vol. 3256, pp. 431–433. Springer, Heidelberg (2004)
4. Belala, N.: Modèles de Temps et leur Intérêt à la Vérification Formelle des Systèmes Temps-Réel. PHD's thesis, University of Mentouri, 25000 Constantine, Algeria (2010)
5. de Lara, J., Vangheluwe, H.: $AToM^3$: A Tool for Multi-formalism and Meta-modelling. In: Kutsche, R.-D., Weber, H. (eds.) FASE 2002. LNCS, vol. 2306, pp. 174–188. Springer, Heidelberg (2002)
6. Fouchal, H., Petitjean, E., Salva, S.: An user-oriented testing of real time systems. In: IEEE Workshop on Real-Time Embedded Systems (RTES 2001). IEEE Computer Society Press (2001)
7. GEF home page, `http://www.eclipse.org/gef/`
8. GME home page, `http://www.isis.vanderbilt.edu/gme`
9. Hachichi, H., Kitouni, I., Saidouni, D.E.: Transforming DATA* with Dotty Format to Aggregate Region Automaton. International Journal of Computer Applications 37(10), 35–42 (2012)
10. Hessel, A., Larsen, K.G., Mikucionis, M., Nielsen, B., Pettersson, P., Skou, A.: Testing Real-Time Systems Using UPPAAL. In: Hierons, R.M., Bowen, J.P., Harman, M. (eds.) FORTEST. LNCS, vol. 4949, pp. 77–117. Springer, Heidelberg (2008)
11. Karsai, G., Agrawal, A.: Graph Transformations in OMG's Model-Driven Architecture. In: Pfaltz, J.L., Nagl, M., Böhlen, B. (eds.) AGTIVE 2003. LNCS, vol. 3062, pp. 243–259. Springer, Heidelberg (2004)

12. Kelly, S., Lyytinen, K., Rossi, M.: MetaEdit+: A Fully Con_gurable Multi-User and Multi-Tool CASE and CAME Environment. In: Constantopoulos, P., Vassiliou, Y., Mylopoulos, J. (eds.) CAiSE 1996. LNCS, vol. 1080, pp. 1–21. Springer, Heidelberg (1996)
13. Kerkouche, E., Chaoui, A., Bourennane, E., Labbani, O.: A UML and Colored Petri Nets Integrated Modeling and Analysis Approach using Graph Transformation. Journal of Object Technology 9(4), 25–43 (2010)
14. Kitouni, I.: Déterminisation des automates temporisés avec durées d'actions pour le test formel. Master's thesis, University of Mentouri, 25000 Constantine, Algeria (2008)
15. Krichen, M., Tripakis, S.: Black-Box Conformance Testing for Real-Time Systems. In: Graf, S., Mounier, L. (eds.) SPIN 2004. LNCS, vol. 2989, pp. 109–126. Springer, Heidelberg (2004)
16. Laurensot, P., Castanet, R.: Integration of Time in Canonical Testers for Real-Time Systems. In: Internationel Workshop on Object-Oriented Real-time Dependable Systems. IEEE Computer Society Press, California (1997)
17. Nielsen, B., Skou, A.: Automated Test Generation from Timed Automata. In: Margaria, T., Yi, W. (eds.) TACAS 2001. LNCS, vol. 2031, pp. 343–357. Springer, Heidelberg (2001)
18. Saïdouni, D.E., Belala, N., Bouneb, M.: Aggregation of transitions in marking graph generation based on maximality semantics for Petri nets. In: Proceedings of the 2nd Workshop on Verification and Evaluation of Computer and Communication Systems (VECoS 2008). University of Leeds, UK (2008)

FSM Based Functional Test Generation Framework for VHDL

Vacius Jusas and Tomas Neverdauskas

Kaunas University of Technology, Software Engineering Department,
Studentų str. 50-406, LT-51368, Kaunas, Lithuania
{vacius.jusas,tomas.neverdauskas}@ktu.lt

Abstract. The major challenge for the semiconductor industry is to design devices in short time with complex logical functionality. At the very top of the list of challenges to be solved is verification. The goal of the verification is to ensure that the design meets the logical functional requirements as defined in the logical functional specification. Verification of the devices takes 40 to 70 per cent of the total development effort for the design. The increasing complexity of hardware designs raises the need for the development of new techniques and methodologies that can provide the verification team with the means to achieve its goals quickly and with limited resources.

We present a framework that enables verification test generation using circuit model presented in VHDL hardware description language. The framework consists of several tools. We use the third party tool VSYML for VHDL description translation. Our tool then extracts finite state machine (FSM) model from translated VHDL description. The goal of the model is to use it for verification test generation. We introduce our software tool and algorithm, as well. The experimental results are presented for the benchmark suite ITC'99. The obtained results demonstrated the viability of the framework.

Keywords: VHDL, FSM, benchmark generation, testing framework, model extraction.

1 Introduction

In the last few years the major challenge, which the semiconductor industry is confronted with, has been to design devices in significantly less time with far more complex logical functionality. At the very top of the list of challenges to be solved is verification. The goal of the verification is to ensure that the design meets the logical functional requirements as defined in the logical functional specifications. Verification of the system-on-chip (SOC) takes 40 to 70 per cent of the total development effort for the design [1]. The increasing complexity of hardware designs raises the need for the development of new techniques and methodologies that can provide the verification team with the means to achieve its goals quickly and with limited resources.

During design process, hardware description languages are used usually for description of the functioning of the SOC. One of these languages is VHDL. It is

T. Skersys, R. Butleris, and R. Butkiene (Eds.): ICIST 2012, CCIS 319, pp. 138–148, 2012.

along with Verilog are the two most popular hardware description languages. VHDL is usually used for higher level description of the design, because it has well developed constructs to describe this level of the abstraction. Meanwhile, Verilog is used for the description of lower level of the design process, because Verilog primarily was used to describe the lower level of the design process and it has well developed facilities for this purpose. Therefore, there is a sense to use the behavioural description presented in VHDL in order to generate the verification test for high level of the design.

In this paper, we present a framework for automated finite state machine (FSM) extraction from VHDL description and verification test generation. Input for this framework is behavioral level of VHDL.

2 Related Work

Verification can be broadly classified into two categories: formal verification and simulation-based verification. Formal verification mathematically analyzes the hardware design and verifies that it is functioning correctly. Simulation-based verification verifies the design by comparing the result of the design with the golden model through simulation.

The simulation is still the most widely used form of device verification, because the formal verification is possible either for smaller projects or small parts of larger projects only [2]. But the simulation needs test suites to validate the design functionalities. Many different approaches are used in order to generate test cases for design verification.

Lichtenstein et al. [3] proposed an approach of verification test generation called as Model Based Test-Generation. This approach allows the incorporation of complex testing knowledge. The architecture model, which is comprised of logical functional blocks, is used. Fournier et al. [4] proposed a pseudo-random test program generator, Genesys, a follow-on of the model based test generation. Genesys enables the combination of randomness and control, thus generating high quality tests. The architecture model is used, as well.

Fine and Ziv [5] addressed one of the main challenges of simulation based verification, by providing a new approach for Coverage Directed Test Generation. This approach is based on Bayesian networks and computer learning techniques. The specification driven and constraints solving based method to automatically generate test programs from simple to complex ones for advanced microprocessors is presented in [6]. Microprocessor architectural automatic test program generator can produce not only random test programs but also a sequence of instructions for a specific constraint by specifying a user constraints file. It is well studied and reported in the literature that for a tool to be scalable with larger designs, it is important to handle the design at higher levels of abstraction. An Automatic Assembly Program Generator that handles the design at the behavioral RTL level is presented in [7]. The Generator is based on logical function-oriented test generation schemes, hence making it scalable and usable for some specific tasks. In recent years special purpose verification languages have been developed to support automatic stimulus generation.

Behm et al [8] reported on experience with a new test generation language for processor verification. Al-Asaad and Hayes [9] presented a simulation-based method for combinational design verification that aims at complete coverage of specified design errors using conventional ATPG tools. All common design errors can readily be mapped into stuck-at faults and a systematic method to perform this mapping is presented. The experimental results show that complete test sets for stuck-at faults detect almost all detectable errors. The experiments demonstrate that high coverage of the modeled design errors can be achieved with small test sets.

Ugarte and Sanchez [10] presented an assertion checking technique for behavioral models that combines a non-linear solver and state exploration techniques and avoids expanding behavior into logic equations. In order to generate proper verification patterns for core-based design, the stuck-at fault model and automatic test pattern generation (ATPG) tools are usually used. In order to reduce the core-based design verification time, a connectivity-based port order fault (POF) model was proposed [11]. The POF assumes that a faulty cell has at least two I/O ports misplaced. In [12], the Event Sequence Coverage Metrics are introduced. The approach is based on an automatic method to extract the control flow of a circuit which can be explored for coverage analysis and ATPG.

The idea of FSM extraction from hardware description languages VHDL or C was presented in [13]. An extended finite state machine (EFSM) model is extracted from the behavioral description and is exhaustively traversed to generate functional tests. This approach analyzes the syntactic structure of the HDL and identifies equivalence relations among parts of the data space thus leading to a sometimes smaller FSM which is equivalent to the original FSM. However, it depends heavily on the syntactic style of the HDL.

We will use the approach similar to the one presented in and we will apply it to nowadays reality.

3 VHDL and FSM

VHDL is Standard defined in IEEE 1076 [14] of the hardware description language with wide range possibilities from specifying circuits wavefronts to large system behavioral models with high-level constructs. That range of flexibility makes standard huge. This paper considers synthesizable subset of VHDL [15].

As programming language VHDL is strongly typed and it borrowed a lot of constructs from Ada [16]. Nevertheless, VHDL is devoted for hardware description. The main block for description of hardware functioning at the high level of the abstraction is a process. The process consists of two parts: declaration and executable. The description part is used to declare the variables. The variables declared within the process are local that can only be accessed from the same scope. Within a process statements are executed sequentially. Another type of variable is a *signal*. Signal cannot be declared within the process. They are declared within the architecture, which encompasses process, part. The difference of signal from variables is that signal values are not updated immediately; new values are assigned either after simulation delta or after defined delay. Circuits can be implemented using many processes, which are executed in parallel. Set of VHDL processes can be described as formal semantics that is cyclic [17].

A finite state machine is a sequential logic circuit which moves between a finite set of states, dependent upon the values of the inputs and the previous state. The state transitions are synchronized by a clock. Unlike the regular sequential circuit, state transition of an FSM is more complicated and the sequence exhibits no simple, regular pattern, as in a counter or shift register. If there is no a priori knowledge the next-state logic has to be constructed from scratch and is sometimes known as "random" logic.

In a synchronous FSM, the transition is controlled by a clock signal (mostly rising) and can occur only at the triggering edge of the clock. All benchmarks described in Section 6 use synchronous clock operations. The main application of an FSM is to realize operations that are performed in a sequence of steps. A large hardware system usually involves complex tasks or algorithms, which can be expressed as a sequence of actions based on system status and external commands. An FSM can function as the control circuit (known as the control path) that coordinates and monitors the operations of other units (known as the data path) of the system.

FSM's can also be used in many simple tasks, such as detecting a unique pattern from an input data stream or generating a specific sequence of output values. So, it is very important part of VHDL semantics and can be used as main part (but not the only) for verification test generating.

There are many ways to describe a finite state machine in VHDL. The most convenient is with a process statement. The logic in a state machine is described using a case statement or the condition (e.g., if-else). All possible combinations of current state and inputs are enumerated, and the appropriate values are specified for next state and the outputs. The state of the machine can be stored in a variable or signal, and the possible states conveniently represented with an enumeration type as showed in the following source code:

```
architecture Explicit of FSM is
  begin
  process
   type StateType is (Idle, Start, Stop, Clear);
   variable State: StateType;
  begin
   wait until RISING_EDGE(Clock);
   if Reset = '1' then
    State := Idle; F <= '0'; G <= '1';
   else
    case State is
     when Idle => State := Start; G <= '0';
     when Start => State := Stop;
     when Stop => State := Clear; F <= '1';
     when Clear => State := Idle; F <= '0';
     G <= '1';
    end case;
   end if;
  end process;
```

Using enumeration type allows you to give symbolic names to the states, but say nothing about the hardware implementation. In practice, it is important that finite state machines are initialized by means of an explicit reset signal. Otherwise, there is no reliable way to get the VHDL and gate level representations of the FSM into the same known state, and thus no way to verify their equivalence.

4 Framework Structure

In order to extract FSM from VHDL high level description and generate functional tests we formed a framework (Fig. 1). The framework consists of the following tools: VSYML, FSM extractor and Test generator.

VSYML [18] is VHDL Symbolic Simulator implemented in OCaml. The main purpose of this tool is extraction of the formal model from hardware description language VHDL. Symbolic simulation method for the analysis of integrated design was proposed by Carter et al [19]. This tool can simulate synchronous, multi-synchronous and timed-asynchronous designs. In VSYML from VHDL source files abstract syntax tree is generated. Next this structure is converted to internal optimized representation for simulation. Symbolic Trajectory Evaluation[20] is method used for the simulation in VSYML. Simulation results are available in couple different formats but XML results are most useful for automated processing software. In order to extract the FSM model for Design-Under-Test, simple benchmark must be created. It consist simple port mapping between design and benchmark. A generated formal model in VSYML is outputted in XML format and it is generally easy to read and transform by any programming language. In the description section of the results, the signals that are assigned inside sequential processes are part of the state vector. They will not be expanded during the simulation while combinational signals (which are signals assigned in combinational processes) will be expanded. This result section shows design inputs and outputs as well.

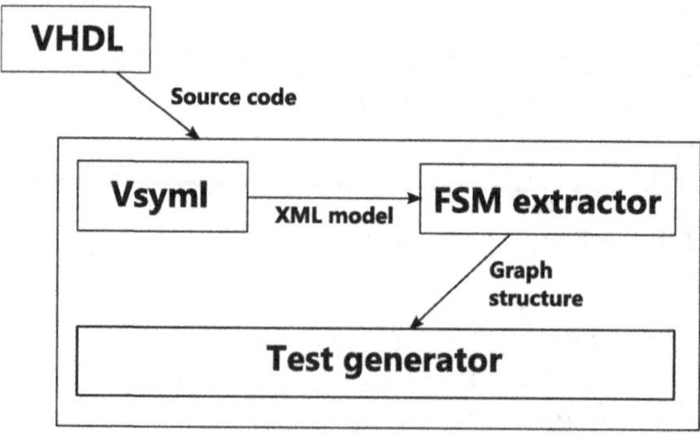

Fig. 1. Framework structure

Our framework is organized as follows (Fig. 1). First the source code of VHDL is read by VSYML tool and simulation is executed. If that step was successful XML file in plain text is read by FSM extraction module and the FSM structure with state and transition between the states is created. This data transformed to graph structure. Next the path generation algorithm is applied and set of a possible paths described in FSM is extracted. Framework not only generates paths but gives some statistical information about FSM's such as state and transition count.

The main purpose of this framework is to generate functional VHDL tests. For now FSM extraction, graph formation and execution paths extraction are completed. Off course with FSM generation approach we are not getting the full set of all available execution paths in given program. As was mentioned in chapter 3 FSM's generated from VHDL gives information about branch operations such as *case-when* (switch operator) or *if-then* (condition operator). Furthermore to get full program execution tree such method as symbolic execution (SE) [21] must be applied. Symbolic execution is a extension of normal execution, providing the normal computations as special case. Computational definitions for the basic operators of the language are extended to accept symbolic inputs and produce symbolic formulas as output. The state of a symbolically executed program includes the symbolic values of program variables, a path condition (PC) and a program counter representing next statement to be executed. The path condition is a (quantifier-free) Boolean formula over the symbolic inputs. It accumulates constraints which the inputs must satisfy in order to follow for an execution the particular associated path. Symbolic execution tree represents the execution paths followed during the symbolic execution of a program. The nodes represent program states and the arcs represent transitions between states. To generate concrete values from execution tree paths Satisfiability Modulo Theories solver will be used [24]. From state exploration and functional test generation point of view path generation from FSM is a subset of symbolic execution tree.

VSYML (GPL licensed) is implemented in Ocaml language. All other parts of framework are implemented in Python.

5 Path Generation Algorithm

FSM extractor in our framework creates nondeterministic finite state machine based on quintuple: N=$(S, \Sigma, q_0, F, \delta)$, where S is a finite, non-empty set of states, Σ – finite, non-empty set of input symbols, q_0 – initial state $q_0 \epsilon S$, F – a (possible empty) set of final states and δ – transition function $\delta : S \times \Sigma \rightarrow \mathcal{P}(\Sigma)$. Each transition is marked with condition that needs to be satisfied for reaching next state.

In the next step N is transformed into directed weighted graph $G = (V, E)$ with $f: s \epsilon S \mapsto v \epsilon V$ and $\forall \delta \mapsto e \epsilon E : e = (u, v, w)$. In this case, w means transition function result. Graph example generated for b01 benchmark is shown in Figure 2. Each vertex represents different state in FSM.

As VHDL execution is cyclic, so the generated graphs have at least one cycle. That's clear from results presented in Table 1. Traditional graph traversing (path-finding) algorithms such as depth-first search or breath-first search without limiting will fail because of lack of end point (endless branching in recursion). We implemented path finder in FSM based on Johnson algorithm [22]. The algorithm outputs every elementary circle exactly once. A circle is a path in which the first and last vertices are identical and is elementary if no vertex appears twice. Johnson's elementary circuit find algorithm proceeds on the graph G. The final result is set of cyclic graphs: $S' = (G'(v : v \in V))$. Every graph G' presents one of execution paths in VHDL.

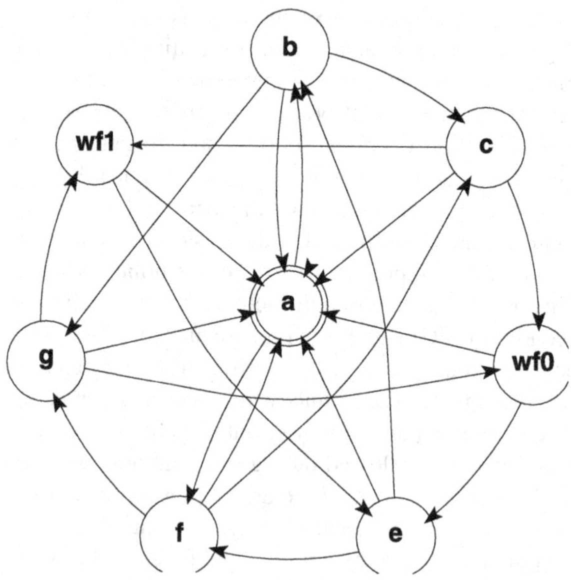

Fig. 2. FSM of b01

Pseudo-code of the algorithm for the path generation from the FSM presented as follows:

1. *Generate set of FSM from the XML file*
2. *For each element in FSM set:*
   2.1. *Add graph vertex $v \in V$*
   2.2. *Add edge between two vertices $e(u, v)$: $e \in E$*
   2.3. *Set δ function result (transition condition) as weight in e(w)*
3. *Evaluate Johnsons cycle find in G*
   3.1. *Create new set S' of cyclic Graphs G'*

6 Results

Well-known ITC'99 [23] benchmarks suite was used to test the framework. Circuits are described in synthesizable VHDL at the RT level. In experiment we used benchmarks from 01 to 15. They are not combined together and represent various VHDL functionalities. The benchmarks code is mainly behavioral, with one or more concurrent processes, but none of used in this experiment contained structural code. For circuits that have more than one FSM results are presented in the same row respectively to each other. For each benchmark separated files with the same name was created. To evaluate results for each benchmark path extraction framework is used.

Results are presented in Table 1. Path generation for two benchmarks (b12 and b14) was unsuccessful because of the source code complexity due to the FSM model generation in VSYML failed. In this case improvement in VSYML symbolic simulation engine is considered as future work as well.

Most significant result of the framework is shown on the last column in Table 1. That is execution path count found in each graph. In other words that is starting point of functional test generation for each VHDL circuit. Generated paths from b01 using proposed algorithm are presented in Table 2 and can be followed in Fig. 2.

Table 1. Results of benchmarked VHDL code

Benchmark	FSM's	FSM states	FSM transitions	Paths
b01	1	8	24	24
b02	1	7	10	5
b03	1	3	2	1
b04	1	2	3	1
b05	1	5	8	3
b06	1	7	13	7
b07	1	7	13	4
b08	1	4	9	3
b09	1	4	8	4
b10	1	11	24	10
b11	1	9	38	7
b12	-	-	-	-
b13	4	8,4,4,10	10,7, 6, 90	3,4,3,11
b14	-	-	-	-
b15	2	8, 10	27, 35	17,8

Table 2. Generated b01 paths

Path
{c, wf1, e, f, c}
{c, wf1, e, f, g, wf0, a, b, c}
{c, wf1, e, b, c}
{c, wf1, e, b, g, wf0, a, f, c}
{c, wf1, a, f, c}
{c, wf1, a, f, g, wf0, e, b, c}
{c, wf1, a, b, c}
{c, wf1, a, b, g, wf0, e, f, c}

Table 2. (*continued*)

{c, wf0, e, f, c}
{c, wf0, e, f, g, wf1, a, b, c}
{c, wf0, e, b, c}
{c, wf0, e, b, g, wf1, a, f, c}
{c, wf0, a, f, c}
{c, wf0, a, f, g, wf1, e, b, c}
{c, wf0, a, b, c}
{c, wf0, a, b, g, wf1, e, f, c}
{e, f, g, wf1, e}
{e, f, g, wf0, e}
{e, b, g, wf1, e}
{e, b, g, wf0, e}
{b, g, wf1, a, b}
{b, g, wf0, a, b}
{a, f, g, wf1, a}
{a, f, g, wf0, a}

7 Conclusions and Future Work

Many of the problems with the functional verification in industry are based on the absence of an effective automation to combat the discouraging growth in the size and complexity of the design. This has forced to rely on manual effort in the development of environments for tests. The goal of the verification is to ensure that the design meets the logical functional requirements as defined in the logical functional specification. Verification takes 40 to 70 per cent of the total development effort for the design. For now, the majority of the efforts are contained in developing and improving specific skills, each of which is excellent in some area of the verification. A common theme of verification effort is to find a comprehensive methodology of verification.

We presented a framework for program execution paths needed for functional test generation. The framework combines VSYML for FSM extraction with our implemented algorithm for path generation from FSM represented as graph structure. The obtained results using ITC'99 series benchmarks demonstrated the viability of the approach.

The future work consists of functional test generation from the framework generated paths using Satisfiability Modulo Theories solver [24] for computing concrete values from FSM transition. Also FSM approach is not enough to get full program execution information, therefore methods used in static software analyze such as symbolic execution is next logical stage of framework development.

References

[1] Bareisa, E., Jusas, V., Motiejunas, K., Seinauskas, R.: The Use of a Software Prototype for Verification Test Generation. Inf. Technol. Control 37(4), 265–274 (2008)

[2] Lam, W.K.: Hardware Design Verification: Simulation and Formal Method-Based Approaches. Prentice Hall PTR (2005)

[3] Lichtenstein, Y., Malka, Y., Aharon, A.: Model-Based Test Generation for Processor Design Verification. In: Proceedings of the Sixth Innovative Applications of Artificial Intelligence (IAAI) Conference, pp. 83–94. AAAI Press (1994)

[4] Fournier, L., Arbetman, Y., Levinger, M.: Functional verification methodology for microprocessors using the Genesys test-program generator. In: Proceedings of the Conference on Design, Automation and Test in Europe, Munich, Germany. ACM (1999)

[5] Fine, S., Ziv, A.: Coverage directed test generation for functional verification using Bayesian networks (2003)

[6] Tun, L., Dan, Z., Yang, G., GongJie, L., SiKun, L.: MA2TG: a functional test program generator for microprocessor verification (2005)

[7] Bhaskar, K.U., Prasanth, M., Kamakoti, V., Maneparambil, K.: A Framework for Automatic Assembly Program Generator (A^2PG) for Verification and Testing of Processor Cores (2005)

[8] Behm, M., Ludden, J., Lichtenstein, Y., Rimon, M., Vinov, M.: Industrial experience with test generation languages for processor verification. In: Proceedings of the 41st Annual Design Automation Conference, San Diego, CA, USA. ACM (2004)

[9] Al-Asaad, H., Hayes, J.P.: Design verification via simulation and automatic test pattern generation. In: Proceedings of the 1995 IEEE/ACM International Conference on Computer-Aided Design, San Jose, California, United States. IEEE Computer Society (1995)

[10] Ugarte, I., Sanchez, P.: Functional vector generation for assertion-based verification at behavioral level using interval analysis. In: Proceedings of the Eighth IEEE International Workshop on High-Level Design Validation and Test Workshop. IEEE Computer Society (2003)

[11] Tung, S.-W., Jou, J.-Y.: Verification Pattern Generation for Core-Based Design Using Port Order Fault Model. In: Proceedings of the 7th Asian Test Symposium. IEEE Computer Society (1998)

[12] Moundanos, D., Abraham, J.A.: 12.1 Using Verification Technology for Validation Coverage Analysis and Test Generation. In: Proceedings of the 16th IEEE VLSI Test Symposium. IEEE Computer Society (1998)

[13] Cheng, K.T., Krishnakumar, A.S.: Automatic functional test generation using the extended finite state machine model. In: Proceedings of the 30th International Design Automation Conference, Dallas, Texas, United States. ACM (1993)

[14] IEEE Standards Interpretations: IEEE Std 1076-1987, IEEE Standard VHDL Language Reference Manual. IEEE Std 1076/INT-19911, 1 (992)

[15] IEEE Standard for VHDL Register Transfer Level (RTL) Synthesis. IEEE Std 1076.6-2004 (Revision of IEEE Std 1076.6-1999) 0_1-112 (2004)

[16] Barnes, J.: Ada 95 Rationale: The Language, the Standard Libraries. Springer (1995)

[17] Maksoud, M.A., Pister, M., Schlickling, M.: An abstraction-aware compiler for VHDL models (2009)

[18] Ouchet, F., Borrione, D., Morin-Allory, K., Pierre, L.: High-level symbolic simulation for automatic model extraction (2009)

[19] Carter, W.C., Joyner Jr., W.H., Brand, D.: Symbolic Simulation for Correct Machine Design (1979)
[20] Bryant, R.E.: Symbolic simulation-techniques and applications (1990)
[21] Cadar, C., Godefroid, P., Khurshid, S., Pasareanu, C.S., Sen, K., Tillmann, N., Visser, W.: Symbolic execution for software testing in practice: preliminary assessment (2011)
[22] Johnson, D.B.: Finding All the Elementary Circuits of a Directed Graph. SIAM Journal on Computing 4(1), 77–84 (1975)
[23] Corno, F., Reorda, M.S., Squillero, G.: RT-level ITC'99 benchmarks and first ATPG results. IEEE Design & Test of Computers 17(3), 44–53 (2000)
[24] Bjrner, N.: SMT Solvers for Testing, Program Analysis and Verification at Microsoft (2009)

Segmentation Algorithm for Algebraic Progressions

Dovile Karaliene[1], Zenonas Navickas[1], and Alfonsas Vainoras[2]

[1] Kaunas University of Technology, Department of Applied Mathematics, Lithuania
dovile.karaliene@gmail.com, zenonas.navickas@ktu.lt
[2] Lithuanian University of Health Sciences, Sport Institute, Lithuania
alfavain@gmail.com

Abstract. Segmentation task can provide important information about the nature of the sequence that is understandable to humans. A new algorithm for sequence segmentation is proposed in this paper. It is shown that it is possible to segment sequence finding a nearest algebraic progression to an each segment of a given sequence. The proposed segmentation technique based of the concept of the rank of a sequence. The rank of a sequence describes exact algebraic relationships between elements of the sequence. Numerical experiments with an artificially generated numerical sequence are used to illustrate the functionality of the proposed algorithm.

Keywords: sequence segmentation, rank of a sequence, algebraic progression.

1 Introduction

Sequence segmentation is a challenging problem in many fields of science and engineering. Application support for large data sequences, such as time series. Sequence segmentation is a partition of the sequence into a number of non-overlapping segments that cover all data points, such that each segment is as homogeneous as possible. Each segment is usually represented by a model that concisely describes the data points appearing in the segment.

A number of algorithms have been proposed for sequence segmentation. Segmentation problem can be solved using the optimal standard dynamic programming algorithm [1]. This algorithm is not satisfactory for data-mining applications for large data sequences. More efficiently are approximation algorithms [2, 3]. Using approximation algorithm [2] each segment is represented by the mean of the points in the segment. The error in this approximate representation is measured using some error function, e.g. the sum of squares. The goal is to find the segmentation of the sequence and the corresponding representatives that minimize the error in the representation of the underlying data. Another approximation algorithm [3] is based on breaking sequences into meaningful subsequences and storing an approximate, compact representation of each subsequence as a mathematical function. Also sequences could be segmented using

T. Skersys, R. Butleris, and R. Butkiene (Eds.): ICIST 2012, CCIS 319, pp. 149–161, 2012.

sliding-window algorithm [4, 6], Markov Chain Monte Carlo algorithm [5, 6] and many other.

Proposed algorithms have been applied for such human sequences as medical cardiology data [3, 4] or times series data. There are proposed a number of algorithms for times series data: frequent patterns finding, structural changes and time series classification and prediction, time series similarities searching [7–12].

The main objective of this paper is to propose an algebraic segmentation algorithm based of the concept of the rank of a sequence [13]. The rank of a sequence just describes algebraic relationships between elements of the sequence without pretending to approximate the analytical model of an underlying dynamical system; moreover, these algebraic relationships are exact. The rank of a sequence is used to express solutions of nonlinear differential equations in forms comprising ratios of finite sums of standard functions [14–16]. Also, it is used for the identification of the skeleton algebraic progression in the time series and use this information to forecast future values of that time series [17]. Application of the rank of a sequence to evaluating complexity of some ECG parameters [18] shows that development of algebraic segmentation algorithm for medical cardiology data is important task.

There exist algorithms of segmentation of numerical sequences which are based on fitting linear recurrent relations to different segments of these sequences. These algorithms belong to the class of change-point detection algorithms for time series. One of these algorithms is described in the paper Moskvina V. G.[19]. Algorithm works well even if the observations are rather noisy. Statistical methods are used in this algorithm. Our goal is using algebraic methods to develop a strategy for finding a nearest algebraic progression to an each segment of a given sequence. We will show that proposed algebraic segmentation algorithm can be effectively exploited for numerical sequences (without noise) segmentation. It is the first step in the direction of these researches. Segmentation of noisy numerical sequences is the futher research object.

2 The Concept of the Rank of a Sequence

Let us consider a sequence: $p_0, p_1, p_2, ... := (p_j; j \in Z_0)$ where elements p_j can be real or complex numbers. Then, a sequence of Hankel matrixes reads:

$$H_n := (p_{i+j-2})_{1 \le i,j \le n} = \begin{bmatrix} p_0 & p_1 & \cdots & p_{n-1} \\ p_1 & p_2 & \cdots & p_n \\ & & \cdots & \\ p_{n-1} & p_n & \cdots & p_{2n-2} \end{bmatrix}, \quad n = 1, 2, ... \tag{1}$$

The Hankel transform (the sequence of determinants of Hankel matrixes) $(d_n; n \in N)$ reads:

$$d_n := \det H_n \tag{2}$$

Definition 1. *The sequence* $(p_j; j \in Z_0)$ *has a rank* $m \in Z_0$; $m < +\infty$

$$Hr(p_j; j \in Z_0) = m, \tag{3}$$

if the sequence of determinants of Hankel matrixes has the following structure:

$$(d_1, d_2, ..., d_m, 0, 0, ...), \tag{4}$$

where $d_m \neq 0$ *and* $d_{m+1} = d_{m+2} = ... = 0$.

Example 1. Let $p_j := j^2$; $j \in Z_0$. Then, $Hr(j^2; j \in Z_0) = 3$ because the sequence of determinants of Hankel matrices reads $(0, -1, -8, 0, 0, \ldots)$.

Definition 2. *Let* $Hr\,(p_j; j \in Z_0) = m$. *Then the characteristic Hankel determinant for the sequence* $(p_j; j \in Z_0)$ *is defined as [13]:*

$$\hat{d}_m := \det \hat{H}_m := \begin{vmatrix} p_0 & p_1 & \cdots & p_m \\ p_1 & p_2 & \cdots & p_{m+1} \\ \cdots & \cdots & \cdots & \cdots \\ p_{m-1} & p_m & \cdots & p_{2m-1} \\ 1 & \rho & \cdots & \rho^m \end{vmatrix} = 0. \tag{5}$$

The expansion of the determinant in Eq.(5) yields an m-th order algebraic equation for the determination of roots of the characteristic equation:

$$A_m\rho^m + A_{m-1}\rho^{m-1} + ... + A_1\rho + A_0 = 0 \tag{6}$$

where $A_m \neq 0$ because $A_m = d_m \neq 0$.

We have assume, that $\mu_{rg}\binom{j}{g}\rho_r^{j-g} = 0$ if $\binom{j}{g} = 0$ what is true when $0 \leq j < g$. Moreover, $0^0 = 1$; $0^1 = 0^2 = ... = 0$. Then the following theorem holds.

Theorem 1. *Let* $Hr(p_j; j \in Z_0) = m$ *and the recurrence indexes of roots* $\rho_1, \rho_2, \rho_3, ..., \rho_c$ *of the characteristic equation (Eq. (6)) are* $m_1, m_2, ..., m_c$ *accordingly;* $\sum_{r=1}^{c} m_r = m$. *Then the following equality holds true:*

$$p_j = \sum_{r=1}^{c}\sum_{g=0}^{m_r-1} \mu_{rg}\binom{j}{g}\rho_r^{j-g} \tag{7}$$

where $\mu_{rg}, \rho_r \in C$; $\mu_{rm_r-1} \neq 0$.

The opposite statement holds also. If Eq. (7) holds true, then

$$Hr(p_j; j \in Z_0) = m_1 + m_2 + ... + m_c$$

Rigorous proof of this theorem is given in [13].

Definition 3. *A sequence* $(p_j; j \in Z_0)$ *is an algebraic progression if elements of that sequence can be expressed in the form of Eq. (7).*

Corollary 1. *Eq. (7) can be rewritten in the following form:*

$$\sum_{r=1}^{c}\sum_{g=0}^{m_r-1}\mu_{rg}\binom{j}{g}\rho_r^{j-g}=\sum_{r=1}^{c}\sum_{g=0}^{m_r-1}\frac{\mu_{rg}}{\rho_r^g}\frac{j!}{g!(j-g)!}\rho_r^j=\sum_{r=1}^{c}\sum_{g=0}^{m_r-1}\hat{\mu}_{rg}j^g\rho_r^j \quad (8)$$

where $\rho_1,\rho_2,...,\rho_c\neq 0$; $\mu_{rm_r-1}\neq 0$ *and* $\hat{\mu}_{rg}$ *do not depend on* j.

Corollary 2. *In case when all roots of the characteristic equation are different, Eq. (7) obtains a more simple form:*

$$p_j=\sum_{r=1}^{m}\mu_r\rho_r^j \quad (9)$$

It can be also noted that coefficients μ_{rg} (or just μ_r) can be found solving the linear algebraic system of equations ($\rho_1,\rho_2,...,\rho_c$ are determined beforehand):

$$\sum_{r=1}^{c}\sum_{g=0}^{m_r-1}\binom{j}{g}\rho_r^{j-g}\mu_{rg}=p_j, j=0,1,...,m-1 \quad (10)$$

This linear system of algebraic equations has one and the only one solution [13].

Example 2. Let $p_j=\sin(0.1j)$; $j\in Z_0$. Let us compute the rank of a sequence p_j and construct its algebraic progression. It is clear that $Hr(p_j;j\in Z_0)=2$ because the sequence of determinants of Hankel matrices reads $(0,-0.01,0,0,\ldots)$. Then the characteristic Hankel determinant (Eq.(5)) takes the form:

$$\hat{d}_2:=\det\hat{H}_2:=\begin{vmatrix}p_0 & p_1 & p_2\\ p_1 & p_2 & p_3\\ 1 & \rho & \rho^2\end{vmatrix}=0$$

and Hankel algebraic equation (Eq.(6)) is: $-0.01\rho^2+0.0198\rho-0.01=0$.

Its roots are: $\hat{\rho}_{1,2}=0.9950\pm 0.0998i$. It can be seen that $\hat{\rho}_{1,2}$ are different. Then, Eq.(9) yields:

$$\hat{p}_j=\mu_1(0.9950+0.0998i)^j+\mu_2(0.9950-0.0998i)^j, j=0,1,2,...$$

Values of parameters $\mu_{1,2}$ are found from the linear system of equations:

$$\hat{\mu}_{1,2}=\mp 0.5i.$$

Then the algebraic progression of p_j reads:

$$\hat{p}_j=-0.5i(0.9950+0.0998i)^j+0.5i(0.9950-0.0998i)^j,\ j\in Z_0. \quad (11)$$

Corollary 3. *Let* $Hr(p_j;j\in Z_0)=m$ *and the first 2m elements of that series are known. Then it is possible to use Eq.(6), Eq.(10) and Eq.(7) to calculate all elements of that sequence.*

Corollary 4. *Let Eq.(3) holds true and roots ρ_r of the characteristic equation Eq.(6) holds:*

$$\rho_r \neq 0, r = 1, 2, ..., m. \tag{12}$$

It can be noted that accordingly to Eq.(8) the following equality holds true:

$$q_j = q_j(k,h) = p_{k+hj} = \sum_{r=1}^{c} \sum_{g=0}^{m_r-1} \hat{\mu}_{rg}(k+hj)^g \rho_r^{k+hj} = \tag{13}$$

$$= \sum_{r=1}^{c} \sum_{g=0}^{m_r-1} \tilde{\mu}_{rg} \rho_r^k \cdot j^g \cdot \left(\rho_r^h\right)^j = \sum_{r=1}^{c} \sum_{g=0}^{m_r-1} \tilde{\mu}_{rg} \tilde{\rho}_r^k \cdot j^g \cdot \tilde{\rho}_r^j, \ \ j \in Z_0,$$

where $\rho_1, \rho_2, ..., \rho_c \neq 0$; $\mu_{rm_r-1} \neq 0$; $\tilde{\mu}_{rg}\rho_r^k$ do not depend on j and

$$\tilde{\rho}_r = \rho_r^h. \tag{14}$$

Then the rank of a subsequence $(q_j; j \in Z_0)$ with all $k \in Z_0$, $h \in N$ is equal to:

$$Hr(q_j; j \in Z_0) \leq m. \tag{15}$$

Example 3. Let sequence $p_j = (1, -1, 1, -1, ...)$. Then $Hr(1, -1, 1, -1, ...) = 2$ but $Hr(p_{2j}, j \in Z_0) = Hr(1, 1, 1, 1, ...) = 1$.

Next will be need the inverse task. It is to obtain the algebraic progression of sequence p_j, $j \in Z_0$ then are known an algebraic progression q_j Eq.(13) and parameters h, k. Then accordingly to Eq.(14) ρ_r can be expressed in the form:

$$(\rho_r)_a = \sqrt[h]{|\tilde{\rho}_r|} \cdot e^{\frac{i(\arg \tilde{\rho}_r + 2\pi a)}{h}} \tag{16}$$

where $|\tilde{\rho}_r| \geq 0$, $\sqrt[h]{|\tilde{\rho}_r|} \geq 0$ and $-\pi \leq \arg \tilde{\rho}_r < \pi$, $a = 0, 1, ..., h-1$.

But values of ρ_r is the only one (it is then $a = a_0$) in the algebraic progression of p_j, $j \in Z_0$:

$$\left(\hat{p}_j\right)_{a_0} = \sum_{r=1}^{c} \sum_{g=0}^{m_r-1} \hat{\mu}_{rg} \cdot j^g \cdot (\rho_r)_{a_0}^j, \tag{17}$$

where values $(\rho_r)_{a_0}$ can be selected minimizing the root mean square error ($RMSE$):

$$R\left(\left(\hat{p}_j\right)_{a_0}\right) = \min_a \sqrt{\frac{1}{\eta} \sum_{j=0}^{\eta} \left(\left(\hat{p}_j\right)_a - p_j\right)^2}, \tag{18}$$

where $\eta \in N$ which allows to estimate a value of a_0.

It can be noted that coefficients $\hat{\mu}_{rg}$ (Eq.(16))) can be found solving the linear algebraic system of equations.

Example 4. Let $p_j = \sin(0.1j)$, $j \in Z_0$. We assume, that subsequence $q_j = p_{k+hj}$, $j \in Z_0$. Let us compute the rank of a subsequence and construct the algebraic progression of this subsequence when $k = 3$, $h = 2$. It is clear that $Hr(q_j; j \in Z_0) = 2$ because the sequence of determinants of Hankel matrices reads: $(0.1987, \ -0.0395, \ 0, \ 0, \ldots)$. Then Hankel algebraic equation Eq.(6) is: $-0.0395\rho^2 + 0.0774\rho - 0.0395 = 0$. Its roots are: $\tilde{\rho}_{1,2} = 0.9801 \pm 0.1987i$.

Then accordingly to Eq.(9) yields:

$$\hat{q}_j = \mu_1 (0.9801 + 0.1987i)^j + \mu_2 (0.9801 - 0.1987i)^j, j = 0, 1, 2, ...$$

Values of parameters $\mu_{1,2}$ are found from the linear system of equations: $\hat{\mu}_{1,2} = \mp 0.5i$. Then the algebraic progression of q_j reads:

$$\hat{q}_j = -0.5i(0.9801 + 0.1987i)^j + 0.5i(0.9801 + 0.1987i)^j, \, j \in Z_0.$$

Now let us to compute algebraic progression of p_j, $j \in Z_0$. Values of $\hat{\rho}_r$ accordingly Eq.(14) reads: $\hat{\rho}_{1,2} = \sqrt{\tilde{\rho}_1} = \sqrt{0.9801 + 0.1987i} = \pm 0.9950 \pm 0.0998i$, $\hat{\rho}_{3,4} = \sqrt{\tilde{\rho}_2} = \sqrt{0.9801 - 0.1987i} = \pm 0.9950 \mp 0.0998i$.

Values of parameters $\hat{\mu}_{1,2}$ are found from the linear system of equations Eq.(9). It was obtained that value of $RMSE$ (Eq.(18)) is minimal when $\hat{\rho}_{1,2} = 0.9950 \pm 0.0998i$ and $\hat{\mu}_{1,2} = \mp 0.5i$. Then accordingly to Eq.(17) can be obtained algebraic progression $\hat{p}_j$ of sequence p_j, $j \in Z_0$. It can be noted that obtained algebraic progression is the same as Eq.(11).

Corollary 5. *It can be noted that given above concept of the rank of a sequence can be applied to finite length sequences in the practice. If is given a sequence* $(p_0, p_1, ..., p_{L-1})$ *of length* L *then sequence of Hankel matrices is:* $H_1, H_2, ..., H_n$, $n \leq L/2$. *We have assume that rank of a sequence is not defined if* $d_n \neq 0$, $n \leq L/2$.

3 An Algebraic Algorithm of Segmentation of Numerical Sequences

Let $P = (p_0, p_1, ..., p_{L-1})$ is the numerical sequence of length L consisted of several segments of algebraic progressions (Eq.(7)). Let construct algorithm for segmentation of sequence P into k non-overlapping contiguous segments $S_l = S_l(u_l, v_l) = (p_{u_l}, p_{u_l+1}, ..., p_{v_l})$, $u_l \leq v_l$ $\left(S := \bigcup_l S_l, \, l = \overline{1, k}\right)$ where u_l is a start position and v_l - end position of each segment S_l.

Let us assume that m_t is the rank of a sequence (then can be applied Theorem 1), k_t is the start position and h_t - the step of the regular grid in the interval of the subsequence $P_t \subset P$. Then can be constructed t different subsequences $P_t = p_{k_t+h_t j}$, $j = \overline{0, b_t - 1}$, $b_t = 2m_t h_t$ with different combinations of parameters m_t, k_t and h_t (generated accordingly to equality: $g_t = k_t + 2m_t h_t - h_t$, where g_t - is the given last position of subsequence P_t).

It can be noted that accordingly to Eq.(13) can be observed t different algebraic progressions of each subsequence P_t:

$$q_j^{(t)} = q_j^{(t)}(k_t, h_t) = p_{k_t+h_t j}, \, j = \overline{0, b_t - 1} \tag{19}$$

Let us construct an algebraic progression Eq.(19) of subsequence P_t. We have assumed that the rank of the algebraic progression $q_j^{(t)}$ is m_t and parameters k_t, h_t are known (it is noted that initial step of the regular grid in the interval of each subsequence must be at least $h_0 = 2$). Then the characteristic Hankel determinant (Eq.(5)) takes the form:

$$\det \begin{bmatrix} q_0^{(t)} & q_1^{(t)} & \dots & q_{m_t}^{(t)} \\ q_1^{(t)} & q_2^{(t)} & \dots & q_{m_t+1}^{(t)} \\ \dots & \dots & \dots & \dots \\ q_{m_t-1}^{(t)} & q_{m_t}^{(t)} & \dots & q_{2m_t-1}^{(t)} \\ 1 & \tilde{\rho}^{(t)} & \dots & \left(\tilde{\rho}^{(t)}\right)^{m_t} \end{bmatrix} = 0 \qquad (20)$$

and yields roots $\tilde{\rho}_1^{(t)}, \tilde{\rho}_2^{(t)}, \dots, \tilde{\rho}_{m_t}^{(t)}$. Linear system of equations is constructed using Eq.(8); its solution produces coefficients $\tilde{\mu}_r^{(t)}$; $r = 1, 2, \dots, m_t$. Finally, the algebraic progression $q_j^{(t)}$ reads:

$$\hat{q}_j^{(t)} = \sum_{r=1}^{d} \sum_{g=0}^{m_{tr}-1} \tilde{\mu}_{rg}^{(t)} \left(\tilde{\rho}_r^{(t)}\right)^{k_t} \cdot j^g \cdot \left(\left(\tilde{\rho}_r^{(t)}\right)^{h_t}\right)^j, \; j = \overline{0, b_t - 1} \qquad (21)$$

It can be noted that accordingly Eq.(21), Eq.(14) and Eq.(17) can be obtained algebraic progression of subsequence P_t:

$$\left(\hat{p}_j^{(t)}\right)_{a_0} = \sum_{r=1}^{c} \sum_{g=0}^{m_r-1} \hat{\mu}_{rg}^{(t)} \cdot j^g \cdot \left(\rho_r^{(t)}\right)_{a_0}^j . \qquad (22)$$

Given algorithm is detailed in Algorithm 1.

Algorithm 1.$(\hat{\rho}_r, \hat{\mu}_r) = ACE\,(P, P_t, m_t, h_t)$ - algorithm of construction of algebraic progression (AEC) of a given subsequence P_t

Input: Sequence P, subsequence P_t and parameters m_t, h_t
Output: Parameters $\hat{\rho}_r, \hat{\mu}_r,\; r = \overline{1, m_t}$
of algebraic progression (Eq.(8)) of subsequence P_t
1. construct the characteristic Hankel determinant $\hat{d}_{m_t} := \det \hat{H}_{m_t}$
2. assign initial values to parameters: $\hat{\rho}_r = Inf, \hat{\mu}_r = Inf$
3. solve Hankel equation $\left(\text{output} : \tilde{\rho}_r^{h_t}, r = \overline{1, m_t}\right)$
4. find all roots $\hat{\rho}(a, r),\; r = \overline{1, m_t}; a = \overline{1, h_t}$

$a = 1$
  while $a \le h_t$
    if $abs(\hat{\rho}(a, r)) \ge 0$ ***then***
    5. construct and solve a linear algebraic system accordingly to Eq.(17); output: $\hat{\mu}(a, r)$
    6. obtain values of algebraic progressions(with parameters $\hat{\rho}(a, r)$ and $\hat{\mu}(a, r)$): $\hat{p}_j, j = \overline{0, n},\;\; n = |P| - 1$

7. compute value of $RMSE$: $\sqrt{\frac{1}{n}\sum_{j=0}^{n}\left(\left(\hat{p}_j\right)_a - p_j\right)^2}$
end if
$a = a + 1$
end while
8. find values of $\hat{\rho}_r, \hat{\mu}_r$, $r = \overline{1, m}$ accordingly to Eq.(18).

Finding the closest algebraic progression of each segment S_l would be an important practical problem which is discussed in details below.

Let us assume that the rank of a sequence of each segment S_l is m_l (we wish to find the closest algebraic progression with the rank equal to m_l of each segment S_l).

We have assumed that Eq.(22) is the closest algebraic progression of segment S_l if the following equality holds true:

$$R_l\left(\hat{P}_l, u_l^0, v_l^0\right) = \min_t \sqrt{\frac{1}{b_t - 1}\sum_{v=0}^{b_t-1}(\hat{p}_v^{(t)} - p_v)^2}. \tag{23}$$

where $R_l(\hat{P}_l, u_l^0, v_l^0)$ - a minimal value of $RMSE$ values;
$\hat{P}_l$=$\hat{p}_{k_l+h_l j}$, $j = \overline{0, v_l^0 - u_l^0 - 1}$; $u_l^0 = k_l$–the start and $v_l^0 = u_l^0 + 2m_l h_l - h_l$- the end position of sequence $\hat{P}_l$ and estimations: $\hat{m}_l = \hat{m}_t$, $\hat{h}_l = \hat{h}_t$, $\hat{k}_l = \hat{k}_t$, where $\hat{m}_t$,$\hat{k}_t$,$\hat{h}_t$ - estimations which were used for the obtainment of the minimized algebraic progression $\hat{p}_j^{(t)}$, $j \in Z_0$. This algorithm is detailed in Algorithm 2.

Algorithm 2. $\left(R_l, \hat{P}_l, u_l^0, v_l^0\right)$ = $MIMIC(P)$ - algorithm of computation sequence $\left(\hat{P}_l = \hat{p}_j, j = \overline{1, v_l^0 - u_l^0}\right)$ of algebraic progression of sequence P.

Input: sequence $P = p_j, j = \overline{1, |P|}$
Output: minimal value (R_l) of $RMSE$; sequence $\hat{P}_l = \hat{p}_j, j = \overline{1, v_l^0 - u_l^0}$, u_l^0 - start position and v_l^0– end position of sequence $\hat{P}_l$
1. assign initial values to parameters: t= 1, $m_0 = 1$, $h_0 = 2$,
$g_{\min} = 1 + 2m_0h_0 - h_0$, $g_t = g_{\min}$, R_l = *Inf*, $\hat{\rho}_r = Inf$, $\hat{\mu}_r = Inf$
while $g_t \leq |P|$
$k_t = 1$
while $k_t \leq g_t - g_{\min} + 1$
2. generate N combinations of parameters m_t, h_t in the interval of $[k_t; g_t]$
$in = 1$
while $in \leq N$
3. construct subsequence of t: $P_t = p_{k_t+h_t j}$, $j = \overline{0, 2m_t}$
4. find $(\hat{\rho}_r, \hat{\mu}_r, r = \overline{1 : m_t}) = AEC(P, P_t, m_t, h_t)$ and calculate $\hat{p}_j^{(t)}$
if $\hat{\rho}_r, \hat{\mu}_r \neq Inf$

5. calculate $RMSE$ values (R_t) accordingly to Eq.(23)
$in = in + 1, \ \ t = t + 1$
else $in = in + 1$
end *if*
end *while*
$k_t = k_t + 1$
end *while*
$g_t = g_t + 1$
end *while*
6. $[R_l, mi] = minR_t, \ m_l = m_t(mi), \ \ h_l = h_t(mi), \ u_l^0 = k_t(im),$
$v_l^0 = u_l^0 + 2m_l h_l - h_l$
7. find $(\hat{\rho}_r, \hat{\mu}_r, r = \overline{1 : m_l}) = AEC\left(P\left(\overline{u_l^0 : 1 : v_l^0}\right), P\left(u_l^0 : h_l : v_l^0\right), m_l, h_l\right)$
and calculate values: $\hat{P}_l = \hat{p}_j, j = \overline{1, v_l^0 - u_l^0}$.

Let $\hat{p}_j, j \in Z_0$ is the algebraic progression of segment S_l and u_l^0 – the start and v_l^0 – the end position of a sequence: $\hat{P}_l = \hat{p}_j, j = \overline{0, v_l^0 - u_l^0 - 1}$. Then it is possible to extrapolate values of the sequence P by using the algebraic progression $\hat{p}_j, j \in Z_0$. Let $\hat{p}l_j$ is values of the extrapolation to the left from position u_l^0 and $\hat{p}r_j$ - to the right from position v_l^0 of sequence $\hat{P}_l$. Then accordingly to conditions:

$$|\hat{p}l_j - pl_j| \leq \varepsilon, \ \ |\hat{p}r_j - pr_j| \leq \varepsilon, \ \ j \in Z_0 \tag{24}$$

(where ε- extrapolation error, pl_j, pr_j - values of sequence P) can be obtained the start $u_l = u_l^0 - sl$ and the end $v_l = v_l^0 + sr$ (sl, sr – counts of values $\hat{p}l_j$,$\hat{p}r_j$ with conditions (24)) positions of segment $S_l = S_l\left(u_l, v_l\right)$. Given algorithm is detailed in Algorithm 3).

The following can be constructed new numerical sequences Q_r: $Q = \bigcup_r Q_r$, $Q \backslash S_l$, $Q \subset P$. Given algorithm runs repeatedly for each new sequence Q_r.

Algorithm 3.(u,v) = AAS (P,ε) - algebraic algorithm of segmentation of numerical sequences

Input: Sequence $P = p_j, j = \overline{1, |P|}$. Parameter: $\varepsilon = \ 1 \cdot 10^{-6}$
Output: Arrays of u - start and v - end position of segments
1. assign initial values to parameters: $Q = P$, $l = 1$
2. compute: $\left(R_l, \hat{Q}_l, u_l^0, v_l^0\right) = MIMIC(Q)$
while $R_l \leq \varepsilon$
3. construct sequences: pl= $Q\left(1 : u_l^0\right)$, pr=$Q\left(v_l^0 : |Q|\right)$ and
$\hat{p}l$= $\hat{Q}_l\left(1 : u_l^0\right)$, $\hat{p}r$=$\hat{Q}_l\left(v_l^0 : |Q|\right)$ and assign $sl = 0$, $sr = 0$
4. ***while*** $abs(\hat{p}l - pl) \leq \varepsilon$ ***and*** $|pl| \geq 1$
$sl = sl \ + 1;$
end *while*

5. ***while*** $abs\,(\hat{pr} - pr) \leq \varepsilon$ ***and*** $|pr| \leq |Q|$
   $sr = sr + 1;$
   end *while*
6. compute $u_l = u_l^0 - sl,\ v_l = v_l^0 + sr,\ \ S_l = (u_l, v_l),\ l = l + 1;$
7. construct a new sequence: Q_r: $Q = \bigcup_r Q_r,\ \ Q \backslash S_l$.
8. compute: $\left(R_l, \hat{Q}_l, u_l^0, v_l^0\right) = MIMIC(Q_r)$

end *while*

4 Computational Experiment

Let's we have a sequence:

$$p_j = (p_1, p_2, ..., p_{93}) = (-0.279, -1.014, -1.615, -1.973, ..., \\ , ..., -0.627, 0.2261, 0.9347),\ \ j = \overline{1, 93} \tag{25}$$

Given sequence p_j is illustrated in Fig. 1.

Let use the proposed algebraic algorithm for segmentation of sequence p_j. First of all there were generated 65177 subsequences of a given sequence p_j using different parameters m, k and h combination. Then with a minimal value of root mean square error $\left(RMSE = 4.70 \cdot 10^{-16}\right)$ and parameters: $\hat{m}_l = 2,\ \hat{k}_l = 35,\ \hat{h}_l = 2$ was obtained an algebraic progression:

$$\hat{p}_j = (-1.37 - 0.60i) \cdot (0.96 + 0.28i)^j + (-1.37 + 0.60i) \cdot (0.96 - 0.28i)^j,\ \ j = \overline{0, 7}.$$

Then accordingly to the condition Eq.(24) (then $\varepsilon = 1 \cdot 10^{-6}$) was found segment: $S_2(u_2, v_2) = S_2(27, 41)$. In such way given sequence p_j was segmented into 4 segments (Fig. 1). Obtained parameters of algebraic progression of each segment are shown in Table 1.

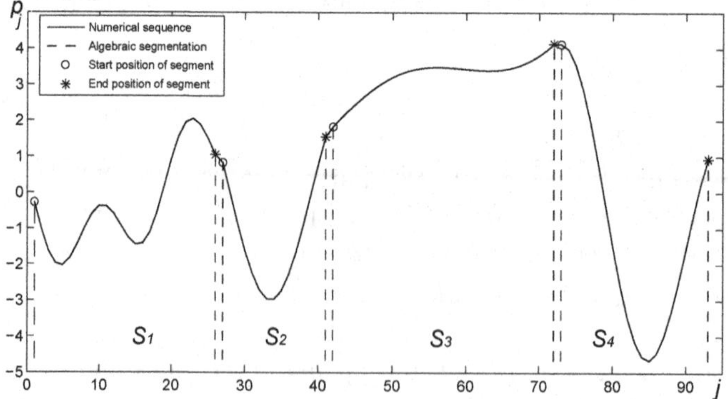

Fig. 1. Segmentation of algebraic progression using proposed algorithm

Table 1. Obtained parameters of algebraic progression of S_l segment

l	R_l	$(\hat{m}_l, \hat{k}_l, \hat{h}_l)$	$\hat{\rho}_r, \hat{\mu}_r,\ r = \overline{1, \hat{m}_l}$	(u_l, v_l)
1	$2.92 \cdot 10^{-15}$	$(4, 2, 2)$	$\hat{\rho}_{1,2} = 0.87 \pm 0.49i,\ \hat{\rho}_{3,4} = 0.98 \pm 0.17i,$ $\hat{\mu}_{1,2} = -0.42 \pm 0.28i,\ \hat{\mu}_{3,4} = -0.39 \pm 0.59i$	$(1, 26)$
2	$4.70 \cdot 10^{-16}$	$(2, 35, 2)$	$\hat{\rho}_{1,2} = 0.96 \pm 0.28i,\ \hat{\mu}_{1,2} = -1.37 \mp 0.60i$	$(27, 41)$
3	$3.68 \cdot 10^{-12}$	$(5, 42, 2)$	$\hat{\rho}_{1,2,3} = 1,\ \hat{\rho}_{4,5} = 0.9913 \pm 0.1488i,$ $\hat{\mu}_1 = 1.3761, \hat{\mu}_2 = 0.0033, \hat{\mu}_3 = 0.0868,$ $\hat{\mu}_{4,5} = 0.2234 \pm 0.4617i$	$(42, 72)$
4	$1.50 \cdot 10^{-12}$	$(4, 59, 2)$	$\hat{\rho}_{1,2} = 0.96 \pm 0.29i,\ \hat{\rho}_{3,4} = 0.99 \pm 0.14i,$ $\hat{\mu}_{1,2} = 1.50 \pm 0.08i,\ \hat{\rho}_{3,4} = 0.49 \pm 0.87i$	$(73, 93)$

Sequence (25) p_j was obtained using following equations:

$$p_j = \begin{cases} \sin\left(\sqrt{3}\,(1.5 + 0.1k)\right) + \cos\left(\sqrt{3}\,(1.5 + 0.1k)\right) + \cos\left(\sqrt{3}\,(4.5 + 0.3k)\right), \\ \qquad k = 0, 1, ..., 25, j = 1 + k; \\ 3\cos\left(\sqrt{2}\,(9.8 + 0.2d)\right), \quad d = 0, 1, ..., 14, j = 27 + d; \\ 0.5(1.7 + 0.05l)^2 + \cos(5.1 + 0.15l), \quad l = 0, 1, ..., 30, j = 42 + l; \\ 2\sin\left(\sqrt{2}\,(12.4 + 0.2g)\right) + 3\cos(18.6 + 0.3g), g = 0, 1, ..., 20, j = 73 + g; \end{cases}$$

It can be seen that sequence (25) was segmented correctly using the proposed algorithm. Also this algorithm can be applied for segmentation of algebraic progressions with a "soft" transition. For example, let apply observed segmentation algorithm (then $\varepsilon = 1 \cdot 10^{-12}$ (Eq.(24))) for sequence p_j:

$$p_j = \begin{cases} \sin(0.1g),\ g = 0, 1, ..., 31,\ j = 1 + g; \\ \sin(3.2 + 0.9999999999k),\ k = 0, 1, ..., 30,\ j = 32 + k; \end{cases}$$

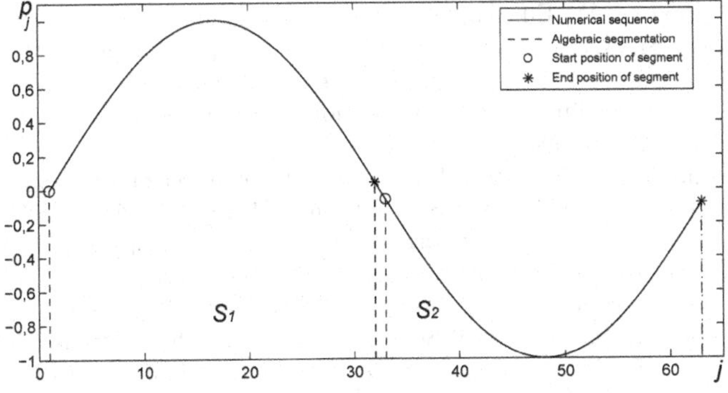

Fig. 2. Segmentation of algebraic progression with a "soft" transition

Segmentation of sequence p_j using the proposed algorithm is illustrated in Fig. 2. It can be noted that segmentation result depends on the approximation error in Eq.(24)).

5 Conclusions

In this paper we proposed a algebraic segmentation algorithm based on the identification of algebraic progression of sequence of each segment. This algorithm was applied for segmentation of artificially generated numerical sequences without noise. It was shown that using the concept of the rank of a sequence the segmented sequence can be efficiently separated into segments. It was noted that algorithm efficiently separating a very similar sequences.

In the future is planned the comparison of algebraic segmentation algorithm with other segmentation algorithms. Also, is planning algorithm improvements for noisy sequences and its application for human sequences, for example, medical cardiology data.

In analysis of medical or biological investigations it is important to separate data sequences into intervals where different physiologic situations could be observed. In living organisms such change of physiologic conditions could be very quick and application of statistical technologies or Furje analysis is not possible in such cases. Proposed matrix analysis could be only technology which can help in analysis of short intervals of data to reveal intervals with stable physiological conditions.

Acknowledgements. The study was supported by Agency for International Science and Technology Development Programs in Lithuania, project VP1-3.1-MM-06-V-01-003 ITEA2 08018 GUARANTEE.

References

1. Bellman, R.: On the approximation of curves by line segments using dynamic programming. Commun. ACM 4(6), 284 (1961)
2. Terzi, E., Tsaparas, P.: Efficient algorithms for sequence segmentation. In: Proceedings of the SIAM International Conference on Data Mining, SDM (2006)
3. Shatkay, H., Zdonik, S.B.: Approximate queries and representations for large data sequences. In: Proceedings of the International Conference on Data Engineering (ICDE), pp. 536–545 (1996)
4. Koski, A., Juhola, M., Meriste, M.: Syntactic recognition of ECG signals by attributed finite automata. Pattern Recognition 28(12), 1927–1940 (1995)
5. Mannila, H., Salmenkivi, M.: Finding simple intensity descriptions from event sequence data. In: Proceedings of the ACM SIGKDD International Conference on Knowledge Discovery and Data Mining (KDD), pp. 341–346 (2001)
6. Dd Ge, X., Smyth, P.: Segmental Semi-Markov models for endpoint detection in plasma etching. IEEE Transactions on Semiconductor Engineering (2001)
7. Eamonn, J.K., Selina, C., David, H., Michael, J.P.: An online algorithm for segmenting time series. In: Proceedings of the IEEE International Conference on Data Mining (ICDM), pp. 289–296 (2001)

8. Fuchs, E., Gruber, T., Nitschke, J., Sick, B.: Online segmentation of time series based on polynomial least-squares approximations. IEEE Trans. Pattern Anal. Mach. Intell. 32(12), 2232–2245 (2010)
9. Fu, A.C., Chung, F.L., Ng, V., Luk, R.: Evolutionary segmentation of financial time series into subsequences. In: Evolutionary Computation, pp. 426–430 (2001)
10. Cohen, P.R., Heeringa, B., Adams, N.M.: Unsupervised segmentation of categorical time series into episodes. In: ICDM, pp. 99–106 (2002)
11. Lemire, D.: A better alternative to piecewise linear time series segmentation. In: SIAM Data Mining, pp. 545–550 (2007)
12. Palpanas, T., Vlachos, M., Keogh, E.J., Gunopulos, D.: Streaming time series summarization using user-defined amnesic functions. TKDE 20(7), 992–1006 (2008)
13. Navickas, Z., Bikulciene, L.: Expressions of solutions of ordinary differential equations by standard functions. Mathematical Modeling and Analysis 11, 399–412 (2006)
14. Navickas, Z., Ragulskis, M.: How far one can go with the Exp-function method? Applied Mathematics and Computation 211, 522–530 (2009)
15. Navickas, Z., Bikulciene, L., Ragulskis, M.: Generalization of Exp-function and other standard function methods. Applied Mathematic sand Computation 216, 2380–2393 (2010)
16. Navickas, Z., Ragulskis, M., Bikulciene, L.: Be careful with the Exp-function method -additional remarks. Communications in Nonlinear Science and Numerical Simulations 15, 3874–3886 (2010)
17. Ragulskis, M., Lukoseviciute, K., Navickas, Z., Palivonaite, R.: Short-term time series forecasting based on the identification of skeleton algebraic sequences. Neurocomputing 64, 1735–1747 (2011)
18. Sliupaite, A., Navickas, Z., Vainoras, A.: Evaluation of Complexity of ECG Parameters Using Sample Entropy and Hankel Matrix. Electronics and Electrical Engineering, Kaunas: Technologija 4(92), 107–110 (2009)
19. Moskvina, V.G., Zhigljavsky, A.A.: An algorithm based on singular spectrum analysis for change-point detection. Communication in Statistics - Simulation and Computation 32(2), 319–352 (2003)

An Approach: A Service-Oriented Functional Business and IT Alignment

Aurelijus Morkevicius[1] and Saulius Gudas[1,2]

[1] Kaunas University of Technology, Faculty of Informatics, Information Systems Department, Studentu 50-313a, LT-51368 Kaunas, Lithuania
aurelijus.morkevicius@stud.ktu.lt
[2] Vilnius University, Kaunas Faculty of Humanities, Muitines 8, LT-44280 Kaunas, Lithuania
gudas@vukhf.lt

Abstract. There are multiple frameworks proposed conceptually defining the business and IT alignment. There are also multiple empirical methods for modeling the business and IT alignment. However, the transition between conceptual definitions and modeling languages still lacks a clear approach and tools for verifying if business and IT are aligned in a particular enterprise model. The paper presents an approach for functional business and IT alignment focusing on its implementation with nowadays enterprise modeling techniques and tools. The suggested approach is based on the SOA, GRAAL, and enterprise modeling techniques such as TOGAF, DoDAF, and UPDM. A real world example is presented to validate the suitability of the approach.

Keywords: Enterprise Architecture, Enterprise Modeling, Business and IT alignment, SOA, Service provisioning.

1 Introduction

The gap between business and IT generally results in expensive IT systems that do not provide expected return on investment (ROI). Many different approaches to the alignment of the business and IT have been spawned in distinct research areas. These are: alignment via architecture, alignment via governance, and alignment via communications [2]. Alignment via architecture utilizes architecture analysis and design techniques to assure proper alignment and is in interest of our research. The scope of this technique could be as broad as the enterprise [2]. The most common technique for the business and IT alignment via architecture is the enterprise architecture (EA).

An Enterprise Architecture is recognized as a blueprint for how an organization achieves the current and future business objectives using IT [5]. Enterprise Architecture despite being a hot topic since 1980-ies was not very widely applied in practices due to the lack of modeling languages and tools [27]. The EA movement has been reinforced with the successful adoption of the Unified Modeling Language (UML) [17] and the Model-Driven Architecture (MDA) [16]. The versatility of UML

T. Skersys, R. Butleris, and R. Butkiene (Eds.): ICIST 2012, CCIS 319, pp. 162–175, 2012.

and its compatibility with its extensions allows integrating enterprise models with the other Object Management Group (OMG) standards based on UML, such as System Modeling Language (SysML), Service Oriented Architecture Modeling Language (SoaML) Object Constraint Language (OCL) etc [13]. The integrity enables creating large and versatile EA models to preserve enterprise knowledge [20] in order to solve a range of problems: business transformation into knowledge-based business, business and IT alignment, and the computerization of business management tasks [6]. Moreover UML allows extending existing and creating new domain specific languages by creating profiles, thus allowing easily bringing in missing concepts to already defined languages [19]. An example of such language is UPDM the Unified profile for MODAF and DoDAF (UPDM) [18]. As UPDM is a profile of UML, it has been easily adopted by the majority of UML tool vendors [14]. UML has also been adopted for the other EA modeling techniques such as TOGAF [21] which evolved significantly over last years.

As business dimensions become part of part of a SOA, the SOA is regarded as "framework for integrating business processes and supporting IT infrastructure as secure, standardized components and services that can be reused and combined to address changing business priorities" [1]. Based on this proposition we are considering SOA as a one of the tools enabling alignment between the business and IT. SOA is becoming a must part of enterprise modeling techniques. TOGAF, DoDAF, MODAF etc provide service oriented architecture viewpoints and integrates SOA concepts all over the business and IT architectures, thus making a binding mechanism between them. SOA also attracts more and more researches in the field of business and IT alignment [23].

According to [11], achieving alignment between business and application architectures is one of the most important drivers for the architecture. For these reasons, enterprise architecture programs are established in enterprises wherein the enterprise architects seek to align enterprise processes and infrastructure with their supporting IT systems [25]. Our interest in this paper is focused to a subset of business and IT alignment problem; the problem of optimally fitting business and information system architectures together. The purpose of our research is to propose a new approach for functional business and IS alignment based on the existing frameworks, theories, UML, and the research of the latest enterprise modeling techniques. The word functional emphasizes the aspect of data input that is focused on structural and dynamic properties of the enterprise in contrast to the performance, cost and other quantitative data [11].

The rest of this paper is structured as follows: in section 2, the related works are analyzed; in section 3, the proposed approach is presented; in section 4, experimental evaluation of the proposed approach on a small real world EA model is described; in section 5, the achieved results, conclusions, and future work directions are indicated.

2 Related Work

One of the most well known projects related to the business and IT alignment is called Guidelines Regarding Architecture Alignment (GRAAL). Its goal is to derive operational guidelines for aligning the IT architecture with business architecture [22].

The GRAAL alignment framework is a conceptual framework providing a collection of concepts and relations among them. It is based on four simple dimensions: system aspects, system aggregation, systems process, and description levels.The first three dimensions analyze system by its observable properties, internal structure, and life cycle and the fourth one concerns a level of granularity.

GRAAL originated from another well know alignment framework of Henderson and Venkatraman [8] which distinguished two alignment dimensions, the service provision and a refinement. Other related frameworks are Zachman Framework [27] and the Kruchten's 4+1 model [9].

In [15] authors identify four essential business and IT alignment components: work, people, the formal organization and the informal organization. Labowitz and Rosansky [10] emphasize the vertical and horizontal business and IT alignment dimensions of an enterprise. The vertical dimension describes the relation between the top strategy and human resources and the horizontal dimension describes the relation between internal processes and external business entities.

Another business and IT alignment framework developed by Wegmann [24] is called Systemic Enterprise Architecture Methodology (SEAM). SEAM is grounded in General System Thinking (GST) [26], and living system theory [12]. The two main SEAM concepts used to express the behavior and construction are: functional level, and organizational level. The functional level represents the behavioral hierarchy and the organizational level represents the constructional hierarchy explaining how to interpret the enterprise reality.

Application of SEAM is presented in [25]. Authors describe the need for having functional and organizational levels in EA frameworks to reason about business and IT alignment. UML models are used to model the example; however the main question of how to identify if model is aligned is not answered.

GRAAL, SEAM, Henderson and Venkatraman, and Zachman are conceptual frameworks mostly defining concepts and high level guidance, however none of them provides a metamodel, methodology, or is linked to use with empirical enterprise modeling languages, frameworks, and methods differently than our indents are.

A research of business and IT alignment has been performed by [28]. Authors analyze GRAAL, Zachman Framework, The Four-Domain Architecture, TOGAF, and RM-ODP. As a result integrated enterprise architecture framework is proposed. It is based on extension of the GRAAL framework. The research however is focusing onto aspects of the analyzed frameworks, but not the business and IT alignment in the concrete enterprise model.

The BITAM [4] is a recent business and IT alignment method based on the SOA that uses a twelve-step process for managing, detecting and correcting the misalignment at the architecture level. The method is an integration of two distinct analysis areas - business analysis and architecture analysis - for aligning elements in three layers of a business system: business strategy, business architecture, and IT architecture [4]. It includes cost-benefit analysis, architectural decision templates, and other success measures, and is targeting both the functional and non-functional architecture analysis aspects. The method is, however, based on the software architecture, but not the enterprise architecture. Besides the fact of the different target it consists of a broad scope of ideas for the enterprise architecture based business and IT alignment method.

Empirical enterprise modeling methods such as DoDAF, MODAF, NAF, TOGAF, and modeling languages such as UML, BPMN, Archimate, EMM [7], and UPDM provide traceability links between business and application models; however they do not provide methodology and tools of how to verify if business and IT is aligned. Study of empirical and mostly used methods gave as a solid background for our research. Our proposed approach is based on the integrated metamodel developed on a basis of these methods. However, our goal is not a new modeling language. Our goal is to propose an approach suitable to use in combination with the majority of existing empirical enterprise modeling techniques.

3 Functional Business and IT Alignment

In this section we describe our proposed approach and techniques related to it.

3.1 Conceptual Metamodel

GRAAL defines two system aspects: a service and quality. A service aspect originates from the behavioral nature, thus we are calling it functional. A quality aspect from its origin is structural, thus we are calling it non-functional. In the scope of this paper we are only focusing on the functional aspect of the business and IT alignment. GRAAL further classifies service aspect into behavior, communication, and data. To be consistent with existing and most popular enterprise architecture frameworks such as TOGAF we have used a little bit different classification. We classify service aspect to the business and information system, and corresponding concepts of a business service and information system service (Fig. 1).

We have defined business service as a service provided by a participant, requested by another participant, and supported by zero or more application services. Participant is a logical business unit that may be either an organization or post. An application service is a service supporting one or more business services. The support relationship is derived from the implementation relationships used to link behavioral constructs of the business and solution architectures. Application service that does not support business service we treat as redundant. Application Service is provided by an application component and requested by a resource configuration comprised of at least one human resource and at least one application component. Human resource is an actor interacting with one or more application components through the user interface.

Application components on the client side and the server side interact according to rules defined by service interfaces. Service interfaces have the operations with the parameters and their types defined. Operations and interfaces can be also defined for the business services; however it is not required in the scope of our method.

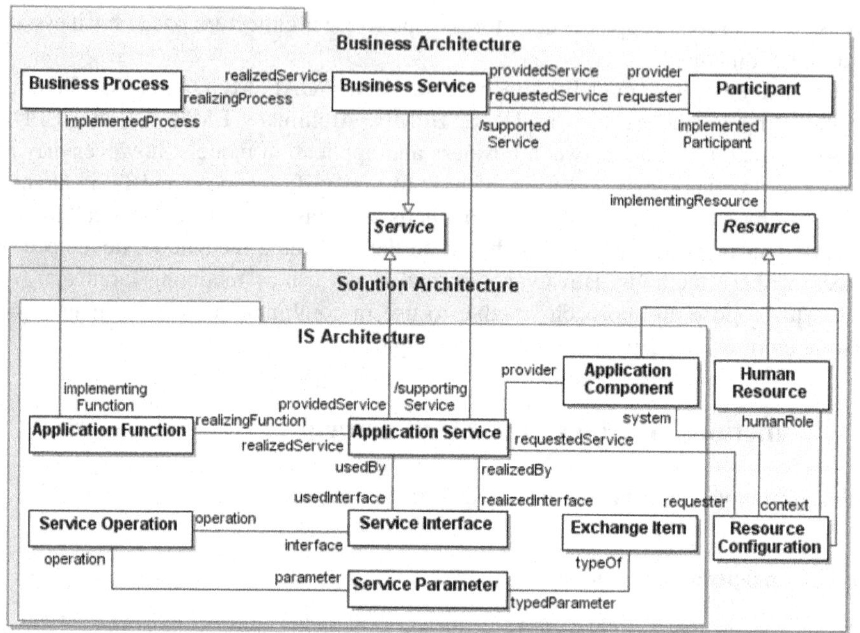

Fig. 1. Conceptual metamodel

Based on the observations made we have built an integrated conceptual model for the business and IT alignment. Further in this paper we are defining vertical and horizontal aspects of the functional business and IT alignment.

3.2 Functional Vertical Alignment of Business and IT

A functional alignment in the enterprise life-cycle is two dimensional: vertical and horizontal.Vertical alignment of the business and IT is of the higher level of abstraction. We have defined a vertical functional business and IT alignment as an alignment of business and application services. Application service must serve business service, by supporting business processes performed; due to a business service would be delivered to a service consumer (Fig. 2).

In the vertical aspect of the business ant IT alignment we come up with the following rules:

1. Application service supports one or more business service.
2. Application function implements one or more business processes.

If rules are satisfied vertical functional alignment is achieved in the scope of a business service. For the rule no. 1 to be satisfied, first, supporting application services needs to be derived for each of the business services. The following

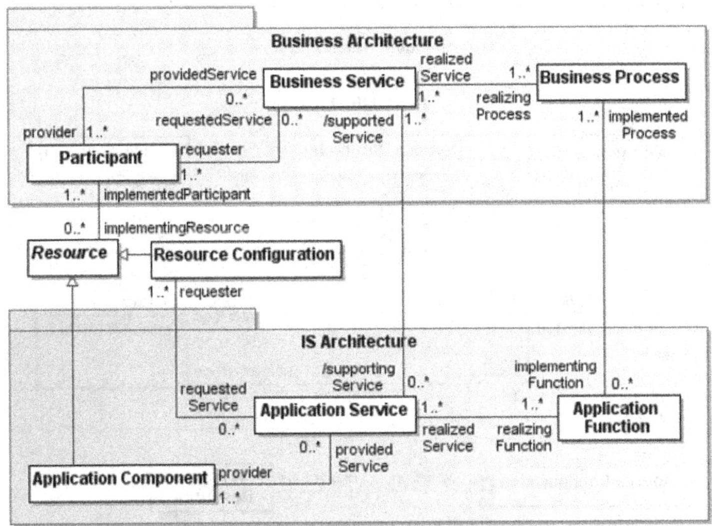

Fig. 2. Vertical functional business and IT alignment aspect

derivation rule applies for supported service derived property of an application service: Application function realizing the application service implements at least one business process that realizes at least one business service. The OCL expression is as follows:

```
Context ApplicationService
inv: self.supportedService-
>collect(self.realizingFunction->forAll(i|
i.oclAsType(ApplicationFunction).implementedProcess-
>forAll(s|
s.oclAsType(BusinessProcess).realizedService)))
```

Only if vertical functional alignment is achieved in the scope of the business service, we can check if horizontal functional alignment is achieved in the same scope.

3.3 Functional Horizontal Alignment of Business and IT

A vertical functional business and IT alignment applies to the interaction between two different layers of the architecture. Vice versa a horizontal functional alignment applies to the interaction of resource configuration comprised of human resource and application component, and an application component (Fig. 3).

Horizontal alignment of business and IT is a detailed interaction between a user and a system. User request has to be satisfied by one or more applications or application component services. At this level details such as service interfaces used, service operations called, and data passed and retrieved are important.

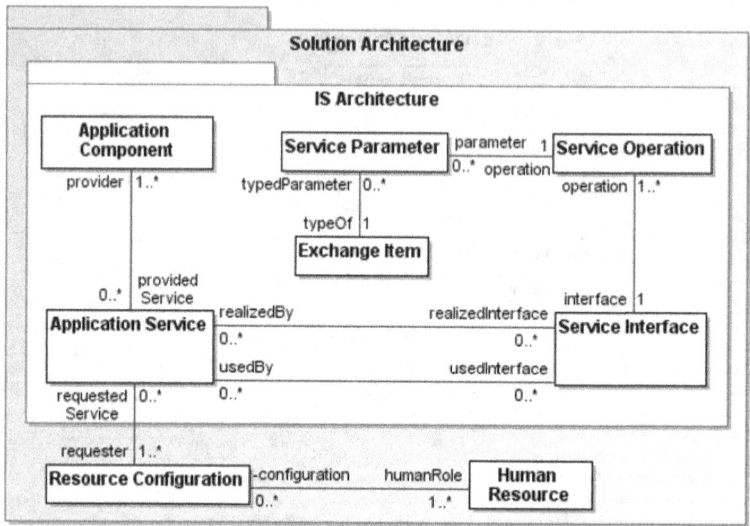

Fig. 3. Horizontal functional Business and IT alignment aspect

For horizontal functional alignment to be achieved a set of rules needs to be satisfied:

- All application service requests from resource configurations must be satisfied.
- Service channel must connect service port with a request port.
- Resource configuration contents should include at least one application component if it's requesting application service. In this case request must be delegated by the included application component.
- Resource configuration contents should include at least one application component if it's providing application service. In this case service provision must be delegated by the included application component.
- Application function realizing an application service must be performed by an application component providing that service.

Table 1. Derived traces for the elements of the horizontal Business and IT alignment

Element	Derived Traces
Human Resource	Application service required by an application component that is directly used by the human resource
Application Component	Provided and requested services
Application Service	Provider and requester
Application Service	Realizing functions

3.4 A Process of Verifying Functional Business and IT Alignment

The framework is incomplete without the methodology and tools. As we encourage using UML based standards for enterprise modeling we have developed:

- A profile for the proposed approach.
- Object Constrain Language (OCL) queries for derived properties.
- A set of constraints in OCL for the verification of the alignment of the business and IT.

For instance checking of whether the application service is supporting at least one business service is performed by executing the following OCL expression:

```
Context ApplicationService
Inv: self.supportingService->isEmpty()
```

Another example OCL expression checks if request of application service is satisfied by the application:

```
Context ApplicationService
Inv: not self.requester->isEmpty()
implies self.provider->isEmpty()
```

A set of executable OCL expressions have been developed. Note that the example expressions are based on the model shown in Fig. 1 and on the derived properties that are also based on OCL queries.

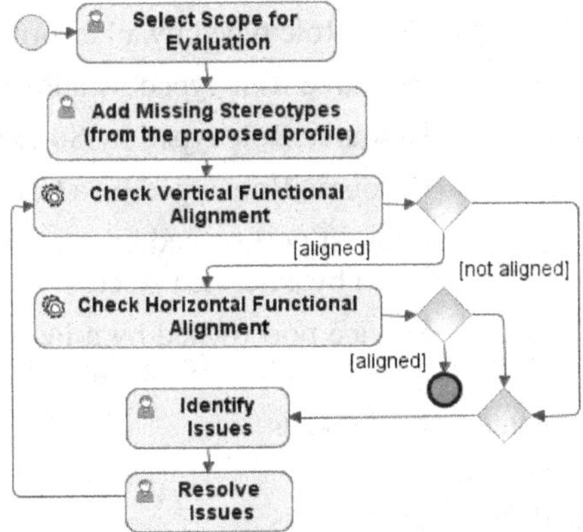

Fig. 4. Business and IS alignment process

As we have already defined the tool, we need to define a process. Functional alignment in architecture based alignment approaches is triggered by the change in the business or application architecture [3]. For instance an IS reengineering or business process reengineering activities. It implies that functional alignment needs to be achieved before the deployment of the changes. Process of the functional alignment of the business and IT starts from defining a model scope we want to check in order to reduce the complexity if checking the whole model at once. We also have to make sure that proposed concepts are well established before proceeding. When these two prerequisites are completed we start with the evaluation of vertical functional alignment in the model. Whole process is provided in the Fig. 4.

As soon as we found issues making the model unaligned, we identify the source for each of the issue and resolve them. We restart the loop to check if all issues have been resolved and if no new issues have appeared. If there are no issues found, the model is treated as completely functionally aligned.

4 Experimental Evaluation

For experimental evaluation we are using the MagicDraw UPDM tool. Our model is based on the UPDM modeling standard [18] with extensions required by the proposed approach of ours and not supported by the UPDM standard by default. We have developed a profile and defined a mapping between the UPDM language and a subset of concepts we are going to use in the case study (Table 2).

Table 2. Mapping of elements of our developed profile and UPDM

Alignment Element	UPDM element
Business Service	Service Access provided in the operational viewpoint
Application Service	Service Access provided in the systems viewpoint
Participant	Node Role typed by a Performer
Human Resource	Resource Role typed by a Post or Organization
Application Component	Resource Role typed by Software.
Resource Configuration	Resource Role typed by a Capability Configuration.
Consumes	Request port owned by a Performer or Software and typed by a Service Access
Provides	Service port owned by a Performer or Software and typed by a Service Access
Business Process implemented by Application Function	Implements
Participant implemented by Resource	Implements

4.1 Case Study

Let us define a simple scenario of the business and IT alignment. We have an e-shop selling goods to private customers. It consists of sales, customer support, and supply chain management departments. It also interacts with external participants such as distribution businesses and banks. We have built the OV-2 model to show the retail logical architecture of the e-shop business (Fig. 5).

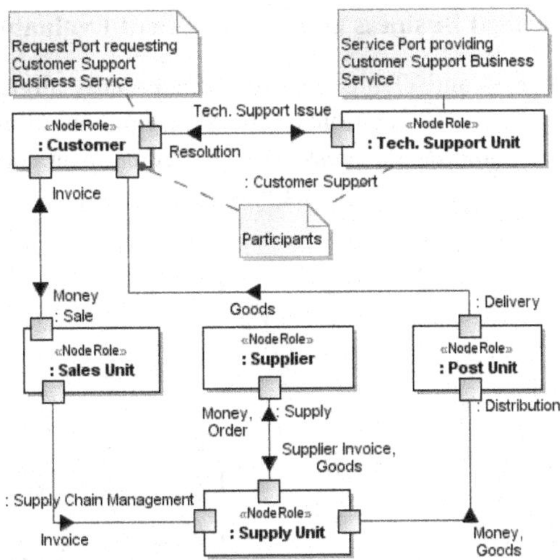

Fig. 5. Architecture of retail business unit

Participants in the example model are providing and requesting services. In other words they are communicating through service channels. For instance in Fig. 5 Customer and Tech. Support Unit are participants where the square on the border of Customer is a request port and the square on the border of Tech. Support Unit is a service port providing business service called Customer Support. Participants are also exchanging information where Issue goes to Tech. Support Unit and Resolution goes to Customer. Data moves along the service channels both ways and usually is a must in order to meet the contract.

This modeling approach of the services is defined by SoaML and a subset of its concepts is used in UPDM modeling language [18]. Here, at the operational level, we define services as business services.

Stimulus for Business and IT alignment analysis has been driven by the adoption of a new customer support information system. Following the process provided in Fig. 4 we have:

1. Selected the *Retail* Business service as a scope for Business and IT alignment verification.
2. Extended model with stereotypes from our developed profile.
3. Built a matrix showing the supported services derived property between business and application services (Fig. 6).
4. Built SV-1 model to show how human resources are interacting with the customer support system (Fig. 7). In systems level we've used application services; we have also defined provided and required interfaces. Interface provision is shown as a lollipop on a service port and a service request is shown as a socket on a request port.

4.2 Functional Vertical Business and IT Alignment Evaluation

To make sure the business and IT are vertically functionally aligned we've validated the model by executing a set of functional vertical alignment validity rules. We come up with the *Customer Support* business service being unsupported by any of the application services.

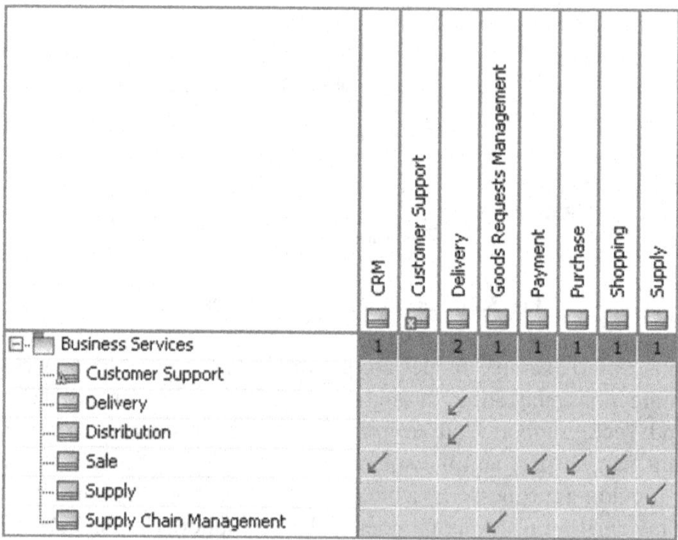

Fig. 6. Business and application services alignment matrix

Based on our proposed approach, business services must be supported supported by one or more application services. We have also built a matrix of services (Fig. 6) vizualizing the mapping between services. We have shown business services as rows and application services as columns. The relationship displayed in the cells is derived property named supported service.

As a result, we have identified that the Customer Support application service is not supporting any of the business services in the architecture. By analyzing a model we have found out that there is a gap between the Customer Support business process and the business service that needs to be investigfated and resolved.

4.3 Functional Horizontal Business and IT alignment evaluation

We have also checked the model by horizontal functional alignment validity rules. As we can see, in the Fig. 7, *Customer* human resource is requesting service from a *Technical Support System*. Based on our proposed approach such service interaction is not possible in the systems layer. The OCL rule is as follows:

```
Context Resource Configuration
inv self.ownedAttribute->exists(e|
e.type.oclIsKindOf(HumanResource) and
self.ownedAttribute->exists(e|
e.type.oclIsKindOf(ApplicationComponent))
```

Human resource is a not a system and using it as a requester for the application service would make the model semanticly incorrect which means non-executable.

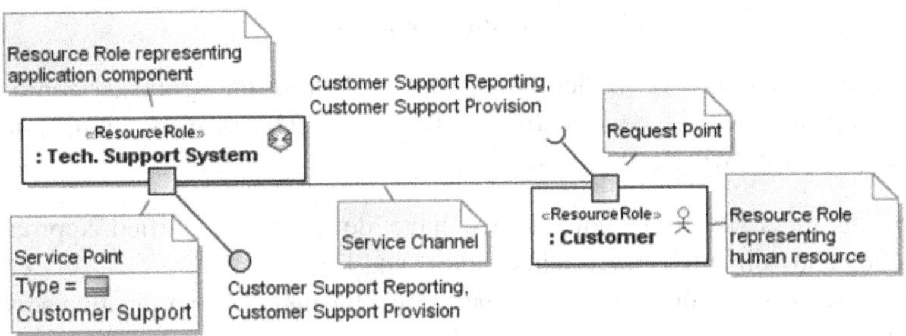

Fig. 7. Systems Interface Description model before alignment

To fix the issue, we have added resource configuration referencing Customer and Tech. Support Web Client application component. The application component is now a requester for a service (Fig. 8), thus allowing to model detailed operation calls from the Customer Support System web service.

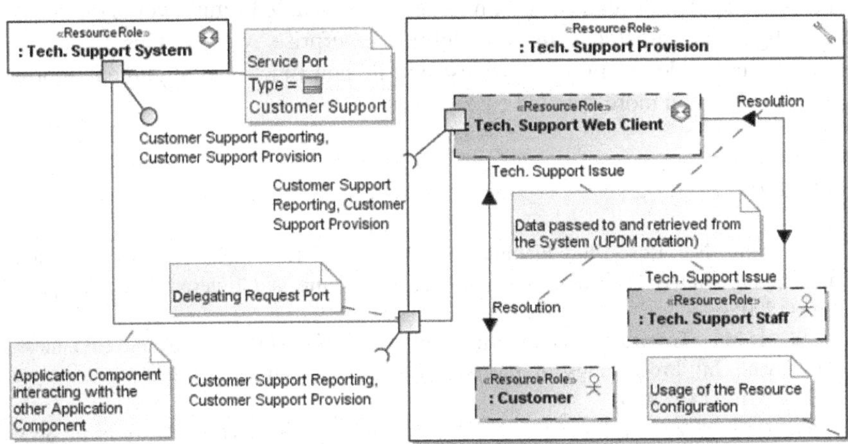

Fig. 8. Systems Interface Description model after alignment

Our proposed approach helped to identify functional missalignments in the enterprise model, at the early phases of the software reengineering process. We have resulted in the aligned model which led to the alignment of the business and IT in a real world enterprise. Further in the lyfecycle of the enteprise non-functional aligment may contribute in verifying if service level agreements are met and Business and IT is completely aligned.

5 Conclusions and Future Works

There have been multiple conceptual business and IT alignment frameworks proposed; however none of them satisfies all of the following:

- Provides methodology.
- Provides approach for verification if business and IT is functionally aligned in the actual enterprise model or its fragment.
- Is based on existing enterprise modeling standards.

Based on the experience in implementing and evaluating the proposed approach on the pilot e-shop model in combination with UPDM enterprise modeling language, we've made the following conclusions:

- Based on the existing techniques we have developed a unified approach for modeling and validating functional business and IT alignment.
- We have identified a derived relation between a business and application services.
- We have identified two different levels of alignment in the enterprise model: vertical and horizontal.
- If both levels of alignment are satisfied for all the business and IT alignment units in the enterprise the business and IT is functionaly aligned.
- Functional alignment of business and IT allows identifying misalignments in the early phase of the software enginerring or reengineering process.

The proposed approach shall be used for even more detailed future works on business and IT alignment researches in well defined enterprise models. Our future tasks consist of detailed description of business and IT non-functional alignment approach followed by the even more detailed case studies.

References

1. Bieberstein, N., Bose, S., Fiammante, M., Jones, K., Shah, R.: Service-Oriented architecture (SOA) Compass: Business Value Planning and Enterprise Roadmap. IBM Press (2005)
2. Chen, H.M.: Towards Service Engineering: Service Orientation and Business-IT Alignment. In: Proceedings of the 41st Hawaii International Conference on System Sciences, p. 114 (2008)
3. Chen, H.M., Kazman, R., Perry, O.: From Software Architecture Analysis to Service Engineering: An Empirical Study of Methodology Development for Enterprise SOA Implementation. IEEE Transactions on Services Computing 3(2), 145–160 (2010)
4. Chen, H.M., Kazman, R., Garg, A.: Managing Misalignments Between Business and IT Architectures: A BITAM Approach. Journal of Science of Computer Programming 57(1), 5–26 (2005)
5. Dahalin, M.Z., Razak, A.R., Ibrahim, H., Yusop, I.N., Kasiran, K.M.: An Enterprise Architecture Methodology for Business-IT Alignment: Adopter and Developer Perspectives. Communications of the IBIMA 2011 (2011)

6. Gudas, S.: Enterprise knowledge modelling domains and aspects. Technological and Economical Development of Economy 15(2), 281–293 (2009)
7. Gudas, S., Lopata, A., Skersys, T.: Approach to Enterprise Modelling for Information Systems Engineering. Informatica 16(2), 175–192 (2005)
8. Henderson, J.C., Venkatraman, N.: Strategic alignment: Leveraging information technology for transforming organizations. IBM Systems Journal 38(2-3), 472–484 (1999)
9. Kruchten, P.: The 4+1 View Model of architecture. Software 12(6), 42–50 (1995)
10. Labowitz, G., Rosansky, V.: The Power of Alignment. Wiley, New York (1997)
11. Lankhorst, M.: Enterprise Architecture at Work. Springer, Berlin (2009)
12. Miller, J.G.: Living Systems. University of Colorado Press (1995)
13. Morkevicius, A., Gudas, S.: Enterprise Knowledge Based Software Requirements Elicitation. Information Technology and Control 40(3), 181–190 (2011)
14. Morkevicius, A., Gudas, S., Silingas, D.: Model-Driven Quantitative Performance Analysis of UPDM-Based Enterprise Architecture. In: Proceedings of the 16th International Conference on Information and Software Technologies, Kaunas, pp. 218–223 (2010)
15. Nadler, D., Gerstein, M., Shaw, R.: Organizational Architecture: Designs for Changing Organizations. Jossey-Bass, San Francisco (1992)
16. OMG: MDA Guide Version 1.0.1. Needham, MA, USA (2003)
17. OMG: Unified Modeling Language (UML) Infrastructure, v2.1.2. Needham, MA, USA (2007)
18. OMG: Unified Profile for the Department of Defense Architecture Framework (DoDAF) and the Ministry of Defence Architecture Framework (MODAF). Needham, MA, USA (2009)
19. Silingas, D., Butleris, R.: Towards customizing UML tools for enterprise architecture modeling. In: Information Systems 2009: Proceedings of the IADIS International Conference, Barcelona, Spain, pp. 25–27 (2009)
20. Silingas, D., Butleris, R.: Towards Implementing a Framework for Modeling Software Requirements in MagicDraw UML. Information Technology and Control 38(2), 153–164 (2009)
21. The Open Group: TOGAF Version 9. Van Haren Publishing, Zaltbommel (2009)
22. Van Eck, P., Blanken, H., Wieringa, R.: Project GRAAL: Towards Operational Architecture Alignment. International Journal of Cooperative Information Systems 13(3), 235–255 (2004)
23. Wang, J., Song, Y., Xiong, Y.: Service Evaluation in SOA: Toward Business/IT Alignment. In: Software Engineering, Artificial Intelligences, Networking and Parallel/Distributed Computing, SNPD 2009, Daegu, pp. 310–315 (2009)
24. Wegmann, A.: On the Systemic Enterprise Architecture Methodology (SEAM). In: Proceedings of the 5th International Conference on Enterprise Information Systems, pp. 483–490 (2003)
25. Wegmann, A., Balabko, P., Le, L., Regev, G., Rychkova, I.: A Method and Tool for Business-IT Alignment in Enterprise Architecture. In: CAiSE 2005 Forum, Porto, Portugal (2005)
26. Weinberg, G.M.: An Introduction to General Systems Thinking. Wiley & Sons, New York (1975)
27. Zachman, J.A.: A Framework for Information Systems Architecture. IBM Systems Journal 26(3), 276–292 (1987)
28. Zarvic, N., Wieringa, R.: An Integrated Enterprise Architecture Framework for Business-IT Alignment. In: Proceedings of Workshops and Doctoral Consortium of the 18th International Conference on Advanced Information Systems Engineering (CAiSE 2006), Luxembourg, pp. 262–270 (2006)

Adaptation of the Presentation in a Multi-tenant Web Information System

Aivars Niedritis and Laila Niedrite

University of Latvia, Faculty of Computing, Raina boulv.19, Riga, Latvia
{Aivars.Niedritis,Laila.Niedrite}@lu.lv

Abstract. We introduced a Web Information System (WIS) adaptation architecture that is based on Software as a Service (SaaS) ideas. It includes adaptation components, which allow adaptation in two levels: the organizations and the users get their own adapted instance of the WIS. The user interface in case of multi-tenancy should be dynamically adapted according to the particular organization and user. The same application component that contains a set of fields, controls and other interface elements should be varied according to the usage context. In this paper we provide a method for adapting the user interface within the proposed adaptation architecture that uses a set of rules describing the sequence of allowed actions generated as a response to the performed user's activities.

Keywords: Multi-Tenancy, Software as a Service, Adaptation, Presentation.

1 Introduction

Web application is a hybrid between a hypermedia and an information system [1]. Customization and dynamic adaptation of content structure, navigation primitives, and presentation styles should be provided as features of a Web application [1].

A Web-based Information System (WIS) is adaptive if the delivery of content and services is dynamically modified according to the context of the client [2]. Personalization requires an adaptation of applications according to preferences of the user and the context of the user [3].

The context is a set of properties that describe the environment where the user interacts with a WIS [3], e.g. time, place, device, user, and environment. An autonomous aspect of the WIS usage context is represented by a profile [2]. Another term used in the adaptation sphere is the definition of configuration as a specification of how the information has to be delivered to the user [2].

There are many approaches [2], [3], [4], [5] for the WIS adaptation based on different understandings of the context, profile, and configuration.

WIS development projects should also take into account the issues of flexibility and cost efficiency in order to deliver the most appropriate system to the user. So, Software product line approach (SPL) [6], Software as a service (SaaS) approach [7] or others could be used.

T. Skersys, R. Butleris, and R. Butkiene (Eds.): ICIST 2012, CCIS 319, pp. 176–186, 2012.

SaaS is "software deployed as a hosted service and accessed over the Internet" [7]. In this case services can be provided to different organizations to support common business processes. Organizations subscribe to use the software and pay for the usage. The provided application is hosted on vendor's servers. One of the possible implementations of SaaS applications is multi-tenant single instance solution [7]. The tenants are different organizations that use the same application instance; however, the data is distinguished between tenants. Architectures for the SaaS applications should solve the problems of how to deliver an adapted application to multiple users using the same application instance and how to support data processing and delivery to an organization and to a particular user. The customization of SaaS application can be performed using the metadata-based configuration.

In our previous research [8] we introduced a WIS adaptation architecture that is based on SaaS ideas. It includes additional adaptation components which allow adaptation in two levels: organizations and users get their own adapted instance of the WIS. We provided also a method for the adaptation of the content [9] where problems concerning data storage, integration, and delivery to the user are solved within the proposed adaptation architecture.

Besides the dynamically provided appropriate data, the user interface in case of multi-tenancy should also be dynamically adapted according to the particular organization and user. The same application component that contains a set of fields, controls, and other interface elements should be varied according to the usage context. In this paper we provide a method for adapting the user interface within the proposed adaptation architecture that uses a set of rules describing the sequence of allowed actions generated as a response to the performed user's activities. The adapted user interface contains elements needed to perform this action sequence.

The rest of the paper is organized as follows. Section 2 presents the adaptation architecture of a Web Information System and describes two levels of adaptation. In Section 3 the profiles that are used to ensure the adaptation are defined. Section 4 describes the presentation metamodel. Section 5 describes how the adapted user interface is constructed based on a presentation metamodel and profiles. In Section 6 the related work is analyzed. Section 7 ends the paper with conclusions.

2 WIS Adaptation Architecture

We will provide a method for user interface adaptation as a part of the adaptation architecture of the Web Information System (WIS) that we presented in our previous work [8]. This architecture could be used for organizations in the same business domain and with the same target user group. This architecture uses the ideas of SaaS, e.g. multi-tenancy.

The adaptation architecture of the WIS consists of following components:

1. Context monitor that determines context properties,
2. An adaptation component that determines the initial configuration of WIS and performs the adaptation of WIS in two levels. Organization level instances of WIS are created during *coarse level* adaptation. The detailed adaptation performs

navigation adaptation and detailed adaptation of content that integrates user's data from all WIS instances available to the particular user.

3. WIS data layer contains profiles that are used in both adaptation levels and business data. Data is physically stored in one database instance, but it consists from virtual data stores owned by particular organizations.

Let's consider an example when the customer is a user of the same WIS used by two different organizations. The adaptation architecture components in this case are shown on the Figure 1.

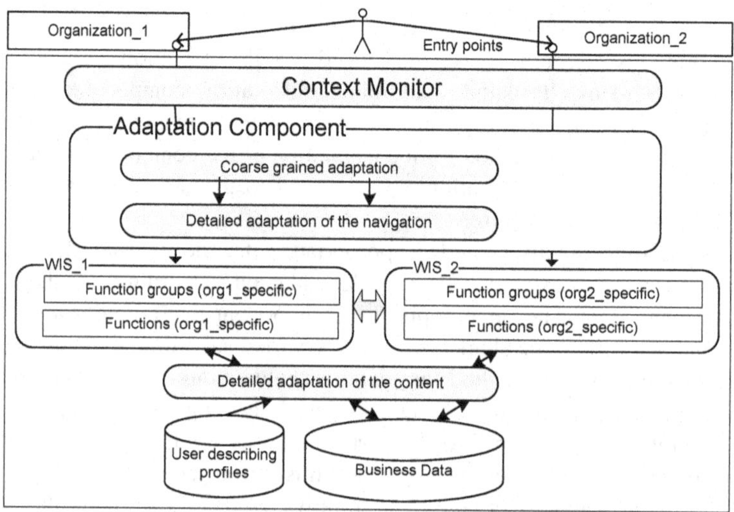

Fig. 1. Adaptation architecture of WIS [7]

The organization level instances of WIS in our example are depicted in Figure 1 as WIS_1 and WIS_2. This is a simplified schema of the architecture. The whole description of the architecture is given in [8].

The architecture allows adapting the initial configuration of the WIS for each particular organization and, moreover, for each particular user, and supports the integration of all functions and all user data from all WIS instances which are used by the particular user into one user interface.

The problems discussed later in this paper are mainly connected with coarse level adaptation of the WIS, but to give an insight of the whole process of adaptation in two levels a short description of adaptation operations is given.

During the coarse level adaptation organization level instances are dynamically built. The adaptation operations of coarse level adaptation are the following [8]: the construction of initial configuration of WIS, the WIS adaptation in organization level, joining of instances of function groups, selection of allowed function groups, and adaptation of layout.

Afterwards, the detailed level adaptation is performed based on the user profile. The detailed adaptation has two operations [8]: detailed adaptation of the navigation and detailed adaptation of the content. The adaptation of the content corresponding to the particular user finds out his restrictions to the data, which are defined in user profile, for example, by using tables, their columns and filters for these columns. The WIS instance with the adapted navigation is supplemented with the content which in default is defined by the data usage of the functions. During the adaptation of the content it is adjusted to the restrictions defined for the user.

3 Extensions of WIS Profiles

The adaptation architecture uses a number of profiles to perform the adaptation: configuration profile, organization profile, and user profile. In our previous research [8] we focused on constructing different adapted instances of web information system from the set of all functions that form the whole WIS. Model diagrams of all profiles in their initial version and more detailed description are given in [8]. In this work we will explain how the different adapted WIS instances are presented to the user. To ensure the adaptation of the presentation we will extend the initial profiles. The already existing classes of profiles are depicted in grey.

3.1 Extended Configuration Profile

Configuration profile describes the structure of the WIS, e.g. components, subsystems, etc., without applying adaptation. Figure 2 represents the extended WIS configuration profile.

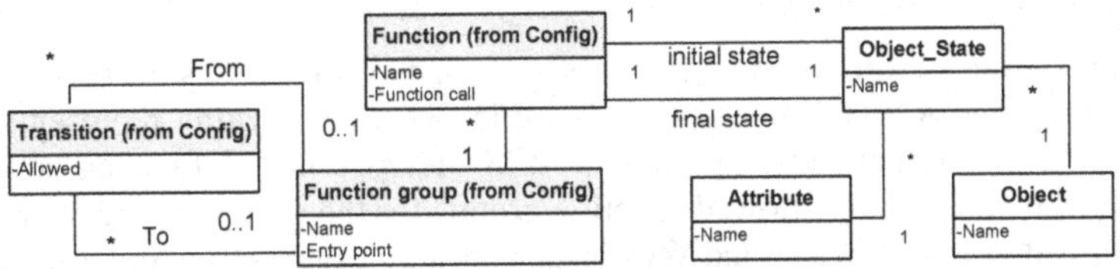

Fig. 2. Extended configuration profile

WIS configuration profile in its initial version consists of such classes as *Function group, Function*, and *Transition*. *Function group* is a grouping of WIS functions defined by an *entry point* to allow different technical implementations of WIS functions. For example, one possible situation where this grouping is necessary is the usage of different authentication methods for different function groups, e.g. authorized part of the system uses the database authentication and the self-service functions use the LDAP authentication. User chooses a link to one of the login forms and then is directed to the corresponding function group of WIS. In the adaptation architecture of WIS different function groups can be joined to allow the user to work with many WIS parts and instances based on the allowed *Transitions* defined in the configuration profile of the system.

The initial profile is extended by the class *Object State* which represents the situation where functions can be state dependent. A function may be allowed in some definite states and forbidden in others. The state in our proposed architecture is introduced as an *Attribute* or set of attributes of an *Object.* If the status allows, the function can perform manipulations with an object that defines the state. A function is allowed according to the initial state of the object. After the function is fulfilled it changes the state of the object to the final state.

3.2 Extended Organization Profile

The organization profile describes properties essential for the organization level instance of the WIS, e.g. local configuration specific for the particular organization, layout, etc.

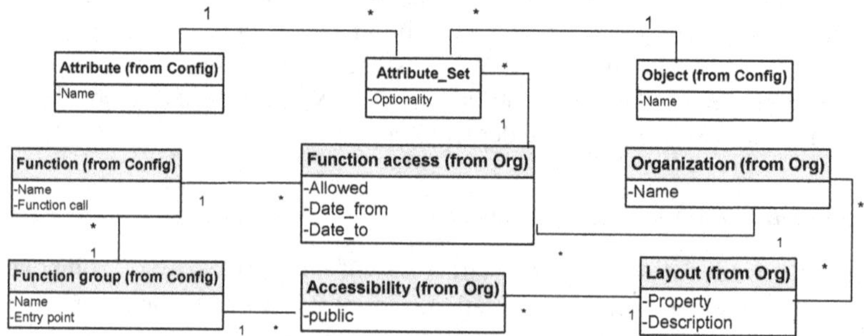

Fig. 3. Extended organization profile

WIS organization profile in its first version consists of classes *Organization, Function access, Accessibility,* and *Layout* (see Fig. 3). *Organization* represents the organizations that have their own instance of WIS. *Accessibility* defines an adapted instance of WIS by describing allowed function groups for the particular organization. *Function access* describes the adapted WIS instance for an organization in more detail by describing the accessible functions in predefined time periods. *Layout* specifies properties of some elements, if a personalized look of the organization level instance of the WIS is needed, e.g. logo, background, font, etc.

For each WIS instance of a particular organization the extended organization profile allows definition of an *Attribute Set* different from the initial attribute set used by a function in original configuration of WIS. The *Attribute Set* has associations with Attributes and Objects from the configuration profile. The feature "optional" of the attribute set describes if an attribute included in the attribute set is mandatory for the function execution logic.

3.3 User Profile

We do not introduce an extended user profile. The initial user profile describes the affiliation of the user in the particular time period in one or more organizations that are tenants of WIS and his access rights to functions and data. The elements of the user model are *User, Affiliation, Table*, and *Row_Access*. The profile uses also the class *Function* from the configuration profile and the class *Organization* from the organization profile. A more detailed description is given in [8].

4 Presentation Metamodel for WIS

To describe how an instance of WIS is presented to the user on the organization level, we described the elements of the user interface with a presentation metamodel (see Fig. 4).

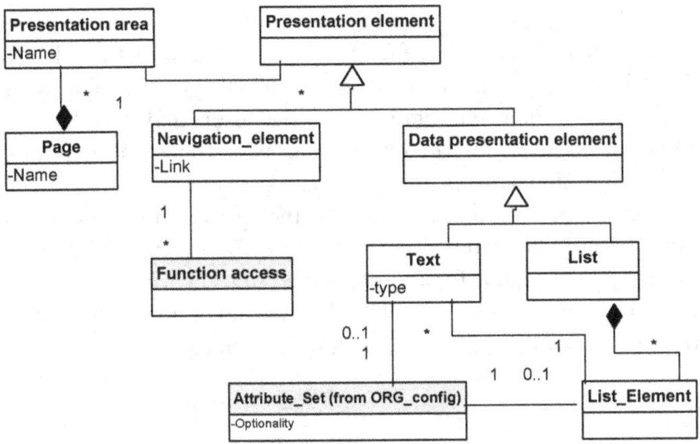

Fig. 4. Presentation metamodel for WIS

Page class is the main presentation element that contains all other user interface elements. Page class presents the Function group from the WIS basic configuration that is described with the configuration profile.

Page consists of at least one *Presentation area* which is provided for grouping of *Presentation elements.* A presentation element can be *Navigation element* or *Data presentation element.*

Navigation element is displayed as a link that represents a function call. In our WIS adaptation architecture the navigation element is not connected directly to the WIS function described in configuration profile, but is associated with a *Function access* class which supports presenting in the user interface only allowed functions of a particular WIS instance for a particular organization.

The data presentation element can be a kind of *Text* or *List* which both are different ways of displaying *Attributes* of the *Objects.* In our WIS adaptation architecture the data presentation elements are not connected directly to the attributes but are associated with an *Attribute Set* class which supports presenting in the user interface only allowed attributes of a particular WIS instance for a particular organization.

A List consists of *List elements* that also can represent attributes from the Attribute Set. The goal of introducing such presentation element is to allow a multiple choice from a set of attribute values. List elements also can be connected with Text presentation elements that can present additional information for each List element.

The property "Type" of the Text element describes whether the given presentation element for a particular WIS instance can only display the attribute value or the updates are allowed.

5 Construction of a Metamodel-Based and Adapted User Interface

The later described workflow (see Fig. 5) performs the construction of the user interface based on the previously described metamodel and uses the extended configuration and organization profiles of WIS adaptation architecture. The interface is generated with a close involvement of the user into the process. The workflow is adjusted to the situation when the choices of the user and the later interface construction depend on statuses of an object that is a focus of activities during business process completion. The user of a web-based business information system in such way gets an interface of WIS that is suited for the specific business situation.

We will consider each step of the process to describe the usage of profiles and adaptation operations, if applicable for the particular step, bearing in mind that only the organization level adaptation is made. The detailed level adaptation that uses the user profile is not the issue of this paper and is described in [9].

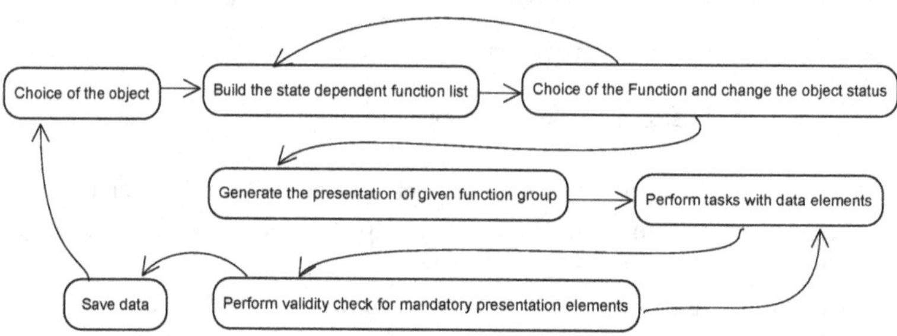

Fig. 5. User development in WIS adaptation

Chose the Object. The user finds the object that will be the focus of activities during the later business process completion. For example, the user finds the record of an existing vehicle to perform later a number of operations with it.

Build the State Dependent Function List. The initial state of the object determines the available operations that can be applied to the object.

Let's see an example (see Fig, 6), which describes a situation with chosen object O1 having a state S1 and a list of allowed three functions F1, F2, and F3 with defined initial and final states. The user can then select either a function F1 or F3 whose description by a parameter 'Initial_state' also contains S1 among other allowed states.

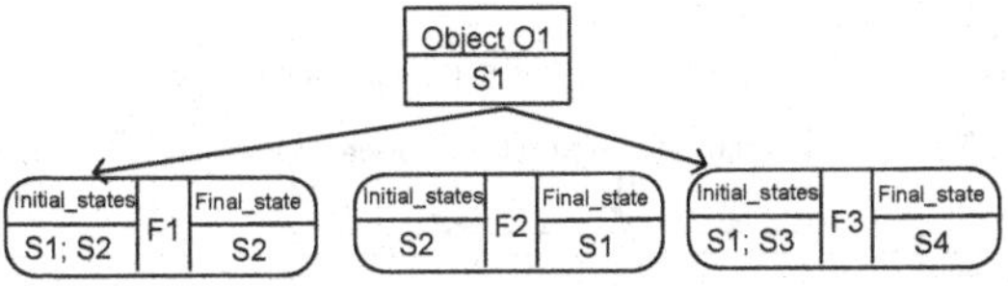

Fig. 6. An example of states of the object and functions

The list of operations allowed for the object (or functions in WIS context) is also based on configuration profile of WIS. The function list is presented in a presentation area as navigation presentation elements.

Chose the Function and Change the Object Status. According to the business needs, the user selects iteratively all necessary operations that should be performed with the object from the list of allowed operations displayed to him. After each choice the potential state of the object, if the operation will be later completed, is registered and it determines the content of the new state dependent function list.

In the previous example (See Fig, 6.) the status of the object is changed according to the value of the parameter 'Final_state' of the function. All possible scenarios of workflow composition for this example are: 1) F1→End 2) F1→F2→End; 3)F1→F2→F3→End; 4) F3→End. The 'End' in this case denotes that the user finishes the selection process.

The chosen functions are presented in a separate presentation area as navigation presentation elements.

Generate the Presentation of the Given Function Group. The user finishes the selection of functions and generates the presentation area that contains data presentation elements. The list of chosen functions and the organization profile of the company where the user works determines the list of attributes for particular WIS instance. The presentation metamodel also influences the look of the generated page. For example, the same attribute can be presented as text presentation element either of type "Input" or "Display" according to different user's choice of functions in presentations of different WIS instances.

For the previous example (see Fig. 6.) the presentation of WIS instance is given in Figure 7, which shows also the decisions of a user and state-dependent dynamic supply of allowed functions to the user, if he follows the workflow scenario 2) F1→F2→End described in previous subsection. Object area contains the presentation element O1, Function area contains the functions allowed according to the state of the selected object O1. Selected functions area contains the user's selection of functions. The data area is built after the user ends the construction of the desired scenario or workflow, and contains the attributes associated with functions also taking into account the configuration and organization profile for constructing an adapted WIS instance. All elements in the Figure 7 are stereotypes according to the presentation metamodel given on Figure 4.

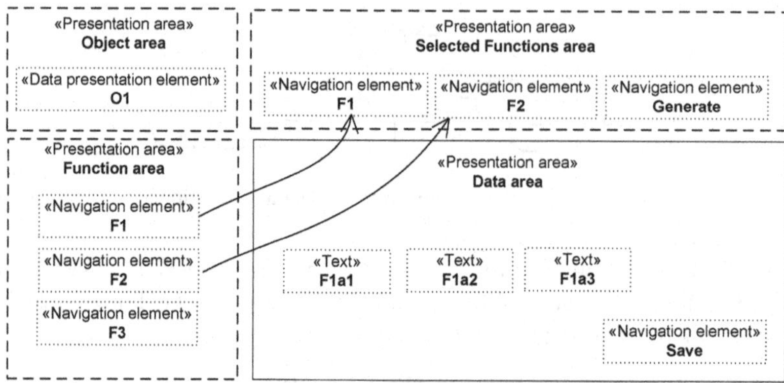

Fig. 7. User interface for the example

Perform Tasks with Data Elements. This step does not influence the user interface and can only influence the values of object's attributes. Also, the attribute (or attributes) that defines the state of the object can be changed.

Perform Validity Check for Mandatory Presentation Elements. Validity check performs evaluation, if all mandatory presentation elements have received their values, and before starting a new operation from the user's selection of functions also the actual state of object is always examined to ensure that a user has fulfilled all tasks from the workflow constructed by himself and has not overlooked any functions, thus, permitting illegal situation according to the objects state.

Save Data. If the validity check is successful, the user can save changed data elements and start constructing a new workflow by selecting a new object.

Principles described in this section and also the whole WIS adaptation framework is implemented in the Vehicle Register. The Object in this implementation is a vehicle. The current status of the vehicle can be, for example, 'active', 'inactive', 'temporary', 'cancelled', etc. The operations allowed for a vehicle in the state 'active' are, for example, 'Rebuilding', 'Change the owner', 'Remove from the register', and many others. Examples of two organizations using the same WIS in form of their adapted instances are in this case Ministry of Transport that holds the vehicle register and certified service centres that among other services also provide technical rebuild possibilities which are later documented in their WIS instance.

6 Related Work

A number of works are published about WIS adaptation. WIS can be adapted according to the context using a profile that corresponds to a configuration [2]. The configuration in this approach defines the information delivery according to the requirements of adaptation for the profile. In [3] different personalization scenarios including preference-based recommendation, context-aware content delivery, and personalized access to multiple contents are presented, which are based on a set of services that implement a personalized access model (PAM). Also, a metamodel is given that defines notions of a profile and context. Personalized presentation layer of WIS is introduced in an architecture proposed in [5]. This presentation layer supports adapted navigation and different views on the presented data.

Also there exist metamodels for Web applications, for example, UWE [10], WebML [11], and many others. These metamodels define semantics of Web applications from different viewpoints.

The research in the fields of SaaS and multi-tenancy is concentrated on configurability issues. Applications can be configured by utilizing the software architecture to build connections between functional elements and configuration [12]. In [13] the authors use patterns to formalize the configuration requirements in seven categories, e.g. data, user type, business rules. Different configurable aspects of SaaS applications are also discussed in [14], and architecture to support configurability is provided.

Our WIS presentation metamodel is provided as a part of WIS adaptation architecture and defines how the adapted WIS instance is presented to the user. Our approach is complimentary to mentioned adaptation approaches and metamodels, and describes specific aspects of Web applications, namely, the aspects connected with SaaS and Multi-tenancy, when many different WIS instances should be provided to the users.

7 Conclusions

Presented approach to the WIS adaptation uses two levels of adaptation – coarse-grained for the organization and fine-grained for the user. The adapted WIS organization level instances are presented to users of different organizations.

We consider in our approach a specific type of business information systems that are implemented as WIS and that support business functions. We consider specific way of performing business processes when the workflow starts with a choice of an object whose state determines the later steps of performing business activities.

The construction of the user interface in our approach is based on a presentation metamodel and uses the configuration and organization profiles of WIS adaptation architecture. The interface is generated with a close involvement of the user into the process. The choice of the user and the interface construction depends on state of an object that is a focus of activities during business process completion. The user of a web-based business information system in such way gets an interface of WIS that is suitable for the specific business situation.

The described architecture and user interface construction according to the presentation metamodel is implemented and is being used in two different WIS; one of them is used for the car registration WIS serving more than 20 regions of the state with approximately 100 different vehicle registrars who all can get their adapted interface to the particular business situation.

Acknowledgments. This work has been supported by ESF project No. 2009/0216/1DP/1.1.1.2.0/09/APIA/VIAA/044.

References

1. Fraternali, P.: Tools and Approaches for Developing Data Intensive Web Applications: a Survey. J. ACM Comput. Surv. 31(3), 227–263 (1999)
2. De Virgilio, R., Torlone, R.: A General Methodology for Context-Aware Data Access. In: Proceedings of the 4th ACM International Workshop on Data Engineering for Wireless and Mobile Access, MobiDE 2005, pp. 9–15. ACM, New York (2005)
3. Abbar, S., Bouzeghoub, M., Kostadinov, D., Lopes, S., Aghasaryan, A., Betge-Brezetz, S.: A Personalized Access Model: Concepts and Services for Content Delivery Platforms. In: Kotsis, G., Taniar, D., Pardede, E., Khalil, I. (eds.) Proc. of the 10th Int. Conf. on Information Integration and Web-Based Applications and Services, iiWAS 2008, pp. 41–47. ACM, New York (2008)
4. Valeriano, D., De Virgilio, R., Torlone, R., Di Federico, D.: An Efficient Implementation of a Rule-based Adaptive Web Information System. In: Frasincar, F., Houben, G.-J., Thiran, P. (eds.) Proc. of Int. CAISE Workshop on Web Information Systems Modeling (WISM 2006). CEUR Workshop Proceedings, vol. 239 (2006)
5. Tvarožek, M., Barla, M., Bieliková, M.: Personalized Presentation in Web-Based Information Systems. In: van Leeuwen, J., Italiano, G.F., van der Hoek, W., Meinel, C., Sack, H., Plášil, F. (eds.) SOFSEM 2007. LNCS, vol. 4362, pp. 796–807. Springer, Heidelberg (2007)
6. Clements, P., Northrop, L.: Software Product Lines: Practices and Patterns. Addison-Wesley (2002)
7. Microsoft, Architecture Strategies for Catching the Long Tail (2006)
8. Niedritis, A., Niedrite, L.: The Adaptation of a Web Information System: a Perspective of Organizations. In: Pokorny, J., Repa, V., Richta, K., Wojtkowski, W., Linger, H., Barry, C., Lang, M. (eds.) Information Systems Development, Business Systems and Services: Modeling and Development, pp. 539–550. Springer (2011)
9. Niedritis, A.: Delivery of Consistent and Integrated User's Data within a Multi-Tenant Adaptive SaaS Application. In: Niedrite, L., Strazdina, R., Wangler, B. (eds.) Perspectives in Business Informatics Research, Local Proceedings of 10th Int. Conf., BIR 2011 Associated Workshops and Doctoral Consortium, pp. 307–314. Riga Technical University, Riga (2011)
10. Koch, N., Kraus, A.: Towards a Common Metamodel for the Development of Web Applications. In: Cueva Lovelle, J.M., Gonzalez Rodriguez, B.M., Joyanes Aguilar, L., Labra Gayo, J.E., Paule Ruiz, M.P. (eds.) ICWE 2003. LNCS, vol. 2722, pp. 497–506. Springer, Heidelberg (2003)
11. Schauerhuber, A., Wimmer, M., Kapsammer, E.: Bridging existing Web modeling languages to model-driven engineering: a metamodel for WebML. In: Workshop Proceedings of the 6th Int. Conf. on Web Engineering. ACM Press, Palo Alto (2006)
12. Wang, H., Zheng, Z.: Software Architecture Driven Configurability of Multi-tenant SaaS Application. In: Wang, F.L., Gong, Z., Luo, X., Lei, J. (eds.) WISM 2010. LNCS, vol. 6318, pp. 418–424. Springer, Heidelberg (2010)
13. Shim, J., Han, J., Kim, J., Lee, B., Oh, J., Wu, C.: Patterns for Configuration Requirements of Software-as-a-Service. In: Proceedings of the 2011 ACM Symposium on Applied Computing (SAC 2011), pp. 155–161. ACM, New York (2011)
14. Nitu: Configurability in SaaS (Software as a Service) Applications. In: Proceedings of the 2nd India Software Engineering Conference (ISEC 2009), pp. 19–26. ACM, New York (2009)

Domain Driven Development and Feature Driven Development for Development of Decision Support Systems

Paulius Danenas and Gintautas Garsva

Department of Informatics, Kaunas Faculty, Vilnius University, Muitines St. 8, LT- 44280 Kaunas, Lithuania
{paulius.danenas,gintautas.garsva}@khf.vu.lt

Abstract. This paper describes adoption of Domain Driven Design and Feature Driven Development paradigms for decision support systems, using credit risk evaluation DSS as a case study. Possible development scenarios using both of these methodologies are discussed, using transformations from previously described development framework. It is concluded that these techniques might be adopted for development of complex DSS.

Keywords: Domain Driven Design, Domain Driven Development, Feature Driven Development, decision support system, credit risk.

1 Introduction

Decision support systems are a tool that enables automation of credit risk evaluation process by integrating models developed using statistical, mathematical and artificial intelligence based techniques into an environment that is acceptable and convenient to use for credit manager. Such systems benefit banks and financial institutions by helping to examine and evaluate financial situation of such companies, performing automated analysis and extraction of structured, detailed and visualized information, and thus supporting credit risk management process. Design and development of such systems is a complex task as it involves development of specific modules and components which is rarely supported by traditional software design approaches. This also requires a lot of expertise from various experts which means their direct involvement into software engineering process that highly increases the complexity of design and development of such software.

Different methodologies have been developed for complex systems development. Domain-driven design and development, an approach extending model driven development has been introduced by Evans [1] and has been widely applied in industrial software engineering. MDA has been applied in development of intelligent systems, for e.g., Megableh and Barrett used their own developed methodology based on MDA for Self-adaptive application for indoor way finding

T. Skersys, R. Butleris, and R. Butkiene (Eds.): ICIST 2012, CCIS 319, pp. 187–198, 2012.

for individuals with cognitive impairments [2]. Mohagheghi and Dehlen [3] developed a survey on applications of model driven engineering in industry which include examples on business applications and financial domain, as well as applications on telecommunications and other domains. Domain driven development for various complex systems has been researched less extensively yet there are papers describing its application for such systems development, for e.g., Burgstaller et al. [4] used domain driven development for monitoring of distributed systems.

However, currently there is lack of research targeted at designing complex decision support systems, especially using object-oriented techniques. The structure of DSS and expert systems in financial and credit risk field has been discussed and proposed in various papers [5-9], as well as agent-based system expert system development[10], yet they only describe high level structure and main components. Zhang et al. [9] present their framework of DSS structured as multilayer system, consisting of information integrated platform layer, utilization layer and information representation layer. This is similar to the framework proposed by the authors in [11]. Thus this paper tries to explore and adopt modern software design and engineering methodologies such as Domain Driven Design and Feature Driven Design in the context of sophisticated DSS framework for credit risk evaluation showing that such approaches might be a proper choice for such systems.

2 Domain Driven Design and Feature Driven Development – Main Concepts

2.1 Domain Driven Design

Domain Driven Design (abbr. as DDD; Evans, 2003) is based on such core concepts as domain, model, ubiquitous language and context. Only basic definitions of artifacts', patterns and concepts are given in this section; for more information of refer to [1]. Domain can be described the subject area of application which can be expressed by ontology, as an influence or activity. The model represents a system of abstractions that describes selected aspects of a domain and can be used to solve problems related to that domain. Ubiquitous language is used by members of development team and helps to express domain model as well as connect all the activities of the team with the software. Context is described as the setting in which a word or statement appears that determines its meaning.

Evans also defines several artifacts to express, create, and retrieve domain models. Fig. 1 shows these artifacts in the context of overall DDD core model, as well as connections between main concepts and artifacts. Table 1 gives the basic definitions of these artifacts together with descriptions of core DDD artifacts.

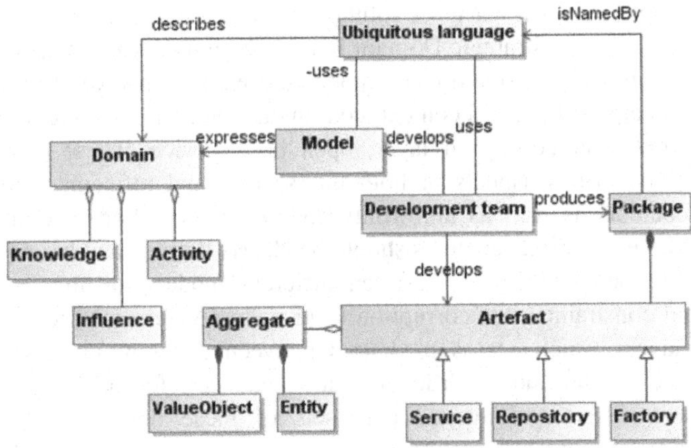

Fig. 1. Concepts of Domain Driven Design

Table 1. Core Concepts of Domain Driven Design

DDD concept/model	Purpose and description
Entity	An abstraction which describes an object or a group of objects a thread of identity that runs through time and often across distinct representations. The objects are not defined primarily by their attributes; entity object might be matched although the attributes might differ.
Value object	Conversely from entity objects, this type of object has no conceptual identity but contains attributes
Aggregates	A set of value objects/entities connected by a root entity (aggregate root). Control all access to the objects inside the boundary is controlled through the root entity.
Service	Services are used when some concepts from the domain commonly are not modeled as objects, i.e., either distorts the definition of a model-based object or adds meaningless artificial objects (Evans, 2003).
Repository	An object that represents storage of domain objects, allowing to easily change storage implementations. According to Evans, they present clients with a simple model for obtaining persistent objects and managing their life cycle and separate application and domain design from data source or persistence technology.
Factory	DDD proposes extensive usage of OO Factory pattern for creating domain objects, which allows to hide complex initialization logic and eliminates to requirement to reference the concrete classes of the objects thus allowing easy switching between several different implementations.
Packages (modules)	Represents separate aspects of implementation reflecting domain. This helps separate the domain layer from other parts of the implementation.

Although single model is an ideal solution, in development practice it is usually split into several models. Strategic Domain Driven Design provides a set of principles to ensure model integrity, refine domain model and work with several models. Evans defines such principles: bounded context, continuous integration, context map, shared kernel, conformity, anticorruption layer, open host service. These context driven patterns describe various aspects of both intersection and refinement for different models and contexts as well as uniformity and integration. For example, bounded context proposes that various contexts should be clearly defined and bounded whereas context map defines interactions between different models together with context boundaries and constraints. Anticorruption layer pattern offers an extensive usage of intermediate layers which act as mediators between different models or systems through interfaces. Thus no modifications are necessary for other systems which might represent different domains or subsets of these domains. Shared kernel facilitates usage of core subsets of each domain which might not be changed independently during the design by each counterpart (development team).

Among these principles, principles of distillation for separating the components and refactoring domain models were also proposed. This includes core domain, defining the most valuable and essential specialized concepts, generic subdomains essential for the full definition of the model and to the system, highlighted, segregated and abstract core, cohesive mechanisms as well as patterns for large scale structures, such as evolving order, responsibility layers, knowledge level and pluggable component framework. The core patterns propose different ways to extract domain core – highlighted core offers this by simplifying core domain description and highlighting its main aspects whereas segregated and abstract core models propose refactoring of core domain in order to obtain clearer models. Responsibility layers pattern offers an interesting system engineering viewpoint as it proposes to refactor the model in a multilayered way such that the responsibilities of each domain object, aggregate and module fit neatly within the responsibility of one layer [1]. Knowledge level pattern extends this approach by implementing such layer system in hierarchical manner, where each level directly depends on lower level. This is an important aspect for design and development of complex decision support systems as they usually include several different domains and aspects which require different kinds of expertise (financial, statistical, machine learning, data source integration); therefore, different experts from various fields are required for development of such system. Pluggable component framework allows uncomplicated substitution of various implementations implementing corresponding interfaces; this is known as one of popular component-based development patterns. Such pattern allows separating and encapsulating several bounded contexts by exposing their functionality as components, with shared kernel as core.

Therefore, as Evans highlights, context, distillation, and large-scale structure design principles are complementary and interact in many ways, for e.g., a large-scale structure can exist within one bounded context, or it can cut across many of them and organize the context map. The combination of these principles will be shown later by a case study of credit risk evaluation DSS.

2.2 Feature Driven Development

Feature-Driven Development (abbr. as FDD) [13] is an iterative and incrementing model-driven software development process, based on short iterations and five activities: overall model development, feature list building, plan by feature, design by feature and build by feature. First two activities are general activities, which define general model and its structure. Other three activities are iterative, where special feature is developed. Palmer and Felsing [13] define feature as small function valued by client, expressed in such form: <action><result><object> (e.g., calculate rating of customer).

Each feature is designed and developed using MDA methodology, specifically UML diagrams. Class, activity and collaboration diagrams (or sets of such diagrams) are usually produced for each feature, as well as for overall model; these models are refined during further development. An exceptional step is domain analysis for each feature done by domain expert.

FDD process usually uses modular structure which defines how various layers communicate with each other; in case of distributed system this architecture also describes inner communication of components. System separation into several layers is useful as it allows forming development teams for different components of such system by their skills, as well as defining interfaces for integration of these components. According to Palmer and Felsing [13], there are 4 layers in their proposed FDD architecture:

- User Interface (UI) layer, which interacts with Problem Domain layer, providing data views and enable users to easily invoke the problem domain features they need to get their desired results. Sub-layers, such as Navigation and Look and Feel sub-layer and Presentation sub-layer are also defined; the first defines how data for problem domain is presented and entered, invokes system functionality, related to problem domain, or navigates on the UI. Presentation sub-layer connects problem domain objects to corresponding objects in the user interface, the management of the user session, and the population of data for the various graphical elements in the user interface; Model-View-Controller pattern can be given as an example of such sub-layer implementation [13].
- Problem Domain (PD) layer – the most stable and independent layer which represents problem domain together with its inner logic and objects. Its development is the most important and therefore time consuming task in FDD architecture development as other layers directly depend on this layer.
- System Interaction (SI) layer – this layer allows to expose problem domain functionality for the external systems and components as well as use their functionality as components or Web Services. Main features which are implemented for this layer are subset of feature list features related with integration or interfacing of such components.
- Data Management (DM) layer, which is responsible of management of business objects. Its implementation might change according to changes in data storage infrastructure, thus it is recommended to separate problem domain and storage logic which is specific for particular implementation. Object-oriented or other inner mappings based persistence mechanisms are usually used to implement this layer.

3 DSS Structure Expressed in Terms of DDD

This section describes integration and application of DDD for development of sophisticated DSS for credit risk domain consisting of several layers. DSS framework described in earlier work of the authors [11] is used as a case study. Their DSS is also described as multilayered structure which makes it easier to integrate and apply DDD by defining mappings between layers of credit risk DSS and corresponding layers in responsibility layer structure of DDD.

The proposed system framework consists of several layers. Only main points such as layer structure are presented here; more information can be found on original paper. The system framework supports intelligent and statistical model development, testing and prediction operations, as well as data analysis using statistical, financial and visual analysis techniques. Credit risk analysis can be viewed as an aggregation of these three as all these activities are present in this process.

The system consists of three core layers which represent each of domains related to the DSS:

- SVM-ML (SVM based machine learning) layer representing machine learning techniques and algorithms for model development, information processing, feature and instance selection;
- Data layer (DL) layer which defines data needed for modeling storage facility such as financial, operational, management, market, statistical, historic and macroeconomic data as well as metadata, such as reference or multilanguage data. Intelligent and statistical model repository together with metadata and execution log is also defined in this layer. The structure of the data is conformant to Basel II requirements as data representing both credit risk, operational risk and market risk is included in this layer.
- Credit risk evaluation layer (CRE layer) represents analysis, modeling, forecasting, visualization and evaluation business logic. Financial Analysis, Modeling and Forecasting modules implement analytics, simulations and forecasting of particular domain.

Such structure provides separation for logic that belongs to different domains and enables reuse of developed components in other intelligent systems where similar problems are solved. Functionality of various supporting services is defined in additional sublayers, which belong to one or more of main three layers:

- Data source interaction layer – it is defined in both SVM-ML and CRE layers. SVM-ML layer interaction sublayer includes database interaction layer with object persistence and database connection frameworks, as well as various data standards including interoperable Predictive Model Markup Language (PMML) standard. It also defines the interfaces for information retrieval using Web Services or intelligent agents. CRE layer extends this layer with financial standards and data sources specifically for finance or credit risk related tasks (e.g., rating information). It also has a mapping package that contains the mappings between XBRL (and other standards) and data stored in Data Layer; structure of such mappings has been discussed in [4].

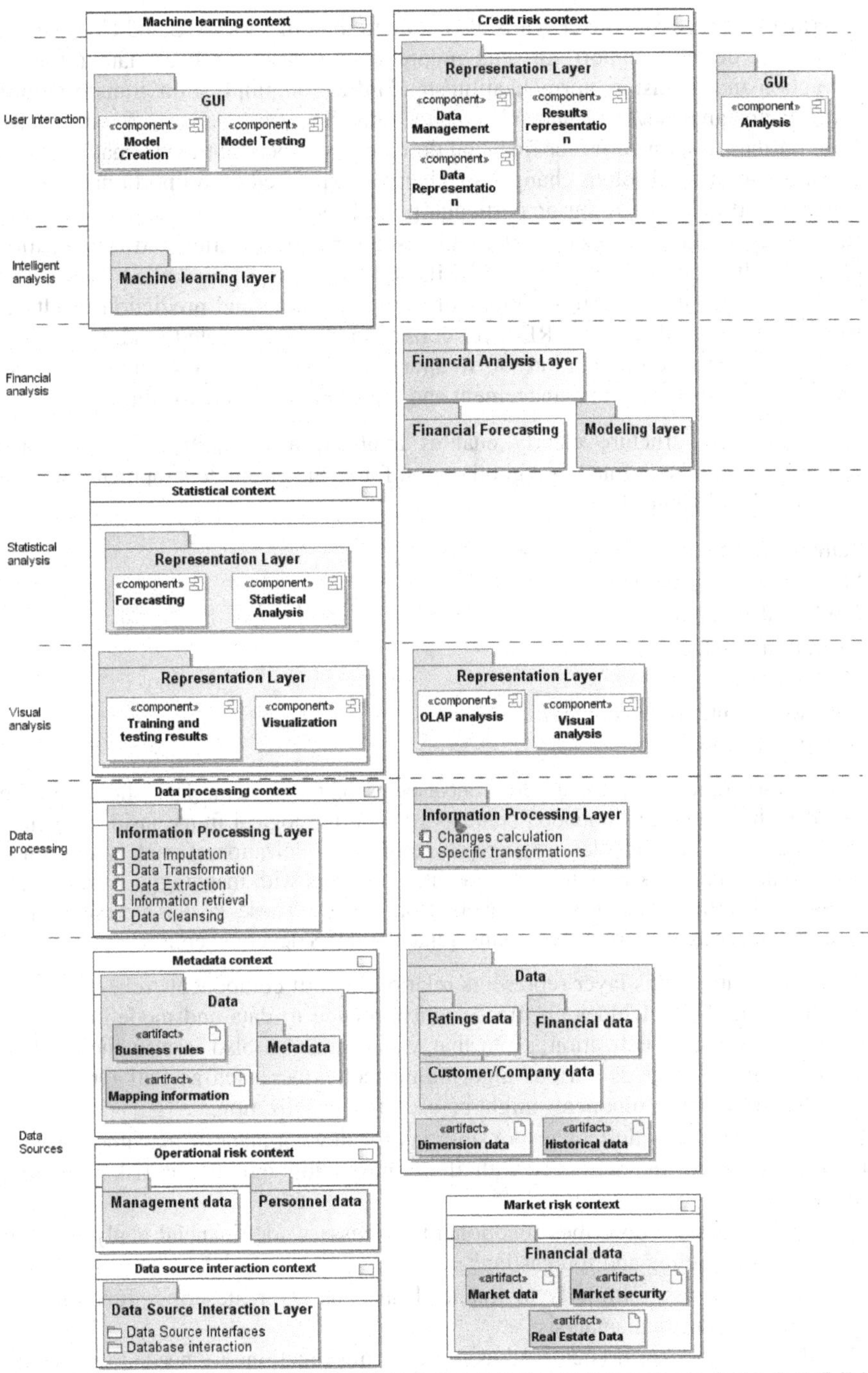

Fig. 2. Responsibility layers for credit risk DSS

- Information Processing layer – it is also defined in both SVM-ML and CRE layers. This layer defines support for data preprocessing tasks, such as data retrieval, extraction and cleansing, normalization/standardization, imputation, transformation using factor analysis/PCA and other algorithms. The same layer defined in CRE layer defines tasks specific for financial domain, e.g., specific transformations, data transformation to absolute changes or changes expressed in proportional manner between particular ratios during particular period and etc.
- Representation layer – describes the logic used for representation and visualization of results. It is defined for both SVM-ML and CR layer. In case of SVM-ML this layer defines standard representations of training, testing and prediction results as well as their visualizations. CRE layer defines more sophisticated modules such as OLAP analysis, representation of financial analysis, simulation/modeling and forecasting as well as data management and representation functionality.

The use of such structure clearly enables application of multicontext approach therefore DDD can be defined as a good option for such system development. Several contexts can be distinguished:

- Statistical context;
- Machine learning context;
- Credit risk context;
- Operational risk context;
- Market risk context;
- Data source interaction context;
- Metadata context.

Each of these contexts represents different aspects of the system. This should not be confused with modules, as bounded contexts provide the logical frame inside of which the model evolves, and modules are more of a tool for organization of models' elements. To extend the framework by introducing additional layers with meaningful semantics, it was extended with 7 responsibility layers from DDD. These layers represent main software engineering and problem domains related to DSS development:

- User interaction – this layer represents relationships of components related to GUI development. This includes all functionality, related to data and modeling results presentation and visualization. Note that visual analysis also is also included in Visual analysis layer as various algorithmic techniques such as Self Organizing Maps or Principal Components might be used for visualization.
- Intelligent analysis – defines responsibilities for development of machine learning based techniques and methods with their integration into credit risk modeling process;
- Financial analysis – describes functionality necessary for financial analysis, such as financial modeling and forecasting;
- Statistical analysis – similarly to financial analysis layer, describes functionality necessary for statistical analysis;
- Visual analysis – here it is defined as representing functionality needed to visually represent modeling results of other analysis layers (intelligent, financial and statistical). Differently from User interaction layer, it is mapped to algorithmic functionality;

- Data processing layer describes implementations of methods for data preprocessing to perform model training and testing tasks;
- Data Sources layer represents data which is needed to perform modeling, analysis and decision support tasks, as well as their interfacing functionality. It includes data for credit, operational, and market risk analysis together with metadata and model repository. This layer describes the responsibilities related to development of data storage implementations.

Avram & Marinescu [12] state that common architectural solution for domain-driven designs contain only four conceptual layers. This is more practical for development, as the complexity of layers in Fig. 2 is simplified to four layers commonly used in almost every system. The simplified architecture according to this suggestion (without bounded contexts described before) is shown in Fig. 3.

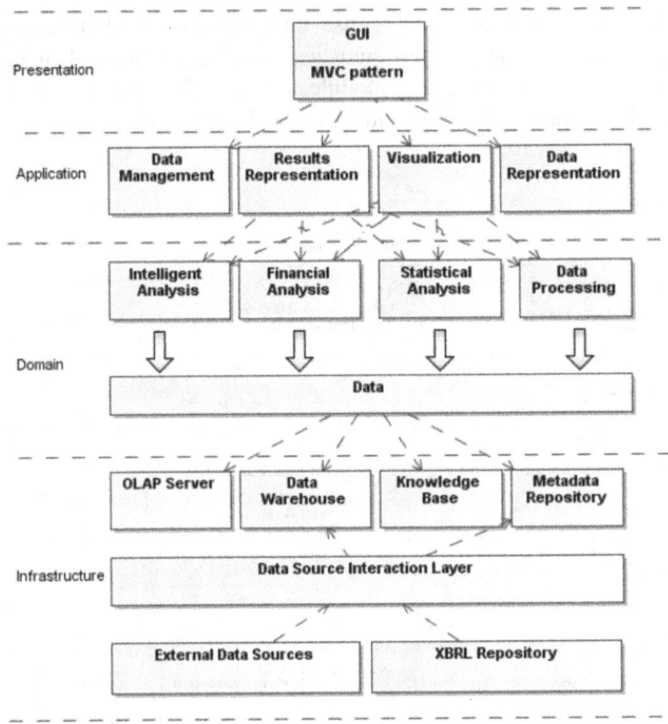

Fig. 3. DSS framework consisting of 4 layers

The main difference is that analysis layers and data processing layer were into single joined domain layer; therefore, the data, used in risk analysis (i.e., defined in credit risk, market risk and operational risk contexts) is moved into Domain layer, while metadata and knowledge base (which also represents model repository) modules defined in Infrastructure layer, together with Data Source Interaction layer. Such distinction separates support, storage implementation and external data source connection functionality from problem domain which is directly dependent on data defined in Data Sources layer. These tasks are defined in Infrastructure layer; note that Infrastructure is defined in software level and is not dependable on the hardware. The presentation layer defines the same set of responsibilities and functionality as in extended model; however, Data Management and Data Representation activities were moved to Application layer, accordingly to MVC pattern. The domain layer is focused on core domain issues; therefore, it is not involved in infrastructure activities, such as management of metadata and external data sources or storage facilities.

4 Feature Driven Development Adopted to Proposed DSS

Feature driven development is also considered as a good choice for development of complex systems, as each feature is developed iteratively. This is especially useful as development and testing of some components is a sophisticated activity requiring a lot of testing iterations; this is a good premise for development of intelligent systems which include machine learning and statistics based techniques. A feature can be represented as a class, component or a module. The technical architecture is described in Section 2.2; Fig. 4 presents its adaptation for credit risk DSS.

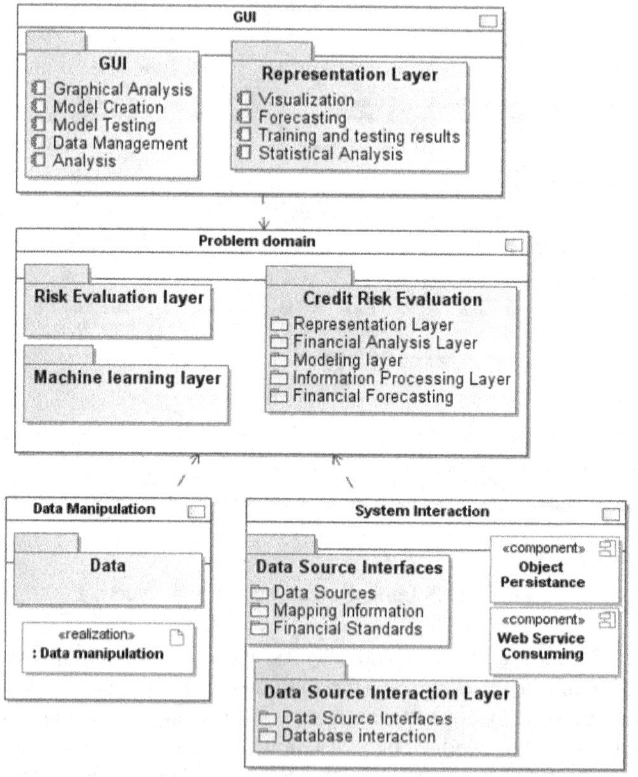

Fig. 4. DSS structure transformed into FDD technical structure

While comparing Fig. 3 and Fig. 4 it can be observed that the layer structure is very similar – both of these models have GUI and Problem domain layers, and System Interaction layer closely resembles Infrastructure layer in simplified DDD. The only difference is that, according to [12], Infrastructure layer contains all libraries and components for other layers (for e.g., persistence frameworks, web application frameworks etc.) as well as provides communication between layers, whereas System Interaction layer is designed mainly for communication with external systems and Web Services. The integration of Web Services is an important criteria as authors of [11] propose implementation for credit risk DSS as distributed system which also increases its complexity. Data manipulation layer in FDD also closely corresponds to Application layer in simplified DDD model as they both represent Data manipulation functionality. Another difference is Data dependency in FDD Data Manipulation layer as, according to its definition, this layer is responsible for managing objects for Data as business objects whereas Data is mapped to Problem Domain layer in simplified DDD. However, this shows that FDD, similarly as DDD, can be applied for development of such systems. Note, that although separate features would be developed by separate development teams, integration of such features requires higher levels experts.

5 Conclusions

Since its development Domain-Driven Design and development was widely applied for software engineering, especially for complex systems. DDD focuses on understanding the customers' needs and the environment in which the customer works and aims to exploit the creativity factor in system development process. However, the analysis of its previous applications and adoptions for design and development of decision support systems showed that it is not widely used in this field. One of the main problems which arise during its adoption is the specific purpose of such systems which requires knowledge from different fields and different experts. Thus different approach from software engineering is needed to be taken. Yet, analysis of DDD patterns and techniques showed that it can be adopted for development of such complex intelligent systems. Usage of multiple contexts and layers helps to ensure proper coordination between several development teams which might involve experts from different domains. This paper analyses a case study of such complex system which involves extensive application of intelligent and statistical techniques for decision support in financial domain. It shows a transformation from previously defined DSS framework to multilayered and multicontext structure. Therefore, we suggest that component-based or other software development methodologies which could be used for development of such DSS might be complemented with initial step based on DDD principles which identifies models and ubiquitous language for inner communication of development team, defines model decomposition levels and develops context mapping, context distillation and anticorruption level models for management of development process.

Another software engineering framework for such systems development, Feature Driven Development, is also discussed for the presented case. Although it does not offer full solution for software development (i.e., it does not comprise early project stages), it is merely concentrated on iterative development using Agile development principles and extensive MDA/UML usage. The analysis of its technical architecture and development capabilities showed that, similarly to DDD, it can also be adopted for development of complex DSS. Therefore, a possible scenario of its adoption for design and development of intelligent credit risk evaluation system is also presented as a case study

References

1. Evans, E.: Domain-Driven Design: Tackling Complexity in the Heart of Software. Addison Wesley (2003)
2. Magableh, B., Barrett, S.: Self-adaptive application for indoor wayfinding for individuals with cognitive impairments. In: 24th International Symposium on Computer-Based Medical Systems (CBMS), Bristol, pp. 1–6 (2011)
3. Mohagheghi, P., Dehlen, V.: Where Is the Proof? - A Review of Experiences from Applying MDE in Industry. In: Schieferdecker, I., Hartman, A. (eds.) ECMDA-FA 2008. LNCS, vol. 5095, pp. 432–443. Springer, Heidelberg (2008)
4. Burgstaller, R., Wuchner, E., Fiege, L., Becker, M., Fritz, T.: Using Domain Driven Development for Monitoring Distributed Systems. In: Hartman, A., Kreische, D. (eds.) ECMDA-FA 2005. LNCS, vol. 3748, pp. 19–24. Springer, Heidelberg (2005)
5. Zopounidis, C., Doumpos, M.: A preference disaggregation decision support system for financial classification problems. European Journal of Operational Research 130, 402–413 (2001)
6. Cheng, H., Lu, Y.-C., Sheu, C.: An ontology-based business intelligence application in a financial knowledge management system. Expert Systems with Applications 36(2), 3614–3622 (2009)
7. Tsaih, R., Liu, Y.-J., Liu, W., Lien, Y.-L.: Credit scoring system for small business loans. Decision Support Systems 38(1), 91–99 (2004)
8. Huai, W.: The Framework Design and Research On Enterprises Group Financial Decision Support System. In: Proceedings of Management and Service Science (MASS), Wuhan, pp. 1–4 (2010)
9. Zhang, M., Gu, Y., Zhu, J.: Analysis of the Framework for Financial Decision Support System. In: Proceedings of 2009 International Conference on Wireless Networks and Information Systems, Shanghai, pp. 241–244 (2009)
10. Guo-an, Y., Hong-bing, X., Chao, W.: Design and implementation of an agent-oriented expert system of loan risk evaluation. In: Proc. of International Conference on Integration of Knowledge Intensive Multi-Agent Systems, pp. 41–45 (2003)
11. Danenas, P., Garsva, G.: SVM and XBRL based decision support system for credit risk evaluation. In: Proc. of the 17th International Conference on Information and Software Technologies (IT 2011), Technologija, Kaunas, Lithuania, pp. 190–198 (2011)
12. Avram, A., Marinescu, F.: Domain-Driven Design Quickly. InfoQ (2006), http://www.infoq.com/resource/minibooks/domain-driven-design-quickly/en/pdf/DomainDrivenDesignQuicklyOnline.pdf
13. Palmer, S.R., Felsing, J.M.: A Practical Guide to Feature-Driven Development. Prentice Hall (2002)

From UML Communication Diagrams to Aspect-Oriented Communication Diagrams Using Graph Transformation

Mouna Aouag, Wafa Chama, and Allaoua Chaoui

MISC Laboratory, Department of Computer Science, University Mentouri Constantine, Algeria
a_mouna25@yahoo.fr, wafachama@gmail.com, a_chaoui2001@yahoo.com

Abstract. UML is a standard modeling language that provides several concepts which are used for different levels of design. The communication diagram is one of UML diagrams used to represent interactions between objects. But it remains an object-oriented model who owns several limits namely the duplication, the difficult resolution and reuse of models. The Aspect Oriented Modeling has shown its usefulness in the design and development of complex systems. There are several studies on the aspects composition. We propose in this paper, an approach for composition aspects. This method is inspired by the approach MATA, graph transformation to automatically integrate aspects models and Object Oriented Communication diagrams and get Aspect Oriented Communication diagrams. To achieve this transformation automatically, we propose two meta-models and from these latter's, we propose a graph grammar. In order to validate our model transformation, we use the meta-modeling tool AToM3. A case study is presented to illustrate our approach.

Keywords: UML, Aspect Oriented Modeling, Communication diagrams, MATA, meta-model, Graph grammar, AToM3.

1 Introduction

Object Oriented Modeling is a paradigm for designing and modeling complex problems since 1990. Several efforts have been invented to improve its techniques and methods of development, from which UML (Unified Modeling Language). UML contains thirteen diagrams, structural and behavioral to represent respectively the static and dynamic views of a system. Communication diagram can describe the dynamic behavior and modeling the interactions between objects by sending messages [1], [15], [16], [17].

However, object-oriented models have several problems and limitations, mainly related to duplication, resolution and reuse of models. The object approach provides no solution. Therefore developers and programmers have thought of a new paradigm that improves and provide solutions to the problems mentioned above, that is Aspect Oriented Paradigm.

In this paper, we develop a formal Framework for automatic transformation from Object-Oriented Communication Diagrams (OOCD) to Aspect Oriented Communication Diagrams (AOCD).It is inspired by the approach MATA (Modeling Aspect using Transformation Approach), the graph transformation and the tool AToM3 is used [2].

T. Skersys, R. Butleris, and R. Butkiene (Eds.): ICIST 2012, CCIS 319, pp. 199–209, 2012.

This paper is organized as follow: Section 2 outlines the major related work and differences between their multiple approaches. In sections 3 we recall some basic concepts about UML communication diagrams, aspect-oriented Modeling and Graph Transformations (GT). In section 4 we describe our approach of transforming Object Oriented Communication Diagram to Aspect Oriented Communication Diagram, it consists on proposing two meta-models associated respectively to OOCD, Aspect oriented model (AOM) and a grammar that deals with the transformation. The meta-models and the grammar are implemented in ATOM3. In section 5 details a case study illustrating our transformation approach through an example. We give an Object Oriented Communication Diagram, aspect model and execute the tool. The final section (Section 6) we give a general conclusion and some perspectives on future work.

2 Related Work

Aspect Oriented Modeling is a new paradigm, developed by kazale and his team in 2000. In [9], the authors presented an approach to achieve the translation of an Object-Oriented model (OOM) to Aspect-Oriented model by using the tool MATA. In [13] the authors have made the modeling of two meta-models of AOM and OOM by the formalism EMF, GMF [4] and they proposed a matching algorithm to perform the translation. However in [7], the authors added the concept of aspect in a single state-transition diagram, but in [14] the addition of the notion of aspects is different, to define one aspect. In fact we must create a profile contains a set of stereotype; thus can, paste this profile on the UML model. In this paper, we propose an automatic approach with tool basing on approach MATA. To realize this transformation of OOCD to AOCD we have using the tool of meta-modeling and graph transformation AToM3.

3 Backgrounds

Our objective is to propose an automatic integration of Aspect Model in Object Oriented Communication Diagram to obtained Aspect Oriented Communication Diagram using graph transformation. The abstract syntax of each formalism is described by means of meta-models. The transformation process is performed by a graph grammar that takes the source model (OOCD, AOM) as an input, execute the rules of the grammar, and generate the target model (AOCD) as output .In the following we recall some basic notions about Communication Diagram, aspect-oriented Modeling and graph transformations.

3.1 Communication Diagram

A diagram of Communication is a simplified representation of sequence diagram [3], [5], [11] and one of UML2.0 interaction diagrams, used to illustrate how objects interact by exchanging messages; it offers a spatial representation of lifelines. Each message is labeled by the name of the operation or signal invoked, a guard condition, allows a number to order the sending of messages and we have several type of message (synchronous, asynchronous, back, lost, etc...). The link in the diagram is a connection between the sender and receiver objects.

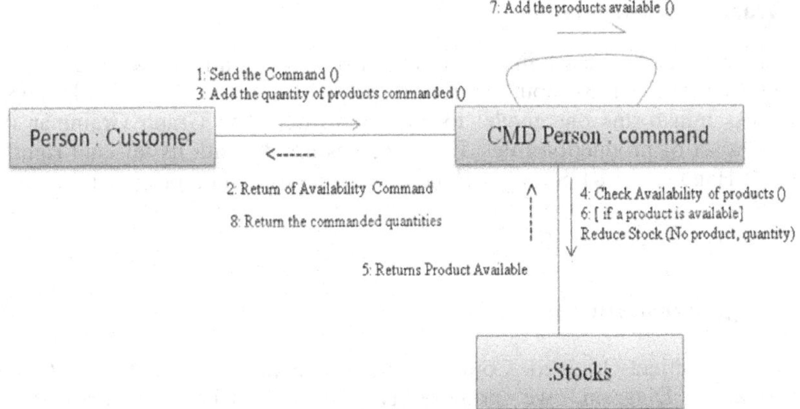

Fig. 1. Shows a simple example of a Communication Diagram; which models a customer commendation system. This figure focuses on the presentation of messages (synchronous, asynchronous, etc...), as shown in this sample caption.

3.2 Aspect-Oriented Modeling

Aspect Oriented Modeling is a new paradigm that allows the separation of a Base Model (BM) and an Aspectual Model (AM). Is an integration of models (Aspect Model and Base Model).For more details, see [13], [6], [12].

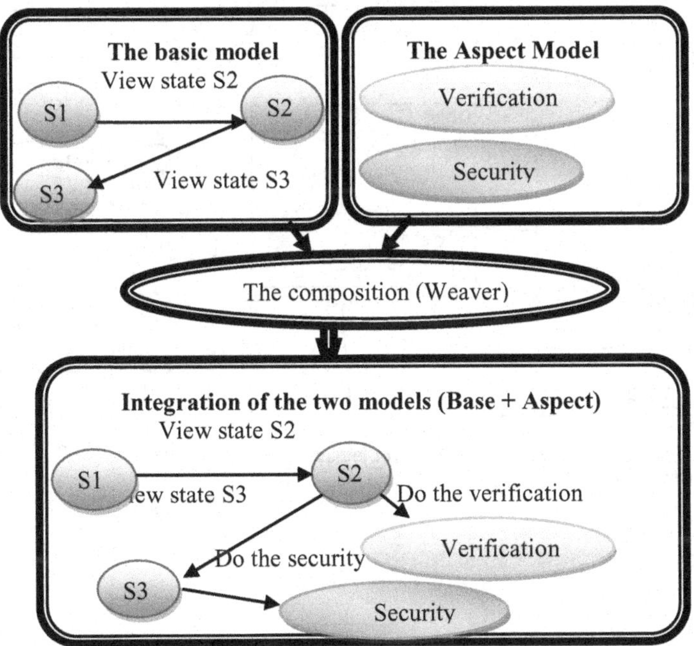

Fig. 2. Shows a simple example of the different tasks of AOM. Where S1, S2, S3 are states. Verification and security are aspect which should be added in BM. as shown in this sample caption.

3.3 Graphs Transformation

The GT is the process of choosing a rule from a specified grammar, applying this rule to a graph (meta-model) as input and repeat the process until no rule can be applied. This process transforms one model to another model. The Graph Grammar (GG) consists of a set of production rules. Each one has graphs with its left and right side (LHS "Left Hand Side" RHS "Right Hand Side") and execution priority in relation to other rules.

For more details, see [10], [8].

4 Proposed Approach

To transform Object-Oriented Communication Diagram to an Aspect Oriented Communication Diagram, we propose two meta-models .The first for the Communication diagram and the second for the aspect model. These meta-models are represented by the formalism of UML class diagram and constraints are expressed in Python. We also propose a set of rules is our graph grammar.

4.1 The Meta-model of the Communication Diagram

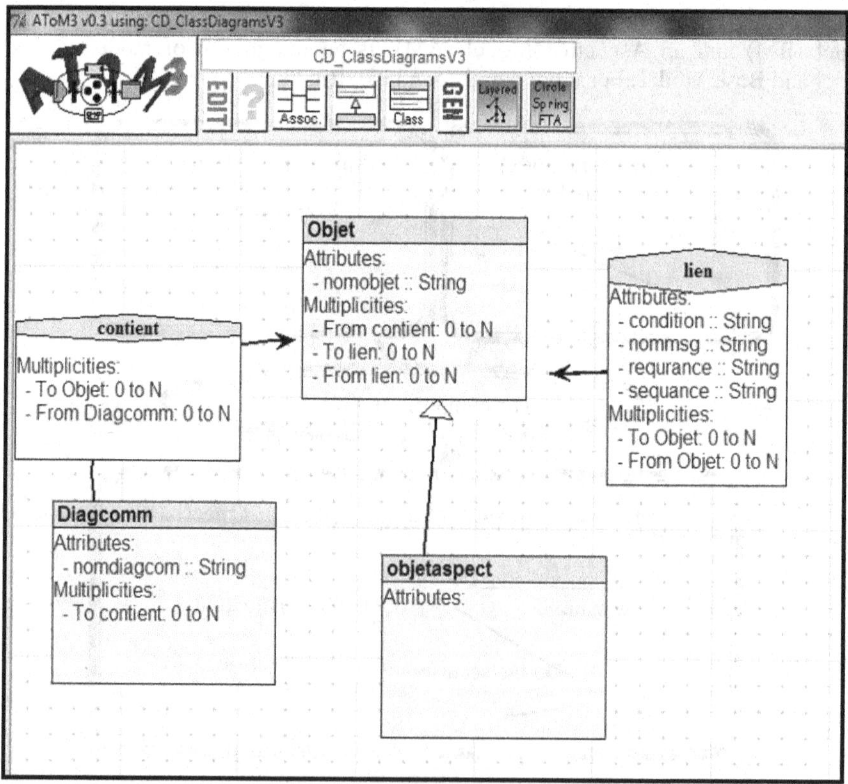

Fig. 3. Our meta-model consists of three classes *(diagcomm, objet* and *objetaspect)* and two associations *(contient, lien),* as shown in this sample caption

- *Diagcomm*: This class is used to represent the communication diagram.
- *Objet*: This class represents objects. Each object has a name and can communicate through connectors.
- *Objetaspect*: This class represents additional objects (aspects) to DCOO. It inherits all its attributes, multiplicities, associations from the object class.
- *Contient*: It is an association of composition. This connects the *Diagcomm* with its *objets*.
- *Lien*: This is a simple association. That permits communication between two objects. In other words, it represents messages sent or received by an object.

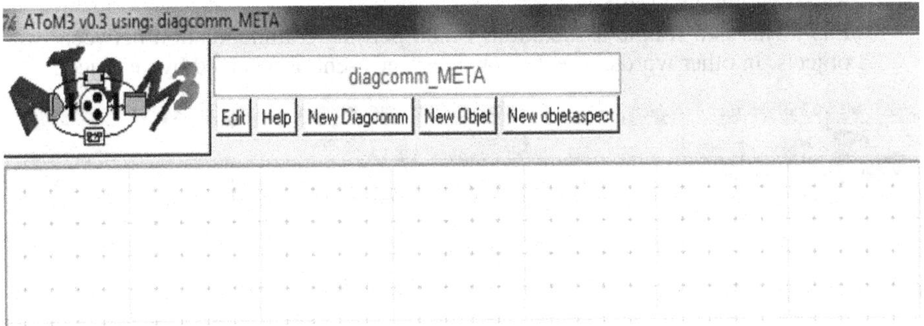

Fig. 4. We generate a tool for manipulating Communication diagrams as shown in this sample caption

4.2 The Meta-model of the Aspect Model

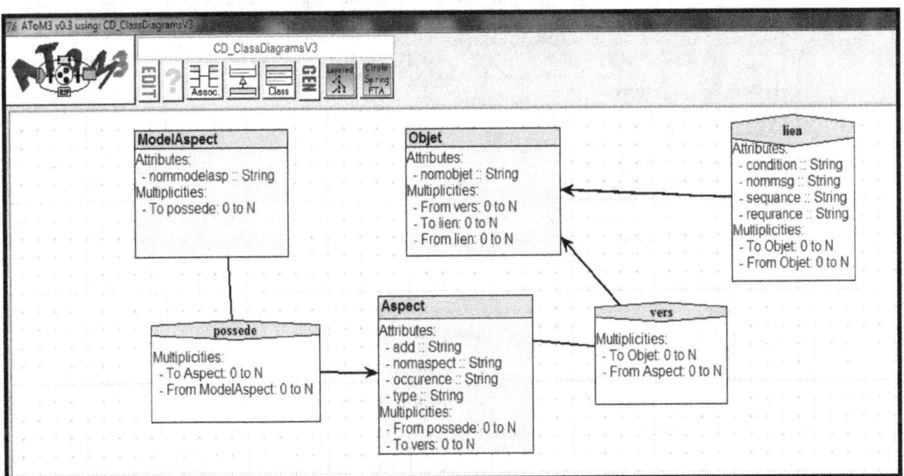

Fig. 5. Our meta-model of AM consists of three classes *(modelAspect, Aspect* and *objet)* and three associations *(possède, Vers* and *lien),* as shown in this sample caption

- *modelAspect*: this class include aspects with their activation points which maybe objects or links between two objects.
- *Aspect*: This class represents aspects according to the given syntax. Each aspect has a name, the activation point and the advice to insert it.
- *Objet*: This class represents objects. Each object has a name and can communicate through connectors.
- *Possède*: It is an association of composition, which connects the *modelAspect* with its *aspects*.
- *Vers*: It is a simple association, linking aspects with the objects on which an aspect should be inserted.
- *Lien*: This is a simple association, which permits communication between two objects. In other words, it represents messages sent or received by an object.

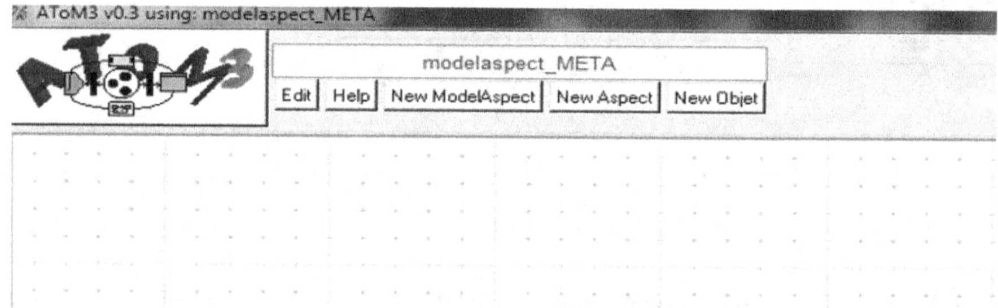

Fig. 6. We generate a tool for manipulating the aspect model as shown in this sample caption

4.3 Our Proposed Grammar

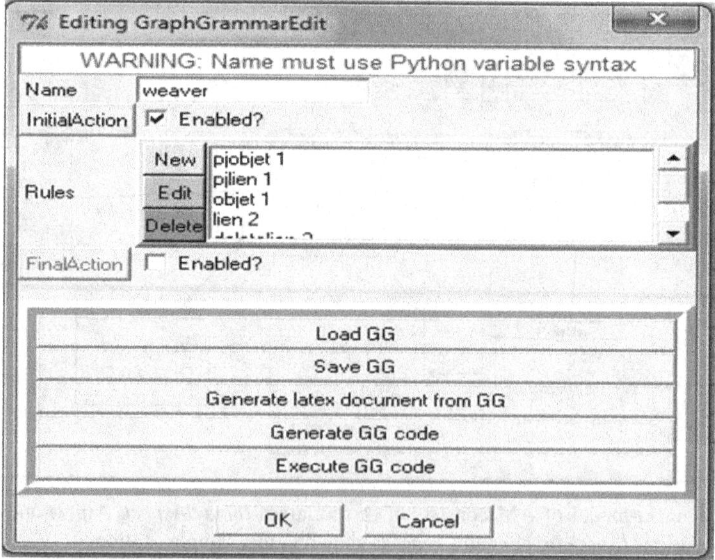

Fig. 7. We have proposed a graph grammar containing of six rules; each rule expresses a particular case, as shown in this sample caption.

Rule 1, 2 *(Resp priority 1, 2):*
These rules are applied to locate an aspect previously untreated (Visited = = 0), and create a linked object to another object or between two objects already communicating in that order.

According to the conditions as follows:

- Aspect.PJ == the name of the object or the link between two objects. To add aspects of type object.
- Aspect.AD== object added (aspect of type objet).
- Aspect. Type == 'create' to create the aspects of type object added.

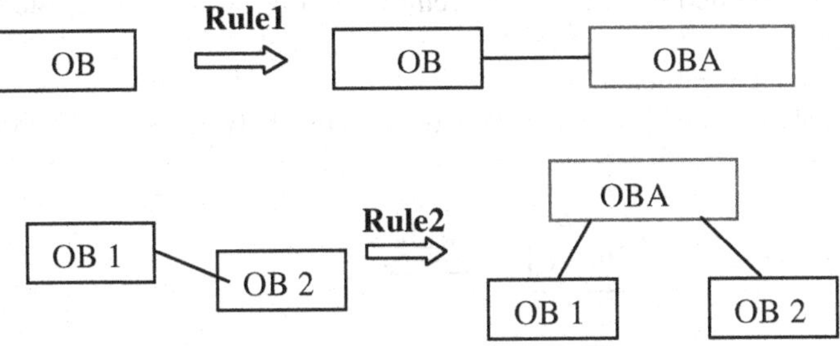

Fig. 8. Shows a simple example of applying the rules 1 and 2, as shown in this sample caption

Rule 3 *(priority 3)*:
This rule is applied to create and add a link connected two objects that do not communicate.
Depending to the condition

- Aspect.AD = = 'link'
- Aspect.Type = = 'create' or 'context); and to mark the aspect as visited.
- Aspect.PJ== the name of the object 1 (OB1) and the object 2 (OB2) which does not communicate.

Fig. 9. Show a simple example of application of the rules 3, as shown in this sample caption

Rule 4 *(Priority 4)*:

This rule is applied to address an aspect not previously visited, and add an object communicating between two other (this object is perfectly adequate to unbound objects).
Depending to the condition:
Aspect.AD = = 'object'
Aspect.Type = = 'create'); and to mark the aspect as visited.
Aspect.PJ== the name of the object 1 (OB1) and the object 2 (OB2) which does not communicate.

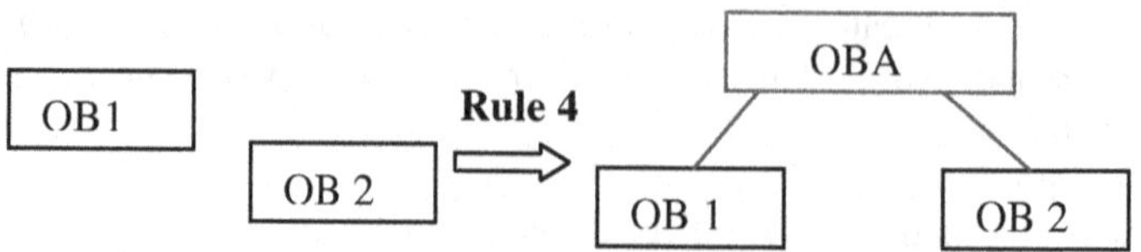

Fig. 10. show a simple example of application of the rules 4, as shown in this sample caption

Rule 5, 6 (*Resp priority 5, 6*):
These rules are applied respectively to remove an object or a link existed according to the condition:

- Aspect.type = = 'delete'.
- Aspect.PJ== object or the name of the link between the two objects to be deleted.

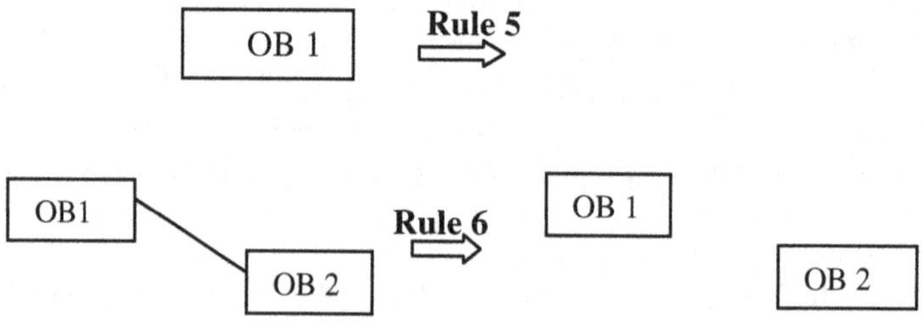

Fig. 11. Shows a simple example of applying the rules 5 and 6, as shown in this sample caption

Remarks:
OB1, OB2: Is objects.
OBA: Is aspect of type objet which should be inserted in BM.
Aspect.PJ: junction points of the aspect.
Aspect.AD: the advice of an aspect.
Aspect.Type: the action of the aspect is creation, deletion or the link between two objects

5 Case Study

To validate the effectiveness of our approach, we have applied to the behavior of an Internet network. Therefore, we have used a Communication diagram, where the objects represent the different machines (Mi) and links represent the communication between the machines (objects).

The Aspect Model represents five aspects (security on a machine, verification of the two machines communicated, adding an object of communication between two machines that do not communicate the addition of a communication link between two machines and the removal of an object in the network).

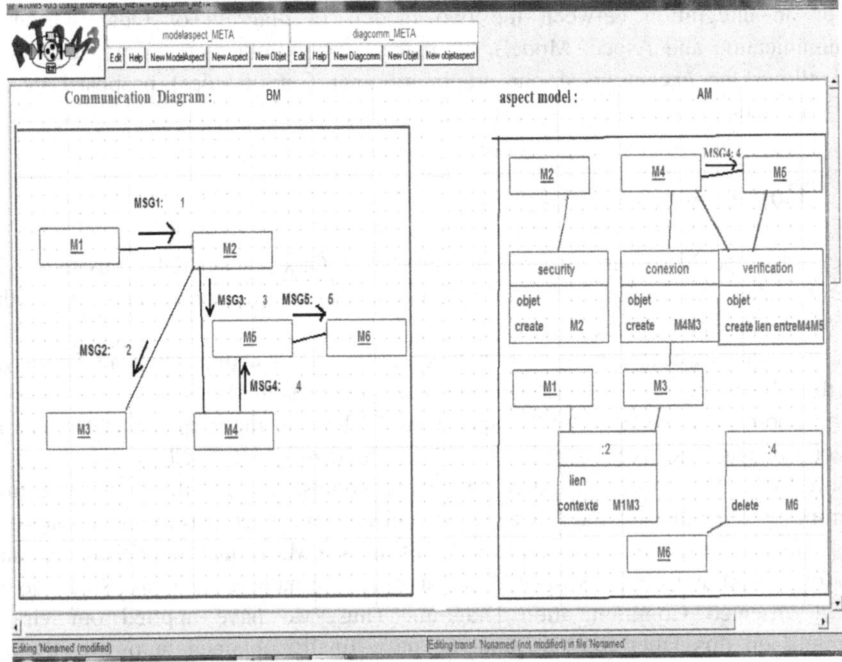

Fig. 12. Encompasses both models, as shown in this sample caption

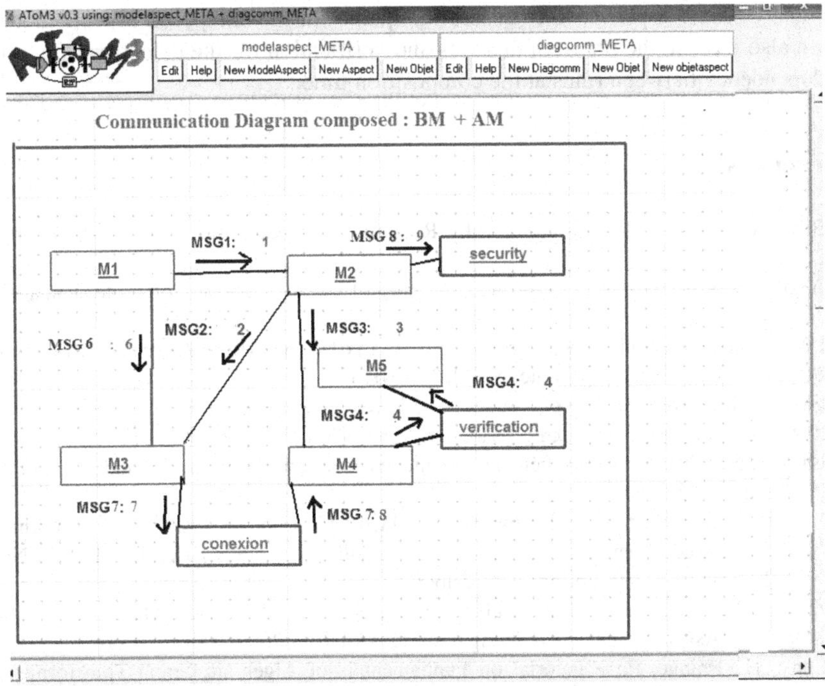

Fig. 13. Gives the result of the composition, as shown in this sample caption

For an integration between the two models (a diagram of Object-Oriented Communication and Aspect Model), we make a simple click on « Trans DCOA ». This allows the execution of our graph grammar (set of rules) proposed in the previous section.

6 Conclusion

Aspect-Oriented Modeling brings new concepts to Object Oriented. Thus there are several studies on the composition of aspect. The graph's transformation is one of the approaches of aspect's composition.

In this paper, we have proposed an approach provided with a new transformation tool that allows the translation of model objects to aspects models.

Our approach is inspired by the approach MATA and the graphs transformation. To achieve our objective, we have used the formalism of UML Class Diagram as a meta-formalism, we have proposed two meta-models, one for the communication diagram and the other for the aspect model and we have a set of rules constitutes our graph grammar. Our work was realized by using AToM3 (a meta-modeling tool and transformation) and for the validated of our work, we have done a case study on an Object Oriented Communication Diagram. Thus, we have applied our Graph Grammar on this latter diagram and we have finally obtained automatically the integrated model which is an Aspect Oriented Communication Diagram.

In future work, we plan to do the same transformation using standard tools like EMF and GMF. We plan also to ensure the quality of the composed aspects models; we can also include the phase of analysis and verification for the detection of conflict and dependency between rules at the composition time.

References

1. Biba, A., Grabherr, F., Larretche, E.L., Richard, Y.: Modélisation avec UML (February 2000)
2. AToM^3, web page, http://atom3.cs.mcgill.ca/ (consultations date: January 18, 2012)
3. UML Diagrams, web page, http://www.iict.ch/Tcom/Cours/OOP/Livre/UML14.pdf (consultations date: March 18, 2012)
4. EMF, GMF, web page, http://www.eclipse.org/gmf, http://www.eclipse.org/emf (consultation date: January 19, 2011)
5. Barbier, F.: UML et MDE Ingénierie des modèlesavec études de cas, Dunod, Paris (2005) ISBN 2 10 049526 7
6. Kiczales, G., Lamping, J., Mendhekar, A., Maeda, C., Lopes, C., Loingtier, J., Irwin, J.: Aspect Oriented Programming. In: Aksit, M., Auletta, V. (eds.) ECOOP 1997. LNCS, vol. 1241, pp. 231–250. Springer, Heidelberg (1997)
7. Zhang, G., Holzl, M.: HiLA: High-Level Aspects for UML State Machines. In: 14th Workshop. Aspect-Oriented Modeling (AOM@MoDELS 2009), Denver (2009)
8. Ehrig, H., Prange, P.: « Tutorial on Fundamentals of Algebraic Graph Transformation. Based on FAGT-Book, EATCS Monographs in TCS. Springer (July 15, 2006)

9. Whittle, J., Jayaraman, P., Elkhodary, A., Moreira, A., Araújo, J.: MATA: A Unified Approach for Composing UML Aspect Models Based on Graph Transformation. In: Katz, S., Ossher, H., France, R., Jézéquel, J.-M. (eds.) Transactions on AOSD VI. LNCS, vol. 5560, pp. 191–237. Springer, Heidelberg (2009)
10. Baresi, L., Heckel, R.: Tutorial Introduction to Graph Transformation: A Software Engineering Perspective
11. Fowler, M.: UML Distilled, brief guide to the standard Object Modeling Langauge, 3rd edn. (October 28, 2003) ISBN 0-321-19368-7
12. Manh, T.: Programmation Orientée Aspect dans Travail d'intérêt personnel (July 2005)
13. Berkane, M.L., Boufaida, M.: Un Modèle De Transformation De Design Pattern Vers Des Programme Orientés Aspects. CIIA (2009)
14. Machta, N., Bennani, M.T., Ben Ahmed, S.: Modélisation Orientée Aspects Des Systèmes Temps Réel. In: 8th International Conference of Modelisation and Simulation - MOSIM 2010, May10-12 (2010)
15. UML webpage, `http://laurent-audibert.developpez.com/Cours-UML/html/Cours-UML.html` (consultation date: June 16, 2011)
16. UML web page, `http://www.uml.org/` (consultation date: June 16, 2011)
17. Xavier, B., Isabelle, M., with the contribution of Cédric, B.: UML2 pour les développeurs. Cours avec exercices corrigés, Paris (2005) ISBN: 2-212-12029-X

Methodology and Experiments to Transform Heterogeneous Meta-program into Meta-meta-programs

Vytautas Štuikys and Kristina Bespalova

Program Software Department, Kaunas University of Technology, Studentų 50, 51368 Kaunas, Lithuania
vytautas.stuikys@ktu.lt, kristina.bespalova@stud.ktu.lt

Abstract. The paper analyzes transformation of a correct heterogeneous meta-program into 2-stage meta-programs. We propose a methodology and describe experiments to solve two tasks: 1) transformation of the 1-stage meta-program into the set of 2-stage meta-programs; 2) checking hypothesis of the transformation equivalence under given transformation rules and constraints. The experimental results have shown that introduced formalism, rules and models ensure correctness of transformations, extend reuse dimension to automatically adapt (through transformations) variants of programs/meta-programs to different contexts of use, enable to better understand meta-program development/change processes and heterogeneous meta-programming per se.

Keywords: meta-program, meta-parameter, meta-programming, multi-stage heterogeneous meta-program.

1 Introduction

A meta-program is a program generator that generates other programs or program parts [1]. Meta-programming is writing of meta-programs. We define meta-programming as an algorithmic manipulation of programs as data aiming to support generative reuse through generalization [2, 3]. The technique enables, at the construction time, to develop a more abstract executable specification (meta-program) from which programs are generated on demand automatically, at the use stage. Heterogeneous meta-programming is based on using at least two languages for the development of a meta-program. The language at a lower-level of abstraction, called target language, serves for expressing the concrete domain functionality. A target program written in the target language is used as data to perform manipulations at a higher-level of abstraction. The language at a higher-level of abstraction, called meta-language, serves for expressing generalization of a target program through transformations according to the pre-scribed requirements for change.

Meta-programming and the development of heterogeneous meta-programs can be dealt with and understood using two general engineering approaches: forward engineering and reverse engineering. The latter approach enables to re-factor a given heterogeneous meta-program and represent it as a k-stage meta-specification aiming

T. Skersys, R. Butleris, and R. Butkiene (Eds.): ICIST 2012, CCIS 319, pp. 210–225, 2012.

at developing meta-meta-programs or meta-generators. Such specifications as higher-level tools are needed to support the broader extent of generative reuse and managing complexity issues as it will be motivated in more details later. In this paper, we address the problem of forward and reverse transformations, i.e., the transformation of a given meta-program into 2-stage meta-programs (meta-meta-programs) and vice versa. We consider two tasks: 1) refactoring of a correct meta-program into the 2-stage one under given constraints and 2) checking hypothesis on the equivalence of the transformations under certain constraints.

We present a methodology and results of dealing with the tasks aiming to test them on simple target languages (*L*-systems, Test frames, etc.) in order we could be able to apply the transformation findings for the real world components (e.g., generative learning objects, web-based meta-components, etc.) on the well-grounded basis later.

The main findings of the paper are as follows: 1) If all meta-parameters are independent (they value are independent) within the parameter space S with n parameters, then any combination of meta-parameters sets consisting of 1 to n-1 parameters can appear at any stage of 2-stage meta-program without violence of the functionality. 2) If two parameters are dependable they should appear at the same stage in order to preserve the same functionality when 1-stage program is transformed into a 2-stage meta-program.

The paper is organized as follows. Section 2 analyzes the related work. Section 3 introduces the concept of multi-stage meta-programming, some formalism and defines the basic terms and rules and formulates the tasks. Section 4 describes the proposed methodology, analyzes the selection of systems to provide experiments and results of experiments. Section 5 provides evaluation of the approach and conclusions.

2 Related Work

Manipulation of the program source code is one of the main aspects of any software development process. As the size and complexity of software is growing continuously, the manual manipulation becomes ever more infeasible. Meta-programming is a higher-level programming paradigm which deals of how manipulating programs as data. The result of the manipulation is the lower-level program. According to Veldhuizen [2], meta-programming can be seen as a program generalization and generation technique. One can learn more about the topic from taxonomies of meta-programming-based concepts. We have found three taxonomies of meta-programming concepts: [3], [4] and [5]. For example, Sheard [4] reviews and summarizes the accomplishments and research challenges in describing formal meta-programming systems.

As it is defined by taxonomies, there are two kinds of meta-programming: homogeneous and heterogeneous. Homogeneous meta-programming – meta-language and domain language are the same languages [4]. Heterogeneous meta-programming – the ones are actually different languages, a target program are written in different languages and has to be interpreted in different environments. The first language is a meta-language. The second one is a domain language. Usually we can use any programming language satisfying a set of minimal requirements in the role of a meta-language (has abstractions for output, looping, etc.) [6]. However, the application domain and designer's flavour are the most decisive attributes for selecting the languages.

Though meta-programming was known and used for a long time in formal logic programming [5], now, however, the scope of the application of the meta-programming techniques is much wider. These include the domains such as programming language implementation [7], including parser and compiler generation [8], application and software generators [9], product lines, program transformations [10], generative reuse, XML-based web applications and web component deployment [11]. Many, if not all of the presented cases, can be summarized as multi-stage programming, i.e., the development of programs in several different stages.

We accept that the term "model transformation" encompasses the term "program transformation" since a model can range from the abstract analysis models, over more concrete design models, to very concrete models of the source code [12]. Program transformation is a wide topic having applications in many areas of software engineering. Formal and semi-formal description of meta-programs, meta-programming and related higher-level programming methodologies and transformations for implementing higher-level programs has been intensively studied by many researchers. Taha was the first to provide a formal description for a multi-stage programming language [13]. The concept is related to the fundamental principle of information hiding through the introduction of a set of abstraction levels (stages) in order to gain a great deal of flexibility in managing the program construction process. This theory can be used to prove equivalency between two staged programs, or between a target program and its staged program or meta-program. Cordy and Sarkar [14] demonstrated that meta-programs can be derived from higher level specifications using second order source transformations. Trujillo, Azanza and Díaz [15] describe ideas to generate meta-programs from abstract specifications of synthesis paths. The execution of such a meta-program code synthesizes a target program of a product line.

Meta-programs as the development artefact can be obtained through forward engineering when meta-programs are developed in a top-down approach from high-level models such as feature models. In this paper, we apply the reverse transformation approach to transform a correct meta-program into its 2-stage representation.

3 Background of the Approach

First, we motivate the need of 2-stage meta-programs (Section 3.1). Next, we explain the concept of a 2-stage meta-program using a simple motivating example (Section 3.2), introduce some formalism and define the basic terms (sub-section 3.3) to understand the approach. Finally, we formulate the tasks considered (sub-section 3.4) and present transformation rules (sub-section 3.5).

3.1 Motivation of the Approach

The main reason of using 2-stage meta-programs is the growth of system complexity. At the domain modelling level, this growth can be observed through the ever-increasing variability to express features of functional, non-functional requirements, context modelling, etc. For example, in e-learning domain content can be represented as generative learning objects (GLOs) [16, 17]. In terms of using meta-programming as a generative technology they can be seen as meta-programs. GLOs have to express not only similar (or related) content variants, but also to represent social variability (students' abilities, age, gender dimension, etc.), environmental variability (to adapt teaching content to various technologies such as learning robots, mobile devices, etc.), and different pedagogical models. Expressing such variability as a 1-stage meta-program may lead to the excessive complexity of the meta-program per se. Managing the over-generalization issues to represent variability though staging the meta-program's structure is a relevant solution because users (teachers) are able to adapt the content variants to different context of use.

The other example of the real application is the development of web-based components [18, 19], where the need for variability modelling and representing it at the higher abstraction level is also a pre-dominant requirement. Evolution of external libraries and the library scaling problem [20] require more and more generators and meta-generators. Finally, examples described in Section 4.1 show the relevance of using higher-level meta-programs. As, in general, the understanding of meta-programs and meta-meta-programs is not an easy task, we present two simple motivating examples below.

3.2 Motivating Examples

Fig. 1 illustrates a simple 1-stage meta-program (or simply meta-program). Here, (a) represents meta-interface of the heterogeneous meta-program and (b) represents meta-body in the dedicated meta-language. This meta-specification specifies the generation of all possible bit strings of length 2. As parameter *p*1 and *p*2 each has two independent values, it is possible to generate 4 different bit strings of length 2 (see Fig. 1 (c)).

```
$
"Enter the value of the 1st bit" {0,1}  p1:=0;
"Enter the value of the 2nd bit" {0,1}  p2:=0;     (a)
$

@sub[p1]@sub[p2]                                   (b)

00 01 10 11                                        (c)
```

Fig. 1. Illustrative example of simple 1-stage meta-program: (a) – meta-interface, (b) – meta-body; (c) – results of generation for all possible parameter values (@sub – means substitution)

Fig. 2 illustrates the 2-stage meta-program of the same functionality as the one given in Fig. 1. The 2-stage specification has the different structure: its meta-interface consists of two stages (a) and processes within the meta-body stages (when the specification is executed) are managed by the label "\". Note that the label before the function (\@sub[*p*2]) de-activates the function during execution of the 2-stage meta-body. After the execution the label is deleted. As a result, the execution of the meta-body produces a 1-stage meta-program (see Fig. 2 (b)).

```
$
"Enter the value of the 1st bit" {0,1} p1:=0;
$
$
"Enter the value of the 2nd bit"{0,1} p2:=0;
$                                                         (a)
@sub[p1]\@sub[p2]
--------------------------------------------
$
"Enter the value of the 2nd bit"{0,1} p2:=0;
$
0@sub[p2]                                                 (b)
1@sub[p2]
-------------------------------------------
00 01
10 11                                                     (c)
```

Fig. 2. (a) – 2-stage meta-program, (b) – result after execution of specification (a), when p1= 0 and 1; (c) – result of execution (b), when p2= 0 and 1

One can learn more details on multi-stage meta-programs from definitions and models given below.

3.3 Nomenclature and Definition of Basic Terms

M^1 – 1-stage meta-program, M^2 – 2-stage meta-program;

$\mu(M_I^1)$ – models of meta-interface, meta-body;

S – the full space of meta-parameters including parameter names and their values;

P – a set of parameters, p_i – the parameter name (identifier), V^i – a set of values of the parameter p_i, $v_{j_0}^i$ – is an initial or default parameter value;

$\mu(B^1)$ – 1-stage a meta-body model, $\mu(B^2)$ – 2-stage a meta-body model;

all R – a full set of target program (instances) derived from M^1;

M_t^2 – a set of 2-stage meta-programs derived from M^2;

$M^1_{s_i}$ – a set of 1-stage meta-program derived from the set M^2_i ; s_i – the number of M^1;

$R(i,s_i,l)$ – a set of target programs derived from $M^1_{s_i}$ which is derived from M^2_i ;

L_M , L_T – a formal notation of meta-language and target language, respectively.

DEFINITION 1. Heterogeneous meta-program model is the structure that consists of the meta-interface model and the meta-body model (see Fig. 1 (a) and 3(a)).

DEFINITION 2. Formally, meta-interface model of a given meta-program M^1 is a n-dimensional (meta-) parameter space $S(S \in M^1)$: $\mu(M^1_l) = S$, where $S = (S_1, S_2, ..., S_n)$, $S_i = (p_i, V^i)$, $S_i \subset S, where\ i \in [1;n]$, $\bigcup p_i = P,\ |P| = n$, $V^i = (v^i_1, v^i_2, .., v^i_{k_i})$, where n - the number of parameters; p_i – the parameter name; P – a set of parameters; V^i – a set of values of the parameter p_i and $v^i_{j_0} \in V^i, (1 \le j_0 \le k_i)$ is an initial or default parameter value (see Fig. 2 (a)).

DEFINITION 3. Meta-body model is a set of meta-constructs expressing manipulations on meta-parameters and target program fragments.

DEFINITION 4. Structurally, heterogeneous meta-program is the two-language specification in which the meta-interface model is coded using a meta-language to specify meta-parameters and the meta-body model is coded using the meta-language to specify modifications on the target program expressed by a target language.

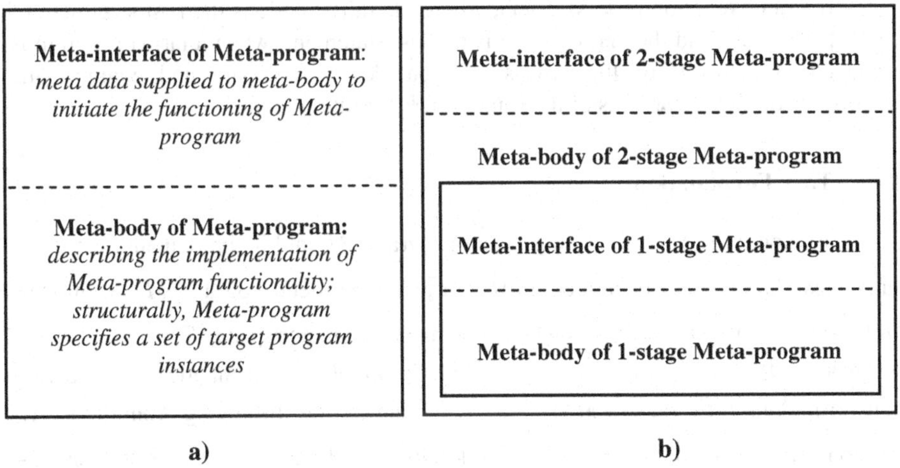

Fig. 3. Structural model of 1-stage (a) and 2-stage meta-programs (b)

DEFINITION 5. Functionality of a heterogeneous meta-program is defined through its execution process. When executed, meta-program produces a set of target programs, each dependent upon the pre-specified meta-parameter values.

DEFINITION 6. Heterogeneous meta-program is the 1-stage meta-program. 2-stage meta-program is the specification the meta-interface and meta-body of which is arranged as 2-stage structures according to pre-defined RULES 1 and 2.

DEFINITION 7. Two 2-stage meta-programs defined on the same meta-parameter space S are equivalent if they produce the equivalent set of 1-stage meta-programs.

DEFINITION 8. Two 1-stage meta-programs derived from the 2-stage meta-program, which is defined on the same meta-parameter space S , are equivalent if they produce the same set of target programs.

DEFINITION 9. Transformation of M^1 into M_i^2 ($M^1 \xrightarrow{T} M_i^2$) is a process of refactoring the meta-program M^1 so that the model $\mu(M^1)$ is transformed into the model $\mu(M^2)$ and the meta-body model $\mu(B^1)$ is transformed into $\mu(B^2)$.

DEFINITION 10. Transform T_i is a result of the transformation process ($M^1 \xrightarrow{T} M_i^2$).

DEFINITION 11. Cyclomatic Index (CI) of a meta-program is the total number of programs that can be derived from the meta-program via the generation process. Cyclomatic Index (CI) of a meta-meta-program is the total number of different meta-programs that can be derived from the meta-meta-program via the one-stage Forward Transformation process.

Formally, CI is computed by enumerating all possible different paths within the meta-program execution process graph, where the initial node is the first statement of the meta-program and the ending node is the last statement, when a target program is produced as a result of the process. CI enables to compare and evaluate the complexity of meta-programs of the same or related functionality.

3.4 Task Formulation

Given: a) model $\mu(M^1)$ of a 1-stage meta-program M^1 and its implementation using languages L_M and L_T; b) model $\mu(M^2)$ of a 2-stage meta-program M^2; c) models $\mu(M^1)$ and $\mu(M^2)$ are defined on the same meta-parameter space S.

Task 1 is to specify all possible semantic preserving transformations $T_i : \forall_i (M^1 \xrightarrow{T} M_i^2)$, $i \in [1, t]$ under the following conditions: (i) M_i^2 conforms the model $\mu(M_i^2)$, (ii) $|T_i| = 2n-2$ (all parameter are orthogonal; n – the number of parameters), (iii) $|T_i| < 2n-2$ (some parameters are dependable).

Pre-conditions. Let E_1 and E_2 be Boolean variables ($E_1, E_2 = \{true, false\}$) indicating a status of transformations in terms of DEFINITIONS 7 and 8, respectively.

Task 2 is to check the hypothesis of transformation equivalence, that is, $E= E_1 \wedge E_2=\{true\}$ under constraints imposed by RULES 4 and 5 (see Section 3.5).

3.5 Transformation Rules

RULE 1. This rule defines the structure of the 2-stage specification. The role of 2-stage specification is to specify the generation process of 1-stage meta-programs. The 2-stage meta-interface of the specification consists of two separable interfaces: 2-stage and 1-stage. Structurally, the 1-stage meta-interface is a part of the whole 2-stage meta-body (see Fig. 3). Meta-functions within the 2-stage meta-body are either active or passive (e.g., having the label "\" before the beginning of a function meaning a de-activating sign).

RULE 2. The 2-stage meta-specification is executed in two stages. The 2-stage is executed first. The process starts with the initiation of meta-parameters values of this stage. Then meta-body of this stage is executed, i.e., all active meta-functions are executed with respect to pre-specified parameter values; all passive meta-functions are activated by removing the label "\". As a result, a 1-stage meta-program that corresponds to the specified meta-parameter values at the 2-stage meta-interface is generated. The process can be repeated from the beginning by specifying the other meta-parameter values. As a result, the other 1-stage meta-program is generated.

RULE 3. If all meta-parameters are independent, then any combination of meta-parameters can be lifted from stage 1 to stage 2 and evaluated at this stage, when M^1 is transformed into M^2.

RULE 4. If there are dependent parameters but they have not the priority relation, then those parameters must appear at the same stage, either 1 or 2, when M^1 is transformed into M^2.

RULE 5. If there is a priority relation among two parameters, then parameters with the higher priority must appear at the stage 2, when M^1 is transformed into M^2.

4 Description of Proposed Methodology

We describe the proposed methodology, which is based on results of Section 3, in Sections 4.1 - 4.3. In Section 4.1, we analyze the selection of domain tasks or systems to provide experiments. In Section 4.2, we formalize the transformation/generation processes to tackle task 1 and task 2. In Section 4.3, we present results of experiments to tackle the tasks.

4.1 Selection of Domain Tasks

As it follows from definitions and motivation the main focus is to be given to meta-program complexity which is measured by the number of different target programs derived from the meta-program. Since this number may be significant (measured in thousands and more), the target program should be as simple as possible. We have selected three systems as a target programs: 1) Abstract string generation from alphabet such as {0, 1} or (a, B) of the pre-defined length such as 0001, 11100 or aB, aaBB; aaaBBBaaa, etc. 2) *L*-system generation; 3) Test frame generation. Though these cases have some conceptual similarity, they differ in semantics and possible applications as follows.

L-systems are a mathematical formalism proposed by the biologist Lindenmayer in 1968 as a foundation for an axiomatic theory of biological development to describe and generate branching structures or geometric objects that exhibit self-similarity [21, 22]. Such structures may be 2D, 3D. *L*-systems are frequently used to generate computer graphic renderings of trees, bushes, grasses, and other plant life. *L*-systems can also be used in the exploration of fractals.

Formally, *L*-systems are a string-rewriting grammar expressed as an ordered triplet (U, ω, H), where: U – alphabet, i.e., a set of symbols (variables) that can be replaced by other symbols; ω – start symbol, also called axiom or initiator, defining the initial state of the system ($\omega \in U$); H – set of production rules defining the way variables can be replaced by a combination of other variables iteratively ($H \subset U \times U^*$).

Example 1. In this illustrative example, parameters are as follows: A, B – variables; A – start symbol; (A → AB), (B → A) – production rules. When applied iteratively (*n* is the number of iterations), production rules produce the following sequences:

n = 0 : A
n = 1 : AB
n = 2 : ABA
n = 3 : ABAAB
n = 4 : ABAABABA
n = 5 : ABAABABAABAAB
n = 6 : ABAABABAABAABABAABABA

Test frame [23] is a set of bit stings composed of symbols from the alphabet {0, 1, X}. The Test frame is used to specify tests for digital circuits compactly. Symbols 'X' within a bit string mean the unknown (unspecified) bit values which are not important in a given context. The following parameters (width, length, the number of unspecified bits and their position within the string) specify the Test frame. Illustrative Example 2 with parameter values (width = 5, length = 8 and number of unspecified bits = 2, position of the bits = (3, 4)) enables to cut the test length from 32 to 8.

Example 2 (Test frame): 00xx0 01xx0 10xx0 11xx0 00xx1 01xx1 10xx1 11xx1

In general, parameters of a *test frame* are highly dependent [23].

The relevance of the cases to our goals is due to:

1. All selected systems are simple enough and can be treated as simple target programs; thus, the use of them simplifies experiments substantially.

2. All selected systems have many parameter values meaning that they can be applied to different contexts of possible applications (e.g., for systems 2 and 3);

3. The use of 2-stage meta-program enables to manage over-generalization of 1-stage meta-programs flexibly.

4. Analysis of system 2 and 3 enables to identify a semantic dependency among some parameter groups and identify the priority condition (parameters with higher priority must be lifted and evaluated at the second, i.e., at the higher stage), which is important to construct 2-stage meta-programs through transformations. In system 2, for example, evaluation of the length parameter has a higher priority then the evaluation of the position for unspecified bits.

5. Simplicity enables to tackle the equivalence checking problem (task 2) more effectively.

6. The relevant use cases to provide experiments enable the use of two different meta-languages (dedicated meta-language and PHP) and identification of some restrictions of the first.

4.2 Formal Description of Processes to Tackle Task 1 and Task 2

As it was assumed previously (Section 3.4), the development of 1-stage meta-programs is not considered in this paper. We accept that the 1-stage meta-program

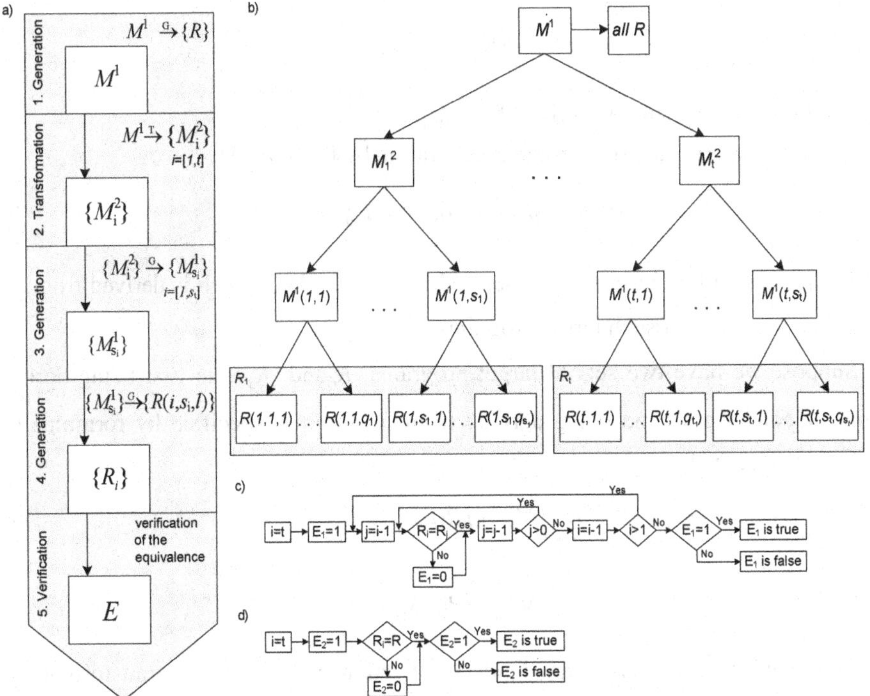

Fig. 4. Transformation/generation processes (a), the produced items (b) and algorithm for checking equivalence of transformations (c) and (d) according to conditions (6) and (7)

M^1 is given and that it is correct. It treats as input data to initiate and describe the processes within the methodology. Here, we use the term *methodology* as a coherent set of methods (procedures) [24]. Fig. 4(a) shows overall processes of the methodology. There are 5 processes. Informally, processes should be understood as follows: $\xrightarrow{G}$ -- means generation of target programs from a meta-program, or meta-programs from 2-stage meta-program; $\xrightarrow{T}$ -- means transformation from 1-stage meta-program to 2-stage meta-programs. Fig. 4(b) illustrates results produced by the processes in more detail.

All domain programs (denoted as a set R) are derived from M^1 as a result of process 1. The set is needed to check hypothesis on transformation equivalence (task 2). To solve task 1, we apply transformation rules (Section 3.5) and perform transformation of the given specification M^1 into a set of specifications M^2 manually (process 2) as it follows from formula (1).

$$M^1 \xrightarrow{T} \{M_i^2\} \quad i = [1, t], \tag{1}$$

(t – number of M^2 subsets).

Using M_i^2 as inputs, we first generate all permissible 1-stage meta-programs according to formula (2):

$$\forall_i M_i^2 \xrightarrow{G} \{M_{s_i}^1\} \quad i = [1, s_t], \tag{2}$$

(s_t – number of M^1 subsets derived from M_i^2).

Next, we describe a target program generation by formula (3):

$$\forall_t M_{s_t}^1 \xrightarrow{G} \{R(i, s_i, l)\}, \quad l = [1, q_{s_t}], \tag{3}$$

$R(i, s_i, l)$ – a set of target programs derived from s_i-th M^1 which is derived from i-th M^2; q_{s_t} – number of such target programs.

Suppose we have two sets of target programs R_i and R_j, the first being derived from M_i^2 and the second being derived from M_j^2 as it is specified by formulae (4) and (5), respectively:

$$R_i = \forall_{s_i, l} \bigcup R(i, s_i, l) \tag{4}$$

$$R_j = \forall_{s_i, l} \bigcup R(j, s_i, l) \tag{5}$$

Let pre-conditions of task 2 are held (see Section 3.4). Then the transformations, when the two 2-stage meta-programs M_i^2 and M_j^2 are derived from the same meta-program M^1 under constraints imposed by RULES 4-5, the condition to checking equivalence is given by formula (6):

$$E_1 = \{true\}, \textit{iff } \forall_{i,j}(R_i = R_j) \text{ ; otherwise } E_1 = \{false\}(i, j \in [1,t]) \quad (6)$$

Let pre-conditions of task 2 are held. The equivalence condition of transformations, when the two 1-stage meta-programs M_i^1 and M_j^1 are derived from the same meta-meta-program M_j^2, and then, R_i (R_j) are derived from M_i^1 (M_j^1), is given by formula (7):

$$E_2 = \{true\}, \textit{iff } \exists_i(R_i = R) \text{ ; otherwise } E_2 = \{false\} \quad (7)$$

Fig. 4(c) and (d) present algorithms to checking the equivalence conditions: $E = E_1 \wedge E_2 = \{true\}$, if (6) and (7) are held.

4.3 Experimental Results of Solving Task 1 and Task 2

The test samples for experiments were selected with regard to results of sub-section 4.1. They have ensured a great deal of flexibility due to conciseness of target programs generated from meta-programs (M^1) or meta-meta-programs (M^2). Two meta-languages were used to specify M^1 and M^2: dedicated and PHP in the role of meta-language. The first gave more concise specifications (Table 1). Results of experiments given in Tables 2-5 have proven the validity of the hypothesis on the transformation equivalence under indicated constraints (Rules 3-5, see sub-section 3.5). It was identified that designer has some choice to identify some varying parameters for the same sample. For example, Test frame 1 had dependent parameters, whereas Test frame 2 had parameters with priorities.

Table 1. Characteristics of 1-stage meta-programs M^1

S #	Name of MP	Dependent meta-parameters (Yes/No)	# of meta-parameters	# of values for each parameter	# of generated instances	Meta-language and (# of CL)
1	Abstract string	No	5	17 (5,4,4,4,4)	1280	Dedicated (8)
2	*L*-system	No	4	13 (5,4,4,4)	320	PHP (52)
3	Test frame 1	Yes	7	14 (2,2,2,2,2, 2-calculated)	32	PHP (86)
4	Test frame 2	Yes	5	21(4,4,4,3,6)	56	PHP (82)

Table 2. Characteristics of 2-stage Abstract string meta-programs and verifying equivalence of transformation

Total # M^2 derived from M^1	# of meta-parameters of M^2	# of generated M^1 from M^2	# of generated instances from M^1	# of tested cases (E)
30	5 cases of M^2 with 1 MP at 2-stage	4 cases of M^2 each giving 4 M^1	320 instances from each M^1	435 (E={*true*})
		1 case of M^2 each giving 5 M^1	256 instances from each M^1	
	10 cases of M^2 with 2 MP at 2-stage	6 cases of M^2 each giving 16 M^1	80 instances from each M^1	
		4 cases of M^2 each giving 20 M^1	64 instances from each M^1	
	10 cases of M^2 with 3 MP at 2-stage	4 cases of M^2 each giving 64 M^1	20 instances from each M^1	
		6 cases of M^2 each giving 80 M^1	16 instances from each M^1	
	5 cases of M^2 with 4 MP at 2-stage	1 case of M^2 each giving 256 M^1	5 instances from each M^1	
		4 cases of M^2 each giving 320 M^1	4 instances from each M^1	
Total:		30 cases – 2469	30 cases – 38400	

Table 3. Characteristics of 2-stage *L*-system meta-programs and verifying equivalence of transformation

Total # M^2 derived from M^1	# of meta-parameters of M^2	# of generated M^1 from M^2	# of generated instances from M^1	# of tested cases (E)
7	3 cases of M^2 with 1 MP at 2-stage	2 cases of M^2 each giving 4 M^1	80 instances from each M^1	21 (E={*true*})
		1 case of M^2 each giving 5 M^1	64 instances from each M^1	
	3 cases of M^2 with 2 MP at 2-stage	1 case of M^2 each giving 16 M^1	20 instances from each M^1	
		2 cases of M^2 each giving 20 M^1	16 instances from each M^1	
	1 case of M^2 with 3 MP at 2-stage	1 case of M^2 each giving 80 M^1	4 instances from each M^1	
Total:		7 cases – 149	7 cases – 2240	

Table 4. Characteristics of 2-stage Test frame 1 meta-programs and verifying equivalence of transformation

Total # M^2 derived from M^1	# of meta-parameters of M^2	# of generated M^1 from M^2	# of generated instances from M^1	# of tested cases (E)
30	5 cases of M^2 with 1 MP at 2-stage	5 cases of M^2 each giving 2 M^1	16 instances from each M^1	435 (E={*true*})
	10 cases of M^2 with 2 MP at 2-stage	10 case of M^2 each giving 4 M^1	8 instances from each M^1	
	10 cases of M^2 with 3 MP at 2-stage	10 case of M^2 each giving 8 M^1	4 instances from each M^1	
	5 cases of M^2 with 4 MP at 2-stage	5 cases of M^2 each giving 16 M^1	2 instances from each M^1	
Total:		30 cases – 210	30 cases – 960	

Table 5. Characteristics of 2-stage Test frame 2 meta-programs and verifying equivalence of transformation

Total # M^2 derived from M^1	# of meta-parameters of M^2	# of generated M^1 from M^2	# of generated instances from M^1	# of tested cases (E)
2	1 case of M^2 with 3 MP at 2-stage	1 case of M^2 each giving 4 M^1	14 instances from each M^1	2 (E={*true*})
	1 case of M^2 with 2 MP at 2-stage	1 case of M^2 each giving 14 M^1	4 instances from each M^1	
Total:		2 cases – 18	2 cases – 112	

S – sample; MP – meta-program; E – Equivalence status; CL – Code lines of M^1; M^1 – 1-stage meta-program; M^2 – 2-stage meta-program.

5 Evaluation of the Approach and Conclusions

We have proposed a methodology and described the experiments to solve two tasks: 1) transformation of the 1-stage meta-program into the set of 2-stage meta-programs; 2) checking hypothesis of the transformation equivalence under given transformation rules and constraints. As the main focus was given to higher-level (meta-) programs and their transformations, we have selected the target programs as simple as possible. The representatives of such programs in our experiments were three types of target programs (Abstract strings, *L*-systems and Test frames). The following results were obtained in this research: 1) formalization of the transformation processes and tasks, 2) overall methodology to consider the processes and tasks, 3) experimental approval of the following statements A and B.

A. If all meta-parameters are independent (their values are independent) within the parameter space *S* containing *n* parameters, then any combination of meta-parameters sets consisting of parameters from 1 to n-1 can appear at any stage of the 2-stage meta-program without the violence of the functionality.

B. If two parameters are dependable, they should appear at the same stage in order to preserve the same functionality when 1-stage program is transformed into a 2-stage meta-program. These statements are treated as constraints to check conditions of the transformations equivalence. Having in mind the statements, meta-designer can select only one transformation, which is relevant to the aims of the design and the tasks dependent on the context of use.

It was also specified that there is no unique way to introduce a parameter space when designer try to generalize the design task for the same domain. In other words, there are many ways to transform a given domain into its abstract (semi-formal) representation by a meta-program. This depends on many factors (domain variability understanding by designer, his/her intention).

The introduced formalisms, rules and models enable (1) to define conditions to ensure correctness of the specified transformations, (2) to manage complexity in using heterogeneous meta-programs, (3) to extend the reuse dimension by flexible adaptation (through automatic generation) of the target program variants and meta-program variants for different contexts of use. Finally, the approach contributes to the better understanding of the meta-program development and change processes and creates some pre-conditions for automatic meta-program transformations.

References

1. Ortiz, A.: An introduction to metaprogramming. Linux Journal (158), 6 (2007)
2. Veldhuizen, T.L.: Tradeoffs in Metaprogramming. In: Proc. of ACM SIGPLAN Workshop on Partial Evaluation and Semantics-Based Program Manipulation, Charleston, SC, USA, pp. 150–159 (2006)
3. Damaševičius, R., Štuikys, V.: Taxonomy of the Fundamental Concepts of Metaprogramming. Information Technology and Control 37(2), 124–132 (2008)
4. Sheard, T.: Accomplishments and Research Challenges in Meta-programming. In: Taha, W. (ed.) SAIG 2001. LNCS, vol. 2196, pp. 2–44. Springer, Heidelberg (2001)
5. Pasalic, E.: The Role of Type Equality in Meta-Programming. PhD thesis, Oregon Health and Sciences University, OGI School of Science and Engineering (2004)
6. Štuikys, V., Damaševičius, R.: Metaprogramming Techniques for Designing Embedded Components for Ambient Intelligence. In: Basten, T., Geilen, M., de Groot, H. (eds.) Ambient Intelligence: Impact on Embedded System Design, pp. 229–250. Kluwer Academic Publishers (2003)
7. Batory, D., Dasari, S., Geraci, B., Singhal, V., Sirkin, M., Thomas, J.: Achieving Reuse with Software System Generators. IEEE Software, 89–94 (September 1995)
8. Terry, P.D.: Compilers and Compiler Generators: An Introduction with C++. International Thomson Computer Press (1997)
9. Batory, D.: Product-line architectures, Invited Presentation, Smalltalk and Java in Industry and Practical Training, Erfurt, Germany, pp. 1–12 (1998)
10. Ludwig, A., Heuzeroth, D.: Metaprogramming in the Large. In: Butler, G., Jarzabek, S. (eds.) GCSE 2000. LNCS, vol. 2177, pp. 178–187. Springer, Heidelberg (2001)

11. Löwe, W., Noga, M.: Metaprogramming Applied to Web Component Deployment. Electronic Notes in Theoretical Computer Science 65(4) (2002)
12. Mens, T., Czarnecki, K., Van Gorp, P.: A Taxonomy of Model Transformations. Electronic Notes in Theoretical Computer Science 152, 125–142 (2006)
13. Taha, W.: Multi-Stage Programming: Its Theory and Applications. PhD thesis, Oregon Graduate Institute of Science and Technology (1999)
14. Cordy, J.R., Sarkar, M.S.: Metaprogram Implementation by Second Order Source Transformation. Position paper at Software Transformation Systems Workshop at Generative Programming and Component Engineering Conference (GPCE 2004), Vancouver, Canada (October 2004)
15. Trujillo, S., Azanza, M., Díaz, O.: Generative Metaprogramming. In: Proc. of 6th Int. Conf. on Generative Programming and Component Eng. (GPCE 2007), October 1-3, pp. 105–114. Salzburg, Austria (2007)
16. Leeder, D., Boyle, T., Morales, R., Wharrad, H., Garrud, P.: To boldly GLO – towards the next generation of Learning Objects. In: Proceedings of World Conference on E-Learning in Corporate, Government, Healthcare, and Higher Education, pp. 28–33. AACE, Chesapeake (2004)
17. Boyle, T.: Layered learning design: Towards an integration of learning design and learning object perspectives. Computers & Education 54, 661–668 (2010)
18. Losh, E.: Assembly Lines: Web Generators as Hypertexts. In: Proc. of the 18th Conf. on Hypertext and Hypermedia, pp. 115–122. ACM Press, New York (2007)
19. Helman, T., Fertalj, K.: A Critique of Web Application Generators. In: Proc. of the 25th Int. Conf. on Information Technology Interfaces (ITI), pp. 639–644 (2003)
20. Biggerstaff, T.J.: The library scaling problem and the limits of concrete component reuse. In: Proceedings of the Third International Conference on Advances in Software Reusability, Rio de Janeiro, pp. 102–109 (1994)
21. Prusinkiewicz, P.: Graphical applications of L-systems. In: Proceedings of Graphics Interface 1986/Vision Interface 1986, pp. 247–253 (1986)
22. Jacob, C.: Modeling Growth with L-Systems & Mathematica. In: Mathematica in Education. TELOS Springer (1995)
23. Bareiša, E., Jusas, V., Motiejūnas, K., Šeinauskas, R.: Functional test generation remote tool. In: 8th Euromicro Conference on Digital System Design (DSD 2005), pp. 192–195 (2005)
24. Roget's 21st Century Thesaurus, 3rd edn. Source location: Philip Lief Group (2009), `http://thesaurus.com/browse/methodology` (accessed: June 26, 2012)

The Business Graph Protocol

Daniel Ritter

SAP AG, Technology Development – Process and Network Integration,
Dietmar-Hopp-Allee 16, 69190 Walldorf, Germany
daniel.ritter@sap.com
http://www.sap.com

Abstract. Business Network Management (BNM) provides companies with techniques for managing their trading partner networks by making (technical) integration, business and social aspects visible within a network view and set them into context to each other. Therefore it computationally links data into business and integration networks as well as computes semantic correlation between entities of both perspectives. The linked real-world data is then captured in a network-centric variant of Business Process Modeling Notation (BPMN), which we call Network Integration Model (NIM).

In this paper, we propose an approach, which features access to the complex inter-connected business and technical perspectives in NIM, called Business Graph Protocol. We define a powerful Resource Graph (RG), which is directly computed from the underlying domain model, e.g. NIM, and allows simple, uniform, but expressive queries and traversal on the linked data. Through embedded, ad-hoc querying techniques, entry points to the network are computed. We present an approach on applying state of the art RESTful WebServices to our domain and report on our experiences with it.

Keywords: Business Network, Graph Query and Traversal, Model-Driven Resource Identification, Network-centric BPMN, Resource Architectures.

1 Introduction

Enterprises are part of value chains consisting of business processes with intra and inter enterprise stakeholders. To remain competitive, enterprises need visibility into their business network and ideally into the relevant parts of partner and customer networks and their processes. However, currently the visibility often ends at the borders of systems or enterprises. Business Network Management (BNM) helps to overcome this situation and allows companies to get insight into their technical, social and business relations [21,22]. For instance, Fig. 1 shows participants in a sample business network.

The model to capture real-world entities constituting such a network, is based on a network-centric BPMN, called Network Integration Model (NIM) [19,20]. NIM covers all relevant aspects of BNM by extending BPMN [15] to the network

T. Skersys, R. Butleris, and R. Butkiene (Eds.): ICIST 2012, CCIS 319, pp. 226–240, 2012.

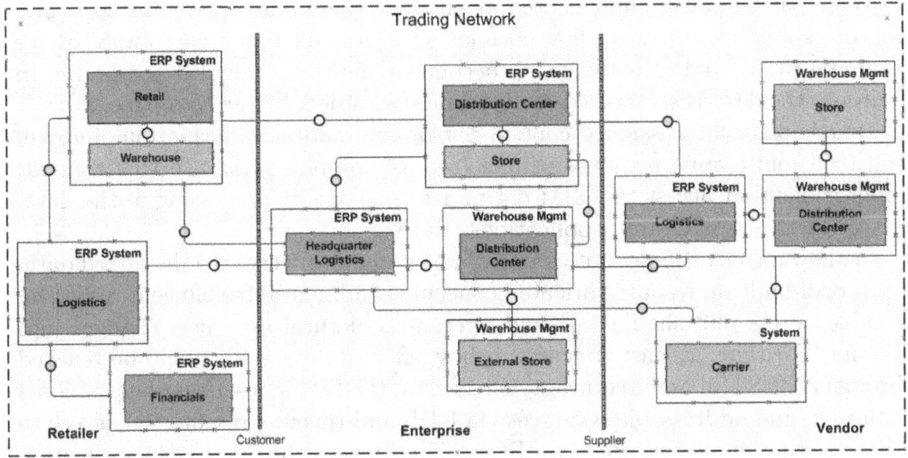

Fig. 1. Sample (cross-) enterprise Business Network showing business participants, denoted as nodes, and business document exchange as edges. Enterprises are characterised by their roles they play within a process.

domain. For that, a *Network* is derived from BPMN *ConversationDiagram* and consists of specializations of BPMN *Participant*, e.g. *BusinessParticipant* and *CommunicationParticipant*, as well as conversations that abstract BPMN *MessageFlow*, e.g. business or technical document flow between participants. Further entities might be named subsequently while defining our approach.

Our approach describes how the NIM logical graph can be automatically translated into a form that sufficiently fulfills all requirements for accessing the complete graph, called the Resource Graph (RG). We show how complex, multi-relational, hyper graph structures with nested object hierarchies or forests are represented in a uniform way using an efficient, standard and easy to use Business Graph Protocol (BGP). For larger networks, ad-hoc entry point computation is introduced to support contextualized traversal. This approach allows all applications interested in BNM data, i.e. Business Graph Applications (BGAs), to build both visualizations and scalable business applications based on NIM.

Section 2 describes the basic RG design principles, which is defined in section 3. Based on that, the Business Graph Protocol is introduced in section 4. Ad-hoc entry-point computation on the Resource Graph is defined in section 5. Related work is discussed in section 7. Section 8 concludes and outlines future work.

2 Design Principles

The Network Integration Model (NIM) is a representative example for data models that cover structurally and semantically complex, linked data describing real-world technical, business and social entities within a business network [19,20]. To capture the relevant aspects of these networks with different perspectives on the data, the single networks are semantically linked, e.g. a *Headquarter*

Logistics participant is implemented by an *ERP* system instance (see Fig. 1) and the corresponding document flow correlates e.g. to a mediated file to web service communication, and thus the graph becomes a multi-relational hyper graph. In addition, the data is structured as deeply nested object hierarchies (tree, forest), e.g. participant with assigned contact person and address information, and will lead to a multi-value response results (sets of complex data). In this context, applications that access the NIM data for visualizing or processing of the data, are called Business Graph Applications (BGA).

To allow a BGA simple, but comprehensive (remote) access to the linked data, a protocol built on resource oriented concepts shall guarantee efficient, uniform, scalable access and should take most recent structural and data changes into account. For that, at least concurrent, best effort data access should be reached through a RESTful architecture style based on HTTP [5], a schema-based model evolution, and addressable resources via URL and their representation as key to a Resource Oriented Architecture (ROA). That means the resource identification shall be derived from the schema of the domain model. The protocol leverages well-known technology to lower the learning curve and allow faster adoption. Resources should be expressed as hypermedia to enable the client to be the engine of application state. Changing domain model entities or data model structures shall not require any source code changes to the interface. Data should be added, changed, removed and queried in a uniform way. For efficient concurrent queries, the communication shall be stateless and the protocol shall allow to define precise and restrictive queries to avoid sending unnecessary data. For that a query and traversal algebra independent of the source model shall be defined, supported by necessary algorithms implemented within the protocol, e.g. graph traversal. Custom or computed entry points for traversal and queries and additional semantic relationships between entities shall be configurable.

3 The Resource Graph

For defining the Business Graph Protocol (BGP), the NIM [20], design principles and related prior art are taken into consideration. The NIM represents a graph of linked data, e.g. connecting participants of different specializations, such as social, business or technical, through message flows of different types. Additionally, there are a variety of supplementary entities, e.g. *Service*, *Group* or *BusinessTerm*. To create the resources in the graph, it is therefore essential to identify the resources in NIM. Subsequently the Resource Graph (RG), a resource representation of NIM, is introduced as foundation of the BGP.

3.1 Defining the Resource Graph

In an abstract view, the business network in the NIM can be seen as a set of participants connected to each other. This cannot be directly found in the actual data, but represents a logical graph. For instance, Fig. 3(a) shows two adjacent participants P_0 and P_1 implicitly through edge S_1, MF_1 and S_2, which represents a normalized, complex edge to the direct neighbor in NIM. The semantic *neighbor* relationship, described later, is depicted by dashed line. Now, a basic logical graph is shown in Fig. 2(a). The graph connects participants (P_0, ..., P_4) with each other. A more formal definition of the logical graph would is given by

$$G = (V, E),$$
$$\texttt{with } V = \{P_0, P_1, P_2, P_3, P_4\},$$
$$\texttt{and } E = \{\{P_0, P_4\}, \{P_0, P_2\},$$
$$\{P_4, P_2\}, \{P_2, P_1\}, \{P_2, P_3\}\}.$$

A simple way to translate such a logical graph into resources would be to take all participants in V and all edges in E and declare them resources. Both, nodes and edges, would know about each other and be addressable as resources. For example, Rexster [18] uses such a representation. Yet this approach is not sufficient to cover the requirements for a network integration model. For that, the logical graph is dissolved to form a suitable resource representation, the Resource Graph.

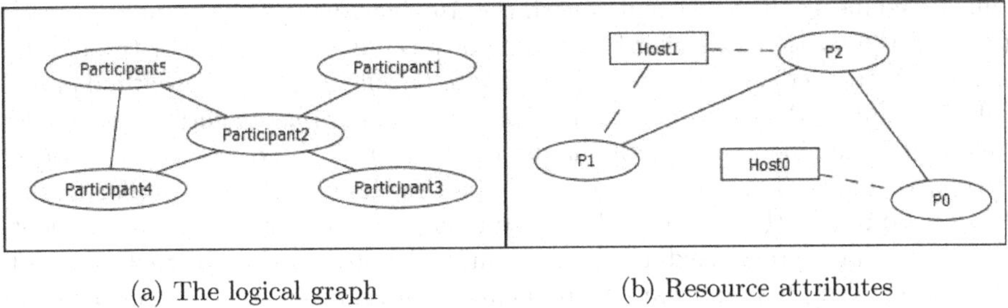

(a) The logical graph (b) Resource attributes

Fig. 2. Dissolving the logical graph

As first step, *attributes* are introduced to the logical graph. Every node in the Logical Graph has an associated set of key-value pairs, called attributes. For example *name*, *description* or *location*. Additionally, every node has the standard attributes *id* and *type*, which make them identifiable. The *type* is always in the most specific form. For instance, a *Participant* in the NIM resolves to *ApplicationParticipant* or *BusinessParticiantWithApplication*, which are specializations of *Participant*. All attributes are automatically identified from the NIM schema. New attributes are introduced into the model without a need for manual updates on the resource graph.

While attributes are a natural concept for nodes, they could not be applied directly to edges. The logical graph is an abstract concept, which means the edges between the nodes are only an abstract representation of a more complex matter. Hence, there is no generic way to find attributes in the NIM that could be applied to these abstract edges.

Another type of attribute can be found in sub-objects that specify participants. For instance, Fig. 2(b) shows a graph with the resource attribute *Host*. The so called *resource attributes* can be compared to 1:n relationships in relational databases. A *Participant* resource does have one host resource assigned for the *host* resource attribute, for example P_0 has $Host_0$, which can be resource attribute of many Participant resources, resp. Aligned with the resource graph, an object that acts as resource attribute can have type-specific normal attributes such as *technicalName*.

Introducing resource attributes leads to semantic differences for edges. While the edge between a *Participant* and a *Host* would be named *host* in accordance with the resource attribute name, the edges between participants could be named *neighbors*. From a data structure perspective, the edge *neighbors* between two participants is more complex than just a "line" between participants. Fig. 3(a) depicts an example of how a possible *neighbors* edge could look like on the underlying data structure of the NIM. This concept is called *connection*, which is indicated by a dotted line that represents the abstract *neighbors* edge, the one that has been drawn as the only edge connecting two participants.

However, there are also two "real" connections between P_0 and P_1. The first one is *MessageFlow* MF_0. Such a flow could be of different types, such as *P2PMessageFlow* or *BusinessFlow*. The second *connection* is more complex, because it connects the participants with the *MessageFlow* MF_1 through *Services* (S_0, S_1), the participants offer for sending or receiving messages. For transforming the abstract edges of the logical graph into resources there are two fundamental techniques: (a) to stay consistent with the logical graph, an entity *Edge* could be created that incorporates all the information of all the connections between two participants. This would allow to shape the Resource Graph similar to the Logical Graph or (b) to leave all entities along the connections as independent resources and therefore extend the Resource Graph, i.e. the abstract edges of the Logical Graph would have to be abandoned and have to be reconstructed manually. Since (b) does not contradict the requirement of generality, we decided to define all entities as independent resources in the Resource Graph. This leads to the final resource design depicted in Fig. 3(b). The resource attributes $Host_0$ and $Host_1$ are shown by connecting two resources through dashed lines. The straight lines are *connections* in the RG, which indicate that any two resources are adjacent to each other. They do not have any attributes attached to them and are stored in a *connection* list attribute on one or both resources they connect to.

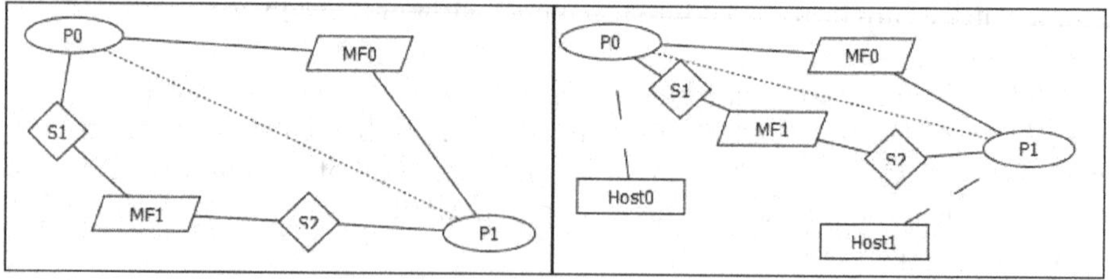

(a) The edges of logical graph dissolved (b) The final Resource Graph

Fig. 3. From logical graph to resource graph

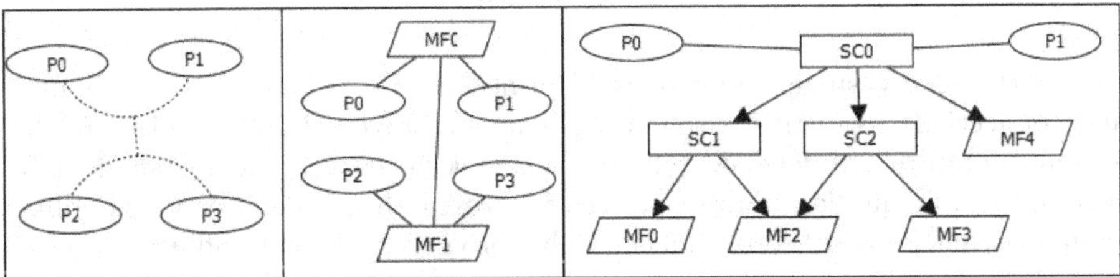

(a) The Logical Graph as a hyper graph (b) The tree structure in NIM

Fig. 4. More complex structures

The definition of the NIM allows to create perspectives for business and integration networks as well as semantic links between participants, and between flows, which builds a hyper graph structure on the logical graph as depicted in Fig. 4(a). However, when using independent resources and connections, the hyper graph can be transformed into a normal graph structure as part of the RG. The concept of *connections* can also be found in the Facebook Graph API [2]. However, it is neither based on a Logical Graph, nor can it handle multi-or hyper graph structures. Another complex construct within NIM are tree/ forest structures. For instance, *MessageFlows* between two participants are grouped by the *SubConversation*, which is also able to nest multiple *SubConversations*. All *MessageFlows* are part of at least one *SubConversation*. Fig. 4(b) shows a possible tree structure in the NIM. In the RG, tree structures are simply resolved as part of the graph. All resources in the tree structures have attributes such as *names*, resource attributes such as *parent* and connections such as *child*.

3.2 Extending the Resource Graph

The Resource Graph has the shortcoming that the information about the Logical Graph is lost. The *neighbor* connection is an abstract concept that is indirectly part of the Resource Graph and there is no direct information about the *MessageFlows* a *Participant* has. All these abstract edges would need manual information on the graph, that contradicts the design principles of the RG. Therefore, the RG allows to deploy custom rules called *shortcuts* while generating the RG from the schema, e.g. the *neighbor* connection. These entities are treated as normal *connections* that exist in NIM. Hence the RG with all resources will always be parsed completely. The shortcuts build a bridge between all the information explicitly contained in the Logical Graph and all the information explicitly contained in the RG. Shortcuts are considered custom, semantic links between entities.

For simplicity and better ease of use, the RG contains metadata associated to the entities, like information about primitive attributes, resource attributes and connections. That is similar to the Facebook API [2]. However for the RG, a semantic description for the entities is added.

3.3 Operations on the Resource Graph

In the RG, every single resource is identified by its unique URL, attributes and connections to further resources. For query, traversal and filtering on the graph, operators are defined. While this might be easy to do for small data sets and simple queries, it raises a need to provide functionalities for handling complex requests. Therefore, a formalized approach to traverse and filter the RG is developed as the concepts of *base identifiers*, *operators* and *attribute filters.*

Base identifiers are part of every query. A base identifier is either a single resource identified by its id, /*resource.id*/, or a set of resources that is predefined on the RG under a given set name, /:*setName*:/ , where $setName = \{resource_1, \ldots, resource_n\}$. Such a query returns all resources in the base identifier set in an abstract resource representation showing type and identifier attributes.

Besides the base identifiers, an unlimited amount of *operators* can be applied to them. Operators can be either connections or resource attributes. For example, an *ApplicationParticipant* has the operator *neighbors* and *host* that could be applied to it. Neighbors in this case is a (shortcut) connection, while host is a resource attribute to the *ApplicationParticipant.* This can be written as /:*setName*:/ `-> neighbors`. Before applying the first operator to the RG, a working set R_0 is created from the base identifier. This working set is then used with the first operator to form the second working set R_1, i.e. $R_0 = resource_1, \ldots, resource_n$, and $R_1 = neighbors(R_0)$. With the working set R_1, the next operator is used to form the next working set R_2. This would be written as

```
/:setName:/
-> neighbors
     -> host
```

and returns a working set R_2 with $R_2 = host(R_1)$.

After applying the operators to the base identifiers, the last part for a formalized query on the RG is to filter the result set. Filtering in this case means showing or not showing particular attributes on resources. Filters are applied as the last part of a query specified by the $\sim$ operator. A query could therefore look like this

$$
\begin{array}{l}
/{:}setName{:}/ \\
\texttt{->}\ operation_0 \\
\quad \sim filter_0 \\
\quad \sim filter_1.
\end{array}
$$

So far filters are defined for primitive attributes. resource attributes, connections and combination of these three. Two important filters are built-in: *deref*, shows all available attributes for all resources of result set R, and *meta*, shows the metadata for all resources in set R.

4 The Business Graph Protocol

The Business Graph Protocol (BGP) is defined as RESful style architecture on HTTP, that allows standard GET, POST, PUT and DELETE access to the resource graph. Accordingly, a base identifier query `/SYSTEM1/` would translate to `http://localhost/SYSTEM1/`. The result can be a standard HTTP response returning data containing a resource identifier, the self-url and type specific attributes and resource attributes. For operations on larger sets, base identifier sets are used as configurable entry-points for queries, like `/:ALLPARTICIPANTS:/`. That is a custom type and is defined to return a set of all specializations of type *Participant*.

Simple queries on the linked data graph start with the *search* keyword and concatenate *query*, for the search term, *type*, for the type of the resource,

```
http://localhost/search?query=term&type=Host&...
```

or *fields*, as field specific search criteria.

```
http://localhost/search?location=Sydney
```

In case of Friend of a Friend (FoaF) queries, like "get all hosts of my neighbors", simple operator graph traversal like

```
/SYSTEM1/
-> neighbors
   -> host
```

translates to `http://localhost/SYSTEM1/neighbors/host/` and results in the required information. The corresponding response, Fig. 5(a), shows the resources connected to *SYSTEM1* as neighbors along the traversal path, but not the resource *SYSTEM1* itself. Consequently *SYSTEM10* and *SYSTEM6* are returned according to the request with their basic attributes and their *Host* resource attribute identifiers. In the same way, the result set could be filtered to return only one attribute of the current base identifier, e.g. *location*, and the name of the resource attribute *host*. The corresponding statement

```
   /SYSTEM1/
      ~ meta
  ~ location
~ host.name
```

translates to

```
http://localhost/SYSTEM1/?show=meta,location,host.name.
```

The resulting response is shown in Fig. 5(b). In this example, the host name and location of the system are requested. The built-in *meta* operator returns all *connections* and field information for all (resource) attributes.

```
[
{"id": "SYSTEM10",
"url": http://localhost/SYSTEM10",
"type": "ApplicationParticipant",
"host":
   [
   {"id": "HOST0",
   "url": "http://localhost/HOST0",
   "type": "Host"
   }
   ]
},
{id: "SYSTEM6"
"url": "http://localhost/SYSTEM6",
"type": "ApplicationParticipant"
"host": [
   {"id": "HOST0"
   }
   ]
}
]
```


(a) FoaF traversal response


```
[{"id":"SYSTEM5",
"host":{"name":"DMU"},
"location":"Hampton",
"metadata":{
   "connections":{
      "neighbors":"no description yet",
      "service":"no description yet",
      "group":"no description yet",
      "flows":"no description yet"
      },
   "fields":{
      "location":{"type":"string",
         "desc":"The location of the Participant"},
      "description":{"type":"string",
         "desc":"A long description of the Participant"},
      "name":{"type":"string",
         "desc":"The name of the Participant"},
      "host":{"type":"resource",
         "desc":"The host of the Participant"}
   }
}]
```


(b) Resource filter response

Fig. 5. Sample Business Graph Protocol responses

In the same way, all modifying operations on the graph, can be performed by using basic HTTP POST, PUT or DELETE requests.

Although the usage of the BGP on the RG is uniform and easy to understand and use, the expressiveness and power of this approach become obvious, when performing more complex queries. For instance, let us consider a BGA that visualizes the complete business network as graph. It shows basic information on the participants within the network, and wants to keep the number of client-server roundtrips at a minimum. For that, there might be at least two ways of doing this with the BGP using entry points to the network: (a) define a custom search set `everything` that translates to `http://localhost/everything/` and returns resources in the graph or a more selective way (b) starting from a search set */:businessnetwork:/*,

```
/:businessnetwork:/
       -> neighbors
            -> host
             ~ name
     ~ description
             ~ type
```

which starts from all participants defined as part of the business network, then traverses all neighbors and returns attributes like *name*, *description* and *type* as well as these fields for resource attribute *host* wihtin one request.

5 Computing Entry-Points to the Network

When working with larger and more complex graphs, entry-points for queries and traversals become important. Entry-points are defined as subsets of a network, i.e. nodes, sharing a common characteristic. Since they might be determined during runtime in an ad-hoc, visual query way, the subsets are generated on-the-fly on the current state of the network. Hence entry-points are transient, ad-hoc, subsets of a network. For that, we introduce a concept called *clustering*, which we define as functional extension to the RG.

5.1 The Basic Clustering Functions

The first clustering function builds clusters based on attributes and resource attributes of a participant in the RG according to their values. For instance, the distribution centers (DC) from Fig. 1 might have a *location* attribute, which allows a grouping according to their geographic location. That means, an entry-point to all Lithuanian warehouses can be easily accessed via a location cluster over the DCs.

In contrast, the second clustering function exploits the structure of the RG. Instead of attribute values or other semantic meaning, the degrees of the nodes are considered. Thereby bridges are edges that keep two segments of a graph connected. Removing a bridge would create two separated segments that could be interpreted as clusters, thus standing for independent subsets in the RG. For finding bridges in a network, we follow the algorithm of [26], which starts by determining a spanning tree T from a random node as the tree root. Then the graph is traversed while creating a tree structure. Every node that had been added to that tree will not be added again. In a second step, T is traversed pre-order to number the nodes. During that, the number of descendants for every node is determined, while every node gets two attributes, the minimum label L and maximum label H. Now all edges within T are determined for which the child's L is greater or equal to its number label and the child's H is smaller than its number label added to the number of descendants. If these two conditions are met, the edge specifies a bridge.

5.2 Clustering Support in the BGP

Allowing cluster computation within the logical graph requires specifying the cluster algorithm(s) and the set of nodes to be clustered. Following the BGP design, the set of nodes is specified the URL path, while the algorithm(s) are given in the query similar to the search concept. A sample query for an attribute clustering on *location* computed for all nodes in the RG would be:

```
http://localhost/allparticipants?cluster=location
```

Since clustering is only defined on nodes, the search set requires the keyword *cluster*. The combination of multiple clustering methods leads to sequential application to the node-set. That means, bridge clustering might structurally put two nodes in different segments, although they could be semantically in the same *location*. A sequentially executed attribute clustering could then never join them into the same cluster again. In other words, with every additional clustering algorithm, the number of clusters would increase.

5.3 On-the-Fly Clustering

The combinatorical explosion of cluster variants according to different single or combined clustering algorithms and the possibly evolving RG, makes a pre-calculation of clusters impractical. Hence, clusters have to be computed on-the-fly. Although the stateless nature of transient clusterings fits to the concepts of the BGP, the overall consistency is ensured by making clusters resources within the RG. For that, they get an addressable *id*, which always points to the same cluster. Due to the transient nature of clusters and the evolving RG, the cluster-query is encoded in its *id* attributes. In addition, clusterings can be versioned, which allows executing different versions of a semantically equivalent clustering, that return equal results.

Technically, a BASE64 encoding is chosen to represent the arguments within an *id*, which produces a URL compatible string with the prefix *cluster_*.

```
http://localhost/cluster_Y2x1c3Rlcj1icmlkZ2U7YWxsc
                 GFydGljaXBhbnRzO3ZlcnNpb249MQ==
```

The BASE64 *id* encoding in the example contains three important clustering parameters: one for the algorithm(s) ("bridge"), one for the set of nodes to be clustered ("allparticipants") and one determining the cluster version ("version=1"). Here, the URL encodes a bridge clustering on all nodes in its first version.

6 Runtime Analysis

The BGP has been implemented based on the RG according to the design principles described in section 2 and tested with respect to runtime performance and scalability on real-world business network data. The original data set contains 72 *Service*, 50 *MessageFlow*, 34 *SubConversation*, 17 *ApplicationParticipant*, 8 *BusinessParticipant* and 40 other RG instances. For testing the original data set is extended structure preserving using a "stamping" algorithm with a strategy that connects the different segments via message flow hubs. We found that this mechanism allows to extend the existing data set most accurately according to the given network structure. Based on that, resource graphs with up to 6000 resources are generated (see Fig. 6) and loaded to the BGP system. The system uses a NIM [20,19] schema based on network-centric BPMN to derive the resource graph from the schema and generically provides the BGP access. All measurements are done via 32-bit Windows Vista OS on an Intel Core2 Duo E8400 with 3.00GHz, 4GB RAM, a SAP JVM version 6.

The first analysis uses a sequential read pattern of the complete graph. That is not the optimal pattern for RG access due to query processing, i.e. the complete graph could be requested at once, but helps to put high, continuous load on the system. The algorithm explores the graph starting from the list of participants (nodes) and *neighbor* shortcut connections (edges). Fig. 6(a) shows the runtime performance in terms of time per request measurement of one client reading

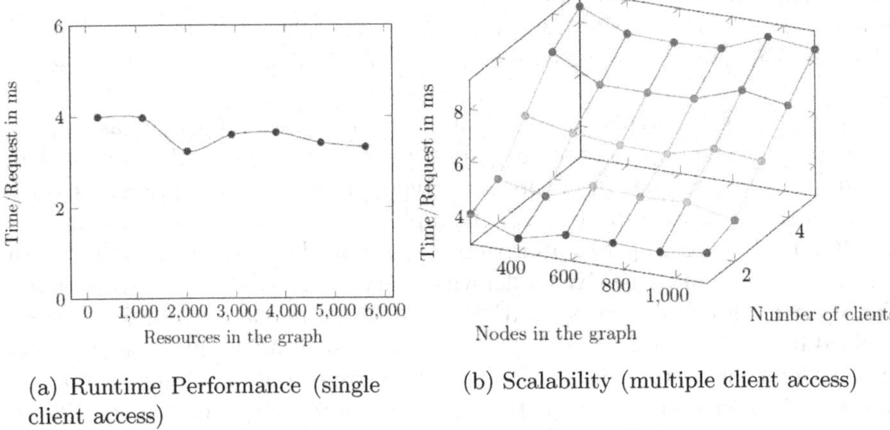

(a) Runtime Performance (single client access)

(b) Scalability (multiple client access)

Fig. 6. Runtime Performance and Scalability

the complete graph. For 220 resources, the algorithm requires 1295 requests and spans to 36425 requests for 5620 resources, which requires between 3 and 4 ms per request. The second analysis shows a load generation scenario with multiple clients querying the complete graph sequentially, while the system is restricted to run on one JVM OS process. Fig. 6(b) again shows that the BGP system is independent of the graph size for a constant number of clients. When increasing the number of clients concurrently accessing the system for sequential read, the response time increases linearly.

7 Related Work

The work on web-based, remote access for the BGP as well as definitions of a resource, representation, etc, is grounded on [5,6], in which architecture styles for resource oriented data access are defined. More recent work on this topic has been conducted in [27,28,16], which connect the theory to state-of-the art system and resource oriented architectures [25].

Based on these concepts, Facebook provides a Graph API [2] and an Open Graph Protocol [3,9], which allows RESTful access to social media data, well suited for social applications. Although it follows similar design principles as the RG in terms of simplicity, ease of use and addressability [3,4], the approach and data model focuses exclusively on social aspects, thus being a simple social graph with flat structures and partially connected data containing e.g. name, personal information, links to friends, etc. The social graph does not support complex business and integration aspects as well as semantics of complex queries or traversal. The notion of semantic, custom extensions as in the resource graph has not been foreseen. For instance, information about people, photos, events, and pages are represented as nodes and the connections between them, e.g. friend relationships, shared content and photo tags, as edges [2]. Thus making it undirected, vertex-labeled, vertex-attributed and edge labeled graph. The concept of connections and metadata within the RG are similar to those of the social graph.

The concepts for hyper graph, multigraph, and tree structures as well as query and traversal operations are partially covered in the work conducted in the graph database domain. There, the HyperGraphDB [13] represents closest known prior art with respect to hyper graph structures, which is one aspect of the RG. The HyperGraphDB approach is based on the work on data models in [1], thus defining an expressive model with n-ary hyperedges to link other edges. Through what is called reification, RDF graph structures can be transformed into a reified form [17]. Apart from that, a rich type system allows programatical extensions for some host languages like Java and more storage near representations. Notably, the modeling as well as type support concentrate more on storage aspects. Important concepts relevant for the RG like uniform traversals, automatic and model-driven resource identification and provisioning are less distinctive.

Query and especially traversal aspects similar to the RG can be found in the Neo4j graph database [14]. There, the work is strongly based on graph traversal patterns described in [23,24]. The different types of graph traversals are formalized on a property graph as operations over power multi set domains and ranges. Only with a graph traversal domain specific language (DSL), called Gremlin [8], the concepts can be conveniently used. Although Gremlin does allow remote queries and traversals on the Neo4j and other graph databases, the patterns are less application domain oriented as the RG. The RG allows traversal on the application domain data directly without expecting to learn a complex path algebra as in [23,24]. Furthermore, while the RG defines a general resource graph over different types of structures, like multi-relational (hyper-) graphs, forest, sets, the work on graph traversal is mainly focused on single-step traversal and content-based similarity.

Other approaches of accessing connected data can be found in Rexter [18] and InfoGrid [12]. Rexter is a system implemented to access data as web service in graph databases similar to InfoGrid. Contrary to the social graph, it works on abstract graphs. That means it is not optimized to work with the semantic meaning of a graph (e.g friendships between people). The specialization on property graphs has two further aspects. Property graphs are directed graphs which is an influential part of the Rexster and InfoGrid design. A business network has undirected edges. Furthermore, property graphs are not hyper graphs as common for multi-perspective business networks. An important principle of the Rexter approach to a graph is its definition of resources and the way of how to expose a graph as a whole. Both are important aids to the BGP. However for the BGP, Rexter's abstract graph comes short due to complexity and nature of business networks.

Generally, the afore discussed technical approaches could partly complement the RG approach by serving as storage variant for compatible concepts or traversal of resources. When looking more into approaches in BNM related domains, the work on Semantic Business Process Management (SBPM) [11] is of interest. SBPM strives to mine business processes semantics mechanically. For that, an ontological approach [10,7] is combined with Semantic Web Services (SWS) and BPM. In general, SBPM and Business Network Management are complementing approaches with combinable technology stacks. However, when it comes to resource definition, representation and access, the approach is more focused on capabilities in the area of SWS instead of RESTful traversal of complex (graph) structures.

8 Discussion and Future Work

In this paper, we presented a model-driven approach to define resources within a business network for uniform query, traversal and filtering, namely the resource graph. The resource graph is automatically generated from the logical graph of the model and provides rich capabilities for custom semantics. The Business Graph Protocol is defined on the resource graph and makes it accessible over a RESTful HTTP interface. Built-in algorithms for ad-hoc entry-point determination to the resource graph allow for good orientation even in larger and more complex graphs. We showed how selective queries and traversals on the linked business network resources can be written by exploiting filtering and custom search sets. Finally, we distinguished our approach from related work. Although there are plenty of approaches for graph storage and traversal, all approaches come short for concepts inherent to business networks.

Future work will be conducted in applying our approach to other domains, like social graphs, and embedding algorithms for different variants of clustering for ad-hoc entry point generation, possibly by user preferences in a machine learning approach. Synergies with related work especially in terms of storage, e.g. replication approaches with eventual consistency, will be analyzed and exploited to ensure availability and scalability for large business networks.

References

1. Angeles, R., Gutierrez, C.: Survey of Graph Database Models. ACM Computing Surveys 40(1), Article 1 (2008)
2. Graph API, Facebook Inc. (2011), `http://developers.facebook.com/docs/reference/api/`
3. Graph Protocol, Facebook Inc. (2011), `http://developers.facebook.com/docs/opengraph/`
4. Fetterman, D.: Data Grows Up: The Architecture of the Facebook Platform. In: Spinellis, D., et al. (eds.), pp. 89–109. O'Reilly Media Inc., Sebastopol (2009)
5. Fielding, R.T.: Architectural Styles and the Design of Network-based Software Architectures. PhD thesis, University of California, Irvine (2000)
6. Fielding, R.T., Taylor, R.N.: Principled Design of Modern Web Architecture. ACM Transactions on Internet Technology 2(2), 115–150 (2002)
7. Filipowska, A., Hepp, M., Kaczmarek, M., Markovic, I.: Organisational Ontology Framework for Semantic Business Process Management. In: Abramowicz, W. (ed.) BIS 2009. LNBIP, vol. 21, pp. 1–12. Springer, Heidelberg (2009)

8. Gremlin: Graph Traversal Language (2012), `https://github.com/tinkerpop/gremlin/wiki`
9. Hagen, A.: The Open Graph Protocol Design Decisions. In: International Semantic Web Conference (ISWC), Shanghai (2010)
10. Hepp, M., Roman, D.: An Ontology Framework for Semantic Business Process Management. Wirtschaftsinformatik, 423–440 (2007)
11. Hepp, M., Leymann, F., Dominigue, J., Wahler, A., Fensel, D.: Semantic Business Process Management – A Vision Towards Using Semantic Web Services for Business Process Management. In: IEEE International Conference on e-Business Engineering (ICEBE), Beijing (2005)
12. Infogrid Web Graph Database. Infogrid (November 2011), `http://infogrid.org/`
13. Iordanov, B.: HyperGraphDB: A Generalized Graph Database. In: Shen, H.T., Pei, J., Özsu, M.T., Zou, L., Lu, J., Ling, T.-W., Yu, G., Zhuang, Y., Shao, J. (eds.) WAIM 2010. LNCS, vol. 6185, pp. 25–36. Springer, Heidelberg (2010)
14. Neo4j Graph Database. Neo Technology (January 2012), `http://neo4j.org/`
15. OMG: BPMN: Business Process Modeling Notation 2.0. Object Management Group (2011)
16. Pautasso, C., Wilde, E.: RESTful web services: principles, patterns, emerging technologies. In: WWW, pp. 1359–1360 (2012)
17. RDF Semantics (2012), `http://www.w3c.org/RT/rdf-mt`
18. Rexster. Rexster (May 2011), `https://github.com/tinkerpop/rexster/wiki/`
19. Ritter, D., Bhatt, A.: Modeling Approach for Business Networks with an Integration and Business Perspective. In: ER 2011 Workshops, Brüssel (2011)
20. Ritter, D., Ackermann, J., Bhatt, A., Hoffmann, F.O.: Building a Business Graph System and Network Integration Model Based on BPMN. In: Dijkman, R., Hofstetter, J., Koehler, J. (eds.) BPMN 2011. LNBIP, vol. 95, pp. 154–159. Springer, Heidelberg (2011)
21. Ritter, D.: From Network Mining to Large Scale Business Networks. In: International Workshop on Large Scale Network Analysis (LSNA), Lyon (2012)
22. Ritter, D.: Towards Business Network Management. In: Confenis: 6th International Conference on Research and Practical Issues of Enterprise Information Systems, Ghent (2012)
23. Rodriguez, M.A., Neubauer, P.: A Path Algebra for Multi-Relational Graphs. In: International Workshop on Graph Data Management (GDM), Hannover (2011)
24. Rodriguez, M.A., Neubauer, P.: The Graph Traversal Pattern. In: Sakr, S., Pardede, E. (eds.) Graph Data Management: Techniques and Applications. IGI Global (2011)
25. Sletten, B.: Resource-Oriented Architectures: Being "In The Web". In: Spinellis, D., et al. (eds.), pp. 89–109. O'Reilly Media Inc., Sebastopol (2009)
26. Tarjan, R.E.: A Note on Finding the Bridges of a Graph. Inf. Process. Lett., 160–161 (1974)
27. Webber, J., Parastatidis, S., Robinson, I.: REST in Practice: Hypermedia and Systems Architecture. O'Reilly & Associates, Sebastopol (2010)
28. Wilde, E., Pautasso, C. (eds.): REST: From Research to Practice. Springer, Heidelberg (2011)

Quality-Oriented Product Line Modeling Using Feature Diagrams and Preference Logic

Paulius Paskevicius, Robertas Damasevicius, and Vytautas Štuikys

Software Engineering Department, Kaunas University of Technology,
Studentų 50-415, LT-51368, Kaunas, Lithuania
paulius.paskevicius@gmail.com,
{robertas.damasevicius,vytautas.stuikys}@ktu.lt

Abstract. Current domain analysis methods for product line engineering usually focus on the implementation of functional requirements for product lines while neglecting the quality aspects. However, in modern software system development the non-functional requirements, such as dependability, maintainability and, especially, quality, have become more important. Furthermore, quality is one of essentials dimensions of variability and there are complex direct and indirect relationships between functional and quality features of systems. The aim of this paper is to extend feature modeling for modeling software quality using elements of preference logic to aid the designer in the decision making process when selecting alternative (optional) features from a feature diagram. Preference logic is used to compactly represent and reason about preference relations between features and quality aspects in integrated feature-quality models represented using extended feature diagrams.

Keywords: quality modeling, feature modeling, feature diagram, product line.

1 Introduction

The increasing pressure for developing software in shorter time and at a lower cost pushes software industry towards adopting the product line methodology for software system development. A software product-line (SPL) is a set of similar software systems that share a common, managed set of features and are developed from a common core of reusable software assets in a prescribed way [1]. Product-line members share common requirements, but also differ in certain variant features. Therefore, modeling commonality and variability in a domain is an essential part of domain analysis for product lines [2]. Product lines are usually modeled using feature models, which are described using Feature Diagrams [3]. Features are user-visible characteristics of software products, while feature models represent admissible combinations of features and can be understood as tools for modeling the configurability aspect of high-variability systems [4].

Current domain analysis methods usually focus on the analysis of functional requirements for product lines with little attention given to product quality. However, in modern software system development the non-functional requirements such as dependability, maintainability and, especially, quality, become more and more important. Quality also is one of essentials dimensions of variability [5].

T. Skersys, R. Butleris, and R. Butkiene (Eds.): ICIST 2012, CCIS 319, pp. 241–254, 2012.

Quality requirements are critical to the success of any application. Even if an application fulfilled all of its functional requirements, it can still be a failure if its availability, capacity, performance, interoperability, security and user interface requirements are not satisfied [6]. Therefore, to support product lines for developing high quality software, software quality modeling is needed.

The aim of this paper is to extend feature modeling for modeling software quality using elements of preference logic to aid the designer in the decision making process when selecting alternative (optional) features from a Feature Diagram. Preference logic [7] can be used to compactly represent and reason about product and feature preference relations. Preference relations are essential for making intelligent choices in complex contexts, e.g., for managing large sets of alternatives or for coordinating decision making process.

The structure of the paper is as follows. Related works are discussed in Section 2. Tools for modeling quality-oriented aspects in software product lines are discussed in Section 3. Extension of feature diagrams for preference logic based modeling of quality aspects is described in Section 4. Case study is given in Section 5. The results are evaluated in Section 6. Finally, conclusions are presented in Section 7.

2 Related Works

In a product line, there are often products with varying degrees of quality attributes. To take necessary decisions during software design and modeling stage, the relationships between different aspects of software quality variability and their influence on the functional aspects of software products must be adequately specified and represented. After analysis of relevant scientific literature, we have discovered several modeling methods that address software quality modeling.

Feature-Oriented Reuse Method (FORM) [8] is an extension of the FODA [3] method with more advanced analysis capabilities. In the feature model, quality attributes are treated similarly to behavioral features, however, complex inter-dependencies among different features and quality attributes cannot be specified effectively.

Definition hierarchy [9] is an AND-function tree where top nodes are design objectives (such as quality attributes) that a system must satisfy. The leaves are design decisions, and an edge between a design objective and a design decision shows that a design objective is (partially) satisfied by a design decision. Each node also has a priority value that means the importance of that node to support the intention of its parent. This value is used to rate products in the definition hierarchy.

Bayesian Belief Network (BBN) [10] can be used to explicitly model the impact of variants (especially design decisions) on system quality attributes. The approach combines the feature model to capture functional requirements and the BBN model to capture the impact of functional variants on quality attributes. The approach is used to perform quality prediction and assessment for a software product line.

Prometheus [11] is a goal-oriented method that integrates quantitative and qualitative approaches to quality control in software product lines. The approach uses the Goal Question Metric (GQM) method to derive quality aspects and BBN to evaluate product quality.

COVAMOF [12] is a framework for variability modeling on all layers of abstraction of the product family. COVAMOF Variability View captures variability in the product family in terms of variation points and dependencies. Quality attributes are modeled with dependencies. A dependency can specify a property that specifies the value of a quality attribute such as performance or memory usage. Association is used to associate variation points and dependencies.

Goal-based modeling [13] proposes to use goal-oriented analysis in product lines. Two sub-models are used: a functional goal model and a soft-goal model. Quality attributes are represented as soft-goals and the operation of those quality attributes is encoded in the functional goal sub-model as tasks. Each soft-goal is assigned a priority to perform analysis and calculate correlations used to represent links among functional goals and soft-goals.

Extended feature model [14] is an extension of feature diagram notation with elements for modeling extra-functional features. Every feature may have one or more measurable attributes such as availability, cost, latency, or bandwidth. Also relations between different attributes can be specified.

Quality Requirements of a Software Family (QRF) method [15] captures and maps the requirements of a product line by analyzing the needs of business and technology development stakeholders and the impact of these needs on the family architecture. QRF includes Quality analysis, where quality requirements are expressed in a way in which they can later be traced, measured and mapped to functionality.

F-SIG [16] provides a framework to register design rationale as interdependencies of variable features and quality attributes using a graph notation that combines feature diagrams with soft-goal interdependency graphs [17]. To express the degree of influence from features to quality attributes, graph branches are the following graph labels are used: Break ("--"; goal is impossible to achieve when implementing quality attribute), Hurt ("-"; goal is easier to achieve without implementing quality attribute), Unknown ("?"), Help ("+"; goal is easier to achieve when implementing quality attribute), Make ("++"; goal is impossible to achieve without implementing quality attribute).

The analysis of support for quality modeling in the related methods for variability modeling is summarized in Table 1.

The novelty of the approach proposed in this paper is the extension of feature modeling with the concepts of preference modeling. Explicit preference modeling provides a declarative way to choose among multiple alternatives of product implementation and allow for fine-grained control over variant selection process.

Table 1. Evaluation of quality modeling in variability modeling methods

Variability modeling method	Support for quality attribute modeling
FORM	... as system features
Definition hierarchy	... as design objectives with priority values
BBN	... as Bayesian Belief Network, a statistical model that represents a set of random variables and their conditional dependencies via a directed acyclic graph
COVAMOF	... as dependencies (properties of quality attributes) associated with variation point
Goal-based modeling	... as soft-goals with priority values
Extended feature modeling	... as feature attributes
QRF	... as requirement graphs
F-SIG	... as soft-goal interdependency graphs

3 Specification and Modeling of Quality Attributes in SPL

Software quality is defined as the degree to which software has a desired combination of attributes [18]. A quality attribute is a property of a software system that has been formulated as a requirement by a stakeholder. Assessment of the system's quality attributes at the modeling stage is essential to justify design decisions early. By selecting the appropriate design decisions before starting the product design and implementation phase, it is possible to reduce development costs and production time. In some domains, such as embedded system design [19, 20], satisfaction quality attributes is even more important than functional requirements. However, most of existing approaches do not integrate quality variability as a part of the systematic variability management of software product lines [21].

In a software product line, different instances of a system may have different quality, or quality characteristics can be optional for some product instance. Furthermore, there can be relationships between functionality features and quality features, so the selection of a functional feature can influence or impact system's quality [6]. Niemelä [22] defined three different types of quality attribute variability:

1. *Optionality* of a quality attribute, when quality requirements are valid only for some members of software product family.
2. *Levels* of quality attribute, when quantitative quality requirements can be assigned to system instances.
3. *Influence* of functional variability on quality, when there is an indirect effect of functional features on the quality requirements.

Variability representation requires the use of diagrams or models to capture all the information. To implement such models, usually, the existing modeling approaches are extended or used in conjunction with other modeling approaches. Firesmith [23] formulated the requirements for developing quality modeling approaches. The quality model must provide:

1. *Taxonomy* of its component quality factors and sub-factors (i.e., aspects, attributes or characteristics); and
2. *Quality criteria and metrics* that can be used to unambiguously specify the associated aspect of quality or to determine software quality during testing.

In general, feature models can be used to capture and model quality attributes, because the definition of feature also covers non-functional properties such as quality. Quality models are defined similarly to feature models as sets of characteristics and relationships between them, so in most cases quality models can be represented as hierarchies (taxonomies, ontologies) of quality attributes [24]. However, the feature modeling approaches usually do not provide any guidance for specifying the quality attribute in a verifiable manner. Furthermore, any quality modeling approach must satisfy the existing industry standards such as ISO 9126 [25], superseded by ISO/IEC 25000 [26]. ISO 9126 introduces a hierarchy of quality characteristics, which can be used when constructing quality models (see Table 2).

Table 2. Product quality characteristics in the ISO 9126-1 quality model

Top-level quality characteristic	Sub-characteristics
Functionality	Suitability, accuracy, interoperability, security
Reliability	Maturity, fault tolerance, recoverability
Usability	Understability, learnability, operability, attractiveness
Efficiency	Time behavior, resource utilization
Maintainability	Analyzability, changeability, stability, testability
Portability	Adaptability, installability, coexistence, replaceability

4 Quality-Oriented Extension of Feature Diagram

A key aspect in product line engineering (PLE) is management of feature variability in product families. Feature variability is usually modeled using Feature Diagrams (FDs): common features among different products are modeled as mandatory features, while differing features may be optional or alternative (see an explanation of the FD notation in Table 3). Optional features represent selectable features for products of a given domain. Alternative features indicate that no more than one feature can be selected for a product.

FD is a directed graph: the root represents the initial concept (component, system), intermediate nodes represent compound features, leaves represent atomic features that may have values (aka variants), and edges represent the parent-child relationships among features. Each FD describes a family (set) of products. The result of the feature selection in a FD is a single product. Basic elements of FD are presented in Table 3.

Table 3. Main elements of a feature diagram

Feature type	Semantics of relationships	Graphical notation (syntax)
Mandatory	Feature B (C, D) is included if its parent A is included: a) *if* A *then* B b) *if* A *then* C *and* D	A, B a) A, C, D b)
Alternative	Feature B (C, D) may be included if its parent A is included: a) *if* A *then* B *or* **<no feature>** b) *if* A *then* C *or* D *or* **<no feature>**	A, B a) A, C, D b)
Optional	At least one feature has to be included if its parent A is included: a) *if* A *then* any-of (B, C) b) *if* A *then* any-of (B, C, D)	A, B, C a) A, B, C, D b)
Constraint <excludes>	Feature K excludes feature F and vice versa	K excludes F
Constraint <requires>	Feature K requires feature F	K requires F

In this paper, we propose the extension of feature diagrams with an additional <prefer> constraint for modeling preference of selection of a feature based on product quality considerations. In a software product line, quality assessment is especially important because an error or an inadequate design decision can be spread into a lot of products. Moreover, in a product line, different members of the line may require different quality attributes. Therefore, a method for quality-aware software product line engineering that takes into account the variability of quality aspects and facilitates quality assessment is presented.

The proposed method is based on preference logic. Preferences [7] are binary relations between objects. There are two fundamental comparison concepts: "better" (strict preference, denoted as $\succ$) and "equal in value to" (indifference, denoted as ~) [24]. Preferences can be considered as expressions of object value:

$$p \succ q \text{, iff } value(p) > value(q)$$

Here p and q are compared objects and *value(.)* is their value function. Further, for simplicity we assume that p and q can be compared directly without we need of the *value* function.

We consider an agent (a software designer, a decision-maker), who tries to select features from a set of alternatives described using feature tree. The features can be compared if some kind of order can be implied between them: either a direct preference (p is preferred to q) or indirect preference induced from a measurement and its associated scale (e.g., p is longer, bigger, faster or more reliable than q).

Let *S* be the set of all software products in a product family. Let S_p be a subset of software products S, where each product in S_p contains feature p. Let S_q be a subset of software products S, where each product in S_q contains feature q. Let $p_{\min}(c) = \min_{S_p} p(c)$ be the minimal value of a product in S_p according to the evaluation criterion c. Let $q_{\max}(c) = \max_{S_q} q(c)$ be the maximal value of a product in S_q according to the evaluation criterion c.

1. *Strict preference* relation '>' on *S* is a binary relation on *S* such that ***p* > *q* iff *p*** is always more preferable as ***q***, i.e., $(p > q) \Leftrightarrow p_{\min}(c) \geq q_{\max}(c)$
2. *Indifference* relation '=' on *S* is a binary relation on *S* such that ***p* = *q* iff *p*** is not preferable to ***q***, and ***q*** is not preferable to ***p***, i.e., $(p = q) \Leftrightarrow \neg(p > q) \cap \neg(q > p)$
3. *Incomparability relation* '<>' on *S* is a binary relation on *S* such that ***p* <> *q* iff** there is not such product there ***p*** can be substituted for ***q*** and *vice versa*, i.e. $(p <> q) \Leftrightarrow (S_p \cap S_q = \varnothing)$.

Given a set of preference relations *R* between the elements of *S* we can define many different orderings of *S* leading to the multi-dimensional choice problem. E.g., for two preference criteria, we can define the following preference relations. The ***p***(c_1,c_2) is preferred over the ***q***(c_1,c_2) **iff** the $p(c_1)$ is preferred over the ***q***(c_1) **and** the ***p***(c_2) is preferred over the ***q***(c_2), where c_1, c_2 are the preference criteria.

For the multi-criteria quality modeling case we can introduce the following preference generalization. Let *C* be the set of all quality criteria for *S*. Then, ***p*** is preferred over ***q* iff p** is preferred over all ***q***(c_i), *where* $c_i \in C$.

Modeling of product preferences in a product line is performed as follows:

1. a list of criteria *C* for evaluating product features *F* is defined;
2. each product feature is evaluating according to each criterion leading to the feature-criterion matrix $F \times C$;
3. using the feature-criterion matrix, each feature is evaluated against other features, and a preference table $F \times F$ is constructed where the results of the evaluation of each quality characteristic against each functional feature is presented denoting the existing preference relationship (if such exists);
4. A combined feature-quality model is constructed, where both feature hierarchy and quality aspect hierarchy are represented as branched of the model's topmost node representing the modeled system itself.
5. Quality and feature hierarchy nodes are related using the preference relations (a dashed line with the <prefer> label leading from a less preferred feature to a more preferred feature, the selection thereof would increase overall quality of a system).

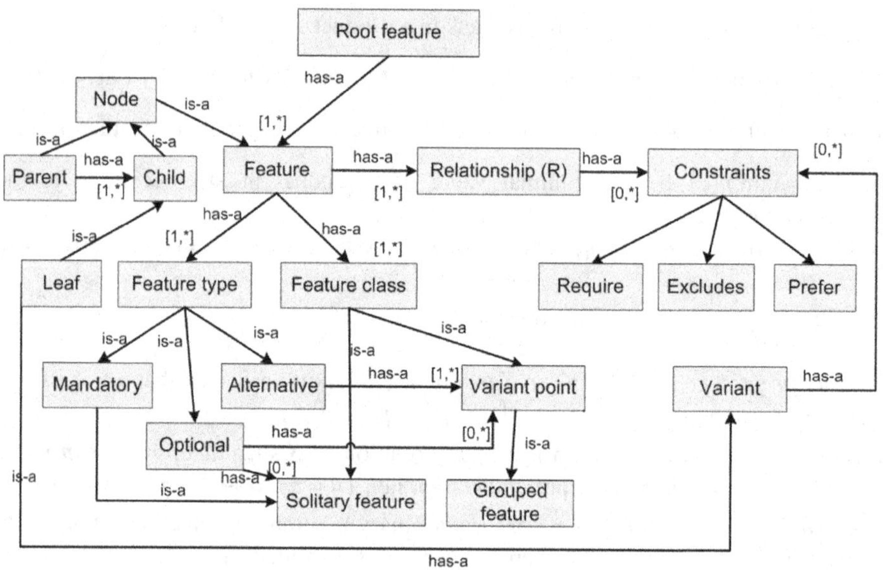

Fig. 1. Meta-model of feature diagram to represent a domain

Finally, to provide a graphical model-oriented description of we present a meta-model of FDs (see Fig. 1) for conceptual explanation of the feature modeling domain with the proposed extension included. In general, a meta-model is the description that specifies all possible model representations of a given class. Here, the task is to obtain the formalism that describes all possible representations of FDs.

5 Case Study

Suppose, we have a set of components of a mobile phone with a similar functionality *P*. We also have a set of selection criteria G that correspond to the quality characteristics of components. Each criterion g_j is a computable function over component $p_i : g_j(p_i) \to R, g_j \in G, p_i \in P$. The aim here is to model a preferable selection of a designer in terms of the earlier selected design criteria and priorities.

In our case study, we analyze the quality-oriented modeling of a mobile phone product line. The features of a mobile phone are summarized in a mobile phone feature model (see Fig. 2). Each mobile phone has a Microprocessor, a Battery (Lithium Ion (LiIon), Nickel-Metal hydride (NiMh) or Nickel-Cadmium (NiCa)), an optional wireless connection (Infrared, Bluetooth, WiFi, or all above), a Display (either color or monochrome), Memory (Flash memory and optional memory card) an optional Touchscreen with Driver and Controller, and an Enclosure. The WiFi connectivity requires LiIon battery, and color display excludes the use of the NiCa battery.

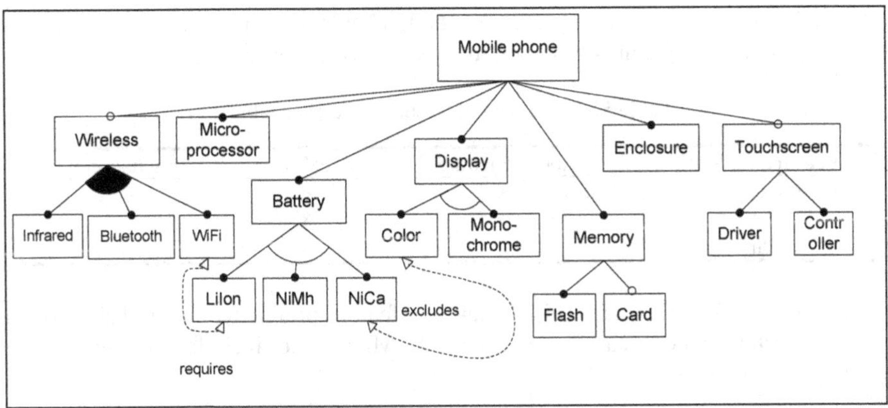

Fig. 2. Feature model of a mobile phone

Here as an example we analyze the use of preferences to extend feature model of a mobile phone with cost and quality relationships. Usability is an important characteristic in the ISO 9126-1 quality model (see Table 2). While cost is also important for assessing attract ability of the phone in the target audiences and markets.

Different quality characteristic tradeoffs of a mobile phone based on their cost and perceived usability are summarized in Table 4. The cost characteristics of the mobile phone components are based on the analysis of mobile phone cost teardowns provided by HIS iSuppli (http://www.isuppli.com/teardowns/). While values of the usability characteristic are based on the comparative analysis of the mobile phone features performed by the authors of this paper.

Table 4. Feature-criterion matrix of cellphone quality characteristics

Feature	Cost, in $	Usability
infrared	5	3
bluetooth	8	3
wifi	23	6
lion	21	8
nimh	15	3
nica	12	2
touchscreen	30	10
color	65	10
monochrome	40	5
microprocessor	20	10
enclosure	32	5
driver	2	1
controller	2	1
flash	30	8
card	7	4

Based on Table 4, a feature preference table (Table 5) can be constructed, which shows preferences of features based on their perceived usability.

Table 5. A fragment of feature preference table

Feature vs. feature	monochrome	color	touchscreen
monochrome	X	<	<
color	>	X	~
touchscreen	>	~	X

Based on the feature model (Fig. 2) and the feature preference table (Table 5), an extended feature model can be constructed, which also includes the preference relations between features.

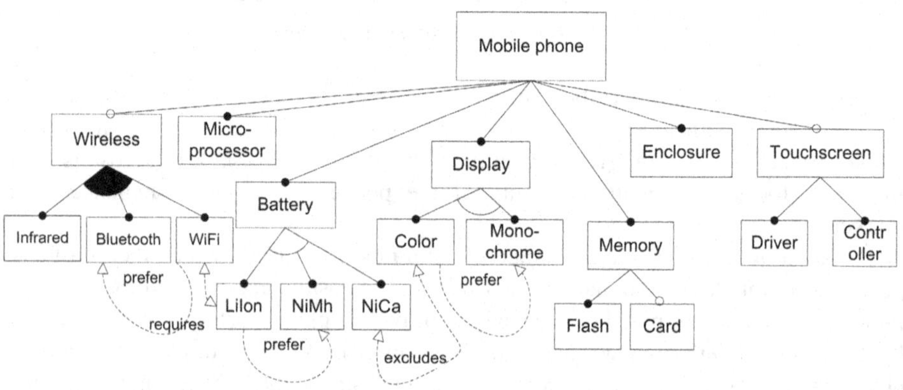

Fig. 3. Extended feature model of a mobile phone: cost view

As we have two quality characteristics (cost, usability), we actually construct two feature models. A feature model depicted in Fig. 3 provides the cost-oriented view towards selection of optional and alternative features of a mobile phone, while Fig. 4 provides the usability-based view.

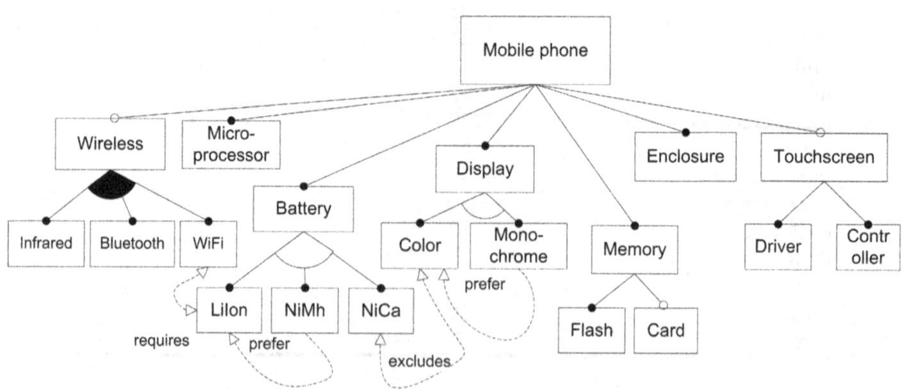

Fig. 4. Extended feature model of a mobile phone: usability view

Finally, we use an extended feature model given in Fig. 3 to find some characteristics of a mobile phone product line such as minimum and maximum cost of a product having a specific optional (or alternative) feature (see Table 6).

Table 6. Product evaluation results in mobile phone product line

Feature	Min. cost of a product having the feature
wifi	166
color	165
lion	148
card	146
touchscreen	143
nimh	142
bluetooth	142
monochrome	139
nica	139
infrared	139

Feature model was described and feature preference was evaluated using a set of PROLOG logic rules [27]. Based on Table 6, we can identify a feature that has the most significant impact on the cost of a product, i.e., the minimal cost of a product having this particular feature in a product line is the highest. We can see that the Wi-Fi connectivity is a most important feature of the mobile phone product line that drives the costs of a mobile phone up.

6 Evaluation

We evaluate the proposed extension of feature modeling with preference logic concepts based on the following requirements for modeling quality attributes [24]:

1. **Specific goals:** the goal is to combine variability modeling of functional system aspects with quality variability modeling.
2. **Models:** the approach uses extended Feature Diagrams with elements of Preference Logic.
3. **Reasoning technique:** existing tools for automatic validation and configuration of feature models could be applied for combined feature-quality variability models.
4. **Case studies:** the approach has been applied for modeling stakeholder requirements for the mobile phone product line.
5. **Tools support:** the feature modeling tool FD2 [28] can be used for modeling quality aspects as well.
6. **Variability representation:** quality aspects may have differing definitions in various domains, thus proper documentation of feature models must be provided.

7. **Optionality:** variability of quality attributes is specified using feature modeling tools.
8. **Levels:** since different priority levels in quality attributes are need, the lower-level quality attributes can be represented at the lower-levels of the feature-quality model.
9. **Impacts:** indirect variations are represented using available relations for the representation of constrains in Feature Diagrams (`<requires>, <excludes>`) as well as the proposed relation for modeling feature-quality relations (`<prefers>`). The group impacts also can be modeled by connecting the lower-level feature model nodes (leaves) with the upper level nodes (quality attribute will apply to a group of features in a feature tree).

7 Conclusions and Future Work

Using the proposed extension of feature diagrams for modeling quality aspects of software systems produces the following benefits for software designers:

1. Important and relevant types of quality requirements are modeled, resulting in a more complete requirements specification and quality assessment.
2. Quality requirements are organized into a logical and understandable hierarchy (taxonomy) that is easy to use and learn.
3. Communication among stakeholders regarding the quality requirements uses Feature Diagrams, which is a common notation in product line engineering, with clearly documented meaning of concepts.
4. Quality aspects are integrated with functional and structural features of a system with relationships between them clearly indicated.

Using Feature Diagrams for large real-world systems, however, can be difficult due to high complexity and lower understandability.

Future work will focus on the integration of the elements of preference logic into the feature modeling tool FD2 to allow reasoning on product quality characteristics, and modularization of Feature Diagrams for easier comprehension.

References

1. Pohl, K., Bockle, G., van der Linden, F.: Software Product Line Engineering. Springer, Heidelberg (2005)
2. Prieto-Diaz, R., Arango, G.: Domain Analysis and Software Systems Modeling. IEEE CS Press (1991)
3. Kang, K.C., Cohen, S.G., Hess, J.A., Novak, W.E., Peterson, A.S.: Feature-oriented domain analysis (FODA) feasibility study. Technical Report CMU/SEI-90-TR-21, Software Engineering Institute (November 1990)
4. Czarnecki, K., Eisenecker, U.W.: Generative Programming - Methods, Tools, and Applications. Addison-Wesley (2000)

5. Liaskos, S., Jiang, L., Lapouchnian, A., Wang, Y., Yu, Y., do Prado Leite, J.C.S., Mylopoulos, J.: Exploring the Dimensions of Variability: a Requirements Engineering Perspective. In: Proc. of First Int. Workshop on Variability of Software-Intensive Systems (VaMos 2007), Limerick, Ireland, January 16-18, pp. 17–27 (2007)
6. Etxeberria, L., Sagardui, G., Belategi, L.: Modelling variation in quality attributes. In: Proc. of First Int. Workshop on Variability of Software-Intensive Systems (VaMos 2007), Lero, pp. 51–60 (2007)
7. Kaci, S., van der Torre, L.W.N.: Algorithms for a Nonmonotonic Logic of Preferences. In: Godo, L. (ed.) ECSQARU 2005. LNCS (LNAI), vol. 3571, pp. 281–292. Springer, Heidelberg (2005)
8. Kang, K.C., Kim, S., Lee, J., Kim, K., Shin, E., Huh, M.: FORM: A feature-oriented reuse method with domain-specific reference architectures. Annals of Software Engineering 5, 143–168 (1998)
9. Kuusela, J., Savolainen, J.: Requirements engineering for product families. In: ICSE 2000: Proc. of the 22nd Int. Conference on Software Engineering, pp. 61–69. ACM Press, New York (2000)
10. Zhang, H., Jarzabek, S., Yang, B.: Quality Prediction and Assessment for Product Lines. In: Eder, J., Missikoff, M. (eds.) CAiSE 2003. LNCS, vol. 2681, pp. 681–695. Springer, Heidelberg (2003)
11. Trendowicz, A., Punter, T.: Quality Modeling for Software Product Lines. In: Proc. of 7th ECOOP Workshop on Quantitative Approaches in Object-Oriented Software Engineering (QAOOSE 2003), p. 7 (2003)
12. Sinnema, M., Deelstra, S., Nijhuis, J., Bosch, J.: COVAMOF: A Framework for Modeling Variability in Software Product Families. In: Nord, R.L. (ed.) SPLC 2004. LNCS, vol. 3154, pp. 197–213. Springer, Heidelberg (2004)
13. González-Baixauli, B., do Prado Leite, J.C.S., Mylopoulos, J.: Visual variability analysis for goal models. In: Proc. of 12th IEEE Int. Conf. on Requirements Engineering (RE), pp. 198–207. IEEE CS (2004)
14. Benavides, D., Trinidad, P., Ruiz-Cortés, A.: Automated Reasoning on Feature Models. In: Pastor, Ó., Falcão e Cunha, J. (eds.) CAiSE 2005. LNCS, vol. 3520, pp. 491–503. Springer, Heidelberg (2005)
15. Niemelä, E.: Quality driven family architecture development. In: Tutorial in Software Product Line Conference, Rennes, France, September 26-29 (2005)
16. Jarzabek, S., Yang, B., Yoeun, S.: Addressing quality attributes in domain analysis for product lines. IEE Proc. - Software 153(2), 61–73 (2006)
17. Chung, L., Nixon, B., Yu, E., Mylopoulos, J.: Non-Functional Requirements in Software Engineering. Kluwer (2000)
18. IEEE Std. 1061-1992. Standard for a Software Quality Metrics Methodology. IEEE, New York (1992)
19. Toldinas, J., Štuikys, V., Damaševičius, R., Ziberkas, G.: Application-level energy consumption in communication models for handhelds. Electronics and Electrical Engineering 6(94), 73–76 (2009)
20. Štuikys, V., Damaševičius, R., Toldinas, J., Ziberkas, G.: Matching DSP Algorithm Transformations for Power, Performance and Memory Trade-Offs. In: Proc. of 15th Conference on Information and Software Technologies, IT 2009, Kaunas, Lithuania, April 23-24, pp. 178–186 (2009)
21. Myllärniemi, V., Männistö, T., Raatikainen, M.: Quality Attribute Variability within a Software Product Family Architecture. In: Proc. of 2nd Int. Conf. on Quality of Software Architecture, QoSA, Vasteras, Sweden, June 27-July 1 (2006)

22. Niemelä, E.: Architecture centric software family engineering, product family engineering seminar. In: Tutorial in 5th Working IEEE/IFIP Conference on Software Architecture, WICSA (2005)
23. Firesmith, D.: Using Quality Models to Engineer Quality Requirements. J. of Obj. Technology 2(5), 67–75 (2003)
24. Etxeberria, L., Sagardui, G.: Quality Assessment in Software Product Lines. In: Mei, H. (ed.) ICSR 2008. LNCS, vol. 5030, pp. 178–181. Springer, Heidelberg (2008)
25. ISO/IEC 9126-1:2001 Software engineering — Product quality — Part 1: Quality model. International Organization for Standardization/International Electrotechnical Commission (2001)
26. ISO/IEC 25000: Software engineering: Software product Quality Requirements and Evaluation (SQuaRE): Guide to SQuaRE (2005)
27. Halldén, S.: On the Logic of Better. Library of Theoria, Lund (1957)
28. Paskevicius, P., Bindokas, M., Kasperavicius, A., Damasevicius, R.: Executable models and model transformations: a framework for research. In: Butleris, R. (ed.) Information Technologies 2011: Proceedings of the 17th International Conference on Information and Software Technologies, IT 2011, Kaunas, Lithuania, April 27-29, pp. 76–83 (2011)

Distributed System Automated Testing Design

Robertas Jasaitis and Eduardas Bareisa

Kaunas University of Technology, Software Engineering Department
Studentu St. 50, LT–51368 Kaunas, Lithuania
jasaitis.robertas@gmail.com, edas@soften.ktu.lt

Abstract. Testing is a very expensive but still very important stage of software development. Most applications today are designed to be networked. Often issues arise in such systems due to the interleaving of the clients and servers as well as resource racing issues. To make testing of distributed systems easier we propose an algorithm that is able to simulate few clients communicating with remote servers and is able to detect resource racing related failures. For clients simulation we use Java Path Finder (JPF). We propose JPF extension which is able to simulate and cover all possible paths threw the distributed system while two clients are interacting with the system at the same time. For resource racing problems we propose to use and extend UML class diagram with 3 additional method stereotypes. From the extended model we generate additional code constraints which are later used in testing as test oracles.

Keywords: Distributed system, automated testing, model checking.

1 Introduction

In our previous work we provided distributed system model checking design [1]. The model checker itself doesn't actually test anything (doesn't solve oracle problem) so we had to come up with some automated solution to extend the proposed method to get rid of the existing drawback.

In order to decide what should we test we need to describe what type of system failures we are trying to solve. In other words we need to know what failures usually happen in the distributed systems. Cristian, Dolev, Strong, and Aghili (1987), and Tanenbaum and Steen (2002) classify distributes system failures and they are listed below [2].

- **Communication Failure** - usually happens when client is not able to locate the server. This includes server crash, fail to response or any kind of lose or damage of the message sent/received. This issue can only be detected on the client side as it might be that the server doesn't even know about the client's attempt to access the server. On a higher level programming languages like Java or C# this type of issue is solved by the connection libraries.

T. Skersys, R. Butleris, and R. Butkiene (Eds.): ICIST 2012, CCIS 319, pp. 255–266, 2012.

- **Byzantine Failure** - "Byzantine Failure relates to the Byzantine Generals Problem which was introduced by Lamport, Shortak, and Pease (1982) and based on the Byzantine army concept" [2]. This is a type of failure when server responds with the incorrect response or doesn't provide any kind of response. So this issue should be detected on both sides: client and server. The client should react to server response with respect to some timeout gracefully. And on the server side incorrect response or empty response should be detected. The timeout situation on a higher level programming languages or systems (like J2EE [3]) are also solved. The incorrect response of the server should still be solved manually.
- **Omission Failure** - this is the type of failure when connection with the server is not possible. This issue should be detected on the client side. It is also solved by the connection libraries of the higher level programming languages.
- **Crash Failure** - this is type of failure when server crashes when handling the request from the client. This is very related to Omission Failure except that this time the issue should be checked on both sides: server and client. Also server crash failure should be manually solved.
- **Timing Failure** - this usually happens when server responds either too early or too late. It is possible that server responds too early and client is not able to handle the data received because of the too small buffer and finally loses some data. Too slow response can provide some issue on the client side as well. So this issue should be checked on both sides: client and server. This failure is also solved by the connection libraries of the higher level programming languages.
- **Response Failure** - this happens when server responds with incorrect response. So obviously only server is responsible for that. And also the issue should be detected manually.

We defined the failures and made a rough partitioning of the issues: some issues should be detected on server side and some on the client side. This doesn't mean that for instance the client doesn't care if server responds with correct answer (in case of Response Failure) as the client may crash in case of some unexpected response but in our case we are focused on the distributed system specific failures so other tests should be used to detect other issues. Also many issues are already solved on a higher level programming languages. And we are only focusing on those languages. So we are focusing on server response failures in this article only.

Some can argue with our failure types stating that it doesn't cover all cases. One of the possible cases that might not be covered is recourse racing issue. But actually this is covered by response failure and may be part of some other failure as well. So our failure division is of a higher abstraction level.

We checked the following existing techniques that focus on automated distributed systems testing [14-19]. None of the provided methods are able to solve resource racing failure. In this article we are focusing on this issue.

Summary of client and server failure detection responsibilities is provided in Table 1.

Table 1. Client and server failure detection responsibilities

Failure Type	*Client Responsibility*	*Server Responsibility*
Communication Failure	Yes	No
Byzantine Failure	Yes	Yes
Omission Failure	Yes	No
Crash Failure	Yes	Yes
Timing Failure	Yes	Yes
Response Failure	No	Yes

We are not focusing on other client or server side failures that can be detected without client/server interaction. Also we are not focusing on non functional failures such as performance or similar.

In this paper we present our second attempt to make a design that is theoretically able to detect issues related to resource racing in a distributed system.

This paper is organized as follows: the determination of the problem and example are given in section 2. The intuition of our solution is given in section 3. Implementation of the design is given in section 4. Limitations of our design are given in section 5. Conclusions and future work are given in section 6.

2 Problem Determination

We start this section with an example distributed system. We analyze "Cinema seat reservation" system. This system is built on J2EE framework [3]. The usual work flow of such application is described by the following sequence:

- User starts client application
- User checks which seats are available
- User selects one seat.

The simplified application implementation is shown below:

```
public static void main(String[] args) {
  ArrayList<Seat> availableSeats = getAvailableSeats();
  displayAvailableSeatsForUser(availableSeats,
    new OnSeatSelectedListener(Seat seat) {
      if (reserveSeat(seat){
        System.out.println("Seat reserved");
      } else {
        System.out.println("Seat reservation failed." +
                "Please try again.");
      }
    }
  );
}
```

Seat class implementation on the client side provided below:

```
public class Seat {
  private int row;
  private int seatNumberInRow;
}
```

We do not go deeper into `getAvailableSeats`, `displayAvailable-SeatsForUser` and `reserveSeat` methods for simplicity. The first `getAvailableSeats` method opens URL connection, sends request to server and waits for the response just to check which seats are not reserved yet. There is a http servlet implemented and running on the server which handles the requests. The second `displayAvailableSeatsForUser` method provides the available seats for user and listens for user selection using OnSeatSelectedListener. The third `reserveSeat` method sends request to server to mark the given seat as reserved. Also we do not provide constructor, setters and getters of the class Seat as they are obvious. We are not interested at server implementation of `getAvailableSeats` functionality at the moment but `reserveSeat` action implementation is important for us. Simplified `reserveSeatServer` method server implementation code provided below (note this is not the same implementation as client `reserveSeat` as client sends request and server just marks the seat as reserved. The `reserveSeatServer` method is called by servlet running on the server):

```
private void reserveSeatServer(Seat seat) {
  if (seat != null) {
    seat.setReserved(true);
  }
}
```

As the `Seat` is the only object that is used in client and server communication the analogue `Seat` class exists on the server implementation as well, except on the server the class communicates with actual database management class:

```
public class Seat {
  private int row;
  private int seatNumberInRow;

  public Seat(int row, int seatNumberInRow) {
      this.row = row;
    this. seatNumberInRow = seatNumberInRow;
  }
  public void setReserved(boolean reserved) {
    if (reserved) {
      DatabaseManager.getInstance().reserveSeat(this);
    }
  }
```

```
  public boolean isReserver() {
    DatabaseManager.getInstance().isSeatReserved(this);
  }
}
```

From the first look the code looks fine. And it actually is fine if there is only one user using the system at a time. But let us provide a situation when the system would fail. Imagine two users interested in the seat 5 in row 5. The actions flow provided below (each following action is started only when the previous one is finished):

- The user A starts application an gets the list of available seats (seat 5 in row 5 is also available)
- The user B starts application an gets the list of available seats (seat 5 in row 5 is also available)
- The user A reserves seat 5 in row 5 and gets response: "Seat reserved".
- The user B reserves seat 5 in row 5 and gets response: "Seat reserved".

This is obvious problem as both users thinks they reserved the seat. So the server implementation in this situation is incorrect. The server never checks if the seat is still available because the developer thought that if the client got the list of available seats and picked one then it means the seat is available. But this is not true if couple of users uses the system concurrently. So let us propose a mechanism to detect this issue using automated testing technique.

First of all we split the detection of the issue into two subtasks:

1. We need to be able to simulate the situation in order to be able to automatically detect the issue;
2. We need to prepare the test which is able to detect the issue in code (so we need a technique which solves oracle problem)

3 Intuition of the Design

The subtask #1 defined in the end of section two is actually solved in our previous work [1]. Our algorithm finds the connection code in the application, simulates two application instances and tries different connection code sequences. Fig. 1 shows all possible sequences of our cinema seat reservation sample system.

The sequence we provided earlier in the end of section two is shown by S2 sequence in the Figure 1. So the model checking algorithm is able to simulate this sequence and other possible sequences. Note that sequences S1 and S4 are not complete because in our situation user notices that seat 5 in row 5 is reserved so user quits application without selecting any of the seats. This means that our distributed system model checking algorithm is able to solve subtask #1.

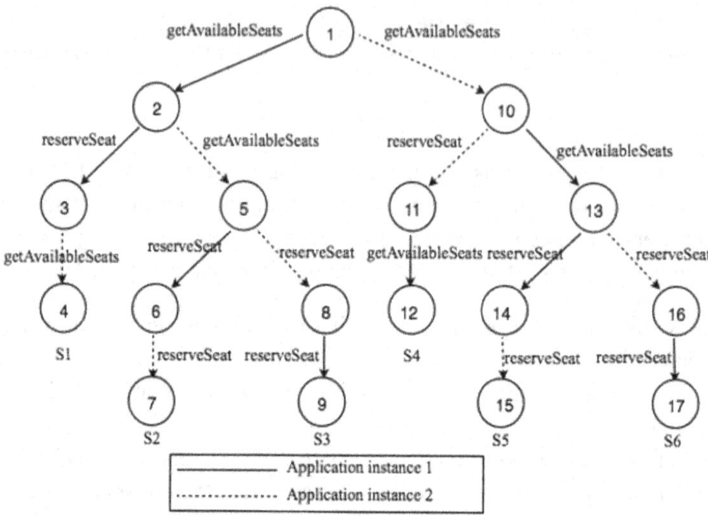

Fig. 1. All possible sequences of cinema seat reservation sample system

To solve our subtask #2 we take advantage of system UML class diagrams. In our case it can be used for both: the client application or the server application. According to object oriented programming encapsulation concept "the data and the implementation code for the object are hidden behind its interface" [4]. "Encapsulation hides internal implementation details from users" [4]. The fragment of possible class diagram of our cinema seat reservation system (server side) provided by Fig. 2.

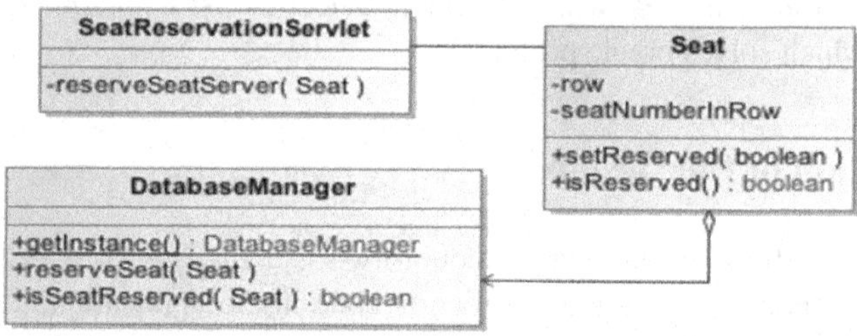

Fig. 2. Cinema seat reservation system class diagram fragment

`SeatReservationServlet` class is a main servlet class which has a private method `reserveSeatServer`. Other methods of the class are not provided for simplicity. The implementation of the `reserveSeatServer` method has been defined earlier in this section. From the implementation and diagram we can see that the method uses `setReserved` setter method of the `Seat` class. The `Seat` class member variables are encapsulated. Also the database operations are handled by DatabaseManager class and `Seat` class uses that functionality. So this model meets object oriented programming requirements.

In the given situation the cinema seat can be reserved only once for given movie. So the situation when two or more users reserve the same seat are treated as failures of the system. The implementation that was provided earlier in this section clearly fails to handle such situation. So this is a task for distributed system testing method to detect such failure and notify the developer of the system.

In order to develop automated testing method which would be able to detect this type of failure we chose to use UML class diagram extension. The proposed extension should be as simple as possible, should not require significant architect input and should be compliant with existing UML 2.0 [5] or above modeling tools. To meet such requirements we chose to use method stereotypes as UML class diagram extension. We propose using new `<<final>>` stereotype for each setter method that could be called only once for the given value. In our case it's `setReserved` method of server `Seat` class. The `Seat` class UML diagram with the stereotype is provided by Fig. 3.

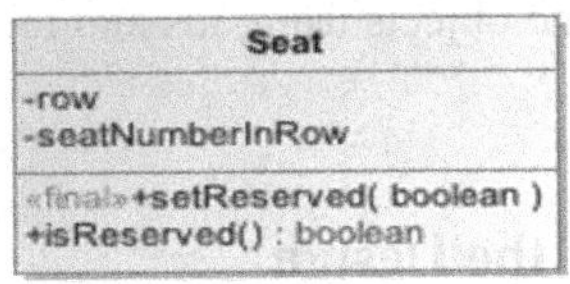

Fig. 3. Seat class diagram with additional `<<final>>` `setReserved` method stereotype

Having this new stereotype set in the diagram we can analyze the class diagram provided in XMI format [6] of the system under test and automatically generate additional constraints for the `<<final>>` method. The constraint checks if any value has been set for the given object. The test oracle: test passes in case some value is being set for the first time and fails vice verse. We will be using assertions provided by Java 1.5 and above for this purpose [7]. In our case the automated test generator can automatically generate the following asserts for `Seat.setReserved` method. Note: the injected code is marked in bold:

```
private static Vector<Object> reserved = new
Vector<Object>();
public void setReserved(boolean reserved) {
  assertFalse(reserved.contains(this));
  reserved.add(this);
  if (reserved) {
    DatabaseManager.getInstance().reserveSeat(this);
  }
}
```

We append static Vector object which is shared between all Seat objects while the server is alive. This shared vector contains all Seat class objects that have been reserved yet. So trying to reserve the same seat again would make an assertion to fail. That is how the tester is notified about the resource racing issue found.

All the system architect had to do is to set the new stereotype for the method and the proposed method done all other work automatically. The generated asserts are invaluable in our sample situation. Now a technique which consists of our distributed system model checking method and the code which includes generated assertions is able to detect the issue when two users reserve the same cinema seat.

In addition to `<<final>>` stereotype we propose to use two more new setter method stereotypes: `<<intermittent>>` and `<<unique>>`.

`<<intermittent>>` failures usually happens when some value is consistently changing. For example a limited number of used discount coupons should always increase until it reaches maximum allowed value, while in a incorrect implementation the number returned which means current number of used coupons can be increased at the same time by two clients and then set on the server as that new number of used coupons (which is increased only by one while should be increased by two).

`<<unique>>`, as it name says, is used in a case when setter method can only be set to a value that have never been set before while executing the test. This can be useful when registering some objects using ids and the same objects (id) cannot be registered twice.

4 Implementation of the Design

Our distributed system model checker algorithm using JPF [8] is provided in our previous work at [1]. So we chose to focus on Java based systems such as J2SE [9] clients and J2EE [3] servers for the implementation of the design. Despite that, similar systems based on other programming languages can be modeled as well.

For setters and getters used in system under test (and of course in the system class diagrams) we require to use JavaBean setters and getters naming convention [10]. We need to know about the naming convention because it is needed for test generation. JavaBeans are widely used worldwide and this naming convention is actually usually used in Java applications.

The implementation of test generator activity diagram is provided by Fig. 4.

Code constraint generation activity depends on the stereotype applied for the method. The pseudo code which is generated for each of the defined stereotypes is provided in Table 2. We use `<methodName>` key in the code which means the method name without "set" suffix and lower case first letter. So the method "setReserved" would become "reserved". We also use `<getter>` key which is the getter of the setter method that we are analyzing as per JavaBean specification. And finally we use `<parameter>` key which means the object's or primitive type's parameter name which is passed in a setter method.

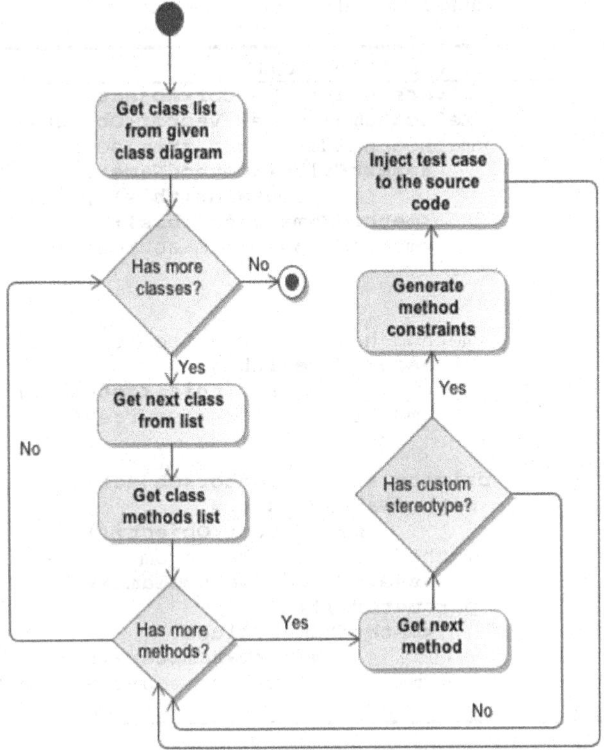

Fig. 4. Test case generator activity diagram

The proposed pseudo code is similar to the <<final>> stereotype one that have been explained earlier in previous section so we do not go into detail on how the injected code is capable of catching resource racing related issues.

Note that each class that contains methods with any of given new stereotypes should override equals method from Java Object class.

When the test case code is injected in the source code the application is compiled. After that we launch our distributed system model checking algorithm which now uses the source with the test cases and simulating two client model checker execute all possible clients and servers communication paths.

This proposed technique is simple to use, versatile and quick to implement for the system architect. All it takes to do is to add required stereotypes for required methods. This does not require any knowledge of any constraint language, just UML basics. This technique is simpler to use comparing to very popular standard OCL constraints [20] or other similar techniques. These techniques tend to become complicated when describing constraints for resource racing issue detection. This is because OCL does not provide such functionality by default. Also existing automated OCL generators are not able to generate OCL constraints for resource racing issue detection [13].

Table 2. Method constrains pseudo code

Stereotype	Generated pseudo code

<<final>>	private static Vector<Object>
	<methodName> = new Vector<Object>();
	<method header taken from source code>{
	assertFalse(<methodName>.
	contains(this));
	<methodName>.add(this);
	<method body from source>
	}

<<intermittent>>	<method header taken from class diagram> {
	assertTure(!this.
	equals(this.<getter>));
	<method body from source>
	}

<<unique>>	private static Vector<Object>
	<methodName>Values =
	new Vector<Object>();
	<method header taken from source code>{
	assertFalse(<methodName>Values.contains(
	<parameter>));
	<methodName>Values.
	add(<parameter>);
	<method body from source>
	}

5 Limitation of the Design

The main limitation of this algorithm currently is the requirement to have slightly customized UML class diagram of the system and slightly adopted methods (if required). If someone would decide to use this technique for any existing project the project manager would have to review all classes in a class diagram and append proposed stereotypes for any of appropriate methods. Also if the setter or getter methods of any class doesn't meet JavaBean requirements, then they should also be changed.

We don't provide any test data generation algorithm in this article. So some of existing techniques should be used. It can be some generator using JPF [11] or genetic algorithms [12] or any other. Test input generation is out of our focus scope at the moment.

6 Conclusions and Future Work

Our previously proposed distributed model checking design [1] has been extended in this paper with the ability to detect resource racing related failures in a networked application. The combination of our two methods provides a testing technique which is able to simulate several users communicating with the same server and is able to detect resource racing related failures between the simulated users. Which means the technique is now able to solve oracle problem.

We proposed to extend UML class diagram method stereotype set with three new stereotypes: `<<final>>`, `<<intermittent>>` and `<<unique>>`. These new method stereotypes allows system architect to describe the resource desired behavior in terms of resource racing. In the future the proposed method stereotype set can be extended with some new stereotypes.

In the future we are planning to implement this method properly and run this technique against some existing distributed system. We are planning on using mutation testing to evaluate how good or bad our technique really is.

Another task for the future is to find new resource racing conditions and provide new methods, classes or member variables stereotypes for these issued detection.

References

1. Jasaitis, R., Bareiša, E.: Distributed system model checking design. In: Information Technologies 2011: Proceedings of the 17th International Conference on Information and Software Technologies, IT 2011, Kaunas, Lithuania, April 27-29 (2011)
2. Le, A.T.: Current Problems and Tools Support for Testing Distributed Systems. A dissertation submitted for the degree of Bachelor of Applied Science with Honours in the Department of Information Science at the University of Otago, Dunedin, New Zealand (2006)
3. Oracle. Java 2 Platform, Enterprise Edition (J2EE) Overview, http://java.sun.com/j2ee/overview.html
4. Oracle. Object-Oriented Programming Concepts, http://docs.oracle.com/javase/tutorial/java/concepts/object.html
5. Object Management Group (OMG). UML Specification, Version 2.0 (2010)
6. Object Management Group (OMG). MOF 2.0/XML Metadata Interchange Mapping Specification, Version 2.1.1 (2007)
7. Brian, A.M., Jeffrey, M.V.: Programming with Assertions: A Prospectus. IT Professional 6(5), 53–59 (2004)
8. Nasa. Java PathFinder Wiki, http://babelfish.arc.nasa.gov/trac/jpf/wiki
9. Oracle. J2SE 5.0, http://www.oracle.com/technetwork/java/javase/index-jsp-135232.html
10. Oracle. JavaBeans Spec, http://www.oracle.com/technetwork/java/javase/documentation/spec-136004.html
11. Visser, W., Pasareanu, C.S., Khurshid, S.: Test Input Generation with Java PathFinder. In: ISSTA 2004, Boston, Massachusetts, USA, July 11-14 (2004)
12. Sun, J., Jiang, S.: An Approach to Automatic Generating Test Data for Multi-path Coverage by Genetic Algorithm. In: 2010 Sixth International Conference on Natural Computation (ICNC 2010), China (2010)
13. Tan, L., Yang, Z., Xie, J.: OCL Constraints Automatic Generation for UML Class Diagram. 978-1-4244-6055-7/10/$26.00, 2010 IEEE (2010)
14. Beyer, D., Chlipala, A., Henzinger, T., Jhala, R., Majumdar, R.: Generating Tests from Counterexamples. In: Proceedings of the 26th International Conference on Software Engineering (ICSE 2004), Scotland, UK, pp. 326–335 (May 2004)

15. Artho, C., Leungwattanakit, W., Hagiya, M.: Cache-based Model Checking of Networked Applications: From Linear to Branching Time. In: ASE 2009, Auckland, New Zealand (November 2009)
16. Tsai, W.T., Chen, Y., Paul, R.: Specification-Based Verification and Validation of Web Services and Service-Oriented Operating Systems. In: 10th IEEE International Workshop on Object-oriented Real-time Dependable Systems (WORDS 2005), Sedona (February 2005)
17. Xiong, P., Probert, R.L., Stepien, B.: An Efficient Formal Testing Approach for Web Service with TTCN-3, http://www.site.uottawa.ca/~bernard
18. Brucker, A.D., Wolff, B.: Testing Distributed Component Based Systems Using UML/OCL, http://citeseer.ist.psu.edu/brucker01testing.html
19. Endo, A.T., da Sima, A., Souza, S.: Web Services Composition Testing: a Strategy Based on Structural Testing of Parallel Programs. IEEE (2008), doi:10.1109/TAIC-.PART.2008.9
20. Object Management Group (OMG). Object Constraint Language Specification, Version 2.2 (2010)

Generating Test Data Using Symbolic Execution: Challenges with Floating Point Data Types

Justinas Prelgauskas and Eduardas Bareisa

Kaunas University of Technology, Software Engineering Department,
Studentu str. 50-406, Kaunas, Lithuania
{justinas.prelgauskas,eduardas.bareisa}@ktu.lt

Abstract. Dynamic compositional symbolic execution is a well-known white-box method for generating unit test data. However there exists certain issues when applying this method for software that heavily depends on floating point data types. In this paper we present these issues and suggest our solution. Our presented method would integrate two techniques: symbolic execution and search-based testing to increase code coverage of software under test. We have implemented it as an extension to tool PEX, that is being developed at Microsoft Research. Our extension implements search-based testing as an optimization technique using AVM method. We present coverage comparison for several benchmark functions.

Keywords: symbolic execution, test data generation, white box testing, search-based testing, floating point data.

1 Introduction

Compositional dynamic symbolic execution[1, 6] is a well-known technique for generating unit test data that would achieve high branch coverage for software with no floating point data types. However, if source code heavily depends on floating point computations, this method is unable to achieve good code coverage results. In this paper we present a method that would integrate both: compositional dynamic symbolic execution[16] and search-based test data generation methods to achieve better code coverage for software that largely depends on floating point computations. We have implemented our method as an extension of a well-know symbolic execution engine – PEX[15]. Our extension implements search-based testing as an optimization technique using AVM[3] method. We present coverage comparison for several benchmark functions.

1.1 Dynamic Symbolic Execution

Static symbolic execution was first proposed by J.C.King [9]. However, in real-world scenarios this method suffers because of external calls, unsolvable constraints and functions that cannot be reasoned about symbolically. This is why dynamic symbolic

T. Skersys, R. Butleris, and R. Butkiene (Eds.): ICIST 2012, CCIS 319, pp. 267–274, 2012.

execution (DSE) was proposed. DSE combines concrete and symbolic execution by providing constraint solver runtime values. Constraints in DSE are simplified in this way so that they become more amenable to constraint solving. However, if source code is analyzed as a single "flat" unit, this method quickly faces the state space explosion problem because its' complexity is exponential in terms of function count in analyzed program.

1.2 Compositional Dynamic Symbolic Execution

Compositional dynamic symbolic execution is an extension to DSE and is currently implemented in several popular tools, such as PEX[15], EXE[5], SMART[6], CUTE[13]. The main idea behind compositional dynamic symbolic execution is to extend DSE with inter- and intra- function call support. Calls to internal functions are analyzed, and every function is augmented with additional meta-data – *function summaries*. Authors of SMART[6] define *function summary* φ_f for a function f as a formula of propositional logic whose propositions are constraints expressed in some theory T. φ_f can be computed by successive iterations and defined as a disjunction of formulas φ_w of the form

$$\varphi_w = pre_w \wedge post_w \tag{1}$$

where pre_w is a conjunction of constraints on the inputs of f while $post_w$ is a conjunction of constraints on the outputs of f. φ_w can be computed from the path constraint corresponding to the execution path w. If we analyze functions in this way we will see that the number of execution paths considered by compositional dynamic symbolic execution will be at most nb (where n is the number of functions f in program P, b is the search depth bound) and is therefore linear in nb. However, this method would end performing random search for floating point constraints that are present in program.

2 Issues with Floating Point Data

In order to reach a branch with some concrete input values, a path constraint for this branch must be passed to constraint solver. Then, a constraint solver must find a counter-example for this constraint or end search with answer "unsatisfiable".

Currently search for a counter-example for floating-point path constraints are implemented in one of the following ways:

1) approximating floating point data types as real types and solving constraint in theory of real numbers [2] (authors' note: no SMT theory of floating point numbers was available at the moment of writing this publication) or

2) performing random search.

However, both solutions have their drawbacks. First option does not take into account specifics of floating point arithmetic (rounding error, normalized forms, etc.) [7]. This method can even sometimes return **incorrect** results. For example when approximating path constraint

$$PC(x) = \{x > 0.0, x + 1.0e^{12} = 1.0e^{12}\} \quad (2)$$

as real constraint (despite x is a floating point variable), constraint solver would not be able to find any solutions that would satisfy this path constraint. However, any floating-point number (represented as defined in IEEE 754 standard[8]) in interval

$$[1.401298464324817e^{-45} \ldots 32767.9990234] \quad (3)$$

is a solution to this constraint. Second option (random search) does not have correctness problem, but is not as effective as some search-based heuristic methods. Furthermore, random search does not have reasonable search termination criteria (it depends only on given time/memory bound of the search). This is why we formulate this problem as an optimization problem and define proper search termination criteria for this type of search (similarly as what was done for hardware testing[4]).

3 Proposed Solution

As soon as our method gets response from constraint solver with answer "unsatisfiable" and constraint contains floating point data types, the corresponding path constraint is forwarded to search-based AVM sub-routine. Entire path constraint *(PC)* can be formulated as a disjunction of individual branch statement constraints in the following way:

$$PC(\vec{x}) = \underset{i \in 0..N}{\wedge} pc_i \quad (4)$$

Vector $\vec{x}$ is what we are trying to find: concrete input values for method under test (MUT). First, we initialize this vector with all random values. Second, using AVM method, we try to move candidate solution towards optimum solution. To do this we first must define what the optimum is by defining the objective function. This function will be used to define whether new generated test input is better or not.

We define the objective (also known as fitness) function Φ as a weighted sum of *branch distance* [17] measures (δ) for each branch statement:

$$\Phi(\vec{x}) = \sum\nolimits_{i \in 0..N} w_i * \delta(\vec{x}) \quad (5)$$

Algorithm goal is to minimize function Φ. When our algorithm starts, all weights w_i for each branch statement pc_i are initialized to 1. The weight is increased if no solution is found for specified number of iterations. This helps algorithm to concentrate on difficult tasks, because whole solution is found only if it satisfies all clauses pc_i.

Distance function δ measures how far current candidate solution $\vec{x}$ is from satisfying the branch constraint pc_i. .NET languages may have various constraint operators in branches. We have defined distance measure function for each of these operators in Table 1.

Table 1. Distance measures for .NET branch operators

Op-code	Examples	δ	Description
BEQ	$a = b$	$N(\|a - b\|)$	Branch on equal.
BGE	$a \geq b$	IF $a \geq b$ THEN 0 ELSE $N(b - a)$	Branch on greater than or equal to.
BGT	$a > b$	IF $a > b$ THEN 0 ELSE $N(b - a)$	Branch on greater than.
BLE	$a \leq b$	IF $a \leq b$ THEN 0 ELSE $N(a - b)$	Branch on less than or equal to.
BLT	$a < b$	IF $a < b$ THEN 0 ELSE $N(a - b)$	Branch on less than.
BNE	$a \neq b$	IF $a \neq b$ THEN 0 ELSE 1	Branch on not equal.
BRFALSE	$a = null$ $a = FALSE$ $a \leq 0$	IF $a = null \mid$ $a = FALSE \mid$ $a = 0$ THEN 0 ELSE 1	Branch on false, null, or zero.
BRTRUE	$a \neq null$ $a = TRUE$ $a > 0$	IF $a = null \mid$ $a = FALSE \mid$ $a = 0$ THEN 1 ELSE 0	Branch on non-false.

Function N denotes a denormalisation function, which normalizes its input into interval [0..1].

We have implemented proposed method as an extension to a well known dynamic symbolic execution tool PEX[15]. Extension was implemented as a custom arithmetic solver using interface *Microsoft.ExtendedReflection.Reasoning. ArithmeticSolving.IArithmeticSolver.* Our extension can be enabled by simply adding custom *AVMCustomArithmeticSolver* attribute to the test assembly containing parameterized unit tests.

4 Evaluation

4.1 Evaluation Subjects

We have evaluated our method with several classical optimization problems [12], manually rewritten into C# language. Details of chosen benchmarks can be seen in Table 2. We have chosen benchmark functions that were previously used in related research by other authors [10, 14].

Table 2. Benchmark functions

Benchmark	C# representation
Brown badly scaled function	(x1 - Math.Pow(10, 6)) == 0 && (x2 - 2 * Math.Pow(10, -6)) == 0 && (x1 * x2 - 2) == 0
Beale function	(1.5 - x1 * (1 - x2)) == 0
Powell singular function	((x1 * 10 * x2) == 0) && (Math.Pow(5, 0.5) * (x3 - x4) == 0) && (Math.Pow((x2 - 2 * x3), 2) == 0) && (Math.Pow(10, 0.5) * Math.Pow((x1 - x4), 2) == 0)
Freudenstein and Roth function	((-13 + x1 + ((5 - x2) * x2 - 2) * x2) == 0) && ((-29 + x1 + ((x2 + 1) * x2 - 14) * x2) == 0)
Rosenbrock function	((1 - x1)==0)&&(10*(x2 - x1 * x1) == 0)

Helical Valley function	(10 * (x3 - 10 * theta(x1, x2))) == 0 &&
	(10 * (Math.Sqrt(x1 * x1 + x2 * x2) - 1)) == 0 &&
	x3 == 0
	
	double theta (double x1, double x2) {
	if(x1 > 0)
	  return Math.Atan(x2 / x1) / (2 * Math.PI);
	else if (x1 < 0)
	  return (Math.Atan(x2 / x1) / (2 * Math.PI) +
	0.5);
	else
	  return 0;
	}

Powell badly scaled function	((Math.Pow(10, 4) * x1 * x2 - 1) == 0) && ((Math.Exp(-x1) + Math.Exp(-x2) - 1.0001) == 0)
Wood function	(10 * (x2 - x1 * x1)) == 0 && (1 - x1) == 0 && (Math.Sqrt(90) * (x4 - x3 * x3)) == 0 && (1 - x3) == 0 && (Math.Sqrt(10) * (x2 + x4 - 2)) == 0 && (Math.Pow(10, -0.5) * (x2 - x4)) == 0

4.2 Experimental Setup

We have implemented simple parameterized test for each benchmark function. Parameterized tests would take function inputs as arguments and have only one "IF" statement. If global optimum for given benchmark function is reached, then test would pass, otherwise, Assert.Fail() will be called. Because of stochastic nature of experiment, we repeated each iteration 100 times. In every iteration for every benchmark function we performed following actions: generated available test inputs, run the generated test and measured block coverage. Average block coverage for each function is given in Fig. 1. In order to have proper results we had to limit exploration bounds. We set maximum exploration time bound for both random and AVM methods to 1 minute in order see a clear distinction between them.

4.3 Evaluation Results

We can clearly see from Fig. 1, that our proposed method outperforms random search in terms of branch coverage for most of benchmark functions. The only function for which average branch coverage was not increased using AVM method was Rosenbrock. Function itself has a long, parabolic shaped flat valley. The global minimum is inside that valley. AVM method finds valley easily, however to converge to the global minimum given previously defined exploration bounds is difficult.

For Beale and Powell badly scaled functions our proposed method was able to find solution, but not for all iterations. This is why average block coverage for those functions was not 100%.

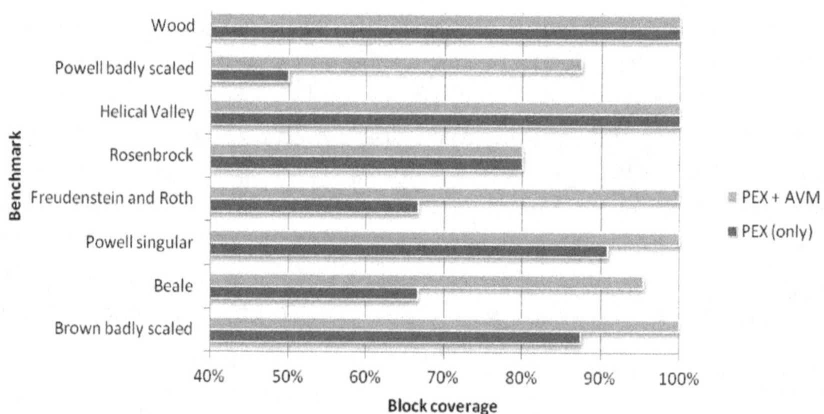

Fig. 1. Average block coverage of generated tests

5 Conclusions

In this article we presented a method for generating test for software that is highly dependent on floating-point expressions and calculations. We have combined two previously well known techniques to solve this problem: compositional dynamic symbolic execution for path exploration and search-based testing (using alternating variable method) for complex floating-point computations.

We have evaluated our proposed method against a suite of benchmark functions. In our future work we plan to implement more search algorithms (e.g. particle-swarm optimization, genetic, etc.) as custom arithmetic solvers, compare their performance and coverage increase. Furthermore, there has been several attempts to integrate floating point arithmetic into several well know SMT solvers (such as Z3). We plan to evaluate same test subjects as soon as any of these SMT solvers gets updated with floating-point solving capabilities. There has recently been issued several studies on real-world software [10, 14] and studies showed, that approximating floating-point types as real types is not always an issue. This is why we plan to perform further experiments with real-world open source projects as well as other optimization algorithms [11].

References

1. Anand, S., Godefroid, P., Tillmann, N.: Demand-driven compositional symbolic execution, pp. 367–381. Springer (2008)
2. Anand, S., Păsăreanu, C.S., Visser, W.: JPF–SE: A Symbolic Execution Extension to Java PathFinder. In: Grumberg, O., Huth, M. (eds.) TACAS 2007. LNCS, vol. 4424, pp. 134–138. Springer, Heidelberg (2007)
3. Arcuri, A.: Full theoretical runtime analysis of alternating variable method on the triangle classification problem, pp. 113–121. IEEE (2009)
4. Bareiša, E., Jusas, V., Motiejūnas, K., Šeinauskas, R.: Defining Random Search Termination Conditions. Electronics and Electrical Engineering 2(66), 26–31
5. Cadar, C., Ganesh, V., Pawlowski, P.M., Dill, D.L., Engler, D.R.: EXE: automatically generating inputs of death. ACM Transactions on Information and System Security (TISSEC) 12(2), 10
6. Godefroid, P.: Compositional dynamic test generation. In: 34th Annual ACM SIGPLAN-SIGACT Symposium on Principles of Programming Languages, pp. 47–54. ACM (2007)
7. Goldberg, D.: What every computer scientist should know about floating-point arithmetic. ACM Computing Surveys (CSUR) 23(1), 5–48
8. Kahan, W.: IEEE standard 754 for binary floating-point arithmetic. Lecture Notes on the Status of IEEE 754. 94720-91776
9. King, J.C.: Symbolic execution and program testing. Commun. ACM 19(7), 385–394
10. Lakhotia, K., Tillmann, N., Harman, M., de Halleux, J.: FloPSy - Search-Based Floating Point Constraint Solving for Symbolic Execution. In: Petrenko, A., Simão, A., Maldonado, J.C. (eds.) ICTSS 2010. LNCS, vol. 6435, pp. 142–157. Springer, Heidelberg (2010)
11. Misevičius, A.: Generation of grey patterns using an improved genetic evolutionary algorithm: some new results. Information Technology and Control 40(4), 330–343

12. Moré, J.J., Garbow, B.S., Hillstrom, K.E.: Testing unconstrained optimization software. ACM Transactions on Mathematical Software (TOMS) 7(1), 17–41
13. Sen, K., Marinov, D., Agha, G.: CUTE: A concolic unit testing engine for C, pp. 263–272. ACM (2005)
14. Souza, M., Borges, M., d'Amorim, M., Păsăreanu, C.S.: CORAL: Solving Complex Constraints for Symbolic PathFinder. In: Bobaru, M., Havelund, K., Holzmann, G.J., Joshi, R. (eds.) NFM 2011. LNCS, vol. 6617, pp. 359–374. Springer, Heidelberg (2011)
15. Tillmann, N., De Halleux, J.: Pex–white box test generation for .net. Tests and Proofs, 134–153
16. Vanoverberghe, D., Piessens, F.: Theoretical aspects of compositional symbolic execution. In: Fundamental Approaches to Software Engineering, pp. 247–261
17. Wegener, J., Baresel, A., Sthamer, H.: Evolutionary test environment for automatic structural testing. Information and Software Technology 43(14), 841–854

Service-Oriented Architecture for Designing of Physical Systems with Efficient Power Consumption

Tomas Blazauskas[1,2], Tomas Iesmantas[2], Robertas Alzbutas[1,2]

[1] Kaunas University of Technology, Studentu str.50, 51368 Kaunas, Lithuania
[2] Lithuanian Energy Institute, Breslaujos str. 3, LT-44403 Kaunas, Lithuania
tomas.blazauskas@ktu.lt

Abstract. A distributed service oriented system which is developed to provide physical system or process monitoring, specification, analysis and simulation services are introduced in this paper. These services in separate components are developed to be used along with computer aided design systems to provide a support for designers in designing physical systems with efficient power consumption. All components of distributed system are presented to describe their role and interaction with Energy Simulator, which is developed by authors of this paper as a key component for simulation of the physical system and for calculation of energy consumption. Then, structure of Energy Simulator and its development process as well as solutions made to create flexible and scalable service oriented architecture is presented. Finally, the implementation of Energy Simulator and a case study devoted for designing of compressed air system is described together with discussion of various constraints of service oriented performance and practical simulation applying MATLAB based tools.

Keywords: Service Oriented Architecture, physical system simulation, power consumption.

1 Introduction

During the last decades the simulation of hybrid and dynamic physical systems was related to the enhancement of modelling capabilities, e.g. applications of combined modelling techniques [2] and specific mathematical oriented languages [3] as well as distributed modelling for physical processes simulation and control [4]. Nowadays, critical issues in designing of advanced physical systems or processes are:

- availability of data and knowledge on actual power consumption;
- balance between requirements regarding performance and efficiency of energy/power use within the manufacturing installations;
- collaborative environment among designers and users.

In addition, the availability of large amounts of computing power, whether in parallel or distributed fashion, enables engineer to investigate large scale modelling problems and to assess various aspects of it, see e.g. [6], where parallel computing was used in order to investigate various aspects of small amounts of information influence on Bayesian statistical inference.

T. Skersys, R. Butleris, and R. Butkiene (Eds.): ICIST 2012, CCIS 319, pp. 275–287, 2012.

So, availability of computational power together with web-based distribution of tasks, which constitute problem at hand, empowers engineer to make more efficient or optimized decisions.

These critical issues in the paper are addressed applying service oriented approach and so called tools of DEMI (Design for AmI Supported Energy Efficient Manufacturing Installations):

- Ambient Intelligent (AmI) systems, which applied for physical systems, on one side, may support energy efficiency of manufacturing processes through various services and, on the other side, can provide the knowledge needed to optimize design from energy efficiency point of view.
- The trade-off between process efficiency and energy use of the designed flexible manufacturing installations, what can be supported by innovative ICT (Information Communication Technology) tools based on TRIZ[1] [1] approach, complex mathematical analysis and simulation techniques.
- The context-sensitive software components were developed following the principles of ICT and based on collaborative working environments, which may be used in order to effectively support collaborative design among the equipment manufacturers and users.

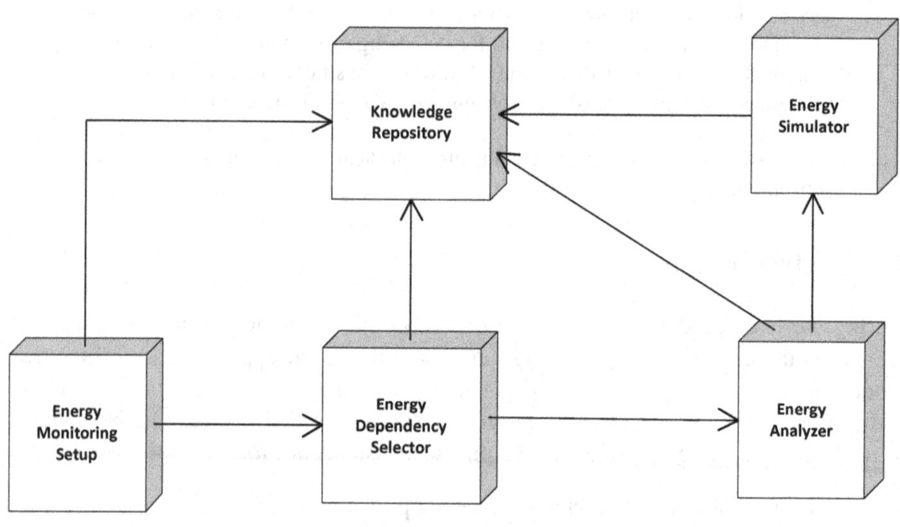

Fig. 1. Components of DEMI system

[1] TRIZ is the Russian acronym for "Theory for Inventive Problem Solving". The work on the Russian Theory for Inventive Problem Solving (TRIZ) began by G. Altshuller in 1946 and continued since then by his students and followers.

The DEMI tools and software could be described as the implementation of different components sharing a mutual knowledge repository[2]. To the user these different ICT components/services provide the ability to assess the energy performance of an existing design or new designs in an effective way. Fig. 1 illustrates how the components are interconnected using service oriented architecture.

The connectors with arrows in Fig. 1 diagram provide information on flows of control tasks. The Energy Monitoring Setup (EMS) component supports the user in a long- and short-term monitoring planning, in the management of monitoring profiles and monitoring orders as well as the monitoring results processing.

The Energy Dependency Selector (EDS) is based on Case Based Reasoning (CBR) / Rule Based Reasoning (RBR) technology enhanced with guidelines from TRIZ [1] principles, which guide the end user in the search for innovative solutions to specific trade-off problems related to the system or process specification and design.

Through multi-objective optimization the Energy Analyser (EA) helps the user to find the optimal design with respect to energy consumption and the user's requirements. The analysis of energy consumption is dependent on an energy estimation and system simulation, which is provided by the simulator.

So called Energy Simulator (ES) is constructed by this paper authors' as an on-the-fly setup and simulation service able to simulate new/innovative manufacturing system or/and process/product designs and estimate energy use for them. It is a key component for simulation of the physical system and calculation of energy consumption.

To establish a joint basis for enabling the information exchange between the DEMI ICT components a joint data model were elaborated, and implemented in the Knowledge Repository (KR). The organization and structure of the repository is dependent on the needs of the other DEMI components, thus KR is considered as a consequence of the other components' design.

As presented before, each of the components is focusing on separate functionalities. However, only by combining components, the full portfolio of the envisaged potentials can be reached. This type of interaction and information exchange between the components requires a harmonization as well as a definition of basic interfaces to enable their integrated usage for designing the physical systems with efficient power consumption.

For implementation of DEMI system, Service Oriented Architecture (SOA) was chosen. One of the SOA benefits which was important to us is that SOA provide the way to define and provision an IT infrastructure, regardless of the operating systems or programming languages underlying those applications [11]. It allows independent development of DEMI components. Also, as notes Gehlen and Pham [5], services oriented architecture and underlying framework enables the simplification of the distributed applications architecture.

---

[2] Knowledge repository is a component, which provide services, although sometimes it is regarded as knowledge database.

2 Energy Simulator

In this section we will describe component called *Energy Simulator*, which is a critical part of the whole DEMI system as it provides physical systems simulation services, and results, which influence all other components. Energy simulator itself consists of several software components which can be used as distributed resources to enable the scalability of the system.

In the first subsection 2.1 we will present service oriented *Energy simulator* architecture and typical workflow (subsection 2.2) for consuming Energy Simulator services. Finally (in subsection 2.3) we will describe operation of simulation software referred as *calculation environment.*

2.1 Service Oriented Energy Simulator Architecture

The simulation of complex physical systems often regarded as expensive [9] in terms of the computational power. Therefore we designed a system which, on the one hand, is flexible and does not require exceptional computer power to handle service requests and, on the another hand, may be implemented by using distributed computer resources or other calculation capability (e.g. supercomputer for parallel calculations).

System deployment scheme is provided in the Fig 2. The system uses three different software components to provide services for client software:

- *SimService*. This software provides actual services, based on SOAP [3] protocol, which communicates with client software and knowledge repository to retrieve specified configurations. It is used to provide services, but does not perform the simulations itself. The main functionality of the service is to add simulation request into the queue, located in local database and provide the results after simulation to the client software.
- *Controller*. This software is used to supervise the task queue, prepare tasks (configurations) for *Calculation Environment* and control calculation environment instances. It also retrieves the results generated by the *calculation environment* and places into the local database.
- *Calculation Environment*. The software performs simulation of the tasks provided by the *Controller* software. In addition to the ability to simulate physical processes, the calculation environment also performs post-processing of simulation results. Operation of calculation environment is described in section 3.

[3] Simple Object Access Protocol for exchanging structured information. Usually used for web service implementation.

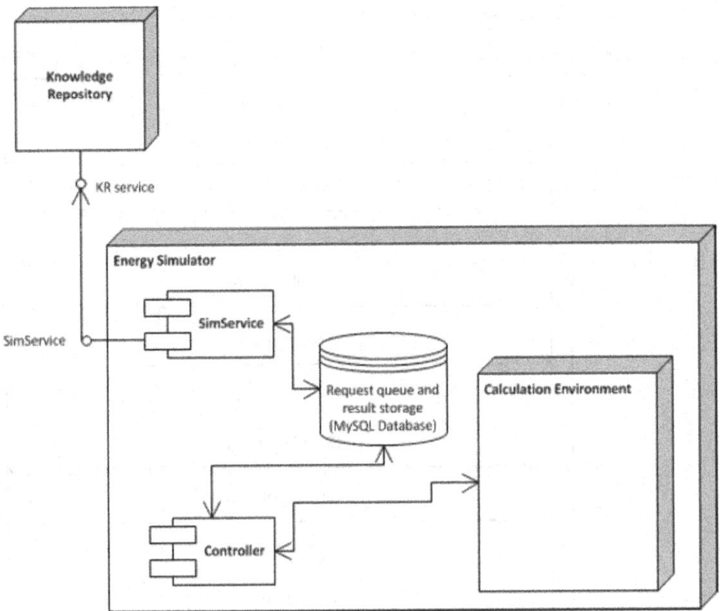

Fig. 2. Current energy simulator service deployment scheme

If energy simulator provider can use distributed or parallel computing resources, *controller* can run a number of parallel calculation environment instances and control them. Therefore the system is scalable, i.e. we can improve overall performance of the system by assigning more computation resources.

Scalability is very important for the system, because it gives the possibility to control the load and effectively use cloud-computing resources. For example, more computing power can be acquired for the short periods of time, when the system is handling increased number of simulation requests. Particularly, when using cloud computing, dynamic scalability becomes more attractive and practical because of the unlimited resource pool [6].

2.2 Client Software Workflow for Consuming Energy Simulator Services

We propose client software workflow illustrated by Fig. 3, although services may be used in different ways.

At the beginning we place simulation request using *InsertSimulationRequest* method, providing API key, configuration ID and boolean value which instructs to store (or not) the result into knowledge repository. Service retrieves configuration parameters as well as used device physical parameters from knowledge repository and stores all the information into the local database.

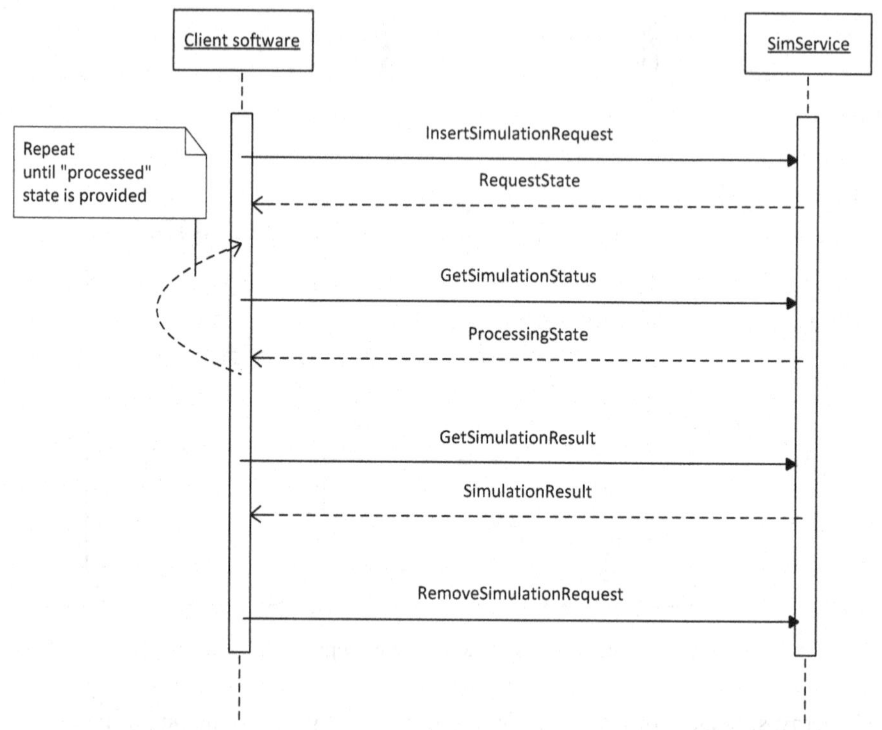

Fig. 3. Client software workflow for consuming energy simulator services

After placing the configurations for simulation, the client software can use polling technique and call method *GetSimulationStatus* repeatedly to see if particular configuration was processed.

When client software receives notification that configuration was processed, method *GetSimulationResult* is used to retrieve simulation results. Client software receives structured data object which contains the values of average/maximal pressure and energy (e.g. electrical power consumed by the working compressors) as well as pressure time series.

Alternatively client software may remove results from simulated configuration list by using *RemoveSimulationRequest*. This function is useful if it is necessary to get updated results after changing simulation algorithms. Also this service is useful when it is necessary to update the results after correcting possible configuration errors.

2.3 Calculation Environment

In our Energy Simulator concept, "calculation environment" refers to a subsystem of ES, which consists of MATLAB (Simulink and SimScape) software and scripts designed for physical systems simulation and results post-processing. Further in this section we will describe how the physical system simulation is carried out within ES.

The simulation of physical system is performed using "block-based modeling" rather than pure "process-based modelling". This means that whole physical system or physical process is decomposed into sub-systems or sub-processes represented by independent blocks (one block for one sub-systems or sub-process).

Sub-system is a specific physical equipment (installation) providing process related output, which itself depends on process related boundary conditions and sub-system parameters (block parameters). Sub-system may be expressed using differential equations with specific parameters.

Sub-process is process variable (output of block) related to physical behaviour of other variables (inputs of block) with their weighting coefficients (block parameters). Sub-process may be expressed as a physical variable or function dependent on other process variables.

The main function is *Calculate Energy Use* (for a specific configuration). The output (response variable) of the system may be any physical variable or/and the energy use, which may be calculated depending on the process variables. This is important in case if Energy Analyser in the specified timescale seeks to obtain the time series or single estimates (e.g. average) of energy use and at certain sub-systems or sub-processes to perform verification of critical values (e.g. maximum) of physical variables, which in turn should confirm that system or process will be operable and compliant with the pre-defined design constraints.

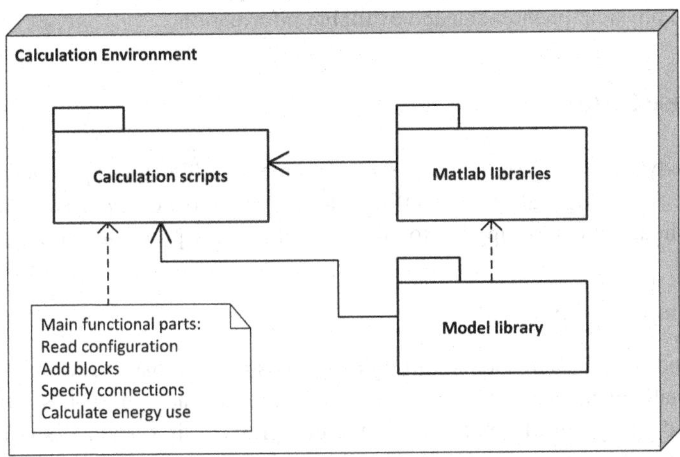

Fig. 4. General overview of calculation environment and its main functions

The list and relation of blocks together with blocks' parameters represents the process configuration, which is the basic information for automatic model generation.

This includes the following four Calculation Environment functionalities: *Read configuration, Add Blocks, Specify Connections* and *Calculate energy use*. The last two functionalities may be related to the application of Model Library, which includes predefined models of possible blocks, i.e. all models of sub-systems or sub-processes.

In accordance to the predefined configuration, initially, whole system or process is modelled automatically connecting all blocks. This can be visualized drawing the lines between the related blocks (see an example in section 3.3). The connected blocks can be mathematically expressed as the system of differential equations or single function, which relates all physical variables. In addition, for the simulation there is a need to perform the evaluation of unknown relations and values, e.g. numerically solve differential equations or evaluate weighting coefficients for physical variables.

In general the process/system modelling and energy use simulation includes the following phases:

- Configuration-based model generation.
- Simulation of process (system).
- Calculation of energy use.

First phase covers first 3 functionalities described above. The last two phases represent the running of the generated model, i.e. simulating the model and performing the calculations, which results are important for Energy Analyser. These phases are covered by the 4th functionality. All three phases depends on the mathematical modelling approach used for specific system or process. For different case the configuration, blocks, modelling, evaluation and simulation is implemented depending on the used mathematical modelling approach, which itself depends on considered physical phenomena and available information.

3 Case Study

In case study we make use of the Service Oriented Architecture approach for Energy Simulator. This application is confined to the case of Compressed Air Systems (CAS), although it can be applied to other manufacturing processes or systems.

3.1 Compressed Air System

Compressed air is used widely throughout industry. Almost every industrial plant, from a small machine shop to an immense pulp and paper mill, has some type of compressed air system. In many cases, the compressed air system is so vital that the facility cannot operate without it.

In many industrial facilities, air compressors use more electricity than any other type of equipment. Inefficiencies in compressed air systems can therefore be significant. Energy saving from system improvements can range from 20% to 50% or more of electricity consumption. A properly managed compressed air system can save energy, reduce maintenance, decrease downtime, increase production throughput, and improve product quality. Compressed Air Systems (CAS) consist of a supply side, which includes compressors and air treatment, and a demand side, which includes distribution and storage systems and end-use equipment.

As an important component for power consumption estimation we will use notion of pressure drop – a term used to characterize the reduction in air pressure from the compressor discharge to the actual point-of use. Pressure drop occurs as the compressed air travels through the treatment and distribution system. Excessive pressure drop will result in poor system performance and excessive energy consumption. Overall pressure drop together with produced flow rate will make essential parts in power consumption estimation.

Even though importance of CAS in industrial applications, still not much research has been done about its power consumption or physical process modelling, e.g. Qin and Mckane [12] reported CAS analysis in terms of energy consumption and Kaya et al. [7] quantified energy losses in CAS.

3.2 Mathematical Model of CAS System

Compressed air system usually consists of several main components: compressors, air dryers, air filters, receivers and connectors. In order to be able to build a mathematical model for whole CAS, one needs to have detailed acting phenomena description. In this case, this phenomenon is a compressed gas flow, which is assumed to be governed by ideal gas thermodynamic laws:

–the energy balance for control volume can be expressed as [10]:

$$\frac{dE_{cv}}{dt} = Q_{cv} - W_{cv} + \sum_i \left(m_i \left(h_i + \frac{1}{2} v_i^2 + gz_i \right) \right) + \sum_o \left(m_o \left(h_o + \frac{1}{2} v_o^2 + gz_o \right) \right),$$

where: E_{cv} - control volume total energy; Q_{cv} - heat energy per second added to the gas through the boundary; W_{cv} - mechanical work per second performed by the gas; h_i, h_o - inlet and outlet enthalpies; v_i, v_o - gas inlet and outlet velocities; z_i, z_o - elevations at inlet and outlet ports; m_i, m_o - mass flow rates in and out of the control volume; g - acceleration due to gravity (all units are in SI system);

–the ideal gas law relates pressure p, density ρ and temperature T as follows:

$$p = \rho RT,$$

where R is specific gas constant.

These laws describe gas flow, temperatures and pressures within each CAS component. Overall pressure drop together with flow demand is then used to estimate compressor power consumption according to the formula:

$$P = \frac{\dot{m} \Delta p}{\eta},$$

where $\dot{m}$ - volumetric flow rate, Δp - overall pressure drop, η - coefficient of efficiency.

However, obtained equations cannot be solved separately, because the thermodynamic processes in one component are determined by the processes in other. To resolve this one needs to treat such systems as a physical network and proceed by solving whole system of equation.

Our numerical experimentations led to the choice of so-called trapezoidal rule with free interpolant for the purpose of solution approximation, because resulting system of differential and algebraic equations are extremely complex and calls for advanced methods.

3.3 Demonstration of Energy Simulator

When ES is invoked by client with new configuration (see *InsertSimulationRequest,* Fig. 3), *GetConfiguration* obtains from database (*KR*) the necessary information about the topology of the CAS system. It is important, that the architecture of ES enables client to provide an array of ID's for different systems and in consecutive order (Fig. 5) it will be processed within ES.

NodeName	AltBlockNames	IN1	IN1 Port	IN2	IN2 Port	Arg1	Arg2
AirSource1	AirSource		0		0		
Compressor1	IRN160K2S	AirSource1	1		0		
Compressor2	IRN160K2S	AirSource1	1		0		
Receiver1	Receiver5000	Compressor1	1	Compressor2	1		
Dryer1	D600INA	flowSensor1	1		0		
Filter1	IRHE1380	Dryer1	1		0		
Dryer2	D600INA	flowSensor1	1		0		
Filter2	IRHE1380	Dryer2	1		0		
Receiver2	Receiver750	Filter1	1	Filter2	1		
Receiver3	Receiver750	Receiver2	1		0		
Receiver4	Receiver750	Receiver3	1		0		
Receiver5	Receiver750	Receiver4	1		0		

Fig. 5. An array of different configurations, supplied to the ES

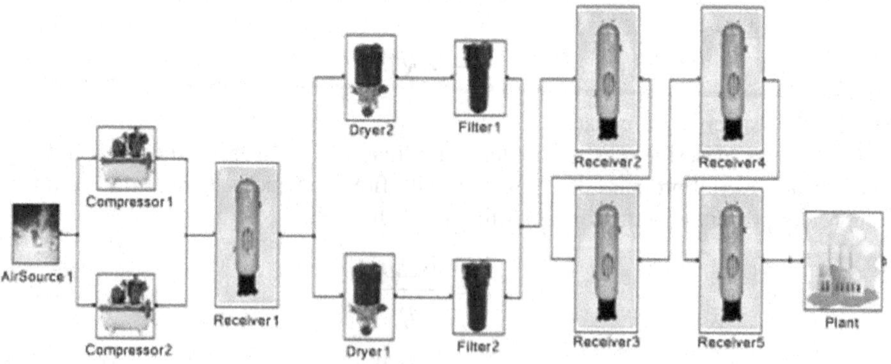

Fig. 6. Example of compressed air system

The top configuration defines real compressed air system, which graphically can be represented as follows:

Once such table-like information is obtained, *AddBlocks* searches within the *Model Library* for necessary blocks and places them in virtual MATLAB environment. If connections defined in table are consistent with those defined within *Library*, this configuration will be triggered, flow rate time series loaded (Fig. 7) and numerical simulation started.

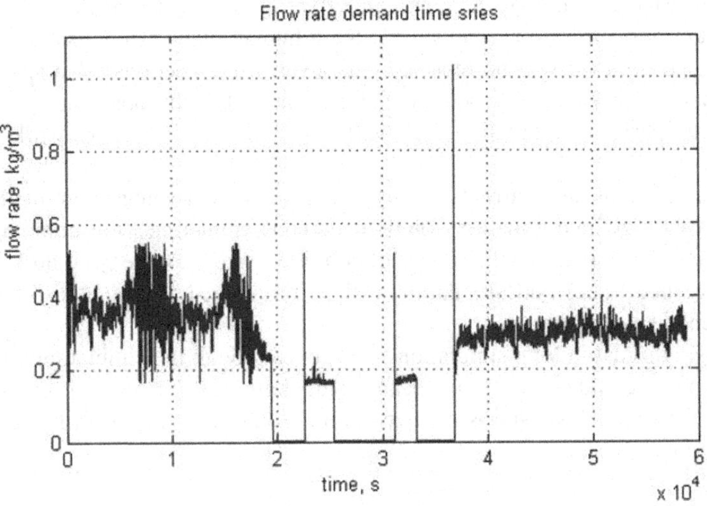

Fig. 7. Flow rate demand in one factory

After the simulation is performed various thermodynamic characteristics as well as energy can be obtained: maximum pressure, average temperature with some particular component (e.g. receiver), etc (Table 1):

Table 1. Energy consumption estimates

Maximum (kW)	Minimum (kW)	Average (kW)
202.88	1.35	58.41

Once required characteristics become available, they will be provided to the client with *SimulationResult*.

3.4 General ES Performance Investigation

Although many configurations can be provided to the ES at one time, the time of simulation of one system varies and depends on many aspects. One such aspect is the complexity or the size of the system. As number of components increases, system of differential and algebraic equations also will increase (in size as well as in complexity). However the size alone is not the most important influencing factor. The system can be made of moderate number of components, but the interdependencies between them can be of various degrees, and such correlations lead to the so-called high stiffness of resulting differential-algebraic equations. This issue can lead to the systems for which numerical simulation will last quite long, sometimes unacceptably long.

Unacceptably long simulation times usually occure, when the physical parameters of particular system are specified to be smaller than the real values, e.g. pressure drop along dryer usually is around 0.2 bars, while typing error can lead to the value 0.02 bars and resulting simulation can "stuck". Such human made errors are not analyzed within ES and no error will be reported. However, if connections (also specified by engineer) are inconsistent (e.g. some component are left with loose end) in this case ES will not perform simulation and will report that physical network are not connected.

Since simulations are carried out by using numerical integration method and gradient-based algebraic equation solution methods, sometimes the combination of physical parameters as well as influence of complex system topology could lead to the non-convergence issues and simulation will be terminated with a note for the user about the encountered error.

Previously discussed long simulation times, even though the simulation will end at some time point, could cause a jam, because other still-unprocessed configurations are waiting in the row. This issue is resolved if more than one instance of computation environment is available.

4 Conclusions

On the basis of the acquired experience in hybrid and dynamic physical systems modelling and applying modern possibilities of ICT, the service oriented software and related simulation methods for designing of physical systems were developed.

Computer aided designing procedure include simulation of physical systems and optimization of power consumption, which require a lot of computational power. Therefore functionally independent ICT components, especially for simulation and analysis, should be identified and implemented for the designing system. Service oriented architecture enables to use these components flexibly and effectively applying distributed computing resources. The case study on designing of compressed air system has shown the physical system dependent constraints of calculation resources and the necessity to run several calculation environments independently.

Service oriented architecture enables one to apply the Energy Simulator to other cases, not just compressed air system, e.g. energy estimation of plastic moulding, the usage of gas in heat treatment process, etc.

Although the proposed and implemented Energy Simulator component is a part of larger DEMI system, it also could be used independently by other computer aided designing systems providing services of physical systems simulation and power consumption calculation.

Acknowledgement. This research was done under the project DEMI (Product and Process Design for AmI Supported Energy Efficient Manufacturing Installations) with partial financing from European Commission under the 7th Framework programme.

References

1. Altshuller, G.: 40 Principles. TRIZ Keys to Technical Innovation. Technical Innovation Center Inc., USA (1997)
2. Alzbutas, R., Janilionis, V.: The simulation of dynamic systems using combined modelling. Mathematical Modelling and Analysis 5, 7–17 (2000) ISSN 1392-6292
3. Alzbutas, R., Janilionis, V.: Dynamic systems simulation using APL2. In: Proceedings of APL 1999 International Conference on all Array Oriented Languages, pp. 20–25. ACM, Scranton (1999)
4. Alzbutas, R., Janilionis, V.: The combined modelling of dynamic system control. Science Works of Lithuanian Mathematicians Association III, 329–335 (1999)
5. Gehlen, G., Pham, L.: Mobile web services for peer-to-peer applications. In: Second IEEE Consumer Communications and Networking Conference, CCNC 2005 (2005)
6. Iesmantas, T., Alzbutas, R.: Age dependent hierarchical Bayesian modelling for reliability assessment under small data sample. To be Presented PSAM 11 & ESREL 2012 Conference (2012)
7. Kaya, D., Phelan, P., Chau, S.: Ibrahim Energy conservation in compressed-air systems. International Journal of Energy Research 26, 837–849 (2002)
8. Mao, M., Li, J., Humphrey, M.: Cloud auto-scaling with deadline and budget constraints. In: Proceedings of GRID (2010)
9. Marzolla, M.: Distributed Simulation of Large Computer Systems. In: Proc. of CHEP 2001, International Conference on Computing in High Energy and Nuclear Physics, Beijing, P. R. China, pp. 477–480 (2001)
10. Moan, M., Shapiro, H.: Fundamentals of Engineering Thermodynamics, 2nd edn. John Wiley & Sons, New York (1992)
11. Newcomer, E., Lomow, G.: Understanding SOA with Web Services. Addison-Wesley (2005)
12. Qin, H.S., Mckane, A.: Improving Energy Efficiency of Compressed Air System Based on System Audit (2008)

Voice Controlled Interface for the Medical-Pharmaceutical Information System

Vytautas Rudzionis[1], Kastytis Ratkevicius[2], Algimantas Rudzionis[2], Rytis Maskeliunas[2], and Gailius Raskinis[3]

[1] Vilnius University, Kaunas Faculty, Muitines str. 8, Kaunas, Lithuania
vytautas.rudzionis@vukhf.lt
[2] Kaunas University of Technology, Information Technologies Institute, Studentu str. 48A-303 Kaunas, Lithuania
kastytis.ratkevicius@ktu.lt
[3] Vytautas Magnus University, Informatics Faculty, Vileikos 8, Kaunas, Lithuania
g.raskinis@if.vdu.lt

Abstract. This paper describes our efforts developing the voice controlled interface for the medical- pharmaceutical information system. It is well known that voice controlled interfaces are of particular importance and may provide significant convenience for healthcare professionals. Many international IT companies provide speech processing by using tools oriented at the physicians or at other professionals working in the related areas. Lithuanian professionals feel a significant lack of speech processing since there are still no attempts to integrate Lithuanian speech processing into medical information systems in this country. The paper presents several IS under development for the use in Lithuanian healthcare institutions. The experimental evaluation shows that it is possible to achieve recognition accuracy (at least 95% of correct recognition) acceptable for the practitioners. The evaluation of system prototypes shows that voice interfaces may lead to the increased convenience of IT systems at the healthcare practitioners.

1 Introduction

Voice technology is potentially of an enormous benefit for the people working in the healthcare industry. This importance is well seen from the fact that companies specializing in the development of products using speech processing technologies include various products particularly aimed at the healthcare practitioners. This trend is clearly seen from the early days of the emergence of voice processing market. Among such products are tools for the automatic transcription of patient case-records, tools for the ubiquitous access to personal medical records (built upon principle "anytime-anywhere") and often using various modern mobile devices, products to get the necessary medical information or to control some of the medical equipment in a hands-free mode (what means using voice commands), or to query the info in the medical databases [1].

T. Skersys, R. Butleris, and R. Butkiene (Eds.): ICIST 2012, CCIS 319, pp. 288–296, 2012.

The importance of voice processing technologies in the medical field may be explained by various factors. One very important factor is the high cost of qualified healthcare practitioners and hence the desire to use the time of these practitioners more efficiently. This means providing the required information as soon as possible or immediately if necessary. Also these include the desire to reduce the amount of subsidiary duties and work (often called "paper work"). In some cases it is important to leave the attention of medical personnel uninterrupted which means providing the possibilities to control the medical equipment by voice, thus reducing the necessity to look at the monitors or to press some keys to control the device. In fact all of this is true for many areas of human activities, but the high costs of healthcare system and the high responsibility facing the people working in this field gives the medical area the priority, especially when developing products utilizing speech processing capabilities [2].

Recent years witnessed at least several important events when developing various speech controlled applications for the different fields of applications. Microsoft, Nuance and some other companies began to distribute speech application programming tools. Such tools provided the developers with a whole set of new and useful tools easing, speeding up and making more economically affordable the development of voice user based interfaces. Researchers usually have their proprietary tools to implement voice user interfaces into the specific types of applications but their implementation into the more universal platforms often makes troubles. Another very important factor was the increased recognition accuracy of available speech recognition engines that made voice user interfaces acceptable for a wide range of users [3].

But all this is true only for the countries were the widely spoken languages (such as English or Spanish) are used as a primary way of communication. The providers of SAPI tools distribute speech recognition engines only for the most popular languages and aren't interested in the development of speech engines for such rarely spoken languages as Lithuanian. Therefore other approaches need to be found in the development of systems for such languages [4]. Our experience with the adaptation of foreign language speech engines to recognize Lithuanian voice commands showed that it is possible to achieve very high recognition accuracy for many Lithuanian voice commands using only the proper selection of phonetic transcriptions for the Lithuanian voice command. Such approach enabled the development of some limited vocabulary applications easier and more economically viable. Earlier research also showed that not all voice commands may be recognized efficiently. It is necessary to use a proprietary recognizer to recognize these specific commands in sufficient quality. The combination of the results provided by two different recognizers requires implementing a so called hybrid approach.

2 Voice Controlled System for the Form Filling of Sick-Lists

Few years ago healthcare institutions in Lithuania moved to the electronic form of sick-lists. Old traditional "paper" sick-lists that were issued by the healthcare institutions (given to the state social security foundation) were replaced by the electronic declarations. It means that instead of the traditional paper sick-list physicians are forced to fulfill electronic declaration form and to send this electronic form to the state social security foundation. The benefits of the electronic forms are clear: those forms reduce the time necessary to check and to evaluate at the state institutions, reduce the possibilities of unintentional errors, etc. In this way it is expected that overall administrative costs of the social security foundation will be reduced as well. Such electronic service could be realized using traditional graphic user interfaces and the desktop computers with Internet connection (e.g. eligible physicians signs in into a website of the social security foundation and fulfills the appropriate fields of the predefined form of the sick-list). Internet based realizations are the most common way to move the service to the electronic media and are used in Lithuanian healthcare institutions most frequently. In practice this approach has several weaknesses. These days there are about 12 thousand doctors that have the rights to issue and are issuing sick-lists to the patients in Lithuania. Of course not all of them are familiar (user friendly) with computers and some estimates show that only 2 thousand of them have a computer at their working place. In this situation some healthcare institutions established special departments were trained personal are filling electronic sick-lists using the data provided by the doctors in that institution. It is not difficult to understand that while lowering the administrative costs of the state institutions such approach will increase the costs of the healthcare institutions. Voice based interface could provide an alternative which is more efficient: doctor can call to the special self-service call center (e.g. using a mobile phone – the device used by the nearly all doctors these days) and tell the necessary data – thus identifying a patient, illness and saying the day of the start and the duration of the sick-leave.

The careful investigation of the vocabulary used in this application showed that most of the commands could be constructed from the digit names or digit strings, e.g. the person could be identified from the personal code, the disease name is coded using a letter name and several digit names, while the other important information for the successful filling of the form is the date when a patient went sick and the duration of the leave. All these considerations allow us to conclude that an effective recognition of digit names is of the essential importance for the successful implementation of this service.

In our previous experiments we've showed that a proper selection of phonetic transcriptions in principle enables achieving high and acceptable (for many practical applications) recognition accuracy of Lithuanian voice commands using foreign language speech engine [5]. The main aim of the new experiments was to establish the limits of possibilities to improve the recognition accuracy of Lithuanian voice commands using a whole word as a main unit and the recognition of words composed from subunits (UPS based phonemic units [6]). Voice controlled information systems were developed and installed on computers running Microsoft Windows'7 operating systems utilizing speech engines designed for this operating system. A Microsoft Spanish/English ASR engine 8.0 was investigated and compared to Microsoft Speech Server MSS'2007 engines. The corpora used contained utterances from 20 different speakers (5 male, 15 female).

Table 1. Average recognition accuracy of Lithuanian digits using English and Spanish engines and different sets of transcriptions

Transcription	*Recognizer and number of digits*			
	ES 8.0 10 digits	ES 8.0 6 digits	EN 9.0 10 digits	ES 9.0 10 digits
Words	93.9	98.0	-	-
Subunits	**94.7**	**98.5**	77.0	**97.0**

Each speaker pronounced the names of each of the 10 digits 20 times. Table 1 shows the obtained results (ES 8.0 means Microsoft Spanish 8.0 engine, EN 9.0 – MSS'2007 English 9.0 engine and ES 9.0 – MSS'2007 Spanish 9.0 engine).

The hybrid approach of recognizer implementation guarantee the recognition accuracy above the target 95 % – in this case the results of 6 digits recognition are estimated eliminating four worst recognition results and taking 4 results from the other recognizer.

Another experiment using MSS'2007 confirmed the assumption that telephony applications could not be implemented in MSS'2007 without the hybrid approach of two recognizers. The technique of proper transcriptions selection, presented in [7], was used in the experiments for recognizing some of the Lithuanian phrases. Nine Lithuanian phrases ("domestic accident", "accident on the way to the work", "donor", "epidemic", "nursing of the patient", "disease", "professional disease", "prosthesis", "observation of healthy child"), used in the internet version of electronic medical documents management system [8], presenting the cases of disability were chosen. Speech corpus consisted of 14 speakers with 60 utterances. Excellent result of phrases recognition was achieved - all phrases were recognized without errors.

3 Voice Controlled Information System for Drug/Pharmaceuticals

The following informative service is oriented at the workplace of physician/ pharmacist and seeks to support and to speed up the search of the necessary information in pharmaceutical databases. In the practice of physician, the problem of getting the information about a particular drug or medicine arises frequently. This problem should often be solved (or at least it is highly desirable to solve it) immediately while performing medical procedures, e.g. during visiting rounds, during inspection etc. The main reason of such queries is the desire to get information about the contraindications of drugs, about a possibility to prescribe the drug in a combination with another drug used by the patient, etc. The necessity to obtain immediate response also means that a doctor must receive the information even in the places without the access to the computer. Today's physicians perform such checks after visitation, meaning that they need to do the same job additionally, sometimes querying the patient additionally. And most importantly the overall productivity of doctor is lower compared to a case, if this information would be available immediately on demand. Voice command interface is a highly convenient solution in this situation: physician may say the name of the drug or medicine of interest using a mobile device (mobile devices are with medical practitioners almost always), this utterance then will be transferred to the speech recognition server, name recognized, appropriate request formed and sent to the pharmaceutical database and consequently response generated and sent to the mobile device of a physician. The important property of this approach is also the fact that the request may be sent without taking the attention of doctor away from other procedures performed. This will enable saving the working time of the physician since he/she will not need to take the attention away from the patient and possibly check for more information if necessary in the same time frame.

There are about 5000 different drugs and medicines registered in Lithuania and all necessary information about them is collected in single publicly available database. It is planned to recognize the names of at least 1000 drugs (and consequently formulate voice queries about 1000 drugs) with the possibility to extend the vocabulary to the bigger number of drug names later. Many names of the drugs are of an international origin but are usually pronounced in a special way: some speakers are using international pronunciation while some Lithuanian pronunciation, e.g. the name of the same drug could be pronounced as "ibumetin" or "ibumetinas". Some drug names have several different pronunciation styles (especially different types of stressing). The good example of such name could be the drug called "cardac" which could be pronounced as "kardak", "kardas", "kardakas", "tsardak" etc. Some names of drugs are usually pronounced using unofficial names. Lexical and morphological rules are often difficult to apply too, since the names of drugs are constructed by the researchers and patent holders and aren't constructed according the rules of Lithuanian grammar and phonetics. Among the other factors complicating the task is the speaker-independent nature of the proposed service: it is aimed to the wide range of healthcare practitioners and the service should help to save the time so it is rather difficult to expect that the user will spend some time adapting the service for the personal use. Important problem is the fact that the drug names aren't a fixed set and may change in time. So it is desirable to develop based on the recognition of a syllable or other phonemic unit's basis and in this way providing the flexibility to the system and to enable the possibility to introduce new names in the future.

All of the above mentioned considerations require and investigation of several recognition factors important to the successful development of this service. Among these factors are the number of speakers used for training and the impact of the number of speakers to the recognition accuracy both using a proprietary recognizer and the adapted foreign language recognizer; the impact of the number of Gaussian mixtures used in the recognition of medicines in the speaker –independent mode, etc. These questions are particularly important since we are aiming to find an optimum choice between the adapted foreign language recognition system and a proprietary recognizer: the more we will train proprietary recognizer the more likely it will perform better, but at the same time this will increase the system development costs. Other problem is that it should be evaluated on how to select the commands to be recognized using an adapted speech recognizer and using a proprietary trained recognizer. Further we will present several experiments aiming to clarify some issues related to these problems.

The first step in the development of the above mentioned service is the collection of the speech corpora containing drug and medicines names. These corpora will be used to adapt a foreign language speech recognizer and to train a proprietary recognizer. This is a costly and a time consuming process.

Trying to evaluate the amount of data necessary to develop such voice interface we carried on several experiments using a corpus of 100 first and family names pronounced in combination. The names and in particular the family names have several properties making them similar with the pronunciation of drug names: sometimes they are pronounced differently by different speakers; sometimes it is unclear which syllable should be stressed and hence different speaker stresses different syllable, etc. From the other point of view names and surnames are non-grammatical lexical constructions and don't have a semantic meaning which could be used to help to recognize the word. The corpora contained the utterances of 36 speakers each pronouncing 100 combinations of name-surname 20 times.

Table 2. The recognition accuracy of 100 Lithuanian names and surnames

Engine type	*Spanish*	*English*
Word error rate %	6.67	68.3

In this experiments validated was corpora used. The first experiment used an adaptation of English and Spanish recognition engines for the recognition of Lithuanian names (not all the names were of Lithuanian origin). Table 2 summarizes the results of this experiment. No optimization of phonetic transcriptions was performed. Experiment clearly showed that a Spanish engine outperformed an English recognizer. In the case of Spanish, relatively good recognition accuracy was achieved especially taking into the account the fact that no optimization of the adaptation was performed. These results also provide the first assumptions on how much the voice commands may be necessary to train the proprietary recognizer for use in hybrid approach.

In the next experiment we've tried to evaluate the importance of the corpora quality for the recognition accuracy using an adapted speech engine. Here two different corpora were used. Both corpora contained the same acoustic-phonetic material (the utterances the name-surname) but one of them was corrected (checking for the accuracy of each pronunciation) while another contained the raw material. It should not be understood that under the raw unchecked data we don't understand rough mistakes: it means that some words were pronounced with indistinct speech. Also parts of some pronunciations weren't pronounced, etc. Such phenomenon is usual in everyday speech. Two different recognition modes were used: one mode treated combination "name-surname" as the single voice command while the other treated it as two separate voice commands spoken in conjunction. Table 3 summarizes the results of the experiments. The Spanish commercial speech recognizer was used for the adaptation purposes.

Table 3. The word recognition error rate using raw and corrected corpora and recognizing the pairs "name-surname" as single command and two commands

Corpora	*Single command*	*Two commands*
Raw	9.38	8.54
Corrected	7.92	6.67

As can be expected, a checked and corrected corpora led to better recognition accuracy than a raw corpora. It could be also seen that the increase in recognition accuracy isn't dramatic. If properly collected even the unchecked speech corpora may be used for the evaluation purposes and may serve as a tool to evaluate voice commands. These results allowed the observation showing that there were no big differences in recognition accuracy if the word pairs were recognized as single command or two consecutive voice commands. In this way such results could serve as indicator for the plans to use single acoustic-phonetic model for the whole voice command or to combine several separate acoustic-models together for the recognition purposes.

Summarizing these results we may conclude that the majority of voice commands necessary to implement voice user interface for the medical-pharmaceutical information system could be successfully recognized using the adapted foreign language recognition system. We could also conclude that the selection of those commands which could be recognized using adapted foreign language engine may be done using corpora with minimum optimization.

4 Prototype of Voice Controlled Medical Information System

The results of the recognition experiments enabled us to begin the development of prototype system aimed to perform the tasks was described above. The basis of the development of this program was our program for computer control by voice commands called "Balsas" which was developed in 2008 [9]. New version of this program – the prototype of voice controlled information system is based on Microsoft SAPI 5.4. NET technology - Microsoft Visual Studio'2010 programming environment with Microsoft .NET Framework 4.0 and Visual C# programming language. Despite the fact that a system is still far from the implementation several aspects of practical implementation became clear and will be implemented in the system. Among them are the next specific features of the program:

- using of separate grammars for voice-controlled programs – it reduces the instantaneous number of voice commands and increases the recognition accuracy of commands (the grammar is reloaded after changing the voice-controlled program);
- control key combinations which simulates the voice commands presented in the grammars as „tag" values – it greatly simplifies the amount of program code;
- the structure of grammars enables using together multiple UPS-based or word-based transcriptions of commands and synonyms of commands according the SRGS grammar specification [10]. This is potential element of implementation of hybrid recognition approach.

The part of the XML code from the developed system is shown below:

```
<item>
<one-of>
<item>baigtidarba</item>
<item>uzdarytiprograma</item>
<token sapi:pron="B A J G T I D A DX B
A">baigtidarba</token> // close the program
<token sapi:pron="U S D A DX T I P DX O G DX A M
A">uzdarytiprograma</token> // end the task
</one-of>
<tag>$._value = "%{F4}"</tag>
</item>
```

As you can see you could use several different commands to perform the same task, the commands could be composed using subword units or a description of command as a single entity. Potentially we could implement the other recognizer using appropriate XML command to the link.

5 Conclusions

Voice based user interfaces could serve as a very useful and desirable element in various services and tools aimed to help healthcare practitioners to perform their duties better. VUI may enable the saving of physician's time, getting the necessary information faster, etc. The countries were non-widely spoken languages are used as the primary way of communication need to look for special strategies developing VUI based services, since major technological companies aren't willing to develop speech recognition engines for such languages. The development of own speech recognizers may be a too expensive solution in many cases. It is possible to adapt a foreign language recognizer and to achieve acceptable system performance for a wide range of applications but this approach can't guarantee a success in every case. The implementation of a hybrid recognition principle – the adaptation of a foreign language commercial recognizer to process the big part of voice commands used in the application and to train a proprietary recognizer to process the rest of commands - may save the time and costs of the systems in development.

A characteristic property of a medical-pharmaceutical information system is that they are characterized by the specific vocabularies where the same semantic term could be used in different phonetic realizations. This means that it is necessary to detect the variety of phonetic pronunciations and to develop the necessary phonetic models for each different phonetic pronunciation.

Experimental evaluation showed that such combined approach may lead to the successful development of voice user interface for medical-pharmaceutical information systems.

Acknowledgment. Parts of this work were done under the research project No.:31V-33/12 funded by "High technology development program for 2011-2013" project "Hybrid recognition technology for voice interface" (INFOBALSAS).

References

1. Sherwani, J., Ali, N., Mirza, S., Fatma, A., Memon, Y., Karim, M., Tongia, R., Rosenfeld, R.: HealthLine: Speech-based Access to Health Information by Low-literate Users. In: Proc. of International Conference on Information and Communication Technologies and Development, ICTD 2007, pp. 34–42 (2007)
2. Mohr, D., Turner, D., Pond, G., Kamath, J., de Vos, C., Carpenter, C.: Speech recogntiion as a transcription aid: a randomized comaprison with standard transcription. Journal of AM Med Inform Assoc. 10(1), 85–93 (2003)
3. Alapetite, A., Andersen, H., Hertzum, M.: Acceptance of speech recognition by physicians: a survey of expectations, experiences and social influence. Int. Journal of Human-Computer Studies 67(1), 36–49 (2009)
4. Schultz, T.: Multilingual Acoustic Modelling. In: Schultz, T., Kirchhoff, K. (eds.) Multilingual Speech Processing. Elsevier, Academic Press (2006) ISBN 13: 978-0-12-088501-5
5. Maskeliūnas, R., Rudžionis, A., Ratkevičius, K., Rudžionis, V.: Investigation of Foreign Languages Models for Lithuanian Speech Recognition. Electronics and Electrical Engineering. - Kaunas, Technologija 3(91), 37–42 (2009)
6. Universal Phone Set (UPS) (2004), http://msdn.microsoft.com/en-us/library/hh361647.aspx
7. System of electronic documents management (2010), http://epts.sodra.lt/bendra-informacija.jsp
8. Speech Recognition Grammar Specification Version 1.0 (2005), http://www.w3.org/TR/speech-grammar
9. Rudžionis, A., Dumbliauskas, T., Ratkevičius, K., Rudžionis, V.: Control of computer by voice commands. In: Information Technologies 2008: Proceedings of the 14th International Conference on Information and Software Technologies, Kaunas, Lithuania, April 24-25, pp. 249–254 (2008)
10. Dunn, M.: Pro Microsoft Speech Server 2007: Developing Speech Enabled Applications with .NET, 275 p. Apress, New York (2007)

Design of a Neural Interface Based System for Control of Robotic Devices

Ignas Martisius, Mindaugas Vasiljevas, Kestutis Sidlauskas, Rutenis Turcinas, Ignas Plauska, and Robertas Damasevicius

Kaunas University of Technology, Software Engineering Department, Studentų 50, LT-51368, Kaunas, Lithuania
ignas_martisius@inbox.com,
{vasiljevasm,kestutissid,rutenisturcinas}@gmail.com,
ignas.plauska@stud.ktu.lt, robertas.damasevicius@ktu.lt

Abstract. The paper describes the design of a Neural Interface Based (NIS) system for control of external robotic devices. The system is being implemented using the principles of component-based reuse and combines modules for data acquisition, data processing, training, classification, direct and the NIS-based control as well as evaluation and graphical representation of results. The system uses the OCZ Neural Impulse Actuator to acquire the data for control of Arduino 4WD and Lynxmotion 5LA Robotic Arm devices. The paper describes the implementation of the system's components as well as presents the results of experiments.

1 Introduction

A brain-computer interface (BCI) is a communication and control channel, which does not require the user to perform any physical action [1]. The BCI systems use the electroencephalogram (EEG) data ("brainwaves") derived from electrodes placed onto the head of the subject, which record the electrical activity of neurons in the brain. The user receives feedback reflecting the outcome of the BCI system's operation, and that feedback can subsequently affect the user's intent and its expression in brain signals [2].

A Neural Interface System (NIS) is a system that uses the EEG data together with data representing other types of neural activity such as muscular or ocular movements [3]. The signals reflecting the activities of nervous system are acquired using the neural signal acquisition device. These signals are evoked by the nervous system as the result of an internal stimulus (thought) or an external stimulus (perception), and can display stable time relationships to a reference event [4]. The acquired data consists of a set of multi-channel signals derived from multiple electrodes and reflects the muscular activity of the head, eye movements, interference from nearby electric devices and electrical grid, skin-electrode impedances and changing conductivity in the electrodes due to the movements of the subject or physicochemical reactions at the electrode sites [5]. Therefore, additional processing (denoising, filtering) of the NIS data is required to remove noise and other unwanted signals. Then the data is used to

T. Skersys, R. Butleris, and R. Butkiene (Eds.): ICIST 2012, CCIS 319, pp. 297–311, 2012.

map the mental states of the subject into the control states (or commands) of a computer program or an external device. This mapping is usually performed using some classifier such as Artificial Neural Network (ANN) or Support Vector Machine (SVM).

The NIS and BCI systems have a wide range of possible practical applications. The main use is to allow communication and operation of electronic devices for physically-disabled people. They include systems for managing basic environmental control (e.g., lights, temperature, television), providing Yes/No questions to answers [6, 7, 8] or driving a wheelchair [4]. Other applications include virtual reality, games, robot control and control of household appliances [9].

In recent years, a number of systems were demonstrated that record the subject's mental state using the motor imagery (MI)-based BCI (e.g., [1]) and map it to the control instructions of a robotics device. For example, Cong *et al.* [10] describes a motor imagery BCI-based robotic arm system to control a robot arm with multiple freedoms. The system consists of the MI-based BCI subsystem which maps EEG data to eight control commands, and robot arm control subsystem, in which the arm only can move toward six directions. The MI-based BCI systems can reliably use only 3-4 control instructions, while increasing the number of instructions means that the accuracy of the BCI system decreases [10]. As usually a few seconds of the data are required for each control decision [11], the approach unsuitable for controlling fast moving object in real-time.

Other approaches for robot control include using the P300 event-related potentials, which produce the response in 300 ms time [12], and using Steady-State Visual Evoked Potentials (SSVEP) to capture the brain's response to flashing symbols [13]. For example, Nawroj *et al.* [14] describe the design, development and test of the BCI system to remotely control the motion of a robot based on identification of P300 response in the EEG data in real-time. Duguleana [15] proposes integrating BCI with other modalities of human-computer interface such as image processing and speech recognition for industrial mobile robot control.

BCI2000 [16] is perhaps the best known example of the BCI system. It has four modules: Source (a data acquisition and storage component), Signal Processing (several components that extract signal features and translate them into device commands), User Application (responsible for stimuli and feedback), and Operator Interface. The modules communicate through a network-capable protocol. BCI2000 also allows communications with other software. Several extensions of the BCI2000 system exist such as [17], which extends BCI2000 with an intelligent graphical user interface (IGUI) and a User Application Interface (UAI). The IGUI has: a two way interface for communication with BCI2000; an interface to user applications for sending of user commands and device identifiers, and receiving notifications of device status. The UAI provides a platform for device interaction by providing a layer of abstraction above different device standards and communication protocols.

In this paper, we describe the development of a NIS system for a control of various external electronics devices. Section 2 describes architecture of the developed system. Section 3 describes functionality and characteristics of the system's components. Section 4 presents an outline of experiments to perform with the system. Finally, Section 5 presents conclusions and considers future work.

2 Architecture of the System

The development of the NIS is based on the principles of *component-based reuse* [18]: we use domain analysis to identify the required components of the system, and then perform code scavenging to search for the open source implementations of the components. The emphasis is on the reuse and adaptation on third-party components rather than implementing the entire system from scratch. The approach allows for rapid prototyping and quality ensurance. The main tasks of the design architect are to perform thorough domain analysis, selection of the programming language based on the availability of third-party components and libraries, identification of components to reuse as needed, if available, and to implement if not available, and definition of interfaces between component to allow communication and exchange of data. The implementation of the system is more about modification, integration and gluing of existing source code, though specific parts of the system such as GU framework will be implemented partly manually, partly from automatically generated code.

After domain analysis, we have identified these components of the system (Fig. 1):

- Data Acquisition Module – reads the neural data from the sensors via USB.
- Data Processing Module – processes data from Data Acquisition Module or from datasets for noise removal, dataset reduction and feature identification.
- Training Module – produces a classification model for identification of mental states.
- Classification Module – identifies mental states in the data using a classification model.
- Device Control Module – maps mental states to control commands and sends them to an external device.
- Evaluation Module – uses feedback from a robotic device to evaluate quality of control.
- Direct Control Module – uses data input from the GUI to control the external device manually rather than using the neural data;
- GUI – user interface to visualize the neural data and device control process.

The system is going to be able to work in three modes of operation:

1) *Offline:* the system uses the existing training and testing datasets to perform classification of neural data and presents its results to the user. The mode is used for evaluating the efficiency of data processing and classification algorithms. The external devices are not connected to the system while working in offline mode.
2) *Data acquisition:* the data acquisition device is connected and the system is used to collect training and testing data for further use. The robotic devices are not connected to the system.
3) *Online:* the data acquisition and robotic devices are connected and the system, after the training session, is used to control the robotic device in real-time.

The system is being implemented in Java as an open source language based on a large availability of third-party libraries, components and tools.

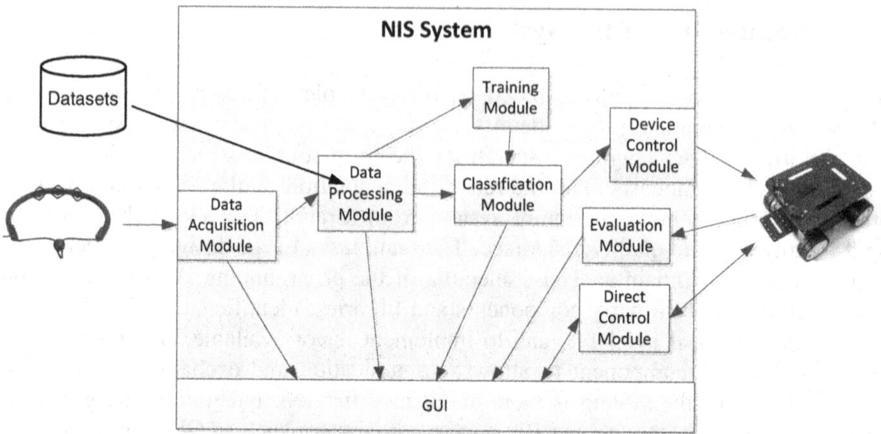

Fig. 1. Architecture of the Neural Interface System (NIS)

3 Description of System's Modules

3.1 Data Acquisition Module

The Data Acquisition Module is implemented to receive data from the OCZ Neural Impulse Actuator (NIA). The NIA is a NIS device that has 3 sensors and uses a USB connector to connect to a computer. The NIA captures three types of signal from the brain and forehead: the neuronal discharges in the brain (alpha, beta and gamma brainwaves), the electrooculogram data (positional differential between the front of retina and the retinal pigmented epithelium which changes relative to the eye orientation), and the electromyograms (neuro-muscular signals along with electrical discharges resulting from depolarization of the muscle cells). The data is wrapped in packets and delivered via interrupt reads. Raw data is provided unprocessed, so we use own methods to map mental states to control commands. Thus, the NIA provides more opportunities for external device control than pure BCI systems providing the EEG data only.

To allow reading of data from the OCZ NIA to the developed system, JavaNiaReader (http://code.google.com/p/eeg4j/wiki/JavaNiaReader) that provides functionality to retrieve and distribute raw data from the NIA was selected for integration into the system. The class diagram of the Data Acquisition Module is given in Fig. 2 and explained below.

The `USBReader` class reads the packets from the USB device and adds to the buffer. To implement the uninterrupted process of data reading from the USB device, parallel programming (`Thread` class) is used. The `NiaSignal` class stores the signal and synchronizes the signal reading thread with program thread. The USBReader's `Clibrary` is an interface for reading USB data. The `NiaDevice2` class is a test class for data reading via USB device.

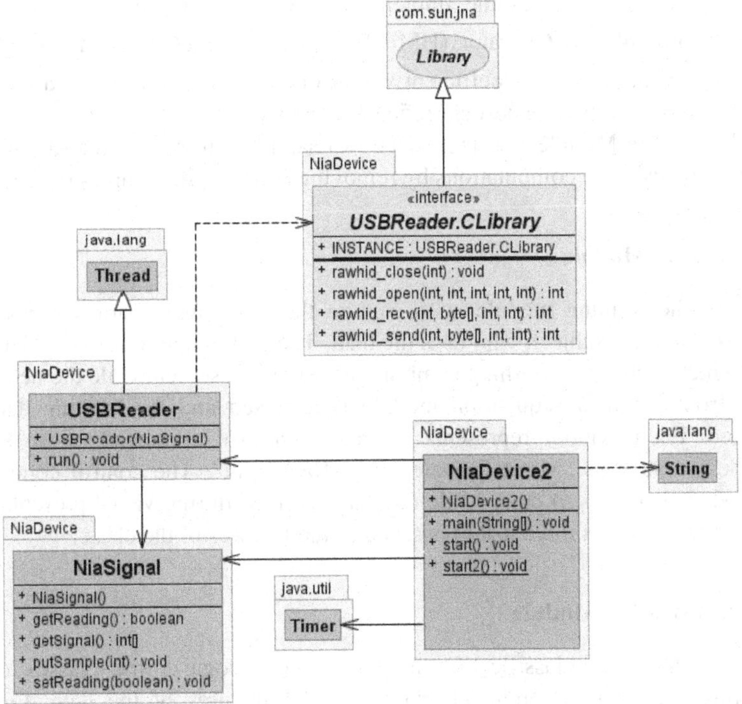

Fig. 2. Class diagram of the Data Acquisition Module

3.2 Data Processing Module

For data processing and denoising we use a custom class-adaptive shrinkage method [19] based on the observation that a limited numbers of the DSP transform coefficients in the lower bands are sufficient to reconstruct the original signal. Therefore, the component is implemented from scratch rather than reused.

The class adaptive denoising algorithm [19] is as follows:

1. Convert the time domain signals to frequency domain signals using a standard DSP transform.
2. For each frequency component f :
   (a) maximize distance between frequency components of positive class and negative class with respect to a set of shrinkage function parameters Λ ,
   (b) save Λ for maximal distance as $\Lambda_{\max}$.
3. Perform shrinkage of the DSP transform coefficients using $\Lambda_{\max}$.
4. Convert the shrinked frequency domain signal to the time domain using an inverse DSP transform.

Our method uses Fisher distance [20] to calculate distance between two data classes, and a smooth sigmoid shrinkage function [21] for signal shrinking.

The system also provides the implementation of the non-linear Homogeneous Multivariate Polynomial Operator (HMPO) $\Psi_m^k[x(n)]$, which is used for removing noise in the signal [22]. The coefficient values of the HMPO are selected during the training session to obtain the best classification results.

Data Processing Module also includes down-sampling to reduce the sampling rate of a signal for real time computations by removing some of the samples of the signal.

3.3 Training Module

The aim of the training module is to capture the individual characteristics of the neural signals of the subject, who uses the data. The component manages the training session, which consists of flashing symbols shown on the screen while the neural data received from the data acquisition module is analysed and the training dataset is constructed. Each symbol represents a specific control command of an external robotic device such as "Move forward" or "Move right". The control command is then encoded as a class of data, while the data received during visual presentation of the command (i.e., neural feedback) is saved as the features of the class.

3.4 Classification Module

The aim of the data classification module is to recognize the classes of data representing the control commands based on the features of the data. First, the classifier is trained using the training dataset constructed by the training module, and the classification model (e.g., a neural network) is constructed. The classification model is used to recognize classes in data received during control of the device.

Based on the analysis of the classification methods used in the NIS applications and, especially, based on the success of methods used in the BCI Competition (http://www.bbci.de/competition), as well as on the availability third-party of source code implementations in Java, we have decided to reuse and modify a specific kind of an Artificial Neural Network, called Voted Perceptron, and a Support Vector Machine. Both methods are explained in detail below.

Voted Perceptron (VP)

Voted Perceptron (VP) was proposed by Freund and Shapire for linear classification [23]. All weight vectors encountered during the learning process vote on a prediction. A measure of correctness of a weight vector, based upon the number of successive trials in which it correctly classified instances, is used as the number of votes given to the weight vector. The output of the VP is calculated as follows:

$$y_i = \operatorname{sgn}\left\{ \sum_{j=0}^{P} c_j \operatorname{sgn}(w_j x_{i,j}) \right\} \quad . \tag{1}$$

here $x_{i,j}$ are inputs, w_j are weights, v_i is the prediction vector, y_i is the predicted class label, d_i is the desired class label and e_i is the error.

The result of training is a collection of linear separators $w_1, w_2 ..., w_P$ along with the w_j survival time c_j, which is a measure of the reliability of w_j.

To make VP suitable for real-time NIS applications, we use the following modification of the training algorithm (see Fig. 3). The algorithm observes the time elapsed from the beginning of the training and cuts the training procedure as soon as the time bound is reached (see a detailed description in [24]).

```
procedure trainClassifier
begin
  let startTime be the current time
  Read and filter data
  Randomize training data
  index := 0;
  i := 0;
  while(true) begin
    instance := 0;
    while(true) begin
      prediction = makePrediction(index, instance);
      if (prediction == classValueOf(instance))
        increaseNeuronWeight(index);
      else begin
        setNeuronWeight(index, i, classValue);
        index := index + 1;
        increaseNeuronWeight(index);
      end;
      let currentTime be be current time
      elapsedTime = currentTime - startTime
      if (elapsedTime >= T)
        finish procedure trainClassifier;
      instance = :instance + 1;
    end;
    i := i + 1;
  end;
end;
```

Fig. 3. Modified training algorithm of Real-Time Voted Perceptron

The advantage of the VP algorithm is its simplicity, which is important for implementing a real-time system.

Support Vector Machine (SVM)

SVM [25] is a binary classification algorithm based on structural risk minimization. SVM training always finds a global minimum. First, SVM implicitly maps the training data into a (usually higher-dimensional) *feature space*. A *hyper-plane* (decision surface) is then constructed in this feature space that bisects the two categories and maximizes the margin of separation between itself and those points lying nearest to it (the *support vectors*). This decision surface can then be used as a basis for classifying vectors of unknown classification.

Consider an input space X with input vectors $x_i \in X$, a target space $Y = \{1,-1\}$ with $y_i \in Y$ and a training set $T = \{(x_1, y_1),..., (x_N, y_N)\}$. In SVM classification, separation of the two classes $Y = \{1,-1\}$ is done by the *maximum margin* hyper-plane, i.e. the hyper-plane that maximizes the distance to the closest data points and guarantees the best generalization on new examples. To classify a new point x_j, function $g(x_j)$ is used:

$$g(x_j) = \text{sgn}\left(\sum_{x_i \in SV} \alpha_i y_i K(x_i, x_j) + b\right), \tag{2}$$

where SV are the support vectors, $K(x_i, x_j)$ is the kernel function, α_i are weights, and b is the offset parameter. If $g(x_j) = +1$, x_j belongs to the Positive class, and if $g(x_j) = -1$, x_j belongs to the Negative class.

SVM is a widely used classification algorithm. However, SVM also has its weaknesses: only binary classification is allowed, therefore for multiple classes an architecture consisting of SVM ensembles [26] must be used, a large parameter space make selection of parameter values a complex task, the algorithm is not a real-time one, i.e., it can not be interrupted early to obtain some intermediate result.

For our implementation of the BCI system, we use the SVM^{light} and SVM^{perf} [27] implementations of SVM.

3.5 Device Control Modules

The device control modules are the implementation of control for two available robotic devices: the Lynxmotion 5LA Robotic Arm and the Arduino 4WD. The detailed description of these robots as well as their control are provided below.

Lynxmotion 5LA Robotic Arm

Starting from the base, the robotic arm has a rotational base joint, a vertical shoulder joint, a vertical elbow joint, a vertical wrist joint, a rotational wrist joint, and a two-fingered end-effector (gripper). In total, it has six degrees of freedom. The structure of robot arm is shown in Fig. 4. The base can rotate 360° horizontally, while other joints can rotate 180° vertically. The grip can do holding and putting action.

To control the arm, a SSC-32 programmable microcontroller is used. The SSC-32 servo control card provides the hardware interface between computer and the robot arm. Programming the microcontroller is done by writing ASCII programs on the PC and transferring them directly to the arm's board via a serial communication (COM) port. The ASCII programs control the servos by specifying the pulse of the signal to each motor: a continuous pulse of 1500 us results in the servo positioning itself in the centre of its range of motion while the pulse width from 500 to 2500 us will position the motor to left or right, respectively [29].

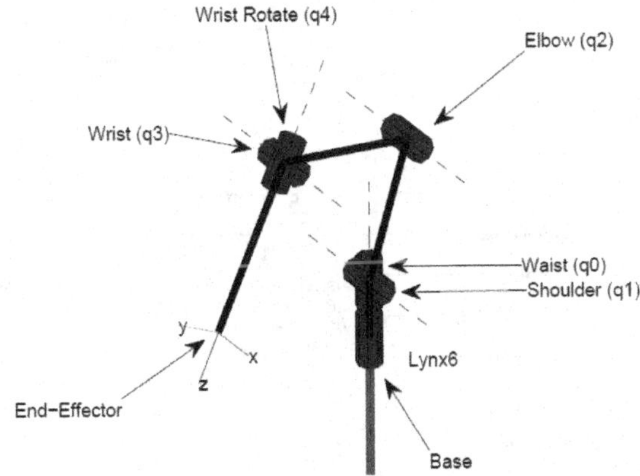

Fig. 4. Model of Lynxmotion Arm [28]

For communication via the COM port, JavaRobots (http://sourceforge.net/projects/javarobots/) is adapted as a third-party Java component. The class diagram of the Direct Control Module is given in Fig. 5.

The `SSC32` class implements the SSC-32 protocol. It uses a third-party component JavaRobots for communication via COM port. The `Controller` class provides methods for servo control. The `HandControl` class is a test class of this module.

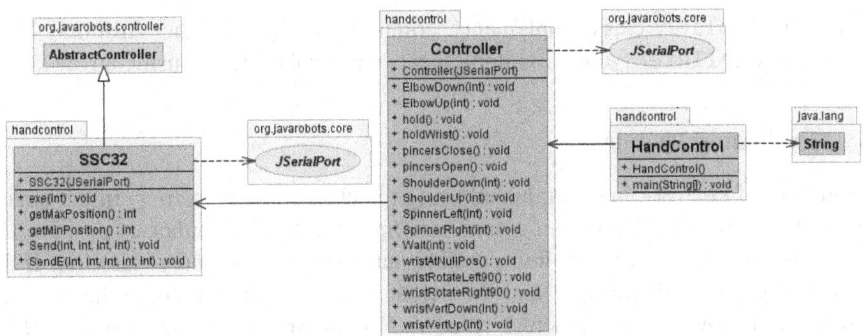

Fig. 5. Class diagram of the Direct Control Module for the Lynxmotion Robotic Arm

Arduino 4WD

The Arduino 4WD Mobile Platform provides a 4 wheel drive system complete with ATmega328 microcontroller board and 4 DC Motors. The platform can be connected to a computer with a USB cable or powered using the AC-to-DC adapter or battery. It has four degrees of freedom (forward, backward, left, right). The control is also implemented using the SSC-32 protocol and the same JavaRobots components as for control of the Lynxmotion robotic arm. The class diagram of the direct control module is given in Fig. 6.

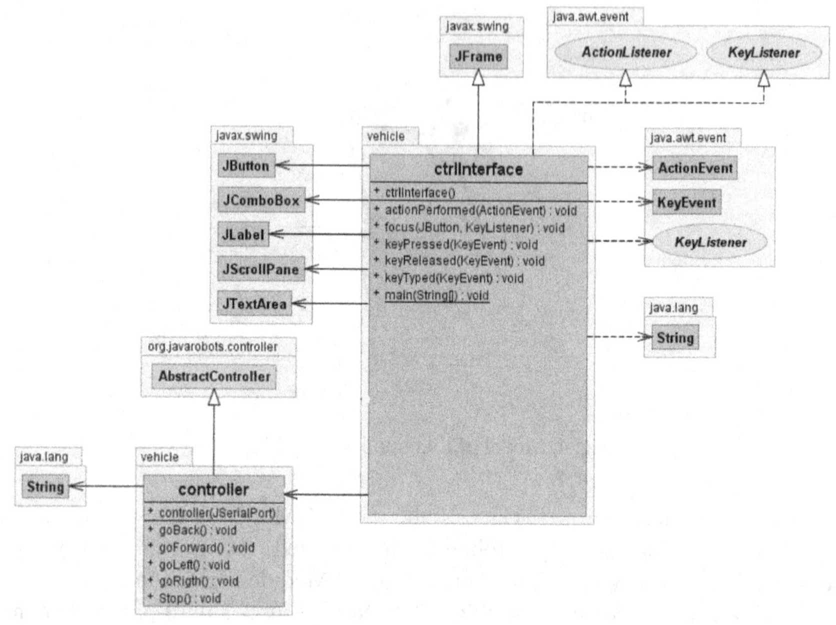

Fig. 6. Class diagram of the Direct Control Module for the Arduino 4WD robot

The `Controller` class implements communication with the Arduino 4WD device. The `CtrlInterface` class implements a control of device using arrow keys.

3.6 Evaluation Module

The success of control can be evaluated using the classification metrics. In the binary classification problem, the classification outcomes are labelled either as positive (P) or negative (N) class. There are four possible outcomes from a binary classifier. If the outcome from a prediction is P and the actual value is also P, then we have a true positive (TP); however if the actual value is N then we have a false positive (FP). Conversely, a true negative (TN) has occurred when both the prediction outcome and the actual value are N, and false negative (FN) is when the prediction outcome is N while the actual value is P. To evaluate the precision of classification the metrics of precision, recall, accuracy, F-measure, AUC and Kappa statistics were used:

4 Outline of Experiments

The NIS applications can be controlled using two alternative approaches: process control and goal (mission) selection. In the process-control approach, the NIS directly controls every aspect of device operation at the low level. In the mission selection, the NIS simply determines the user's intent to select one of possible missions, which is then executed by the system [2]. The mission is a high-level global task that can be decomposed to elementary behaviours or tasks. We provide the descriptions of exemplary missions using both Arduino 4WD and Lynxmotion 5LA below.

4.1 Arduino 4WD

Mission No. 1. Room Visiting

The mission of a robot consists of visiting the rooms (see Fig. 7) in the desired order. The mission starts in the start position ('S'). Then the robot has to visit all rooms by driving around the token placed in each room and go back to start position ('S'). The blue trace shows possible path of room visiting. Three subjects were trained to perform the mission using direct control and the time required to complete the mission was taken. The results of the experiments are presented in Table 1.

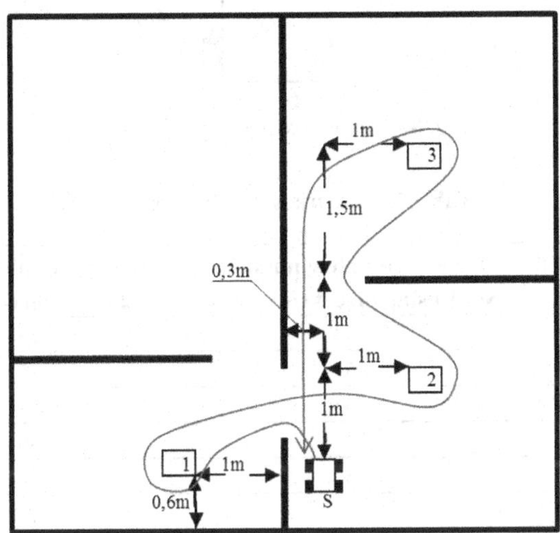

Fig. 7. Plan of the room visiting mission

Mission No. 2. Box Pushing

The mission of a robot consists of pushing the box from the start position (position No. 1) to the end position ("the gates", position No. 3) (see Fig. 8). To make a mission more difficult an obstacle is placed on the path of the robot, which the robot has to avoid. To change a direction of pushing, a robot has to retreat, when to approach a box from a different side, and to start pushing again (position No. 2). The size of the box used in the experiments is 17 x 34 cm, and the width of the gates is 48 cm. The distance between the start position of the robot and the gates is 2 m, however the real path of the robot is longer and depends upon a sequence of control commands issued. The robot also has to avoid obstacles when driving. Three subjects were trained to perform direct control of the robot and the time required to complete the mission was taken. The results of the experiments are presented in Table 1.

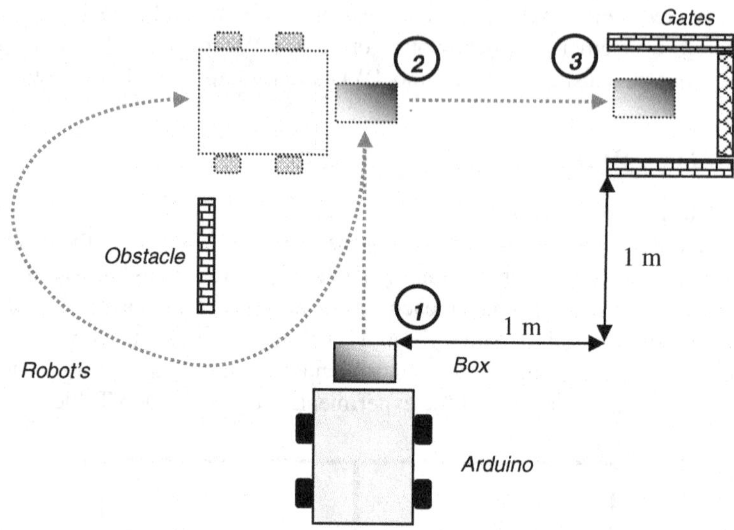

Fig. 8. Plan of box-pushing mission

Table 1. Time trials of robot control

Subject	Trial no.	Time to complete mission No. 1 using direct control, s	Time to complete mission No. 2 using direct control, s
1	1	93	44
	2	85	37
	3	92	41
2	1	92	36
	2	85	34
	3	81	46
3	1	82	40
	2	82	38
	3	76	33
Average:		*85*	*39*

4.2 Lynxmotion 5LA Robotic Arm

Mission. Draw a Figure on a Sheet of Paper

The mission is a variant of the trajectory following problem [30]. We assume that a sheet of paper is placed horizontally on top of a table. Therefore, the grip of the robotic arm has only 2 degrees of freedom while drawing. To implement the control of the robotic arm during drawing, one must compute the positions of all servos during arm's operation.

The success of the mission is evaluated by measuring the relative difference (measured at the reference points) between the geometrical shape of the known figure and the shape of the figure drawn using the robotic arm.

In our experiment we used a pre-programmed script that executed a sequence of robot control commands for drawing a square, and the relative distance was calculated using a formula:

$$\Delta = \sum_{i=1}^{n} d_i \Big/ L \cdot 100\% , \tag{3}$$

here d_i is the distance between the corresponding reference points of the ideal and drawn figures, n is the number of the reference points, and L is the dimension (length) of the figure. The experimental results for drawing a square (5 cm x 5 cm) using the robotic arm are presented in Table 2.

Table 2. Results of drawing mission using robotic arm

Trial no.	**Relative distance using pre-programmed script, %**
1	8,0
2	9,6
3	5,4
4	9,0
5	6,0
Average:	*7,6*

5 Conclusions and Future Work

In this paper, we have described the design of a Neural Interface Based (NIS) system for control of external robotic devices. We have started to implement the system using the principles of component-based reuse to allow rapid prototyping and reuse of existing code for interoperability with external devices. The architecture has common components used in similar systems, however, our system can operate in three different operational modes thus allowing to perform data acquisition, scientific research using the existing datasets (offline mode) as well as perform online control of robotic devices in real time. Currently, we system can work only in the offline mode of operations and has components implemented for data acquisition and working in the online mode. To validate the system at the current stage of development, we have performed experiments in direct robot control to implement three different missions using two robotic devices.

In further work, we aim to solve the component integration problems, to implement system training and to receive feedback from external devices for evaluation to have the system fully operational. We plan to repeat the robotic missions using the neural data based control and to compare the obtained experimental results with the ones given in this paper. We also intend to improve the quality of the robotic mission executed by the robotic arm by applying the methods of inverse kinematics for calculating the exact rotational positions of each joint.

References

1. Millán, J.R., Renkens, F., Mouriño, J., Gerstner, W.: Non-Invasive Brain-Actuated Control of a Mobile Robot. IEEE Trans. on Biomedical Engineering 51(6), 1026–1033 (2004)
2. Wolpaw, J.R., Birbaumer, N., McFarland, D.J., Pfurtscheller, G., Vaughan, T.M.: Braincomputer interfaces for communication and control. Clinical Neurophysiology 113, 767–791 (2002)
3. Hatsopoulos, N.G., Donoghue, J.P.: The science of neural interface systems. Annu. Rev. Neurosci. 32, 249–266 (2009)
4. Iturrate, I., Antelis, J., Kuebler, A., Minguez, J.: Non-Invasive Brain-Actuated Wheelchair based on a P300 Neurophysiological Protocol and Automated Navigation. IEEE Trans. on Robotics 25(3), 614–627 (2009)
5. Bartošová, V., Vyšata, O., Procházka, A.: Graphical User Interface for EEG Signal Segmentation. In: Proc. of 15th Annual Conf. Technical Computing, Prague, 22/1-6 (2007)
6. Miner, L.A., McFarland, D.J., Wolpaw, J.R.: Answering questions with an EEG-based brain–computer interface (BCI). Arch. Phys. Med. Rehabil. 79, 1029–1033 (1998)
7. Birbaumer, N., Ghanayim, N., Hinterberger, T., Iversen, I., Kotchoubey, B., Kübler, A., Perelmouter, J., Taub, E., Flor, H.: A spelling device for the paralysed. Nature 398, 297–298 (1999)
8. Pfurtscheller, G., Neuper, C., Müller, G.R., Obermaier, B., Krausz, G., Schlögl, A., Scherer, R., Graimann, B., Keinrath, C., Skliris, D., Wörtz, M., Supp, G., Schrank, C.: Graz-BCI: state of the art and clinical applications. IEEE Trans. Neural Sys. Rehabil. Eng. 11, 177–180 (2003)
9. Escolano, C., Antelis, J., Minguez, J.: Human Brain-Teleoperated Robot between Remote Places. In: IEEE Int. Conf. on Robotics and Automation, ICRA 2009, pp. 4430–4437 (2009)
10. Cong, W., Bin, X., Jie, L., Wenlu, Y., Dianyun, X., Velez, A.C., Hong, Y.: Motor imagery BCI-based robot arm system. In: 7th Int. Conf. on Natural Computation, ICNC, pp. 181–184 (2011)
11. Sepulveda, F.: Brain-actuated Control of Robot Navigation. In: Advances in Robot Navigation, ch. 8 (2011)
12. Rebsamen, B., Burdet, E., Cuntai, G., Chee, L.T., Qiang, Z., Ang, M., Laugier, C.: Controlling a wheelchair using a BCI with low information transfer rate. In: IEEE 10th Int. Conf. on Rehabilitation Robotics, ICORR 2007, Noordwijk, Netherlands, pp. 1003–1008 (2007)
13. Gao, X., Xu, D., Cheng, M., Gao, S.: A BCI-based environmental controller for the motion-disabled. IEEE Trans. Neural Syst. Rehabil. Eng. 11, 137–140 (2003)
14. Nawroj, A., Wang, S., Yu, Y.-C., Gabel, L.A.: A Brain Computer Interface for Robotic Navigation. In: IEEE 38th Annual Northeast Bioengineering Conference (NEBEC), Philadelphia, PA, March 16-18 (2012)
15. Duguleana, M.: Developing a brain-computer-based human-robot interaction for industrial environments. In: Annals of DAAAM for 2009 & Proceedings of the 20th International DAAAM Symposium, vol. 20(1), pp. 191–192 (2009)

16. Schalk, G.: Effective brain-computer interfacing using BCI2000. In: IEEE Int. Conf. of the Engineering in Medicine and Biology Society, EMBC 2009, pp. 5498–5501 (2009)
17. McCullagh, P.J., Ware, M.P., Lightbody, G.: Brain Computer Interfaces for inclusion. In: 1st Augmented Human International Conference (AH 2010), Article 6, 8 p. ACM, New York (2010)
18. Sametinger, J.: Software Engineering with Reusable Components. Springer (1997)
19. Martišius, I., Damaševičius, R.: Class-Adaptive Denoising for EEG Data Classification. In: Rutkowski, L., Korytkowski, M., Scherer, R., Tadeusiewicz, R., Zadeh, L.A., Zurada, J.M. (eds.) ICAISC 2012, Part II. LNCS, vol. 7268, pp. 302–309. Springer, Heidelberg (2012)
20. Ince, N.F., Arica, S., Tewfik, A.: Classification of single trial motor imagery EEG recordings with subject adapted nondyadi arbitrary time-frequency tilings. J. Neural Eng. 3, 235–244 (2006)
21. Atto, A.M., Pastor, D., Mercier, G.: Smooth Sigmoid Wavelet Shrinkage For Non-Parametric Estimation. In: IEEE Int. Conf. on Acoustics, Speech, and Signal Processing, ICASSP 2008, Las Vegas, Nevada, USA, pp. 3265–3268 (2008)
22. Martisius, I., Damasevicius, R., Jusas, V., Birvinskas, D.: Using higher order nonlinear operators for SVM classification of EEG data. Electronics and Electrical Engineering 3(119), 99–102 (2012)
23. Freund, Y., Schapire, R.E.: Large Margin Classification Using the Perceptron Algorithm. Machine Learning 37(3), 277–296 (1999)
24. Damasevicius, R., Martisius, I., Sidlauskas, K.: Towards Real Time Training of Neural Networks for Classification of EEG Data. International Journal of Artificial Intelligence (IJAI)
25. Cristianini, N., Shawe-Taylor, J.: An Introduction to Support Vector Machines. Cambridge University Press (2000)
26. Sun, B.-Y., Zhang, X.-M., Wang, R.-Y.: On Constructing and Pruning SVM Ensembles. In: 3rd Int. IEEE Conf. on Signal-Image Technologies and Internet-Based System, SITIS 2007, pp. 855–859 (2007)
27. Joachims, T.: A Support Vector Method for Multivariate Performance Measures. In: Proc. of 22nd Int. Conf. on Machine Learning, ICML 2005, pp. 377–384 (2005)
28. Filippi, H.: Wireless Teleoperation of Robotic Arms. Master Thesis, Luleå University of. Technology, Kiruna, Espoo-Finland (2007)
29. Blakely, T.M., Smart, W.D.: Control of a Robotic Arm Using Low-Dimensional EMG and ECoG Biofeedback Technical Report WUCSE-2007-39, Department of Computer Science and Engineering, Washington University in St. Louis (2007)
30. Appin Knowledge Solutions: Robotics, 1st edn. Jones & Bartlett Publishers (2007)

Influence of Network Communications to the Final Performance of Grid Visualization Software

Arnas Kaceniauskas and Ruslan Pacevic

Laboratory of Parallel Computing, Vilnius Gediminas Technical University, Sauletekio al. 11, 10223 Vilnius, Lithuania
{arnka,ruslan.pacevic}@vgtu.lt

Abstract. Influence of network communications to the final performance of grid visualization software VisPartDEM is investigated. Distributed architecture of VisPartDEM is designed for interactive visualization of large particle systems simulated by the discrete element method on the gLite-based grid. Performance analysis of VisPartDEM is made on the geographically distributed gLite grid infrastructure. The attention is focused on the data transfer from storage elements, image transfer to clients and their contribution to the total benchmark time. The discussed issues are important for all researchers interactively visualizing results on gLite-based remote grid infrastructures.

Keywords: network communications, interactive grid visualization, gLite middleware, distributed visualization software, VisPartDEM.

1 Introduction

Visualization is a powerful tool for analyzing the data across a wide range of disciplines [1]. Grid computing [2] represents one of the most promising advancements in modern computational science. Distributed grid visualization allocates different parts of the machine processing to different components like Working Node (WN) of Computing Element (CE), Storage Element (SE) and User Interface (UI). However, this leads to very complex software systems, handling visualization on remote heterogeneous infrastructures [2]. Network communications have significant influence for the final performance of the developed software.

Visapult [3] is a visualization framework with the ability to render a huge amount of datasets of the order of 1-5 Tb. Visapult uses parallel rendering hardware to carry out the high speed rendering processes and can transfer huge amount of data through the network. Using Cactus [3] the data are distributed amongst many parallel nodes for volume rendering.

Cactus [3] is an open source problem-solving environment designed for scientists and engineers. Cactus consists of a central core component, called the flesh, and a set of modules called thorns. Cactus builds on the Globus [4] Toolkit to provide secure access to remote resources as well as secure communications and job scheduling on remote resources. The data is stored in HDF5 format [5]. Visualization is provided via

T. Skersys, R. Butleris, and R. Butkiene (Eds.): ICIST 2012, CCIS 319, pp. 312–323, 2012.

standard products such as OpenDX [6], Amira [7] and IRIS Explorer [8]. These systems effectively operate as thorns connected to the Cactus system via special modules that are able to read the data formats exported by Cactus.

VisAD [9] is a Java component library for interactive and collaborative visualization and analysis of numerical data. It makes use of Java's RMI technology, which allows methods of remote Java objects to be invoked from other Java virtual machines, possibly on different hosts. The construction of distributed applications in VisAD is facilitated by its event-driven design.

Grid Visualization Kernel (GVK) [10] based on the Globus middleware [4] has been developed in the CrossGrid project. The interface to GVK is established via the available visualization software such as OpenDX [6]. The difference between the traditional approach and the GVK visualization services is that some modules of the data-flow graph are replaced by the corresponding GVK modules. A module called GVid provides grid-enabled video streaming for scientific visualization [11].

More complete environments for collaborative and remote scientific visualization include the Scalable Adaptive Graphics Environment (SAGE) [12] and the Visualization Interface Toolkit (VisIT) [13]. The functionality of each of these tools is more powerful than the features provided by GVK.

RAVE (Resource-Aware Visualization Environment) [14] is a collaborative visualization environment that scales across visualization platforms, ranging from large immersive devices all the way down to handheld the partial differential equations. RAVE is based on web service technologies, and provides distributed rendering on remote machines.

Grid visualization e-service VizLitG [15] is designed for convenient access and interactive visualization of remote data files located in SE. Partial dataset transfer from the experimental SE of the gLite-based grid infrastructure is developed in order to reduce the communication time [16], [17], [18]. However, the visualization engine of VizLitG is not parallel, therefore, time consuming visualization filters can hardly be applied on large datasets.

Grid portals are widely employed to provide end users with the customized views of hardware resources, the available software and visualized results specific to their particular problem domain [2]. The P-GRADE Portal [19] is a workflow-oriented grid portal supporting all stages of grid workflow development and execution processes. It enables the graphical design of workflows created from executable components and executing these workflows in Globus-based [4] grids.

The most of the overviewed grid environments for visualization are based on the Globus middleware [4]. Visualization software can be highly integrated with working environment. BalticGrid [20] is built on gLite middleware [21]. The important Globus functionality like Grid Resource Allocation and Management service cannot be accessed in the considered grid environment, therefore, most of the available visualization software cannot be applied.

The paper presents the development of grid visualization tool VisPartDEM and the investigation of the network communication between the remote parts of the software. Section 2 presents the distributed architecture of VisPartDEM. The performance analysis of the VisPartDEM and the investigation of its network communications are discussed in Section 3, while the concluding remarks are presented in Section 4.

2 The Architecture of VisPartDEM

The distributed visualization tool VisPartDEM [18] was developed at the Laboratory of Parallel Computing of Vilnius Gediminas Technical University (VGTU). The distributed architecture of VisPartDEM (Fig. 1) was designed for grid infrastructures build by gLite middleware. Client software including a GUI and a Remote Viewer was downloaded by using Java Web Start technology [22]. VisPartDEM client implemented as Java application connected to any UI by means of JSCH library [23]. Traditional gLite commands for user authentication and authorization, job submission and monitoring were enwrapped by Java programming language. Considered visualization pipelines, JDL files and shell scripts for running visualization engine were generated automatically in order to submit job to grid. Parallel visualization engine of VisPartDEM ran on WNs of any CE while the compressed video stream was efficiently transferred from the zero MPI node through the network and displayed on the client by the Remote Viewer.

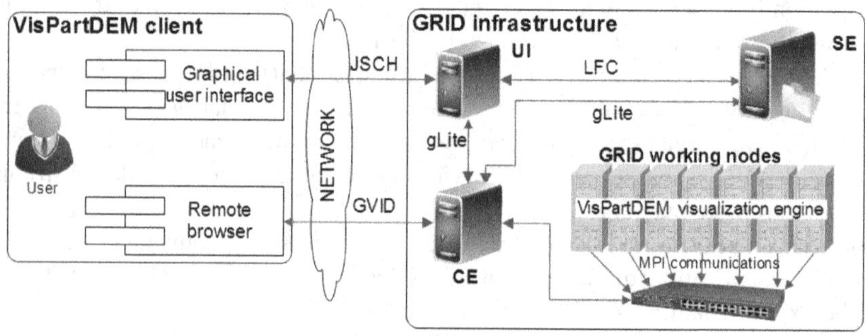

Fig. 1. The architecture of VisPartDEM

Distributed visualization engine of VisPartDEM is based on VTK [24]. VTK applications are platform independent which is very attractive for heterogeneous grid architectures. Data parallel model of VTK is employed for visualization of large particle systems. A large dataset is partitioned into many independent subsets that are processed in parallel. Data parallel modules are usually followed by a data parallel merge module that gathers the independently computed results and merges them into a final result on a single processor. A sort-last parallel rendering class inputs a z-buffer and image pair from each process by using MPI communication and outputs a single composite result image to MPI process zero.

GUI of VisPartDEM is designed to cover from user unnecessary details and complexities of heterogeneous grid infrastructure. The GUI (Fig. 2) is implemented as Java application. Tabular design of GUI is developed by using Java Swing [25]. The considered visualization pipelines are described by XML language [17]. Valid XML documents are automatically generated on a client and transferred to computing element by gLite means. Resulting XML documents govern assembling of visualization pipelines from VTK filters in visualization engine.

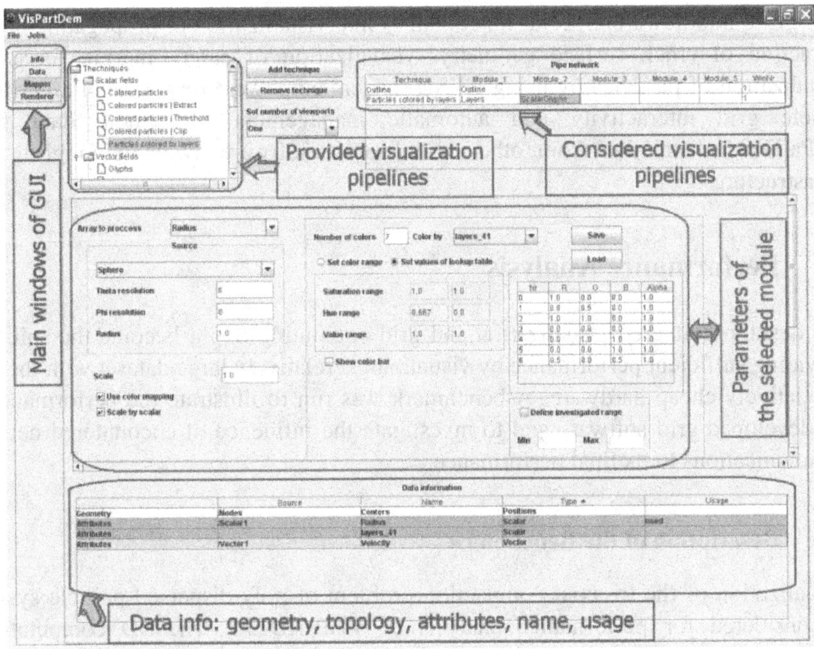

Fig. 2. GUI of VisPartDEM

Many advances in modern science today depend on the capability of visualization software interactively to access vast amounts of remote data. The GUI of VisPartDEM allows interactive browsing of storage element (SE) content and automatic data management. The HDF5 [5] is employed as a basic data format for VisPartDEM because of its universality and efficient data reading/writing for large discrete particle systems. Moreover, HDF5 is platform-, operating system-, and application-independent format, which is very attractive for distributed visualization in grid. In order to process HDF5 files automatically, datasets are stored in predefined structure allowing the software to interpret the structure and contents of a file without any outside information. HDF5 groups and datasets are automatically processed considering values of HDF5 attributes. XML interface for remote data is developed to provide grid users with the interactive dataset selection. Inter alia it allows easy implementation of readers for other formats. Usually, large HDF5 file containing data is dislocated in remote storage element, while small XML file containing metadata on the data structure can be stored in any convenient location (client PC, UI or even SE).

The Remote Viewer of VisPartDEM employs GVid software [11] as video streaming module to provide grid users with the high interactivity level. As a result the video stream is transferred through the network from the working node and displayed on the client. Thus, remote grid user has full interactivity provided by the Remote Viewer based on GVid software and VTK widgets.

Distributed VisPartDEM software has functionality for visualization of large particle systems, which is not available in other visualization software compatible with gLite middleware. Special functionality like visualization of propagating cracks, extraction of crack surface geometry, visualization of safety margin force, fast visualization of particles by using GLSL shaders empowered by parallel algorithms, remote grid interactivity and automatic management of remote data make VisParDEM distinctive from other visualization software available in gLite grid infrastructures.

3 Performance Analysis

The desktop-delivered visualization and grid computing might become the solutions providing sufficient performance by visualizing a relatively large dataset with the help of relatively cheap hardware. A benchmark was run to illustrate the performance of the developed grid software and to investigate the influence of encountered network communications to its final performance.

3.1 Description of the Benchmark

Visualization of the tri-axial compaction problem of poly-dispersed particle systems is considered for performance analysis of VisPartDEM. The 3D computational domain imitates a representative macroscopic volume element containing particles and presents a box in the form of rectangular parallelepiped. Agglomerate is formed by tri-axial compression of initially loose packing of spherical particles. Numerical solution of tri-axial compaction helps to evaluate unknown material properties. Fig. 3 illustrates visualization of tri-axial compaction problem containing 100036 particles. Heterogeneous particles are coloured according to process Id to illustrate the employed domain decomposition for 8 processes.

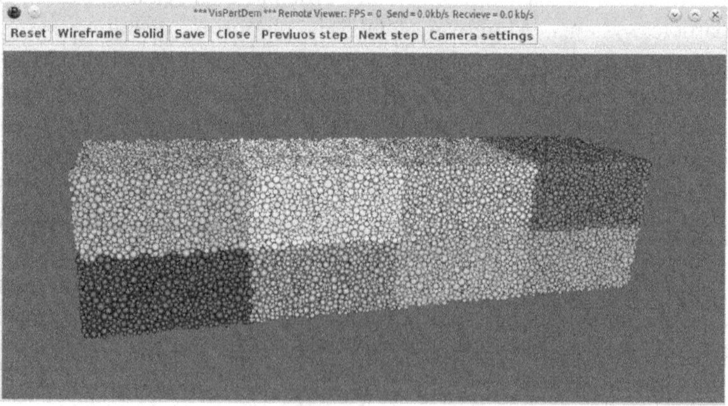

Fig. 3. Tri-axial compaction problem: particles coloured according to process Id

The visualization benchmark is based on the glyph generation, because particles, computed velocities and obtained forces are often represented by glyphs that can be coloured by investigated scalar values or oriented by the examined vectors. The examined datasets contain 100036, 150119 and 200194 heterogeneous particles. Meaningful data are composed from the positions of particles and their radius, therefore, the real sizes of the visualized data are quite small (3.13 MB in case of 100036 particles). Numerical results include a lot of values of variables that are written in HDF5 files, therefore, the size of complete HDF5 file is equal to 21.39 MB in case of 100036 particles. The total size of partitioned result files is up to 21.63 MB, which is close to the size of the single file. The size of the single file containing the results of 150119 particle system is equal to 32.09 MB, while the total size of 16 partitions is equal to 32.37 MB. In case of the particle system containing 200194 heterogeneous particles, the size of the single file is equal to 42.79 MB, while the total size of partitioned files is up to 43.07 MB. Particles are represented by generated spherical glyphs. The size of the object, which encapsulates data of generated glyphs, is equal to 326 MB in case of 100036 poly-dispersed particles. It makes the described benchmark very specific, because a generated geometry is larger than the initial dataset.

The tests were repeated up to ten times and the averaged values were investigated. The main attention was focused on the performance of the data transfer from SE, speed-up of visualization procedures and the interactive performance. Mapping was not considered because it took a very short time equal approximately to 0.0001 s. In the performed benchmark, MPI communication for message passing between working nodes is employed for composition of the final image. Detailed investigation of MPI communication is not presented because it lasts negligible time (less than 0.002 s). HDF5 files were transferred from the SE to WNs by using LFC means. Each process of VisPartDEM transferred its data file independently, in asynchronous fashion. In case of the considered datasets asynchronous data transfer can be up to 11 times faster than the synchronous one.

3.2 Employed Grid Infrastructure

The benchmark was performed on BalticGrid-II site ce2.grid.vgtu.lt collected from ordinary PCs equipped by GPUs. This gLite CE maintained by VGTU was considered for benchmark, because it supported direct GPU rendering and it was based on the multi-core architecture. The CE consisted of 14 HP Compaq dc7900 personal computers (nodes) including Pentium(R) Dual-Core CPU E5300 (bus frequency equal 2.60 GHz), 4 GB DDR2 RAM 800 MHz, 500 GB HDD. Each node is equipped by GPU (Nvidia GeForce 9600GT 512 MB 256 bit). Nodes are connected to 1 Gbps Ethernet LAN by 3Com Baseline Switch 2928-SFP Plus (24 auto sensing 10/100/1000Mbps Base-TX ports). Hardware characteristics of the storage element se.grid.vgtu.lt (SE-1) maintained by VGTU are listed below: AMD Athlon X2 Dual Core BE-2300 1.9 GHz CPU, 2 GB DDR2 800 RAM, 3 x 500GB SATA II Extensions, Software Raid0 and 1 Gbps LAN. The SE-1 was connected to the same switch as the ce2.grid.vgtu.lt. In geographically distributed environment, the data transfer tests were performed employing the storage element se.bg.ktu.lt (SE-2) located at Kaunas Technical University (KTU). Hardware characteristics of the SE-2 are listed below: Intel®Xeon 5130 2.00 GHz CPU, 2 GB DDR2 800 RAM, 3 x 200GB SATA II Extensions, Software Raid5, 1 Gbps LAN.

3.3 Data Transfer from SE to WNS

The asynchronous data transfer is investigated in geographically distributed grid. Each process independently transfers its data file from the SE to its WN. The longest transfer time is picked up from times consumed by all parallel processes. The round-trip time from the CE to SE-1 at VGTU was 0.161/0.229/2.218 ms (Min/Average/Max) during the benchmark. The network bandwidth measured by using Iperf [26] was equal to 583 Mbit/s. The average system load of the SE-1 was equal to 10 %. The round-trip time from the CE to SE-2 at KTU in Kaunas was 1.00/2.06/4.39 ms (Min/Average/Max) during the benchmark. The measured network bandwidth was equal to 184 Mbit/s. The average system load of the SE-2 was equal to 30 % during the geographically distributed benchmark.

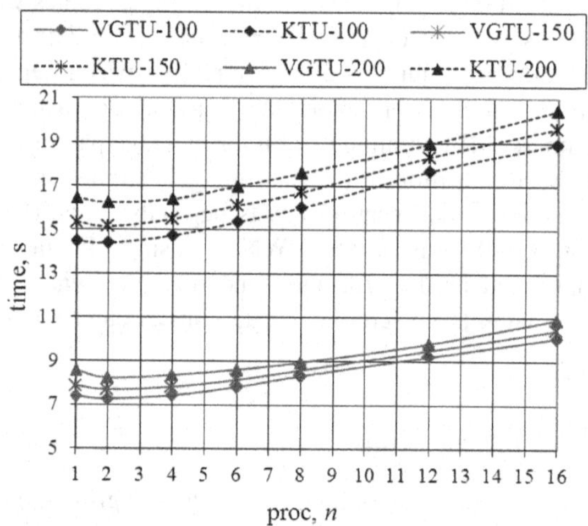

Fig. 4. Time consumed by the data transfer from SEs to WNs

Fig. 4 shows the time consumed by the asynchronous data transfer. The curves VGTU-100, VGTU-150 and VGTU-200 represent time consumed by transferring datasets of 100036, 150119 and 200194 particles, respectively, from SE-1 to WNs of ce2.grid.vgtu.lt. The dotted curves KTU-100, KTU-150 and KTU-200 represent transferring datasets of 100036, 150119 and 200194 particles, respectively, from SE-2 located at KTU to CE located at VGTU. The asynchronous data transfer helps to reduce transferring time in case of very small number of processes. All parallel processes use the same network equipment and the same hardware of the employed

SE. Encountered bottlenecks do not allow attaining parallel speed-up in data transfer. The distant data transfer strongly depends on the network load, therefore, the curves representing datasets of different size are not so gradually distributed. As expected, data transfer from the distant SE-2 was slower than that from SE-1 located in the same building as CE.

3.4 Interactive Communication Between Client Computer and WN

The performance of interactivity was also investigated in the case of the geographically distributed grid. The Remote Viewer is based on the GVid software, which transports the efficiently compressed standard video stream to the remote output device and handles interactive events. Video stream is encoded by using XviD codec [27]. The transfer of the encoded frame of 302.6 kB size was investigated, which consists of 1100 x 600 pixels. The image encoding (Encode), frame sending (Send) and receiving (Receive) as well as decoding (Decode) and displaying (Display) were considered in the performed benchmark. The image encoding and frame sending time is measured on CE in VGTU, while receiving, decoding and displaying time was measured on two different clients. Interactive events were captured and transferred very quickly, therefore, their time consumption was not included. The round-trip time from CE to the client C-1 located in the VGTU building was 0.171/0.199/0.219 ms (Min/Average/Max) during the benchmark. The network bandwidth measured by using Iperf [26] was equal to 933 Mbit/s. The round-trip time from CE to the client C-2 located in Alytus was 1.755/9.253/71.642 ms (Min/Average/Max) during the benchmark. The network bandwidth measured by using Iperf was equal to 1.95 Mbit/s. A low quality network was tested to simulate extreme cases representing a bottleneck for interactive visualization. The benchmark tests were repeated up to one hundred times and the averaged values were presented.

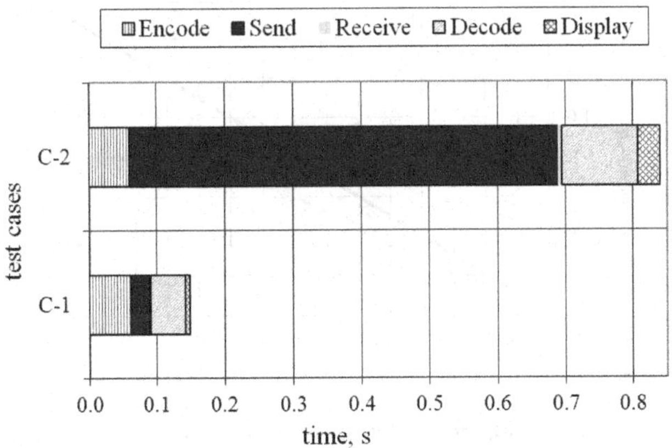

Fig. 5. Image coding and frame transfer for remote interactivity

Fig. 5 shows the time consumed by GVid on two clients (the curves C-1 and C-2) and the CE. The encoding was performed on the server, therefore, it consumes almost the same amount of time for the defined frame. Different time values were measured transferring the frames to different clients, while the receiving time was negligibly small in all cases. Frame decoding strongly depended on the client hardware. The C-1 equipped by the Intel® Core2Quad Q6600 2.40 GHz CPU was significantly faster than the other client. Displaying of the decoded frame lasted about 0.01 s. However, in the case of the low end graphics cards like ATI Radeon X1200 installed on the client C-2, a longer time was observed. It is evident, that frame sending strongly depends on the network connection and the frame size. It is not suitable for interactive purposes in the case of the low bandwidth and high latency networks like the connection between the CE and C-2 located in Alytus. However, the GVid is well designed for a variable or low bandwidth, because of the efficient compression codec XviD and rate adaptation to the current network bandwidth. Thus, the frame rate was automatically adapted to a low bandwidth, and the transferred data was reduced.

3.5 Final Performance

Fig. 6 illustrates parallel speed-up of VisPartDEM. The curves G-200, G-150 and G-100-2P represent visualization of 200194, 150119 and 100036 particles employing GPU rendering performed by two processes per multi-core node, respectively. The curve G-100-1P represents visualization of 100036 particles employing GPU rendering performed by one processes per node while the curve G-100-CPU represents visualization of 100036 particles employing CPU rendering. The special curve Ideal shows the ideal speed-up.

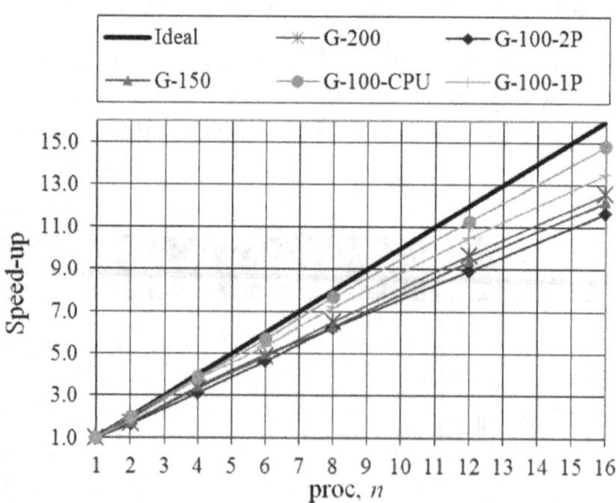

Fig. 6. Parallel speed-up attained

Parallel speed-up of visualization employing GPU rendering is lower than that of visualization based on CPU rendering. However, execution time of visualization employing GPU is significantly shorter than that of using CPU rendering. Higher speed-up was measured visualizing larger particle systems. It becomes obvious that in usual grid conditions, when two processes use one GPU on multi-core architecture, parallel speed-up achieved by GPU rendering is moderate. It can be concluded, that Fig. 6 proves sufficient speed-up of visualization performed on grid testbed based on multi-core architecture.

In Fig. 7, the chart compares the contribution of data transfer (Transfer), visualization (Visualize) and interactive session (Inter) to the total visualization time of 200194 particles measured on the CE. Visualization includes data reading, glyphs and parallel GPU rendering, while interactive session consists of image encoding, frame sending, receiving, decoding and displaying as well as processing interactive events. The stacked columns G-1, G-2, G-4, G-8, G-12 and G-16 represent visualization time on grid site by using 1, 2, 4, 8, 12 and 16 processes, respectively. Fig.7 shows that visualization time was significantly reduced employing parallel processing. Moreover, performing glyphs-based benchmark the time consumed by interactive session is negligible. However, the overall problem is not scalable because of the data transfer from SE, which is insignificantly growing.

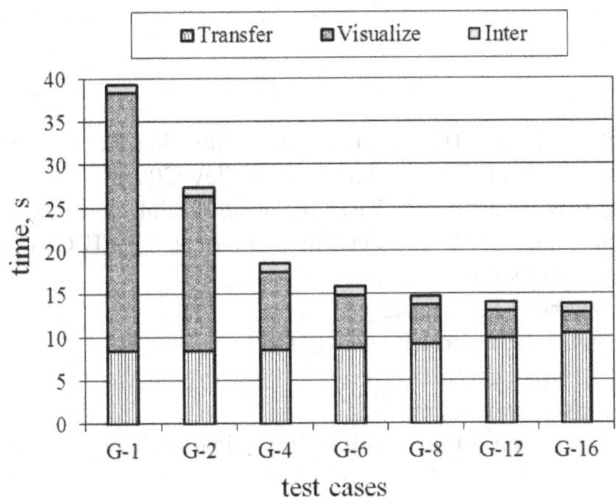

Fig. 7. Contribution of visualization procedures to the total benchmark time

4 Conclusions

Distributed grid visualization tool VisPartDEM was developed and tested on multi-core grid testbed build by gLite middleware. Based on the investigation of network communications to the final performance of grid visualization software, some observations and concluding remarks may be drawn as follows:

- Developed software VisPartDEM is successfully applied to visualize poly-dispersed particle systems on multi-core grid testbed build by gLite.
- The time consumed by interactive GVid communication and MPI message passing between working nodes can be treated as negligibly small.
- The asynchronous data transfer helps to reduce data transferring time for very small number of processes. However, in case of number of processes exceeding 4, encountered bottleneck does not allow attaining parallel speed-up in data transfer from SE.
- Time of visualization procedures including GPU rendering was significantly reduced employing parallel processing. However, the speed-up of overall benchmark problem is diminished by the data transfer from SE, which hardly reducible by software means.
- The performance analysis reveals that developed VisPartDEM software is well designed for distributed visualization of considered datasets in the real grid environment based on the multi-core architectures.

Acknowledgements. The research was supported by the Ministry of Education and Science of the Republic of Lithuania through the VP1-3.1-ŠMM-08-K program, project "Research and development of technologies for virtualization, visualization and security e-services".

References

1. Hansen, C.D., Johnson, C.R.: The Visualization Handbook. Elsevier (2005)
2. Li, M., Baker, M.: The Grid: Core Technologies. Wiley (2005)
3. Shalf, J., Bethel, E.W.: Cactus and Visapult: an ultra-high performance grid-distributed visualization architecture using connectionless protocols. IEEE Computer Graphics and Applications 23(2), 51–59 (2003)
4. Globus, `http://www.globus.org/`
5. HDF5, `http://www.hdfgroup.org/HDF5/`
6. OpenDX, `http://www.opendx.org/`
7. Amira, `http://www.amira.com/`
8. Foulser, D.: IRIS Explorer: a framework for investigation. Computer Graphics 29(2), 13–16 (1995)
9. VisAD, `http://www.ssec.wisc.edu/~billh/visad.html`
10. Kranzlmuller, D., Kurka, G., Heinzlreiter, P., Volkert, J.: Optimizations in the Grid Visualization Kernel. In: Proc. of the Workshop on Parallel and Distributed Computing in Image Processing, Video Processing and Multimedia, Ft. Lauder-dale, Florida (2002)
11. Gvid, `http://www.gup.jku.at/gvid/`
12. Jeong, B., Jagodic, R., Renambot, L., Singh, R., Johnson, A., Leigh, J.: Scalable graphics ar-chitecture for high-resolution displays. In: Proc. of IEEE Information Visualization Workshop, Minneapolis, MN, USA (2005)
13. Eickermann, T., Frings, W., Gibbon, P., Kirtchakova, L., Mallmann, D., Visser, A.: Steering UNICORE applications with VISIT. Philosophical Transactions of the Royal Society A 363, 1855–1865 (2005)

14. Grimstead, I.J., Avis, N.J., Walker, D.W., Philp, R.N.: Resource-aware visualization using web servines. In: Proc. of the UK e-Science All Hands Meeting, Nottingham, UK. EPSRC (2005)
15. VizLitG, http://lsl.vgtu.lt/vizlitg/en/
16. Kačeniauskas, A., Kačianauskas, R., Maknickas, A., Markauskas, D.: Computation and visualization of discrete particle systems on gLite-based grid. Advances in Engineering Software 42(5), 237–246 (2011)
17. Kačeniauskas, A.: Solution and analysis of CFD applications by using grid infrastructure. J. Information Technology and Control 39(4), 284–290 (2010)
18. Kačeniauskas, A., Pacevič, R., Markauskas, D., Kačianauskas, R.: VisPartDEM: grid visualization tool for particle systems. In: Civil-Comp Proceedings, Proc. of 2nd International Conference on Parallel, Distributed, Grid and Cloud Computing for Engineering. Stirlingshire: Civil-Comp. Proceedings, vol. 95, pp. 1759–3433 (2011)
19. Kacsuk, P., Sipos, G.: Multi-grid, multi-user workflows in the P-GRADE grid portal. J. Grid Computing 3(3-4), 221–238 (2006)
20. BalticGrid, http://www.balticgrid.eu/
21. gLite, http://glite.cern.ch/
22. Marinilli, M.: Java Deployment with Jnlp and Webstart. Sams Publishing (2001)
23. JSCH, http://www.jcraft.com/jsch/
24. Schroeder, W., Martin, K., Lorensen, B.: Visualization Toolkit: An Object-Oriented Approach to 3D Graphics, 4th edn. Kitware Inc. (2006)
25. Zukowski, J.: The Definitive Guide to Java Swing. Apress (2005)
26. Iperf, http://sourceforge.net/projects/iperf/
27. The XviD project, http://www.xvid.org/

Influence of Blended Learning on Outcomes of Postgraduate Studies

Algimantas Venckauskas, Audrone Janaviciute, Stasys Maciulevicius, and Irena Mikuckiene

Kaunas University of Technology, Computer Department, Studentu str. 50, LT-51368, Kaunas, Lithuania
{Algimantas.Venckauskas,Audrone.Janaviciute, Stasys.Maciulevicius,Irena.Mikuckiene}@ktu.lt

Abstract. Information and communication technologies are an integral part of modern society. The need of highly qualified professionals with a master's degree is growing. Universities are faced with major challenges in organizing postgraduate studies. For a variety of reasons, very high percentage of postgraduate studies isn't completed. The obvious forces the need for innovative forms of education. One of the ways to solve problems in postgraduate studies are using of blended learning.

Keywords: blended learning, postgraduate studies.

1 Why Do Postgraduate Studies Require for an Innovative Form of Education?

Manufacturing, services, information and communication technologies (ICT) become more complex in modern society. This causes growing demand for highly skilled professionals with a master's degree. According to long-term occupational employment projections, published by The Bureau of Labour Statistics of the U.S. Department of Labour, employment and total job openings for professionals with master's qualification, demand up to 2018 will increase by 18.3% [1]. The same Bureau of Labour Statistics projects growth of computer networks and systems professionals, which include those specialized in computer security, by 30%, and highly skilled Systems Analysts – by 53% [2]. The same trends in growth of security professionals are expected in the European Union and Lithuania. Master's training needs and issues are examined in the study "The systematic evaluation of matching of supply and demand for most highly qualified professionals (masters)", carried out by the Labour and Social Research Institute of the Lithuanian Ministry for Social Security and Labour [3].

In the evaluation of studies one of the most important indicators is rate of study discontinuation (drop out), which, especially in the light of the current university funding model ("baskets"), is very painful for universities and students, brings significant financial and moral losses. Master's level of training partly can be reflected by average mark of studies. We will investigate postgraduate studies taking into account these aspects and linking outcomes with learning forms.

T. Skersys, R. Butleris, and R. Butkiene (Eds.): ICIST 2012, CCIS 319, pp. 324–331, 2012.

The authors didn't find aggregate statistical data about scale of postgraduate studies discontinuation. The study "The professional training of top-level specialists, scientific research and experimental development, science-intensive business development in the field of laser" [4] presents details about discontinued postgraduate study dynamics in the Vilnius University, Faculty of Physics. This rate in 2004 - 2006 ranged from 32.35% to 45.83%. The study "The professional training of top-level specialists, scientific research and experimental development, science-intensive business development in mechatronics" [5], presents details about discontinued postgraduate study dynamics of mechatronics and electronic and telecommunication system technology in Kaunas University of Technology (KUT), Vilnius Gediminas Technical University (VGTU), Klaipeda and Siauliai Universities from 2004 to 2006. Discontinued postgraduate studies in KUT graduates yearly wastage by up to 18%, Vilnius Gediminas Technical University– 20%, with 27% – at Klaipeda University – 11%. However, data in this study include dropout data for all postgraduate courses per year. It does not reflect the number of postgraduate study dropout. As the postgraduate studies last two years, mainly wastage becomes in the first study year, the dropout part of the study is about one and a half times higher, and reaches over 30% and is close to the VGTU figures. Data on dynamics in the KTU Informatics Engineering postgraduate studies (Software Engineering, Information Systems Engineering and Single Chip Systems) in 2005-2008 are presented in Table 1. This figure varies from year to year from 34% to 47%.

Table 1. Dynamics of discontinued postgraduate studies in Informatics Engineering (KUT)

Admission year	Number of adopted postgraduate students	Drop out after 1st year (%)	Drop out after 2nd year (%)	Number of graduates	Number of discontinued (%)	Average rating of study subjects
2005	122	26	18	74	39	8,6
2006	135	36	17	72	47	8,6
2007	116	26	12	76	34	8,3
2008	102	38	13	55	46	8,7

The data show the drop out figures presented for all universities and education programs examined are similar and high – more than a third of matriculated graduates discontinue their postgraduate studies.

Drop out in the postgraduate studies is governed by the peculiarities in countries economics, politics, education and culture, as well as economic and social status of the individual, personal characteristics, motivation, and so on.

Large parts of the postgraduate have some job. According to research "Masters integration into the labour market" [6], the Lithuanian universities' students begin to work early enough. Half of the surveyed postgraduates (51%) began to work at bachelor studies or immediately after graduating (before postgraduate studies). One fifth (19.4%) of postgraduate student in 2001-2005 started to work during the postgraduate studies. Only a little over a tenth (13.4%) started to work after the master's degree. More than two-thirds of surveyed postgraduates (69.5%) combine the education and work. Some other studies [4, 5] also noted that up to 80% of postgraduates are working. Part of postgraduates are living (and working) in another city than universities.

Every year part of postgraduate students who received scholarships [7] is decreasing: from 65% in 2000-2001 down to 58% in 2004-2005, and this trend continues.

The analysis [8] of study discontinuation reasons in higher education related to the organization of the study process, showed that the reasons most frequently given are too high learning load, hastily chosen study program, poor learning motivation.

In summary such the main reasons for discontinuation of study can be listed:

- high level of business (employment) – the majority of postgraduate work and have family concerns),
- large learning load,
- economic and social problems (declining part of postgraduates – scholarship recipients),
- the geographic spread of postgraduate students (they are working or/and living in a different city than the University location),
- individual learning problems (speed, time, location).

For solving of these problems innovative ways and forms of organizing of studies can be used [9]. High hopes have been associated with distance learning. But the reality proved far different things.

2 Distance Learning. Problems of Distance Learning

Joergen Bang in his publication [10] asks "Have e-learning and virtual universities met the expectations?" and considers in detail e-learning problems and prospects. Trying to answer the question he provides such data.

"In the late nineties, several US universities formed commercial companies alone or in collaboration with other universities, cultural institutions and providers of e-solutions. Among others, New York University invested $20m in NYU Online and Columbia University formed Fathom together with 14 universities, libraries and museums, using $40m. None of these ever launched an e-learning course. At the same time, Cornell University invested $12m in eCornell without registering any significant numbers of students. Also, the attempt by the Open University of the UK to deliver education on the US marked failed with a loss of approximately $20m.

One of the few successful e-learning providers in the USA is University of Phoenix, and its success seems to be related to a focus on a limited and specialized market in the business and health field.

Many national European projects for e-learning were launched, e.g. the UK e-University (UkeU), the Digital University in the Netherlands, the Bavarian Virtual University, the Virtual University in Finland and the Net-University in Sweden.

Five years later, the UKeU has ceased operations. What was launched as a worldwide 21st century successor of the Open University never attracted financial support from commercial partners and recruited only 900 students at a time when 5000 were expected? £60m of public money was spent on the operation."

One of the reasons why e-universities faced the financial failures is the great drop out of students. Various sources [11, 12] show the data drop out in e-studies is 10-25% higher than in traditional studies, and reaches as much as 70-80%.

The difficulties encountered by many of the above e-education and training using the Internet initiatives appeared on the approach to learning, especially to e-learning as the transfer of knowledge rather than knowledge creation process. Too much attention was paid to self-contained courses and sources based learning. Distance education creates many challenges for students: autonomy, the ability to organize their own learning process, self-discipline, initiative, motivation and sense of isolation, lack of interaction and support, self-control and so on.

3 Blended Learning

The best results are achieved by combining traditional training with e-educational technology. Combination of traditional training with e-learning is called blended learning [13, 14]. Studies [15, 16, 17] show that the training results using the hybrid training method is better than the traditional or e-learning mode. Blended learning model ("Time and Space") presented in Figure 1.

Teaching and learning time

Teaching and learning place		Same	different
	different	synchronous Student interaction with the lecturer in ICT support real-time	asynchronous Student self-learning, using ICT tools
	Same	traditional Face to face communication with the student teacher	traditional Student self-study

Fig. 1. Blended learning model ("Time and Space")

There are three main components of the overall instructional design:

- face-to-face training – a form of traditional classroom education (teacher-student),
- self-study learning – an independent student's work: literary studies, project development, information retrieval on the Internet and so on,
- online collaborative learning – an interactive teaching and student's work using ICT tools: e-conferencing, E-mail, audio and video IP telephony, etc.

Table 2 below outlines the main differences between e-learning (distance learning) and blended learning solutions.

Table 2. The differences between e-learning and blended learning solutions

E-learning	Blended learning
"Distance learning" – upon request, at anytime, anywhere	Traditional classroom sessions conducted – class + e-learning + self-study. "Freely chosen" and fixed learning time
Learning process control, consistency of content and pace of learning in this case depends almost entirely on the learner	Learning process control, consistency of content and pace of learning depends on both the teacher and the learner
Self-discipline and all responsibility for the learning organization rests solely with the learner	Responsibility for organizing learning share teacher and the learner, and learners together

4 Blended Learning of Postgraduate Studies in KTU Informatics Faculty

In 2008 a new postgraduate study program "Information technology and information security" was prepared [18] at Faculty of Informatics. In preparation process the needs of postgraduates and teaching methods (traditional, e-learning and blended learning) advantages and disadvantages were evaluated. The decision was made – to apply a blended learning format. Model of the learning activities (distribution in time and space) is shown in Figure 2.

Teaching and learning time

Teaching and learning place	Same	different
different	Synchronous (student online interaction with the lecturer using ICT): e-lectures, e-laboratory, e-guidance, e-seminar, e-tests	asynchronous (student self-study using ICT tools): Records of the e-lectures, e-learning materials, e-mail, e-forums, e-teamwork
same	Traditional (Face to face student's communication with the teacher): Lecture in auditorium, work in the laboratory, seminars, consulting, exams, tests, defending a work	traditional (Self-dependent study): Self-dependent work in laboratory, teamwork, working in a library

Fig. 2. Blended learning activities in postgraduate studies (in time and space)

Proper learning methods and the combination of technologies has great importance for quality and performance of education [19]. Since all learning activities have to be carried out in classroom and distance, proper learning means and tools were chosen for teaching activities as is shown in Figure 3.

Teaching and learning time

Teaching and learning place	Same	different
different	synchronous (student online interaction with the lecturer using ICT) KUT ViPS, Adobe Connect DimDim, Skype Moodle	asynchronous (student self-study using ICT tools) KUT ViPS, Adobe Connect Moodle MS Live@edu
same	traditional (Face to face student's communication with the teacher) Auditorium, Laboratory	traditional (Self-dependent study) Laboratory Library

Fig. 3. Blended learning means and tools in postgraduate studies

Lectures are delivered according to schedule in classroom and are broadcasted over the Web using ViPS KUT or Adobe Connect system. Lecture records can be viewed at any time. Practical work is carried out in University laboratories in face to face sessions or using remote access tools. Consulting and seminars are organized in the University as well as using Adobe Connect support. Exams, term papers, defending a thesis are organized in the University. All learning materials needed are presented in printed form or in the virtual learning environment Moodle.

Postgraduate student may choose what study activities he carries out traditionally and what - remotely. Since all study activities (except for credits, exams, defending a thesis) can be performed in both ways – traditionally and by distance, a postgraduate student can choose the study form – traditional, distance or blended.

Master's study program "Information and Information Technology Security" is conducted since 2008. Three master's graduates completed this program and even more are currently studying. Results of their studies are presented in Table 3.

Table 3. Study results (master's degree program in Information and IT Security)

Admission year	Number of adopted postgraduate students	Drop out after 1st year (%)	Drop out after 2nd year (%)	Number of graduates	Number of discontinued (%)	Average rating of study subjects
2008	26	15	0	22	15	9,1
2009	15	13	0	13	13	9,2
2010	20	25	0	15	25	8,9

The study program "Information and Information Technology Security" is still carried out only four years and we have only three graduates, it is too early make wider conclusions, but early results are encouraging. Drop-out in postgraduate studies for adopted in 2008 – 2010 is 18%, while average rating of study subjects is 9.1. This much better as in the traditional form of ongoing programs in Computer Engineering master study programs: drop-out in postgraduate studies for adopted in 2005-2008 is 42%, while average rating of study subjects – 8.6. We can't confirm unambiguously that the results are better only because of the forms of innovative studies. The drop out depends on other causes as well, but certain trends can be seen – blended studies have positive effect on postgraduate study results.

5 Conclusions

Continuing spread of Information and Information Technologies demands of highly skilled professionals with a master's degree. This is confirmed by studies in countries with high developed economy. Lithuanian also is facing this challenge. However our universities preparing masters face significant challenges – in last year's more than a third of matriculated graduates discontinue their postgraduate studies. And this is great material and moral losses.

The high dropout is due to various reasons – economic (a large part of the postgraduates have some job to earn means of subsistence) and subjective (personal qualities, insufficient motivation) as well.

In order to solve these problems of organization postgraduate studies, a lot of expectations were associated with distance learning technology. However, it is not entirely justified; dropout in distance studies is 10-25% higher than in conventional studies and reach in some cases 70-80%.

For a new master study program "Information technology and information security" at Faculty of Informatics blended learning format was chosen. Lectures are delivered in classroom and are broadcasted over the Web using ViPS KUT or Adobe Connect system. Practical work is carried out in University laboratories in face to face sessions or using remote access tools. Consulting and seminars are organized in the University as well as using Adobe Connect support. All learning materials needed are presented in printed form or in the virtual learning environment Moodle

First results are encouraging – drop-out in postgraduate studies for adopted in 2008 – 2010 is 18%, while average rating of study subjects is 9.1. We hope the blended learning is the right way in solving our problems in postgraduate studies.

References

1. Lacey, T.A., Wright, B.: Occupational employment projections to 2018, The Bureau of Labor Statistics of the U.S. Department of Labor (2009), \
   `http://www.bls.gov/opub/mlr/2009/11/art5full.pdf`
2. Occupational Outlook Handbook, 2010-11 Edition, The Bureau of Labor Statistics of the U.S. Department of Labor (2010),
   `http://www.bls.gov/oco/pdf/ocos305.pdf`

3. Ruževskis, B., Blažienė, I., Pocius, A., Zabarauskaitė, R.: ir kt.: Aukščiausios kvalifikacijos specialistų (magistrantų) pasiūlos ir paklausos atitikimo sisteminis įvertinimas. (The systematic evaluation of matching supply and demand of highly qualified specialists (masters)). Vilnius (2008) (in Lithuanian)
4. Sirutkaitis, V., Piskarskas, A., Račiukaitis, G., Kuprionis, Z.: Aukščiausios kompetencijos specialistų rengimas, moksliniai tyrimai ir eksperimentinė plėtra, mokslui imlaus verslo vystymas lazerių srityje (The professional training of top-level specialists, scientific research and experimental development science-intensive business development in the laser field). LR SMM. Vilnius (2007) (in Lithuanian)
5. Aukščiausios kompetencijos specialistų rengimas, moksliniai tyrimai ir eksperimentinė plėtra, mokslui imlaus verslo vystymas mechatronikos srityje (The professional training of top-level specialists, scientific research and experimental development, science-intensive business development in mechatronics). KTU. Vilnius (2007) (in Lithuanian)
6. Beresnevičiūtė, V., Poviliūnas, A.: Magistrų integracija į darbo rinką: magistrantūros studijų absolventų sociologinės apklausos analizė (Master's integration into the labor market: analysis of postgraduates sociological survey). Sociologija. Mintis ir veiksmas. 2007/1(19), 88–103 (2007) (in Lithuanian)
7. Barkauskaitė, M., Gudžinskienė, V.: Studentų išstojimo iš aukštųjų universitetinių ir neuniversitetinių mokyklų dinamika 1999–2004 metais. Pedagogika. T. 84, 53–58 (2006) (in Lithuanian)
8. Gaigalienė, M.: Studentų išstojimo iš aukštosios mokyklos priežastys, susijusios su studijų proceso organizavimu (Student withdrawal from the university and non-high-school dynamics in 1999-2004). Pedagogika. T. 83. pp. 122–127 (2006) (in Lithuanian)
9. Targamadzė, A., Petrauskienė, R.: Impact of Information Technologies on Modern Learning. Information Technologies and Control 39(3), 169–175 (2010)
10. Bang, J.: eLearning reconsidered. Have e-learning and virtual universities met the expectations? (2006), `http://www.elearningpapers.eu`
11. Betts, K.: Online Human Touch (OHT) Instruction and Programming: A Conceptual Framework to Increase Student Engagement and Retention in Online Education, Part 1. MERLOT Journal of Online Learning and Teaching 4(3), 399–418 (2008)
12. Lorraine, M.A., Williams, F.K., Natvig, D.: Strategies to Engage Online Students and Reduce Attrition Rates. The Journal of Educators Online 4(2), 1–14 (2007)
13. Sharpe, R., Benfield, G., Roberts, G., Francis, R.: The undergraduate experience of blended e-learning: a review of UK literature and practice. The Higher Education Academy (2006)
14. Butrimė, E., Jarmakovienė, J., Zuzevičiūtė, V.: Mišraus mokymo poreikiai socialinių mokslų studentų ir dėstytojų požiūriu (Blended learning needs of social science students and teachers). Acta Paedagogica Vilnensia 23, 43–51 (2009)
15. Hughes, G.: Using blended learning to increase learner support and improve retention. Teaching in Higher Education 12(3), 349–363 (2007)
16. Stacey, E., Gerbic, P.: Success factors for blended learning. In: Proceedings Ascilite Melbourne, pp. 964–968 (2008)
17. Hameed, S., Fathulla, K., Thomas, A.: Extent of e-learning effectiveness and efficiency in an integrated blended learning environment. Newport CELT Journal 2, 52–62 (2009)
18. Venčkauskas, A., Maciulevičius, S., Toldinas, J.: Informacijos ir informacinių technologij saugos magistrantūros programa (Master study program Information and Information Technology Security). XV kompiuterininkų konferencijos mokslo darbai. Vilnius, Žara. pp. 196–204 (2011) (in Lithuanian)
19. Targamadzė, A., Petrauskienė, R., Rubliauskas, D.: Influence of Technologies on Quality of Distance Learning. Electronics and Electrical Engineering. Kaunas: Technologija 6(102), 131–134 (2010)

Two-Stage Generative Learning Objects

Vytautas Štuikys and Renata Burbaite

Program Software Department, Kaunas University of Technology, Studentų 50, 51368 Kaunas, Lithuania
vytautas.stuikys@ktu.lt, renata.burbaite@gmail.com

Abstract. Generative Learning Objects (GLOs) introduced by Boyle *et al.* in 2004 extend the reuse dimension and create conditions for better quality in learning and teaching. We motivate the benefits of GLOs for e-learning and extend the scope of understanding GLOs by introducing the concept of the two-stage GLOs (TS GLOs). The aim of the paper is to show how this new kind of GLOs can contribute to the advanced e-learning through e-learning variability (social context, content variants, e-learning environment characteristics, etc.) modelling. GLOs and TS GLOs are seen as tools to further enhance reuse, to ensure a great deal of flexibility for teachers, and to manage complexity in the LO domain. Our case study has also showed the benefit for students in using the approach for self-learning by selecting different tasks or variants with respect to students flavour or abilities.

Keywords: e-learning, learning object, generative learning object, one-stage generative learning object, two-stage generative learning object.

1 Introduction

The content and e-learning environment plays a decisive role in learning. The content, which is delivered by teacher and consumed by students, fuels the whole learning process. The e-learning environment, on the other hand, can be seen as supporting tools to better managing the content preparation, storing, distributing, representing, changing, sharing and interacting with consumers. The content is more flexible and better suited for changes and adaptations. The need for content management was growing along with technology expansion, adoptions of various pedagogical approaches, maturity of e-learning environments and better understanding of e-learning per se.

We consider two periods of e-learning evolution here. The first period was nominated by the Internet expansion in the decade (1990 – 2000). As a result, the e-learning community clearly understood the need to re-evaluate the new capabilities of technology and its impact on learning. The aim was to resolve the problem of interoperability of learning content and extend the scope of reuse. By introducing the concept of learning objects (LOs) into e-learning in 1992-1994 [1], there was made the move from the *concrete understanding* to the *abstract* (i.e., more general) *understanding* of the teaching content. The paradigm change has fuelled a wide

T. Skersys, R. Butleris, and R. Butkiene (Eds.): ICIST 2012, CCIS 319, pp. 332–347, 2012.

stream of research, initiatives for standardization and created conditions for lifting the e-learning domain to a higher maturity level as it will be explained in detail by analysis of the related work in Section 2.

The second period is characterized by efforts to extend the LO concept. The result was the appearance of generative learning objects (GLO) in 2004-05 due to the works [2, 3]. The aim (as defined by pioneers of the concept) was to extend the reuse dimension, create conditions for better quality in learning and teaching, to enhance productivity in preparing, sharing and using of the teaching content. Though the number of proponents of this approach is constantly growing up (see Section 2), this concept could not be regarded as well-understood by the e-learning community yet due to the restricted number of subjects and users involved.

The aim of this paper is not only to motivate the benefits of GLOs for e-learning but also to further extend the scope of understanding GLOs by introducing the concept of the *two-stage* GLOs (TS GLOs). More specifically, the aim of the paper is to show how this *new kind* of GLOs can contribute to the advanced e-learning through e-learning variability (social context, content variants, e-learning environment characteristics, etc.) modelling.

The paper is structured as follows. Section 2 analyses the related work. Section 3 motivates usefulness of GLOs and TS GLOs. Section 4 explains meta-programming-based GLOs models and motivating examples. Section 5 presents a case study explaining how GLOs are used in teaching/learning process within the robot-based e-learning environment. Section 6 provides summary, evaluation and conclusions.

2 Related Work

We categorize the analyzed work as related to LO research into two categories according to the introduced periods of e-learning evolution as follows: 1) the relevant papers and works published in 1994-2003; 2) papers on generative LOs published after 2003.

The learning content is a core part of e-learning along with the pedagogical approaches used. The first period of e-learning is characterized by these educational characteristics: 1) distributed constructivist and cognitive models, 2) internet-based flexible courseware, 3) online multimedia courseware, 4) increased interactivity and 5) remote user-user interactions [4, 5]. In this period the concept of LO was introduced. The basic properties of LO, such as granularity, compositionality and adaptability, help better understand the importance of LO in e-learning [6, 7, 8, 9]. The content granularity is an extremely important characteristic of LOs because it enables to aggregate higher-level compounds (e.g., lessons, courses) from smaller parts [10, 11, 12]. Wiley states that "LO granularity can be viewed as a trade-off between the possible benefits of reuse and the expenses of cataloguing" [13]. Indeed, the smaller in size a LO is, the easier is to transfer it for reuse in another context of use. This is because we are usually expressing essential knowledge units at the lowest level [14, 15]. Compositionality of LOs entails the sequencing problem of lower-level LOs to form a larger LO such as a lecture topic, or entire course [13, 16, 17, 18].

More abstractly, the composites are viewed as structural models of LOs. Though adaptability, as an underlying attribute of LOs, is well-understood in the community and is exploited in a variety of different contexts, however, it is yet little known on mechanisms how to implement automatic or semi-automatic adaptation. To understand such mechanisms we need to look at the existing models of LOs.

As learning/teaching is a multi-target and multi-level process (ranging from planning to delivery and assessment), the traditional LO models, such as metadata – content [19], or hierarchical models based on content granularity [19, 20] are not enough, because: 1) e-learning domain is rapidly advancing and we need to have more flexible, more adaptable, more personalized, and more contextualized LOs to support advanced learning; 2) the traditional component-based view to LOs has limited capabilities for adaptation and further extension of reuse; 3) with the expansion of LO domain, digital libraries are growing rapidly in volume and this situation may lead to serious managing and maintenance problems [21, 22]; 4) for advancement, e-learning has practically unlimited technological support due to the variety of choice and capabilities (mobility, networking, tools, methodology, etc.). As a response to IT advances and capabilities, the adequate LO models should be relevant to new challenges.

A significant contribution to address these challenges has been the concept generative learning object (further GLO) introduced by Boyle and his colleagues [2]. In a wider context, a LO is an abstraction or a model to support reusability across large e-learning communities [23]. However, the GLO model as "a next generation of LO" has new capabilities such as generativity and flexible adaptation. Separation of the LO structure from its content is the basic idea, based on which a GLO works [2, 3, 24, 25, 26]. This separation is introduced in advance (within the model) and it is implemented with the use of a generative technology (hence the name 'generative LO').

Though there are a variety of generative technologies as indicated in [27] they can be grouped into two large groups according to this factor: template-based [2] and meta-programming-based [28]. Technology is also influential to tools that support the GLOs. As a technology may have many implementations, thus a variety of different approaches are applied to support GLOs.

For example, knowledge-based GLO model [28] consists of three basic parts: name, knowledge-based interface and knowledge-based body. Name is for identification and referencing or the learning objective statement. Interface is for communicating and transferring knowledge to the LO and from it. Interface is separated from body. The body defines structural and functional aspects of a LO. This model gives a basis for systematic construction of courses from LO instances since the model describes interaction explicitly. Han and Krämer suggest developing content, called information objects (IOs), independently from pedagogical context, such as learning objectives and scenarios, and connecting both ad hoc at reuse time to form meaningful LOs "keeping content and educational context separate at design time and connecting both facets of LOs only at reuse time" [29]. Oldfield implemented a template-based GLO model in accounting teaching process [30].

We summarize the trends of GLO evolution as follows: a) GLO models have a great potential for e-learning domain to extend reusability with productivity aspects; b) the analysis also have showed the expending reuse dimension in different learning subjects (medicine, accounting, computer science); c) despite the works of GLO pioneers and other researchers the maturity level of the approach is still low, and as a result, the research efforts should be extended. Thus, we consider and research in this field by introducing a new concept of GLOs called two-stage GLO (TS GLO).

3 Motivation of the Need of GLOs and TS GLOs

In this section, we introduce a new term *learning variability* to better understand e-learning and learning content expressed through learning objects. In general, variability is defined as a property of a process, a system, an entity, etc. that has multiple variants. By learning variability we mean the variability that relates to any aspect of learning (pedagogy, social, content, environment, etc.). We motivate the need of GLOs TS GLOs by learning variability as it is explain below.

3.1 Understanding of e-Learning Domain through Learning Variability

Learning variability for teachers serves to plan content variants for different groups of students, to introduce different models of teaching, to select different types of e-learning facilities with the e-learning environment. All these may be dependent on social aspects (student's age, student's abilities, gender, etc.), teaching/learning goals (knowledge delivery, knowledge assessment), and technology capabilities to represent the content in various forms, to motivate the students and to increase their engagement into learning. Learning variability is also important for students. Students are able to select the content, the teaching model, the characteristics of a facility on own flavour or depending upon abilities of learning, teaching and knowledge assessment and gain a great deal of flexibility in learning.

What is most important to understanding the learning variability is that different kinds (features) of variability are dependent meaning that they *interact among themselves*. For example, teaching goals may dictate the selection of teaching model and scenario used. All these may be influential on the selection of content variants. The content variants may be dependent on representation forms and technology used within the e-learning environment. In our view, ever-growing technology capabilities and the better understanding of its role to e-learning are the main sources which enlarge the variability space and make the learning variability interaction more feasible.

The *learning variability modelling* is the process that enables to identify the learning variability *features and the interaction among* them. There are two general forms to represent (learning) variability: the *implicit* and *explicit* representation. The implicit representation is the one in which variants of some learning features are kept in actors mind or they are introduced not directly but are visible from the context. For example, it may appear when teacher introduce the learning scenario together with the teaching content. The first is based on the intention and knowledge of the course designer or teacher. In the most cases, variability in learning is represented implicitly. Especially it is true when the variability space is small. In early e-learning systems, variability aspects were represented either implicitly or the explicit representation was restricted.

The explicit representation requires specific means. It is more powerful as compared with the implicit representation. It is applicable to larger variability spaces. As the variability spaces are constantly expanding due to technology advances and e-learning evolution, the learning variability modelling is the big issue. It should be treated as a separate task. In the context of this paper, we can formulate the following finding. The recognition of the learning variability problem brings the methodological foundation of using generative learning objects (GLOs) because, in fact, GLOs are the technology-driven representation of learning variability as it will be explained in detail below.

3.2 Variability Example in Computer Science Teaching

Assume the following topic ("*Loops in computer programs*") for secondary school students is to be presented. We consider the pedagogy-based, content and environmental variability aspects. We focus on the following pedagogy-based variability aspects: *pedagogical model* (constructivist, cognitive, behaviourist), *means for students' engagement* (low, middle, high), *learning goal* (to learn basics, advanced learning). We focus on the following content variability features: *one-loop structure* (simple, conditional), *nested loop structure* (two-loops without condition, with condition), *problem domain task* (data summation, data sorting, ornament constructing, etc.), *language to specify the program* (C, Pascal, PHP), *mode of representation of teaching content* (to see the program specification text only, result of the program execution), *representation of the problem result* (by computer, by printer, by teaching robot, etc.), *e-learning environment* (stand-alone computer, Internet + computer, stand-alone robot, robot + computer + Internet).

Note that variability aspects first can be expressed through features at a higher abstraction level, and then they are represented by parameters at the GLO specification level as it will be showed in presented examples.

4 Meta-Programming-Based GLOs Models and Motivating Examples

In this section, we explain our approach, i.e., meta-programming-based GLOs and their derivatives TS GLOs in detail. To do that we first define related terms, provide examples of two kinds of GLOs (one-stage and two-stage) along with their models. Then we analyze properties of the GLOs.

4.1 Basic Definitions

DEFINITION 1. Learning object (LO) is "*any digital entity, which can be used, reused or referenced during technology-supported learning*" (adapted from [6]).

DEFINITION 2. Generative LO (GLO) is *a reusable LO (RLO) which entails a multi-level structure for implementing the content flexibly using a generative technology* (adopted from Boyle *et al.* works [2]).

DEFINITION 3. Template-based GLO is the structure "*where the form of the learning object can be shaped and adapted through a generative process, rather than just being captured in a surface template form*" (Adapted from Boyle paper [31]).

DEFINITION 4. Meta-programming is a generative technology that uses higher-level functions (meta-functions) *to manipulate a target program as data* [32]. Meta-program is a program generator – the product of meta-programming [33]. The functions are introduced by a meta-language to specify variability aspects.
In the case of using the technology in e-learning, LO is treated as a target program and GLO is treated as a meta-program.

DEFINITION 5. Meta-programming-based GLO is *a generative technology-driven entity that specifies a family of related LO instances to generate and deliver on demand the variants of teaching content and relevant pedagogical features.*

DEFINITION 6. One-stage GLO is a meta-programming-based GLO having the model as specified by Fig. 1.

DEFINITION 7. Model of the one-stage GLO is the structure consisting of meta-interface and meta-body. The first specifies metadata to be transferred to the meta-body which implements functionality of the GLO.

DEFINITION 8. Metadata are meta-parameters to specify the variability aspects of a GLO to perform anticipated manipulations within the meta-body.

DEFINITION 9. Two-stage GLO is a derivative object derived from the one-stage GLO under pre-specified constraints and conditions using the model (see Fig 2). The model of two-stage GLO consists of the staged meta-interface and the staged meta-body. The functionality of the staged meta-body is based on the use of active and passive meta-functions to specify anticipated manipulations.

DEFINITION 10. A meta-function is *active* if it performs its pre-scribed action as a construct of a meta-language at the current stage of GLO execution. It does not contain the de-activation label ('\') written before the beginning of the function.

DEFINITION 11. A meta-function is *passive* if it has been deactivated and is treated as a part of a target language text at the current stage of GLO execution. For example, \@sub[x] is the passive function in the given stage of its interpretation because the function contains the de-activation label.

DEFINITION 12. *De-activation process* of a meta-function is the labeling of the function by the de-activation label "\". *Activation process* is deleting of the de-activation label. The activation process takes place during the second stage of the GLO execution.

4.2 One-Stage GLOs Model with Example

The model of GLO (see Fig.1 and DEFINITIONS 6-8) consists of two interrelated parts: *meta-interface* and *meta-body*. Meta-interface specifies metadata expressed by meta-parameters (shortly parameters) to manage variability aspects or features implemented into the meta-body. Meta-interface is visible for learner/teacher to perform managing procedures. Meta-body specifies implementation details of a GLO. The implementation is described using a higher-level language (called meta-language). Constructs of meta-language specify various types of operations called meta-functions. Meta-body is hidden for the user because it contains technology-related details woven together with content and context information.

Meta-interface of GLO: *meta-data supplied to meta-body to initiate the functioning of GLO*
Meta-body of GLO: *describing the implementation of GLO functionality; structurally, GLO is a set of related LO instances woven together by means of generative technology, such as meta-programming*

Fig. 1. Meta-programming-based one-stage GLO model

As a motivating example to explain the specification of GLOs, we have chosen the assignment statements that can be met in different programming languages (e.g., PASCAL, C, and PHP). The variants of representing the statements as LOs are presented in Fig. 2 (here variability is defined by the coefficient type (scalar, element of array), by the coefficient value (=1, =/ 1), by the variable type (scalar, element of array), and by the assignment notation (=, :=).

```
y := x1 + x2;
y := x[1] + x[2];
y := a1*x1 + a2*x2;
y := a[1]*x1 + a[2]*x2;
y := a[1]*x[1] + a[2]*x[2];
y = x1 + x2;
y = x[1] + x[2];
y = a1*x1 + a2*x2;
y = a1*x[1] + a2*x[2];
y = a[1]*x1 + a[2]*x2;
y = a[1]*x[1] + a[2]*x[2];
```

Fig. 2. Motivating example: variants of assignment statement in programming languages

Below we present a specification of the one-stage GLO (or simply GLO) to implement the variability aspects given in Fig. 2. For simplicity reasons, the content variability aspects are described only (programming language aspects are ignored). The GLO is implemented using a Open PROMOL meta-language (see Fig. 3). Comments within specifications (@-…for a Open PROMOL meta-language) explain the details of the specifications.

```
$
@--this is a meta-interface of GLO
"Select assignment statement type: 1--:=, 2--=" {:=,=}                p1:= :=;
"Select type of coefficient a:1--null,2--scalar,3--indexed" {1,2,3 } p2:=2;
"Select type of variable x: 1--scalar, 2--indexed" {1,2}              p3:=2;
$
@--this is a meta-body of GLO
y@sub[p1] @case[p2, { }, {a1}, {a[1]}]*@case[p3, {x1 },{x[1]}]  +
          @case[p2, { }, {a2}, {a[2]}]*@case[p3, {x2 },{x[2]}];
```

Fig. 3. Illustrative example of simple one-stage GLO implemented by Open PROMOL programming language: @sub[*p*1] – when executed the function will be substituted by its pre-specified argument value, i.e., by :=; @case[*p*2, { }, {a1}, {a[1]}] – when executed the function will return the value a1 because *p*2=2 (second item, i.e., a1 will be selected)

The result of the GLO execution with respect to pre-specified parameter values is as follows:

```
y := a1*x[1] + a2*x[2];
```

To design any GLO teacher or designer has to use the following set of functions (see Table 1), if Open PROMOL programming language has been selected as a meta-language to specify GLO.

Table 1. List of basic Open PROMOL programming language functions: their syntax and semantics [34]

Function name	Examples of the usage	Parameter value	The returned value
@sub	V := **@sub**[n*2+1];	n := 2	V := 5;
@if	X: bit**@if**[n>1, { _vector (0 to **@sub**[n-1]) }];	n := 4	X: bit_vector (0 to 3);
@case	Y <= **@case**[n, {B1}, {B2}, {B3}];	n := 2	Y <= B2;
@for	**@for**[i, 0, n-1, {L(**@sub**[i]) }]	n := 5	L(0) L(1) L(2) L(3) L(4)
@gen	Y <= **@gen**[n, { AND }, {X}, 0];	n := 3	Y <= X0 AND X1 AND X2;
@move	**@move**[f, {NOT}]	f := NOT	<null>
@rep	X <= "**@rep**[n, {**@sub**[sym]}]";	n := 4; sym := 0	X <= "0000";
@include	**@include**[gate]		<null>
@macro	**@macro**[gate, {AND}, n]	n := 2	2-input AND gate instance

4.3 Two-Stage GLO Model with Example

Fig. 4 illustrates the two-stage GLO model of the same functionality as the one given in Fig. 1. The model should be analyzed and understood along with DEFINITIONS 9-12.

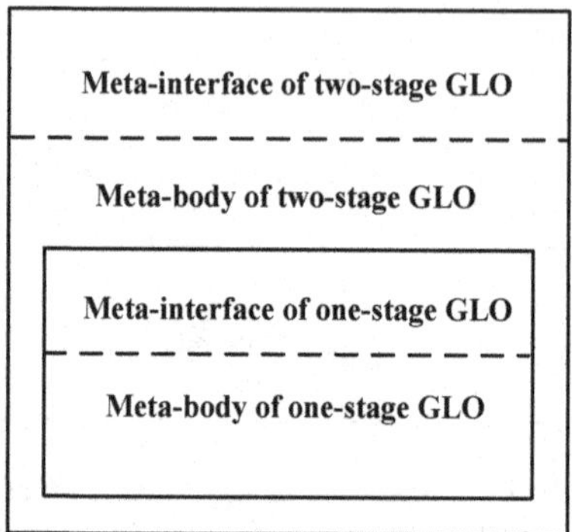

Fig. 4. Model of two-stage GLO

```
$
@--this is a meta-interface of second-stage GLO
"Select assignment statement type: 1--:=, 2--=" {:=,=}                    p1:= :=;
$
     @--this is the meta-body of the second stage GLO
     @--the meta-body also includes interface of the first stage GLO (see Fig. 3)
     $

    "Select type of coefficient a:1--null,2--scalar,3--indexed" {1,2,3 } p2:=2;
    "Select type of variable x: 1--scalar, 2--indexed" {1,2}               p3:=2;
     $

    y@sub[p1] \@case[p2, { }, {a1}, {a[1]}] * \@case[p3, {x1 },{x[1]}]  +
              \@case[p2, { }, {a2}, {a[2]}] * \@case[p3, {x2 },{x[2]}];
```

a)

```
$

    "Select type of coefficient a:1--null,2--scalar,3--indexed" {1,2,3 } p2:=2;
    "Select type of variable x: 1--scalar, 2--indexed" {1,2}               p3:=2;
$

    y:=@case[p2, { }, {a1}, {a[1]}] * @case[p3, {x1 },{x[1]}]  +
       @case[p2, { }, {a2}, {a[2]}] * @case[p3, {x2 },{x[2]}];
```

b)

```
y := a1*x[1] + a2*x[2];
```

c)

Fig. 5. a) Two-stage GLO, b) its derivative one-stage GLO, c) LO derived from one-stage GLO

The two-stage specification has the different structure: its meta-interface consists of two stages (Fig. 5 a)) and processes within the meta-body stages (when the specification is executed) are managed by the label "\". Note that the label before the function (e.g., \@case[*p*2, { }, {a1}, {a[1]}])de-activates the function during execution of the two-stage meta-body. After the execution the label is deleted. As a result, the execution of the meta-body produces a one-stage GLO (see Fig. 5 b)). The result of the one-stage GLO execution with respect to pre-specified parameter values is presented in Fig. 5 c).

As it is seen from the Figs. 4 and 5, the result is identical in using of one-stage or two-stage GLOs within the same meta-parameter space. We present more properties of the introduced GLOs and TS GLOs below.

4.4 Basic Properties of GLOs/TS GLO

1. The structural model of two-stage GLO can be derived through refactoring of the one-stage GLO model in the following way: a) meta-interface of the one-stage GLO is splitted into two parts (the higher (see Fig. 5 a) to be evaluated at the second stage and the lower to be evaluated at the first stage).
2. The lower-level part (see Fig. 5 b)) of the meta-interface is a constituent of meta-body of the two-stage GLO.
3. The result of the interpretation (execution of two-stage program) is a set of one-stage GLOs defined on the pre-scribed higher-level meta-parameter values (see Fig. 5 b)).
4. The process of the two-stage GLO interpretation has also two stages (as a result of the structural model implementation). In the higher stage, the result is as it is defined by property 3. In the lower stage, the result is either a single LO (if it was derived according one possible parameter values) or a set of LO instances (if different one-stage LOs set were used for the space of possible parameter values). Fig. 5 c) specifies only a single LO.
5. Meta-functions appear within meta-body and govern its functionality. The meta-functions are of two types: either active or passive (see DEFINITION 10 and DEFINITION 11).
6. The two-stage meta-body contains both kinds of meta-functions, while the one-stage meta-body contains the active functions only (see Fig. 5 a) and b)).
7. If all n meta-parameters are orthogonal any combination of $(n\text{-}1)$ meta-parameters can be lifted to the second stage. If some parameters are dependent, then such parameter must appear at the same stage, either at stage 2 or 1.
8. The most important property to implement two-stage GLOs is the activation and de-activation process of a meta-function within the meta-body as it is explained by DEFINITIONS 10-12 and can be seen in Fig 5.

5 Case Study: The Teaching/Learning Process Using GLOs/TS GLOs and LEGO-Based DRAWBOT Tools

The case study demonstrates the ability to solve and visually represent a set of related graph-based tasks (given as LOs) in teaching programming. A particular LO adapted to the learning context is derived from the GLO's / TS GLO's automatically. The overall process using the Lego-based DRAWBOT tools is summarized below.

5.1. Learning/teaching subject: *Computer Science.*
5.2. LO topic: *Loops and Nested Loops in a Computer Program.*
5.3. e-learning environment: *Lego-based DRAWBOT (drawing robot).*
5.4. Learning content: *an LO derived from One-stage GLOs and two-stage GLOs.*
5.5. Learners: *10-11th grade secondary school students at J. Balčikonis Gymnasium.*
5.6. Pedagogical model used: *Constructivist.*
5.7. Learning objectives: *Visualization of the process and learning content.*
5.8. Process description by teacher: *a) design and testing of the e-learning environment; b) design and testing one-stage GLO; c) testing-generating LO instances from GLO to apply them to different context of use; d) design of two-stage GLO, transforming of one-stage GLO to the two-stage one and testing/generating.*
5.9. Learning activity by students: *a) design of the robot mechanics under the teacher guidance b) identification of robot characteristics relevant for teaching tasks; c) participation in the development of GLOs, including robot control programs as GLOs and content visualization programs as GLOs (see Fig. 6).*
5.10. Learning evaluation: *a) teacher makes observes and records students' activity actions, feedback and on this basis evaluated the gained knowledge.*

We analyze two GLOs/TS GLO. The first is "The measurement of technical parameters of DRAWBOT", because these parameters are used for the robot control program. Motors are controlled for specifying a power level to apply to the motor. The programming language RobotC uses parameter named "Power level". Power levels range from –100 to +100. Negative values indicate reverse direction and positive values indicate forward direction. The distance driven by the robot per time depends on the motor's Power level. The movement of the robot depends on robot's construction and motor's technical parameters. To ensure the smooth movement there are three operating modes: 1) manual adjustment by the motor command "Power level" for the straight robot's move, 2) use of the PID (Proportional-Integral-Derivative) speed control algorithm, 3) use of the motor synchronization to ensure that both motors run at the same speed [35]. This GLO is described using 3 parameters: 1) operating mode, which takes 3 values, 2) DRAWBOT's speed with 5 power levels: 30, 50, 70, 90, 100 and 3) DRAWBOT's movement time with 3 values equal 1, 3 and 5 seconds. 45 LO instances can be generated in 1-stage GLO and 2-stage GLO (see Table 2).

The second GLO is "Ornaments' drawing by DRAWBOT". It is described using 7 parameters. 4 parameters are used for drawing a single ornament: 2 motor's power level can have values 30, 50, 70; movement's time can be chosen 0,5, 1 or 2 seconds;

number of parts of ornament is 1..12. 3 parameters define the distance between ornaments (2 motor's power level also can have values 30, 50, 70) and number of ornaments (1..10). 29160 LOs can be generated in this case (see Table 2, Fig. 6).

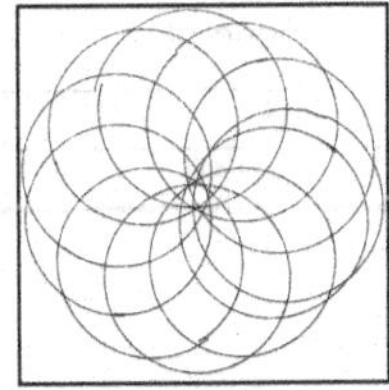
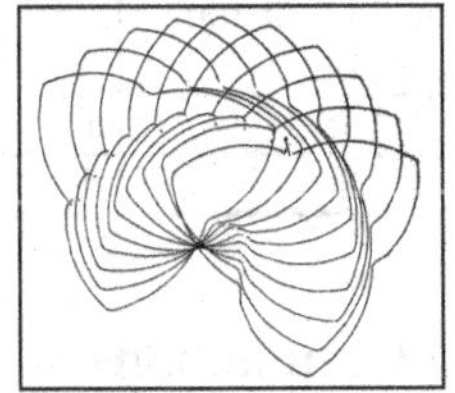

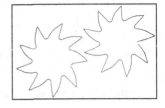

Fig. 6. Ornaments with different parameters as a result of nested loops – GLOs obtained using the DRAWBOT e-learning environment

Pedagogical effectiveness of using one-stage and two-stage GLO can be evaluated, e.g., by "engagement levels" using the methodology described in [36]. Fig. 7 explains assessment of the student engagement levels:

1. *Viewing*: Students view the ornaments given by teacher passively and are passive LO consumers.
2. *Responding*: Students use the visualization of ornaments actively as a resource for answering questions given by teacher and are active LO consumers.
3. *Changing*: Students themselves modify ornaments by changing meta-parameter values using the pre-specified meta-interface and the tool and are LO designers.
4. *Constructing*: Students construct their own ornaments introducing new meta-parameter values not anticipated by the meta-interface and are LO co-designers and testers.
5. *Presenting*: Students present to the audience for discussion new ornaments and are GLO co-designers.

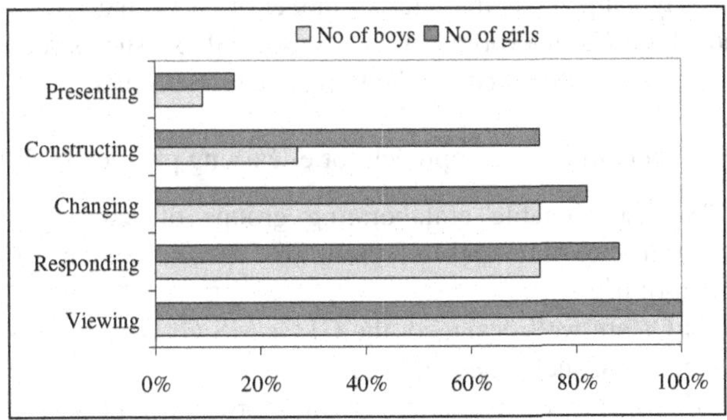

Fig. 7. Student engagement levels using one-stage and two-stage GLO within DRAWBOT environment

Table 2. One-stage GLO vs. Two-stage GLO for the same GLO

GLO	One-stage GLO		Two-stage GLO			
	Parameter number (#)	LO instances generated	# parameters at stage 2	# 1-stage GLO generated	# parameters at stage 1	LO instances generated
1	3	45	2	15	1	45
2	7	29160	3	90	4	29160

6 Summary, Evaluation and Conclusions

We have identified the following benefits of the approach based on using GLO /TS GLO for e-learning theory.

1. As the concept of GLOs extends reusability aspects (content adaptability to different context of use, flexibility of use through automatic generation, etc.), GLOs contribute to LO research in general.
2. The two-stage GLOs further extend the scope of reusability aspects in LO research due to the explicitly defined stages in the model structure of the GLO and within the process when the meta-specification is executed.
3. As e-learning domain has an extremely wide context (social, pedagogical, technological) and content is directly dependent upon its context, the content variability has a great potential to expand. As a result, a problem to manage the complexity issues arises. GLOs and TS GLOs are seen as tools to manage complexity in LO domain. Specifically, TS GLOs are seen also as tools to manage the complexity growth of GLOs per se.
4. As digital libraries (DSL, etc.) for e-learning to support wide-scale reuse and intellectual property sharing have tendency to increase in volume (due to the expansion of e-learning domain), the library scaling problem identical to software libraries [37] may happen. As the internal model of GLOs incorporates a set of LO instances and TS GLOs incorporate related sets of GLOs, such structures benefit to predicting negative consequences of the library scaling problem.

We have identified benefits of the approach for e-learning practice as follows:

1. The GLOs/TS GLOs enable collaborating groups of teachers such as Lego Engineering Group to plan and represent the related content as generics for multiple context of use.
2. If GLOs/TS GLOs are well-designed, the GLOs/MS GLOs can be maintained and flexibly changed when such a need arises.
3. The pre-specified generative content in the form of GLOs/TS GLO ensures productivity and resource saving through automatic tools and technology support.
4. As our case study (experience) have shown, a solitary teacher can be largely benefited in using GLO/TS GLOs in the concrete e-learning setting to manage the following issues:

  - automatic generation of related LOs that are designated to different groups of learners,
  - automatic adaptation of the content to different e-learning environments or different characteristics of the same environment, such as ones based on using mobile devices, or learning robots, etc.,
  - flexible change of the pre-specified generic specifications.
5. Our case study (experience) has also showed the benefit for students in using the approach, for self-learning by selecting different tasks or variants with respect to students flavor or abilities (of course, if the GLO are designed to support such features).
6. As GLOs/TS GLOs are technology-driven structures, the gains come at the larger extent to computer science students because they obtain knowledge in modern technology such as meta-programming.
7. Though we apply the approach in teaching of Informatics topics (as our case study summarizes), we believe the soundness and applicability of the approach for other topics too, if teachers providing the courses (e.g., physics, engineering, mathematics) are assisted by generative technology knowledgeable assistants.

As experience and maturity level is low, we recognize the need for wider research efforts. The foregoing benefits of the proposed approach are not for free. The development of GLOs/TS GLOs is much more complicated, but this topic is beyond the scope of this paper. The concept of TS GLO can contribute to the methodology in designing GLOs too.

References

1. Jacobsen, P.: Reusable learning objects: What does the future hold? e-Learning Magazine (2002), http://www.mcli.dist.maricopa.edu/ocotillo/retreat02/rlos.php
2. Leeder, D., Boyle, T., Morales, R., Wharrad, H., Garrud, P.: To boldly GLO – towards the next generation of Learning Objects. In: Proceedings of World Conference on E-Learning in Corporate, Government, Healthcare, and Higher Education 2004, pp. 28–33. AACE, Chesapeake (2004)
3. Morales, R., Leeder, D., Boyle, T.: A case in the design of generative learning objects (GLOs): applied statistical methods. In: Proceedings of World Conference on Educational Multimedia, Hypermedia and Telecommunications, pp. 2091–2097. AACE, Chesapeake (2005)
4. Keengwe, J., Kidd, T.T.: Towards Best Practices in Online Learning and Teaching in Higher Education. MERLOT Journal of Online Learning and Teaching 6(2) (2010), http://jolt.merlot.org/vol6no2/keengwe_0610.html
5. Anderson, T., Dron, J.: Three Generations of Distance Education Pedagogy. The International Review of Research in Open and Distance Learning 12(3), http://www.irrodl.org/index.php/irrodl/article/view/890/1663
6. IEEE Learning Standards Committee, WG 12: Learning Object Metadata, http://ltsc.ieee.org/wg12
7. LOM working draft v4.1, http://ltsc.ieee.org/doc/wg12/LOMv4.1.html

8. Polsani, P.R.: Use and abuse of reusable learning objects. Journal of Digital Information 3 (2003), `http://journals.tdl.org/jodi/article/view/89/88`
9. Silveira, I.F., Araújo, C.F., Amaral, L.H., Alcântara de Oliveira, I.C., Schimiguel, J., Ledôn, M.F.-P., Ferreira, M.A.G.V.: Granularity and Reusability of Learning Objects. In: Koohang, A., Harman, K. (eds.) Learning Objects and Instructional Design, pp. 139–170. Informing Science Press (2007)
10. Pitkänen, S.H., Silander, P.: Criteria for Pedagogical Reusability of Learning Objects Enabling Adaptation and Individualized Learning Processes. In: Proceedings of the IEEE International Conference on Advanced Learning Technologies (ICALT 2004), pp. 246–250 (2004)
11. Štuikys, V., Damaševičius, R.: Development of Generative Learning Objects Using Feature Diagrams and Generative Techniques. Informatics in Education 7(2), 277–288 (2008)
12. Štuikys, V., Brauklytė, I.: Aggregating of Learning Object Units Derived from a Generative Learning Object. Informatics in Education 8(2), 295–314 (2009)
13. Wiley, D.A.: Connecting learning objects to instructional design theory: A definition, a metaphor, and a taxonomy. In: Wiley, D.A. (ed.) The Instructional Use of Learning Objects (2000), `http://reusability.org/read/chapters/wiley.doc`
14. Merrill, M.D.: Knowledge Objects. CBT Solutions, 6–11 (March/April issue 1998)
15. Redeker, G.: An educational taxonomy for learning objects. In: Third IEEE International Conference on Advanced Learning Technologies (ICALT 2003), pp. 250–251 (2003)
16. Parrish, P.: The trouble with learning objects. Educational Technology Research and Development 52(1), 49–67 (2004)
17. Karampiperis, P., Sampson, D.: Adaptive instructional planning using ontologies. In: Proceedings of the 4th IEEE International Conference on Advanced Learning Technologies, ICALT 2004, pp. 126–130 (2004)
18. Damaševičius, R., Štuikys, V.: Specification and Generation of Learning Object Sequences for e-Learning Using Sequence Feature Diagrams and Metaprogramming Techniques. In: Proceedings of the 9th IEEE International Conference on Advanced Learning Technologies, Riga, Latvia, July 14-18, pp. 572–576 (2009)
19. Balatsoukas, P., Morris, A., O'Brien, A.: Learning Objects Update: Review and Critical Approach to Content Aggregation. Educational Technology & Society 11, 119–130 (2008)
20. Verbert, K., Duval, E.: Towards a global architecture for learning objects: a comparative analysis of learning object content models. In: Proceedings of World Conference on Educational Multimedia, Hypermedia and Telecommunications, pp. 202–208. AACE, Chesapeake (2004)
21. Dreher, H., Krottmaier, H., Maurer, H.: What we Expect from Digital Libraries. Journal of Universal Computer Science 10, 1110–1122 (2004)
22. Nash, S.: Learning Objects, Learning Object Repositories, and Learning Theory: Preliminary Best Practices for Online Courses. Interdisciplinary Journal of Knowledge and Learning Objects 1, 217–228 (2005)
23. Liber, O.: Learning objects: conditions for viability. Journal of Computer Assisted Learning 21, 366–373 (2005)
24. Boyle, T.: Generative learning objects (GLOs): design as the basis for reuse and repurposing. In: First International Conference on e-Learning and Distance Learning, Riyadh, Saudi Arabia, March 16-18 (2009), `http://ipac.kacst.edu.sa/eDoc/2009/173839_1.pdf`
25. Boyle, T.: Layered learning design: Towards an integration of learning design and learning object perspectives. Computers & Education 54, 661–668 (2010)

26. Ravenscroft, A., Boyle, T.: Deep Learning Design for Technology Enhanced Learning. In: Proceedings Ed-Media (2010), http://altc2010.alt.ac.uk/attachments/0001/1840/DLD-AR_TB_fsub1_d_.pdf
27. Damaševičius, R., Štuikys, V.: Taxonomy of the fundamental concepts of metaprogramming. Information Technology and Control 37(2), 124–132 (2008)
28. Štuikys, V., Damaševičius, R.: Towards knowledge-based generative learning objects. Information Technology and Control 36(2), 202–212 (2007)
29. Han, P., Krämer, B.J.: Generating interactive learning objects from configurable samples. In: International Conference on Mobile, Hybrid, an On-Line Learning (ELML 2009), Cancun, pp. 1–6 (2009)
30. Oldfield, J.D.: An implementation of the generative learning object model in accounting. In: Proceedings of ASCILITE, Melbourne (2008), http://www.ascilite.org.au/conferences/melbourne08/procs/oldfield.pdf
31. Boyle, T.: The design and development of second generation learning objects. Invited talk given at Ed Media 2006, World Conference on Educational Multimedia, Hypermedia & Telecommunications, Orlando, Florida (2006), http://www.rlo-cetl.ac.uk/press/news_events/docs/second%20generation%20learning%20objects.doc
32. Veldhuizen, T.L.: Tradeoffs in Metaprogramming. In: Proc. of ACM SIGPLAN Workshop on Partial Evaluation and Semantics-Based Program Manipulation, Charleston, SC, USA, pp. 150–159 (2006)
33. Ortiz, A.: An introduction to metaprogramming. Linux Journal (158), 6 (2007)
34. Štuikys, V., Damaševičius, R., Ziberkas, G.: Open PROMOL: An Experimental Language for Domain Program Modification. In: Mignotte, A., Vilar, E., Horobin, L. (eds.) System on Chip Design Languages, pp. 235–246. Kluwer Academic Publishers, Boston (2002)
35. Carnegie, M.: RobotC – Improved movement, pp. 1–19 (2007), http://www.doc.ic.ac.uk/~ajd/Robotics/RoboticsResources/ROBOTC%20%20Improved%20Movement.pdf
36. Urquiza-Fuentes, J., Velázquez-Iturbide, J.Á.: Pedagogical Effectiveness of Engagement Levels – A Survey of Successful Experiences. Journal Electronic Notes Theoretical Computer Science 224, 169–178 (2009)
37. Biggerstaff, T.J.: The library scaling problem and the limits of concrete component reuse. In: Proceedings of Third International Conference on Software Reuse: Advances in Software Reusability, pp. 102–109. Microsoft Corp., Redmond (1994)

Usability Evaluation of a LMS Mobile Web Interface

Daniel Ivanc, Radu Vasiu, and Mihai Onita

Communications Department, "Politehnica" University of Timisoara
Bv, V. Parvan nr. 2, Timisoara, Romania
{dan.ivanc,radu.vasiu,mihai.onita}@cm.upt.ro

Abstract. The growth in the use of mobile devices in everyday life determined an increasing demand to access educational information using mobile technology. Nevertheless, most existing computer based Learning Management Systems still do not have advanced access support for mobile devices. This paper presents the basis of an in-progress research, aiming to enhance our understanding of mobile learning usability considerations and measurement. It also provides the starting point for performing a usability evaluation of the MyMobile web interface of our university's Moodle LMS. The main contribution of this paper is our proposed approach, based on four perspectives that have to be considered when designing or testing a mobile learning solution: Pedagogical usability, Usability of the device, Usability of the content and Usability of the mobile web interface. Additionally, metrics, methods and guidelines for usability testing are given. The main goal of the paper is to provide an overview on a proposed framework for testing and optimizing a LMS mobile web interface from a usability perspective.

Keywords: mobile learning, usability, metrics, mobile devices.

1 Introduction

Mobile technology is recognized to be one of the most significant directions of nowadays knowledge based society concept. The growth in the use of mobile devices as mobile phones, smartphones, tablets, netbooks and notebooks in everyday life determined an increasing demand to access educational information, instruction and tools using mobile technology. Many studies have given encouraging results for using mobile technologies to support students in the teaching and learning process. Nevertheless, most existing computer based Learning Management System still do not have advanced access support for mobile devices, and there are deficiencies in cross-platform these solutions. Even more, many mobile device's browsers do not support scripting or plug-ins, and do not have available memory to display desktop web-pages and graphics. This influences a lot the usability of mobile learning systems. Also, web content that is mostly the format of electronic learning content is not always suited for mobile browsers and the ability to display information in various multimedia formats is limited. These usability issues of mobile devices and learning must be considered when different types of interfaces and device oriented applications are developed and tested [1].

T. Skersys, R. Butleris, and R. Butkiene (Eds.): ICIST 2012, CCIS 319, pp. 348–361, 2012.

Moodle is one of the most popular open-source e-Learning platforms. It has proven to be a serious competitor to other paid worldwide-known solutions and is usually the first choice when a low-cost, robust eLearning solution is needed. It has been used for several years in the eLearning Centre of our university and several add-ons and tools have been developed.

Because very few open source mobile extensions for Moodle were available and none complied with our needs, the first option was to develop a new mobile user interface for Moodle. This was needed not only for obtaining a functional access to the platform by using mobile devices, but also in order to test and to analyze usability issues in mLearning and especially to develop a usability testing methodology for mLearning because our research revealed that there is a lack of studies on this aspect. However the release of the 2.0 version of Moodle provided a new way of developing mobile friendly interfaces and the release of MyMobile Moodle mobile-optimized interface, based on jquerymobile was considered and later adopted for providing mobile access to the eLearning platform and for continuing the research on mLearning usability testing.

Starting from thequestion of whetherthere arespecificmethods and metrics for mLearning usabilitytesting, the goal of this paper is to provide an overview on our work in progress on developing a framework for testing and optimizing a LMS mobile web interface from a usability perspective. It provides an introduction to mobile learning usability testing, presents several usability testing methods and metrics, selected or adapted from literature review, the setup needed for the testing, and the proposed framework for the design and implementation of usability testing of a LMS mobile web interface.

2 Mobile Learning and Usability

2.1 Defining Usability

ISO/IEC 9126-1 defines usability as "the capability of the software product to be understood, learned, used and be attractive to the user, when used under specified conditions". This definition is primarily concerned with a software product; however, it can be applied to mobile learning software taking into consideration features specific to mobile phones and eLearning aspects.

ISO 9241-11 defines usability as: "the extent to which a product can be used by specified users to achieve specified goals with effectiveness, efficiency and satisfaction in a specified context of use" and suggests the possibility of using specific metrics for measuring performances.

A challenge with definitions of usability is that it is very difficult to specify what its characteristics and its attributes should be, in particular because the nature of the characteristics and required attributes depend on the context in which the product is used [2]. Three critical elements are also revealed: usability of the product relates to specific users, the ones that it was designed for; these specific users have to follow some specified goals for the product was designed for; a specific context of use.

2.2 Mobile Learning Usability Testing

Most of the mobile devices that are used in mobile learning were not designed for educational purpose, and usability issues continue to be the most serious restraining.

Frequent approaches to usability incline to be limited to metrics relating to time taken to complete a task, effort, throughput, flexibility and the user's satisfaction and attitude. Usability has to be considered in a different manner when it is being evaluated in the context of teaching and learning, and the concept of pedagogical usability can be helpful when considering the close relationship between usability and pedagogical design.

2.3 A Four Perspectives Approach

The usability is reviewed as a determinant factor of success of an educational platform and it should be given special attention also when talking about accessing it on mobile devices that were not designed for educational purposes. Based on the fact that the device's and UI usability issues influence in different ways the user experience [19], and on the fact that mobile learning is usually considered an extension to eLearning and have similar characteristics, we consider that the usability of a mLearning platform has to be regarded from four different perspectives that are presented in Table 1 and described in the following paragraphs.

Table 1. A four perspectives usability testing approach

Device Usability	Mobile Learning Usability Testing	Web User Interface Usability
Pedagogical Usability		Educational Content Usability

2.4 Pedagogical Usability

Pedagogical usability is the analysis of the way an educational application (tools, content, tasks and interface) supports students in their learning process within various learning contexts according to learning objectives. It should be especially concerned with educational aspects such as the learning process, purposes of learning, user's needs, the learning experience, learning content and learning outcomes [3].

When developing or improving a mobile learning application is not sufficient to intend that people can use it, they must want to use it [4].

Some relevant pedagogical usability metrics and a description of what each of the usability metrics measures are provided in Table 2. Our research on pedagogical usability testing needs to go further and establish practical methods for evaluating the mLearning platform from the pedagogical point of view.

Table 2. Pedagogical usability metrics and their measurements [3]

Metric	Measurement
Instruction	Whether the application's instruction is clear or if it needs a lecturer's intervention.
Learning content relevance	The extent to which the content of the application supports students in their learning.
Learning content structure	The degree to which the content of the application is organized in a way [clear, consistent and coherent] that supports learning.
Tasks	The extent to which the tasks performed on the application help students to achieve their learning goals.
Learner variables	The degree to which learner variables are considered in the application.
Collaborative learning	The extent to which the application allows students to study in groups.
Ease of use	The provision by the application of clear directions and descriptions of what students should do at every stage when questions to the mobile class activities are answered.
Learner control	The characteristics possessed by the application that allow students to make instructional choices. The extent to which the learning material is broken down into meaningful units. The extent to which the learning material in the application is so interesting to students that it compels them to participate.
Motivation	The degree to which the application motivates students.

2.5 Usability of the Device

Any usability testing methodology has to account for the current limitations of mobile devices that are supposed to be used as learning mediums and has to provide information on the ease-of-use, effectiveness and efficiency of the mobile user interface. There are a series of known usability issues of the mobile devices that can affect the overall usability of the mLearning system: small screen sizes, low screen resolution or the form factor, low storage capacity and network bandwidth, limited processor performance, compatibility issues, lack of data input capability, short battery life, the use of the devices more often on the move. There are also a multitude of mobile user interfaces types with their own usability issues: scroll-and-select interfaces, tilting/sensor based interfaces, speech-based user interfaces, interfaces that use a stylus, and nowadays most common touch interfaces. Other specific characteristics are provided by the different operating systems interaction facilities and navigation scheme of the applications. There are a wide variety of devices, possessing different characteristics, which the application must be adaptable to all of them. These usability issues of mobile devices must be considered and carefully examined during the usability testing of a mobile learning interface in order to select an appropriate research methodology and reduce the effect of contextual factors in the usability testing outcomes [5].

2.6 Usability of the Educational Content

There could be usability issues regarding the content delivered by the mLearning application or web user interface. The format of electronic learning content is not always compatible to most mobile browsers, scripts and plug-ins are usually not supported and the ability to display information in various multimedia content is limited. Integrated graphics and animation should be provided in compatible mobile formats as well as audio and video files. Placing large images, video, PDF, MS Office files and usually any types of similar resources directly on the front of course pages should be avoided, links to images and video via activities, resources and pages is recommendable to be used. These and similar multimedia content compatibility issues must be considered when structuring the mLearning content.

As a result of the usability testing of the content/courses provided by the mobile web interface we intend to elaborate a guideline for designing, developing and especially organizing content in a Moodle course for best use on mobile devices.

2.7 Usability of the Mobile Web Interface

In this case, the mobile web interface strictly refers to the elements and structure of the mobile-friendly MyMobileMoodle interface. The usability testing can be similar to any other mobile web-page or application, and unlike the other perspectives, it can be evaluated using heuristic methods. The goals of the usability testing, in this case are: discovering navigation issues, improving the positioning and use of the menu elements, discovering bugs and verifying compatibility and interoperability of the UI elements on different devices, assuring efficiency, learnability and satisfaction in using the system and completing the tasks.

3 Research Questions and Test Preparations

Our first research question was if we could use the classical methods and techniques used in computer web interfaces usability testing for mLearning web interface usability testing. Even if there is not much literature on this topic, the main answer was that these methods are usually used with the observation that some need to be adapted to be used for mobile devices and some cannot be used at all because of the lack of technical solutions or specific software. There is a need in developing specific methods in evaluating mobile learning applications and we are looking forward to researching and providing such methods.

The second research question was if the metrics used in computer web interfaces usability testing could be used for our purpose. The review of mobile UI usability testing guidelines from the research literature reveals some specific metrics that we proposed to use for mLearning user interface testing.

The third research question is what metrics of the above are best to be used in order to evaluate the usability of a mobile web interface of LMS?

3.1 Users, Materials, Devices and Location

Usability testing of the mLearning MyMobile web interface for our Moodle eLearning platform will be performed by four groups of students and one group of experts:

- students that are already using our university's Moodle eLearning platform, that are used with the eLearning platform's characteristics and with the course format
- future users of the mLearning platform which are not used with the existing eLearning platform
- students that use their own mobile devices (used with the specific UI)
- students that use the provided mobile devices
- experts from the eLearning department with professional background in the domain

There are three types of devices that are proposed to be used for the evaluation:

- old-generation smartphones with medium-size display and normal or full keyboard
- new-generation smartphones / superphones with full touch-screen displays
- new-generation tablets

We also want to test the ability of these devices to support technologies used by the MyMobile UI. Their features also dictate whether certain UI features will be rendered, identified and visible on these devices.

The usability test must set up in a way that is as close to the normal context as possible. Testing in a usability lab offers some benefits because it can be designed to create the ideal testing environment by using specific equipment for recording the session, controlled logging software, special equipment for testing mobile devices. On field and remote testing is much closer to the normal context of use and requires special applications that have the ability to automatically collect user interface events as the user interacts with the application, to capture screenshots and eventually, make an audio-video recording of the user. Even if closer to the real life use of the final product, testing out of the lab has specific disadvantages [6][7].

The testing will take place in one of the universities laboratories, a quiet and air-conditioned room, equipped with audio-video recording system.

One of the difficulties was to find a mobile and tablet usability testing kit [8] wishing to capture the full context of usage. There are some testing methods which use a static camera, telling the user to put a mobile device on a table, operating it within a designated area (where the camera is pointing). Such testing fails to capture the true experience of real usage context. It does not allow the user to hold the device in his hand, and operate it as he or she would do in real life scenarios. More than that: the fact that the user is instructed not to move the device from a designated area, adds on stress during testing, which in itself is an un-wanted cognitive load, thus being a negative interference.

The conditions considered when building a homemade mobile and tablet usability testing kit are:

- the testing device should allow users to hold the mobile device (smartphone, tablet) the way they would hold it in real life

- the testing device should be flexible to fit many types of mobile devices, which differ in size, and in screen resolution.
- the device should look professional and communicate trust

The solution that meets the challenges:

- GPS mounts and mobile device holders
- a high-end HD camera, which proves to produce high quality outcome in various light conditions, with autofocus
- a glass-fiber lead to be used as a camera mount which gives both stability and flexibility. This allows to adjust the camera to fit many screen sizes, and also keeps a steady picture when the user moves the device around while using it.

3.2 Methods

User-based evaluation methods are mostly used in mLearning usability testing. These methods involve collecting quantitative and qualitative data from users while or after running through well prepared scenarios. Users are invited to do typical tasks with a

Table 3. Usability evaluation methods [11]

User testing	Thinking aloud protocol	User speaks aloud about what he is thinking throughout the evaluation.
	Wizard of Oz	
	Log file analysis	
	Observation	This is done to watch the action in its setting, and recording as many details as possible, without obstructing the experience of the subjects being studied.
	Measuring performance	
Inquiry	Cognitive walk-through	This aims to complement observation, in order to get more insight into what is observed.
	Heuristics evaluation	This involves Usability Experts and requires an interactive prototype.
	Guidelines review	
	Interviews	The researcher formulates questions about the product, based on the issues of interest. Interview representative users are then asked these questions, in order to gather desired information
Inspection	Questionnaires for satisfaction	
	Questionnaires for preferences	
	Questionnaires for cognitive workload	

product, or simply asked to explore it freely, while their behaviors are observed and recorded in order to identify design flaws that cause user errors or difficulties. During these observations, the time required to complete a task, task completion rates, and number and types of errors, are recorded. [9]. Users are also asked to complete questionnaires/surveys that provide useful qualitative data from users. Although the data collected is subjective, it provides valuable information on what the user wants. Professional observers and audio-video recording are also used to provide useful information by using the "think aloud protocol" and by measuring performance data. Traditional laboratory testing can be complemented by using UI event logging systems that provide useful information for measuring performance data and usability metrics [10].

3.3 Metrics

Upon review of the measures' relative appearance in the reviewed literature the core constructs for the measurement of usability appear to be:

- Efficiency: Degree to which the product is enabling the tasks to be performed in a quick, effective and economical manner or is hindering performance
- Effectiveness: Accuracy and completeness with which specified users achieved specified goals in particular environment
- Satisfaction: The degree to which a product is giving contentment or making the user satisfied

These three dimensions also reflect the ISO 9241 standard making a strong case for its use in related future studies. [12]

Based on the GQM model, Table 4 provides a list of usability characteristics, goals, guidelines and metrics that can help to collect quantitative or qualitative data during the usability evaluation process [13].

Table 4. Measures, goals, guidelines and metrics

Measure	Goal	Guideline	Metric
Effectiveness	Accessibility	Ease of understanding content	Time taken to understand the content
	Help	Ease of navigation of help topics	Is/ not easy to learn how to navigate help topics
	Interactivity	Ease of interaction	Amount of interaction required
		Ease of use Ease of customization	Is or not easy to use Allow/ not allow customization
	Navigation	Ease of navigation	Provide/ not provide easy navigation

Table 4. (*continued*)

	Time taken Effort required	Loading application Time to learn Time taken to respond Amount of task effort	Time taken to load the application Time taken to learn the application Number of mistakes made before knowing how to use Time taken before to respond Amount of task effort required Amount of time taken before knowing what to do Time taken to complete a task Number of time the user follows the wrong path when attempting a task
	Features	Provision of task related clues. Provision of error recovery Provision of help. Allow personalization Organize content appropriately. Coherent multimedia usage. Use of appropriate controls. Narratives to structure the content.	Provide/not task related clues Provide/not error recovery assistance Provide/not help Allow/ Not cater for personalization Rating scale of content organization Rating scale of multimedia usage Use or not appropriate controls Use or not narratives for content structure Rating scale of narratives appropriateness
Satisfaction	Familiarity	Mental models	Use or not familiar mental models Rating scale of user familiarity with user interface
	Consistency	Navigation	Rating scale of consistency during navigation across system Is or not easy to navigate
	Attractiveness	Use appropriate font style, size, and colors	Rating scale on whether the system is attractive Is or not attractive
	Help	Sufficient help information Organization of help topics	Provide or not sufficient help information Rating scale of usefulness of help information
	Preciseness	Messages precision	Provide or not precise messages Rating scale of message preciseness
	Feedback	Helpful messages Suitability for all users	Provide or not helpful feedback messages Provide or not suitable feedback messages for all categories of users.

Usability can also be defined by other several quality components [14][15]:

- Learnability: how easy users accomplish their basic tasks the first time they encounter the design.
- Efficiency: number of steps it takes for a user to complete a task
- Memorability: how easy is to memorize how to use the interface of the system and how easily users can reuse the system after a break
- Errors: how many errors do users make using the interface of the system and how serious are these errors?
- Satisfaction: how do users like using the system's interface
- Understandability (display load, clarity of operation possibilities, completeness of operation menu)
- Operability (ease of input entering, display self-adjustment possibilities, messages conciseness, ease of output use, parameters self-adjustment possibilities, tasks based on user location)
- Attractiveness (ease of use - displays per output, ease of use - displays per task)

Mathematical formulas, the methods they were obtained and methods of application for some of the listed usability metrics can provide the source for developing new personalized metrics [16][17].

Based on testing methods and metrics, a usability testing framework for developing or testing mobile learning applications or mobile web interfaces can be structured and useful usability design guidelines can be modeled [18].

This paper presents a work in progress and the reviewed and listed metrics have to be also analyzed from a pedagogical perspective so that only relevant metrics are used.

The final step would be the analysis and interpretation of the collected data and the use of the results in improving the mobile web user interface of the LMS and the educational content provided.

4 Usability Testing Framework

In this section, the authors are proposing a generic framework (Figure 1) for the design and implementation of the usability testing of a LMS mobile web interface.

The design of the usability testing should start with identifying research questions and objectives, as these determine the selection of the methods, location, tools and metrics used during the test.

A survey should be done before choosing the mobile devices to be used for the test as they should be representative for the majority of the users of the system and should include different types of devices in terms of operating system, keyboard, display size and multimedia characteristics.

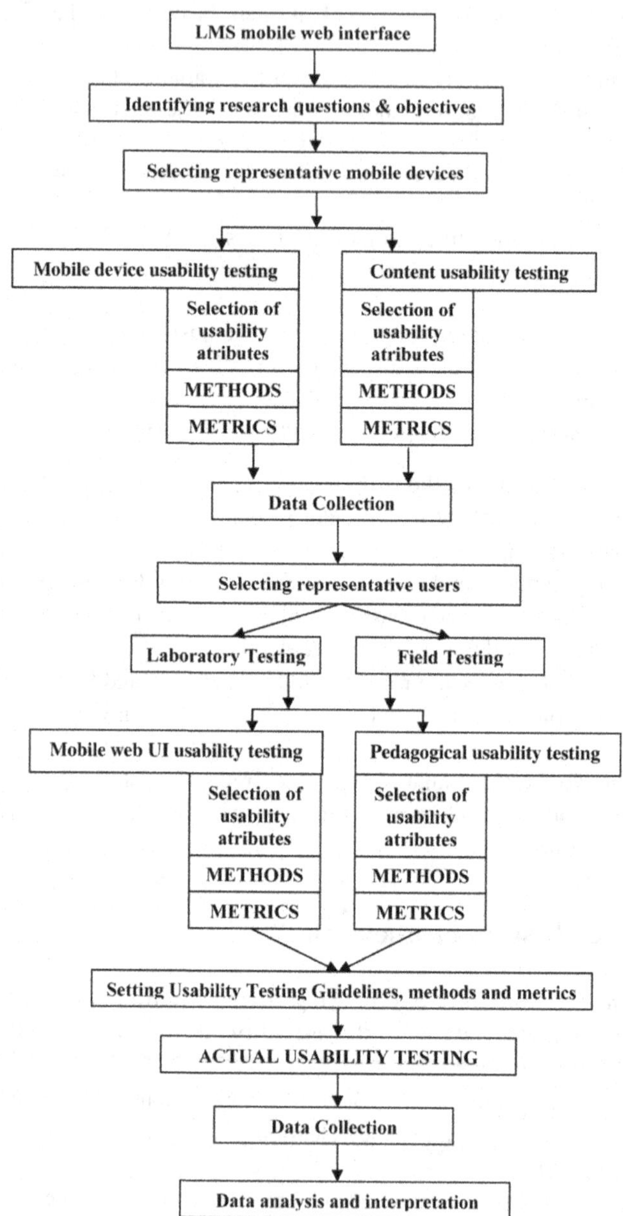

Fig. 1. A Framework for the Design and Implementation of Usability Testing of a LMS mobile web interface

The selected representative mobile devices should be used in the first stage for testing their own usability issues and the possibility to display the educational content provided by the learning platform. Experimented users should be used in identifying the main usability issues of the devices and educational content that could influence the UI usability testing and the pedagogical usability testing. Furthermore this is the step where experts are selecting the usability attributes to be measured, methods and metrics that should be used in the further main usability test, that are best to answer the research questions and objectives.

After deciding if a laboratory or a field testing is required, and after determining the representative user profile of the learning platform, the next important step is selecting the usability attributes to be measured, methods and metrics that are best for answering the research questions and objectives from the UI and pedagogical usability testing points of view.

The guidelines for the main usability test, the setup of the environment and equipment, the preparing of questionnaires and all the necessary preparations can be done based on the results of the previous steps.

Running the actual usability testing, data collection, analysis and interpretation, are the last steps, followed by required changes of the mLearning platform.

As this is a research in progress paper, the proposed framework still has to be improved, detailed and validated by a real test.

5 Discussions

The first contribution of this paper is an usability testing approach based on four perspectives that have to be considered when designing or testing a mobile learning web interface: Pedagogical usability, Usability of the device, Usability of the educational content and Usability of mobile web interface.

There certainly are direct usability influences among the four domains. For example, usability issues of mobile devices accentuate usability issues of the UI [19]. Therefore, because the school cannot ask the students to change their mobile devices, usability improvements should be done to improve the user experience on the existing devices.

The existing educational content cannot be easily changed, but changes can be easily done in the way courses are structured, and multimedia content can be adapted be used both on eLearning or mLearning web interfaces.

Further research should be done on understanding the connections and influences between the usability issues that belong to each of the four usability testing perspectives and identify the methods and metrics that can reveal best results when used in a realistic usability test.

Concerning usability metrics that were mentioned in this paper, the next step should be the selection of the measuring formulas, or developing specific ones based on quality metric frameworks [16] for learning environments, and also the preparation of specific questionnaires elements, as our review of the literature indicates a lack of specific usability metrics for mobile learning environments.

6 Conclusions

Even if it is one of the most popular open-source eLearning platforms, Moodle is still in its beginnings in providing educational content on mobile devices. One of the biggest challenges that it has to overcome is the usability issue that mobile devices, mobile applications and web interfaces reveal.

As the usability is reviewed as a determinant factor of success of an educational platform, it is very important to achieve a high usability level also on the mobile web interface.

This research-in-progress presents the basis of a continuing research, which aims to enhance our understanding of mobile learning usability considerations and measurement and it provides the starting point for performing a usability evaluation of the MyMobile web interface of Moodle LMS. The proposed framework still has to be improved, detailed and validated by a real test.Additionally, metrics, methods and guidelines for usability testing were given. However, in order to test their applicability, they have to be applied on the real mLearning web interface with real users in the form of an actual evaluation.

Research progress in usability design and testing guidelines, focusing on pedagogical usability also, rapidly improvements in the usability of mobile devices and their performances will influence in a good way the development of mobile learning.

Acknowledgments. "This work was partially supported by the strategic grant POSDRU/88/1.5/S/50783(2009) of the Ministry of Labor, Family and Social Protection, Romania, co-financed by the European Social Fund–Investing in people."

References

1. Fetaji, B., Fetaji, M.: Analyses and review of M-learning feasibility, trends, advantages and drawbacks in the past decade (2000-2010). In: Proceedings of the 5th European Conference on European Computing Conference (ECC 2011), World Scientific and Engineering Academy and Society (WSEAS), Stevens Point, Wisconsin, USA, pp. 474–479 (2011)
2. Abran, A., Khelifi, A., Suryn, W., Seffah, A.: Consolidating the ISO usability models. In: Proceedings of 11th International Software Quality Management Conference, Glasgow, Scotland, UK, April 23-25, Springer (2003)
3. Kukulska-Hulme, A.: Mobile usability in educational contexts: What have we learnt? International Review of Research in Open and Distance Learning 8(2), 1–16 (2007)
4. Khomokhoana, P.J.: Using mobile learning applications to encourage active classroom participation: Technical and pedagogical considerations, Department of Computer Science and Informatics, University of the Free State, Bloemfontein - South Africa, p. 58 (May 2011)
5. Fetaji, B., Fetaji, M.: Analyses and review of M-learning feasibility, trends, advantages and drawbacks in the past decade (2000-2010). In: Leandre, R., Demiralp, M., Tuba, M., Vladareanu, L., Martin, O. (eds.) Proceedings of the 5th European Conference on European Computing conference (ECC 2011), pp. 474–479. World Scientific and Engineering Academy and Society (WSEAS), Stevens Point (2011)

6. Barnum, C.M.: Usability Testing Essentials: Ready, Set..test! Elsevier (2011) ISBN: 978-0-12-375092-1
7. Kaikkonen, A., Kekäläinen, A., Cankar, M., Kallio, T., Kankainen, A.: Usability testing of mobile applications: A comparison between laboratory and field testing. Journal of Usability Studies 1(1), 4–17 (2005)
8. Spotless Interactive (January 2012), `http://www.spotlessinteractive.com/news/mobile-usability-testing-kit.php`
9. Kunjachan, M.A.C.: Evaluation of Usability on Mobile User Interface. University of Washington, Bothell
10. Ma, X., Yan, B., Chen, G., Zhang, C., Huang, K., Drury, J.: A Toolkit for Usability Testing of Mobile Applications, Computer Science Department, University of Massachusetts, MobiCase 2011 (2011)
11. Bernhaupt, R., Mihalic, K., Obrist, M.: Usability Evaluation Methods for Mobile Applications. In: Lumsden, J. (ed.) Handbook of Research on User Interface Design and Evaluation for Mobile Technology, pp. 745–758. IGI Global
12. Coursaris, C., Kim, D.: A Qualitative Review of Empirical Mobile Usability Studies. In: Proceedings of the Americas Conference on Information Systems (AMCIS), Acapulco, Mexico, August 4-6 (2006)
13. Kantore, A., van Greunen, D.: Metrics for m-learning usability evaluation. In: WWW 2010, Durban (September 2010)
14. Nielsen, J.: Usability 101: Introduction to Usability (2003), `http://www.useit.com/alertbox/20030825.html`
15. Gafni, R.: Usability Issues in Mobile-Wireless Information System. Issues in Informing Science and Information Technology 6 (2009)
16. Gafni, R.: Framework for quality metrics in mobile-wireless information systems. Interdisciplinary Journal of Information, Knowledge, and Management 3, 23–38 (2008)
17. Gafni, R.: Quality Metrics for PDA-based M-Learning Information Systems. Interdisciplinary Journal of E-Learning and Learning Objects 5 (2009)
18. Majlinda, F., Bekim, F.: Devising M-learning Usability Framework. In: Information Technology Interfaces (ITI), Proceedings of the ITI 2011 33rd International Conference, pp. 275–280. IEEE, New York (2011) ISBN 978-1-61284
19. Hussain, A., Kutar, M.: Apps vs Devices: Can the Usability of Mobile Apps be Decoupled from the Device? IJCSI International Journal of Computer Science Issues 9(3), 11–16 (2012)

Interdisciplinarity in e-Learning Platforms Based on Textual Annotation

Andrei Marius Gabor and Radu Vasiu

"Politehnica" University of Timisoara, Department of Communications
{marius,radu.vasiu}@cm.upt.ro

Abstract. Interdisciplinarity will become, not only a way of content restructuring, but also a new way to organize learning. This paper proposes a framework for building ontology for e-learning and aims for a navigation and efficient retrieval and reuse content in the "virtual university". The framework used the content annotation Learning Object (LO), and the content structure by exploiting Learning Object Metadata (LOM). Ontology can be used for content analysis, recognition of concepts, the relationship between them and allows search and retrieval of content produced by query and the reuse of it in different subjects, using the MP7QF framework specific to MPEG-7.

Keywords: ontology learning, OWL, semantic search, MPEG-7, MP7QF.

1 Introduction

Currently, the e-learning domain is given a special attention due to the number of users and their diversity, from large companies to educational institutions. E-learning platforms have a unitary structure, they use specific procedures for administration, maintenance and upgrading, while providing interaction between users and/or groups of users.

A typical e-learning platform consists of: LMS (Learning Management System), LCMS (Learning Content Management System) and a Web portal [1]. The LMS is a software application for managing, documenting, verifying and reporting courses, classrooms, events, and users. So, the main purpose of an LMS is to provide the management of courses and users. The LCMS (Learning Content Management System) is a related technology and management system focused on developing, managing and publishing content that will be delivered via the LMS. The LCMS creates, stores, manages digital content, but also allows to create, import, manage and search for parts of the digital content, referred to as learning objects (LO). These objects are including media files, evaluation elements, text, graphics or any other objects that forms the content of a course.

Most of times, these objects may be re-used in the content and context of different courses. This is, in fact, the philosophy behind educational software portability through the SCORM standard, implemented by the IEEE Learning Technologies Committee [2].

T. Skersys, R. Butleris, and R. Butkiene (Eds.): ICIST 2012, CCIS 319, pp. 362–372, 2012.

Distance education has started to become familiar and to develop based on computers` performance, increasing communication and video [3]. Videos have a strong pedagogical impact because multiple media elements such as: text and sound are skillfully put together. Many institutions such as schools, associations, distribute audio and video material through electronic devices, the Internet. Such institutions or "virtual universities" are described as organizations, which provide programs of higher learning and offer the possibility of online learning technologies using various media.

Videos have become the most popular multimedia data due to high volume of information transmitted. In this case, the main challenge is given by the indexing video signal, which provides facilitation in the content retrieval. This requires an endorsement of the content, which can be carried out manually or automatically via algorithms, so that there is a more concise description of the characteristics of multimedia content. Searching for a video sequences according to relevant semantic content provides the ability (of the teacher or learner) to reuse some of the contents. However, users are often unable to locate a specific area of information in a video presentation, and most of the times, the manual search for this information is needed. Indexing task related to the content is more complex as this content is semantically richer. Within the e-learning platforms the accuracy of search and retrieval of the content may be increased by using ontology. Thus, there have been identified many types of concept-related ontologies, domain-related ontologies, all these being specific to the teaching and learning process. There have also been identified ontologies related to the physical structure of the objects (Mahan and Brooks 2003) [4].

The usage of ontology in e-learning domain has increased in the last few years. Researches have resulted in more than one study; therefore, I will mention Trial Solution, the study of Dragan G., J. Jovanovic & Vladan D. (2007) [5], and also with applicability in the medical field, the work of S. Colantio et al (2009) [6]. Semantic web technologies used in the context of e-learning has been applied as Panteleyev et al (2002) [7], but also by making smart spaces for e-learning's work in Dolog et al (2004) [8].

2 Ontology Construction

At the same time with the development of semantic WEB, specific ontologies have also been developed, in order to annotate and represent the multimedia content. [9] Gruber (1993) [10] has described the development of such formal and explicit ontologies, which describe the representations of the conceptualized world. These ontologies are an important and useful tool for representing, sharing and re-use of knowledge.

The purpose of the work is to develop an ontological model specific to "virtual universities" and to annotate of the videos on the platform of e-learning of the university, in order to ensure interdisciplinary between the different courses. Ontologies have been developed for the video documents based on the content (domain), context and structure, (Stojanovic, and Studer Stoab 2001) [11] and that may be compatible with other instruments of indexing and navigation. In this respect MPEG-7 also known as "The interface for the description of multimedia content", is able to fulfill this role.

2.1 Ontology

Learning Object Metadata describes the contents of a course using metadata attributes of high level (semantic descriptions). LOM is specific to e-learning through the providing of learning specific attributes such as a course difficulty, the learning time of a course, vocabulary, and the structure course. Learning Object Metadata describes learning object and similar resources used in order to support the learning technology.

There have been proposed a few standards of metadata such as in Isaac study (2004) [12] as well as Dublin Core [13], LOM [14], VRA Coreh [15] that are directly linked to the representation of the multimedia content for a specific domain and provides diagrams of description and standardized syntax well defined.

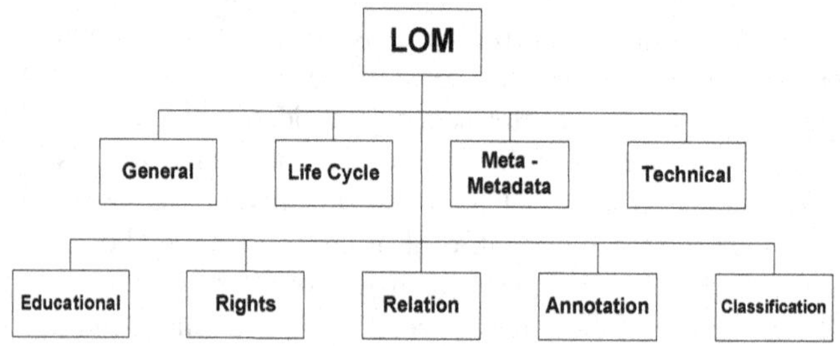

Fig. 1. LOM Elements Hierarchy

LOM includes a hierarchy of elements represented in Fig. 1 in the form of the nine categories, each of them containing sub-elements that can be simple or may contain sub-elements to their other sub-elements, the semantic of each element being determined by the context.

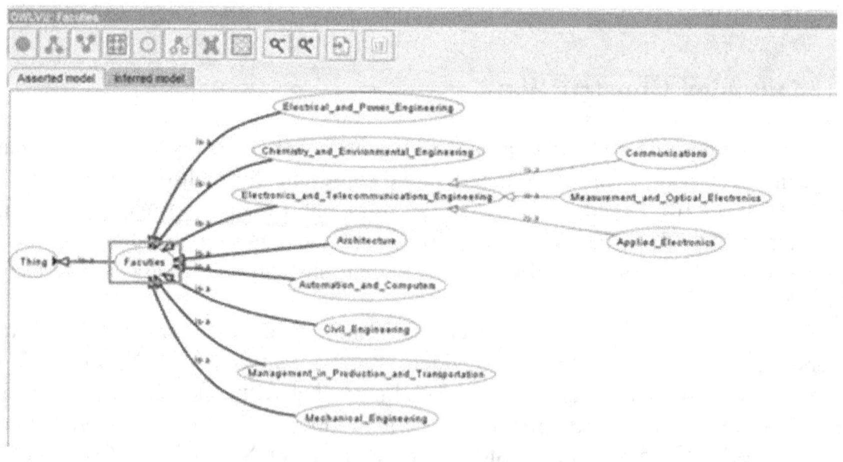

Fig. 2. Ontology structure in Protégé

SCORM (Sharable Content Object Reference Model) uses XML to define Course Structure format, which represent the structure of the courses so that educational videos may interfere with other platforms.

We have accomplished ontology by grouping on domains, and the faculties, described in Fig. 2, in the framework of the "virtual university", so that there is possibility to reuse the resources in various disciplines in the ROI, so that the author may establish new courses (interdisciplinary).

Metadata ontology refers to an ontology representation intended to describe LOM using metadata (Fig. 3).

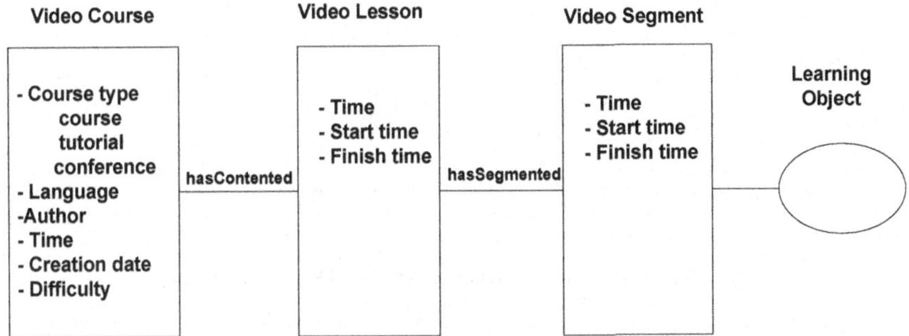

Fig. 3. LOM. Ontology description

XML file related to Fig. 4 outlines the ontology that establishes the relations between video courses, lessons and video segments.

```
- <rdf:RDF xml:base="http://www.cv.upt.ro/ontology/video_ontology.owl">
  - <owl:Ontology rdf:about="">
      <rdfs:comment rdf:datatype="http://www.w3.org/2001/XMLSchema#string"/>
    </owl:Ontology>
  - <owl:Class rdf:ID="CourseType">
    - <rdfs:subClassOf>
        <owl:Class rdf:ID="VideoCourse"/>
      </rdfs:subClassOf>
    </owl:Class>
  - <owl:Class rdf:ID="StartTimeSeg">
    - <rdfs:subClassOf>
        <owl:Class rdf:ID="VideoSegment"/>
      </rdfs:subClassOf>
    </owl:Class>
  - <owl:Class rdf:about="#VideoCourse">
    - <owl:disjointWith>
        <owl:Class rdf:about="#VideoSegment"/>
      </owl:disjointWith>
    - <owl:disjointWith>
        <owl:Class rdf:ID="VideoLesson"/>
      </owl:disjointWith>
    </owl:Class>
  - <owl:Class rdf:ID="Language">
      <rdfs:subClassOf rdf:resource="#VideoCourse"/>
```

Fig. 4. OWL. Multimedia ontology.

2.2 Ontology Domain

According to IEEE Learning Technology Standards Community (LTSC), IEEE P1848.12.1-2002 Learning Object Metadata Working Group [16], learning object (LO) is defined as any digital or non-digital entity, which can be used or reused in e-learning technology. Also, a learning object may be considered a collection of elements of independent media (interactivity, architecture, context) and metadata. These metadata can be enriched with concepts specific ontology of the domains, so that each LO is assigned a structure description based on ontology (Fig. 5). More than one learning objects, are assembled by authors to form the rates, and then they are released for consumption.

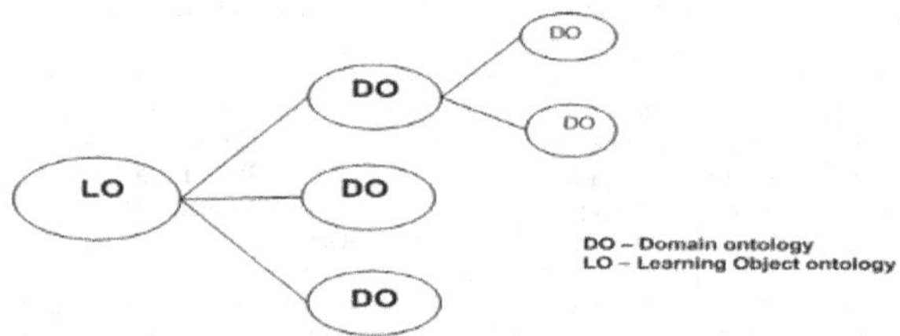

Fig. 5. Relation between LO ontology and Domain ontology

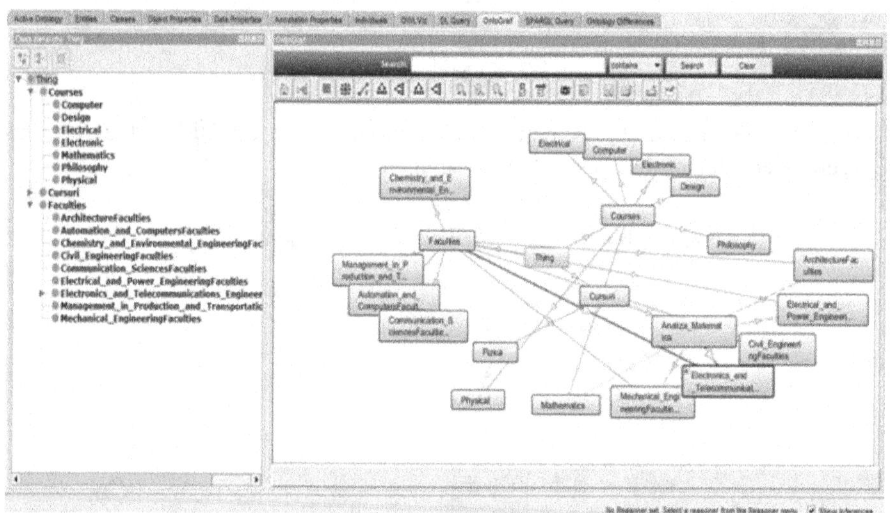

Fig. 6. Ontology domain

Being created, the ontology for learning object (LO) can be integrated so as to allow efficient retrieval of the content and the ability to be re-attached (Fig. 6). SCORM reflects the tendency of unification of the metadata specifications as a specialized subset that describes RLO (Reusable Learning Object) based on the content, by the RIO (Reusable Information Object). RIO may be parts of the video streaming which, through combining, will form the RLO structure [17]. A management and modeling pattern of data, is used by the Memorae [18] project, according to two ontologies that describe and specify the concepts used in annotation.

3 Video Annotation

For video documents extra annotations are required. These extra annotations compared to those based on text, are necessary to perform searches and retrievals of the content. Similar research for using the semantic annotation of the lesson of the teaching process has been made by Carbonara and Ferini. (2005)[19]

An important step in effective handling and visual retrieval is represented by semantic information in such a way that the system through ontology may express entities and relations between them [20]. Thus it is permitted to change and create descriptions of the contents in order to represent the domain as good as possible and to annotate it efficiently. The basic idea for indexing platforms file in e-learning video is based on different types of ontology, which define the context, the structure of the file and the ontologies specific to teaching and learning.

The video annotation process has been defined by Charhad in [21] as a process through which the text is associated with the video clip, in order to improve the content. Thus, Charhad`s research focused on constructing a model based on tools so as to produce concepts and features.

Videos annotation has a special role because it helps you to retrieve content efficiently. The process of annotation is performed in two steps. First step is a video segmentation where entire video file is divided into smaller pieces, which are representative for the user, using automatic stabilizers algorithms or by making this segmentation manually. The next step is the annotation one, which allows the annotation of the video segments. Each segment (video clip) that belongs to the video sequence is annotated based on the basis ontology described above. These descriptions are labeled for each clip. There are two approaches for video segmentation, the first being in the process of the pixels, and the other being the process in the field of compression.

3.1 Experiment

The algorithms for temporal segmentation detect sudden or gradual changes from a video sequence. Examples are techniques of detection by Zhang [22], as well as the fast techniques in the domain of compression [23]. The frames are divided into a number of blocks, and after that they are compared between successive frames, so is the approach proposed by Nagasaka and Tanaka [24].

The segments or video clips are, at the same time, parts of the course and presents the lessons, which define an idea or a subject, that is important for the user.

Polysema application helps the user to annotate video sequences by selecting desired ontology, so that every clip to be annotated. All the video clips are displayed (shown) and there is the possibility to eliminate, to unite and then to annotate, process by which the text will be associated with these clips. Once the annotation is done, the application will generate a MPEG-7 file in the form of some descriptions, in an XML file.

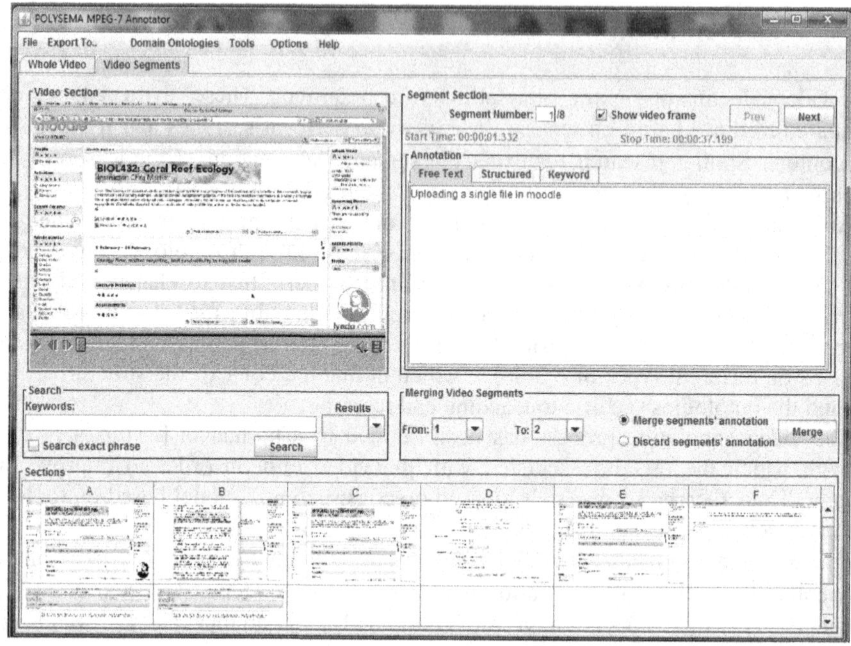

Fig. 7. Polysema, video annotation MPEG-7

```
        <Name xml:lang="en">School_programs</Name>
      </Genre>
    </Classification>
  </CreationInformation>
- <TemporalDecomposition>
  - <VideoSegment id="segment1">
    - <MediaTime>
        <MediaTimePoint>T00:00:00:0F1000</MediaTimePoint>
        <MediaDuration>PT04S0N1000F</MediaDuration>
      </MediaTime>
    </VideoSegment>
  - <VideoSegment id="segment2">
    - <MediaTime>
        <MediaTimePoint>T00:00:04:0F1000</MediaTimePoint>
        <MediaDuration>PT04M57S666N1000F</MediaDuration>
      </MediaTime>
    </VideoSegment>
  - <VideoSegment id="segment65">
    - <TextAnnotation>
        <FreeTextAnnotation>Uploading a single file in moodle</FreeTextAnnotation>
      - <KeywordAnnotation>
          <Keyword>computers</Keyword>
          <Keyword>moodle</Keyword>
          <Keyword>uploading</Keyword>
        </KeywordAnnotation>
      </TextAnnotation>
    - <MediaTime>
```

Fig. 8. MPEG-7 file

MPEG 7 developed by Movie Picture Expert Group (MPEG) is one of the most widely accepted standards to describe multimedia content. MPEG-7 provides not only a rich set of tools for the description of content, content management, navigation and access but also the interaction with the user (Fig. 8). In this respect there have been developed standard ontologies specific to MPEG-7 as described in the studies of Hunter [25] and Tsinaraki [26].

4 MP7QF for e-Learning Platforms

Within the system that is proposed, the multimedia queries on the e-learning platforms are based on the MP7QF framework specifications for text, audio, video, images and semantic annotation.

A general architecture for the system of interrogation of databases in MPEG-7 is described and shown in Fig. 9, where IQF (Input Query Format) explains the syntax and structure of the query, and OQF (Output Query Format) specifies the syntax and structure of the set of results. [27]

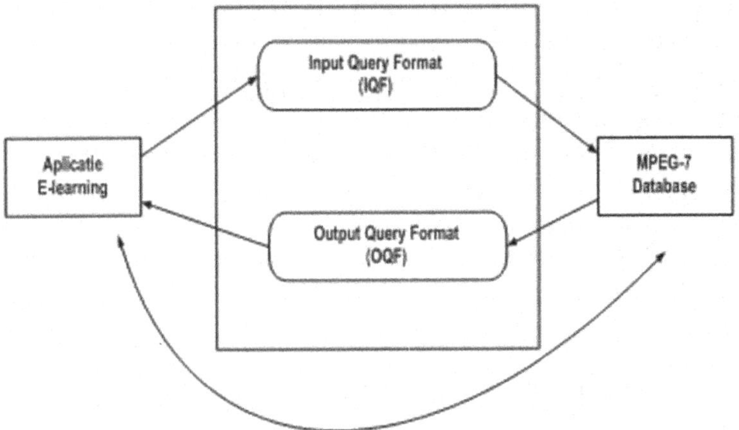

Fig. 9. MP7QF standard

Because there is not a query standard format of the metadata for MPEG-7, the MPEG Commission has decided that the query format should be the MP7Qf framework (standardized ISO/IEC 15938-12) together with a set of requirements (N8219). The objective of the MP7QF framework is to provide an interface for the MPEG-7 databases, in order to allow multimedia data retrieval by users. The Student signed up for a specific course may make queries to multiple databases, and the result of the query to be based on their preferences and the history of use. The MP7QF framework must meet the following expectations in order to be used on the e-learning platforms:

- to allow simultaneous search in the multiple databases
- to accept media formats returned by query in the process of retrieving data multimedia

Teachers and students can use MP7QF query results, results that can be RIO (Reusable Information Object) to create another course, respectively, for the consumption content. The user must be able to choose, select and group the video data according to the e-learning context and content as a result of the query and the retrieval. The MP7QF framework must ensure support for the different query: [28]

- description queries, which are based on text descriptions (described in Fig. 10), but also using the description and the MPEG-7 description schemes.
- queries based by examples, in which the space and time relations will be used as well as the low level features and the semantic features. The user may select the needed image from the returning results, and if he/she is not satisfied, may reformulate the query.
- queries based on the MPEG-7 standard specification. Color and texture descriptors will be used for query as well as the description schemes.
- queries based on the preferences and the history of the user.

```
<m7qf:Query >
  <m7qf:Input >
    < m7qf:QueryCondition >
      < m7qf:QueryExpression >
        < m7qf:SingleSearch xsi:type =" m7qf:TextQueryType "retrieval =" contains ">
            < m7qf:FreeTextQuery >
              < m7qf:SearchTerm >Search object learning
              </ m7qf:SearchTerm >
            </ m7qf:FreeTextQuery >
        </ m7qf:SingleSearch >
      </ m7qf:QueryExpression >
    </ m7qf:QueryCondition >
  </ m7qf:Input >
</ m7qf:Query >
```

Fig. 10. MP7QF query based on text descriptions

5 Conclusion and Future Researches

The paper describes the proposed process for segmenting and annotating video content on e-learning platforms, within the framework of the "virtual universities". During the annotation process, the user has the possibility to select the ontology that is specific to the domain and the structure of content. The queries that are carried out, use the MP7QF framework and they return (give back) the video parts of interest, (Reusable Information Object) which can be used either in the process of creation of new courses on for consumption.

Our contribution to this study in theory has been materialized by carrying out ontologies to annotate the content, creating possibilities to select them, possibilities which are specific to the domain and contribution has generated the text annotation of more video documents. After annotation, we created different queries specific to the courses and the subjects involved in this process.

Future research will focus on describing new video retrieval algorithms, based on semantic requests and on the exploitation of the low-level features. We are, also, taking into consideration the idea of incorporate the results of queries based on probabilistic algorithms, needed for delimitating areas of interest.

Acknowledgment. "This work was been partially supported by the strategic grant POSDRU 107/1.5/S/77265, inside POSDRU Romania 2007-2013 co-financed by the European Social Fund – Investing in People."

Reference

1. `http://www.fluidpower.ro/itfps/Etapa1ITFPS.pdf`
2. IEEE Learning Technology Stardardization Committee Draft Standard for Learning Object Metadata (April 18, 2001)
3. Harting, K., Erthal, M.J.: Hystory of Distance Learning, Information Technology. Learning and Performance Journal 23(1) (May 2010)
4. Mohan, P., Brooks, C.: Learning objects on the Semantic Web. In: Procedings of the 3rd IEEE International Conference on Asdvanced Learning Technologies, pp. 195–199. IEEE Compuer Society Press, Los Alanitos (2003)
5. Gorevic, D., Jovanovic, J., Devedzic, V.: Ontology-based annotation of learning objevt contecnt. Interactive Learning Enviromments, 1–26
6. Colantio, S., Salvetti, O., Gurevich, I.B., Trusova, Z.: An Ontological Franework for Media Anal'ysis and Mining. Pattern Recognition and Image Analysis 19(2) (2009)
7. Panteleyev, M., Puzankov, D., Sazykin, P., Sergeyev, D.: Intelligent educational enviroments based on the Semantic Web technologies. In: Proceeding of the IEEE International Conference on Artificial Intelligence Systems, pp. 457–462. IEEE Computer Society Press, Los Alamitos (2002)
8. Dolog, P., Henze, N., Nejdl, W., Sintek, M.: Personalization in distributed e-learning enviroments. In: Proceeding of the 13th Inernational Word Wide Web Conference on Altenate Track Paper & Posters, New York, USA, December 4, pp. 170–179 (2004)
9. Hyv Aonen, E., Styrucu, A., Saarela, S.: Ontology – based image trievals. Poster Proceedings, the 12th International Word Wide Conference (2008)
10. Gruber, T.R.: Towards principles for the design of ontologies used for Knowledge sharing. In: Guarino, N., Poli, R. (eds.) Formal Ontology in Conceptual Abalysis and Knowledge Reprezentation. Kluwer Academic Publishers, The Netherlands (1993)
11. Stojanovic, L., Stoab, S., Studer, R.: eLearning in the Semantic Web. In: Proceeding of the Word Conference on the WW and the Internet (WebNet 2001), pp. 1174–1183. AACE, Chesapeake (2001)
12. Isaac, A., Trancy, R.: Designing and Using an Audio-visual Description Care Ontology. In: Proceeding of the 14th International Conference on Knowledge Engineering and Knowledge Managemnet (October 2004)
13. Dublin Care Metadata Element Set Version 1.1, `http://dublincare.org/documents/1999/07/02/dces`
14. LOM, IEEE Learning Technology Standards Committeé's Learning Object Meta-data Working Group (2002), `http://Ptsc.ieee.org/wg12/`
15. Vra Coreh (1999), `http://www.vraweb.org/projects/cracore4/index.html`

16. Buffa, M., Dehors, S., Farov-Zucker, C., Sander, P.: Towards a Corporate Semantic Web Approach in Designing Learning System. In: Workshop Conference AIED Revien of the TRIAL Solution Project (2005)
17. Aroyo, L., Pakraev, S., Brussee, R.: Preparing SCORM for the semantic web. In: Proceesing of International Conference on Ontologies, Databases, and Applications of Semantics, Catania, Italy (2003)
18. Benayache, A.: Construction d'une mémoire organisationnelle de formation et évaluation dans un contexte elearning: le projet MEMORAe, Ph. D. Theses, l'UTC (2005), http://tel.archives-ouvertes.fr/docs/00/21/19/76/PDF/rapport-HDR-MHA-publie.pdf
19. Carbonaro, A., Ferrini, R.: Considering semantic abilities to improve a Web Based Distance Learning System. In: ACM International Workshop on Combining Intelligent and Adaptive Hypermedia Methods/Techniques in Web-based Education Systems (2005)
20. Blohdorn, S., Petridis, K., Simon, N., Tzonnaras, V., Aurithis, Y., Handstchh, S., Kompatriaris, Z., Staab, S., Stintzis, M.: Knowledge Reprezentation for Semantic Multimedia Content Analysis and Reasoning. In: Proceedings of the European Workshop on the Integration of Knowledge, Semantics and Digital Media Technology
21. Charhad, M.: Modèles de Documents Vidéo basés sur le Formalisme des Graphes Conceptuels pour l'Indexation et la Recherche par le Contenu Sémantique, Ph.D, Thesis, University Joseph Fourier, Grenoble, France (2005), http://www-mrim.imag.fr/publications/2005/CHA05/These_MC.pdf
22. Zang, H., Kankahalli, A., Smoliav, S.W.: Automatic partitioning of full motion video. Multimedia Systems 1(1), 10–28 (1993)
23. Meng, J., Juan, Z., Chang, S.F.: Scene change detection in a MPEG compressed video seqvrence. In: ISA T/SPIE Symposion Proceeding on Electronic Imaging: Science & Technology, vol. 2419, pp. 14–25 (February 1995)
24. Nagasaka, A., Tanaka, Y.: Automatic video indexing and full search for video apperances. In: Visual Database Systems, Amsterdam, vol. II, pp. 113–127 (1992)
25. Hunter, J.: Adding Multimedia to the Semantic Web Building an MPEG-7 Ontology. In: The 1st International Semantic Web Working Symposium (SWWS 2001), pp. 261–281 (2001)
26. Tsinaraki, C., Polydoros, P., Christodoulakis, S.: Interoperability suport for Ontology-based Video Retrieval Applications. In: Proceeding of 3rd International Conference on Image and Video Retrieval, pp. 582–591
27. Doller, M., Wolf, I., Gruhne, M., Kosch, H.: Towards an MPEG-7 Query Language. In: Proceedings of the International Conference on Signal-Image Technology and Internet Based Systems (IEEE/ACM SITIS 2006), Hammamet, Tunesia, pp. 36–45 (2006)
28. Renner, K.: Specification of an MPEG-7 Query Language. University of Pasau, Germany (2007)

ICT Architecture for Online Learning Approach

Danguole Rutkauskiene[1], Daina Gudoniene[1], Gytis Cibulskis[1], and Oleksandr Suk[2]

[1] Kaunas University of Technology, Kaunas, Lithuania
{danguole.rutkauskiene,daina.gudoniene,gytis.cibulskis}@ktu.lt
[2] National Technical University "Kharkiv Polytechnic Institute", Kharkiv, Ukraine
afs@kpi.kharkov.ua

Abstract. The use of information communication technologies (ICT) in education has introduced a new set of technological and educational opportunities for educators and students. That is why it is so important to understand the attitudes of educators towards e-learning in education as well as ICT based learning.

Information and Communication Technologies are important enablers of the new social structure. We are experiencing the first generation of truly portable ICT removable memory chips, diaries, email, Web, basic word processing and spreadsheets, and data input, storage, and transfer what is used in nowadays education process. The aim of the papers is to present the new architecture based on the open source technological solutions to be used in e-learning and social networking systems.

Keywords: technologies, e-learning, social networking.

1 Introduction

Currently not only in Lithuania and Ukraine but also in the whole world social and economic changes have evolved, which require more and more skills from various specialists. In the rapidly changing society a person, who is trying to gain more knowledge and experience in his field of work due to trace of the social situations and adapts to modern life, becomes a successful one.

An increasing number of web-based software packages have been developed to enhance the teaching and design of control systems [5]. Rapid development of a permanent information and communication technology (ICT) changes and diversity also impacts society changes. The developments and use of ICT is an important element of the European Union's strategy in order to ensure the educational effectiveness and competitiveness. Since 2007 the use of ICT in education has become one of the key issues. Digital excellence is recognized as one of the eight skills necessary for all knowledge communities.

The aim of the papers is to present the new architecture based on the open source technological solutions to be used in e-learning and social networking systems for online learning approach.

T. Skersys, R. Butleris, and R. Butkiene (Eds.): ICIST 2012, CCIS 319, pp. 373–387, 2012.

2 Educational Aspects to Use ICT Tools in Practice

2.1 New Methods to Use ICT in Education

ICT is one of the driving forces for socio-economic change. On the technological side, trends towards high-quality, converging, mobile and accessible technologies, together with more sophisticated, user-friendly, adaptable and safe applications and services will integrate technology more and more into everyday life. Eventually more advanced technologies, such as ambient technologies, immersive 3D environments and strong AI, may become a reality. As a consequence, technology will be more smoothly integrated into our daily lives and become a basic commodity [15].

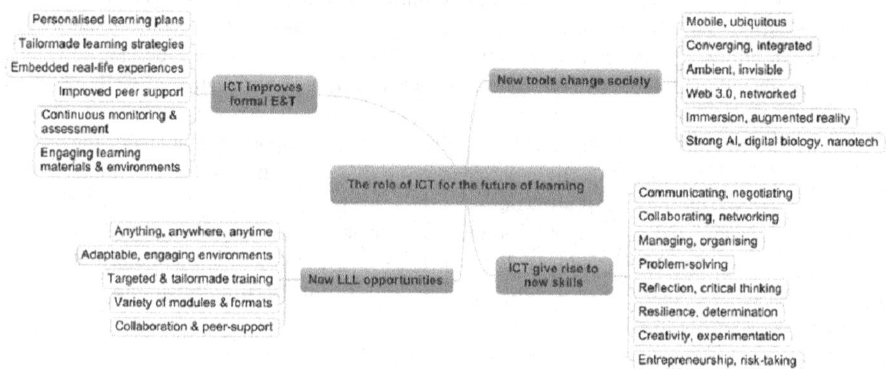

Fig. 1. The role of ICT for future learning strategies

There is growing evidence that innovative ICT tools can enhance the learning delivery for learners and their engagement with mainstream education. The great strength of such learning tools is their capacity to support informal learning, which provides a secure environment for acquiring knowledge and rebuilding confidence among learners.

The innovation of web technologies will transform the teaching process into a student centred learning process. Technology should allow learners to upgrade themselves from being a passive knowledge consumer (to whom knowledge is pushed) into an active contributor in a social constructionist process (knowledge building) [12].

However for new technologies of informatics and computer sciences a different approach is needed. For scientific collaboration the possibility to run software developed by colleagues by internet is essential. One can test directly results of other researchers by running their software with different data. Therefore algorithms, software and results published in the scientific papers can be investigated independently [5].

Training provision, quality of schools and universities, ensure not only the available equipment, broadband internet / intranet connection or support systems, but also services that meet a wide-ranging educational needs, quality and performance, i.e. very important and high-quality digital educational content and applications of new ICT tools and the increasing use of different technologies in teaching / learning process [3]. Other critical conditions associated with the successful development of innovative ICT-based teaching and learning methods is the fact that teachers must have ICT usage skills and be able to transfer them to students [4]. It is also important to assess whether ICT is utilized and what its impact on teaching and learning outcomes is.

Current use of ICT: Social computing applications are currently not deployed on a large scale in formal education and training in Europe. However, there are a vast number and variety of locally-embedded Web 2.0 initiatives all over Europe, which illustrate the variety and scope of web 2.0 approaches in formal education and training. The following general approaches towards using social computing in formal educational settings are distinguished by the European Commission Joint Research Centre in the E-Learning 2.0 Report [1] :

Opening Up to Society. Many educational institutions use social computing as a means of facilitating access to information by current and prospective students, making institutional processes more transparent and facilitating the technological distribution of educational material. In some cases, social computing tools are used to encourage the involvement of third parties, e.g. teachers, parents, prospective future employers or external experts.

Embracing Diversity. Social computing applications are used as a means of integrating learning into a wider community, reaching out to virtually meet people from other age-groups and socio-cultural backgrounds and linking to experts, researchers or practitioner in a certain field of study and thus opening up alternative channels for gaining knowledge and enhancing skills. From this point of view, Web 2.0 enables students to broaden their horizons, and collaborate across borders, language barriers, and institutional walls, thus anchoring their learning experiences in a rich world of diverse cultures, traditions, languages and opinions.

Networking. Social computing applications are primarily conceived of as communication tools among students or teachers and between students and teachers. The social networking tools assure the exchange of knowledge and material as well as facilitate community building, providing teachers and learners with social environments that offer assistance and (emotional) support; and provide platforms for collaboration, allowing teachers and learners to jointly develop (educational) content.

Achieving. It can be used as a means to increase academic achievement. Social computing provides learners and teachers with a wide variety of didactical and methodological tools that can be adapted to their respective learning objectives and individual needs with a positive effect on their performance and achievement. Research evidence suggests that Web 2.0 strategies can be used successfully to enhance individual motivation, improve learner participation and foster social and learning skills. They can further contribute to the development of higher order cognitive skills like reflection and meta-cognition, increase self-directed learning skills and enable individuals to better develop and realise their personal potential.

Learning. In many cases, social computing tools are used to implement pedagogical strategies intended to support, facilitate, enhance and improve learning processes. As the paper presents Web 2.0 tools are very versatile in accommodating diverse learning needs and preferences by addressing different sensory channels; by supplying more engaging (multimedia) learning environments; by supporting personalised ways of retrieving, managing and transforming information; by equipping learners and teachers with a variety of adaptable tools; and by integrating students into collaborative networks that facilitate the joint production of content and offer peer support and assistance. They thus allow implementation of learning strategies that are tailored to each learner's individual preferences, interests and needs; providing learning environments which are better suited to accommodating individual differences, and supporting differentiation in heterogeneous learner groups.

In open source software no clear boundaries between users and developers are defined. The software developed by a user often is applied by many others. Therefore open source software is important tool for academic studies and scientific collaboration [5]. The technological solutions presented in the paper below are based on the open source.

2.2 Web Based Technological Solutions for Education

One can read a lot of articles on innovation, which suggests a set of tools that are considered to be innovative and thus makes believe that the use of which would result in innovation. Web 2.0 tools are referred to as such, but very often even the description of this set of tools is unclear to the public as well as teachers who are supposed to achieve innovation by using them in their daily routines [12]. Information and communication technology - the digital ways and means created for educational purposes to collect, store, transform and disseminate information [4]. Note that these technologies are used for information transmitting purposes - communication, collaboration, cooperation, information sharing, which is very often provided by various ICT tools. In educational context, ICT purpose is to be viewed more as a joint, cooperative learning, reflection, etc.

E-learning organizing, video lectures, e-content development of courses and similar systems can be enriched with social networking tools adapted to e-learning, social software, systems, where users or groups can interact and share information in this way extending learning activities.

Curriculum planning and delivery process is very important together with new technologies in a variety of individualized constructive learning strategies and social skills that are acquired through constant communication, active knowledge and experiences sharing, joint activities in various groups, teamwork, training (learning) environments and social networks by jointly developing and evaluating the results of individual work. ICT changes causes differences in teacher and student relationship, resulting from new information and knowledge management techniques and other student activities. Information technology teaching represents student directed approach, providing technological knowledge and skills to better understanding of all subjects and developing the ability and willingness to communicate in a society, not only with the surrounding community, school, family, but also with their peers around the world.

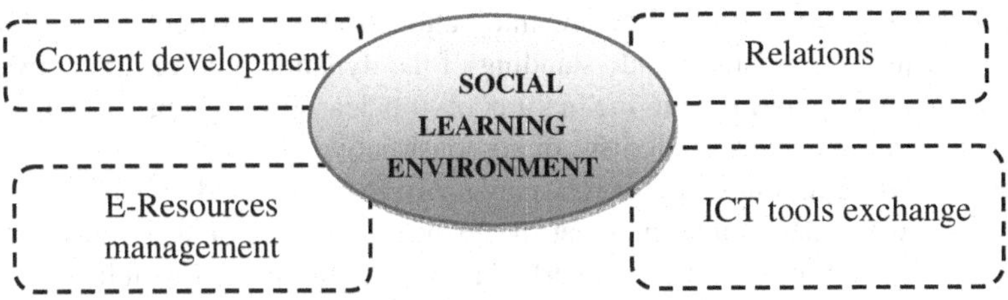

Fig. 2. Social Learning Environment

ICT encourages learners' creativity, the ability to work in a team, ability to communicate in the global IT space. We can say that for the majority of respondents communication and collaboration online is crucial. ICT knowledge provided and consistently developed in schools should be integrated with a variety of subjects and topics to improve the quality of modern learning competences. ICT can be very effective in developing communication, cognitive, labour and business skills and competencies, to help students gather information (knowledge), to develop skills and abilities and creatively apply them in practice for achieving the teaching (learning) goals.

E-learning environments are becoming ubiquitous and can be accessed not only on the computer but also on mobile devices what brings so-called mobile learning (m-learning) to the next level.

Smart phones and tablet computers lets you move freely and learn together, by receiving information and communicating wirelessly. So mobile learning is a further step towards an active student studying in its own pace. New generation of smart phones equipped with variety of sensors (cameras, GPS, compass, accelerometer, gyroscope, etc.) and having permanent internet connection have enabled development of new services such as Augmented Reality that are actively entering to e-learning market. This allows contextualising information to learners by providing learning objects alongside with the real environment.

Social networking platforms on the web are actively developing services, that unleashing the power of social interaction in many new ways. Mobile devices make this interaction and sharing of information even more accessible and results in new innovative applications. Social and mobile tools can bring added value not only to e-learning courses, but also in blended or "face to face" learning setting.

Social networking can help to bring personalized learning experiences regardless of institutional setting. Still it is the most popular among university and college students, as far as they are more eager to meet with peers and other people, to share information and their experiences on learning, hobbies as well as develop friendships, find job. Topics and interests are as varied and rich as our society and human history [1].

The knowledge and skills that teachers require in order to implement technology-based learning designs successfully and emphasize the importance of the intersections between Technological Knowledge, Pedagogical Knowledge and Content Knowledge, and propose that effective integration of Web 2.0 technology into the curriculum requires a sensitive understanding of the dynamic relationship between all three components, pointing out the nature of the learning design as being more transmissive, dialogic, constructionist or co-constructive [13].

At the same time mindless use of ICT may provoke unexpected effects.

Students and teachers sometimes get the feeling that a set of ICT tools, which is especially organized into a social network, can operate by itself. Just tell the students where and how to log in, and half the way is passed. The rest, i.e. the actual learning process, is reduced to the technically correct use of ICT tools proposed by the teacher. In other words, learning technology can substitute the content of education. The consequence of this effect is unreasonably high formalization of training and the fall of the quality of education.

Another negative effect is seeming availability of any information. Today's students often do not want to remember the instructional information, citing the fact that in any search engine you can find it in a split second. They often did not even occur to him that the information is necessary not only to see / hear, but also to understand. As a result such student becomes an individual that is functionally illiterate, not amenable to further study. The other side of the same coin is the abundance of poor quality and / or false information on the internet.

Mentioned and some other negative effects may severely decrease the quality of education. The experience of the Distance Education Center of National Technical University “Kharkiv Polytechnic Institute” (CDE NTU KhPI) Experience has shown that successful educational use of ICT tools, especially from the arsenal of web 2.0, requires careful theoretical and experimental investigation of all their strengths, weaknesses, opportunities and risks that are associated with their use. This was the way how, for instance, Consulting e-Learning Services, educational blogs and other ICT tools have been implemented into the educational process of the University (see details on CDE site http://cde.kpi.kharkov.ua/cdes/LMNP.htm).

3 Integrations of e-Learning and Social Networking Platforms

Moodle is the most commonly used e-learning platform in Universities. It belongs to the category of Learning Management Systems and does not provide with the social networking features. Learning process in Moodle is centered on the course and this prevents from spontaneous interactions with other learners that are not involved in the course. Trying to solve this problem we have chosen to implement University social networking platform based on most popular open source social networking system Elgg. It was obvious that we need some kind of integration of Moodle and Elgg but trying to find solution we have quickly discovered that integration of those two systems is not enough and we should look at much broader perspective. After careful analysis of students, teachers and faculty administration needs we have defined the main patterns of users' interactions and have identified a list of systems that handles data related to this interaction.

User's central directory provides with the Single-Sing-On user authentication service (LDAP + SAML) and with the basic profile information about the user (Name, Surname, e-mail, student/teacher ID, etc.)

Academic Information System contains data about study programs, study modules, responsible teachers, students, their division into academic groups, chosen study programs and courses, etc.

Learning Management System Moodle contains learning material and activities of specific courses. It is completely depends upon the teacher if he or she decides to use Moodle or not. As far as the same course may be taught in different study programs by different teachers, it is quite common that courses have several instances on Moodle dedicated to different student groups and curetted by different teachers. Access to the courses is typically managed by setting up enrolment key and sending it to the students via e-mail.

Video Presentation and Lecturing System ViPS provides with facilities for the teachers to deliver and record video lectures Records are organised into the courses/channels and courses can be included into study programs. Similar to the Moodle students' access to the recorded lectures can be limited by setting up enrolment key for the course channel and sending it via e-mail.

Social Networking System Elgg provides with main functionality of most social networking platforms: setting up users profiles, managing own connections with friend and peers, creating and joining groups of interests, sharing files, collecting resources, writing blogs, collaboratively publishing pages, etc.

Having all those systems we were missing solution that would allow to coordinate data exchange among all systems and would provide with group communication and notification services to all university users.

In order to bridge this gap we have decided to build a custom portal Mano.ktu.lt (My KTU) for personalised services to all university members. Mano.ktu.lt serves as intranet solution and connects main systems dedicated to accommodate study process.

Bellow we provide with some use case scenarios for the teachers and students.

Teachers when connected to this portal are provided with list of courses from Academic Information System they are responsible for. By selecting one of the courses teacher can publish a message to specific group of students that is subscribed to this course, he can also activate course virtual learning environment on Moodle platform and/or to record lectures for this course on ViPS system. After activation of the course environment on Moodle or ViPS, teacher can invite students to join Moodle course, ViPS channel and/or group on Elgg by indicating from what academic groups students are allowed to connect to subscribed course.

Students when connected to the system, see the list of messages published by teachers in the courses they are subscribed to. They can see the links to course environment on Moodle, ViPS and Elgg systems in case they are used with selected course. Students can also communicate with their peers on Elgg within their academic group, can join other open groups and can request creation of new group.

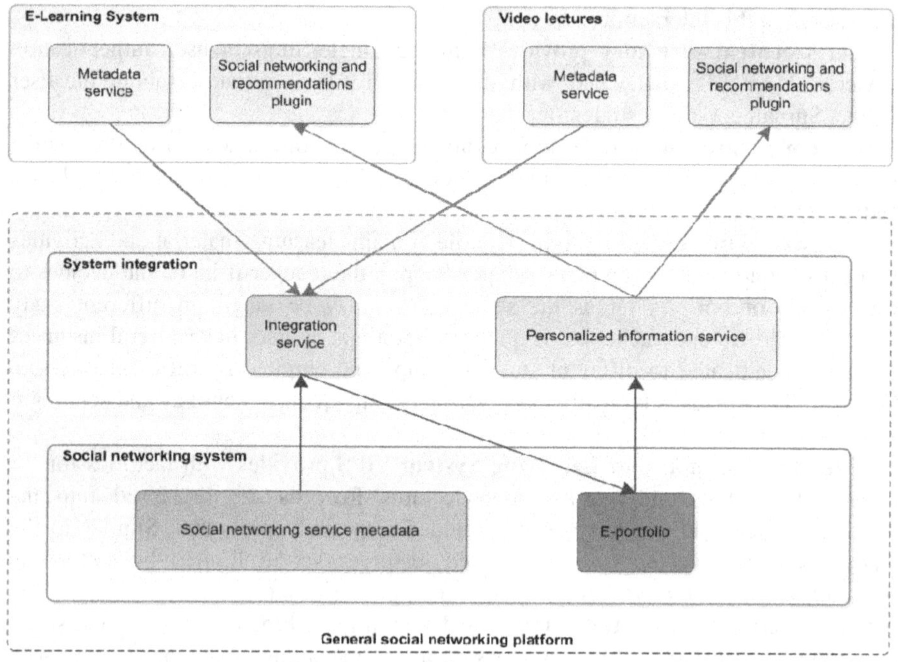

Fig. 3. General integration schema

All systems used in KTU are connected through Single-Sign-On (SSO) solution provided by KTU Information Technology Centre. Thus, there are no integration problems between different student's data basis, e-learning environments and social networking system. When user is connected to one of the services, other systems do not require logging in because the system automatically checks online users and authorizes it.

Using this code example system can connect to user directory and connect user to the system. This code snippet requires simplesamlphp libraries, than connects to user directory SAML service ant loads user. When user is loaded code tries to get all required user fields – email, username, id and other user attributes. When all information is gathered script authenticates user.

3.1 The Scheme of e-Learning Systems Extension by the Social Means of Communication

Arrows in diagram (fig. 3) illustrate the flows of information. Metadata Service transmits meta-information to integration service components. Integration and

```
require_once ($simplesamlpath);

$as = new SimpleSAML_Auth_Simple($simplesaml_sp);
$as->requireAuth();
$attributes = $as->get Attributes ();

$mail = $attributes['mail'][0];
$name = $attributes['eduPersonPrincipalName'][0];
$secureid = $attributes['eduPersonTargetedID'][0];
$parts = explode(":", $attributes['schacPersonalUniqueCode'][0]);
$vidko = $parts[8];

$account = user_load(array('name' => $mail));
```

Fig. 4. Script authenticates user

information service transforms the data to e-learning portfolio. Personalized information service, upon request from the social networking and recommendation service provides personalized recommendations based on learner e-portfolio.

General social networking platform allows integrating social networking tools to e-learning content management and supply systems. Single-platform flexibility allows integrating a number of e-learning systems and accumulation of these systems provides the content meta-information to an e-learning portfolio.

General Social Networking Platform Includes

- social networking system;
- the learner's e-portfolio;
- integration with:
  - metadata integration service;
  - personalized information Service;
- social networking and recommendations plugins.

3.2 E-portfolio. Issues and Challenges of Institutional Portfolio

Artefacts collected during social networking activities reflect the student's interests. An electronic portfolio can be used for such artefacts organized accumulation. E-portfolio can be supplemented with other learning systems, accumulated information from various student learning activities. It also helps to develop and review the meta-object information:

- E-learning system of meta-information describes the learner's artefacts:
  - the courses and modules attended,
  - completed tests,
  - received certificates.

- Video lectures meta-information system for multimedia learning objects:
  - created video presentations,
  - reviewed video presentations of other authors,
  - participation in conferences.

E-portfolio is an organized source of information about student interests. It is organized and structured way to gather information from other information systems for e-learning metadata and integration services. Rich e-portfolio better reflects the student's interests and allows systems to provide accurate personalized services.

In essence e-portfolios are serving students to become critical thinkers and aiding in the development of their writing and multimedia communication skills. E-portfolios can help students learn information and technology literacy skills and how to use digital media. Beyond academic evidence, they give students the opportunity to create a digitized showcase of their work and skills that can be presented to prospective employers. Some career services offices are providing an e-portfolio tool to students (and more recently to alumni). These e-portfolios [13] may link students to their alma mater after graduation, provided they receive temporary or lifetime access to their e-portfolios housed on the institution's servers. This can be a free or fee-based (typically through alumni membership) alumni service, depending on the institution.

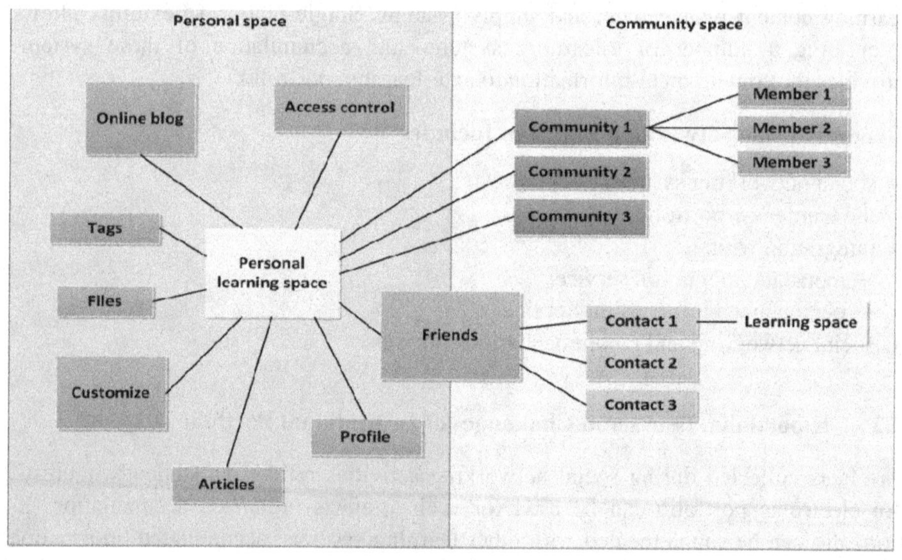

Fig. 5. E- portfolio

An e-portfolio is more than a collection of information and technological resources however it can also serve as an administrative tool to manage and organize work created with different applications and control. The definition of an e-portfolio typically derives from the exchange of ideas and feedback between the users and those who view and interact with the e-portfolio. In addition, the user's personal reflection on the work inside an e-portfolio helps create a meaningful learning experience. E-portfolios can also be defined as personalized, Web-based collections of work, responses to work, and reflections that are used to demonstrate key skills and accomplishments for a variety of contexts and time periods. While it is impossible to precisely determine how many institutions have adopted e-portfolio systems, their adoption continues to grow.

There are three broad categories emerge: student e-portfolio, teaching e-portfolio, and institutional e-portfolio. E-portfolio have several functions what are used to plan educational programs, document knowledge, skills, abilities, and learning, track development within a program, find a job, evaluate a course, and monitor and evaluate performance.

The issues and challenges of institutional e-portfolios go beyond those for individual e-portfolios.

Using authentic examples of student and faculty work inside an institutional e-portfolio raises confidentiality and permission concerns. These issues can be addressed through subject release forms in which students and faculty grant the university permission to use samples of their work. Permanent files of the release forms are then maintained in an electronic database of the participants' names and their contributions.

Institutional e-portfolios require significant organizational development and maintenance efforts. Different organizations, spanning academic affairs and IT, must be involved. And those efforts must be sustained over time and across departmental lines.

Building an effective institutional e-portfolio requires the active participation of institutional research staff, knowledgeable Web developers, graphic designers, and a technical staff with multimedia expertise, as well as strong database construction and maintenance skills.

3.3 The Extension of e-Learning Systems with Recommendation Plug-In

The integration system is designed to mediate between the e-learning and social networking systems. It also integrates social networking tools in e-learning systems. Integration includes system integration service and personalized information service.

Service Integration and Metadata Services. Integration Service applies to the metadata service that brings together existing systems and protocols in the metadata of the information received about the student artefacts e-portfolio. Metadata Services use e-learning environments application programming interface from the database to extract the learner's interests in defining the content and transfer it to the integration services company.

Personalized information service. Personalized information service gathers on request from the e-learning environment with plug-in interest-related e-learner profile information. According to the E-learning environment plug-in, taking advantage of that environment, application programming interface to provide personalized content and thus expanding opportunities for social interaction.

Social networking and recommendations Plugin. This particular learning environment and social networking plug-in is a module that complements the

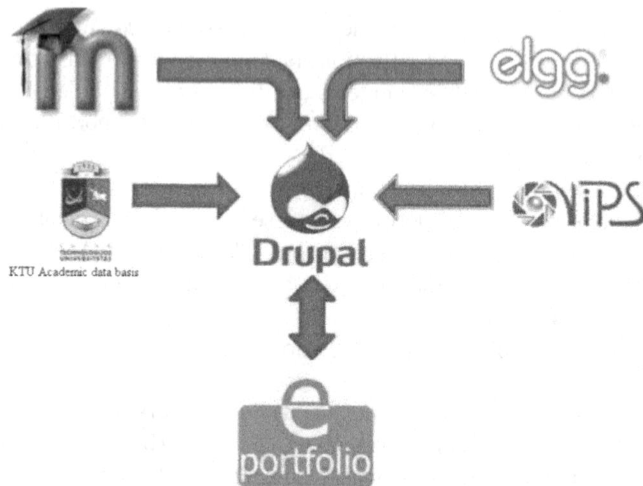

Fig. 6. Integration e-portfolio to academic data basis

environment of e-learning content by social networking capabilities and provides additional personalized content recommendations. E-learning systems allow users to share e-learning systems content, to write web content by sharing the link with other learners. Opportunities to leave comments, discuss, evaluate, designate and in accordance with this later on get personalized recommendations for content.

3.4 Intelligent Service of Frequently Asked and Answered Questions (iFAQ)

One of the problems have always existed in the educational process based on ICT is duplicated information transmitted from teacher to students (typical questions on discipline and the same typical answers). ICT tools can significantly reduce the amount of such information and, thus, release time of teachers and students for another, more interesting and creative work.

This innovative tool is integrated into the Information Management System (IMS) – e-learning environment that is using in NTU KhPI (http://cde.kpi.kharkov.ua/). It's iFAQ – intellectual knowledge base (expert system), which allows the teacher in the learning process to form the base of questions and answers to them, the most frequently encountered in this or that distance course (FAQ-FAA). In fact, it is about creating with joint efforts of students and teachers a dynamic knowledge base on selected topics.

iFAQ is an intellectual FAQ. iFAQ works similar to regular FAQ system. You can find an answer on your question in regular FAQ system by using search engine or open certain section of FAQ. iFAQ unlike FAQ have substantially more advanced functions. iFAQ utilizes semantic, but not lexicographic system for information treatment and search in knowledge base. iFAQ uses "analogies" - semantic linguistic constructions for accumulating knowledge in the knowledge base. The wider the

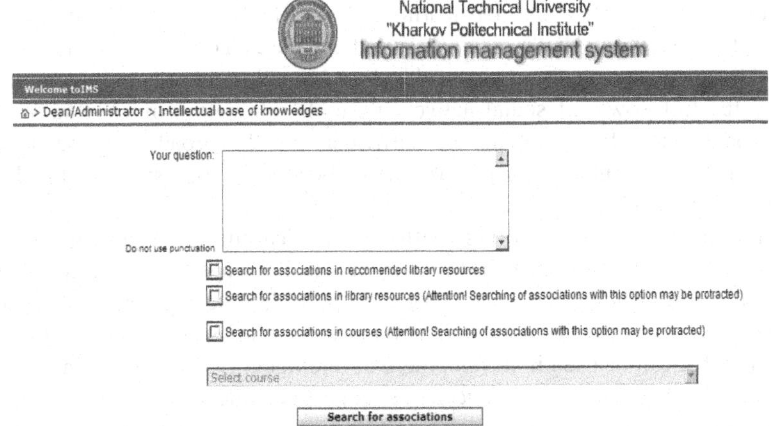

Fig. 7. iFAQ main screen

sense of analogy the wider range of possible questions from the users it can cover. iFAQ is teachable system that means that so called "teacher" of the system can collect, sort, add, delete, summarize, unite, unify analogies. Besides learning with "teacher" iFAQ can teach itself by collecting and sorting pairs of FAQ-FAA (Frequently Asked Questions-Frequently Answered Answers) that produces by users of SIM in different conversation tools (SIM mail, SIM forums, SIM chats). Also iFAQ can search in courses content for semantic coincidences with iFAQ user question. iFAQ receives not only keywords for search but also regular questions instead keywords requests. For example you can use full sentence: "What is magnetron and how it works?" instead keyword request: "magnetron work action". In case when you use question you will get exactly an answer about how magnetron works and only when the information about magnetron construction and principle of action you will get separate information block about magnetron. In case when you use keywords you will get a lot of information about different magnetrons and different works which can be connected with magnetron and other can no be. So in conclusion iFAQ can be described as a "semantic teachable searching server of the distributed database".

4 Conclusions

Methods of education are changing rapidly, facing new challenges both at institutional and at individual levels. Due to the increase in national and international competition, institutions are struggling to offer attractive programmes for learners by employing modern ICT based e-learning.

E-learning programmes trying to leverage full potential of communication and collaboration technologies by involving Web 2.0 applications, social networking tools and mobile devices.

We can see rapid changes in E-learning market and tendency towards an open source and free solutions that can be integrated and extended with additional modules provided by open source community or developed to tailored needs of institution. Still to unveil the full power of social networking tools integration of existing solutions (e.g. Moodle with Elgg) may not be sufficient and the broader perspective with analysis of existing interaction patterns and inventory of all systems involved is highly recommended.

Integration of social networking platform with learning management, academic information and other systems allows to exchange information among them and to collect user's artefacts into personal learner's e-portfolio. Accumulation of other data about learner's activities and communication patterns allows creating a pool of meta-information that can be used in development of intelligent recommendation widgets.

Still full implementation of educational concepts/models and new learning and teaching methods by using modern ICT needs involvement of competitive teachers and support staff. This is particularly very important at a secondary education level where investments to infrastructure and new equipment should planned together with the large scale teachers trainings on how to use ICT based innovative learning and teaching methods in their teaching practices.

Acknowledgements. This paper has been partially supported by EUREKA scientific programme ITEA 2 Call 4 09020 (European Structural Funds project No. VP1-3.1-ŠMM-06-V-01-003, FFCC, VICAM).

References

1. Redecker, C.: Learning 2.0: The Impact of Web 2.0 Innovation on Education and Training in Europe, Spain, 122 p. (2009)
2. Burneikaitė, N., Jarienė, R., Jašinauskas, L., Motiejūnienė, E., Neseckienė, I., Vingelienė, S.: Informacinių komunikacinių technologijų taikymo ugdymo procese galimybės, Vilnius, 231 p. (2009)
3. Gray, D.E., Ryan, M., Coulon, A.: The Training of Teachers and Trainers: Innovative Practices, Skills and Competencies in the use of eLearning. European Journal of Open, Distance and E-learning, `http://www.eurodl.org/?p=archives&year=2004&halfyear=2&article=159`
4. Rutkauskienė, D., Gudonienė, D.: E. švietimas: tendencijos ir iššūkiai. Konferencijos pranešimų medžiaga: Web 2.0 saitynas, Vilnius, 110 p. (2005)
5. Mockus, J.: Investigation of Examples of E-education Environment for Scientific Collaboration and Distance Graduate Studies. Informatica 19(1), pt. 2, 45–62 (2008)
6. Kuzucuoglu, A.E., Gokhan, E.: Development of A Web-Based Control and Robotic Applications Laboratory for Control Engineering Education. Information Technology and Control 40(4) (2011)
7. Vitiutinas, R., Silingas, D., Telksnys, L.: Model-driven plug-in development for UML based modelling systems. Information Technology and Control 40(3) (2011)
8. Pečiuliauskienė, P.: Kompiuterizuoto mokymo metodai pradedančiųjų mokytojų edukacinėje praktikoje, 89 p. (2008)
9. Grodecka, K., Wild, F., Kieslinger, B.: How to Use Social Software in Higher Education, 130 p. (2009)

10. Rutkauskienė, D., Gudonienė, D.: Socialinė tinklaveika ir iššūkiai. Konferencijos pranešimų medžiaga (2010)
11. Rutkauskiene, D., Huet, I., Gudoniene, D.: E-Learning in Teachers and Tutors Training Using ICT Based Curriculum (2010)
12. Turcsányi-Szabó, M.: Aiming at Sustainable Innovation in Teacher Education – from Theory to Practice. Informatics in Education 11(1), 115–130 (2012)
13. Bower, M., Hedberg, J.G., Kuswara, A.: A framework for Web 2.0 learning design. Educational Media International 47(3), 177–198 (2010)
14. Lorenzo, G., Ittelson, J.: An Overview of E-Portfolios, 29 p. (2005)
15. Redecker, C., Leis, M., Leendertse, M., Punie, Y., Gijsbers, G., Kirschner, P., Stoyanov, S., Hoogveld, B.: The Future of Learning: Preparing for Change, 94 p. (2011) ISSN: 1831-9424

Competition Based Online Social Learning

Tomas Blazauskas, Virginija Limanauskiene, and Vitalija Kersiene

Kaunas University of Technology
Kaunas, Lithuania
{tomas.blazauskas,virginija.limanauskiene,
vitalija.kersiene}@ktu.lt

Abstract. In this paper we introduce a framework for providing competition based social learning. We discuss that competition in learning activities, especially paired with social learning, is very well accepted still the existing solutions lack tools for directing and organizing learning activities. We provide a description of a social learning portal www.arzinai.lt which implements competition in learning, also has features of personal and group learning environments. Some usage statistics, which confirm that competitions provide a strong motivation for learners, are provided as well.

Keywords: Computers And Education, Learning Systems, Social Computing, Knowledge Sharing, Collaborative Learning, Learning Environment, web2.

1 Introduction

Despite lots of research done in the field of e-learning, researches are still trying to understand how people learn, why some learning platforms and tools are rejected or not being used as supposed to. It is noted that the technological means by themselves do not ensure effective learning process, social environment is necessary.

Popular social software such as Facebook, MySpace, Twitter and LinkedIn has attracted a large number of young users at 21'st century. Pupils and students use these tools to share information with each other, to blog, to online communicate, to tag, to rate, to comment and so on. Students of Net Generation [6, 10] consider computers a natural part of their environment; the virtual world is an extension of their real world. Therefore new models of learning should be used now. We propose use social software and competition based learning model to attract people of all ages to share their knowledge and learn from each other's.

Social learning appears when learning that takes place in a social context, observing other people, using discussions, direct interactions with experts and peers, working within team-based projects. Social environment provides strong motivation for learning. Motivation is usually based on fun, competition, reputation and social creativity. Competition is arguably the strongest aspect which influence all other.

There are reports [5, 3] that competition based learning (CBL) is successfully integrated in usual learning environments and facilitates effective learning. Even more

T. Skersys, R. Butleris, and R. Butkiene (Eds.): ICIST 2012, CCIS 319, pp. 388–396, 2012.

important competition based learning should be for the e-learning and self-organized learning as motivation becomes very important in these cases.

The aim of the paper is to overview of successful non-formal CBL portals, implemented models and pedagogical aspects which facilitate learning, to provide concepts and model of competition enhanced learning which is implemented in social portal www.arzinai.lt, to present brief overview on some implementation details and tools for self-directed learning. The paper is organized as follows. We analyze the related works in Section 2. We describe competition enhanced learning concepts and implementation in Section 3. We present a case study in Section 4.

2 Related Works

In this section we analyze the related work by categorizing it into two streams as follows: (1) analysis of learning as a process; (2) best practice examples of the competition based learning.

Learning could be thought of as "a process by which behaviour changes as a result of experience" [8]. It is significant, are people conscious of what is going on? Are they aware that they are engaged in learning? Such questions have appeared in debates around the "informal learning".

Social cognitive theorists [15, 16] use the term self-motivation which assumes that learners' continuing motivations derived from their self-efficacy perceptions and use of self- regulatory processes during learning such as goal setting. Zimmerman and Martinez-Pons found students who reported using self-regulated learning strategies were significantly more likely to volunteer for special projects. Pintrich and De Groot found that learners require more than task-oriented strategies, they need learning strategies that focus on self-regulatory processes [11]. Self-regulated learners are significantly more likely to organize or restructure their place of study than regular learners and they are more likely to seek help from the persons who is known to be capable. In this sense, seeking information from social sources is not different from seeking it from written sources [15].

It is necessary to construct the rules that encourage users to explore and learn the properties of their possibilities through the use of feedback mechanisms and make learning more engaging. It is necessary to investigate the learners' audience, not just the subject matter, but to research the brands, hobbies, and media (television, films, games, websites, etc.) that target audience enjoys. This should give a better idea of the aesthetics and interactions that learners like and want [12].

One-fifth (20%) of college students in 2002 (Net generation) began using computers between the ages of 5 and 8. By the time they were 16 to 18 years old, all of today's current college students had begun using computers and the Internet was common place [6].

Brown predicates that "Net Generation students are achievement and goal oriented. Their question is not "What does it mean?" or "How does it work?" (as previous generations were inclined to ask), but rather "How do I build it? "This predilection maps to learning theory's emphasis on active learning. Discovery, exploration, experimentation, criticism, analysis—all represent active learning, a style that suits the Net Gen well" [2].

Meece analyses the role of motivation in self-regulated learning [9]. She writes that some students seek to increase their competences, whereas others seek to demonstrate high ability. Self-regulated learning could be examined in the context of achievement goal theory and implicit theory of intelligence. The achievements goals individuals pursue create "the framework within which they interpret and react to events" [9]. Research indicates that learners benefit the most from learning situations when they focus on mastering the task at hand rather than commetting with others with grades and teacher approval. It is necessary to privide for participants learning activities that are meaningful and relevant, provide opportunities for learners' choice and decision-making, rewarding and recognizing personal improvement, and reduce emphasis on social competition and comparisons [9].

Reed et al argue that to be considered social learning, a process must: (1) demonstrate that a change in understanding has taken place in the individuals involved; (2) demonstrate that this change goes beyond the individual and becomes situated within wider social units or communities of practice and (3) occur through social interactions and processes between actors within a social network either through direct interaction, e.g., conversation, or through other media, e.g., mass media, telephone, or Web 2.0 applications [13]. Social software has ignited a shift toward social learning and collaboration.

Cob emphasizes that in the learning 2.0 paradigm, the old teacher-centric, expert-dominated learning model breaks down, and the remaining constraints on time and geography are loosened to the point of almost disappearing entirely. Learning dialogs and collaborations become dramatically more prevalent not just between teacher and learner, but between learner and learner [4].

People engage competition all the time, engaging in wide variety of sports (golf, tennis) and games (bridge, chess) as well as musical recitals, drama auditions and talent shows. Tjosvold argues, that the constructiveness of competition may be reflected in (a) the experience of engaging in competition and (b) the consequences resulting from the competition [14]. Internal motivation to compete and the strategy of competing fairly were found to be the most powerful influences on the constructiveness of competition. Constructiveness in competition may be reflected in enjoying the competition, wanting to participate, and interacting positively with competitors.

Competitions as the means to provide effective learning have a long history. Some believe competitions are a part of the natural learning. Elara et al provide the example of CBL implementation in students projects in the Soccer humanoid robotics area. The results of the experiment showed that these projects helped in enhancing student's interest and motivation in learning engineering topics [5].

At the beginning of learning environment (platform) era such the natural learning methods were forgotten or not implemented properly. A lack of student interest towards learning by using learning environments stimulated lots of research in the area and a major trend, built upon ideas of fun, competition and challenges, appeared "serious games".

During last decade various sites, which are not dedicated to serve as learning platforms, successfully implemented the idea of competitions. Many of these sites (like hackits.de[1], hackthissite.org, hackquest.com and other) were dedicated to ethical hacking field. Creators usually provided safe playgrounds (sandbox) so that competitors could solve real-world hacking tasks (for example - to hack a pre-maid site with a known security hole). For solving these tasks competitors were awarded by points and ranks. Forums were organized in order to give directions for the people who could not solve problems by themselves. Elements of problem and competition based learning made these sites so addictive that these sites counted tens of thousands of users. Learning model of such sites can be described in the Fig. 1.

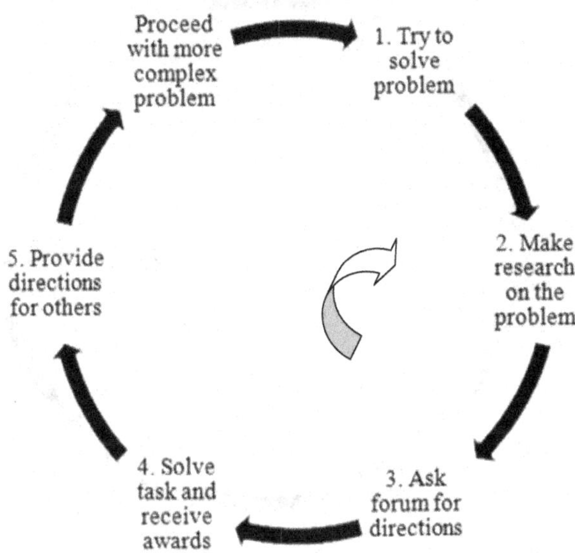

Fig. 1. Problem based and competition enhanced learning process (model) with directions in forums

It should be noted, that directions (No. 3 in Fig. 1) in forum could not be direct answers, just hints which competitors could use to make further research on the problem. Also, providing directions for other competitors has another pedagogical aspect: self-reflection. By providing a non-direct hint people have to formulate solution in other words (for example by using analogies) as the same concepts could give away the solution.

Being so popular some of such web-sites started to provide learning paths for its users as well as learning materials. For example, learning path for the specific ethical hacking field in website hackits.de included a set of incremental difficulty tasks which could be solved in sequential order only.

[1] This website ceased to exist approximately in the year 2009.

Arguably following success of these sites, other sites appeared which included wider range of disciplines. One of the most known websites which focus is on computational mathematics - projecteuler.net [7]. This project retained some aspects as rewarding points and ranks, but also has a different approach influencing self-reflection and perfection.

In projecteuler.net website competitors can post solution for a problem, but these solutions are hidden for the people who didn't solve that specific problem. After solving a problem competitor may see other solutions, improve his own solution and post his improved solution (learning model is provided in Fig.2).

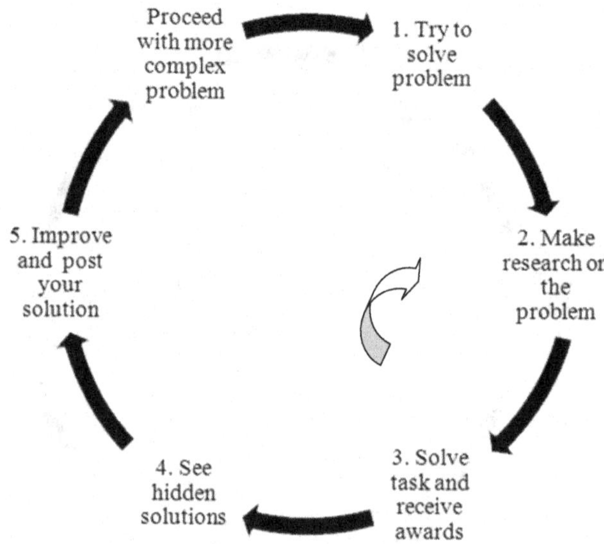

Fig. 2. Problem based and competition enhanced learning process (model) with solutions sharing between competitors

Differently from previously discussed sites, projecteuler.net does not have forum where competitors can get hints. It is discussed that because of this more people are involved in cheating activities which distort competition to some point. Still projecteuler.net has a good name and is viewed as very successful example of competition and problem based learning. Interesting to note that despite the competition people are willingly sharing their solutions and social environment facilitates it.

3 The Concept and Implementation of the Competition Based Social Learning

The initial idea is to create bottom-up community driven, competition based social learning completely free portal. Such portal supports the learning from the community members by building content on other people's ideas or products. This project unites the ideas of different competition based websites as well as includes tools for self-directed learning and group work. This idea is implemented in the portal arzinai.lt [1]. The portal provides for participants the possibilities of the learning activities that are meaningful and the opportunities for learners' choice and decision-making rewarding and recognizing personal improvement.

The whole problem solving (learning) cycle at arzinai.lt is provided in Fig. 3.

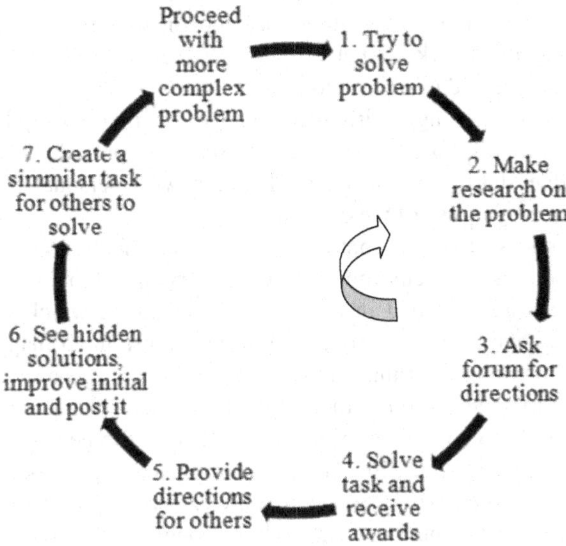

Fig. 3. Problem based and competition enhanced learning process (model) implemented in the portal arzinai.lt

The main aspect of our system is maintaining motivation for learning. As one can see, the problem solving as well as pedagogy aspects are very similar to described cases in Fig. 1 and Fig. 2. One new activity - the task creation activity (No. 7 in Fig. 3) is added, which is optional, but it occurs frequently as social environment favors it. Community members (learners) act as designers of articles, tasks (quizzes and puzzles), they gain reputation by creating new tasks for their competitors, they are eager to receive comments, feedback and assessment.

Motivation is based on four key elements: fun, competition, reputation and social creativity.

Participation in learning process enhanced by competition usually evolves through the following phases:

- users are having fun by playing their favourite educational games and solving tasks;
- members earn points by solving tasks, they are ranked and begin to compete with other community members;

- after achieving a certain level, they are gaining the reputation which should be maintained by continuing task solving activities and helping others;
- some members create tasks by themselves what also indirectly influences reputation;
- optionally for more effective collaboration users create the groups of interests or hobbies.

Learners working with social software not only learn a specific topic, but they are equipped with tools for their future activities and acquire communication and design skills. After the end of the learning, the social networks continue to exist. Continued participation in social networks and creation of new networks give participants access to communities, people and other resources.

Using of the social learning environment changes the relationship between learners and learners themselves. Social learning environment provide additional value - extends knowledge sharing by providing learners with personal and collaborative tools and by enhancing re-use of the content.

The learning process could be controlled to be more effective. For that purpose the personal and group learning environments with respective tools are provided in the portal. These tools are provided in a form of applications which can be added to personal or group environment. Among such tools we use mind mapping application to describe and organize learning flow, provide links to learning materials and competition tasks to solve. Another tool which is frequently used – competition map which gives quick overview of the progress made. Environment also includes usual applications such as discussions, file sharing, communication and other. Also, there is a possibility for a teacher (or learner) to add external applications into learning environment in the same manner one can do it in igoogle and similar environments.

4 Case Study: Results of Using Social Learning Portal

Portal arzinai.lt was created at the beginning of 2008 by one of the authors of this paper and is in continuous improvement [1]. It is based on the open source framework Joomla. Users can use their own Facebook accounts to access portal. The language of the portal is Lithuanian.

Personal learning environment is implemented in user spaces. Users can customize and enhance their spaces by adding various applications including tools which can facilitate learning: learning path application which uses mind mapping tool, solved task tool which provides a quick look at the progress, forum comments tracking application and blogging application to share and discuss the experiences.

Group learning environment shares the same concepts and tools as the personal environment (space) and adds tools for managing the group users and resources. For example, users may create private learning groups and the competition tasks created by the group users may be assigned only for that particular group.

We analyze the impact of the competition approach to the vitality of community, content quality. Here we provide the results of the analysis with the respect to the competition influence to the learning content and achievements.

During 20 month period (from January of 2010 to September of 2011), the portal community created 147 reviewed tasks and 398 lower quality tasks.

These tasks were viewed and solved approximately 326 thousand times by anonymous and nearly 7 thousand by registered users.

Only 140 tasks of 513 (27%) are created by website authors (learning mentors), other comes from users (learners). Proposed tasks are evaluated by portal referees and only accepted tasks are published for the competition. Other, lower quality tasks or the tasks which do not add any new aspects to the existing are published separately. The language of the portal is Lithuanian. Majority of the users come from the Lithuania, United States and UK. The users are from 8 to 55 years of age, with a peak at age 18-19. No correlation was found between age and number of materials created or tasks solved. 70 percent of users are male, no correlation was found between gender and the number of content created.

5 Conclusions and Future Work

This paper introduces a model for competition based social learning and its implementation in the Lithuanian portal arzinai.lt.

Successful experience of the competition based social learning portal once again proves that discussed four elements (fun, competition, reputation and social creativity) can be used to maintain motivation for self-directed or casual learning.

The results (described in section 4) of the experience analysis indicate that use of friendly competitions provide a strong motivation and increase the learners performance and creativity. But group environments were not used often as a tool for group learning as was expected. Likely, successful examples and case studies are necessary to promote the usage of group environments for learning purposes.

We plan to investigate how the provided group environment of the social portal can be effectively used for the directed group learning.

The next step will be testing the proposed problem based learning concept and implemented portal in a formal education courses. The idea is to ask the learners to use the portal as a basis for the competitive tournaments and to evaluate the impact of the learning method and environment to the learning achievements.

References

1. Blazauskas, T.: Ar zinai? (in Lithuanian), `http://www.arzinai.lt`
2. Brown, M.: Learning Spaces. EDUCAUSE (2012)
3. Burguillo, J.C.: Using Game Theory and Competition-Based Learning to Stimulate Student Motivation and Performance. Computers & Education 55(2) (2010)
4. Cobb, J.: Crowd sourced predictions for your 2012 education strategy (2011)
5. Elara, M.R., Acosta Calderon, C.A., Zhou, C., Zhang, L., Yang, Y., Yang, T.: Experimenting Competition Based Learning of Engineering Topics With Soccer Playing Humanoid Robots. In: 10th Asia Pacific Conference on Giftedness, Singapore (2008)

6. Jones, S.: The Internet Goes to College: How Students are Living in Future with Today's Technology. In: Pew Internet and American Life Project, Washington, DC (2002), http://www.eric.ed.gov/PDFS/ED472669.pdf
7. Hughes, C.: Project Euler, UK, http://projecteuler.net
8. Maples, M.F., Webster, J.M.: Thorndike's Connectionism. In: Gazda, G.M., Corsini, R.J. (eds.) Theories of Learning, F. E. Peacock, Itasca (1980)
9. Meece, J.L.: The Role of Motivation in Self-Regulated Learning. In: Schunk, D.H., Zimmerman, B.J. (eds.) Self-Regulation of Learning and Performance: Issues and Educational Applications, p. 40. Library of Congress Cataloging-in-Publication Data (1994)
10. Oblinger, D., Oblinger, J.: Is It Age or IT: First Steps Toward Understanding the Net Generatio. EDUCAUSE (2012)
11. Pintrich, P.R., De Groot, E.: Motivational and Self-Regulated Learning Components of Classroom Academic Performance. Journal of Educational Psychology 82, 33–40 (1990)
12. Raymer, R.: Gamification: Using Game Mechanics to Enhance eLearning, eLearn Magazine (2011), http://elearnmag.acm.org/featured.cfm?aid=2031772
13. Reed, M.S., Evely, A.C., Cundill, G., Fazey, I., Glass, J., Laing, A., Newig, J., Parrish, B., Prell, C., Raymond, C., Stringer, L.C.: What is social learning? Ecology and Society 15(4), r1 (2010)
14. Tjosvold, D., Johnson, D.W., Johnson, R., Haifa Sun, T.: Competitive Motives and Strategies. Group Dynamics: Theory, Research, and Practice 10(2), 87–99 (2006)
15. Zimmerman, B.: Dimensions of Academic Self-regulation: A Conceptual Framework for Education. In: Schunk, D.H., Zimmerman, B.J. (eds.) Self-Regulation of Learning and Performance: Issues and Educational Applications, Library of Congress Cataloging-in-Publication Data (1994)
16. Zimmerman, B.J., Martinez-Pons, M.: Construct Validation of a Strategy Model of Student Self-Regulated Learning. Journal of Educational Psychology 80, 284–290 (1988)

Agent System as Complex Support for the Learning Process

Aleksandras Targamadze[1] and Ruta Petrauskiene[2]

[1] Kaunas University of Technology, Faculty of Informatics, 50 Studentu Str., Kaunas LT-51368, Lithuania
aleksandras.targamadze@laba.lt

[2] Alytaus Kolegija University of Applied Sciences, Distance Study Centre, 1C Ligonines Str., Alytus LT-62114, Lithuania
ruta.petrauskiene@akolegija.lt

Abstract. Implementation of agent based intelligent technologies in the environment of distance learning can individualise learning, enable an optimal use of learning resources and ensure effective interaction with all participants of the learning process. In recent scientific literature, however, only descriptions of individual agents or small agent groups that support one learning activity may be found. The article describes a designed system of pedagogical software agents that integrally supports the learning process and that is adapted to virtual learning environment Moodle.

Keywords: distance learning, virtual learning, information technologies in learning, agents.

1 Introduction

Information technologies (ITs) used in a modern learning process have many possibilities to render learning content, yet individualised learning is still not supported sufficiently. There is a need for technologies that can intellectualise the process of learning, activate interactions among a student, learning content and tutor (teacher, coach). These drawbacks may be eliminated using technologies based on pedagogical software agents. Agents release human from any trouble, they work in background regime without a human influence therefore are more convenient comparing to plugins. Agents can work when servers work at a minimum regime.

The purpose of pedagogical software agents is to facilitate the learning process while supporting the activities of a learner and a teacher and assisting them. In the learning environment, software agents may be given various roles that realise such assistance: course tutors [6], teachers-informers [5], fellow-students [2], learning help [4], assistants [1], learning through cooperation agent [10], etc. Social context and interaction among process participants are essential for learner development [7]; thus pedagogical agents may enhance learning motivation while simulating interaction with a learner [6].

T. Skersys, R. Butleris, and R. Butkiene (Eds.): ICIST 2012, CCIS 319, pp. 397–405, 2012.

Agents may collect information, for example, about student learning achievements, behaviour in the course of learning; they can accumulate information and send a report of a certain form to a teacher or tutor via email. If needed, an agent may send a warning signal or other reminder to a teacher or a student about the study situation via email. During the period of accounting for assignments, an agent may follow assignment evaluations and send messages to the students whose assignments received a negative evaluation and inform a teacher about the students who have not turned in their assignments. Besides, an agent may solve one more problem: people make plenty of mistakes in their routine activities, while agents do not.

[11] suggest the classification of pedagogical software agents based on a distance learning model at the level of study subject proposed by Anderson and Garrison [2]. There are some cases proposed how to use pedagogical software agents to perform certain functions, yet there is no complex agent system, the activity of which would be based on the analysis of learning/teaching activities and support the entire learning process.

The article is to discuss the possibilities of pedagogical software agents to integrally support the process of distance studies. The *object* of the article is the learning process in virtual learning environment (VLE). The aim of the article is to introduce the design process of agent system that integrally supports the learning process.

The learning process will be analysed at the level of study subject. We will assume that subject content has already been entered into VLE and does not change throughout the learning process; and that the schedule of learning events (work plan) has already been posted into VLE and students have already been enrolled to a study subject.

2 Learning Process and Types of Learning Events

The learning process may be analysed as a sequence of student's actions and tutor's pedagogical impacts in a certain environment distributed in time. We will analyse the learning process in VLE and will identify events that appear during the process because of the actions of a student, lecturer and VLE. We will assume that a study subject consists of themes. To realise each of them, all types of 8 learning/teaching activities identified by Leclercq and Poumay [9] are suitable.

Themes are distributed in time coherently in the order they are mastered. In individual cases, students may choose the order of themes themselves. Presumable start and end time is indicated for each them, and it is set which themes the theme may follow. The ending is *strict* if it is forbidden to perform actions related to the theme after the end time (students cannot turn in an assignment, take a test, participate in discussion, etc.). The ending is *lenient* if it is allowed to perform actions related to the theme after the end time (students are allowed to perform a task, take a test, etc.)

We will assume that time is not indicated for individual sections of themes, but they have to be completed in a period of time allocated for the theme. Students may do theme sections repeatedly; for some theme sections, the order may be indicated. For example, tasks may be performed only when the theoretical section has been covered. A student's knowledge is evaluated by intermediate (IntT) and final (e. g. examination)(FT) tests. Graphically, this may be shown in a time axis (Fig. 1).

As during the learning process the content does not change, learning/teaching events are triggered by student or tutor actions (logging in to the course, performing a task, sending a message, participating in discussion, etc.). Over the course of the learning process, the main participant of the process is a student, and it is he/she who mostly triggers learning events. Teacher's role is that of an assistant or mentor (material, tasks, tests and etc. have already been put into VLE); they usually performs assisting functions, although their actions also trigger learning events, for example, evaluated assignment, answered question. Despite the fact that in this case tutor's role is narrower, he must follow the majority of students' actions in the learning process and respond to them. VLE may help both a student and a tutor in the process.

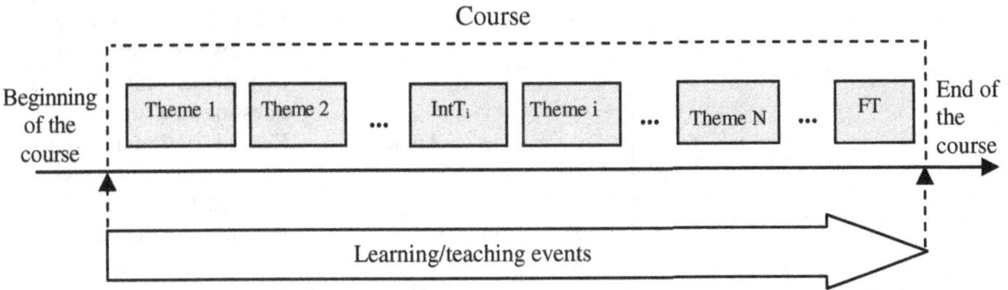

Fig. 1. The sequence of learning process events during the course

Many commercial and open code VLE have been created: Blackboard Vista, Moodle, FirstClass, Learning space, TopClass, Dokeos, Cyber Extension and others. Each VLE has slightly different attributes and functions. In order to expand the possibilities to help a student and a tutor, let's analyse possible student and tutor actions in VLE. We will realise subject themes through learning events, each of which belongs to one of activity types according to [9]. A study subject theme may not necessarily contain all activity types.

Learning events related to possible student and tutor actions and characteristic of each activity type will be discerned. Apart from activity types, we will distinguish events of more general nature (the beginning of course, the end of the course, final evaluation, etc.) that are indispensable to the learning process. VLE may take over part of student and tutors tasks; therefore, let's analyse a desirable VLE response to learning events as well (part of them shown in Table 1). Sequences of events related to assignment reports and questions repeat themselves, so we will distinguish them separately and use, when needed, to realise other activity types. Routine tutor actions may be passed to VLE where possible.

Table 1. Fragment of the table of types of learning/teaching activities, learning events characteristic of them, and desirable VLE response are presented

	Possible learning/teaching events		
Sequences of recurrent learning/ teaching events	***Student***	***Tutor***	***VLE***
'Report'	Submits report		Sends a message to a tutor, records time
		Assesses	Sends a message to a student, records action and time
	Views assessment		Records action and time
'Question'	Asks questions		Records action and time, suggests question templates, analyses frequently asked questions (FAQ), if the question is already there, provides an answer from FAQ. Otherwise, directs the question to a tutor.
		Answers	Records action and time, suggests including recurrent questions to FAQ.
	Views answers		Records action and time
Activity types			
1. Imitation and modelling	Logs in to the programme		Records action and time
	Works with the programme, observes the process, records data		Records action and time
	Determines parameters		Records action and time, comments on parameters
	'Report'		
	'Question'		
	Logs out		Records action and time
2. Reception and transmission 3. Exercising and guidance 4. Exploration and documenting 5. Experimentation and reactivity 6. Creation and facilitation	*[Details are not provided due to large size]* *[Details are not provided due to large size]*		

Table 1. *(continued)*

7. Meta-reflection and co-reflection 8. Debate and animation			
General events			
Beginning of subject	Fills in an initial form Views information	 Views information	Records action and time Organises information about a student, fills in a student model, fills in a group model. Sends summarised information to a student and a tutor. System settings are revised
End of subject Beginning of theme End of theme Beginning of session (login) End of session (login) Theme time is about to finish Theme time has finished Missed theme or material section Tutorial Intermediate/final test New event in the schedule Tutor's announcement No login to the subject (for a set period of time for a student and/or a tutor) Task/assessment was not performed (for a set period of time or number for a student and/or a tutor) No participation in discussion/forum (for a set period of time or number) Message was not viewed (for a set period of time or number for a student and/or a tutor) List of problematic students and their description No login to the course	*[Details are not provided due to large size]*		

Table 1 presents possible learning/teaching events that happen while a student is learning and a tutor is working in VLE and a desirable VLE response to them. Not all indicated events are necessary to happen over the course of each learning process; however, some events recur many times with new content. Events presented in the table show the key steps in the learning process.

3 System of Pedagogical Agents

Real VLE realise only a part of the functions indicated in Table 1. Existing VLE do not fully guarantee realisation of such important activities as timely student and tutor notification, supervision of student learning, its coordination, etc. VLE could support a more active distance learning process while following student and tutor actions, providing information and support, recording time and duration and supporting other learning events. It would be purposeful to expand their possibilities when installing the system of VLE agents that would realise the lacking yet desirable functions.

Function distribution between VLE and agent depends on a particular VLE. The less required functions VLE performs, the more work has to be done by agents. Consequently, agent system is designed for a particular VLE. We will choose an open code VLE, since it is easier to supplement it with new possibilities and thus to insert agents.

[8] presents a technological analysis of the open code learning environment, which showed that from a technological point of view, Moodle is the best among popular open code technological environments. The environment has a convenient possibility for extensions, and therefore it was chosen for designing the set of agents.

When planning the system of agents that integrally supports the study process and determining agent roles and responsibilities, the functions of VLE with agents presented in Table 2 were evaluated and it was assessed what the VLE Moodle performs on its own and what actions are left for agents to perform. The list of 16 planned agents is presented in Table 2.

Table 2. List of pedagogical agents and agent functions

Agent title	Description of functions
Active participation agent	Organises information on student's activity in discussions and during conversations, questions asked. Composes a report to the tutor. Processes information to achievement agent.
Environment agent	Restores the state of the session that was true before a user logged out. Registers the state at the end of the session, at the beginning of the session, if it is not the first log in, navigates to the state at the time of log out.
Tutor agent	Collects student's data relevant to the tutor: passed/failed tests, submitted/not submitted assignments, reviewed/non-reviewed material, active participation, achievement
Discussion board agent	Registers the number of student's comments.

Table 2. (*continued*)

Agent title	Description of functions
Group model agent	Organizes information about the group (achievements of all students): collects data from students' models, keeps the record of short-term and long-term statistics of students' control test results, determines students with best results.
Timetable agent	Records a new timetable event added by a tutor. Records an event if there is a certain period of time left until it (e.g. less than two weeks). Forms a notice about an upcoming or new event in the schedule and repeats it according to the settings.
Question agent	Records how many times a student posted questions. If a question being written by the student is similar to those contained in Frequently Asked Questions (FAQ) database, the agent compares it to the FAQ and proposes model questions If a posed question is similar to that in FAQ, an answer is sent to it; if not, the question is directed to a tutor. If a student poses a question to the tutor and the type of question is frequent, it is included into FAQ with tutor's permission.
Time recording agent	Records the type of learning event, times of beginning and end and duration.
Setting agent	Helps a student to set parameters, comments on them.
Achievement agent	Analyses student test results and active participation. Organises information. Prepares information for a tutor.
Chat room agent	Records the number of student's posts.
Overdue agent	Analyses the events that have been scheduled yet not fulfilled, creates a message for a tutor.
Message agent	Accepts the text created by other agents and an addressee (reads from the data base) and sends it to a student or to a tutor: on to his/her desktop (if he/she is logged in), into VLE e-mail or external e-mail or as an SMS (if it is set by default).
Student model agent	Organises information about a student (questionnaire data, grades, active participation), fills the student model, refreshes information in student data base, provides information to a group model; generalised information is rendered to the student or a tutor. Informs group model agent about problematic students.
Test analysis agent	Analyses test results; with reference to test results, suggest a topic or a section for revision, if required.
Content tracking agent	Ensures the succession of tasks. Records student's actions with content. Does not allow students to log on to the topic if the student has not covered previous required topics. If the end date is exact, does not allow overdue students to log on to the topic.

Depending on the use simulation programs and Moodle version is not necessary to implement all the agents. For instance, *Setting agent* depends on a particular software or specialised application program of simulation virtual model; therefore it is not purposeful to realise it without the model or program itself. *Time recording agent* is not necessary in the latest versions of Moodle, since the records of all system users' actions are stored in *logs* component.

VLE Moodle performs many functions that record users' actions: the systems records (in *logs* block) each student's click for navigation purposes, presents extensive visual report, etc. A tutor may find reports about each student's individual activity. Nevertheless, when working with a large number of students, the abundance of information becomes inconvenient and thus is rarely used. The system of agents may present the tutor with processed and organised information about students.

4 Agent System Implementation

The performed evaluation of the model of pedagogical software agents system according to quality characteristics of ISO/IEC 9126 standard, while comparing VLE Moodle with agents and VLE Moodle without agents in terms of final users, showed that the installed agent system for a final user may increase the functionality, usability and efficiency of the learning environment. The system of pedagogical software agents acting as assistants to students and tutors complements VLE Moodle with necessary functions determined during the analysis of the learning process according to possible types of learning activities and learning events.

The described system of pedagogical software agents has been presented to be implemented by Master students at Informatics Faculty of Kaunas University of Technology. Currently, the agent system realisation is about to be completed, it is being tested and since autumn term of 2012, the pilot exploitation with one group of distance learning students who use VLE Moodle in their studies is planned.

The pilot exploitation will highlight advantages and disadvantages of realised pedagogical software agents. Prior to the exploitation of pedagogical software agent system, it is planned to improve them and eliminate the noticed defects.

References

1. Amandi, A., Campop, M., Armentano, M., Berdun, L.: Intelligent Agent for Distance Learning. Informatics in Education 2, 161–180 (2003)
2. Anderson, T.D., Garrison, D.R.: Learning in a networked world: New roles and responsibilities. In: Gibson, C.C. (ed.) Distance Learners in Higher Education: Institutional Responses for Quality Outcomes, pp. 1–8. Atwood Publishing, Madison (1998)
3. Chan, T.W.: Artificial Agents in Distance Learning. International Journal of Educational Telecommunications 1(2/3), 263–282 (1995)
4. Chen, W., Wasson, B.: Intelligent Agents Supporting Distributed Collaborative Learning. In: Lin, F.O. (ed.) Designing Distributed Environments with Intelligent Software Agents, p. 311. Idea Group Publishing (2004)

5. Jaques, P., et al.: Using Pedagogical Agents to Support Collaborative Distance Learning. In: CSCL 2002, January 7-11, pp. 1–9. University of Colorado, Boulder (2002)
6. Johnson, W.L., Rickel, J.W., Lester, J.C.: Animated pedagogical agents: Face-to-face interaction in interactive learning environments. International Journal of AI in Education (11), 47–78 (2000)
7. Kim, Y., Baylor, A.L., Shen, E.: Pedagogical agents as learning companions: the impact of agent emotion and gender. Journal of Computer Assisted Learning 23(3), 220–234 (2007)
8. Kurilovas, E., Dagienė, V.: Multiple Criteria Comparative Evaluation of E-Learning Systems and Components. Informatica. Institute of Mathematics and Informatics 20(4), 499–518 (2009)
9. Leclercq, D., Poumay, M.: The 8 Learning Events Model and its principles. LabSET, University of Liège (2005), http://www.labset.net/media/prod/8LEM.pdf
10. Suh, H.J., Lee, S.W.: Collaborative Learning Agent for Promoting Group Interaction. ETRI Journal 28(4), 461–474 (2006)
11. Targamadze, A., Petrauskiene, R.: Classification of Distance Learning Agents. In: Information Technologies' 2010: Proceedings of the 16th International Conference on Information and Software Technologies, IT 2010, April 21-23, pp. 316–323. Kaunas University of Technology, Kaunas (2010)

Methodology for Developing Topic Maps Based on Principles of Ontology Engineering

Gintare Bernotaityte, Lina Nemuraite, and Milda Stankeviciene

Kaunas University of Technology, Department of Information Systems, Studentu 50-313a
{gintare.bernotaityte,lina.nemuraite,
milda.stankeviciene}@ktu.lt

Abstract. Topic Maps is knowledge representation and exchange model having rich verbalization possibilities for improving navigation-based search and understanding for human and interpretable by machine. Despite increasing usage of Topic Maps in knowledge-based information networks and portals, the flexibility of the representation often leads to disability to judge on correctness or completeness of a Topic Map model, or simply gives no rule how to model problematic actualities. The paper presents the methodology for developing Topic Maps on the base of the principles of developing ontologies extending them with recommendations for solving some problems specific to Topic Maps development: creating normalized schema; representing association properties and names, multidimensional classification hierarchies, and so on. The suitability of the methodology is analyzed via a case study for developing a topic map of Information System Development Methodologies with Ontopia tools.

Keywords: Topic Maps, ontology, Tolog, OWL.

1 Introduction

Topic Maps [1] is a knowledge representation and management model, initially intended for representing indexes and references, but later mainly applied in content management systems and large information portals, especially in Norway, Finland and other outstanding European countries. Currently, there are interests for this technology in Lithuania.

Creating of Topic Maps confronts with problems as the theoretical Topic Maps model allows unlimited flexibility of representation, close to human thinking. It is a knowledge model for human, along with possibility of processing by machine. Computer supported processing of universal Topic Maps models is not easy; consequently, existing editors of Topic Maps have limited capabilities. Creators of Topic Maps often have a lot of problems with representing particular things as there is not so much experience in the field of Topic Maps as, for comparison, in creating databases using SQL, or ontologies using Web Ontology Language (OWL, currently, OWL2).

The main motivation behind this work is the assumption that methodology for engineering ontologies may be applied for developing Topic Maps, supplementing

T. Skersys, R. Butleris, and R. Butkiene (Eds.): ICIST 2012, CCIS 319, pp. 406–419, 2012.

that methodology with aspects relevant to specifics of Topic Maps. In the current paper, we present such a methodology and analyze its suitability via a case study where the methodology was applied for implementing a topic map for UML-based Information System Development (UISD) using Ontopia tools.

The rest of the paper is structured as follows. Section 2 analyses related work. Section 3 presents the proposed methodology for developing Topic Maps. Section 4 provides a case study for applying the methodology and evaluating its suitability. Finally, we summarize conclusions and envisage future works.

2 Related Work

Topic Maps is a knowledge representation model for describing information resources about subjects in the form of networks comprised of topics, their occurrences and associations among them. "Subject" is understood as any object of reality or a node representing that object in a global network, uniquely identifiable by its URI.

According to Pepper [2], Topic Maps have much in common with ontology. OWL2 class, object or data properties coincide with Topic Maps concepts "topic", "association", and "occurrence". Both ontologies and Topic Maps have XML interchange formats; both belong to the realm of semantics and comprise graphs of concepts; both are concerned with identity; both have some (though unequal) means for inference and querying.

In addition, Pepper [2] noticed differences. On creating ontology, the fundamental matter is class generalization hierarchy and inference. Associations play the essential role in Topic Maps. Topic Maps allow define various types of names for topics, associations, and roles, therefore relations between concepts may be red as expressions in natural language. If supplemented with linguistic processing, Topic Maps technology may become an interface for semantic communicating between human and computer in natural language while in OWL2 ontology these capabilities are more restricted – there is no possibility to give separate names for roles and relations. However, Topic Maps yet have no means for defining constraints and, consequently, no Topic Map reasoners are implemented. OWL2 is well suited for computer processing, whereas semantics of Topic Maps is devoted for human. Topic Maps can help to analyze information but their inference may be made only by a query language.

There are many methodologies for creating Topic Maps [3] but they mostly are incomplete. Usually, they present guidelines, similar to principles for creating conceptual models, or are oriented to Topic Maps development process, e.g. [4], which is similar to a common process for developing software. Other methods are focused on technological aspects as generating Topic Maps from ontologies, RDF or XML documents; multilinguality; joint development, and similar. These aspects are certainly important; however, none of methodologies for developing Topic Maps are based on quality criteria, which would allow evaluate correctness, completeness and other desirable features of Topic Maps.

For these reasons we have analyzed the quality criteria used for developing ontologies, such as correctness, consistency, extendibility, minimality, competence, completeness, and normalization [5–9]. Different authors were focused on different criteria in ontology development: competence and completeness of ontology [8]; normalisation, modularity and reuse [9]. For making methodology for developing Topic Maps, we used the methodology [10], generalized on the base of the mentioned works and consisting of 8 steps. It starts on formulating requirements in the form of competence questions, creating concept model, creating instances and validating model, defining multidimensional classification hierarchies, formalizing competence questions, evaluating quality criteria, and evolving the initial model.

For applying ontology development methodology for Topic Maps, the suitability of ontology quality criteria for our purpose was analyzed and noted that these criteria could be equally applied for Topic Maps. Ontology (Topic Map) is correct, if interpretation of classifications (associations between topics) corresponds to intention of the developer; normalized, if generalization hierarchy of classes (topics) comprises homogeneous tree, consisting of disjoint sets of subtrees; consistent, if it has no conflicting features and is validated by a reasoner (Topic Map editor); complete, if includes all concepts required for answering competence questions; minimal, if includes only concepts required for answering competence questions; competent if it is able to answer all competence questions; extensible, if allows introduction of new hierarchies of classes (topics) without violating existing hierarchies. While the same criteria may be applied to ontologies and Topic Maps, their processing peculiarities are different.

Ontology individuals are classified (i.e. assigned to classes according axioms defining their properties and restrictions) by reasoners. OWL2 also has a query language SPARQL that gives the possibility to retrieve information unobtainable by reasoners. Only a query language Tolog, which capabilities are weaker in comparison with OWL2 reasoners and SPARQL (especially SPARQL 1.1), may assess topic Maps. Topic Maps have less means for ensuring their consistency, as Topic Map editors are only partially able of doing this.

The essential problem in developing Topic Maps is to understand and define associations. The most general associations describe meronymy (part and whole), generalization and specialization, causal and sequel relations, and others. There have been various attempts to define universal or specific sets of semantic relations, e.g. Universal Network Language (UNL) [11], relations for organizing knowledge [12], linguistic relations [13], and strands [14].

Universal Networking Language (UNL) is a computing language allowing processing a natural language by reflecting its functions. Nodes in UNL graph represent so called universal words, edges define relations between them [11]. UNL authors argue that their defined set of relations is able to express everything needed for formalizing natural languages. Strand concept described in [14] supports the idea that for creating meaningful information content it is desirable highlighting the reading scenario so helping readers to understand it better.

Analysis of the mentioned works allowed complementing the methodology for developing ontologies with aspects insufficiently addressed in a case of applying the same methodology to Topic Maps, i.e. formulating association names; reusing information resources; ensuring multiple classifications without violating consistency of Topic Maps; defining properties of associations; ensuring efficient navigation; ensuring identity of user interface and Topic Map etc.

3 Methodology for Developing Topic Maps

The methodology obtained by applying principles of ontology engineering for Topic Maps consists of 7 steps (Fig. 1.).

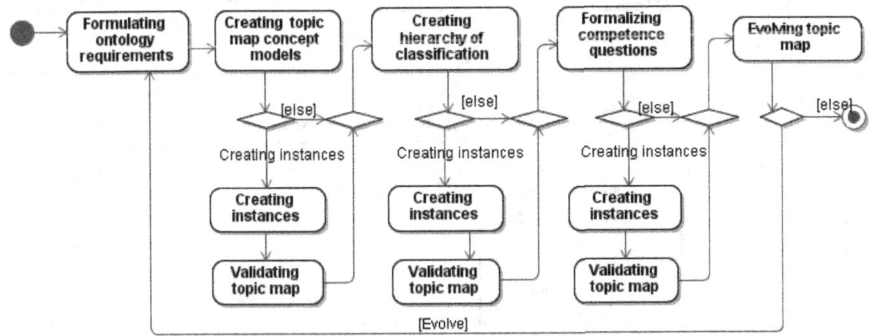

Fig. 1. Process for developing Topic Maps

1st Step. Defining requirements (competence questions). The purpose of Topic Maps is to answer all questions relevant for a domain under investigation, e.g.: What terms are used in the domain (topic, subtopic, …)? What concepts are fundamental (alternate, auxiliary, …) in the domain? What definitions (explanations, examples, and exceptions) are used for these concepts? What concepts refine them? What causes the need for these concepts? What topics are related to the concept? What are synonyms of the concept? What order is meaningful for analyzing these topics (subtopics, concepts, …)? The list of questions is constructed similarly as for ontology: on the base of user needs, general knowledge, opinion of experts etc.

2nd Step. Creating Topic Maps ontology (or schema), comprised of essential topics of domain under investigation. For representing ontologies of Topic Maps, we have used UML profile created according Topic Maps metamodel [15] (Fig. 2.), the example of applying the profile can be seen in Fig. 6.

For creating schema, the following rules should be applied.

Ontology Normalization Rule. For developing schema, identify topics essential for a domain and not derivable from other topics. These topics may comprise a single generalization hierarchy based on permanent characteristics of topics where all subtopics of one topic are disjoint. In other words, topic map's ontology must define primitive, non-derivable elements, comprising taxonomy of topics in domain under investigation. The taxonomy plays the essential role in ontologies but in Topic Maps associations among topics are much more important. The set of associations is identified from competence questions including both general, universal associations and specific ones characteristic only for the specific domain.

Reusing Resources Rule. Essential topics of the schema must be atomic, undivided elements of content, and may be reused in various application scenarios.

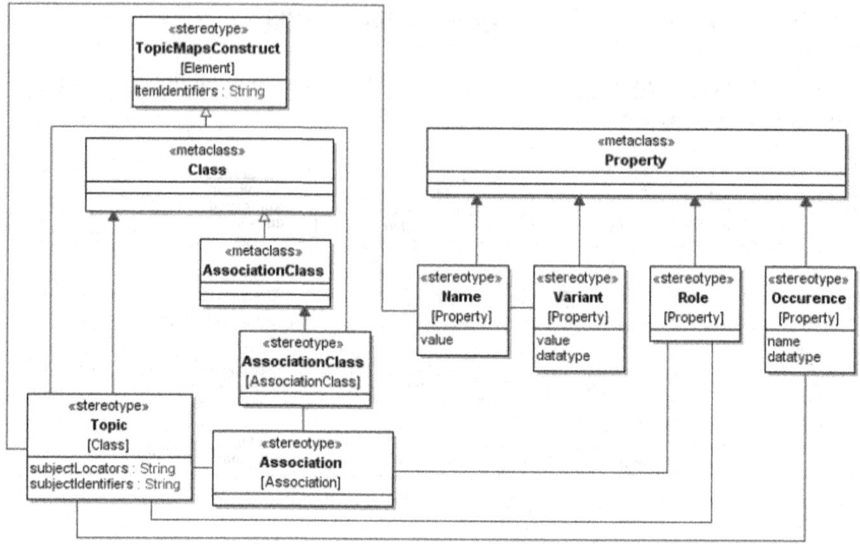

Fig. 2. Topic Maps profile

User Interface and Topic Map Identity Rule. Topic map's ontology should ensure that information content is constructed and presented according the same knowledge model, i.e. user interface is identical to the topic map.

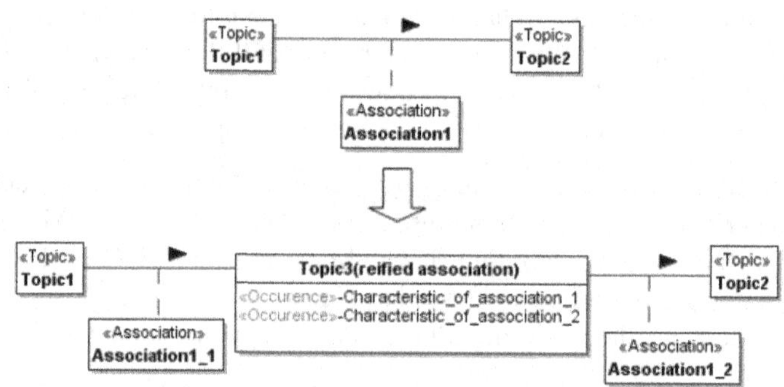

Fig. 3. Principle of defining properties of association

Association Naming Rule. For defining schema, association and role names are important. Their formulation is problematic in Lithuanian language for Topic Maps without linguistic processing due to inflection, form (plural or singular), and gender. The decision was taken to apply laconic style of naming that relates two topics using „/" symbol, e.g. "author/book" and "book/author" instead of "author has_written book" and "book is_written_by author". The chosen style allows acceptable representation of Topic Maps, but does not use all flexibility that would be possible in Topic Maps enhanced with linguistic processing.

Association Property Defining Rule. We often need to define properties of associations, e.g. for evaluating the strength of relations, their duration, place etc. (Fig. 3.).

For this purpose, we propose creating a new topic type e.g. *Topic3* that reifies the association (e.g. *Association1*) type. The new topic type should have associations with topic types playing roles in the reified association type, and occurrences representing the desired properties of the reified association. Then properties of the reified association could be accessed by queries.

3rd Step. Creating instances. The step is performed every time when new constructions are introduced into a Topic Map. Instances are attributed for elements of schema only. Instances allow checking correctness of a Topic Map, compatibility of new constructs with existing elements, and suitability for the intended purpose. Topic Maps tools do not have reasoners alike ontology processors; therefore, checking is based on an available Topic Maps editor and remains in the responsibility of developers. For automatically assuring correctness of Topic Maps, it is desirable to create and store instances by means of Database Management Systems.

4th Step. Creation of inferable topics. In Topic Maps, the problem of multiple generalization and classification arises. Usually, it is desirable to classify information resources according several topics under several criteria. In ontologies, multiple generalization / classification hierarchies are achieved by defining inferable classes. Ontology reasoners assign instances to these classes according defined axioms.

In Topic Maps, assignment of instances to new topics is possible by using queries [16], based on associations or occurrences specified. Often it is desirable classifying topics according their importance (primary, main, supplementary, auxiliary); usage (often, average, rarely used topics); complexity (elementary, middle, complex, extra complex); specific keywords, etc. Using classifying associations or occurrences allow creating of multiple virtual classifications and generalizations avoiding inserting them into schema what would burden maintenance and evolution of Topic Maps.

```
select $TOPIC4 from value($TOPICNAME1,"Section"),
topic-name($TOPICTYPE1,$TOPICNAME1),instance-of($TOPIC1,$TOPICTYPE1),

value($TOPICNAME2,"1.2.Object-oriented methodology"),
topic-name($TOPIC11,$TOPICNAME2),$TOPIC1=$TOPIC11,
value($ASSOCNAME3,"Used_in/Term"),topic-name($ASSOCTYPE3,$ASSOCNAME3),
type($ASSOC3,$ASSOCTYPE3),

value($TOPICNAME4,"Term"),topic-name($TOPICTYPE4,$TOPICNAME4),
instance-of($TOPIC4,$TOPICTYPE4),

role-player($ROLE1,$TOPIC4),association-role($ASSOC3,$ROLE1),
association-role($ASSOC3,$ROLE2),role-player($ROLE2,$TOPIC1),
$ROLE1/=$ROLE2?
```

Fig. 4. Example of Tolog query for the Topic Map presented in Fig. 6

5th Step. Formalizing competence questions. It is possible by constructing Tolog queries [17] that allow selecting information according associations. Tolog query language does not have such rich possibilities as ontology query language SPARQL 1.1 or SQL; it would not allow e.g. performing calculations. It is possible to avoid such shortcomings by keeping Topic Map instances in a database and using database means. Tolog query for a competence question "What terms are used in the topic "Object-oriented methodology"?" would look like the one in Fig. 4.

Answers to competence questions are accessible via navigating a topic map. Such navigating is based on three types of rules: association, hierarchy, and projection. Algorithm for navigating Topic Maps according these rules is presented in Fig. 5.

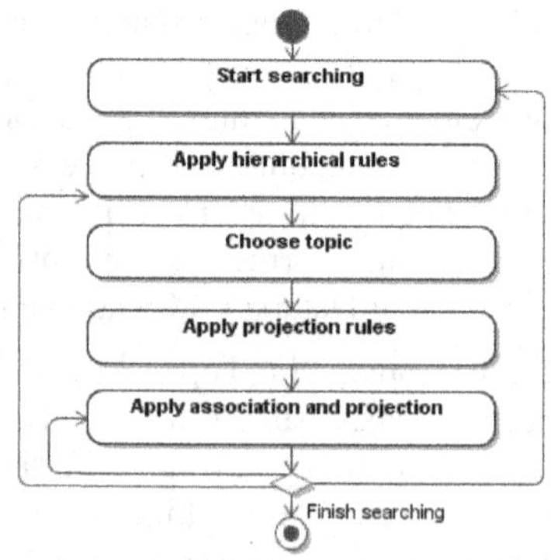

Fig. 5. Algorithm for navigating in Topic Maps

6th Step. Validating Topic Maps. Such a step is performed after every updating a topic map during its creation or maintenance. For validating a topic map, instances should be created for reflecting made decisions.

For example, after introducing a new classification hierarchy, new instances are created and correctness of their classification is analyzed. Validation encompasses the growing set of criteria; all criteria should be reached at the end of creation.

7th Step. Topic Maps evolution. Evolution should be monotonic: new topics, associations and occurrences should not conflict with existing ones but extend and refine them. New elements are inserted into topic maps following the same methodology used for their creation. For extending topic maps, merging could be applied that allows adding new instances as well as augmenting schema [18–22]. There are various possibilities for merging topic maps: identical subject identifiers, names, or even their similarity. The latter requires applying similarity-estimating rules.

4 Case Study

The purpose of the experiment, which was performed according methodology [23], is to assure the suitability of the methodology for creating topic maps according desirable criteria. The experiment should give answers to the following questions: 1) Does methodology help defining requirements for Topic Maps? 2) Does it support constructing Topic Maps schemas fulfilling requirements of normalization and reuse;

giving names for associations? 3) Does it advise introducing instances? 4) Does it help defining inferable topics, multiple classifications, properties of associations? 5) Does it advise formalizing competence questions? 6) Does it allow validating Topic Maps according correctness, completeness, consistency, normalization, minimality; does it ensure effective navigating, identity of user interface and Topic Map's content? 7) Does it support evolution of Topic Maps?

1st Question. Requirements for a desirable UISD Topic Map, as methodology suggests, were stated via the following competence questions:

What are chapters of a book? Who are authors of a book? What terms are used in a book (chapter, section, topic)? What are main/auxiliary topics of a book? What are frequently asked questions of a book? What modules use a book? What terms are used in section (chapter, book)? What terms are main (auxiliary, advanced) w.r.t. the topic, etc.

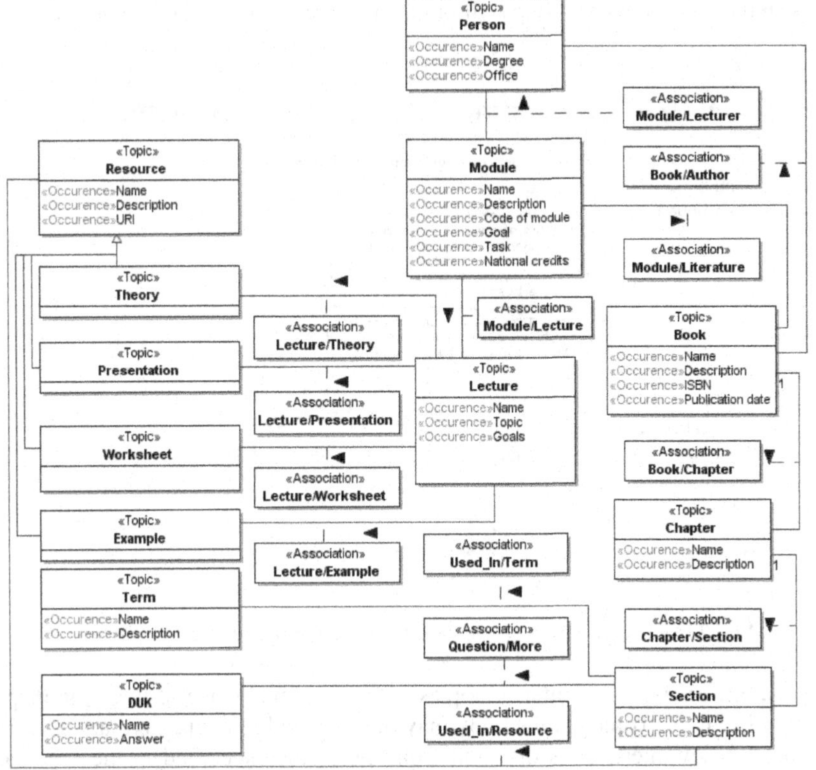

Fig. 6. Part of schema of the Topic Map of UML based Information System Development

2nd Question. A schema of the topic map created for answering aforementioned questions (Step 2) is presented in Fig. 6 where a topic "Resource" represents elements of information content (theory, presentations, worksheets), which may be used for making books or modules for studies. Resources are accessible via URIs, which may point to a local Internet server or an external source; so a topic map is able to use resources of farther topic maps and is accessible by other topic maps.

The schema (Fig. 6. satisfies requirements of normalization: it has a single hierarchy of resource types, which are non-inferable from other topics; it has all required concepts and associations, and has no redundant topics. The proposed laconic style was suitable for giving names to associations, and these names were suitable not only for the schema, but also for exposing the topic map in the user interface. The requirement for reusing resources is fulfilled as well. All types of resources are independent topics that may be used in contexts of various other topics.

Associations corresponding to the competence questions are: „Book/Author" (representing roles of a book and an author of the book in the association "Book authorship"; „Book/Chapter"; "Chapter/Section"; "Used_in/Term", etc.

3rd Question. Instances were regularly created for every topic, association and occurrence, and their correctness and suitability for representing the problem domain and purpose of the topic map were continually verified. An example of an instance of a book in the Ontopia Topic Maps editor and a Topic Map's portal is presented in Fig. 7 and 8.

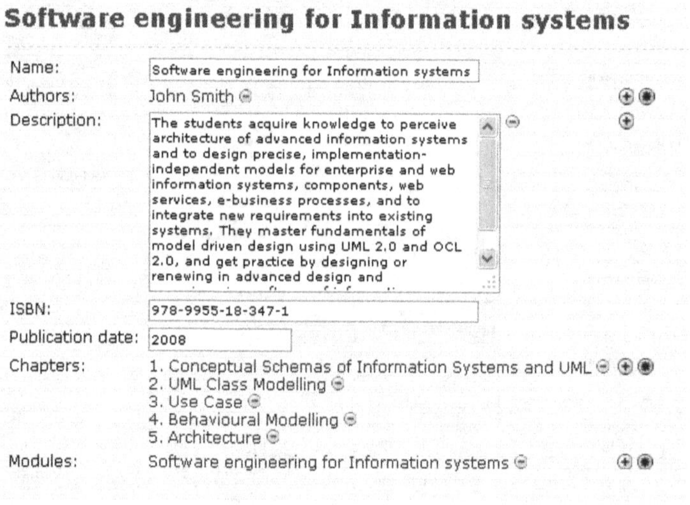

Software engineering for Information systems

Name: Software engineering for Information systems
Authors: John Smith
Description: The students acquire knowledge to perceive architecture of advanced information systems and to design precise, implementation-independent models for enterprise and web information systems, components, web services, e-business processes, and to integrate new requirements into existing systems. They master fundamentals of model driven design using UML 2.0 and OCL 2.0, and get practice by designing or renewing in advanced design and
ISBN: 978-9955-18-347-1
Publication date: 2008
Chapters: 1. Conceptual Schemas of Information Systems and UML
2. UML Class Modelling
3. Use Case
4. Behavioural Modelling
5. Architecture
Modules: Software engineering for Information systems

Fig. 7. An instance of the topic "Book" in the Ontopia Topic Maps editor

4th Question. Examples of inferred topics extending knowledge of the topic map are presented in Fig. 9. Topics of the book may be classified to main, auxiliary, advanced ones making new hierarchies different from hierarchies specified in the schema. In this way, it becomes possible to create multiple virtual classifications without explicitly introducing them into a schema as the latter would burden the maintenance of Topic Maps and even is not allowed by Topic Maps tools as Ontopia.

5th Question. For formalizing competence questions, Tolog queries are used. An example of Tolog query for classifying topics is presented in Fig. 10 where all main topics are retrieved by using basic predicates and validated during the 6th step for ensuring that a topic map is able to answer all competence questions. The view of the topic map in the portal with classified topics is presented in Fig. 11.

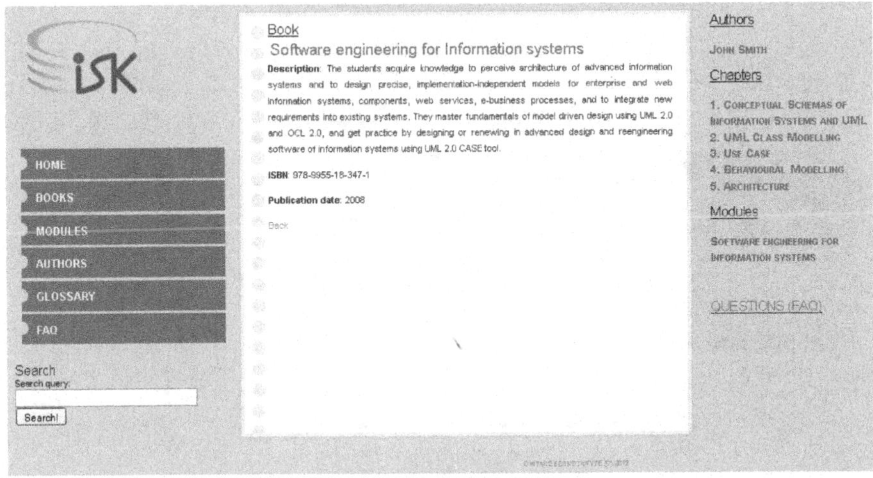

Fig. 8. An instance of the topic "Book" in the portal of the UISD Topic Map

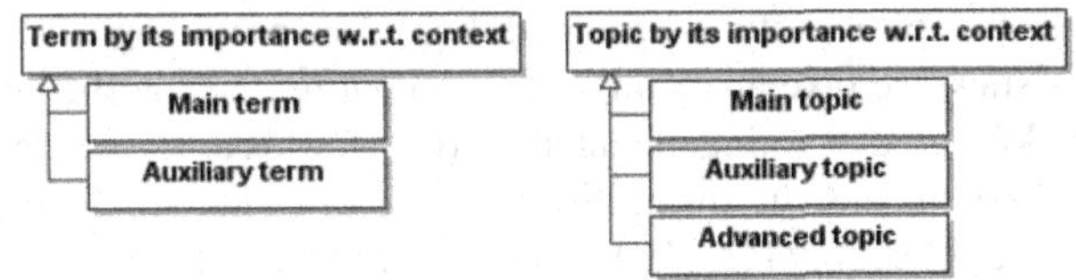

Fig. 9. An example of an inferred hierarchy in a topic map

```
select $TOPIC3  from value($ASSOCNAME1, "Book/Chapter"),
topic-name ($ASSOCTYPE1, $ASSOCNAME1), type($ASSOC1, $ASSOCTYPE1),
value($ASSOCNAME2, "Chapter/Section"), topic-name ($ASSOCTYPE2,
$ASSOCNAME2), type($ASSOC2, $ASSOCTYPE2),
value($TOPICNAME1, "Book"), topic-name($TOPICTYPE1, $TOPICNAME1),
instance-of($TOPIC1, $TOPICTYPE1), topic-name(%book%, $TOPICNAME2),
topic-name($TOPIC11, $TOPICNAME2), $TOPIC1=$TOPIC11,
role-player($ROLE1, $TOPIC11), association-role($ASSOC1, $ROLE1),
association-role($ASSOC1, $ROLE2), role-player($ROLE2, $TOPIC2),
$ROLE1/=$ROLE2,
value($TOPICNAME3, "Section"), topic-name($TOPICTYPE3, $TOPICNAME3),
instance-of($TOPIC3, $TOPICTYPE3), value($TOPICNAME4, "Chapter"),
topic-name($TOPICTYPE4, $TOPICNAME4), type($ROLE4, $TOPICTYPE4),
role-player($ROLE3, $TOPIC3), association-role($ASSOC2, $ROLE3),
association-role($ASSOC2, $ROLE4), role-player($ROLE4, $TOPIC2),
$ROLE3/=$ROLE4,
value($ASSOCNAME3, "Main topic/Resource"), topic-name($ASSOCTYPE3,
$ASSOCNAME3), type($ASSOC3, $ASSOCTYPE3),
role-player($ROLE5, $TOPIC3), association-role($ASSOC3, $ROLE5),
association-role($ASSOC3, $ROLE6), role-player($ROLE6, $TOPIC2),
$ROLE5/=$ROLE6 order by $TOPIC3 asc?
```

Fig. 10. An example of a Tolog query with classification of topics

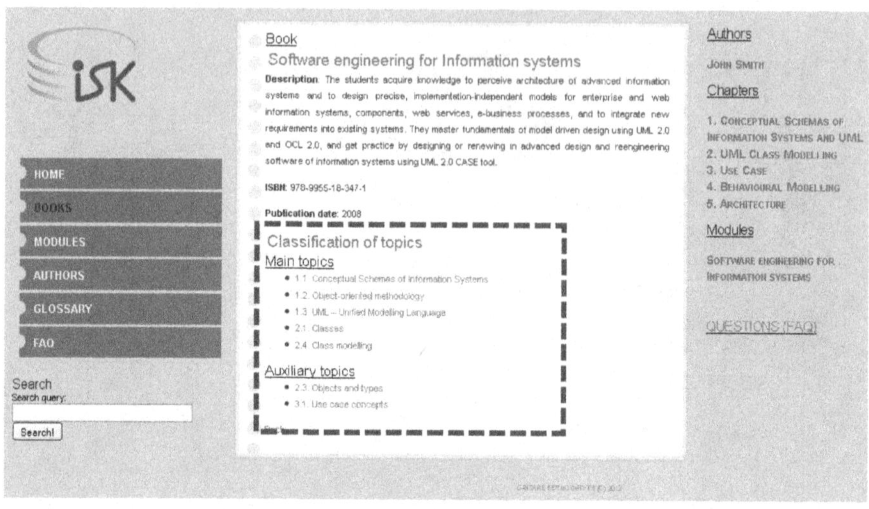

Fig. 11. An example of Topic Maps with classification of topics

For assessing the possibility of methodology for providing associations with certain characteristics, we take an example for evaluating the significance of the term for some topic. We used a rating in interval [0; 1] where "1" means the greatest significance, and "0" means the insignificance. The association "Section/Term" was reified by a topic "Section/Term", having occurrence "Term_Rating" and two associations with topics "Section" and "Term". For visualizing ratings, the Tolog query (Fig. 12) returns all terms of a section sorted by their ratings (Fig. 13).

```
select $TOPIC2, $TOPIC3, $occ FROM
value($ASSOCNAME1, "Section/Term_Rating"),
topic-name($ASSOCTYPE1, $ASSOCNAME1), type($ASSOC1, $ASSOCTYPE1),

value($TOPICNAME1, "Section"),topic-name($TOPICTYPE1, $TOPICNAME1),
instance-of($TOPIC1, $TOPICTYPE1),
topic-name(%topic%, $TOPICNAME2), topic-name($TOPIC11, $TOPICNAME2),
$TOPIC1=$TOPIC11,
role-player($ROLE1, $TOPIC11), association-role($ASSOC1, $ROLE1),
association-role($ASSOC1, $ROLE2),role-player($ROLE2, $TOPIC2),
$ROLE1/=$ROLE2,
value($TOPICNAME3, "Term"), topic-name($TOPICTYPE3, $TOPICNAME3),
instance-of($TOPIC3, $TOPICTYPE3),
value($ASSOCNAME3, "Source/Term_Rating"),
topic-name($ASSOCTYPE3, $ASSOCNAME3), type($ASSOC3, $ASSOCTYPE3),
role-player($ROLE3, $TOPIC3), association-role($ASSOC3, $ROLE3),
association-role($ASSOC3, $ROLE4),  role-player($ROLE4, $TOPIC2),
$ROLE3/=$ROLE4,
occurrence( $TOPIC2, $occ ), type( $occ, $type) order by $occ desc?
```

Fig. 12. Tolog query for sorting terms of a section according to their significance

TOPIC2	TOPIC3	occ
1.1. Conceptual model	Conceptual model	[basic.Occurrence, 4290 <0.9>]
1.1. Conceptual schema	Conceptual schema	[basic.Occurrence, 4288 <0.5>]
1.1. Concept	Concept	[basic.Occurrence, 422 <0.1>]

(a)

Terms by relevance

1. Conceptual model
2. Conceptual schema
3. Concept

(b)

Fig. 13. Results of the query in Fig. 12: (a) – in Omnigator; (b) – in portal

6th Question. The created Topic Map of Information System Development Methodologies (TM UISD) is correct as it was recognized such by the developer herself and by authors of presented modules and books. In addition, the TM UISD is complete as it gives answers to all competence questions.

The TM UISD is consistent, as the Ontopia editor has exhibited no errors for introduced instances. However, the Ontopia editor checks only data types and cardinalities; assurance of other integrity constraints is on the responsibility of the developer.

The TM UISD ontology is normalized, as it has a single specialization hierarchy based on permanent properties; all instances were created only for elements of schema, but not for inferable topics or associations.

The TM UISD also conforms to requirement of minimality, as it has no redundant topics or associations.

Finally, the user interface of TM UISD is identical to the TM UISD as you can see, e.g., in Fig. 7 and Fig. 8. No additional elements were used for representing the created Topic Map in the portal.

7th Question. The methodology supports evolution of Topic Maps, as we can evolve the developed Topic Map by applying the same steps as for its initial creation. E.g., let us introduce the additional competence question "What papers are published by persons?" We should create a topic "Paper", an occurrence "Paper_title", roles "Author" and "Publication", and association "Publication/Author". Then we should insert instances and validate the Topic Map. If we additionally introduce questions "What journal has published the paper?", "What is the ISSN, the volume and the year of the journal?" we should create a topic "Journal", occurrences "ISSN", "Journal_title", "Journal_volume", "Journal_year", and association "Journal/Paper".

Extending the Topic Map (7th Step), it is desirable to apply the concept of strands for refining current atomic elements of the content. It would be useful to adapt a certain pattern for analyzing the content of the TM UISD: the relevance of a topic; its concepts; definitions and explanations of concepts; problems, solved by the topic; goals and tasks of the topic; solving methods; criteria, applied to solutions; examples; applications; exceptions; tips; references; related topics, etc. It would allow analyzing the content in more detail and providing the way for learning it.

In addition, we can use the merging as means for extending the Topic Map with local or external Topic Maps for augmenting its schema or enlarging a number of instances.

5 Conclusion and Future Works

Analysis of methodologies for developing Topic Maps and ontologies has shown that methodologies for developing Topic Maps are immature; they do not provide rules for solving problems arising during construction of Topic Maps, and do not allow evaluate their correctness, completeness, normalization, etc. In other words, it is not clear from what to start developing a Topic Map and how to arbitrate about its goodness.

Due to similarity of Topic Maps and ontologies, the hypothesis was raised about the legitimacy of applying for Topic Maps the same set of criteria as for ontology engineering. During analysis, the methodology of ontology engineering was supplemented with specific solutions needed for Topic Maps: giving names and properties for associations; assuring identity of user interface and Topic Map's content; implementing efficient navigation; making inference, and so on.

The created methodology was systematically analyzed in a case study for implementing the Topic Map of UML based Information System Development. The case study has shown that the methodology was suitable for creating the Topic Map, validating its competence, consistency, normalization and completeness. In addition, it allowed evolving the Topic Map after finalizing its development.

The presented methodology is substantial for starting creation of reasonable Topic Maps; however, it is not an exhaustive solution for all cases of applying Topic Maps. Our nearest future work will be devoted for refining Topic Maps content with learning patterns but the major challenges are concerned with automation of creating and evolving Topic Maps, and enhancing them with linguistic processing.

References

1. Pepper, S.: Topic Maps. In: Encyclopedia of Library and Information Sciences, 3rd edn., pp. 1–19. Taylor & Francis (2010)
2. Pepper, S.: Topic Maps and the Semantic Web, `http://topicmaps.wordpress.com/2008/05/11/topic-maps-and-the-semantic-web/`
3. Ellouze, N., Metais, E., Ahmed, M.: State of the Art on Topic Maps Building Approacher. In: Kutsche, R.D., Milanovic, N. (eds.) MBSDI 2008. CCIS, vol. 8, pp. 102–112. Springer, Heidelberg (2008)
4. Garshol, L.M.: Towards a Methodology for Developing Topic Maps Ontologies. In: Maicher, L., Sigel, A., Garshol, L.M. (eds.) TMRA 2006. LNCS (LNAI), vol. 4438, pp. 20–31. Springer, Heidelberg (2007)
5. Cordi, V., Mascardi, V.: Checking the Completeness of Ontologies: a Case Study from the Semantic Web. In: Proceedings of the Italian Conference on Computational Logic (CILC 2004), vol. 390, pp. 1–15. Quaderno del Dipartimento di Matematica, University of Parma (2004)
6. Cornet, R., Abu-Hanna, A.: Two DL–based methods for auditing medical terminological systems. In: AMIA Annu. Symp. Proc., pp. 166–170 (2005)
7. Gruber, T.R.: Toward Principles for the Design of Ontologies Used for Knowledge Sharing. Technical report, KSL–93–04, Knowledge Systems Laboratory, Stanford University (1993)

8. Grüninger, M., Fox, M.S.: Methodology for the Design and Evaluation of Ontologies. In: Proceedingsofthe IJCAI Workshop on Basic Ontological Issues in Knowledge Sharing, pp. 1–10. AAAI Press, Menlo Park (1995)
9. Rector, A.L.: Normalisation of ontology implementations: Towards modularity, re-use, and maintainability. In: Proceedings of Workshop on Ontologies for Multiagent Systems (OMAS) in Conjunction with European Knowledge Acquisition Workshop, pp. 1–16 (2002)
10. Nemuraite, L., Paradauskas, B.: A Methodology for Engineering OWL 2 Ontologies in Practise Considering their Semantic Normalisation and Completeness. Electronics and Electrical Engineering 4(120), 89–94 (2012)
11. UNL Foundation. The Universal NetworkingLanguage (UNL) Specifications. Version 3 Edition UNL Center (December 2004)
12. Green, R.: Relationships in the Organization of Knowledge: An Overview. In: Bean, Green (eds.) Relationships in the Organization of Knowledge. Information Science and Knowledge Management, vol. 2, pp. 3–18. Kluwer Academic Publishers, Dordrecht (2001)
13. Loos, E.E., Anderson, S., Day Jr., D.H., Jordan, P.C., Wingate, J.D.: Glossary of linguistic terms. SIL International (2003)
14. Delcambre, L., Archer, D., Price, S., Britell, S.: Superimposing a strand map over lectures and text book content. Journal of Computing Sciences in Colleges 27(1), 143–151 (2011)
15. OMG. Ontology Definition Metamodel. OMG Document Number: ptc/2008-09-07
16. The Built-in tolog Predicates, Reference Documentation, `http://www.ontopia.net/omnigator/docs/query/predicate-reference.html#p-less-than`
17. Garshol, L.M.: Tolog. A Topic Maps Query Language. Ontopia, `http://www.ontopia.net/topicmaps/materials/tolog.html`
18. Chung, H., Kim, J.: Conflict Detection and Resolution in Merging of Topic Maps. In: Proceedings of International Conference on Convergance Infromation Technology, pp. 907–912 (2007)
19. Kim, J., Shin, H., Kim, H.: Shema and Constraints-based Matching and Merging of Topic Maps. Information Processing and Management 43, 930–945 (2007)
20. Maicher, L., Witschek, H.F.: Merging of Distributed Topic Maps based on the Subject Identity Measure (SIM) Approach. In: Proceeding of LIT, vol. 4, pp. 229–238 (2004)
21. Moore, G., Ahmed, K.: An Introduction to Topic Maps, `http://msdn.microsoft.com/en-us/library/aa480048.aspx`
22. Xue, Y., Feng, W.L.B., Cao, W.: Merging of Topic Maps Based on Corpus. In: 2010 International Conference on Electrical and Control Engineering, pp. 2840–2843 (2010)
23. Runeson, P., Host, M.: Guidelines for conducting and reporting case study research in software engineering. Empirical Software Engineering 14(2), 131–164 (2009)

Requirements for Semantic Business Vocabularies and Rules for Transforming Them into Consistent OWL2 Ontologies

Jaroslav Karpovic, Lina Nemuraite, and Milda Stankeviciene

KaunasUniversity of Technology, Department of Information Systems, Studentu 50-313a
jaroslav.karpovic@stud.ktu.lt,
{lina.nemuraite,milda.stankeviciene}@ktu.lt

Abstract. Structured language, based on Semantics of Business Vocabulary and Business Rules (SBVR), can be seen as domain expert friendly means for developing OWL2 ontologies, which are becoming more and more important in Semantic Web and Enterprise applications. The goal of the paper is to present transformations from SBVR specifications to ontologies and to describe conditions for creating "right" vocabularies in order to obtain consistent ontologies without losing information. The need for such approach is caused by several reasons. Concept models rely on the closed world assumption, whereas ontologies rely on the open one where every constraint should be explicitly specified. Both SBVR and OWL2 have terminology related part, desirable being separated from the substantial ontology. We suggest rules that can help creating meaningful SBVR vocabularies regarding consequences of affecting the behavior of ontology reasoners, taking advantages of ontologies and retaining terminological information separately from the main ontology.

Keywords: Semantics, ontology, business vocabulary, business rules, transformations, consistency, SBVR, OWL2, ATL.

1 Introduction

Semantics of Business Vocabulary and Business Rules (SBVR) is the OMG metamodel [1] for raising the abstraction level of descriptions and meaning of business concepts and business rules, and making them understandable for business experts as well as for software systems. It was designed for describing business for business people but later it was recognized that SBVR is rather suitable for describing software artefacts supporting that business. SBVR is not oriented to specification of specific technologies, but we cannot neglect the fact that we need specific vocabularies having some additional peculiarities for describing business concepts and rules that should be transformed into database schemas, UML models [2], Web Services [3] or ontologies.

SBVR can act as a human understandable interface between business participants and semantic technologies, such as Web Ontology Language OWL2 [4], which have capabilities for reasoning and querying semantic specifications. In our previous work

T. Skersys, R. Butleris, and R. Butkiene (Eds.): ICIST 2012, CCIS 319, pp. 420–435, 2012.

[5], we have considered transformations of main SBVR concepts into Web Ontology Language OWL2. The current paper presents the next version of transformations from SBVR into OWL2, which regards several new aspects that have emerged in the course of applying obtained ontologies for querying and reasoning.

For enabling reasoning and querying, SBVR business vocabularies and rules should produce consistent ontologies. What additional axioms should be specified and what should be prohibited in SBVR vocabulary for ensuring such consistency?

Second, SBVR business vocabularies and rules should be considered from ontology point of view: what is reasonable to specify if we are seeking for usage of ontologies obtained from SBVR specifications. Should the same SBVR specification be equally suitable for transforming into OWL2 and, e.g., UML? SBVR metamodel allows to represent meanings exclusively typical for OWL2 ontology language as specialization of roles and fact types but, for example, has no direct concepts for defining transitive, reflexive and other characteristics of fact types – such properties are meaningful in OWL2. From the other side, OWL2 is limited to binary relations, while SBVR allows specifying n-ary ones etc.

Third, SBVR to OWL2 transformation should be lossless – how is it possible to achieve? SBVR models are focused on meaning and multiple representations of meaning, i.e., they have terminological and linguistic elements. OWL2 is rather focused on representation of meaning. Practically, linguistic ontologies are far from mature; therefore there is no predefined solution for that problem. Several possibilities exist – separating linguistic ontologies and substantial concept ontologies obtained from non-linguistic SBVR elements; mixing linguistic and non-linguistic elements, or representing linguistic information in annotations. In our point of view, SBVR representations should be separated from meanings and presented in a special ontology.

The rest of the paper is structured as follows. In Section 2, the related work is considered. Section 3 presents an example, which is used in SBVR into OWL2 transformations, described in Section 4. Section 4 present requirements for creating SBVR vocabularies that are intended for transforming into OWL2 ontologies. Section 6 describes principles of implementing transformations from SBVR into OWL2. Finally, Section 7 draws conclusions and outlines future works.

2 Related Works

Currently, explicitly specified SBVR transformation into OWL2 does not exist, but there are some close works. SBVR and OWL2 were created to be compliant with Common Logics [6]; therefore, SBVR concepts can be mapped to OWL2 concepts. The correspondences between SBVR and the previous version of Web Ontology Language (OWL) concepts are presented in SBVR specification itself [1] but such mapping is insufficient for OWL2. SBVR metamodel was created on the base of Object Role Modelling (ORM2), authored by Halpin [7], and works of Business Rule Group. There are ORM2 mappings to Description Logics (DL) [8] and even direct mapping to OWL2 [9], but the latter is mostly incorrect. The most exhaustive ORM2 mapping to First Order Logic (FOL) is described in [10] where the essential theoretical backgrounds are presented that are needed in order to provide a formally consistent translation of ORM2 conceptual schema into the OWL2 ontologies. Formalization in [10] is close to [8] with several improvements. The mapping [10] is used for transforming SBVR into OWL2, however, SBVRToOWL2 transformations are not explicitly presented, and their implementation is enclosed in commercial software. Besides, ORM2 and SBVR mappings to OWL2 are not exactly the same. SBVR has surface semantics beyond deep semantics [11], which may be formalized in FOL or DL. This surface semantics involves both terminological and linguistic concepts. It is desirable to involve that semantics into OWL2 ontologies for applications of Semantic Web.

The terminological knowledge in SBVR is presented by synonyms and synonymous forms; preferred, non-preferred and prohibited representations. It should be mentioned that synonyms in ontologies usually are modelled as classes related by synonym relation (e.g. synsets in WordNet ontology) thus mixing conceptual semantics with terminology. In SKOS ontology [12], preferred, hidden or alternative labels are modelled as subproperties of annotation property "Label", and notations are modelled as data properties. Linguistic knowledge in SBVR is expressed by representations that may be designations, placeholders and definitions for concepts; fact type forms for fact types, and statements for propositions. Statements have the most complex structure constructed from various combinations of designations and fact type forms that depend on logical formulations of propositions. Besides arguments of predicates, SBVR allows to recover structure of sentences and word collocations. However, it does not specify morphological and syntactic characteristics appropriate for complete lexical semantics.

In OWL2 models, annotation labels often are used for expressing naming of classes, object and data properties, and individuals. Labels are insufficient for presenting linguistic knowledge extracted from SBVR vocabularies and rules. There are several possibilities to map SBVR terminological and linguistic information to ontology concepts using simplified [13] or complex [14] linguistic models. The most relevant approach for expressing linguistic, terminological and ontological information is presented by Cimiano et al. [15] where it is stated that linguistic and ontological levels should be clearly separated aiming at clearly associating linguistic information to ontological entities. Such separation should allow to associate different lexicons with one and the same ontology, to specify the meaning of linguistic constructions with respect to ontologies of various domains, and to support representation of complex lexical entries for multiple languages. The approach overlaps with SBVR in many aspects though SBVR lacks complete linguistic representations. Therefore, we will regard the principle of separation in defining SBVR transformations into OWL2 by creating separate ontologies for domain concepts (meanings) and representations.

For transforming SBVR into OWL2, we have chosen the OWL2 metamodel based on its direct semantics [16] for its conceptual clarity. OWL2 also has RDF based semantics [17] but RDF based metamodel of OWL2 still does not exist; it is expected to be finalized in a new version of ontology definition metamodel [6]. A mapping from OWL2 to RDF graphs is defined in [18], and it is possible to convert OWL2 Functional style ontologies into RDF documents [19]; but the reverse is not always true. The RDF format is more flexible, capable representing the OWL2 FULL, whereas OWL2 Functional style ontologies are limited to Description Logics (DL). Consequently, our transformations are limited to Description Logics, but we do not consider this as a shortcoming as current ontology reasoners are able to work with OWL2 DL compatible ontologies only. Therefore, SBVR vocabularies under transformation should conform to Description Logics as well as to regard particularities of OWL2 ontologies allowing efficient reasoning, maintenance and evolution.

3 Running Example

For illustrating SBVR into OWL2 transformations, we will use SBVR Vocabulary "Citations". SBVR vocabulary is presented in Fig. 1 as UML class diagram.

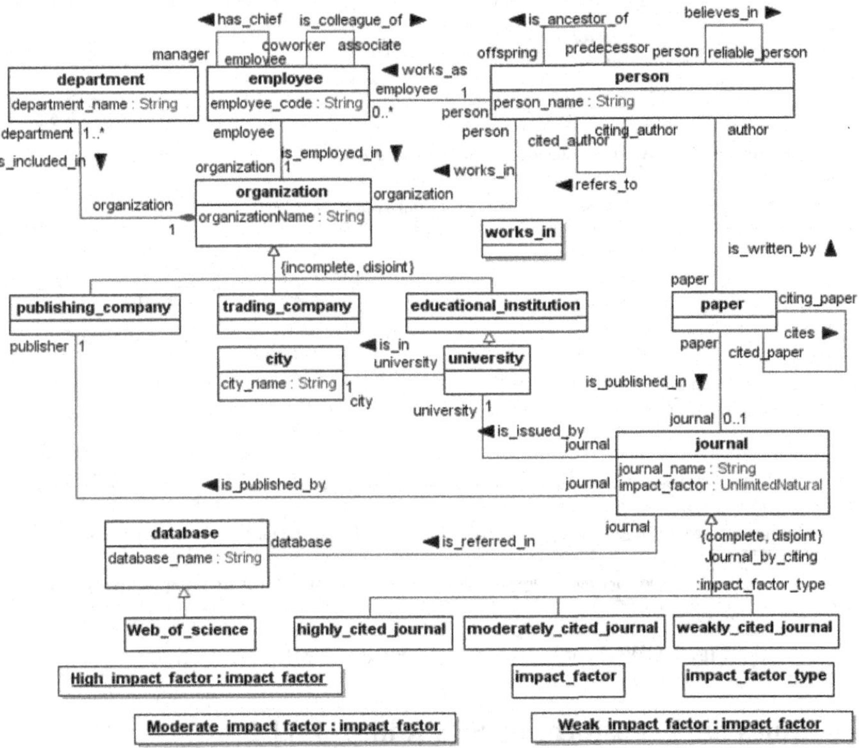

Fig. 1. SBVR vocabulary for Citations represented as UML class diagram

In Fig. 1, UML classes correspond to SBVR object types, UML associations (compositions) represent SBVR associative (partitive) fact types, and UML attributes render SBVR roles related to object types via `is_property_of` fact types; generalization sets represent categorization schemes or segmentations.

OWL2 ontologies obtained from SBVR vocabularies and presented as UML diagrams would have almost the same appearance where OWL2 classes would correspond to UML classes, OWL2 object properties to UML associations or compositions, and OWL2 data properties to UML attributes; however, object properties may differ by constructions of names. Therefore, we will use Fig. 1 for explaining the considered problem domain represented in SBVR, and Fig. 2 for its representation in OWL2. Part of SBVR business rules as well as OWL2 axioms are not seen on UML class diagrams and they will be additionally explained.

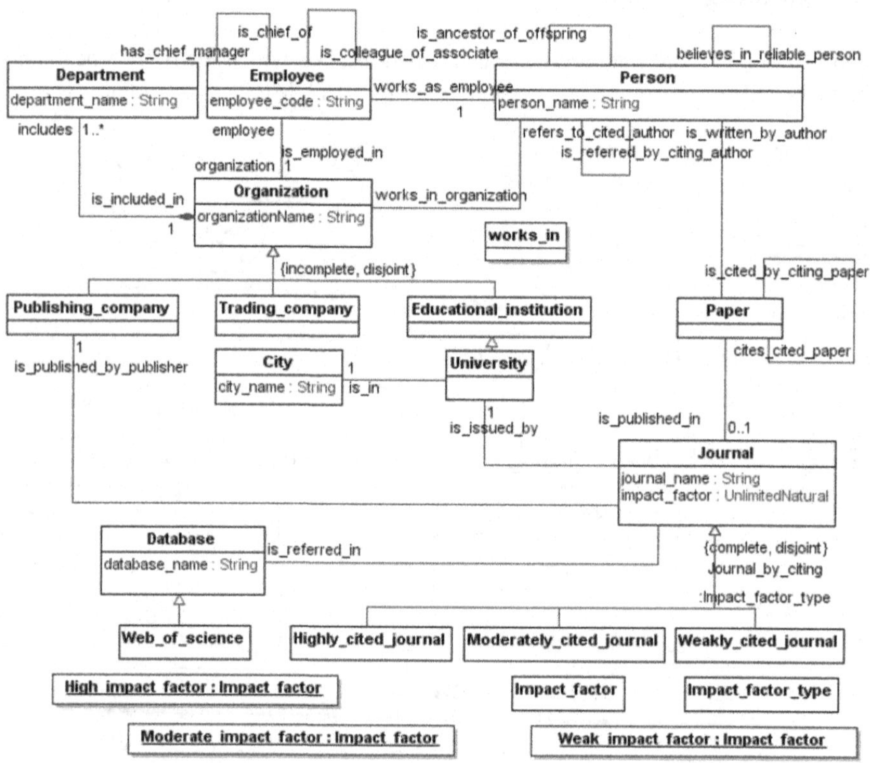

Fig. 2. OWL2 for Citations represented as UML class diagram

4 Rules for Transforming SBVR into OWL2

For the sake of comprehension, we will shortly present main transformation rules described in [4], appended with additional rules, giving more attention for previously unconsidered factors. For SBVR specifications, we use the SBVR style for `terms`, *`verbs`*, Names and `keywords` [1]. For OWL2, we use its abstract syntax [4].

Rule 1. Transforming SBVR Vocabulary into OWL2 Ontology, e.g.:

```
Citations
General concept: vocabulary → Ontology (Citations)
```

Rule 2. Transforming SBVR primitive concepts into XSD data types used in OWL2. SBVR integer is transformed into OWL2 integer; "number" is transformed into OWL2 "real"; "text" – into "string", "boolean" – into "boolean". In practise, SBVR metamodel may be extended by other primitive concepts required by a domain under consideration.

Rule 3. Transforming SBVR object types into OWL2 classes, e.g.:

```
paper →  Declaration (Class (Paper))
```

Rule 4. Transforming SBVR binary associative fact type AFT into OWL2 object property OPE. If the AFT (represented by its preferred fact type form) has a second fact type role different from an object type it ranges over then a name of OPE is obtained by concatenating the preferred representation of the verb phrase of AFT with a preferred representation of that fact type role. Otherwise, the AFT verb phrase is transformed into the name of OPE. Object type the first fact type role ranges over is transformed into a domain of OPE and object type the second fact type role ranges over is transformed into its range.

Example for case 1:

```
paper is_published_in journal →
  Declaration(ObjectProperty(is_published_in))
  ObjectPropertyDomain (is_published_in Paper)
  ObjectPropertyRange(is_published_in Journal)
```

Example for case 2:

```
paper is_written_by author →
  Declaration(ObjectProperty (is_written_by_author))
  ObjectPropertyDomain (is_written_by_author Paper)
  ObjectPropertyRange(is_written_by_author Person)
```

In a reverse transformation, concatenated names may be restored from specifications of fact type forms, representing fact types, in representation ontology, which is not presented in current paper. A fact type form consists of a verb phrase and placeholders, representing fact type roles. Therefore, it is possible to preserve the original SBVR representation of OWL2 object properties by creating ontology for representations.

Rule 5. Transforming a SBVR partitive fact type PTF is analogous to ATF. However, for expressing all semantics of partitive fact types additional axioms should be introduced for relating life cycles of things related by such an inclusion. Various forms of inclusions are defined in upper ontologies such as e.g. Dolce; a more deep analysis of transforming partitive fact types is not considered in current paper. .

Rule 6. Transforming specialization between a pair of object types into `SubClassOf` axiom between more specific and more general object types:

```
university
  General_concept: educational_institution →
    SubClassOf(University Educational_institution)_
```

Rule 7. Transforming specialization between a pair of SBVR (associative or partitive) fact types into OWL2 `SubObjectProperty`. (Examples for this rule are not presented in Fig. 1–2).

Case 1. If a generalised AFT (represented by its preferred fact type form) has a second fact type role the same as the object type it ranges over and its verb phrase (in its preferred form) is the same as of its general concept type then the `SubObjectPropertyOf` axiom is not created and the specialization between a pair of SBVR fact types should be replaced by specializations between object types. `ObjectUnionOf` of ranges, obtained by transforming object types of the second fact type roles of both AFTs. Also, if the first fact type role of the generalised AFT is same as the object type it ranges over the `ObjectUnionOf` of domains obtained by transforming object types of the first fact type roles of both AFT is created.

```
university
  General concept: organization
city
  General concept: location
university is_in city
  General concept: organization is_in location →
   Declaration(ObjectProperty (is_in))
   ObjectPropertyDomain (is_in(ObjectUnionOf(Organization University))
   ObjectPropertyRange(is_in(ObjectUnionOf(Location City))
   ObjectUnionOf(University Organization))
```

Case 2. If a generalised AFT (in its preferred fact type form) has a second fact type role SFTR different from the object type OT it ranges over and the concatenation of representations of the SFTR and OT is different from the corresponding concatenation of the corresponding ones of the generalizing AFT then the `SubObjectPropertyOf` axiom is created, e.g.:

```
producer
  Concept type: role
  General concept: organization
publisher
  Concept_type: role
  General_concept: publishing_company
journal is_published_by publisher
  General concept: product is_produced_by producer →
SubObjectPropertyOf(is_published_by_publisher is_produced_by_producer)
```

Case 3. If a generalised AFT (in its preferred fact type form) has a designation of the second fact type role the same as the object type it ranges over but its verb phrase (in its preferred form) is different from the representation of its general concept type then the `SubObjectPropertyOf` axiom is created, e.g. (the case is not presented in Fig.1):

```
organization
publishing_company
 General concept: organization
journal is_published_by publishing_company
 General concept: product is_produced_by organization →
  SubObjectPropertyOf(is_published_by is_produced_by)
```

Rule 8. Transforming SBVR alethic or deontic business rule having "at most one" quantification over associative or partitive fact type into OWL2 functional property (*Case 1*). The alternative is to transform "at most one" quantification into OWL2 cardinality (*Case 2*) though a definition of an object's property as functional is much simpler.

```
It is necessary that paper is_published_in at most one journal. →
  Case 1.
  FunctionalObjectProperty(is_published_in)
  Case 2.
  SubClassOf(Paper ObjectMaxCardinality(1 is_published_in Journal))
```

Rule 9. Transforming SBVR alethic or deontic business rules expressing existential ("at least one") quantifications over associative or partitive fact types into OWL2 existential class expressions `SomeValuesFrom` (*Case 1*). The alternative is to transform "at least one" quantification into OWL2 cardinality restriction (*Case 2*).

```
It is obligatory that organization includes at least one department. →
  Case 1.
  SubClassOf(Organization ObjectSomeValuesFrom(includes Department))
  Case 2.
  SubClassOf(Organization ObjectMinCardinality(1 includes Department))
```

Rule 10. Transforming SBVR alethic or deontic business rules having "at most n", "at least n", "exactly n", "numeric range" quantifications into corresponding OWL2 cardinality restrictions is similar as in rules 8 or 9.

Rule 11. Rules for transforming quantifications, expressed over *`is_property_of`* fact types, into restrictions on OWL2 data properties are similar as in Rules 8 – 10.

Rule 12. Transforming SBVR business rule into OWL2 inverse property. As only preferred representations are used for transforming SBVR meanings, a resulting OWL2 ontology would not have inverse properties. It does not mean a loss of meaning. However, it may be desirable having inverse properties. For such cases, a dedicated alethic SBVR business rule should be explicitly defined that would be transformed into inverse object property, e.g.:

```
It is necessary that cited_paper is_cited_by citing_paper
  if citing_paper cites cited_paper.→
InverseObjectProperties(is_cited_by_citing_paper cites_cited_paper)
```

Such a rule may be directly transformed into SWRL rule (as well as 13–15 rules), but we give the priority to applying OWL2 concepts, and transformations into SWRL rules would be used only when it would be impossible to express an intended meaning in OWL2.

Rule 13. Transforming SBVR business rule into OWL2 symmetric property. The rule holds for SBVR alethic or deontic business rule of the form as, e.g.:

```
It is necessary that thing_1[coworker]
 is_colleague_of  thing_2[associate]
 if thing_2[associate] is_colleague_of thing_1[coworker].→
   SymmetricObjectProperty(is_colleague_of_associate)
```

Rule 14. Transforming SBVR business rule into OWL2 asymmetric property is similar to Rule 13, e.g.:

```
It is impossible that thing_1[employee] is_chief_of thing_2[manager]
  if thing_2[manager] is_chief_of thing_1[employee].→
AssymmetricObjectProperty(is_chief_of)
```

Rule 15. Transforming SBVR business rule into OWL2 reflexive property. The rule holds for SBVR alethic or deontic business rule of the form as, e.g.:

```
It is necessary that thing_1[person] believes_in thing_2
[reliable_person] if thing_1 is thing_2.→
   ReflexiveObjectProperty(believes_in_reliable_person)
```

Rule 16. Transforming SBVR business rule into OWL2 irreflexive property. The rule holds for SBVR alethic or deontic business rule of the form as, e.g.:

```
It is impossible that thing_1[employee] is_chief_of thing_2[manager]
  if thing_1 is thing_2.→
    IrreflexiveObjectProperty(is_chief_of)
```

Rule 17. Transforming SBVR alethic or deontic business rule into OWL2 transitive object property. For identifying transitive object properties, complex condition should be verified but a result is simple, e.g.:

```
It is necessary that thing_1 [predecessor]
  is_ancestor_of thing_3 [offspring]
  if thing_1[predecessor] is_ancestor_of thing_2[offspring]
  and thing_2[precessor] is_ancestor_of thing_3[offspring]. →
   TransitiveObjectProperty(is_ancestor_of_offspring)
   ObjectPropertyDomain (is_ancestor_of_offspring Person)
   ObjectPropertyRange(is_ancestor_of_offspring Person)
```

Rule 18. Transforming SBVR associative fact types "concept1 is_coextensive_with concept2" into OWL2 equivalent concepts (classes or object properties). Equivalence may be used for objectification of fact types, e.g.:

```
 employee is_coextensive_with works_in →
   EquivalentClasses(Employee works_in)
```

Rule 19. Transforming SBVR business rules into OWL2 object property chains, e.g.:_

```
It is necessary that person works_in organization if person works_as
  employee that is_employed_in that organization →
    SubObjectPropertyOf(ObjectPropertyChain(works_as is_employed_in)
      works_in)
```

Rule 20. Transforming SBVR negations into OWL2 complement, e.g.:

```
It is impossible that trading company is educational institution. →
SubClassOf(Trading_company ObjectComplementOf(Educational_institution))
```

Rule 21. Transforming SBVR categorization schemes and segmentations, that allow defining multiple specializations of the same object type, e.g.:

```
Journal_by_citing
 Necessity: segmentation for general_concept journal
   that subdivides journal by impact_factor_type
highly_cited_journal
 General_concept: journal
 Necessity: is_included_in Journal by citing
moderately_cited_journal
 General_concept: journal
 Necessity: is_included_in Journal by citing
weakly_cited_journal
 General_concept: journal
 Necessity: is_included_in Journal by citing
```

We present a single segmentation, but other segmentations or categorization schemes may be defined for the concept, e.g., journals by field, journals by periodicity, etc. All segmentations or categorization schemes are equivalent to a general concept they categorize; all specializing concepts in the same categorization scheme or segmentation are disjoint; and disjoint union axiom is defined for specializing concepts of the same segmentation:

```
EquivalentClasses(Journal Journal_by_citing)
SubClassOf(Highly_cited_journal Journal_by_citing)
SubClassOf(Moderately_cited_journal Journal_by_citing)
SubClassOf(Weakly_cited_journal Journal_by_citing)
EquivalentClasses(Journal_by_citing ObjectUnionOf
(Highly_cited_journal Moderately_cited_journal Weakly_cited_journal))
DisjointUnion(Journal_by_citing Highly_cited_journal
  Moderately_cited_journal Weakly_cited_journal)
```

Rule 22. All OWL2 concepts (classes, object and data properties), obtained from SBVR concepts (object types, fact types, roles) and specializing the same general concept, should be made disjoint. According the closed world assumption, all individuals should be made different if the opposite is not asserted, e.g.:

```
DisjointClasses (Educational_institution Publishing_company
   Trading_company)
DifferentIndividuals (Paper1 Paper2 Paper3)
```

Rule 23. SBVR individual concepts are transformed into OWL2 individuals along with their assertions, e.g.:

```
Paper1
  General concept: Paper
Paper2
  General concept: Paper
Paper1 cites Paper2 →
  Declaration(NamedIndividual(Paper1))ClassAssertion(Paper Paper1)
  Declaration(NamedIndividual(Paper2))ClassAssertion(Paper Paper2)
  ObjectPropertyAssertion(cites_cited_paper Paper1 Paper2)
```

5 Requirements to SBVR Vocabularies and Business Rules for Creating Consistent Ontologies

SBVR vocabularies should correctly represent a problem domain under consideration. That means they should correspond to semantics of the domain intended by developer to present. There are several basic well-formedness rules applicable for concept models and ontologies [20], [21], [22]; other rules were formulated on the base of investigating results of SBVR into OWL2 transformations.

Concept Hierarchy Formulating Rules. Primitive, non-inferable domain concepts should not have more than one primitive parent. Non-inferable generalization hierarchies of the domain should comprise homogeneous disjoint trees, where specializations are based on the same criteria. All sub-concepts of the same parent concept should be disjoint but not necessarily covering the parent whereas values are disjoint and value types may be disjoint or overlapping.

Such rules in SBVR are supported by categorization schemes and segmentations. Moreover, they may be used for multiple specializations into inferable hierarchies that are often needed in ontologies for classifying concepts according various criteria. However, disjointness or equivalence of segmentations and categorization schemes is not explicitly defined by dedicated rules. Such implied rules should be addressed during constructing SBVR into OWL2 transformations.

Individual Creation Rules. Each individual concept must be an instance of exactly one most specific self-standing primitive concept; business rules should be defined in such a way that inferences should never result in making individuals instances of several non-inferable concepts. For ensuring desired inferences, inferable concepts should be defined. Currently, we have yet not given a sufficient attention for inferable concepts, i.e. for formulating SBVR business rules and definitions for concepts.

Naming Rules. SBVR metamodel allows using the same preferred names for different concepts, e.g. for roles related via `is_property_of fact` type with several object types. It means that a corresponding OWL2 data property will have several domain classes what leads to undesirable classifications and inconsistencies during inference performed by ontology reasoners. The safe solution is to give unique preferred names, or purposely formulate right subsumption hierarchies for object types, roles, fact type roles, and fact types for avoiding undesirable classifications.

Rules for Defining Characteristics of Fact Types. In OWL2, object properties may have characteristics such as functional, transitive, reflexive, irreflexive, symmetric and asymmetric ones that are important for inference. In SBVR, there are no direct means for defining such characteristics. Therefore, it is desirable to explicitly define such rules in SBVR vocabulary and to define proper transformation rules for identifying such characteristics.

6 Implementation

SBVR into OWL2 transformation consists of several steps (Fig. 3): creating SBVR XMI schema from SBVR Structured English text; transforming SBVR XMI document into to OWL2 XMI, and transforming OWL2 XMI into the OWL2 document in functional style syntax. The SBVR into OWL transformation is executed by ATL engine, and OWL2 XMI transformation into OWL2 functional style syntax – by XSLT transformation.

The source model for a transformation is provided by the SBVR editor [2], implemented in Eclipse environment, which supports creating, editing and validating syntax of SBVR Business Vocabularies and Business Rules, presented in a textual format, and generates SBVR specifications in the XMI format.

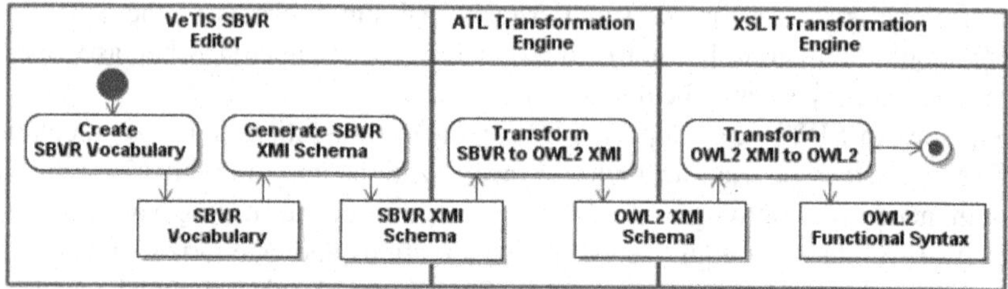

Fig. 3. Transformation from SBVR into OWL2

The generated XMI model conforms to SBVR Ecore metamodel and can be used in ATL transformations. The final OWL2 document structure and syntax depends on the XSL transformations implemented according Zedlitz et al. [23]. ATL transformations are defined in a straightforward way using helpers for constructing names of OWL2 entities and reusing main transformations for various cases by applying additional conditions. The examples of ATL transformations are given in Fig. 4–6.

```
rule Vocabulary2Ontology {
  from s : SBVR!Vocabulary
  to o2 : OWL2!Ontology(ontologyIRI <- t_iri),
   t_iri : OWL2!IRI(lexicalValue <- thisModule.getIriLexValue(''))}
```

Fig. 4. ATL rule for transforming SBVR Vocabulary into OWL2 ontology

Two additional helpers are constructed with purpose to attain ontology IRI and create IRIs for every element in ontology). These helpers add a SBVR Vocabulary textual representation (value) as a part of global IRI for the ontology themselves and for every ontology concept (e.g. Class, ObjectProperty, etc.).

```
helper def: getOntologyName() : String =
  let text : SBVR!Text = SBVR!Text.allInstances()->
   select(i|i=SBVR!Name.allInstances()->first().expression)->first() in
     text.value;
helper def :getIriLexValue(val:String):String =
  'urn:'+thisModule.getOntologyName()+if val<>''then '#' +val
   else '' endif;
```

Fig. 5. Additional helpers for IRI creation

```
rule ObjectType2Class {
  from s : SBVR!ObjectType (not s.isPrimitiveDataType())
  to o : OWL2!Class(
     declaration <- t_declaration,
     entityIRI <- t_iri),
     t_iri : OWL2!IRI(lexicalValue <- thisModule.getIriLexValue(
     s.getClassName(s.getObjectTypeTerm()))),
     t_declaration:OWL2!Declaration(ontology <-
       thisModule.getOntology())}
```

Fig. 6. ATL rule for transforming SBVR object type into the OWL2 class

For separating SBVR terminological, linguistic and conceptual parts, several ontologies should be obtained from SBVR specification: a substantial ontology for meanings and ontology for representations. Individuals also should be kept in separate files importing the main ontology representing schema of a problem domain. For reasoning and querying tasks, individuals may be merged with the main ontology. For making linguistic analysis or annotating electronic resources, ontology of representations may be merged with ontology models under consideration. Such approach has several advantages: the main ontology holds only concepts of meaning that may be efficiently used in various ways; representation ontologies can relate reasoning and querying ontologies with linguistic processing tasks. During SBVR into OWL2 transformation, decomposing a resulting ontology to separate parts can be done in the XSL transformation step without influencing the transformation from SBVR into OWL2 in XMI.

7 Conclusion and Future Works

The main findings following from investigating results of SBVR into OWL2 transformations are the following: there are some regularities implied in SBVR specifications that should be explicitly specified in ontology (e.g. various cases of disjointness), and, vice versa, there are some features desirable to have in OWL2 ontologies that should be defined in SBVR specification (e.g. functional, transitive, and other characteristics of fact types). Constructing names in SBVR requires a special attention as it may lead to undesirable and inconsistent classifications. Such factors should be regarded during creating SBVR specifications and constructing SBVR into OWL2 transformations.

The contribution of the paper is 23 rules for transforming SBVR concepts into OWL2 ontologies, and some considerations about requirements for creating SBVR vocabularies for obtaining consistent OWL2 ontologies. SBVR into OWL2 transformations also can serve for gradual development of SBVR vocabularies using obtained ontologies for validating their consistency.

Our future work will be devoted for more deep analysis of SBVR definitions and logical formulations for creating some kind of methodology how to specify OWL2 ontologies using SBVR structured language. Also, we will give efforts to elaborating ontology for representations in a way suitable for relating SBVR with linguistic processing means.

References

1. OMG: Semantics of Business Vocabulary and Business Rules (SBVR), Version 1.0., OMG Document Number: formal/2008-01-02 (December 2008)
2. Nemuraite, L., Skersys, T., Sukys, A., Sinkevičius, E., Ablonskis, L.: VETIS tool for editing and transforming SBVR business vocabularies and business rules into UML&OCL models. In: Targamadze, A., et al. (eds.) Information Technologies' 2010: Proceedings of the 16th International Conference on Information and Software Technologies, IT 2010, April 21-23, pp. 377–384. Kaunas Technologija, Kaunas (2010)

3. Demuth, B., Liebau, H.-B.: An Approach for Bridging the Gap Between Business Rules and the Semantic Web. In: Paschke, A., Biletskiy, Y. (eds.) RuleML 2007. LNCS, vol. 4824, pp. 119–133. Springer, Heidelberg (2007)
4. Motik, B., Patel-Schneider, P.F., Parsia, B.: OWL 2 Web Ontology Language Structural Specification and Functional-Style Syntax. W3C Proposed Recommendation (September 22, 2009)
5. Karpovic, J., Nemuraite, L.: Transforming SBVR business semantics into Web ontology language OWL2: main concepts. In: Butleris, R., et al. (eds.) Information Technologies' 2011: Proceedings of the 17th International Conference on Information and Software Technologies, IT 2011, April 27-29, pp. 231–238. Kaunas Technologija, Kaunas (2011)
6. OMG: Ontology definition metamodel. OMG Document Number: ptc/2008-09-07 (2008)
7. Halpin, T.: ORM 2 Graphical Notation. Neumont University, Technical Report ORM2-01 (September 2005)
8. Keet, C.M.: Mapping the object-role modeling language ORM2 into description logic language DLR. Technical Report KRDB07-2, KRDB Research Centre, Faculty of Computer Science, Free University of Bozen-Bolzano (2007)
9. Wagih, H.M., ElZanfaly, D.S., Kouta, M.M.: Mapping Object Role Modeling 2 schemes to OWL2 ontologies. In: Proceedings of the 3rd IEEE International Conference on Computer Research and Development (ICCRD), Shanghai, China, March 11-13, vol. 4, pp. 126–132. IEEE Press (2011)
10. Franconi, E., Mosca, A.: Reasoning on ORM2 Conceptual Schema: Theoretical Backgrounds. EU-IST Integrated Project (IP) 2009-231875 (2009)
11. ter Hofstede, A.H.M., Proper, H.A.: How to formalize it? Formalization Principles for Information Systems Development Methods. Information and Software Technology 40(10), 519–540 (1998)
12. W3C: SKOS. Simple Knowledge Organization System Reference. W3C Recommendation (August 18, 2009)
13. Kleiner, M., Albert, P., Bézivin, J.: Parsing SBVR-Based Controlled Languages. In: Schürr, A., Selic, B. (eds.) MODELS 2009. LNCS, vol. 5795, pp. 122–136. Springer, Heidelberg (2009)
14. Buitelaar, P., Cimiano, P., Haase, P., Sintek, M.: Towards Linguistically Grounded Ontologies. In: Aroyo, L., Traverso, P., Ciravegna, F., Cimiano, P., Heath, T., Hyvönen, E., Mizoguchi, R., Oren, E., Sabou, M., Simperl, E. (eds.) ESWC 2009. LNCS, vol. 5554, pp. 111–125. Springer, Heidelberg (2009)
15. Cimiano, P., Buitelaar, P., McCrae, J., Sintek, M.: LexInfo: A declarative model for the lexicon-ontology interface. Web Semantics: Science, Services and Agents on the World Wide Web 9, 29–51 (2011)
16. Horrocks, I., Parsia, B., Sattle, U.: OWL 2 Web Ontology Language Direct Semantics. W3C Recommendation (October 27, 2009)
17. Carrol, J., Herman, I., Patel-Schneider, P.F.: OWL 2 Web Ontology Language RDF-Based Semantics. W3C Recommendation (October 27, 2009)
18. W3C: OWL 2 Web Ontology Language Mapping to RDF Graphs. W3C Recommendation (October 27, 2009)
19. The University of Manchester. OWL Syntax Converter, `http://owl.cs.manchester.ac.uk/converter/`
20. Rector, A.L.: Normalisation of ontology implementations: Towards modularity, re-use, and maintainability. In: Proceedings Workshop on Ontologies for Multiagent Systems (OMAS) in Conjunction with European Knowledge Acquisition Workshop, pp. 1–16 (2002)

21. Rector, A.L.: Modularisation of domain ontologies implemented in description logics and related formalisms including owl. In: Genari, J. (ed.) Proceedings of the 2nd International Conference on Knowledge Capture, K-CAP 2003, pp. 121–128. ACM (2003)
22. Rector, A.L., Drummond, N., Horridge, M., Rogers, J., Knublauch, H., Stevens, R., Wang, H., Wroe, C.: OWL Pizzas: Practical Experience of Teaching OWL-DL: Common Errors & Common Patterns. In: Motta, E., Shadbolt, N.R., Stutt, A., Gibbins, N. (eds.) EKAW 2004. LNCS (LNAI), vol. 3257, pp. 63–81. Springer, Heidelberg (2004)
23. Zedlitz, J., Jörke, J., Luttenberger, N.: From UML to OWL2. In: STAKE 2011 - 3rd Semantic Technology and Knowledge Engineering Conference, pp. 2011–2013. UNITEN Putrajaya Campus, Malaysia (2011)

Representing and Transforming SBVR Question Patterns into SPARQL

Algirdas Sukys, Lina Nemuraite, and Bronius Paradauskas

Kaunas University of Technology, Department of Information Systems, Studentu 50–308
{algirdas.sukys,lina.nemuraite,bronius.paradauskas}@ktu.lt

Abstract. The goal of the paper is to present question patterns in structured natural language and their transformations into ontology query language SPARQL for allowing business participants to communicate with business software services and data in more flexible and friendly way. The structured language is based on Semantics of Business Vocabulary and Business Rules (SBVR) metamodel, which allows creating and managing business vocabularies and business rules in specific domains. The current paper is focused on transforming question patterns, including usage of synonyms and synonymous forms; projecting formulations constrained by atomic formulations based on facts and fact types; projections on several variables; restricting query results by auxiliary variables constrained by various logical formulations; supplementing questions with derivation rules from SBVR vocabulary of business rules, etc. Patterns are followed by examples, proved by implemented SBVR query editor and SBVR to SPARQL transformations.

Keywords: SBVR, SBVR question, business vocabulary, business rule, ontology, OWL2, SWRL, SPARQL.

1 Introduction

The goal of the paper is to present question patterns, formulated in structured natural language, along with transformations into ontology query language SPARQL, for allowing business participants to communicate with business software services and data in more flexible and friendly way.

The structured language is based on Semantics of Business Vocabulary and Rules (SBVR) metamodel [1], which was designed for creating and managing business vocabularies and business rules in specific domains. SBVR vocabularies and rules are translatable into Web Ontology Language (OWL 2) [2] and Semantic Web Rules (SWRL), which may be analysed by ontology reasoners and SPARQL query engines.

Currently, SBVR has gaining an attention both in commercial applications and academic world. There are many SBVR related applications, for example, generation of software models and code [3], creation of terminological vocabularies for various fields [4], auditing compliance between governmental regulations and business actualities [5], etc. However, SBVR questions have not attained a great attention yet. The possibility of querying business data on the base of SBVR questions was noticed

T. Skersys, R. Butleris, and R. Butkiene (Eds.): ICIST 2012, CCIS 319, pp. 436–451, 2012.

by Kriechhammer [6] but no further research in that direction was done. Ontology query language SPARQL [7] was proposed for applying SBVR rules in compliance checking [5], but the implementation was not automated. Our work is directed towards automating SBVR support for analysing business information – i.e., formulating SBVR questions and transforming them into SPARQL for immediate access to business data from various sources (databases, business process management and enterprise resource planning (ERP) systems, documents), supported with ontological descriptions.

The preliminaries of implementing the SBVR question approach were studied in our previous works [8], [9]. The current paper is focused on particularities of transforming typical question patterns, including usage of synonyms and synonymous forms; projecting formulations constrained by atomic formulations based on facts and fact types; binding fact type roles to individual concepts; projections on several variables; restricting query results by auxiliary variables constrained by various logical formulations; logical operations such as disjunctions and negations, and supplementing simple questions with derivation rules from SBVR vocabulary of business rules. Patterns, transformations and SPARQL queries are followed by examples, proved by implemented SBVR editor, ATL transformations from SBVR questions into SPARQL, ontology reasoners and SPARQL query engines.

The rest of the paper is structured as follows. Section 2 analyses related work. Section 3 and 4 present SBVR and SPARQL metamodels used for transforming question patterns, and generic transformation rules. Section 5 is devoted to question patterns along with transformation details and examples. Section 6 presents their implementation. Finally, Section 7 draws conclusions and outlines the future work.

2 Related Work

The SPARQL is ontology query language oriented to computer processing on the Semantic Web and, as such, is not suitable for supporting immediate access to business data for business people. SBVR metamodel, concentrated on specifying the meaning of knowledge in terms of concepts, propositions and questions, is devoted for filling this gap by proposing the abstract syntax, expressible in structured languages, understandable by human and having formal interpretation based on first order logics. It may be treated as multilingual representation of meaning in structured language intermediate between natural languages and executable software specifications [10]. However, SBVR lacks inference [11, 12], and SBVR transformations into logics based languages as OWL 2 are yet under investigation [13]. Currently there are no widely available means for availing potential SBVR possibilities in business practise. Our work is based on our own previously created SBVR editor [14] and a tool for transforming SBVR into OWL 2 [13, 15] which is under contemporaneous development with our transformations.

Transforming of SBVR vocabularies and rules into OWL 2 has the great importance for expressing SBVR questions in SPARQL as SPARQL queries are executed over RDF and OWL 2 ontologies. SBVR and OWL 2 were created to be compliant with Common Logics [16]; therefore, SBVR concepts can be mapped to OWL 2 concepts. Rough correspondences between SBVR and first OWL version were declared in SBVR specification, but OWL was overridden by more expressive OWL 2, and existing references in [1] became not enough. Existing implementations of SBVR into OWL 2 transformations are encapsulated in commercial products [17, 18] and directly unusable for other research projects or applications. Therefore, we are developing our own framework for applying SBVR [19].

SBVR transformations into SPARQL are dependent on SBVR transformations into OWL 2 [13, 15], which are created using OWL 2 abstract (Functional style) syntax metamodel based on its direct semantics [20]. OWL 2 also has RDF based semantics [21], but standard RDF metamodel of OWL 2 is not finalized though OWL 2 ontologies can be mapped into RDF graphs and vice versa using special mapping rules [22], which are implemented in a converter created by the Manchester University.

SPARQL also has two kinds of syntaxes: RDF syntax and SPARQL Abstract Syntax (SPARQLAS) [23], which is directed towards querying and two-way transforming of UML and OWL 2 models. SPARQLAS directly includes part of OWL 2 metamodel, so the advantage of using the SPARQLAS is a conceptual clarity and decidability of reasoning and querying tasks; its shortcoming – the limitation to OWL 2 Description Logics (DL). Users can fast write SPARQLAS queries, which are automatically translated into SPARQL and executed using an OWL 2 reasoner and a SPARQL engine. SBVR to SPARQLAS transformations also would be much simpler but such transformations may be not suitable for all cases because the newest version, SPARQL 1.1, has dependencies on OWL 2 Full. As SBVR semantics also is not limited to OWL 2 DL, we have given the preference to RDF based SPARQL metamodel against OWL 2 Functional Syntax based one regarding the fact that the latter solution could be not applicable in a general case for SBVR questions that are considerably more expressive and should not be limited to OWL 2 DL capabilities.

Our SBVR into SPARQL transformations use SPARQL RDF based metamodel. They map SBVR concepts to ontology concepts with the requirement that SBVR transformation into OWL 2 should preserve the same semantics as SBVR into SPARQL. For providing querying capabilities suitable to SBVR questions, the SBVR transformation into OWL 2 should represent in domain ontology SBVR related meanings separated from terminological concepts such as preferred, not-preferred and prohibited designations; synonyms and synonymous forms; taking into account meaning of predefined fact types etc. Terminological concepts should not make impact on behaviour of reasoners and other ontology processing means. Therefore, terminology and linguistics related SBVR elements should be separated from conceptual knowledge for efficient querying using synonyms or synonymous forms and getting correct answers. Consequently, transforming SBVR questions into SPARQL should be done only on the base of meanings represented by preferred representations while asking questions may be done using various representation forms.

3 Metamodels for Representing SBVR Questions and SPARQL Queries

Transformation from SBVR to SPARQL query is executed by two steps: model to model transformation from SBVR to SPARQL, and translation of SPARQL model into textual representation. The first step is executed by automatic model to model transformation. It requires SBVR question model as input and produces SPARQL model as output. Both models conform to corresponding metamodels.

3.1 SBVR Metamodel for Representing Questions

SBVR metamodel fragment actual for our purpose is presented in Fig. 1.

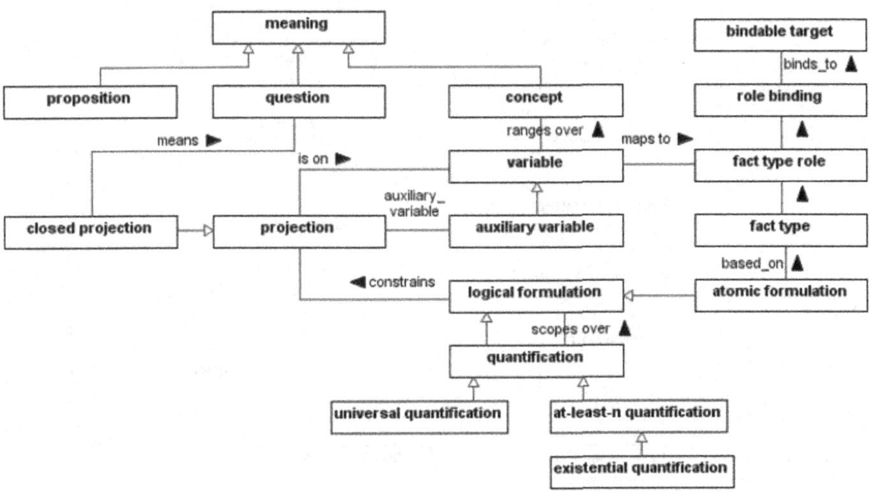

Fig. 1. SBVR metamodel for representing meanings and questions

SBVR metamodel allows formulating several types of meanings – concepts (noun concepts, fact types), propositions (facts), and questions. Noun concepts and fact types describe business concepts and their relations. They are used to compose conceptual schema that is a basis for defining propositions about a problem domain. Propositions are used to describe business facts, and questions are used to formulate queries against SBVR models.

The meaning of a question is meant by the SBVR semantic formulation – *closed projection*. According to SBVR specification [1], the basic meaning of the projection is a set of things that are valid referents of projection variables in actualities that satisfy logical formulations constraining the projection. Each projection variable represents a result of the certain concept type (ranges over that concept). For example, if one wants to see a list of cars in results, variable that ranges over object type “car” should be created.

Projection projects variables to semantic domains, constrained by a logical formulation that is scoped over an atomic formulation based on fact types. Depending on the question formulation, fact type roles can be bound to particular bindable targets – variables or individual concepts. Projection may have auxiliary variables that further constrain projection results by other logical formulations. In such a way, we are able to construct various question patterns.

3.2 SPARQL Metamodel

The SPARQL metamodel used in SBVR into SPARQL transformation was taken from the EMFText project [24].

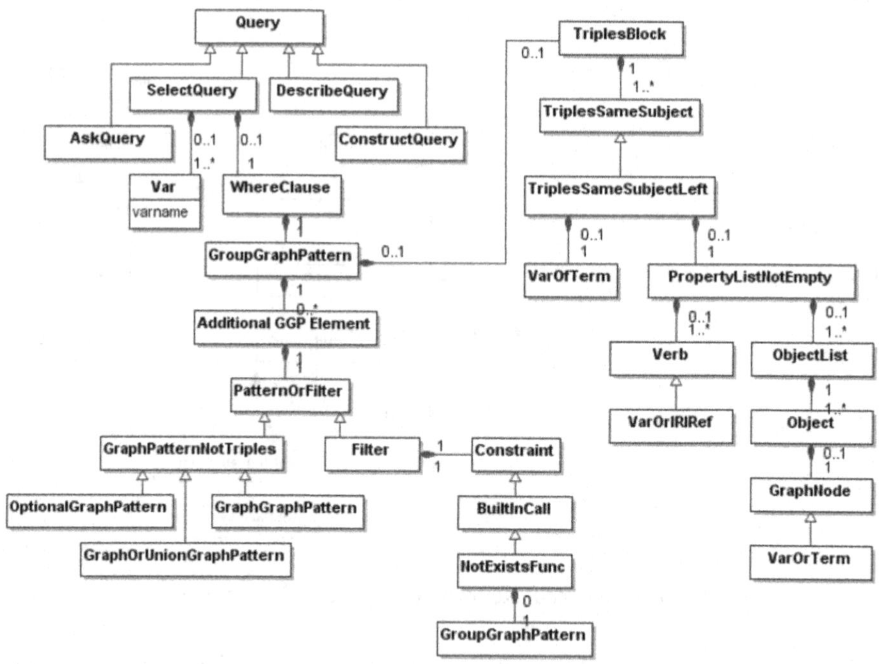

Fig. 2. Part of SPARQL metamodel (supplemented from [24])

It has a possibility to express all types of SPARQL queries (SELECT, ASK, DESCRIBE and CONSTRUCT), FILTER conditions, UNION, LIMIT, OFFSET solution modifiers. On the other hand, metamodel lacks capabilities to express SPARQL 1.1 constructions, such as property paths, negation or subqueries. It was supplemented with NotExistFunct element but more extensions are needed.

SELECT query (Fig. 2.) consists of two main parts – at least one variable and a conditional element – WHERE clause, containing a graph pattern. The graph pattern consists of TriplesSameSublectLeft elements, which represent SPARQL triple patterns. TriplesSameSublectLeft elements consist of subject, predicate and object.

Subject and object are represented by element VarOrTerm, and predicate is represented by VarOrIRIRef. Group graph pattern can also contain additional group graph pattern elements to express SPARQL FILTER, OPTIONAL or UNION keywords.

4 Generic Transformation Rules from SBVR into SPARQL

For transforming SBVR questions into SPARQL, semantic SBVR formulations that mean questions are transformed into SPARQL query model which is translated into textual representation of SPARQL. In this section we present transformation rules for transforming SBVR into SPARQL.

- Rule I. Closed projection that means question is transformed into the skeleton of SPARQL query (*Sparql Query*, *Group Graph Pattern* and *Triples Block* elements).
- Rule II. Each variable that is in the closed projection is transformed into *Var* element of SPARQL query; the name of the variable is derived from concept, that variable ranges over; SPARQL triple pattern having predicate *rdf:type* is created to define type of variable.
- Rule III. The atomic formulation that constrains a closed projection or auxiliary variable of the closed projection is transformed into SPARQL triple pattern element. Subject, predicate and object elements of the triple pattern are defined by a fact type the atomic formulation is based on:

– if the first role of the fact type binds to variable, SPARQL *Var* element in a position of subject is created; the name of the variable is derived from the concept that variable ranges over; SPARQL triple pattern having predicate *rdf:type* is created for defining the type of the variable;
– if the role of the fact type binds to individual concept, *RDF Literal* element is created. The name of the element is derived from the name of the individual concept.
– the second role of the fact type is transformed into the element in a position of object using the same principles as for the first fact type role;
– the verb of the fact type is expressed by a fact symbol element. It is transformed into the predicate element of the triple pattern.

5 SBVR Question Patterns

In this section, we present various patterns of SBVR questions and rules for transforming them into SPARQL. The description of the first pattern is most comprehensive, including basic principles of representing questions and rules of transforming them. For remaining patterns, only specific aspects are considered. The patterns are presented using examples of questions based on SBVR vocabulary, which describes persons and their workplaces. The ontology, generated from this vocabulary is presented in Fig. 3.

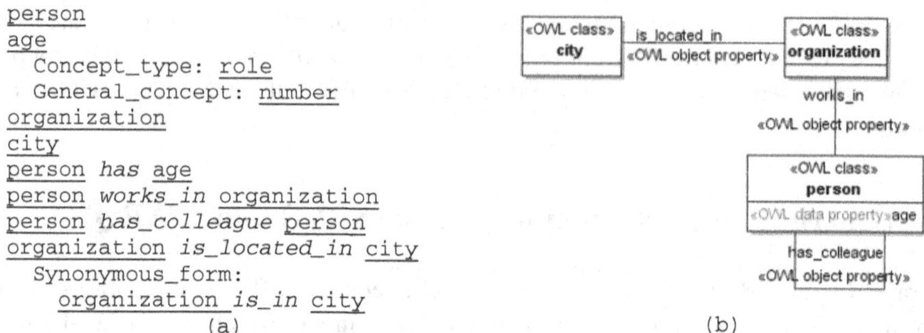

Fig. 3. The SBVR vocabulary and corresponding ontology model represented as UML class diagram with stereotypes

5.1 Questions, Using Projections Constrained by Atomic Formulations Based on Fact Types

An example of such a question may be getting all persons that work in some organization. Logical formulation constraining a projection on a variable of type "person" is a universal quantification (all persons) scoped over an existential quantification (some organization). Existential quantification is scoped over the atomic formulation based on the fact type person *works_in* organization.

SBVR question "What persons *work_in* some organization?" in **First Order Logics (FOL)**:

$\forall v1 \exists v2 (Person(v1) \cap Organization(v2) \cap works\_in(v1, v2))$ is formulated by semantic formulation:

Semantic formulation in SBVR

```
The question q is defined by a closed projection. (s1)
. The closed projection is on a variable v1. (s2)
.. The variable v1 ranges over a concept 'person'.
. The closed projection is constrained by a universal quantification.
.. The universal quantification binds to a variable v1
.. The universal quantification scopes over an existential
   quantification.
... The existential quantification introduces a variable v2.
.... The variable v2 ranges over a concept 'organization'.
... The existential quantification scopes over an atomic
      formulation. (s3)
.... The atomic formulation is based on a fact type
        'person works_in organization'. (s4)
.... The atomic formulation has a role binding. (s5)
..... The role binding is of the role 'person' of the fact type.
..... The role binding binds to the variable v1.
.... The atomic formulation has a second role binding. (s6)
..... The second role binding is of the role 'organization'.
..... The second role binding binds to the variable v2.
```

Transformation into SPARQL model is accomplished according rules:

Rule I. The closed projection (s1) transformed into select query (t1), where clause (t3), group graph pattern (t4) and triples block (t5) elements;

Rule II. The variable (s2) that is in closed projection is transformed into var (t2) element. The name of the variable inherited from ranged over concept 'person'; to define type of the result SPARQL triple pattern *person rdf:type :person* created (t6);

Rule III. The atomic formulation (s3) is transformed into triples same subject left named element (t7) (SPARQL triple pattern). The subject, predicate and object elements of triple pattern are composed as follows:

– the first role binding of the fact type that atomic formulation (s5) is based on is transformed into variable element (t8) in a position of subject;

– the fact type (s4) that atomic formulation is based on is transformed into property list not empty element (t9). The name of the element (t10) is derived from the verb of the fact type;

– the second role binding of the fact type that atomic formulation (s6) is based on is transformed into variable element (t11) in a position of object.

SPARQL query model

```
Select Query (t1)
. Var, varname: '?person' (t2)
. Where Clause (t3)
.. Group Graph Pattern (t4)
... Triples Block (t5)
.... Triples Same Subject Left NE (t6)
..... Var, varname: '?person'
..... Property List Not Empty
...... PNAME LN
....... PN LOCAL, pn_local: 'rdf:type'
...... Object List
....... Object
........ PNAME LN
......... PN LOCAL, pn_local: ':person'
.... Triples Same Subject Left NE (t7)
..... Var, varname: '?person' (t8)
..... Property List Not Empty (t9)
...... PNAME LN
....... PN LOCAL, pn_local: ':works_in' (t10)
...... Object List
....... Object (t11)
........ Var, varname: '?organization'
```

Textual representation of SPARQL query

```
SELECT ?person {?person rdf:type :person .
   ?person :works_in ?orgnization}
```

5.2 Questions with Fact Type Roles Bound to Individual Concepts

A question for finding all persons that work in organization "KTU" differs from the previous one in that the fact type has role binding to individual concept. In SPARQL, it is expressed in a same way, using multiple triple patterns.

SBVR question "What persons *work_in* organization KTU?" in **FOL**:

$$\forall v1(Person(v1) \cap works\_in(v1, KTU))$$

Transformation into SPARQL follows the same principles as the previous one. The main aspect of transforming this question is that the second role of the fact type has role binding to individual concept "KTU", which is transformed into SPARQL RDF literal element.

Semantic formulation of question in SBVR

```
.... The atomic formulation has a second role binding.
..... The second role binding is of the role 'organization'.
..... The second role binding binds to the individual concept 'KTU'.
```

SPARQL query model

```
Select Query
. Var, varname: 'person'
. Where Clause
.. Group Graph Pattern
... Triples Block
.... Triples Same Subject Left NE
..... Var, varname: '?person'
..... Property List Not Empty
...... PNAME LN
....... PN LOCAL, pn_local: 'rdf:type'
...... Object List
....... Object
........ PNAME LN
......... PN LOCAL, pn_local: ':person'
.... Triples Same Subject Left NE
..... Var, varname: 'person'
..... Property List Not Empty
  ...... PNAME LN
  ....... PN LOCAL, pn_local: ':works_in'
  ...... Object List
  ....... Object
  ........ RDF Literal
  ......... String Literal, string: 'KTU'
```

Textual representation of SPARQL query

```
SELECT ?person {?person rdf:type :person .
  ?person :works_in 'KTU'}
```

5.3 Questions with Projections Having Auxiliary Variables

Auxiliary variables are used to introduce restrictions to fact type roles using additional logical formulations. Such questions are expressed in SPARQL by "Where" clauses using multiple triple patterns.

SBVR question "What persons *work_in* organization that *is_located_in* city Kaunas?" in **FOL**:

$$\forall v1(Person(v1) \cap works\_in(v1, aux1) \cap is\_located\_in(aux1, Kaunas)$$

Semantic formulation of question in SBVR

The fact type role organization is restricted by introducing auxiliary variable that is constrained by atomic formulation, based on fact type organization *is_located_in* city:

```
The question q is defined by a closed projection.
. The closed projection is on a variable v1.
.. The variable v1 ranges over a concept 'person'.
. The closed projection has auxiliary variable aux1.
.. The auxiliary variable ranges over concept 'organization'.
. The closed projection is constrained by a universal
  quantification.
.. The universal quantification binds to a variable v1.
.. The universal quantification scopes over an atomic formulation.
... The atomic formulation is based on a fact type
    'person works_in organization'.
.... The atomic formulation has a role binding.
..... The role binding is of the role 'person' of the fact type.
...... The role binding binds to the variable v1.
.... The atomic formulation has a second role binding.
...... The second role binding is of the role 'organization'.
....... The second role binding binds to the auxiliary variable aux1.
........ The auxiliary variable aux1 is constrained by atomic
         formulation.
......... The atomic formulation is based on fact type
          'organization is_located_in city'.
.......... The atomic formulation has a role binding.
........... The role binding is of the role 'organization' of
            the fact type.
............ The role binding binds to the auxiliary variable aux1.
.......... The atomic formulation has a second role binding.
........... The second role binding is of the role 'city'.
............ The second role binding binds to the individual
             concept Kaunas.
```

Textual representation of SPARQL query

```
SELECT ?person {?person rdf:type :person .
?person:works_in ?organization.?organization:is_located_in 'Kaunas'}
```

5.4 Questions, Using Synonyms and Synonymous Forms

SBVR standard allows a flexible way of asking questions using synonyms and synonymous forms. During transforming SBVR business vocabulary and business rules into OWL, only meanings expressed in preferred designations are used. The same rules apply to transformations SBVR questions into SPARQL. E.g. a question "What organizations *are_in* city Kaunas?" using synonymous form organization *is_in* city, should be replaced by statement using the preferred designation "What organizations *are_located_in* city Kaunas?"

5.5 Questions with Restrictions on Fact Type Role Values

To restrict fact type roles, predefined SBVR fact types can be used: *is_greater_than*, *is_less_than*, *is_equal_to*. These restrictions can be applied to roles of fact types, which correspond to OWL data properties. Consider concept person having attribute age. Using restrictions one can find persons of certain age. In SBVR model such a restriction is expressed by an auxiliary variable, restricted by atomic formulation, based on binary fact type "number1 *is_greater_than* number2". In SPARQL model it is expressed using filter.

SBVR question Find persons that *has* age *greater_than* 25 in **FOL**:
$\forall v1 \exists age(Person(v1) \cap has\_age(v1, age) \cap is\_greater\_than(age, 25))$

Semantic formulation of question in SBVR

```
. The closed projection has auxiliary variable aux1.
.. The auxiliary variable ranges over concept 'age'.
... The auxiliary variable is constrained by an atomic formulation.
.... The atomic formulation is based on fact type 'number1 > number2'
..... The atomic formulation has a role binding.
...... The role binding is of role 'number1' of the fact type.
....... The role binding binds to the auxiliary variable aux1.
..... The atomic formulation has a second role binding.
...... The second role binding is of the role 'number2'.
....... The second role binding binds to the individual concept 25.
```

SPARQL query model

```
Select Query
. Var, varname: 'person'
. Where Clause
.. Group Graph Pattern
... Triples Block
... Additional GGP Element
.... Filter
..... Bracketted Expression
...... Expression
```

Textual representation of SPARQL query

```
SELECT ?person {
   ?person rdf:type :person .
   ?person :age ?age .FILTER (?age > 25)}
```

5.6 Questions with Projections on Several Variables

If a question has several types of results, the closed projection has a variable for each of them. E. g. a question "Find organizations and persons that *work_in* those organizations" will be presented by a closed projection on two variables ranging over organization and person.

5.7 Questions Using Disjunction or Conjunction

SBVR metamodel supports logical operations: disjunctions and conjunctions. Disjunction has two logical operands and is indicated using keyword "or" in SBVR SE syntax. In SBVR question model, disjunction constrains projection and has two atomic formulations as operands. In SPARQL disjunction is expressed using keyword UNION. Consider the following question to find people who work in organizations KTU or VDU:

SBVR question "What person *work_in* organization KTU or *work_in* organization VDU?" in **FOL**:

$$\forall v1(Person(v1) \cap ((work\_in(v1, KTU) \cup work\_in(v1, VDU)))$$

Semantic formulation of question in SBVR

```
. The closed projection is constrained by a universal quantification.
.. The universal quantification bind to a variable v1
... The universal quantification scopes over disjunction.
.... The first logical operand of disjunction is atomic
formulation.
..... The atomic formulation is based on a fact type 'person works_in
organization'.
......
.... The second logical operand of disjunction is second atomic formu-
lation.
..... The second atomic formulation is based on a fact type 'person
works_in organization'.......
```

SPARQL query model

```
Select Query
. Var, varname: '?person'
. Where Clause
.. Group Graph Pattern
... Triples Block
.... Triples Same Subject Left NE
... Additional GGP Element
.... Group Or Union Graph Pattern
..... Group Graph Pattern
...... Triples Block
....... Triples Same Subject Left NE
..... Group Graph Pattern
...... Triples Block
....... Triples Same Subject Left NE
```

Textual representation of SPARQL query

```
SELECT ?person {?person rdf:type :person .
  {?person :works_in 'KTU'} UNION {?person :works_in 'VDU'}}
```

5.8 Questions Using Negation

SBVR negation is a logical operation, having one logical operand, which constrains the projection. Negation is restricted by universal quantification that scopes over atomic formulation. In SPARQL, negation is expressed using NOT EXISTS keyword. For transforming such questions, SPARQL metamodel was extended by an element NotExistsFunct for expressing negation.

SBVR question "What persons not *work_in* organization KTU?" in **FOL**:

$\forall v1(Person(v1) \cap \sim work\_in(v1, KTU))$

Semantic formulation of question in SBVR

```
. The closed projection is constrained by a logical negation.
.. The logical operand of the logical negation is a universal
quantification.
... The universal quantification binds to a variable v1.
... The universal quantification scopes over atomic formulation.
..... The atomic formulation is based on a fact type 'person works_in
organization'.......
```

Textual representation of SPARQL query

```
SELECT ?person {?person rdf:type :person .
  FILTER NOT EXISTS {?person :works_in 'KTU'}}
```

5.9 Questions Using Derivation Rules from SBVR Vocabulary of Business Rules

Sometimes one needs to find facts that are not defined in a question but inferred by derivation rules (implication formulations) in SBVR vocabulary of business rules. Derivation rules should be defined by SBVR implication formulations and transformed into SWRL rules supplementing OWL ontology. E.g. facts of type "person1 *is_colleague_of* person2 may be inferred using the business rule: "It is necessary that person1 *is_colleague_of* person2 if person1 *works_in* organization1 and person2 *works_in* organization1." After applying this rule one can find colleagues of a certain person:

What person *are_colleague_of* person Tadas_Gudas?

6 Implementation of SBVR into SPARQL Transformations

Fig. 4 presents the question transformation process along with other processes required for its implementation: creating SBVR business vocabulary and business rules, transforming them into OWL 2 and SWRL, and executing SPARQL queries.

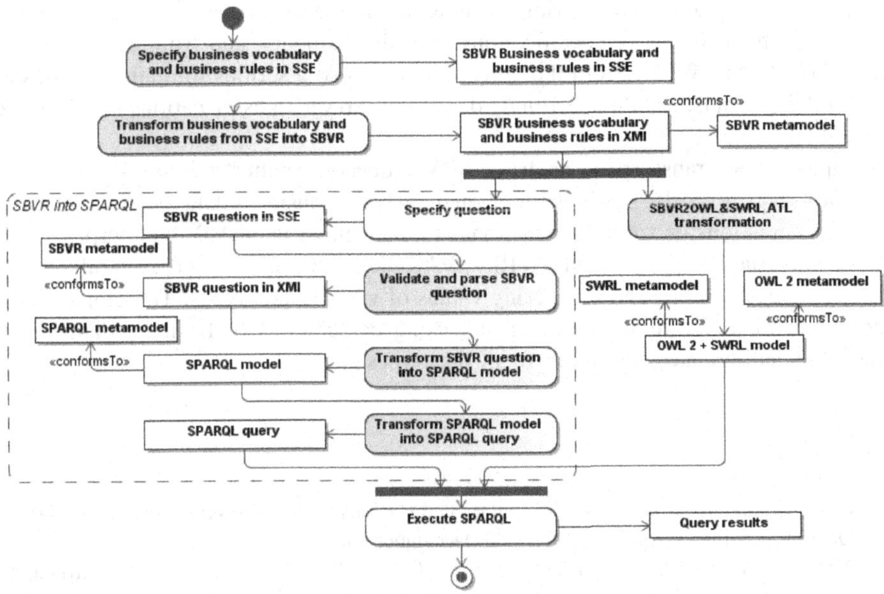

Fig. 4. Process of transforming and executing SBVR questions (shadowed components are implemented by authors of the paper and authors of [13, 14])

It is a part of a whole framework for querying business data using SBVR structured natural language, which contains various transformations from SBVR specifications to software models, data storage environments, and query execution engines.

OWL 2 ontology and SWRL rules comprise a data source for executing SPARQL queries. SBVR specification is also used to validate SBVR questions to keep conformance between ontology and SPARQL queries. I.e. questions must contain only concepts, specified in SBVR business vocabulary. Unidentified concepts or unrecognized questions (non-conforming to predefined question patterns) are marked as errors. Synonyms and synonymous forms used in questions are replaced by their preferred forms from SBVR business vocabulary. Finally, when a question is validated and parsed, it is transformed into SPARQL query. SBVR question patterns are implemented using ANTLR grammar. The transformation from SBVR question into SPARQL query is divided into two steps: model transformation from SBVR into SPARQL using ATL language and SPARQL model transformation into textual representation of SPARQL.

7 Conclusions and Future Work

The main idea behind this work was that the same language based on SBVR metamodel is suitable for automated developing business supporting software artefacts and querying business data produced or captured by using these artefacts. Moreover, transforming SBVR questions into SPARQL may be easy as they can inherit all experience gained during defining and implementing transformations from SBVR structured language specifications into SBVR model, and from SBVR model into OWL 2 and SWRL. From the other side, it is also a serious limitation as SBVR into SPARQL transformations strongly depend on SBVR transformations into OWL 2 and SWRL.

Implemented transformations from SBVR question patterns into SPARQL are only first steps towards real questioning and analysing business data. Expressing even simple calculations or value comparisons is a hard thing in SBVR. Not surprisingly, the same is true for OWL 2 and SWRL. SPARQL 1.1 has much more capabilities for processing calculations and comparing values of various data types. Therefore, it is a hard work for a future for defining and using calculations of business data under interest including dates, measures, fuzzy data types etc.

References

1. OMG: Semantics of Business Vocabulary and Business Rules (SBVR). Version 1.0. OMG Document Number: formal/2008-01-02 (December 2008)
2. Motik, B., Patel-Schneider, P.F., Parsia, B.: OWL 2 Web Ontology Language Structural Specification and Functional-Style Syntax. W3C Proposed Recommendation (September 22, 2009)
3. Marinos, A., Krause, P.: An SBVR Framework for RESTful Web Applications. In: Governatori, G., Hall, J., Paschke, A. (eds.) RuleML 2009. LNCS, vol. 5858, pp. 144–158. Springer, Heidelberg (2009)
4. OMG: Date-Time Vocabulary (Date-Time). OMG Document Number: bmi/2011-08-01 (2011)
5. Bouzidi, K.R., Faron-Zucker, C., Fies, B., Le Thanh, N.: An Ontological Approach for Modeling Technical Standards for Compliance Checking. In: Rudolph, S., Gutierrez, C. (eds.) RR 2011. LNCS, vol. 6902, pp. 244–249. Springer, Heidelberg (2011)
6. Kriechhammer, M.: Querying Systems for business models, `http://www.kriechhammer.com/?English_Portfolio:my_Documents:Finals`
7. W3C: SPARQL 1.1 Query Language. W3C Working Draft (October 14, 2010)
8. Sukys, A., Nemuraite, L., Paradauskas, B., Sinkevicius, E.: Querying ontologies on the base of semantics of business vocabularies and business rules. In: Information Technologies' 2011: Proceedings of the 17th International Conference on Information and Software Technologies, IT 2011, Kaunas, Lithuania, April 27-29, pp. 247–254 (2011)
9. Sukys, A., Nemuraite, L., Paradauskas, B., Sinkevičius, E.: SBVR based representation of SPARQL queries and SWRL rules for analyzing semantic relations. In: The First International Conference on Business Intelligence and Technology (Bustech 2011), Rome, Italy, IARIA, September 25-30, pp. 1–6 (2011)
10. Kleiner, M., Albert, P., Bézivin, J.: Parsing SBVR-Based Controlled Languages. In: Schürr, A., Selic, B. (eds.) MODELS 2009. LNCS, vol. 5795, pp. 122–136. Springer, Heidelberg (2009)
11. Spreeuwenberg, S., Healy, K.A.: SBVR's Approach to Controlled Natural Language. In: Fuchs, N.E. (ed.) CNL 2009. LNCS, vol. 5972, pp. 155–169. Springer, Heidelberg (2010)

12. Spreeuwenberg, S., Gerrits, R.: Business Rules in the Semantic Web, Are There Any or Are They Different? In: Barahona, P., Bry, F., Franconi, E., Henze, N., Sattler, U. (eds.) Reasoning Web 2006. LNCS, vol. 4126, pp. 152–163. Springer, Heidelberg (2006)
13. Karpovic, J., Nemuraite, L.: Transforming SBVR business semantics into Web ontology language OWL2: main concepts. In: Information Technologies' 2011: Proceedings of the 17th International Conference on Information and Software Technologies, IT 2011, Kaunas, Lithuania, April 27-29, pp. 231–238 (2011)
14. Nemuraite, L., Skersys, T., Sukys, A., Sinkevicius, E., Ablonskis, L.: VETIS tool for editing and transforming SBVR business vocabularies and business rules into UML&OCL models. In: Information Technologies' 2010: Proceedings of the 16th International Conference on Information and Software Technologies, IT 2010, Kaunas, Lithuania, April 21-23, pp. 377–384 (2010)
15. Karpovic, J., Nemuraite, L., Stankeviciene, M.: Requirements for Semantic Business Vocabularies and Rules for Transforming them into Consistent OWL2 Ontologies. In: Skersys, T., Butleris, R., Butkiene, R. (eds.) ICIST 2012. CCIS, vol. 319, pp. 420–435. Springer, Heidelberg (2012)
16. OMG: Ontology definition metamodel. OMG Document Number: ptc/2008-09-07
17. Collibra: Data governance software, `http://www.collibra.com`
18. Ontorule project: Ontologies meet business rules, `http://ontorule-project.eu`
19. Sukys, A., Nemuraite, L., Paradauskas, B., Sinkevičius, E.: Transformation Framework for SBVR based Semantic Queries in Business Information Systems. To appear in: the Second International Conference on Business Intelligence and Technology, Bustech 2012 (2012)
20. Horrocks, I., Parsia, B., Sattle, U.: OWL 2 Web Ontology Language Direct Semantics. W3C Recommendation (October 27, 2009)
21. Carrol, J., Herman, I., Patel-Schneider, P.F.: OWL 2 Web Ontology Language RDF-Based Semantics. W3C Recommendation (October 27, 2009)
22. W3C: OWL 2 Web Ontology Language Mapping to RDF Graphs. W3C Recommendation (October 27, 2009)
23. Schneider, M.: SPARQLAS – Implementing SPARQL Queries with OWL Syntax. In: Proceedings of the 3rd Workshop on Transforming and Weaving Ontologies in Model Driven Engineering, Málaga, Spain, June 30, pp. 1–7 (2010)
24. EMF Text SPARQL metamodel, `http://emftext.org/index.php/EMFText_Concrete_Syntax_Zoo_SPARQL`

The Ten Best Practices for Test Case Prioritization

Cagatay Catal

Istanbul Kultur University
Department of Computer Engineering
34156, Istanbul, Turkey
c.catal@iku.edu.tr

Abstract. In this study, test case prioritization approaches that are used to execute the regression testing in a cost-effective manner were investigated. We discussed the critical issues and best practices that a software company should focus on before and after the implementation of test case prioritization techniques inside the company. Due to the increasing complexity of today's software intensive systems, the number of test cases in a software development project increases for an effective validation & verification process and the time allocated to execute the regression tests decreases because of the marketing pressures. For this reason, it is very crucial to plan and setup test case prioritization infrastructures properly in software companies to improve the software testing process. Ten best practices for a successful test case prioritization are introduced and explained in this study.

Keywords: Software testing, regression tests, test case prioritization, process improvement.

1 Introduction

The modifications made on the software source code can negatively adverse the execution of existing software components and can prevent them to work properly. Therefore, we should ensure that existing features and components are not destroyed when new features are added to the software or when modifications are made to correct the faults. To ensure the consistency of the components, one may think that execution of all test cases is a good option. However, while it seems an appropriate approach theoretically, it is not feasible practically when we consider the necessary time and the overall cost.

An industrial collaborator of a researcher [1] stated that a test suite of software having 20,000 lines of code requires seven weeks to run. Another industrial collaborator that runs tests continuously in a test cycle requires over 30 days completing the testing activity [1]. In another study, it has been stated that a regression test suite includes 30,000 functional test cases and regression tests take 1000 machine-hour. As it can be seen from these examples, it is necessary to prioritize test cases when there are many test cases even if the number of lines of code does not reach to millions of lines of code. In addition to the required time to execute

T. Skersys, R. Butleris, and R. Butkiene (Eds.): ICIST 2012, CCIS 319, pp. 452–459, 2012.

the test cases, there are several activities which consume the resources of the company such as the preparation of test environment, the documentation of test results, and the evaluation of testing activities for software process improvement. For this reason, researchers proposed the following approaches [3] to implement the regression testing in a cost-effective manner:

- Test Suite Reduction (TSR),
- Regression Test Selection (RTS),
- Test Case Prioritization (TCP).

While test suite reduction and regression test selection reduce the number of test cases, test case prioritization approaches do not affect the number of test cases. Because this paper is only related with TCP, we will skip the details of TSR and RTS approaches. When test cases are reduced with TSR and RTS, some faults may not be identified due to the missing test cases and faulty products may be deployed to the field. Therefore, TCP seems more reliable and more efficient approach compared to the other approaches. We may sort the test cases based on their priority, start testing activities with the test case that has highest priority, go on testing with the prioritization list, and stop when the allocated testing time finishes. In this study, we propose effective best practices for the companies that need to implement a successful TCP. There are hundreds of TCP papers that introduce and validate several methods in literature, but we did not see any paper that provides best practices for the companies.

The remainder of this paper is structured as follows: Section 2 introduces test case prioritization. Section 3 presents ten best practices and Section 4 shows the related work. Section 5 explains APFD metric and TCP with examples. We conclude the paper with conclusions section.

2 Test Case Prioritization

During the testing process, it is possible to detect faults earlier and identify more faults with some test cases. Most of the TCP papers are code coverage-based. For example, “total method coverage prioritization” sorts the test cases in the order of the number of methods they cover. The logic behind this approach is that the test cases executing more methods will eventually detect more faults. In addition to the method coverage-based methods, researchers showed that prioritization can be performed in terms of the number of statements, branches, and basic blocks test cases cover. Solution space is very large for TCP problem. For example, a test suite of 20 test cases will have 20! = 2,432,902,008,176,640,000 different orderings. No algorithm can provide the optimal solution for such a huge solution space, but very useful algorithms such as genetic algorithms can be developed. Several authors empirically showed that prioritization techniques improve the regression testing [4]. Rothermel et al. [5] defines the test case prioritization problem as follows:

Given: T , a test suite; PT , the set of permutations of T ; and f , a function from PT to the real numbers.

Problem: Find $T' \in PT$ such that $(\forall T'')(T'' \in PT)(T'' \neq T')[f(T') \geq f(T'')]$

Yoo and Harman [3] categorized 49 TCP papers published between 1999 and 2009 into the following groups:

- *Coverage-based prioritization:* The assumption is that the maximization of structural coverage will increase the chance of maximization of fault detection.
- *Distribution-based approach:* It prioritizes test cases based on the distribution of the profiles of test cases. Clustering test cases show that similar test cases are redundant and isolated clusters may cause failures.
- *Human-based approach:* Human tester is used in this kind of approaches. Prioritization is based on the comparisons made by the tester.
- *Probabilistic approach:* Probabilistic theory is applied. Bayesian Network-based approaches are shown in this category.
- *History-based approach:* Historical data such as execution history or change information is used in this approach.
- *Requirement-based approach:* Requirement properties are used.
- *Model-based approach:* Different models such as UML sequence or activity diagrams are used instead of code blocks.
- *Cost-aware approach:* The costs of test cases are taken into account because the costs of all the test cases cannot be equal.
- *Other approaches:* Authors showed the other techniques such as interface-contract mutation, relevant slices, and call-tree paths in this category.

Some researchers used feedback for TCP. For example, "additional method coverage prioritization" first selects a test case that provides the greatest method coverage, and then successively adds test cases that cover the most yet uncovered parts. It has been proved that simple coverage-based methods perform better than feedback-based methods [5]. Rothermel et al. [4] introduced APFD (average percentage of faults detected) metric to evaluate the effectiveness of prioritization techniques. Higher APFD metric implies better fault detection rate and it ranges from 0 to 100. Most of the researchers use this metric to evaluate their techniques.

3 Best Practices

In this section, we introduce the best practices and explain how we can use TCP methods for a successful implementation in a software company.

- *Start with a well-known, simple TCP method:* If companies start using TCP with complex methods, it will be very difficult to understand how the identified order is computed. Rothermel and Sebastian [5] showed that all the TCP methods they identified performed better than not prioritizing. Also, they had shown that simple coverage-based approaches are better than feedback-based and change-based approaches.

- *Decide whether TCP is necessary or not:* Rothermel and Sebastian [5] stated that TCP is not meaningful if the time spent to execute the test cases is short and if test cases are executed automatically. However, if the testing consumes so much time, if the tester has to check the intermediate results of tests, or the time allocated for testing is very limited, TCP will help a lot for software quality engineers and testers [5].
- *Always update the test suite:* When new features are implemented and added to the version control system, it is necessary to develop the relevant test cases and add these new test cases to the test suite. If this update mechanism is not setup properly, test cases to detect software faults will not be enough to detect all the faults for the whole product, and faults will not be detected as requested. Therefore, a proper update of test cases is a crucial issue for successful TCP.
- *Use automated tools:* When there are thousands of test cases, and millions of lines of code, it is not possible to compute the order of test cases manually. Instead, an automated tool should be preferred. If there is no such a tool, this may cause several computational problems or de-motivate the implementers of TCP. Companies may develop their own TCP tool if there is no specific tool for their needs.
- *Evaluate the effectiveness:* The performance of TCP methods may change based on the test suite granularity, modification location, and analysis level [5]. Therefore, the approach chosen at the first release should be evaluated for its effectiveness. The faults identified at the first release should be recorded. Researchers who work on TCP area access the repository SIR (Software-artifact Infrastructure Repository) [6] to get the datasets. SIR repository includes software artifacts that can be used by researchers who work on software testing methods and program analysis methods.
- *Build the enterprise repository:* Building a repository in a company is much more appropriate rather than using SIR repository. Therefore, SIR can be investigated in order to build a similar enterprise repository in the company.
- *Define the responsibilities:* Who will prioritize the test cases? When will they be prioritized? Who will evaluate the effectiveness of TCP method and when will it be evaluated? All these questions must be answered in the company for a successful TCP. Systematic approach for prioritization answers all of these questions.
- *Avoid subjective information:* Subjective information should not be used inside the TCP methods. For example, customer prioritization information may be very misleading for this problem because customers may not know which test case can detect more faults.
- *Document the experience and share:* A pilot project is a good starting point for the implementation of TCP in a company and results should be shared with the other groups in the company. Otherwise, the experience will not be known by all the employees.
- *Focus on available data instead of best method:* Instead of looking for the best approach in literature, implementers should look at what the available data is in the company. This will help them to start using TCP in a very short duration.

4 Related Work

There are many TCP papers that propose and validate prioritization approaches in literature, but we did not see any paper that suggests several success factors as performed in this study. Rothermel et al. [4] performed several experiments with the following prioritization techniques to improve the rate of fault detection: total statement coverage prioritization, additional statement coverage prioritization, total branch coverage prioritization, additional branch coverage prioritization, total fault-exposing-potential (FEP) prioritization, and additional fault-exposing-potential (FEP) prioritization. They showed that each of these prioritization techniques improved the rate of fault detection of test suites. They reported that additional FEP prioritization may not be as cost-effective as coverage-based techniques. On the Siemens programs, branch-coverage-based techniques were better than statement-coverage-based techniques but on the Space program, this difference did not occur.

Elbaum et al. [7] performed several experiments with prioritization techniques. They showed that fine-granularity techniques outperform course-granularity techniques by a small margin and incorporation of fault-proneness techniques provided small improvements. 18 test case prioritization techniques were examined and classified into three groups: comparator group (random, optimal), statement level group, and function-level group. Experimental results showed that version-specific prioritization improves the rate of fault detection, function-level and statement-level techniques provided similar results, and incorporation of fault-proneness into prioritization provided small improvements. Also, they reported that the best technique may vary across programs.

Rothermel and Elbaum [5] provide their own experiences on test case prioritization (TCP) techniques and summarize their previous studies in this paper. They stated that every prioritization technique they've investigated has created prioritized test suites that provide better performance than not prioritized test suites until now. They reported the following cost-effectiveness factors for TCP techniques: Test suite granularity, modification location, and level of analysis. They started that in many cases, performance varied with characteristics of test suites, programs, and faults. Also, they reported that simple coverage techniques outperformed techniques that incorporate feedback and techniques that utilizing modification information. To choose the best technique, authors suggest first to decide the data types that can be collected such as coverage effectively and then use historical data for the system. Average Percentage of Faults Detected (APFD) metric was widely used by authors to evaluate the effectiveness of techniques. They reported that if regression testing takes significant time to complete, requires expensive human intervention, or is performed under limited periods, prioritization will help a lot. However, if tests cases are executed fully automatically and short-lived, TCP might make no difference in testing processes. They mentioned about one company that has a regression test suite for a system of 20,000 lines of code that takes seven weeks and costs several hundred thousand dollars to execute. Therefore, it is very critical to prioritize test cases and increase a test suite's rate of fault detection.

Do et al. [8] performed experiments to examine the effectiveness of prioritization techniques on Java programs tested under JUnit. They showed that prioritization improves the rate of fault detection of JUnit test suites but there exists several differences compared to the previous studies. Nine techniques were considered and classified into three groups: Control techniques (no prioritization, random, optimal), block-level techniques, method-level techniques. They reported that test suite granularity did not affect the rate of fault detection.

5 APFD Metric and an Example

APFD (Average Percentage of Faults Detected) metric is used to evaluate the effectiveness of TCP methods. Companies may use this metric to evaluate the method they use and then, depending on the results, they may go on or switch to another method.

Let's assume that a program has 10 faults and there is a test suite including 5 test cases (A, B, C, D, and E). In Figure 1.1, each test case is shown with the fault that can be detected with that test case. Sign x indicates that this fault can be detected with this test case. For example, test case A can detect fault 1 and fault 5. While Figure 1.2 shows the rate of fault detection when the test case order is A-B-C-D-E, Figure 1.3 shows the rate of fault detection when the test order is C-E-B-A-D. As noted in the figures, APFD is 84 for Figure 1.3 and 50 for Figure 1.2. Therefore, C-E-B-A-D order is much more appropriate for this program. While axis y shows the percentage of detected faults, axis x shows the rate of applied test cases. For example, let's look at the figure of A-B-C-D-E order. When test case A is executed, two faults are detected and only one test case is executed in total. Therefore, value y will be 20% (2/10=20%) and value x will be 0.2 (1/5=0.2). When test case B is executed after test case A, fault 6 and fault 7 are detected. Therefore, y value will be 40% (4/10=40%) and value x will be 0.4 (2/5=0.40). Let's look at the figure of C-E-B-A-D order. When test case C is executed, seven faults are identified in total. For this reason, value y will be 70% (7/10=70%) and value x will be 0.2 (1/5=0.2). When we plot all the (x, y) points on the figure, we will see that the area under Figure 1.2 will be 50% and the area under Figure 1.3 will be 84%. According to these numerical values, the approach that provides the order C-E-B-A-D is much more efficient than the approach used for the A-B-C-D-E order.

We show how TCP works in a scenario by using the Table 1. Table 1 shows the statements covered by each test case (1, 2, and 3). Let's assume that we use total statement coverage prioritization and additional statement coverage prioritization techniques. According to the total statement coverage prioritization, Test Case-3 should be executed first because it covers the highest number of statements (eight statements). Later Test Case-1 and finally Test Case-2 should be executed. Therefore, the ordering should be 3-1-2 according to the total statement coverage prioritization.

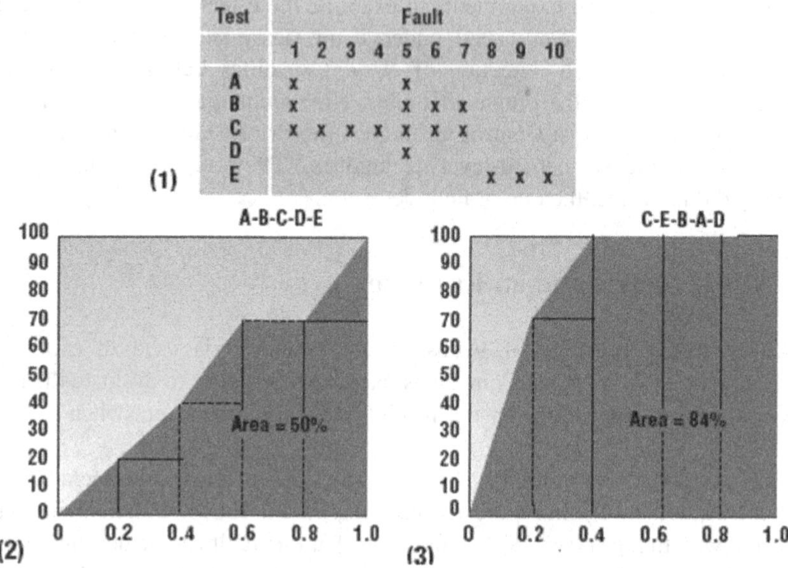

Fig. 1. APFD metric and rate of fault detection [5]

According to the additional statement coverage prioritization, Test Case-3 will be executed first because of the number of statements covered by this test case. Statement 4 will not be covered by Test Case-3 and therefore, the second test case should cover this test case. For this reason, Test Case-2 will be executed to cover Statement 4. Finally, Test Case-1 will be executed. The ordering will be 3-2-1 according to the additional statement coverage prioritization. This example was not taken from a real scenario and it is possible to see that additional statement coverage prioritization (an example of feedback-based approaches) performed better than the simpler approach. As we specified in previous chapters, researchers showed that simple coverage-based approaches perform better than feedback-based approaches in real projects. This simple example can be contradictory to that evidence, but this example is too simple for empirical evidence.

Table 1. Statements covered by test cases.

Statement	*Test case 1*	*Test case 2*	*Test case 3*
1	X	X	X
2	X	X	X
3		X	X
4		X	
5			X
6			X
7	X		X
8	X		X
9	X		X

6 Conclusion

Test case prioritization is one of the techniques that can help to execute the regression tests in a cost-effective manner and it has been quantitatively shown in literature that this method is very effective to improve the rate of fault detection. It is not enough to know the general issues of TCP for software companies. Companies should also be aware of the best practices that we introduced in this study for a successful implementation of TCP approaches. Future work could focus on investigating these practices for a very large scale software development project that consists of large number of test cases to get empirical evidence of the effectiveness of these practices.

References

[1] Elbaum, S., Kallakuri, P., Malishevsky, A.G., Rothermel, G., Kanduri, S.: Understanding the Effects of Changes on the Cost-Effectiveness of Regression Testing Techniques. Journal of Software Testing, Verification, and Reliability 13(2), 65–83 (2003)

[2] Do, H., Mirarab, S., Tahvildari, L., Rothermel, G.: The Effects of Time Constraints on Test Case Prioritization: A Series of Controlled Experiments. IEEE Trans. Software Eng. 36(5), 593–617 (2010)

[3] Yoo, S., Harman, M.: Regression Testing Minimization, Selection and Prioritization: a Survey. Software Testing, Verification and Reliability (published online in 2010), doi: 10.1002/stvr.430

[4] Rothermel, G., Untch, R.J., Chu, C.: Prioritizing Test Cases For Regression Testing. IEEE Trans. Softw. Eng. 27(10), 929–948 (2001)

[5] Rothermel, G., Elbaum, S.: Putting Your Best Tests Forward. IEEE Softw. 20(5), 74–77 (2003)

[6] http://sir.unl.edu/portal/index.html (accessed on December 5, 2011)

[7] Elbaum, S., Malishevsky, A.G., Rothermel, G.: Test Case Prioritization: A Family of Empirical Studies. IEEE Transactions on Software Engineering 28(2), 159–182 (2002)

[8] Do, H., Rothermel, G., Kinneer, A.: Prioritizing JUnit Test Cases: An Empirical Assessment and Cost-Benefits Analysis. Empirical Software Engineering 1(1), 33–70 (2006)

[9] http://selab.fbk.eu/swat/slide/test-case-prioritization.ppt (accessed on December 5, 2011)

Using a Semantic Wiki to Improve the Consistency and Analyzability of Functional Requirements

Jing Ma, Wuping Yao, Zheying Zhang, and Jyrki Nummenmaa

School of Information Sciences, University of Tampere 33014 Tampere, Finland
{Jing.Ma,Wuping.Yao,Zheying.Zhang,Jyrki.Nummenmaa}@uta.fi

Abstract. Even though the software industry seems to have matured from the initial stage, the software projects' success rates are still low. This is mainly because of lack of correct, unambiguous, complete, consistent description on software requirements. How to specify and represent requirements correctly, unambiguously, completely and reach a common understanding among stakeholders in software projects, have become high priority issues. The aim of this paper is to study the ways of specifying and representing the semantic information of functional requirements in software projects. We propose a meta-model and implement it into semantic forms in Semantic MediaWiki. Our approach enables the building of functional requirements on a common semantic basis, thereby improving the analyzability and consistency of the requirements. The wiki environment also enables asynchronous collaboration to create and maintain the functional requirements.

Keywords: Requirement Engineering, Functional Requirements, Semantic MediaWiki.

1 Introduction

Requirements analysis is an essential and critical task for software development success. Typically, software analysis models are manually produced from requirements specified in natural language (NL). Even though diverse techniques for requirements analysis and model derivation have been developed, problems still remain in this process, mainly related with the ambiguity, incompleteness and inconsistency of the documented requirements. Documenting high-quality software requirements [1] that efficiently support the follow-up software analysis and design remains a classical challenge to the requirements engineering research community.

Even if requirements are specified as a good quality document, transforming knowledge from requirements to software analysis and design is not easy. The NL processing techniques can help in parsing the text and analyzing the semantic content of the statements [2-4], but they are inherently brittle and limited [5, 6]. The analysis process involves great manual effort. If a common semantic basis can be established for the requirements, a lot of effort can be saved during the analysis and design processes.

T. Skersys, R. Butleris, and R. Butkiene (Eds.): ICIST 2012, CCIS 319, pp. 460–473, 2012.

In our work, we limit our scope to functional requirements (FRs), and study an approach to precisely specify a FR with its associated semantic information. We propose a meta-model as a basis for the description of semantic information. Our meta-model is similar to the one used by Guo et al [7], which was also used to unify the semantic information of FRs. The meta-model is based on identification of different linguistic elements of FRs. A typical FR contains a description of an action expected of the system, and can be simply specified by a verb-object pair, e.g., "confirm an order", along with further information such as who confirms the order? Where? How? etc. The information has different semantic roles within the action. We present a FR meta-model which adapts semantic cases [8] to specify the contextual information. The classification of linguistic elements is based on the classic Fillmore's case grammar theory [8] which analyzes the link between a verb and its semantic valency.

In order to follow the FR meta-model to specify the semantic information in a consistent and unambiguous way, a flexible and open platform for asynchronous collaboration to create and maintain FRs is required. Wikis in general provide such platforms that allow users to follow predefined templates to create and edit contents [9, 10]. More specifically, semantic wikis like Semantic MediaWiki (SMW) support semantic annotations of wiki pages and of the relations between wiki pages [11, 12], which makes it possible to specify and document the semantic information in a FR. Taking the advantage of the SMW, we develop semantic forms and templates for documenting the information expressed in FRs.

The idea of using semantic wikis to specify and manage requirements is not new. Many applications or research prototypes such as ReqMan [13], Moki [14], ReqWiki [15], etc. have provided support for requirements development and management. These tools, however, remain on a coarse-grained level to specify and manage requirements, which is insufficient to support requirements analysis for software modeling. The information embodied by individual FRs cannot be explicitly represented to support the follow-up software development activities. Our solution is the first attempt to combine the representation of the information of a FR with the functionality of a semantic wiki to specify requirements in a clear and consistent manner.

The remainder of the paper is organized as follows. Section 2 reviews different ways of requirements representation, and discusses their limitations in support of requirements analysis. Section 3 presents the meta-model for the FR specification and the reasoning behind it. On the basis of the meta-model, in Section 4 we develop semantic forms for the SMW. Section 5 discusses some benefits and limitations of our approach to FR specification. Section 6 concludes the paper.

2 Functional Requirements Representation

Requirements are specifications of the services that the system should provide, the constraints on the system and the background information that is necessary to developing the system [16]. Services of the system are commonly specified as FRs, which define the fundamental actions of a software application in accepting and processing the inputs and generating the outputs [1]. Besides, there are further concerns about the actions, such as validity checks on the inputs, exact sequence of operations, responses to abnormal situations, effect of parameters and relationship of outputs to inputs [1]. Together with actions, they form the essential data which reflects customer's needs and supports requirements analysis and software modeling.

FRs are commonly written in NL. The informal textual representation may be easy to understand, but it often contains ambiguous expressions and expressions with ill-defined syntax [17]. Moreover, it is much harder to validate FRs in NL than FRs embodied by prototypes [18]. And if the textual document becomes larger, the consistency and maintenance becomes even harder [19].

Well-defined and correct requirements have traditionally been seen as a critical factor behind software project success [1, 20]. The ambiguity of textual representation lies in the implicit and ambiguous semantic roles implied by data expressed in requirements. Even if a FR was specified correctly and precisely, the action and its associated information might not be equally obvious for heterogeneous groups of stakeholders to achieve a common and correct understanding [17, 20-22]. In many situations, requirements are represented as use cases or user stories which are often documented using templates [23-25] which specify information such as "who", "what", "why", "how" in software features and functions. Although there is no standard template, and users typically choose the template that works for them or is requirements by a project or a CASE tool, information documented in use cases or user stories can serve as a basis to elicit refined FRs. Further information such as the objects which are affected by actions, the constraints on actions, the conditions that enable an action, etc. can be achieved by analyzing textual requirements.

Pohl [20] addressed that the desired output of a requirements engineering process is a complete system specification expressed using a formal language on which all people involved agree. In order to represent the semantic meaning of a FR in an explicit manner, formalized representation is needed. The formal representations, such as mathematical expressions, have a precise syntax and rich semantics and, thus, provide a better basis for reasoning and verification, but they are hardly understood by non-technical users. Formal representations of just certain aspects of the system, such as ER diagrams or state diagrams, can provide a clear and more understandable view of the system. They are often applied in modeling domain concepts and context. These models and their semantic contents, however, are mainly derived by analyzing textual requirements.

The textual requirements have no deliberate separation of actions and the associated semantic information. It is tedious to parse the text to automate the analysis of information in different semantic roles. There is hence a need to develop a suitable approach to specifying and representing FRs and their structural information without ambiguity, and to better supporting the follow-up software analysis and design.

3 A Meta-model of Functional Requirements

Every FR is a complete sentence that expresses an action, the entities performing or affected by the action, the conditions and constraints on action, etc. It is natural to apply a linguistic analysis system such as Fillmore's case grammar theory [8] to assign semantic roles to the information specified in a FR. Many recent researches on domain engineering [7, 26-29] adapted semantic cases [8] to analyze and document requirements variability in software product line engineering. For example, Guo et al. [7] define a meta-model for product FRs. Their meta-model comprises a set of semantic cases such as Agentive, Dative, Objective, Instrumental, Factitive, Temporal, Locative, and Conditional to represent action-oriented concerns of a FR.

Even though linguistic analysis can serve as a meaningful framework to analyze the semantic information in a FR, it is difficult to precisely identify the distinct semantic cases expressed in every requirement statement. Many approaches on NL requirements analysis are inherently brittle and limited to a subset of NL [5, 6]. Instead of analyzing the semantic elements in a requirement, it is possible to proactively specify a FR into an action, associated with structural information in different semantic roles. In this way, the specified information can be directly used in requirements formalization and model derivation.

On the basis of the meta-model by Guo et al [7], we further clarify the description of semantic elements in a FR, and define the meta-mode for FRs specification. As shown in Fig. 1, every FR has a unique identifier (id), a name, a verb (action), and a free-text description (description). The verb simply represents an action implemented in the given FR. It is the core of a FR.

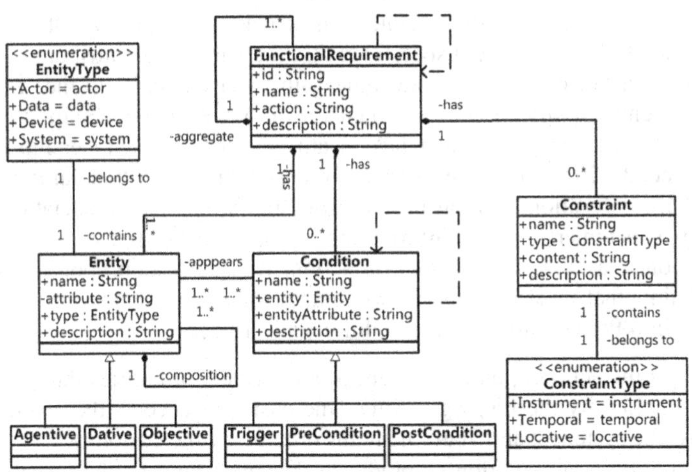

Fig. 1. Functional requirement meta-mode

FRs can be specified at different abstraction levels. A higher level requirement can be decomposed into a set of refined ones. During this recursive process, lower level requirements are derived from higher level feature or user requirements. The aggregation relationship associated with the FR helps to illustrate the hierarchical structure of requirements. Besides, the dependency relationship, represented in a dashed arrow, represents the sequence of operation between requirements.

The elaborate semantic information is further specified into entities, conditions and constraints.

An entity is a thing with distinct and independence existence. It is a person, object, place or event associated with an action implied by a FR. A FR statement can include a number of entities, with different roles. Some entities perform the action, while some are affected by the action. Even the same entity can take a dynamic role in different FRs, i.e. an entity can be an initiator of an action, and be a beneficiary of another action. Therefore, an entity is specialized into an Agentive, a Dative, or an Objective, as discussed in [7].

- *Agentive* is the semantic role of an initiator of an action. It is usually the grammatical subject of the verb in an active clause. An agentive is typically the system or its subsystem, an external actor or a combination of actors, e.g. "The $\{\text{system}\}_{Ag}$ shall show the product catalog to the customer".
- *Dative* is the concern of an object that is conscious of being affected by the action. It is typically the external actor or combinations of actors in an interaction between users and systems, e.g. "The system shall show the product catalog to the $\{\text{customer}\}_{D}$".
- *Objective* is the concern of an object that is advantaged or disadvantaged by the action. In contrast to Agentive and Dative, it is often inanimate, e.g. "The system shall show the $\{\text{product catalog}\}_{O}$ to the customer".

The attribute of an entity specifies the particular quality or status of the entity associated with the given requirement. It is usually an adjective of an entity in a clause. Instead of referring to a specific entity, the value of an attribute can indicate a set of entity instances that have the same value. For example, in the statement "a system shall send a notification email to customers whose membership is expired on Dec. 31 2012", the entity Customer has an attribute that his membership expiration date is on Dec. 31 2012. It implies a group of customers rather than an individual. In addition, the composition relationship specifies the whole-part association between entities, e.g. a customer's contact information is a part of an order.

A condition is a kind of constraint on action. It is the action upon the system or state constraints that must be satisfied while an action is activated or completed. We can refine it into Pre-condition, Post-condition and Trigger.

- *Trigger* is the action upon the system or an attribute of entities that activates the action implied by the FR, e.g. "After $\{\text{the customer accepts the changes on the order}\}_{T}$, the system shall list all the items ordered by the customer".
- *Pre-condition* is a condition or predicate that must be satisfied just prior to the execution of an action. Typically, a pre-condition can be represented as objects associated with their states, and placed before the trigger, e.g. "If $\{\text{the user is authenticated}\}_{PC}$, the system shall show the product catalog to the customer".
- *Post*-condition *is* a condition or predicate that must be satisfied just after the execution of an action. A post-condition represents the state resulting from the action, e.g. an accepted order is the post-condition of an action that a customer accepts his changes on the order. It is similar to the factitive case [7, 8] which concerns the object(s) that is/are resulting from an action or understood as a part of the meaning of the action. Pre-condition(s) and Post-condition(s) often imply the sequential order of actions.

No matter what specialized type a condition is, the predicate in a condition can be always interpreted as an entity, associated with a specific state or attribute, i.e. entityAttribute. Therefore, the condition can be specified as a composition of predicates which are combined with logical connectives, such as negation, conjunction or disjunction. In the meta-mode, the dependency relationship connects condition using such connectives.

A constraint defines the means how the action is implemented. Similar to what are presented in [8], the means of implementation is classified into different types, i.e. Temporal, Instrumental and Locative.

- *Temporal* defines the frequency or duration of an action, e.g. "The system shall automatically log the customer off after $\{10\text{ minutes}\}_T$ of inactivity".
- *Locative* identifies the location or spatial orientation of an action, e.g. "The customer can add one or more items in the $\{\text{order}\}_L$."
- *Instrumental* concerns the tool(s) or method(s) used by the Agentive to implement an action. It is usually nouns occurring in the noun phrase of a clause, e.g. "The system shall send the confirmation to the customer by $\{\text{an email and a short message}\}_I$".

The meta-mode explicitly defines semantic elements within an action of a FR. Individual statement can be prepared by following the definition in the meta-mode. Taking an online shopping application as an example, there is a set of FRs related to the process of placing an order and making changes, as shown in Fig. 2.

... ...
Order.Creation: *The customer can select one or more items from product catalog list, define the quantity of the selected items, and create an order.*
Order.Modification.Add: *Before confirming an order, the customer can add items into the order.*
Order.Modification.Remove: *......*
Order.Modification.Change: *... ...*
Order.Modification.Acceptance_Prompt: *The system shall prompt the customer to initially accept his changes before he proceeds to the next page.*
... ...

Fig. 2. An Excerpt of functional requirements for an online shopping web application

Instead of specifying requirements in NL, we can specify the structural information of the above FRs by following the meta-mode definition, as shown in Table 1. The information assigned by different semantic roles is explicitly presented in a simplified form. The properties of each element like the type of entity, etc. will be illustrated in the later section. Following the definition of the meta-model, we can easily identify concepts (i.e. entities) that are used in the application domain, analyze the properties possessed by entities (i.e. attributes of an entity), and analyze the possible sequence of operation by checking the conditions of an action. It is intuitive to further generate data structure models and behavior models for software analysis and design.

Table 1. Examples of contextual information in functional requirements

Name: Order.Creation **Action:** Create **Objective:** Order **Agentive:** Customer **Pre-condition:** items are selected AND their quantity is defined **Post-condition:** an order is initially accepted **Locative:** product catalog list page	**Name:** Order.Modification.Add **Action:** Add **Objective:** Product Item(s) **Agentive:** Customer **Pre-condition:** the order is initially accepted **Post-condition:** new items are added into the order **Locative:** order page (attribute: current)	**Name:** Order.Modification.Acceptance_Prompt **Action:** Prompt **Objective:** Change acceptance prompt **Agentive:** System **Dative:** Customer **Trigger:** Customer proceeds to the next page **Pre-condition:** items are added into the order OR items are removed from the order OR the quantity of items changes **Post-condition:** an order is initially accepted **Locative:** Order page (attribute: current)

4 Using Semantic Forms to Specify Functional Requirements

Wikis provide a flexible and open platform for asynchronous collaboration to create content in general [9, 10]. They are useful in projects for organizing, tracking, and publishing the work, especially in the distributed projects. In order to retrieve relevant knowledge and make structured data more accessible for users, Semantic wikis combine semantic web technologies with the functionality of a wiki, and use RDF for semantic annotations of wiki pages and of the relations between wiki pages [11, 12]. The semantic annotations provide improved navigation and search, context dependent presentation, and are increasingly used in knowledge management and ontology engineering [30]. For example, AceWiki [31] is a semantic wiki to manage knowledge representations by using a predictive editor to construct sentences following often used sentence patterns. Semantic MediaWiki (SMW) is an extension to MediaWiki [32] that allows for annotating semantic data within wiki pages. It has gained traction in creating domain terminologies and ontology. Kiwi [33] provides a flexible and adaptable platform to implement and integrate many different kinds of social software services. KnowWE [34] defines and maintains ontologies and problem-solving knowledge to support collaboratively build decision-support systems.

4.1 Semantic Wikis for Requirements Engineering

Taking the advantage of semantic annotation in the context of software development, a lot of researchers utilize the feature to develop applications for creating, maintaining and managing software artifacts, especially at the requirements stage. Many applications use the SMW extension to provide a technical platform with semantic support for requirements development and management. For example, ReqMan [13] represents a reference model of wiki-based support at different stages of requirements engineering process. The concepts are further implemented in SOP [35], which is partly based on SMW. Moki [14] supports enterprise modeling, with a focus on the domain ontology models and process models. ReqWiki [15] includes NL processing assistants to support the creation of requirements and the derivation of traceability matrices. In addition, SoftWiki [36] is a plug-in for a semantic data wiki, Ontowiki, It enables stakeholders to collaboratively specify, query and rearrange requirements.

The semantic annotation in the above applications improves the navigation, search, and contextual information representation in requirements for software development. They, however, hardly provide precise support for analyzing and representing the semantic knowledge express inside individual requirements. Even though ReqWiki [15] provides pre-defined semantic form to help users in creating various requirements artifacts and the required metadata, the analysis of semantic knowledge in individual requirements remains on a coarse-grained level. The semantic annotation shall be further refined to specify entities, conditions, constraints, etc. in a requirement. In this way, it is possible to provide efficient support for domain analysis and model generation.

4.2 Representing Functional Requirements in Semantic Forms

In order to analyze and represent the semantic concerns in a FR, we elaborate on SMW and seek for solutions to FRs specification. SMW organizes the structure of data into *category*, *form*, *template* and *property*. *Forms* are created to add and edit wiki pages. Each wiki page holds one and only one *form*. A *form* contains a (set of) *template(s)* and every *template* can be used more than once. A *template* sets the display of the semantic data on a page, and the data is specified by *properties*. *Properties* can be viewed as categories for values in wiki pages.

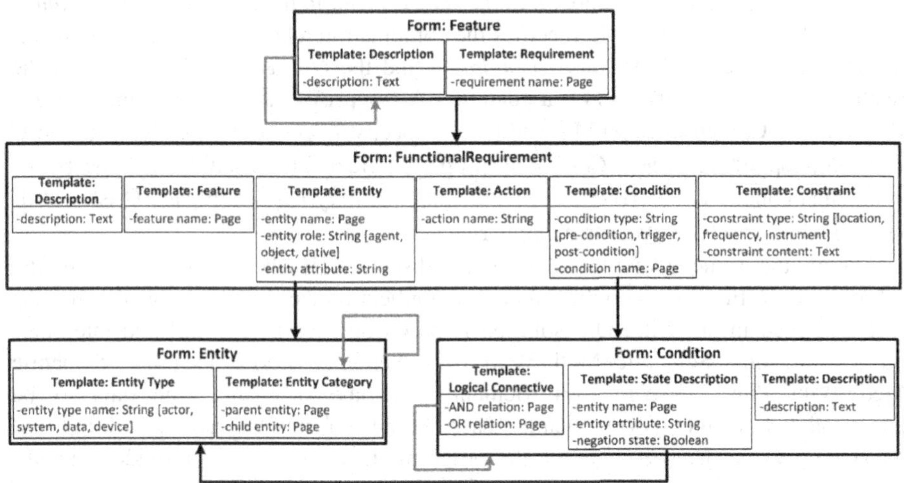

Fig. 3. Mapping from meta-model to wiki pages

According to the meta-model defined in section 3, we define four forms, i.e. *Feature*, *FunctionalRequirement*, *Entity* and *Condition,* as shown in Fig. 3. Every form contains a template *Description* to describe the contents of the form in a free text. A link between a template and a form indicates the value of a property of type Page linked to another page in the wiki, and the page name is the value of the property.

A *Feature* contains a list of FRs, as shown in the template *Requirement* in which the property *requirement name* is a Page type and links to another page which has a default form *FunctionalRequirement.* The order of requirements can be adjusted by dragging the FRs up and down in the *feature* form.

A *FunctionalRequirement* contains templates specifying the action implied by the given requirements and its related information, i.e. *Action*, *Entity*, *Condition* and *Constraint.* Properties in every template define the input that will show up in the form. A Page type property links the value of the property to a default page, e.g. the property *entity name* in the template *Entity* links to the page which has the default form *Entity*.

An *Entity* has property *entity type*, which has four default values: *actor*, *system, data* and *device*. The properties *parent entity* and *child entity* have a Page type linking to another *Entity* page. The link shows the composition relationship represented in the meta-mode.

A *Condition* contains a *Logical Connective* template and one or more *State Description* template. The *state Description* template specifies the state of the system that shall be satisfied. It consists of an entity (i.e. *entity name*) and its state (i.e. *entity attribute)* that shall be satisfied in a given requirement. Normally, an adjective is used to represent the state of an entity. If a condition is a trigger and it expresses the action upon the system, it shall be interpreted as a state of an entity. Besides, the Boolean property *negation state* indicates the unary negation connective. If its value is true, it means that the corresponding entity shall not be in the state defined in the property *entity attribute*. A *Logical Connective* template specifies the combination relationship of conditions, i.e. binary connectives such as the *AND relation* and the *OR relation. The* usage of the relations follows two rules: (1) if a condition A comprises of a binary connective, *i.e.* $B\wedge C$ or $B\vee C$, then there will be two links respectively connect to condition B and C in the corresponding *Logical Connective* property field; (2) if a condition A appears in a compound condition, *e.g.* $(B\wedge C)\ \vee D$, then an auxiliary *Condition* page *D'* should be used to replace $(B\wedge C)$. After that, apply rule (2).

Taking the same example as what we discussed in the previous section, the information of FRs for the online shopping application can be documented using the forms defined in our wiki. Our solution is based on MediaWiki [32] and integrates three extensions: Semantic MediaWiki [37], Semantic Forms [38] and Semantic MediaWiki Plus (SMW+) [39]. Semantic MediaWiki enables the data to be interrelated. Semantic Forms enables users to have forms for adding, editing and querying data on the wiki without any programming. [38] SMW+ provides friendly user interface and convenient user operation support. Fig. 4 shows the screenshots of FRs documented for the online shopping application. Page 1 is a form-based interface that lets the user enter FRs to wiki pages. Semantic forms then generate presentations of this form-entered data for each wiki page in tables, e.g. Page 3 presents the requirement "Create an order" that is edited in page 1. The semantic elements of the requirement are represented in tables. Page 2 presents the view of the feature "place an order" which contains a list of requirements such as "Create an order". The link of requirements leads to the corresponding requirement representation form. Page 4

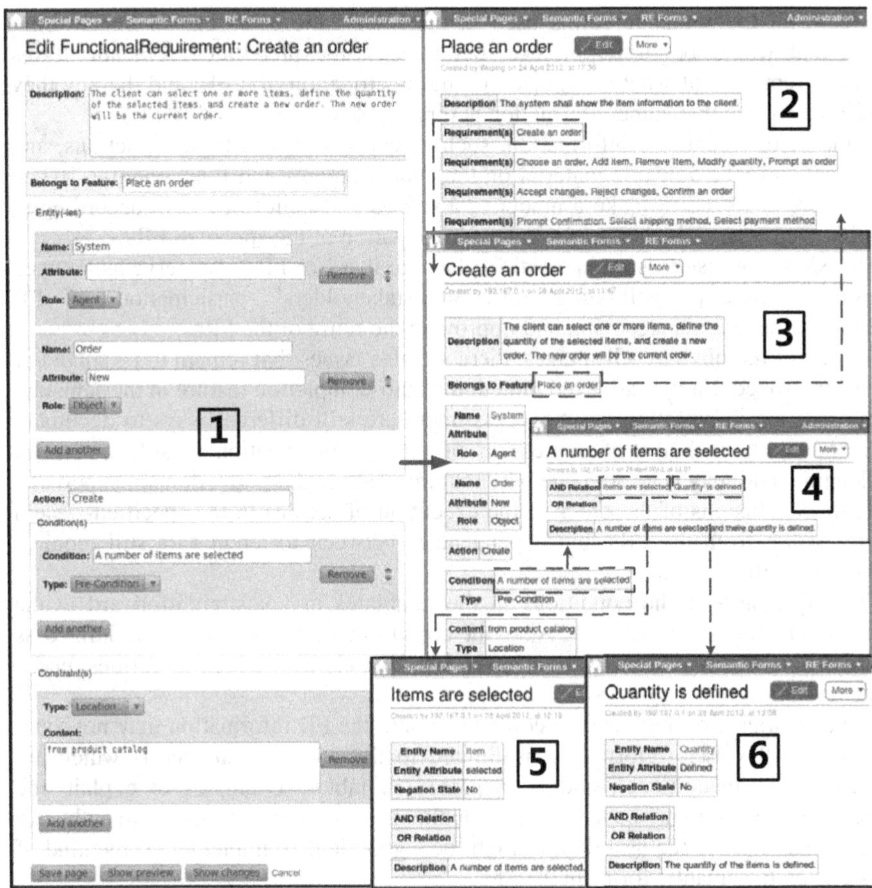

Fig. 4. Representation of "Place an order"

shows the AND relation of two conditions in the requirement "Create an order", i.e. items are selected and quantity is defined. Details of the conditions are further presented in Condition pages 5 and 6.

5 Discussion

We propose an approach, where the FRs are documented using the SMW. The use of SMW is based on the definition of related templates and forms, which, in turn, are based on a meta-model for FRs, also developed as a part of this work.

There are clear advantages of using our approach. First of all, it is easier to analyze the FRs, because they are already presented based on a meta-model that separates different aspects of the FRs. Also, the related data items, conditions, etc., are linked to each other in the SMW's data model. This improves the semantic consistency of the FRs, documented in the SMW according to the meta-model.

Even with the semantic forms used in the SMW, the users can of course omit details that would be of importance, but at least the predefined semantic forms provide a reminder of what is expected in the specification of a FR, and thereby they reduce the chance that some information is forgotten.

Some of the identified information, such as entities, their attributes, actions, and conditions, provide valuable material on the data structures and functionalities, when the FRs are analyzed to make a model of a software system to be built according to the FRs. One way to do this is by further formalization of the specified FRs.

The SMW, by itself, is an interesting platform that, for FRs, can serve as an open repository, thereby facilitating different stakeholders' participation in FR documentation and management, and improving the reuse of the FRs.

In spite of the obvious advantages, there are also issues that remain to be solved or at least improved. First of all, even though the auto-completion feature in the semantic form eases the information input process, there are still different ways to document FRs, and a good choice of expression of the FR information is still somewhat challenging, and may need some help by requirements analysts and domain experts.

Some conclusions of the order of the execution of actions in the specified system can be drawn from the FRs, but dependencies between different FRs still requires further in-depth analysis.

The expression of the conditions in the templates in not straightforward at the moment, and needs further work. Also, the constraints are, at the moment, defined as separate elements, and their relationships with other elements, such as entities, needs further attention.

The appearance of the forms to edit and present the FR information may not seem intuitive for the user. Information is limited to the concepts and terms which are defined in the meta-model, and is presented in tables. Examples to explain the concepts in the form may be useful to guide the user to understand the form and enter the data. To improve the usability, it might be a good idea to implement some kind of an extension to semantic forms in the SMW.

6 Conclusions

In this paper, we propose a meta-model and SMW-based solution for specification of the information in a FR. Our work has yielded two main contributions. First, we propose a meta-model for the representation of FRs in the SMW, based on a set of semantic roles. The meta-model supports documentation of FRs to express and the FRs and their structural information in a precise manner. Secondly, based on the meta-model, we define semantic forms for the presentation of FRs in the SMW. The structured semantic forms facilitate the identification and documentation of the information contained in a set of FRs in a consistent manner. The SMW is a flexible platform, and enables asynchronous collaboration to create and maintain FRs.

In spite of the obvious advantages of using the proposed SMW forms, based on our meta-model, there are still many open issues to resolve, as discussed in the previous section. It will be our objective to tackle these issues in the future. The SMW is an open and flexible platform for collaboration to create and manage requirements. Besides specifying requirements, we can take the advantage of the platform and propose extensions that can utilize our current requirements specification to better support requirements analysis and the follow-up design activities. Moreover, developing a set of practices in requirements specification involves application and validation across a variety of domains and organizations. In the future, we would seek to develop and validate our ideas in different contexts on an on-going basis. A further topic for future work is the development of methods to utilize the requirements collected using the SMW.

The true value of the proposed method is hard to evaluate, because of the pros and cons associated: for many users, additional effort is needed to document the requirements using such a systematic way, and the added value of the improved documentation is not realized immediately, but over time when the system analysis and implementation takes place. Further, the system development methodology needs to be adapted to fully utilize the improved semantic information, including automated or semi-automated methods utilizing the semantic information that can be made available about the desired system. This area provides challenges for further work.

References

1. IEEE: In IEEE Recommended Practice for Software Requirements Specifications. Technical report, IEEE Std 830-1998 (1998)
2. Luisa, M., Mariangela, F., Pierluigi, I.: Market research for requirements analysis using linguistic tools. Requirements Engineering 9, 40–56 (2004)
3. Mu, Y., Wang, Y., Guo, J.: Extracting Software Functional Requirements from Free Text Documents. In: Proceedings of the International Conference on Information and Multimedia Technology. IEEE Computer Society, Washington, DC (2009)
4. Zhang, Z., Nummenmaa, J., Guo, J., Ma, J., Wang, Y.: Patterns for Activities on Formalization Based Requirements Reuse. In: Wang, Y., Li, T. (eds.) Knowledge Engineering and Management. AISC, vol. 123, pp. 695–707. Springer, Heidelberg (2011)
5. Ambriola, V., Gervasi, V.: Processing natural language requirements. In: Proceedings of the 12th IEEE International Conference on Automated Software Engineering, pp. 36–45. IEEE Press (1997)
6. Mate, J.L., Silva, A.: Requirements Engineering for Sociotechnical Systems. Information Science Publishing (2005)
7. Guo, J., Wang, Y., Zhang, Z., Nummenmaa, J., Niu, N.: Model-driven approach to developing domain functional requirements in software product lines. IET Software (to appear, 2012)
8. Fillmore, C.: The Case for Case. In: Bach, E., Harms, R. (eds.) Universals in Linguistic Theory, pp. 1–88. Holt, Rinehart and Winston, New York (1968)
9. Louridas, P.: Using Wikis in Software Development. IEEE Software 23, 88–91 (2006)
10. Decker, B., Ras, E., Rech, J., Jaubert, P., Rieth, M.: Wiki-Based Stakeholder Participation in Requirements Engineering. IEEE Software 24, 28–35 (2007)
11. Oren, E.: SemperWiki: a semantic personal Wiki. In: Proceedings of Semantic Desktop Workshop on The Semantic Desktop, 4th International Semantic Web Conference, Galway, Ireland (2006)
12. Kousetti, C., Millard, D.E., Howard, Y.: A Study of Ontology Convergence in a Semantic Wiki. In: Proceedings of the 4th International Symposium on Wikis. ACM, New York (2008)

13. Pedersen, M.G.: `http://www.requirementone.com/` (access date: April 2012)
14. Rospocher, M., Ghidini, C., Pammer, V., Serafini, L., Lindstaedt, S.: MoKi: the Modelling Wiki. In: Knowledge Management. CEUR Workshop Proceedings, vol. 464, pp. 113–128 (2009)
15. Concordia University: ReqWiki, `http://www.semanticsoftware.info/reqwiki` (access date: April 2012)
16. Zave, P.: Classification of Research Efforts in Requirements Engineering. ACM Computing Surveys 29, 315–321 (1997)
17. Lamsweerde, A.V.: Formal specification: A roadmap. In: ICSE 2000: Proceedings of the Conference on The Future of Software Engineering, New York, USA, pp. 147–159 (2000)
18. Ravid, A., Berry, D.M.: A method for extracting and stating software requirements that a user interface prototype contains. Requirements Engineering 5, 225–241 (2000)
19. Davis, A., Overmyer, S., Jordan, K., Ceruso, J., Dandashi, F., Dinh, A., et al.: Identifying and measuring quality in a software requirements specification. In: Proceedings of the 1st International Software Metrics Symposium, Baltimore, MD, pp. 141–152. IEEE Computer Society Press, Los Alamitos (1993)
20. Pohl, K.: The Three Dimensions of Requirements Engineering. In: Rolland, C., Cauvet, C., Bodart, F. (eds.) CAiSE 1993. LNCS, vol. 685, pp. 275–292. Springer, Heidelberg (1993)
21. Young, R.R.: Recommended Requirements Gathering Practices. Crosstalk 15, 9–12 (2002)
22. Nummenmaa, J., Zhang, Z., Nummenmaa, T., Berki, E., Guo, J., Wang, Y.: On the Generation of DisCo Specifications from Functional Requirements. Department of Computer Sciences, University of Tampere (2010)
23. Jacobson, I., Booch, G., Rumbaugh, J.: The Unified Software Development Process. Addison-Wesley Professional, USA (1999)
24. Cockburn, A.: Writing Effective Use Cases. Addison-Wesley, Boston (2001)
25. Cohn, M.: User Storeis Applied: for Agile Software Development. Addison-Wesley Professional (2004)
26. Moon, M., Chae, H.S., Yeom, K.: An approach to developing domain requirements as a core asset based on commonality and variability analysis in a product line. IEEE Transactions on Software Engineering 31, 551–569 (2005)
27. Liaskos, S., Lapouchnian, A., Yu, Y., Yu, E., Mylopoulus, J.: On Goal-based Variability Acquisition and Analysis. In: Proceedings of the 14th IEEE International Conference of Requirements Engineering, USA (2006)
28. Niu, N., Easterbrook, S.: Extracting and modeling product line functional requirements. In: Proceedings of the 16th IEEE International Requirements Engineering Conference, pp. 155–164. IEEE Computer Society, Washington, DC (2008)
29. Guo, J., Zhang, Z., Wang, Y.: Model-Driven Derivation of Domain Functional Requirements from Use Cases. Journal of Software Engineering and Applications 3, 875–881 (2010)
30. Maedche, A., Staab, S.: Learning Ontologies for the Semantic Web. Journal IEEE Intelligent Systems 16 (2001)
31. Tobias, K.: AceWiki: A Natural and Expressive Semantic Wiki. In: Proceedings of the Fifth International Workshop on Semantic Web User Interaction. CEUR Workshop Proceedings, vol. 543 (2009)
32. WikiMedia Foundation, `http://www.mediawiki.org/` (access date: April 2012)
33. Schaffert, S., Eder, J., Grunwald, S., Kurz, T., Radulescu, M.: KiWi - A Platform for Semantic Social Software Demonstration. In: The Semantic Web: Research and Applications, Proceedings of the 6th European Semantic Web Conference, Heraklion, Greece, pp. 888–892 (2009)

34. Baumeister, J., Reutelshoefer, J., Puppe, F.: KnowWE: A Semantic Wiki for Knowledge Engineering. Applied Intelligence 35, 323–344 (2011)
35. Weber, S., Thomas, L., Armbrust, O., Ras, E., Rech, J., Uenalan, O., et al.: A Software Organization Platform (SOP). In: The 10th Workshop on Learning Software Organizations, Rome, Italy (2008)
36. Riechert, T., Berger, T.: Leveraging Semantic Data Wikis for Distributed Requirements Elicitation. In: Proceedings of the 4th Workshop on Wikis for Software Engineering Wikis4SE at 31st International Conference on Software Engineering, pp. 12–19. IEEE Computer Society, Vancouver (2009)
37. Semantic MediaWiki, http://semantic-mediawiki.org/ (access date: April 2012)
38. Yaron, K., Stephan, G.: Extension: Semantic Forms, http://www.mediawiki.org/wiki/Extension:Semantic_Forms (access date: April 2012)
39. Semantic MediaWiki Plus, http://www.smwplus.com (access date: April 2012)

Towards Software Testing Process Improvement from Requirements

Kristina Smilgyte[1] and Rimantas Butleris[2]

[1] Kaunas University of Technology, Department of Information Systems, Studentu st. 50-309, LT-51368, Kaunas, Lithuania
kristina.smilgyte@gmail.com
[2] Kaunas University of Technology, Centre of Information Systems Design Technologies, Studentu st. 50-313a, LT-51368, Kaunas, Lithuania
rimantas.butleris@ktu.lt

Abstract. Software requirements are the concurrent part of any project. However, these requirements are not effectively used in the testing process. The solutions founded in literature not only confirm the relevance of the software requirements and testing, but also reveal the absence of better solution combining software requirements and testing in a single element. The solution how to minimize the gap between requirements and testing is presented in this paper, since it is especially significant in a change of requirements. The idea of solution is based on gathering the useful data for information system testing from requirements and transforming it into structural models.

Keywords: Software Process Improvement, Software Testing, Requirement Engineering, Models Transformation, Requirements-Based Testing.

1 Introduction

Rising the demand of customers, the created software becomes more complicated and greater, influencing its advanced testing. The question how not to lose between volatile software requirements and maintain the appropriate software testing becomes more relevant while implementing various IT projects.

Software testing or its wider idea – software quality closely correlates with requirement engineering and requirements. The requirement is one of the essential attribute of the software. Requirements are usually formulated by sentences identifying software abilities, characteristics or quality factors, providing the benefit for software users [1]. Requirements specify the possibilities of information systems, whereas the testing have to certain that the software satisfies the specifications. The insufficient and inappropriate coherence of requirements and testing functions are frequent problems in order to obtain the high quality of the created product and its development. Performing the testing it is significant to know whether the requirements influencing the particular test are not being modified. Information concerned with changed requirements helps analyzing defects found during the testing, since it indicates the requirement to update tests and minimizes the reporting of incorrect defects. Also, there is a lack of information related to the effective organization of test development with reference to particular requirements of the software.

T. Skersys, R. Butleris, and R. Butkiene (Eds.): ICIST 2012, CCIS 319, pp. 474–481, 2012.

In literature, authors analyzing similar problems represent two aspects of reviews and suggestions. The ones analyze the direct linking and traceability between requirements and testing [2], [3], while the others – the methods how to obtain the required elements for testing using the available requirements [4], [5], [6]. Elements include the test scenario (test scenario is an account or synopsis of a projected course of events or actions, commonly used for groups of test cases [7]), test, model or other result influencing the testing process. It is chosen to improve the gathering of information from requirements, to add requirements with their design requirements and to compose the test scenarios while evaluating the relevant demand to have closer link between requirement engineering and testing range. This demand is also confirmed by the analysis in 2011 paper [3] of Barmi et al, which includes the researches of the last decade in this area.

The paper represents an idea for information systems, which allocates to minimize the gap between requirements and testing, to improve the tester's work organizing the scenarios of tests in accordance with the requirements indispensable for the software, to give some concreteness when necessary to evaluate which part of requirements is covered with tests. The gap between requirements and testing is minimized by creating the patterns (models) of requirement, which are transformed into structural models providing their adaptability in testing.

The related work review is presented in chapter 2. The development idea of the testing process using requirements is presented in chapter 3. The conclusions and further work are given in the last part of the paper.

2 Related Work

The requirement engineering and testing have a synergistic relationship. Using good requirements the better tests are developed, whereas the accomplished good analysis of tests improves the quality of requirements. Analyzing the solutions presented in literature the greater consideration is given to works proposing the suggestions how to apply the requirements in the process of testing more effective. The detection of various mistakes in a process of development cost much cheaper than finding the mistake when the product is already given to customers. The timely correction of mistakes requires less effort, since it is possible to avoid the fundamental changes of the software reliant on the mistake type. Implementing the software to the customer and finding the mistake it is essential not only to correct it, but also to update or implement the software once more [8].

It is possible to improve the general quality of requirements and testing having complete, well defined and qualitative documents of the software. The checking idea of the project documents (e.g. specification of requirements, design documents, test plans) introduced by Dautovic et al can be applied in both mentioned cases [9]. Automated document quality defect detection approach is used for popular types of document formats such as doc, pdf, ppt, xls [9]. The checking of documents is based on the usage of quality rules. For example, using such method, it is possible to check whether all pictures have reference in the text or not. The particular description of the picture in the text gives more accuracy and concreteness in order to minimize the interpretations while analyzing the document by various project members, since the pictures are rarely self-explanatory. Dautovic et al who adapted document defect detection approach confirmed that the defect detection tool of natural language text is not fully able to replace the human work [9]. Subject to the particularity of the project documents the time committed to the application of rules or configuration buys off only when the rules are properly applied without modifying.

In order to improve the defect detection in the software requirements and in the developing software, the preliminary works of the testing are started before the developed software or its part is prepared to the testing. According to the accuracy and explicitness of the requirements, both, the programmer and the tester interpret them diversely regarding the human factor. The automated test generation from the diagrams of use cases introduced in the paper [4] can minimize this factor. The flow of events is made from elaborate sequence diagram and additional information for each use case if it is necessary. The text file from the obtained information is generated and test cases are presented for each of the use case. Managing these test cases both, the programmer and tester manually check the accordance of software or its part with the requirements and indicate the tested situations of the given list. Test case is documentation specifying inputs, predicted results and a set of execution conditions for the test item [7]. McGregor maintains that the use cases for testing have to be selected according to the priority [10]. There is no great difference while working with small projects. However, for large projects it gives security that the main project parts will be tested in short terms. The detected defects are eliminated in a period of project assurance performing minor software updates. Applying use cases introduced as UML notation the MATE (Methodology for Automated model-driven testing) methodology is presented in the paper [6]. This methodology describes how to obtain the executable test code for the particular use case by transforming the models. From requirements given as diagram of use case the UML sequences and states diagrams are created and the test code is obtained by performing the transformations. The diagram of sequences expands the use case while the state diagram gives the finite states of it. The methodology framework based on the standards of Object Management Group (OMG), therefore it is realized in almost all supportive tools of UML.

The next method to reduce the human factor is the semi automated generation of UML models from natural language. It is called UMGAR [5]. Before performing the generation of UML models (use case, class and collaboration model for each use case), the requirements expressed in natural language are normalized. UMGAR additionally uses Stanford Parser, WordNet2.1 and JavaRAP tools and human interaction during elimination of irrelevant classes and identification of aggregation/composition relationship among objects. UMGAR in contradistinction to other similar approach solutions can process the considerable amount specification files of requirements. The final result of UMGAR is the generated XML Metadata Interchange (XMI) files. The visual model form is obtained while XML files are imported into the UML modeling tool, which supports the XMI importing possibility.

It is possible to achieve more unanimous conception of requirements not only by generating the models from natural language, but also like Silingas et al are state [11], while composing the models it is required to comply with one common UML of software modeling standard and to use its possibilities more effective. The idea in the paper presents how coherently to model the software requirements using various UML diagrams and gives illustrative examples. It encourages not restricting with the use cases and sequencing diagrams, which are prevalent as initial sources for the test generation.

Some solutions give the direct benefit to the testing. For example, the link between particular requirements specified by use case diagram and test verifying them. The other solutions improve testing process in an indirect way. In this way the design possibilities of UML models from requirements or quality improvement of document requirements are analyzed. Table 1 represents the way how various solutions influence the testing process. In order to minimize the gap between requirements and testing the more general guidelines indicating the presentation of the requirements, test design and influence evaluation of requirement change are necessary. The existing solutions are committed to individual details; however, the detailed integration analysis of them is not given.

Table 1. The direct and indirect influence of requirements for testing

Solution	The influence of requirements for testing	
	Direct	Indirect
Quality improvement of document requirements [9].	-	The more detailed requirements are described, the more obvious details of testing object are.
Test generation from use case diagram [4]	The test case list is received for each use case. In such way it is known what to check.	Minimizes the different interpretation of requirements concerning the human factor.
Priority assignment for use cases [10]	The use cases having high usage or risk importance are tested primarily.	Reduces the risk that the main parts would be left untested.
MATE methodology application [6]	The test code is received for particular use case.	Requirements and testing are related to UML models.
UML models generation from natural language [5]	-	The generated UML models can be used in developing tests.
The application of general standard designing models such as UML [11].	-	It is stimulated to have various assortments of models using the same UML standard. In such way the UML and other models designing the tests can appear (not only use case or sequence diagrams).

3 Proposed Solution

The idea of the testing process improvement based on requirements mentioned in a literature is introduced considering the solutions for improvement of requirements or the usage in a testing of their single parts. The main parts of the developing project are introduced as the UML activity diagram in Fig 1.

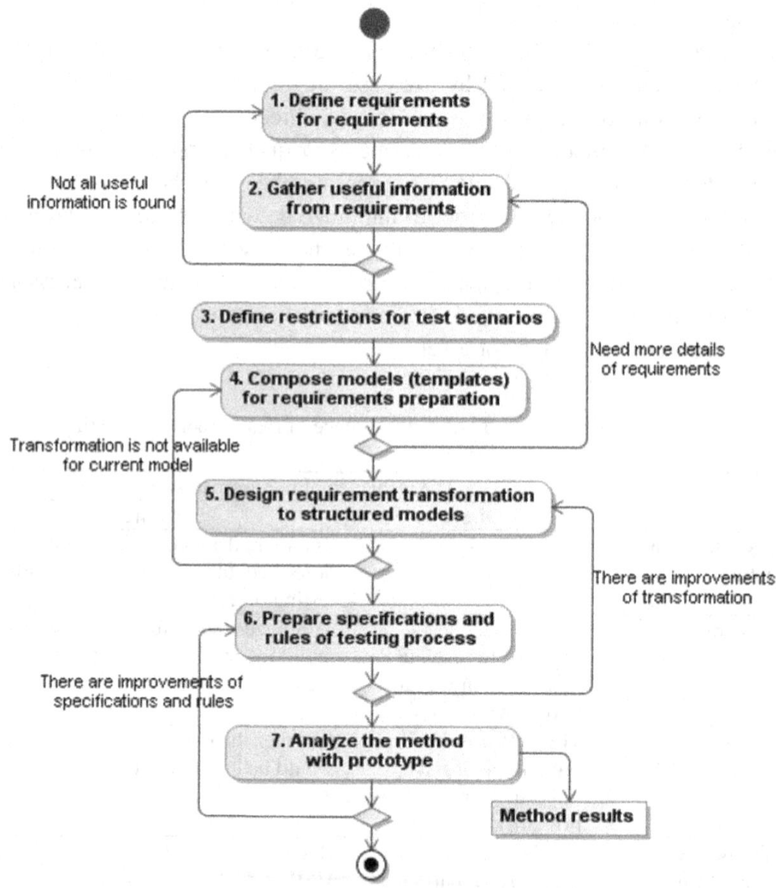

Fig. 1. The idea of software testing process improvement from requirements

Define Requirements for Requirements. Initial project requirements have to be defined because of the different methods of specification of requirements and the particularity of the presentation. The components of requirements are outlined according to the rules [9] defined by Dautovic et al in order to minimize the defects in documents and represent them as more complete. Rules of requirements are going to enhance the confidence that the required information for testing is in the document of project requirements. The rules are expressed with the sentences if-then and with the restrictions defining the composition of requirements. For example, the restriction – *„recommendations for the testing environment have to be defined in the specification"*. The usage of if then – *„if the internet browsers are assigned to software environment, then the oldest supportive version has to be indicated to each of them"*.

Gather Useful Information from Requirements. Gathering the useful information from requirements involves the representation of requirements UML models in order to give them particularity and quicker conveyance of information [12]. For example, the software users have to be named by project members. In accordance with the diagram of use cases identifying the users it is simpler and quicker (since they are already excluded as actors) than finding them in natural language text.

Define Restrictions for Test Scenarios. The outline of test scenarios limitations includes the exclusion of the main differences of business scenarios and test cases. It is essential to define the definitions, since their use would be equally understood, without personal interpretations or the lack of the knowledge by persons not particularly working with the requirements and/or testing processes.

Compose Models (Templates) for Requirements Preparation. The composition of models (templates) appends and elaborates the second clause outlining how to prepare the requirements which would maintain the compatibility with testing process and its further parts. The greater amount of requirements have to be reflected in the models (templates) applying them in a software testing in order to enhance the coverage of software requirements with the tests. Designing the models (templates) the evaluation in which form the given requirements can be related to automated test development and which requirements can't be related in further stages is made.

Design Requirement Transformation to Structured Models. Having the composed models (templates) from the previous stage the algorithms and rules allowing the requirements to be transformed from the second stage into the defined structured models in a fourth stage are prepared. The tester or other person of the project should not be burden with transformation. It has to enhance the integrity of the requirements and testing.

Prepare Specifications and Rules of Testing Process. Evaluating the results and testing process from previous stages the specifications and rules are in order to automate the testing process in accordance with models of requirements. The results and evaluation of testing process from previous stages are performed in accordance with adaptability of existing software tools, integration possibilities of received results for individual testing parts (test planning, development, and organization), software testing maintenance changing the specifications of requirements and etc. During the time the specification and rules are prepared, the determination which particular parts of testing process are being automated and which ones need tester's manual help is identified.

Analyze the Method with Prototype. The method is generalized and experimental analyses are made using the prototype implementing automated testing process on the basis of requirements specifications. The systemized description of the method is formulated when the experimental analyses are made.

The suggested solution is oriented towards the user of information systems, therefore could be used in the verification of requirements, functional, acceptance testing or similar testing methods. The major attention is given to the implemented functionality which is tangible by user in accordance with requirements, but not to the unit testing of single source code.

Evaluating the present situation of requirements and testing the idea of the practical benefit is general improvement of requirements quality, the reduction of the test scenarios and cases in order to refund the developed requirements. The secondary work benefit is the reduction of manual work automating the process of testing (or its parts), which would enables tester to concentrate his attention to the different various testing problems.

4 Conclusion and Future Work

The accomplished review of software testing, integration of requirements and usage revealed the existence of various solutions such as document quality development of requirements, UML design of models from the text given in natural language, tests and their source code development from single UML models (generally, the diagrams of sequences and use cases). However, the following problems still remain: how to use the requirements more effective in a testing process, how to minimize the gap between them, so as the testing would transform accordingly to the change of requirements. The main idea of the solution presented in this paper is the more effective information gathering from requirements and more expedient usage of it in order to apply the information in testing. The transformation of appropriate requirements for testing into the structural models minimizes the complexity of the requirements variety in order to sort out the required information for testing.

In future, the usage offering the interaction solutions of requirements and testing integration are going to be analyzed. The purification and specification of single stage of the suggested solution is also going to be pursued.

References

1. Young, R.R.: The Requirements Engineering Handbook, p. 254. Artech House (2004)
2. Uusitalo, E.J., Komssi, M., Kauppinen, M., Davis, A.M.: Linking Requirements and Testing in Practice. In: Proceedings of the 2008 16th IEEE International Requirements Engineering Conference (RE 2008), pp. 265–270. IEEE Press, Washington (2008)
3. Barmi, Z.A., Ebrahimi, A.H., Feldt, R.: Alignment of Requirements Specification and Testing: A Systematic Mapping Study. In: Proceedings of the 2011 IEEE Fourth International Conference on Software Testing, Verification and Validation Workshops (ICSTW 2011), pp. 476–485. IEEE Press, Washington (2011)

4. Ismail, N., Ibrahim, R., Ibrahim, N.: Automatic Generation of Test Cases from Use-Case Diagram. In: Proceedings of the International Conference on Electrical Engineering and Informatics (ICEEI 2007), pp. 699–702 (2007)
5. Deeptimahanti, D.K., Sanyal, R.: Semi-automatic Generation of UML Models from Natural Language Requirements. In: Proceedings of the 4th India Software Engineering Conference (ISEC 2011), pp. 165–174. ACM Press, New York (2011)
6. Lamancha, B.P., Polo, M.: MATE: Methodology for Automated Model-Driven Testing. Testing Experience Magazine (17), 28–32 (2012)
7. IEEE Std 829-2008. IEEE Standard for Software and System Test Documentation. IEEE Press, New York (2008)
8. Smilgyte, K., Nenortaite, J.: Artificial Neural Networks Application in Software Testing Selection Method. In: Corchado, E., Kurzyński, M., Woźniak, M. (eds.) HAIS 2011, Part I. LNCS, vol. 6678, pp. 247–254. Springer, Heidelberg (2011)
9. Dautovic, A., Plosch, R., Saft, M.: Automatic Checking of Quality Best Practices in Software Development Documents. In: Proceedings of the 11th International Conference on Quality Software (QSIC 2011), pp. 208–217. IEEE Press (2011)
10. McGregor, J.: Form over Substance. Journal of Object Technology 6(8), 9–17 (2007)
11. Silingas, D., Butleris, R.: Towards Implementation a Framework for Modelling Software Requirements in MagicDraw UML. Information Technology and Control 38(2), 153–164 (2009)
12. Lopata, A., Ambraziunas, M., Gudas, S.: Knowledge Based MDA Requirements Specification and Validation Technique. Transformations in Business & Economics, 11(1(25)), 248–260 (2012)

Extracting Business Rules from Existing Enterprise Software System

Kestutis Normantas and Olegas Vasilecas

Information Systems Research Laboratory, Vilnius Gediminas Technical University,
Sauletekio al. 11, LT-10223, Vilnius, Lithuania
{kestutis.normantas,olegas.vasilecas}@isl.vgtu.lt

Abstract. As software systems evolve, it becomes increasingly complex for maintainers to keep them aligned with rapidly changing business requirements. Therefore the cost of software maintenance often exceeds the cost of its initial development or adaptation. As a result, automated approaches for software comprehension emerge providing valuable improvements and cost-savings for the software maintenance. This paper presents an approach that facilitates software comprehension by enabling traceability of implementation of business rules and business scenarios in the software system. It also describes a case study on application of this approach for comprehension of business logic implemented in the enterprise content management system and reports obtained results.

Keywords: Business Knowledge Extraction, Business Rules Discovery, Knowledge Discovery Meta-Model, Architecture-Driven Modernization, Model-Driven Reverse Engineering.

1 Introduction

Modern enterprises are characterized by a large amount of integrated software systems, designed using heterogeneous technologies to fulfill flexible business processes. Over time, software systems evolve and it becomes increasingly complex for maintainers to correct faults, improve performances or other attributes, or adapt to a changed environment [1]. Canfora and Cimitile [19] reveal that the cost of maintenance consumes 60% to 80% of the total life cycle costs while Seacord et al. [14] observe that the relative cost for maintaining and evolving the software has been steadily increasing and reached more than 90% of the total cost. At the same time, the Standish Group study [15], [22] shows that only one-third of code in applications contained business logic, while the remaining code was intended to support infrastructure and design activities. It follows that by identifying business logic implementing code parts, the costs of maintenance could be lowered significantly.

Recently, the Object Management Group (OMG) within the Architecture-Driven Modernization (ADM) Task Force initiative [8] provides a number of standards [10] for representation and analysis of existing software systems in order to support modernization activities. The Knowledge Discovery Meta-model (KDM) [9] plays the

T. Skersys, R. Butleris, and R. Butkiene (Eds.): ICIST 2012, CCIS 319, pp. 482–496, 2012.

fundamental role as it defines representation of all aspects of the software system and enables interoperability for tools that captures and analyses information about the existing system. A number of modernization projects [17] report significant cost savings by applying architecture-driven approaches in the modernization of information systems. However, not many works have been done in order to facilitate business logic extraction from the KDM representation of the software system. Therefore, in our research we aim to develop a method for business specific knowledge segregation from the knowledge about the existing software system represented within the KDM. In this paper we address related issues and present our approach for the discovery of business logic from existing software systems. We apply this approach in a case study of enterprise content management system used in several governmental organizations of Lithuania. The cost of the system maintenance has already exceeded its budged; therefore, automation of system comprehension is essential to reduce the maintenance costs.

The rest of this paper is organized of follows. In the next section we give an overview to related work in the field of BR extraction from the source code. After, we explain our approach by presenting the process of BR discovery. Then, we present a case study from our on-going project and discuss on the obtained results.

2 Related Work

Numerous methods and techniques for business rules discovery from existing software systems have been contributed in the field of reverse engineering. Though they differ by their objectives, application domains and scopes, it can be seen that most of them are concerned with certain kind of program slicing[1] to identify parts of code that implement business rules.

Chiang [3] presents a static program slicing based approach, which for any data output determines functions that create or change it, locations of those functions, and conditions that affect the execution of functions. For this reason, a control flow graph (CFG), representing program code statements and their control dependence, is sliced in accordance with criterion $C=<p,W>$, where p – is a program point (statement) of interest, and W is a set of output data variables. A slice S_C is a set of executable statements that contribute to the values of W just before statement p is executed. The approach considers selection of program point p to be the last statement of program slice contributing to the computation of a business rule. It follows that a number of slices become extremely large in case of large software system. For this reason, the program code is separated into the three categories: user interface; business logic; and data access. The starting point for slicing user interface is considered as a statement reading or displaying the data. Data I/O statements such as read, write, rewrite, open, or close are considered as candidates for the starting point of slicing data access layer. During the analysis of business logic category, code parts that affect data variables are separated and presented for software developers for validation.

[1] The term *program slicing* has been introduced by Mark Weiser [20], as a method for program comprehension using data flow analysis [6].

Another program slicing based approach for business rules extraction from legacy code is proposed by Huang et al. [5]. They define a number of heuristic rules for domain variables identification, slicing criteria identification, and slicing algorithm selection. Domain variables are identified considering every input and output variables of the system, arguments and return parameters of procedures. Slicing criteria involves input and output statements of the program, dispatch centers and return statements of procedures. A slicing algorithm is selected according formulated slicing criteria: for input variables and dispatch centers forward slicing is used; for output variables backward slicing is used to extract the relevant computation logic. Extracted business rules are represented in three ways: code-view; formula-view (three parts formulae – left hand side for a variable, right hand side for an expression that modifies variable, and conditions under which modifications may be executed); and input-output dependence view (bidirectional data flows between input and output parameters).

An extension to Huang et al. [5] solution is proposed by Wang et al. [1]. The approach proposed by them consists of five steps as follows. First, the program is sliced into multiple slices. Then, two types of domain variables are identified: pure domain variables that represent system's input and output; and derived domain variables that depend on pure domain variables. Dependences are established using forward slicing algorithm proposed by Bergeretti and Carre [2]. Having extracted domain variables and their dependences, the next step, called data analysis, identifies business items that are actually implemented in the selected slice. According to the obtained information, a set of business rules is extracted and represented using multiple views in order to be validated with stakeholders. An improvement to Wang et al. work is proposed by Gang [4]. The approach computes backward slices from a program dependence graph (PDG). Resulting slices are presented for validation with stakeholders as code fragments. However, code views requires deep understanding of technological aspects of the software system, therefore they are difficult to be validated with stakeholders.

Putrycz and Kark [13] emphasize the fact that business analysts require more than just code snippets referring the business rules. For this reason, they propose an approach that use document (in HTML format) content extraction and key phrase analysis to link the source code implementing business rules with technical and other related documentation. To separate business processing logic from infrastructure related, they focus on single program statements that carry a business meaning, such as calculation and branching, since they most often represents high level processing. Resulting production rules in the form of <Condition><Action> are represented using business vocabulary and business rules (SBVR).

From this we can see that many important issues must be taken into account: what intermediate representation of a software system should be chosen for the software comprehension; what algorithm to employ for the source code analysis; how to identify starting points for the analysis; and finally, how to represent extracted business rules in order to evaluate them with stakeholders. In contrast to related works, our research concentrates on software systems that are built using heterogeneous technologies, and aims to gather any kind of information about the software system to facilitate the comprehension of business logic implemented in the system. We therefore rely on the KDM standard to represent the knowledge about the software system and apply source code analysis to abstract the business logic.

3 An Approach

An approach for business rules discovery in existing software systems is based on reverse engineering process that obtains intermediate representation of different aspects of the software system using the KDM and abstracts the business logic from this representation (fig. 1). It consists of the three main stages that will be overviewed in this section.

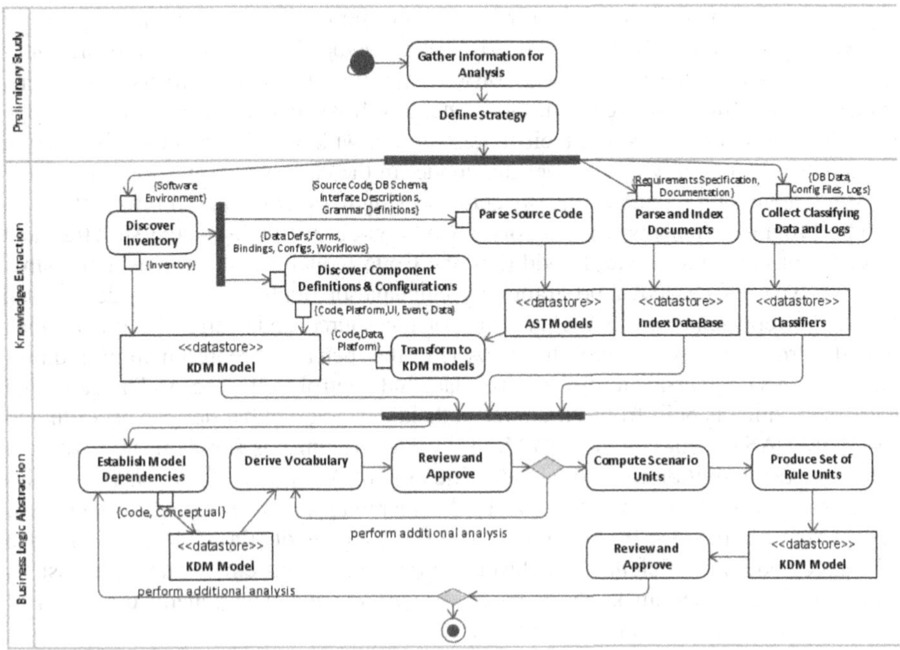

Fig. 1. The process of business logic discovery from existing software systems

3.1 Preliminary Study

The first phase of business rules discovery process involves preliminary study of the existing software system and it consist of the following steps: gather initial information; and define the strategy for knowledge extraction and representation within KDM. During the first step, the present architecture of software system is reviewed, the architectural components are identified, and the high-level dependencies between them are established. Based on the acquired initial knowledge about the software system, a strategy for obtaining the representation within KDM is defined. The strategy establishes the list of software artifacts that will be processed, the ways they will be processed, and the time expected for delivery of each representation.

3.2 Knowledge Extraction

This phase involves several steps whose purpose is to build knowledge base used as the main source for business logic abstraction. The knowledge base consists of a set of KDM models that represent software system (referred thereafter as KDM representation), the data base of indexed software documentation, and the data base of classifiers (i.e. lookup table values) and system log information.

KDM defines representation of the software system at several layers of abstraction: Infrastructure, Program elements, Runtime resources, and Conceptual layers. Within each layer, one or more architectural views on certain aspects of software system might be produced. The Infrastructure layer involves the Inventory model that is intended to represent software system's physical artifacts: containers, folders, source files, resource definitions, etc. The Inventory model serves as a bridge between physical artifacts and their representation within higher level of abstraction. Therefore it is naturally to discover this model in the early steps, and we employ file system scanning or version control system querying to obtain required information.

The Program elements layer involves Code model to represent the structure and behavior of the source code. In addition, the Code model might serve as a container for data types of particular programming language or platform resource definitions. While the representation of the structure of the source code might be transformed directly from abstract syntax trees (AST), the behavior representation requires numerous AST traversals to discover the data and control flow. The AST is generated by parser, which is built from the source code language grammar defined according to specialized AST meta-model (ASTM, [11]). The grammar is supplemented with the software API definition to facilitate identification of API usage. Transformation rules are defined according to ASTM-to-KDM mapping rules specified in [11] and considering MicroKDM [9] semantics. The latter allows obtain KDM representation of source code at sufficiently low level of granularity – statements and expressions represented using certain kinds of KDM *ActionElements*. The general principles of this process are illustrated in the figure 2.

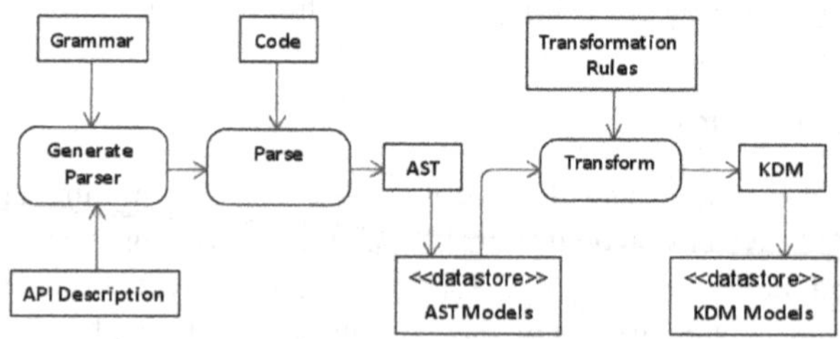

Fig. 2. Process for obtainment of source code representation within KDM Code model

The Runtime Resources layer involves several kinds of models to represent resources of the system: UI, Data, Platform, and Events models. Depending on the software system, there may be different types of resource definitions, including user interface, data, workflow, system job, task, or component definitions. During runtime, these definitions are processed by the software platform to create runtime objects (e.g. form instances) that might be manipulated by the application code using software API. In order to establish dependencies between source code and runtime resource objects, we additionally create a set of Code models containing elements that represents structural composition of resources as *ClassUnit* element consisting of either other *ClassUnit* or *MemberUnit* elements. The content of resource definition files is structured according to particular schema definition. However, the definition of schema not always may be available; therefore, it might be reversed automatically from the content [7] or defined manually by considering only relevant parts of the content. Then, according to the predefined set of mapping rules between the schema elements and elements of particular KDM model, the content of resource definitions is parsed and corresponding KDM representation is created.

KDM runtime resource models are augmented with representation of content of configuration files. While discovering their content, it is possible to discover platform resources other than previously identified. It should be noted that such information does not necessary mean that they are actual, because the configuration data may be obsolete, written by resources that are changed or removed in time.

The creation of database of software documentation is built in several steps. Digital documents are parsed using specialized document parsing libraries to retrieve trees representing logical structure of document content: document, chapter, section, subsection, and body. Depending on type of document, it may be retrieved directly from the structure definition (e.g. TOC in word documents), bookmarks that links to different pages within a PDF, or considering a set of rules established regarding the properties of physical content (i.e. blocks) of document. Retrieved information is further tokenized, supplemented with corresponding attributes and indexed with full-text index engine to be available for linking with elements of KDM representation.

Finally, a database of classifiers and log information is built by reviewing known lookup tables, files containing classifying data definitions, log files or tables. For each resource, a local copy of data is created and stored in the database to be available for further analysis. The data in this database is later used to define base facts from the established business terms.

3.3 Business Logic Abstraction

Having extracted all the available and relevant knowledge about the software system into the KDM representation, the next phase of the recovery process involves activities to separate KDM model parts that represent business logic implementation from the infrastructure related ones. For this reason, we first of all establish dependencies between model elements. Then, we derive initial set of term and fact units, and validate it with maintainer of the system. We follow the SBVR standard [12] as guidance to classify the business rules and to enable their formal definition. We further apply static source code analysis techniques to refine this set and to identify the implementation logic of business rules, and to extract particular business scenarios. Finally, extracted knowledge is reviewed and approved with the maintainers of the system.

The aim of dependencies establishment step is to build a system-level control flow graph (SCFG) from the KDM representation. SCFG consists of collection of procedure control flow graph (CFG). A CFG is a graph containing nodes that represent statements and predicate expressions (KDM *ActionElement*), and directed edges between nodes representing the flow of control (KDM *ControlFlow* subclasses). To obtain system-level graph, CFGs are interconnected by traversing call dependencies. Call dependencies between runtime resources and source code are established considering the following:

- Source code handling software platform events (e.g. periodical event, application starting/stopping);
- Source code handling user interface events (e.g. form event or form control event);
- Source code handling object instantiation or access events (e.g. create, update, delete);
- Source code handling events produced due to access to particular software platform functionality (e.g. user login, user management event);
- Source code handling events of workflow activities and transitions between them (e.g. on enter to activity or exit from it, on transition);
- Source code accessing runtime resources that produce particular kind of event (source code that sends signal to runtime resource invokes execution of source code that handles the event of signal receive, e.g. setting form field value programmatically invokes execution of source code that handles *OnSetFieldText* event).

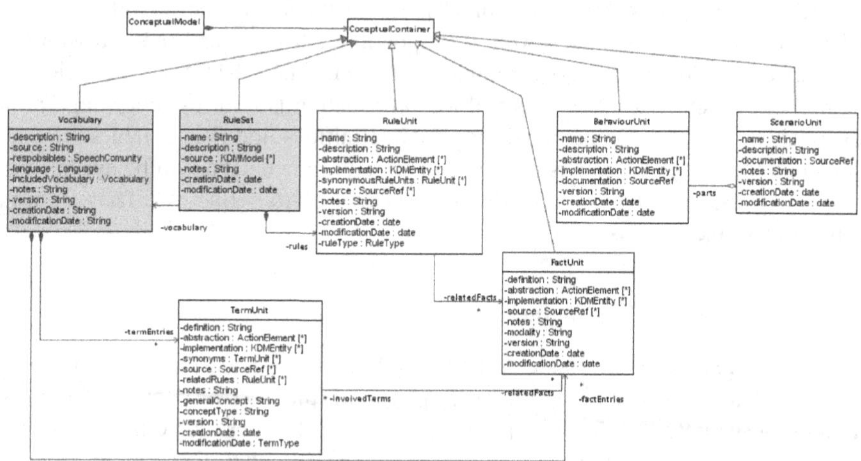

Fig. 3. A fragment of extended KDM representing conceptual model elements for definition business rules

Having established dependences and built a SCFG, source code analysis techniques may be applied to identify the business logic implementing source code and related resources, and to represent it within the KDM Conceptual model. The Conceptual model enables mapping of KDM compliant model to models compliant to other specifications. Currently, KDM provides "concept" classes – *TermUnit*, *FactUnit* and *RuleUnit* facilitating mapping to SBVR [9]. We slightly extend this representation (fig 3) in order to facilitate further mappings.

A vocabulary containing a set of term units and fact units is derived by primarily considering the representation of structural elements of runtime resources. We first refer to the *Data* and *UI* models, because they contain elements that convey business terms explicitly and therefore may be merely understood by the maintainer. Thus, for each *KDMEntity* which is an instance of specific type of *AbstractDataElement* or *AbstractUIElement* a *TermUnit* is created and added to *ConceptualModel*. A reference to that entity is added to the collection of elements representing implementation of *TermUnit* (property "*implementation*"). The collection is further supplemented with references to elements that bind with UI elements (i.e. data definition fields upon which form and report fields are built). Then, the set of *TermUnit* elements is augmented with elements that correspond to instances of specific types of *AbstractPlatformElement* (extracted from the configuration files).

To facilitate definition of business terms, we reference TermUnits with indices from the data base of software documentation. For each TermUnit, we construct several types of search queries: the first one limits the search scope to a title of structural elements of indexed documents (i.e. chapter, section, subsection); the second one limits search scope to a body of document's structural element. Search results ranked by relevance are referenced with TermUnit element as source property containing a set of references for each matching index.

Table 1. Fact Types derivation

Fact Type	Derivation principles
1) Associative fact type *fact type that has more than one role.*	**References to objects**; e.g. lookup fields (foreign keys) within data structure definitions; object properties containing a collection of references to another objects;
1.1) is-property-of fact type *fact type that involves two concepts, where the first concepts define essential quality of the second concept.*	**Primitive object properties or references to another objects**; e.g. fields within data structure definitions; form fields; object properties;
2) Partitive fact type *fact type determining the whole-part relationship*	**Object composition**; e.g. nested objects; groups of UI controls (framed, tabbed);
3) Specialization fact type	
3.1) Categorization fact type *fact type declaring concept dependence on certain categorization concept*	**Classifying properties**; e.g. lookup table values that defines particular categories, such as a kind, type, etc.
3.2) Contextualization fact type *is-role-of fact type and is-facet-of fact type*	**Data type instantiation**; e.g. object instantiation; object reference assignment to a certain variable;
4) Assortment fact type *fact type that is defined with respect to a given general concept and a given individual concept.*	**Object inheritances**; e.g. class inheritances; properties that defines object dependence to certain general concept;

In order to derive *FactUnits* from the software system we refer to SBVR fact types categorization scheme that classifies facts based on their semantic nature. The SBVR distinguishes fact types into the following categories: associative fact type, partitive fact type, specialization fact types, and assortment fact types. The table 1 presents general principles for derivation of certain types of *FactUnits*.

Having derived initial set of candidates to business terms and related facts (*TermUnits* and *FactUnits*), the vocabulary is reviewed and validated to separate design specific *TermUnits* and *FactUnits* from the business specific ones. To identify how particular *TermUnit* is derived, static inter-procedural backward slicing [16] of the SCFG is performed with respect to slicing criterion $C_{Der}=<DE, ae_{out}>$, where *DE* is a set of KDM *DataElements* representing implementation of this *TermUnit*, and ae_{out} is a kind of KDM *ActionElement* representing output of these data elements to user interface, database or other kind of data repository. A resulting slice $S_{Der}=\{ActionElement\}$ containing a set of control and data dependent *ActionElements* is added to the property *abstraction* of derived *RuleUnit*.

ScenarioUnits are derived to represent behavioral paths from platform or user interface events through the SCFG. They are computed by traversing SCFG along the control flow and call edges [6]. *ActionElements* representing conditional statements (i.e. *if* or *switch statements*) within those paths and their intermediate successors are considered as candidates to *RuleUnits*.

4 A Case Study

So far we have discussed on general principles of the approach for business logic abstraction from the representation of the existing software systems. In this section we will present a case study from our on-going research project, where we apply it to abstract business logic from the commercial-off-the-shelf (COTS) Enterprise Content Management (ECM) system.

4.1 An Overview of the Software System

The system is used for document management, records management, web content management, and collaboration in several governmental organizations of Lithuania. It is designed using multi-tiered Client/Server architecture (fig. 4). The software system serves as a platform for development of business specific solutions: it provides customization capabilities by enabling to define specific data objects (using data definitions); create forms and reports; specify workflows that may be assigned to data objects; configure periodic server jobs. It also provides application programming interface (API) allowing automation of particular system events using a dialect of the Visual Basic for Application (VBA) language and integration with other software systems using the Component Object Model (COM) interface. Internally the system may be considered as a black-box – the logic behind the interface may be understood only from software technical documentation, or from experience gained by using API in the development of business specific solutions.

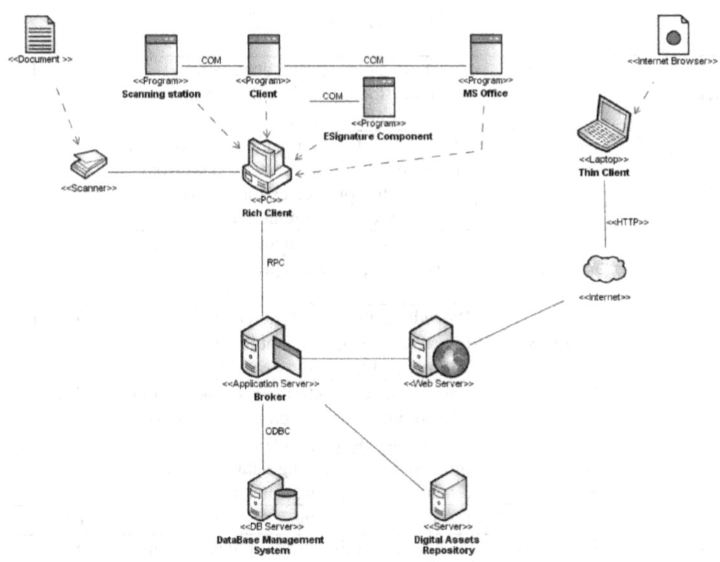

Fig. 4. Architecture of Enterprise Content Management System

Table 2. Overview of gathered initial information about the software system

Component	Resources	Description	Format	Qnt
Client *-is a desktop application that interacts over network with broker server using RPC; with external applications over COM API.*	*Local configs*	Client specific configurations: defined actions, application window setting, etc.	INI	200
	Log files	Client specific log information.	CSV	200
	Folders	User specific collection of documents.	XML	155
Broker Server *-is a service component containing subcomponents for interaction with clients (by distributing its resources to client applications), database management system (ODBC), web server (Gateway Server), and stores document objects in repository.*	*Application files*	Platform components	DLL, EXE, etc	132
	Macros	Visual Basic for Application script modules containing module level constants, external library declarations, procedure and function declarations (that handles certain resource event).	VBA	57 (>40K LOC)
	Defs	Document, lookup and audit table definitions.	XML	187
	Reports	Data representation and data source definitions that are based on one or more Defs.	XML	16
	Forms	Definitions of forms for data editing or querying; are based on one or more Defs.	XML	83
	Workflows	Workflow definitions: activities, transitions, decision points; events corresponding to these workflow elements (on entry, on exit, etc)	XML	5
	Config. files	Platform specific configuration.	INI, XML	3
	Log files	Server log information.	CSV	3

Table 2. (*continued*)

Database Management System *-used to store and retrieve document metadata, lookup table values, audit, and other system data.*	*DB Tables*	Database tables storing document metadata, lookup table values, audit values, or custom data.	T-SQL	80
	DB Views	Stored SELECT statements that associate one or more tables to retrieve data from them, applies predicates for data filtering, calls functions for output data formatting.	T-SQL	92
	DB Procedures	Stored procedures that are called from VB script over application provided interface to database connectivity component.	T-SQL	30
	DB Triggers	Procedures that are executed in response to particular events on table; used for internal audit, temporary tables.	T-SQL	10
	DB Functions	User Defined Functions that process input data to produce required output, and are called from stored procedures or views.	T-SQL	26
	Lookup table data	Information classifying data, such as document kind, type, status and etc.	Data	20
	Log	Database specific log.	Data	2
ScanStation *-scans physical document, performs optical recognition, and transfers textual information to client.*	*Templates*	Template definitions for optical content recognition.	XML	23
	Config. files	Fields mapping definitions	INI, XML	2
Office Integration *-transfers user filled document templates to client.*	*Config. files*	Configuration mapping Fields mapping definitions	INI	1
	Document templates	Word document templates containing fields mapped to document fields.	doc, docx	20

In order to meet the requirements of the organization and the rules of management of electronic documents, it has been greatly customized (table 2 summarizes the results of our initial study on what artifacts contains software system). However, over the time, requirements change and the software system must be updated to reflect those changes. It leads to many undocumented modifications, and even worse, because the impact of these modifications to other parts of the system is very difficult to evaluate, they usually tend to be not fully tested. The maintenance cost exceeds its budged; therefore, the approach for automated system comprehension is essential to reduce the maintenance costs.

4.2 The Strategy

Having identified the artifacts of the software system and its integration components, we defined the strategy for the knowledge extraction. Within the strategy it was identified that 8 custom parsers and 13 transformation rules sets must be developed in order to obtain the "as-is" KDM representation of the system. For the implementation of these tools set, we chose the Eclipse platform, because of numerous reasons: it is an open-source; there is already developed the KDM framework for this platform; it supports model-driven engineering (i.e. model driven parser generators, meta-model based transformation tools, model graphic editors, etc.); and finally, it is extendable and allows additional tools integration.

To process documentation of the software system and store it in full-text search database, we selected to use *Apache Lucene* and *Solr* technologies in combination with *PDF* and *DOC(X)* document parsers (all available documentation has been provided in these formats). We have not considered any specific kind of phrase comparison algorithm to obtain more results in search queries, because the number of documents was not so large (less than 30, including platform documentation, requirements specifications, manuals, etc.), and it was clear that most of identifiers obtained from definitions of platform resources would have identical terms used in the documentation.

4.3 Discovering Knowledge about the Software System

In order to evaluate the feasibility of our approach, we selected to discover artifacts of Client and Broker Server components. Their interaction with other components we decided to represent as external calls and leave the analysis of these components for the further research. By discovering analyzed components content, we obtained a set of KDM models representing architectural views on platform components, UI composition, automation, and data structure of the ECM system.

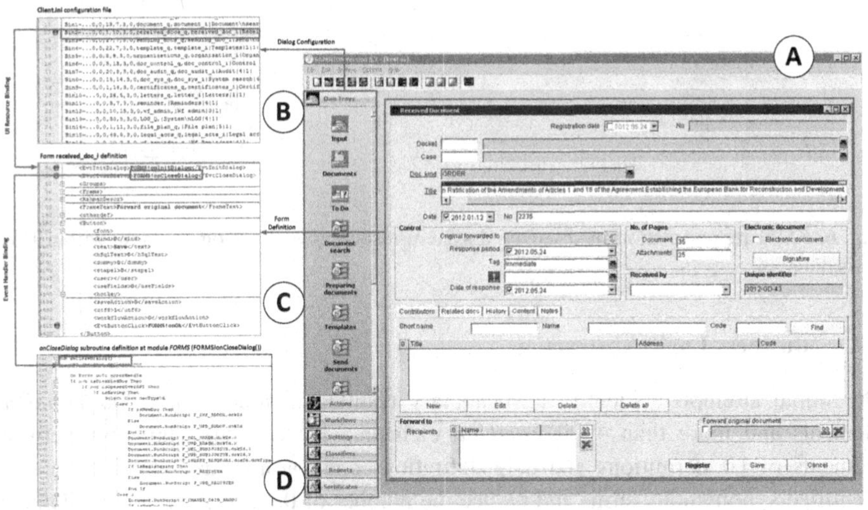

Fig. 5. The main dialog of ECM and the form to fill document metadata (A); a snippet of configuration file that defines left side tray bar (B); a snippet of form definition (C); a fragment of code module containing subroutine that handles form event (D).

The picture above presents a fragment of ECM: the main application dialog and the form to fill metadata of receivable document (fig. 5, A). The structure of document object is defined within the data definition file that maps to database object (table or view). The configuration of trays for the particular client is predefined within client.ini configuration file (fig. 5, B). A configuration of tray is a key-value pair that reference to form definitions, which are opened due to action performed by a user of the system (drag-and-drop document object and a double click). The form definition (fig. 5, C) contains a description of UI elements within the form and references to the form or its controls event handling code procedures declared within macro modules (fig. 5, D).

The left side of figure 6 shows the snippet of tree view of KDM representation discovered from the software resources and code. The right side represents it logical view with UML Class diagram (where stereotypes correspond to KDM element types).

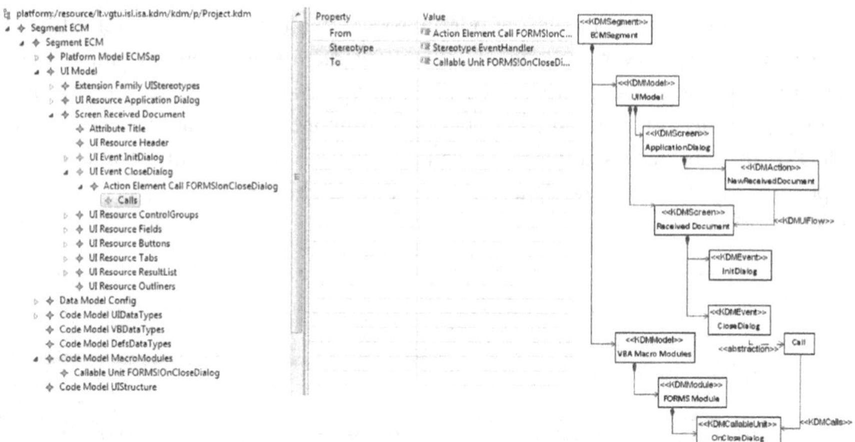

Fig. 6. KDM representation of discovered system resources and its logical view within UML class diagram

4.4 Business Logic Abstraction

Our initial attempt to identify a vocabulary resulted in more than 2000 *TermUnit* elements and more than 4000 *FactUnit* elements. By analyzing bindings between elements of UI definitions and data definitions and variable assignments we have identified synonymous terms and reduce the number of the actual *TermUnit* elements to 884. From the data definitions we obtained about 321 structural *RuleUnit* elements (mandatory fields, unique indices, default values, etc.). The picture below presents the vocabulary entry for *TermUnit* Receivable Document.

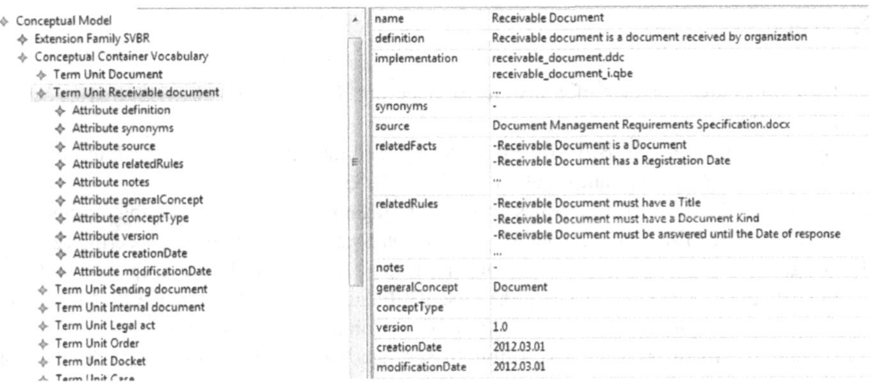

Fig. 7. Vocabulary entry representation of TermUnit

Identification of scenario units was relatively straightforward, because almost each business use case could have been traced from the system actions (menu and trays functionality). We have sliced KDM representation and identified 32 scenario units in total, which actually corresponded to functionality of the system: document registration, preparation, forwarding, notifying, assigning tasks and execution control, etc. Then, we traversed obtained slices to identify implementation of *RuleUnit* elements that has affect to the flow of control within the scenario unit (*ActionElement* representing control statement that uses a subset of *TermUnits* in conditional predicate expression). The *CodeModel* we have analyzed contained many *ActionElements* representing nested *if* and *select case* statements (nesting level more than *10*); however, after preliminary study we have found that a relatively large number of conditional *if* statements are platform specific or introduced for technical purposes, e.g. check object instantiation, check if document object is loaded or locked, etc. We have identified that at an average the number of such conditional elements for each scenario unit was up to *60%*. By eliminating these elements we reduced the number of candidates to operational *RuleUnits* from more than *2000* to *800*.

5 Conclusions and Further Research

In this paper we have presented the approach for business logic discovery from existing software systems. Within this process-centric approach we identified the activities for knowledge extraction and representation with KDM, and determined the steps for business logic separation from this representation. We have presented a case study from our on-going research project, and discussed on our initially obtained results. The vocabulary and related rules as well as business scenario units identified within this case study facilitate the maintenance of the software system providing traceability to the business logic implementation parts representing KDM elements.

However, KDM representation is only intermediate format valuable for automated analysis. Seeking to produce more comprehensive representations of views of particular software system aspect, the conversion to static and dynamic UML models must be considered in the further research. In order to be able to validate discovered knowledge with stakeholders, candidates to business rules should be transformed to SBVR templates, decision tables or trees, or other acceptable format.

References

1. IEEE Standard Glossary of Software Engineering Terminology, IEEE Std 610.12-1990. IEEE (1990)
2. Bergeretti, J.-F., Carré, B.A.: Information-flow and data-flow analysis of while-programs. ACM Trans. Program. Lang. Syst. 7(1), 37–61 (1985)
3. Chiang, C.-C.: Extracting business rules from legacy systems into reusable components. In: 2006 IEEE/SMC International Conference on System of Systems Engineering (2006)
4. Gang, X.: Business Rule Extraction from Legacy System Using Dependence-Cache Slicing. In: Proceedings of the 2009 First IEEE International Conference on Information Science and Engineering, pp. 4214–4218. IEEE Computer Society (2009)
5. Huang, H.: Business Rule Extraction from Legacy Code. In: Proceedings of the 20th Conference on Computer Software and Applications, pp. 162–168. IEEE Computer Society (1996)
6. Khedker, U., Sanyal, A., Karkare, B.: Data Flow Analysis: Theory and Practice. CRC Press, Inc. (2009)
7. Nečaský, M.: Reverse engineering of XML schemas to conceptual diagrams. In: Proceedings of the Sixth Asia-Pacific Conference on Conceptual Modeling, vol. 96, pp. 117–128. Australian Computer Society, Inc. (2009)
8. OMG. Architecture Driven Modernization Task Force (2012), `http://adm.omg.org`
9. OMG. Knowledge Discovery Metamodel Specification Version 1.3 (2011), `http://www.omg.org/spec/KDM/1.3/PDF/`
10. OMG. Architecture driven modernization standards roadmap (2009), `http://adm.omg.org/ADMTFRoadmap.pdf`
11. OMG. Abstract Syntax Tree Metamodel v1.0 (2009), `http://www.omg.org/spec/ASTM/1.0/`
12. OMG. Semantics of Business Vocabulary and Business Rules v1.0 (2008), `http://www.omg.org/spec/SBVR/1.0/`
13. Putrycz, E., Kark, A.W.: Connecting Legacy Code, Business Rules and Documentation. In: Bassiliades, N., Governatori, G., Paschke, A. (eds.) RuleML 2008. LNCS, vol. 5321, pp. 17–30. Springer, Heidelberg (2008)
14. Seacord, R.C., Plakosh, D., Lewis, G.A.: Modernizing Legacy Systems: Software Technologies, Engineering Process and Business Practices. Addison-Wesley Longman Publishing Co., Inc. (2003)
15. Standish, T.A.: An Essay on Software Reuse. IEEE Trans. Software Eng., 494–497 (1984)
16. Tip, F.: A Survey of Program Slicing Techniques. Journal of Programming Languages 3, 121–189 (1995)
17. Ulrich, W.M., Newcomb, P.: Information Systems Transformation: Architecture-Driven Modernization Case Studies. Morgan Kaufmann Publishers Inc. (2010)
18. Wang, X., Sun, J., Yang, X., He, Z., Maddineni, S.: Business Rules Extraction from Large Legacy Systems. In: Proceedings of the Eighth Euromicro Working Conference on Software Maintenance and Reengineering (CSMR 2004), pp. 249–254. IEEE Computer Society (2004)
19. Canfora, G., Cimitile, A.: Software Maintenance. In: Proc. 7th Int. Conf. Software Engineering and Knowledge Engineering, pp. 478–486 (1995)
20. Weiser, M.: Program slicing. IEEE Transactions on Software Engineering SE-10(4), 352–357 (1984)
21. The Standish Group, The Internet Goes Business Critical (2009)

Author Index